Business
Plans
Handbook

Business Plans

A COMPILATION
OF BUSINESS
PLANS DEVELOPED
BY INDIVIDUALS
THROUGHOUT
NORTH AMERICA

Handbook

VOLUME

22

Michelle Lee,
Project Editor

GALE
CENGAGE Learning™

Detroit • New York • San Francisco • New Haven, Conn • Waterville, Maine • London

GALE
CENGAGE Learning™

Business Plans Handbook, Volume 22

Project Editor: Michelle Lee

Product Manager: Jenai Drouillard

Product Design: Jennifer Wahi

Composition and Electronic Prepress: Evi Seoud

Manufacturing: Rita Wimberley

Gale, a part of Cengage Learning
27500 Drake Rd.
Farmington Hills, MI 48331-3535

ISBN-13: 978-1-4144-6834-1
ISBN-10: 1-4144-6834-2
1084-4473

Printed in Mexico
1 2 3 4 5 6 7 13 12 11

Contents

CONTENTS

Highlights

Business Plans Handbook, Volume 22 (BPH-22) is a collection of business plans compiled by entrepreneurs seeking funding for small businesses throughout North America. For those looking for examples of how to approach, structure, and compose their own business plans, *BPH-22* presents 20 sample plans, including plans for the following businesses:

- Burger Stand
- Church
- Commercial Diving Service
- Concession Equipment Rental Business
- Cosmetics Manufacturer
- DVD Kiosk Rental Business
- Grant Writer
- Inflatable Amusement Rental Business
- Infusion Therapy
- iPhone App Developer
- IT Network Installer
- Medical Practice
- Mobile Oil Change Business
- Online Job Service
- Nonprofit Concession Stand Business
- Personal Loan Company
- Pressure Washing Business
- Record Company
- Self Storage Business
- Used Car Business

FEATURES AND BENEFITS

BPH-22 offers many features not provided by other business planning references including:

- Twenty business plans, each of which represent an attempt at clarifying (for themselves and others) the reasons that the business should exist or expand and why a lender should fund the enterprise.
- Two fictional plans that are used by business counselors at a prominent small business development organization as examples for their clients. (You will find these in the Business Plan Template Appendix.)

- A directory section that includes: listings for venture capital and finance companies, which specialize in funding start-up and second-stage small business ventures, and a comprehensive listing of Service Corps of Retired Executives (SCORE) offices. In addition, the Appendix also contains updated listings of all Small Business Development Centers (SBDCs); associations of interest to entrepreneurs; Small Business Administration (SBA) Regional Offices; and consultants specializing in small business planning and advice. It is strongly advised that you consult supporting organizations while planning your business, as they can provide a wealth of useful information.

- A Small Business Term Glossary to help you decipher the sometimes confusing terminology used by lenders and others in the financial and small business communities.

- A cumulative index, outlining each plan profiled in the complete *Business Plans Handbook* series.

- A Business Plan Template which serves as a model to help you construct your own business plan. This generic outline lists all the essential elements of a complete business plan and their components, including the Summary, Business History and Industry Outlook, Market Examination, Competition, Marketing, Administration and Management, Financial Information, and other key sections. Use this guide as a starting point for compiling your plan.

- Extensive financial documentation required to solicit funding from small business lenders. You will find examples of: Cash Flows, Balance Sheets, Income Projections, and other financial information included with the textual portions of the plan.

Introduction

Perhaps the most important aspect of business planning is simply doing it. More and more business owners are beginning to compile business plans even if they don't need a bank loan. Others discover the value of planning when they must provide a business plan for the bank. The sheer act of putting thoughts on paper seems to clarify priorities and provide focus. Sometimes business owners completely change strategies when compiling their plan, deciding on a different product mix or advertising scheme after finding that their assumptions were incorrect. This kind of healthy thinking and re-thinking via business planning is becoming the norm. The editors of *Business Plans Handbook, Volume 22 (BPH-22)* sincerely hope that this latest addition to the series is a helpful tool in the successful completion of your business plan, no matter what the reason for creating it.

This twenty-second volume, like each volume in the series, offers business plans used and created by real people. *BPH-22* provides 20 business plans. The business and personal names and addresses and general locations have been changed to protect the privacy of the plan authors.

NEW BUSINESS OPPORTUNITIES

As in other volumes in the series, *BPH-22* finds entrepreneurs engaged in a wide variety of creative endeavors. Examples include a proposal for a Church, a Commercial Diving Service, and a Medical Practice. In addition, several other plans are provided, including a Record Company, an iPhone App Developer, and DVD Rental Kiosks, among others.

Comprehensive financial documentation has become increasingly important as today's entrepreneurs compete for the finite resources of business lenders. Our plans illustrate the financial data generally required of loan applicants, including Income Statements, Financial Projections, Cash Flows, and Balance Sheets.

ENHANCED APPENDIXES

In an effort to provide the most relevant and valuable information for our readers, we have updated the coverage of small business resources. For instance, you will find: a directory section, which includes listings of all of the Service Corps of Retired Executives (SCORE) offices; an informative glossary, which includes small business terms; and a cumulative index, outlining each plan profiled in the complete *Business Plans Handbook* series. In addition we have updated the list of Small Business Development Centers (SBDCs); Small Business Administration Regional Offices; venture capital and finance companies, which specialize in funding start-up and second-stage small business enterprises; associations of interest to entrepreneurs; and consultants, specializing in small business advice and planning. For your reference, we have also reprinted the business plan template, which provides a comprehensive overview of the essential components of a business plan and two fictional plans used by small business counselors.

SERIES INFORMATION

If you already have the first twenty-one volumes of *BPH*, with this twenty-second volume, you will now have a collection of over 452 business plans (not including the updated plans); contact information for hundreds of organizations and agencies offering business expertise; a helpful business plan template; more than 1,500 citations to valuable small business development material; and a comprehensive glossary of terms to help the business planner navigate the sometimes confusing language of entrepreneurship.

ACKNOWLEDGEMENTS

The Editors wish to sincerely thank the contributors to *BPH-22*, including:

- BizPlanDB.com
- Paul Greenland

COMMENTS WELCOME

Your comments on *Business Plans Handbook* are appreciated. Please direct all correspondence, suggestions for future volumes of *BPH*, and other recommendations to the following:

Managing Editor, Business Product
Business Plans Handbook
Gale, a part of Cengage Learning
27500 Drake Rd.
Farmington Hills, MI 48331-3535
Phone: (248)699-4253
Fax: (248)699-8052
Toll-Free: 800-347-GALE
E-mail: BusinessProducts@gale.com

Burger Stand

Bob's Burger Shack

1200 High St.
Brooklyn, New York 11219

BizPlanDB.com

The purpose of this business plan is to raise $60,000 for the development of a food stand that will sell burgers, hot dogs, and beverages to customers in its targeted market. The Company was founded by Robert Bergeon.

1.0 EXECUTIVE SUMMARY

The purpose of this business plan is to raise $60,000 for the development of a burger stand while showcasing the expected financials and operations over the next three years. Bob's Burger Shack ("the Company") is a New York-based corporation that will provide burgers, hot dogs, and beverages to customers in its targeted market. The Company was founded by Robert Bergeon.

1.1 The Services

Our vision for Bob's Burger Shack is to operate a small location that will provide a wide selection of burgers, hotdogs, beverages, and ice cream.

Bob's Burger Shack, vis-a-vis food and beverage sales, will generate substantial gross margins that will allow the business to generate profitable revenue throughout the course of the calendar year.

The third section of the business plan will further describe the services offered by Bob's Burger Shack.

1.2 Financing

Mr. Bergeon is seeking to raise $50,000 from a bank loan. The interest rate and loan agreement are to be further discussed during negotiation. This business plan assumes that the business will receive a 10 year loan with a 9% fixed interest rate. The financing will be used for the following:

- Development of the Company's location.
- Financing for the first six months of operation.
- Capital to purchase the Company's equipment.

Mr. Bergeon will contribute $10,000 to the venture.

1.3 Mission Statement

The Company is committed to providing customers with quality burgers, hot dogs, ice cream, and beverages at reasonable prices while conforming to all laws regarding the sale of food on both the state and local level.

1.4 Management Team

The Company was founded by Robert Bergeon. Mr. Bergeon has more than 10 years of experience in the retail food establishment industry. Through his expertise, he will be able to bring the operations of the business to profitability within its first year of operations.

1.5 Sales Forecasts

Mr. Bergeon expects a strong rate of growth at the start of operations. Below are the expected financials over the next three years.

Proforma profit and loss (yearly)

Year	1	2	3
Sales	$430,122	$473,134	$520,448
Operating costs	$219,454	$227,558	$236,028
EBITDA	$124,644	$150,950	$180,330
Taxes, interest, and depreciation	$ 60,209	$ 66,510	$ 77,263
Net profit	$ 64,434	$ 84,440	$103,067

Sales, operating costs, and profit forecast

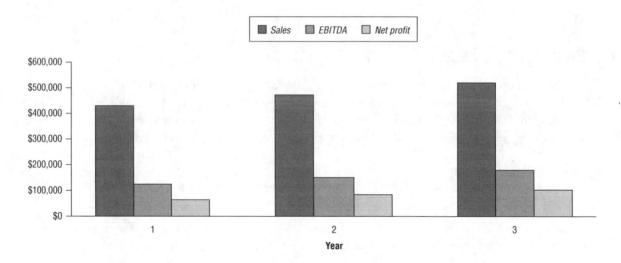

1.6 Expansion Plan

The Founder expects that the business will aggressively expand during the first three years of operation. Mr. Bergeon intends to implement marketing campaigns that will effectively target individuals within the target market.

2.0 COMPANY AND FINANCING SUMMARY

2.1 Registered Name and Corporate Structure

The Company is registered as a corporation in the State of New York.

2.2 Required Funds

At this time, Bob's Burger Shack requires $50,000 of debt funds. Below is a breakdown of how these funds will be used:

Projected startup costs

Initial lease payments and deposits	$ 5,000
Working capital	$17,500
FF&E	$12,500
Leasehold improvements	$ 2,500
Security deposits	$ 2,500
Insurance	$ 1,250
Cooking equipment	$10,000
Marketing budget	$ 3,750
Miscellaneous and unforeseen costs	$ 5,000
Total startup costs	**$60,000**

Use of funds

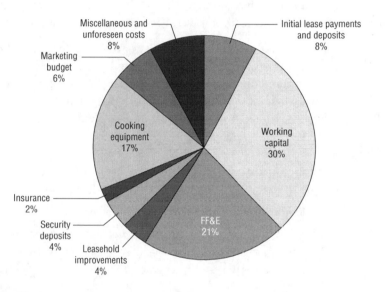

2.3 Investor Equity

Mr. Bergeon is not seeking an investment from a third party at this time.

2.4 Management Equity

Mr. Bergeon owns 100% of Bob's Burger Shack.

2.5 Exit Strategy

If the business is very successful, Mr. Bergeon may seek to sell the business to a third party for a significant earnings multiple. Most likely, the Company will hire a qualified business broker to sell the business on behalf of Bob's Burger Shack. Based on historical numbers, the business could fetch a sales premium of up to 3 times earnings. There are moderate risks associated with operating a restaurant business, and as such Mr. Bergeon will need to properly train a new owner for at least 30 to 60 days after the sale is complete.

3.0 PRODUCTS AND SERVICES

Bob's Burger Shack will sell a variety of hamburgers, hot dogs, ice cream, smoothies, and other products that are common within Burger Stands.

The Owner's top priority (along with serving quality food) is to comply with all state and local laws regarding the sale of food and beverages to the general public. Within Bob's Burger Shack's facility, the Company will always properly handle dairy and meat products, which have higher incidences of spoilage. The Owner will ensure, at all times, the Company's facility is in compliance with all health and food safety laws.

He intends to further the support for the business by sourcing inventories of meat, ice cream, and other food products from local stores that will provide Bob's Burger Shack with bulk discounts. This will allow the business to further its ties to the local economy.

Mr. Bergeon is sourcing a number of inventory and equipment suppliers for the ongoing and one time costs associated with this business.

4.0 STRATEGIC AND MARKET ANALYSIS

4.1 Economic Outlook

This section of the analysis will detail the economic climate, the burger stand quick service food industry, the customer profile, and the competition that the business will face as it progresses through its business operations.

Presently the economic market condition in the United States is moderate. The meltdown of the sub prime mortgage market coupled with increasing gas prices has led many people to believe that the US is on the cusp of a double dip economic recession. This slowdown in the economy has also greatly impacted real estate sales, which has halted to historical lows. However, due to the low pricing point of the food products offered by Bob's Burger Shack, the business should be able to remain profitable despite any future economic declines.

4.2 Industry Analysis

There are over 640,000 restaurants in the United States. Gross annual receipts total more than $193 billion dollars per year. The industry also employs over 10.5 million people, and generates an average annual payroll of more than $40 billion dollars per year.

As it pertains to relationships that specifically focus on selling hamburgers and similar products, there are approximately 75,000 businesses that operate within this sub-segment of the general restaurant industry. Each year, these businesses typically generate 15% to 19% of all revenues generated by restaurants within the United States.

4.3 Customer Profile

As the business offers an expansive menu of burgers, hot dogs, ice cream, and other products, it is difficult to categorize the average customer of Bob's Burger Shack as many people, of all walks of life, enjoy the products offered by the Company.

Management expects that the average customer will be a middle to upper middle class man or woman (usually with children) living in the Company's target market. Common traits among clients will include:

- Annual household income exceeding $30,000

- Lives or works no more than 5 miles from the Company's location.

- Will spend $5 to $15 per visit to Bob's Burger Shack

In the Company's target market radius (approximately 5 miles), there are more than 100,000 residents. Among these residents, the annual household income is $42,000 while median family income is approximately $50,000. The 10 year population growth of the area has been 3%.

4.4 Competition

As with any metropolitan area, there are always many businesses that operate in a similar or identical capacity. The Company's burger stand will face competition from other restaurants as well as with major franchised locations that serve similar fare. Management intends to differentiate itself by operating in a burger stand capacity while serving the freshest quality products.

5.0 MARKETING PLAN

Bob's Burger Shack intends to maintain an extensive marketing campaign that will ensure maximum visibility for the business in its targeted market. Below is an overview of the marketing strategies and objectives of Bob's Burger Shack.

5.1 Marketing Objectives

- Implement a local campaign with the Company's targeted market via the use of coupons that will be provided with all mailed advertisements.

- Build a large word-of-mouth referral network through existing customer base once the business becomes popular within the local community.

- Establish connections with local suppliers and vendors.

5.2 Marketing Strategies

Direct marketing will be the most difficult portion of the marketing strategy. This is because one of the essential elements to reaching a retail food and beverage purchasing audience is that the Company must build a brand affinity with the customer. Bob's Burger Shack will maintain a moderate level of traditional print and media advertising among local channels. These promotional campaigns will provide customers with coupons and special savings deals that will entice consumers to come to the Company's location.

Prior to opening the Company's location, Management intends to send mailing and circulars to local residents within the target market so that the business has instant traffic and visibility upon its grand opening. Every mailing undertaken by the business will include a coupon.

As stated earlier, the business will also heavily benefit from the high visibility location which Mr. Bergeon is currently sourcing. Management anticipates that a vast majority of the Company's revenues will come from passers-by and shoppers.

5.3 Pricing

The Company intends to price its food products between $1.50 to $3.50 per hamburger, hot dog, ice cream, or beverage. Management anticipates gross margins of approximately 80% on each dollar generated.

6.0 ORGANIZATIONAL PLAN AND PERSONNEL SUMMARY

6.1 Corporate Organization

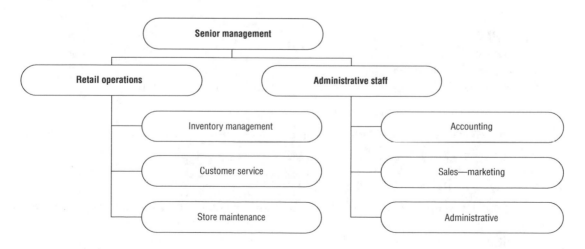

6.2 Organizational Budget

Personnel plan—yearly

Year	1	2	3
Owner	$ 35,000	$ 36,050	$ 37,132
Store manager	$ 29,000	$ 29,870	$ 30,766
Customer service	$ 46,500	$ 47,895	$ 49,332
Bookkeeper (P/T)	$ 12,500	$ 12,875	$ 13,261
Administrative	$ 22,000	$ 22,660	$ 23,340
Total	**$145,000**	**$149,350**	**$153,831**

Numbers of personnel

Year	1	2	3
Owner	1	1	1
Store manager	1	1	1
Customer service	3	3	3
Bookkeeper (P/T)	1	1	1
Administrative	1	1	1
Totals	**7**	**7**	**7**

Personnel expense breakdown

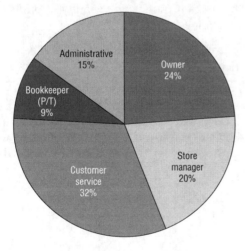

7.0 FINANCIAL PLAN

7.1 Underlying Assumptions

The Company has based its proforma financial statements on the following:

- Bob's Burger Shack will have an annual revenue growth rate of 10% per year.

- The Owner will acquire $50,000 of debt funds to develop the business.

- The loan will have a 10 year term with a 9% interest rate.

7.2 Sensitivity Analysis

The Company's revenues are somewhat sensitive to the overall conditions of the economy. During times of economic recession, the Company may have a decrease in its top line revenues as people will demand fewer beverages/food products from retail locations. However, the Company's revenues provide high levels of operating income for the business, and Bob's Burger Shack would need to have a significant decrease in its top line income before the Company becomes unprofitable.

7.3 Source of Funds

Financing

Equity contributions	
Management investment	$ 10,000.00
Total equity financing	**$10,000.00**
Banks and lenders	
Banks and lenders	$ 50,000.00
Total debt financing	**$50,000.00**
Total financing	**$60,000.00**

7.4 General Assumptions

General assumptions

Year	1	2	3
Short term interest rate	9.5%	9.5%	9.5%
Long term interest rate	10.0%	10.0%	10.0%
Federal tax rate	33.0%	33.0%	33.0%
State tax rate	5.0%	5.0%	5.0%
Personnel taxes	15.0%	15.0%	15.0%

7.5 Profit and Loss Statements

Proforma profit and loss (yearly)

Year	1	2	3
Sales	**$430,122**	**$473,134**	**$520,448**
Cost of goods sold	$ 86,024	$ 94,627	$104,090
Gross margin	80.00%	80.00%	80.00%
Operating income	**$344,098**	**$378,507**	**$416,358**
Expenses			
Payroll	$145,000	$149,350	$153,831
General and administrative	$ 13,200	$ 13,728	$ 14,277
Marketing expenses	$ 4,301	$ 4,731	$ 5,204
Professional fees and licensure	$ 5,219	$ 5,376	$ 5,537
Insurance costs	$ 5,987	$ 6,286	$ 6,601
Travel and vehicle costs	$ 7,596	$ 8,356	$ 9,191
Rent and utilities	$ 14,250	$ 14,963	$ 15,711
Miscellaneous costs	$ 2,151	$ 2,366	$ 2,602
Payroll taxes	$ 21,750	$ 22,403	$ 23,075
Total operating costs	**$219,454**	**$227,558**	**$236,028**
EBITDA	**$124,644**	**$150,950**	**$180,330**
Federal income tax	$ 41,132	$ 47,130	$ 57,044
State income tax	$ 6,232	$ 7,141	$ 8,643
Interest expense	$ 8,738	$ 8,131	$ 7,468
Depreciation expenses	$ 4,107	$ 4,107	$ 4,107
Net profit	**$ 64,434**	**$ 84,440**	**$103,067**
Profit margin	**14.98%**	**17.85%**	**19.80%**

Sales, operating costs, and profit forecast

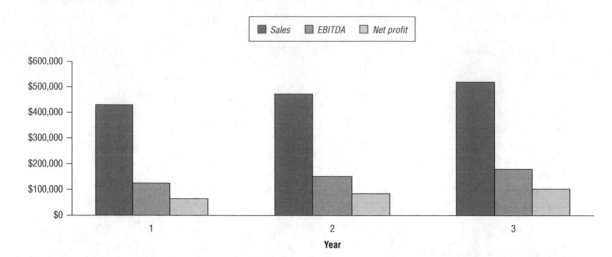

7.6 Cash Flow Analysis

Proforma cash flow analysis—yearly

Year	1	2	3
Cash from operations	$ 72,910	$ 91,068	$109,489
Cash from receivables	$ 0	$ 0	$ 0
Operating cash inflow	**$ 72,910**	**$ 91,068**	**$109,489**
Other cash inflows			
Equity investment	$ 10,000	$ 0	$ 0
Increased borrowings	$ 50,000	$ 0	$ 0
Sales of business assets	$ 0	$ 0	$ 0
A/P increases	$ 37,902	$ 43,587	$ 50,125
Total other cash inflows	**$ 97,902**	**$ 43,587**	**$ 50,125**
Total cash inflow	**$170,812**	**$134,655**	**$159,615**
Cash outflows			
Repayment of principal	$ 3,232	$ 3,535	$ 3,866
A/P decreases	$ 24,897	$ 29,876	$ 35,852
A/R increases	$ 0	$ 0	$ 0
Asset purchases	$ 32,000	$ 22,767	$ 27,372
Dividends	$ 51,037	$ 63,748	$ 76,643
Total cash outflows	**$111,166**	**$119,926**	**$143,733**
Net cash flow	**$ 59,646**	**$ 14,729**	**$ 15,882**
Cash balance	**$ 59,646**	**$ 74,376**	**$ 90,258**

Proforma cash flow (yearly)

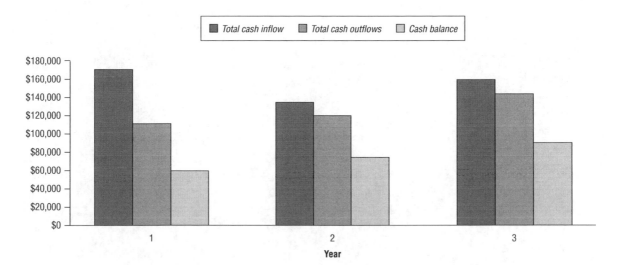

7.7 Balance Sheet

Proforma balance sheet—yearly

Year	1	2	3
Assets			
Cash	$59,646	$ 74,376	$ 90,258
Amortized development/expansion costs	$ 9,500	$ 16,330	$ 19,067
Burger stand equipment	$10,000	$ 15,602	$ 22,535
FF&E	$12,500	$ 22,745	$ 35,063
Accumulated depreciation	($ 2,286)	($ 4,571)	($ 6,857)
Total assets	**$89,361**	**$124,571**	**$160,065**
Liabilities and equity			
Accounts payable	$13,005	$ 26,716	$ 40,990
Long term liabilities	$46,768	$ 43,233	$ 39,699
Other liabilities	$ 0	$ 0	$ 0
Total liabilities	**$59,773**	**$ 69,949**	**$ 80,688**
Net worth	**$29,587**	**$ 54,622**	**$ 79,377**
Total liabilities and equity	**$89,361**	**$124,571**	**$160,065**

Proforma balance sheet

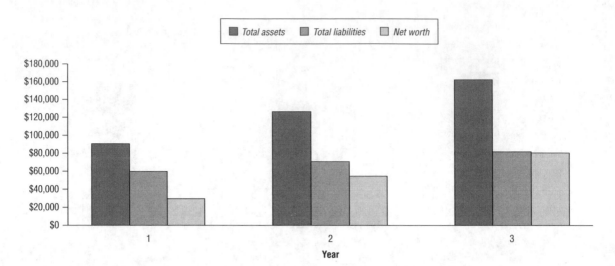

7.8 Breakeven Analysis

Monthly break even analysis

Year	1	2	3
Monthly revenue	$ 22,860	$ 23,704	$ 24,586
Yearly revenue	$274,317	$284,447	$295,035

Break even analysis

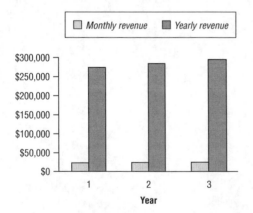

7.9 Business Ratios

Business ratios—yearly

Year	1	2	3
Sales			
Sales growth	0.00%	10.00%	10.00%
Gross margin	80.00%	80.00%	80.00%
Financials			
Profit margin	14.98%	17.85%	19.80%
Assets to liabilities	1.25	1.43	1.59
Equity to liabilities	0.25	0.43	0.59
Assets to equity	5.03	3.31	2.70
Liquidity			
Acid test	0.75	0.80	0.85
Cash to assets	0.60	0.56	0.54

7.10 Three Year Profit and Loss Statement

Profit and loss statement (first year)

Months	1	2	3	4	5	6	7
Sales	$26,600	$26,733	$26,866	$26,999	$39,900	$49,875	$53,200
Cost of goods sold	$ 5,320	$ 5,347	$ 5,373	$ 5,400	$ 7,980	$ 9,975	$10,640
Gross margin	80.00%	80.00%	80.00%	80.00%	80.00%	80.00%	80.00%
Operating income	$21,280	$21,386	$21,493	$21,599	$31,920	$39,900	$42,560
Expenses							
Payroll	$12,083	$12,083	$12,083	$12,083	$12,083	$12,083	$12,083
General and administrative	$ 1,100	$ 1,100	$ 1,100	$ 1,100	$ 1,100	$ 1,100	$ 1,100
Marketing expenses	$ 358	$ 358	$ 358	$ 358	$ 358	$ 358	$ 358
Professional fees and licensure	$ 435	$ 435	$ 435	$ 435	$ 435	$ 435	$ 435
Insurance costs	$ 499	$ 499	$ 499	$ 499	$ 499	$ 499	$ 499
Travel and vehicle costs	$ 633	$ 633	$ 633	$ 633	$ 633	$ 633	$ 633
Rent and utilities	$ 1,188	$ 1,188	$ 1,188	$ 1,188	$ 1,188	$ 1,188	$ 1,188
Miscellaneous costs	$ 179	$ 179	$ 179	$ 179	$ 179	$ 179	$ 179
Payroll taxes	$ 1,813	$ 1,813	$ 1,813	$ 1,813	$ 1,813	$ 1,813	$ 1,813
Total operating costs	$18,288	$18,288	$18,288	$18,288	$18,288	$18,288	$18,288
EDITDA	$ 2,992	$ 3,099	$ 3,205	$ 3,311	$13,632	$21,612	$24,272
Federal income tax	$ 2,544	$ 2,556	$ 2,569	$ 2,582	$ 3,816	$ 4,770	$ 5,088
State income tax	$ 385	$ 387	$ 389	$ 391	$ 578	$ 723	$ 771
Interest expense	$ 750	$ 746	$ 742	$ 730	$ 734	$ 730	$ 726
Depreciation expense	$ 342	$ 342	$ 342	$ 342	$ 342	$ 342	$ 342
Net profit	−$ 1,029	−$ 934	−$ 838	−$ 742	$ 8,162	$15,047	$17,345

Profit and loss statement (first year cont.)

Month	8	9	10	11	12	1
Sales	$56,525	$43,225	$26,600	$26,733	$26,866	$430,122
Cost of goods sold	$11,305	$ 8,645	$ 5,320	$ 5,347	$ 5,373	$ 86,024
Gross margin	80.0%	80.0%	80.0%	80.0%	80.0%	80.0%
Operating income	**$45,220**	**$34,580**	**$21,280**	**$21,386**	**$21,493**	**$344,098**
Expenses						
Payroll	$12,083	$12,083	$12,083	$12,083	$12,083	$145,000
General and administrative	$ 1,100	$ 1,100	$ 1,100	$ 1,100	$ 1,100	$ 13,200
Marketing expenses	$ 358	$ 358	$ 358	$ 358	$ 358	$ 4,301
Professional fees and licensure	$ 435	$ 435	$ 435	$ 435	$ 435	$ 5,219
Insurance costs	$ 499	$ 499	$ 499	$ 499	$ 499	$ 5,987
Travel and vehicle costs	$ 633	$ 633	$ 633	$ 633	$ 633	$ 7,596
Rent and utilities	$ 1,188	$ 1,188	$ 1,188	$ 1,188	$ 1,188	$ 14,250
Miscellaneous costs	$ 179	$ 179	$ 179	$ 179	$ 179	$ 2,151
Payroll taxes	$ 1,813	$ 1,813	$ 1,813	$ 1,813	$ 1,813	$ 21,750
Total operating costs	**$18,288**	**$18,288**	**$18,288**	**$18,288**	**$18,288**	**$219,454**
EBITDA	**$26,932**	**$16,292**	**$ 2,992**	**$ 3,099**	**$ 3,205**	**$124,644**
Federal income tax	$ 5,405	$ 4,134	$ 2,544	$ 2,556	$ 2,569	$ 41,132
State income tax	$ 819	$ 626	$ 385	$ 387	$ 389	$ 6,232
Interest expense	$ 722	$ 718	$ 714	$ 710	$ 706	$ 8,738
Depreciation expense	$ 342	$ 342	$ 342	$ 342	$ 342	$ 4,107
Net profit	**$19,643**	**$10,472**	**−$ 993**	**−$ 897**	**−$ 801**	**$ 64,434**

Profit and loss statement (second year)

Quarter	Q1	2 Q2	Q3	Q4	2
Sales	$94,627	$118,284	$127,746	$132,478	$473,134
Cost of goods sold	$18,925	$ 23,657	$ 25,549	$ 26,496	$ 94,627
Gross margin	80.0%	80.0%	80.0%	80.0%	80.0%
Operating income	**$75,701**	**$ 94,627**	**$102,197**	**$105,982**	**$378,507**
Expenses					
Payroll	$29,870	$ 37,338	$ 40,325	$ 41,818	$149,350
General and administrative	$ 2,746	$ 3,432	$ 3,707	$ 3,844	$ 13,728
Marketing expenses	$ 946	$ 1,183	$ 1,277	$ 1,325	$ 4,731
Professional fees and licensure	$ 1,075	$ 1,344	$ 1,451	$ 1,505	$ 5,376
Insurance costs	$ 1,257	$ 1,572	$ 1,697	$ 1,760	$ 6,286
Travel and vehicle costs	$ 1,671	$ 2,089	$ 2,256	$ 2,340	$ 8,356
Rent and utilities	$ 2,993	$ 3,741	$ 4,040	$ 4,190	$ 14,963
Miscellaneous costs	$ 473	$ 591	$ 639	$ 662	$ 2,366
Payroll taxes	$ 4,481	$ 5,601	$ 6,049	$ 6,273	$ 22,403
Total operating costs	**$45,512**	**$ 56,889**	**$ 61,441**	**$ 63,716**	**$227,558**
EBITDA	**$30,190**	**$ 37,737**	**$ 40,756**	**$ 42,266**	**$150,950**
Federal income tax	$ 9,426	$ 11,783	$ 12,725	$ 13,196	$ 47,130
State income tax	$ 1,428	$ 1,785	$ 1,928	$ 1,999	$ 7,141
Interest expense	$ 2,092	$ 2,053	$ 2,013	$ 1,973	$ 8,131
Depreciation expense	$ 1,027	$ 1,027	$ 1,027	$ 1,027	$ 4,107
Net profit	**$16,217**	**$ 21,090**	**$ 23,063**	**$ 24,070**	**$ 84,440**

Profit and loss statement (third year)

Quarter	Q1	3 Q2	Q3	Q4	3
Sales	$104,090	$130,112	$140,521	$145,725	$520,448
Cost of goods sold	$ 20,818	$ 26,022	$ 28,104	$ 29,145	$104,090
Gross margin	80.0%	80.0%	80.0%	80.0%	80.0%
Operating income	$ 83,272	$104,090	$112,417	$116,580	$416,358
Expenses					
Payroll	$ 30,766	$ 38,458	$ 41,534	$ 43,073	$153,831
General and administrative	$ 2,855	$ 3,569	$ 3,855	$ 3,998	$ 14,277
Marketing expenses	$ 1,041	$ 1,301	$ 1,405	$ 1,457	$ 5,204
Professional fees and licensure	$ 1,107	$ 1,384	$ 1,495	$ 1,550	$ 5,537
Insurance costs	$ 1,320	$ 1,650	$ 1,782	$ 1,848	$ 6,601
Travel and vehicle costs	$ 1,838	$ 2,298	$ 2,482	$ 2,574	$ 9,191
Rent and utilities	$ 3,142	$ 3,928	$ 4,242	$ 4,399	$ 15,711
Miscellaneous costs	$ 520	$ 651	$ 703	$ 729	$ 2,602
Payroll taxes	$ 4,615	$ 5,769	$ 6,230	$ 6,461	$ 23,075
Total operating costs	$ 47,206	$ 59,007	$ 63,728	$ 66,088	$236,028
EBITDA	$ 36,066	$ 45,082	$ 48,689	$ 50,492	$180,330
Federal income tax	$ 11,409	$ 14,261	$ 15,402	$ 15,972	$ 57,044
State income tax	$ 1,729	$ 2,161	$ 2,334	$ 2,420	$ 8,643
Interest expense	$ 1,932	$ 1,889	$ 1,846	$ 1,802	$ 7,468
Depreciation expense	$ 1,027	$ 1,027	$ 1,027	$ 1,027	$ 4,107
Net profit	$ 19,970	$ 25,745	$ 28,081	$ 29,272	$103,067

7.11 Three Year Cash Flow Analysis

Cash flow analysis (first year)

Month	1	2	3	4	5	6	7
Cash from operations	−$ 312	−$ 218	−$ 125	−$ 31	$ 8,871	$15,755	$18,051
Cash from receivables	$ 0	$ 0	$ 0	$ 0	$ 0	$ 0	$ 0
Operating cash inflow	−$ 312	−$ 218	−$ 125	−$ 31	$ 8,871	$15,755	$18,051
Other cash inflows							
Equity investment	$10,000	$ 0	$ 0	$ 0	$ 0	$ 0	$ 0
Increased borrowings	$50,000	$ 0	$ 0	$ 0	$ 0	$ 0	$ 0
Sales of business assets	$ 0	$ 0	$ 0	$ 0	$ 0	$ 0	$ 0
A/P increases	$ 3,159	$ 3,159	$ 3,159	$ 3,159	$ 3,159	$ 3,159	$ 3,159
Total other cash inflows	$63,159	$ 3,159	$ 3,159	$ 3,159	$ 3,159	$ 3,159	$ 3,159
Total cash inflow	$62,847	$ 2,940	$ 3,034	$ 3,128	$12,030	$18,913	$21,209
Cash outflows							
Repayment of principal	$ 258	$ 260	$ 262	$ 264	$ 266	$ 268	$ 270
A/P decreases	$ 2,075	$ 2,075	$ 2,075	$ 2,075	$ 2,075	$ 2,075	$ 2,075
A/R increases	$ 0	$ 0	$ 0	$ 0	$ 0	$ 0	$ 0
Asset purchases	$32,000	$ 0	$ 0	$ 0	$ 0	$ 0	$ 0
Dividends	$ 0	$ 0	$ 0	$ 0	$ 0	$ 0	$ 0
Total cash outflows	$34,333	$ 2,335	$ 2,337	$ 2,339	$ 2,341	$ 2,343	$ 2,345
Net cash flow	$28,513	$ 605	$ 697	$ 789	$ 9,689	$16,570	$18,864
Cash balance	$28,513	$29,119	$29,815	$30,604	$40,293	$56,863	$75,727

Cash flow analysis (first year cont.)

Month	8	9	10	11	12	1
Cash from operations	$20,347	$ 11,173	−$ 294	−$ 200	−$ 106	$ 72,910
Cash from receivables	$ 0	$ 0	$ 0	$ 0	$ 0	$ 0
Operating cash inflow	**$20,347**	**$ 11,173**	**−$ 294**	**−$ 200**	**−$ 106**	**$ 72,910**
Other cash inflows						
Equity investment	$ 0	$ 0	$ 0	$ 0	$ 0	$ 10,000
Increased borrowings	$ 0	$ 0	$ 0	$ 0	$ 0	$ 50,000
Sales of business assets	$ 0	$ 0	$ 0	$ 0	$ 0	$ 0
A/P increases	$ 3,159	$ 3,159	$ 3,159	$ 3,159	$ 3,159	$ 37,902
Total other cash inflows	**$ 3,159**	**$ 3,159**	**$ 3,159**	**$ 3,159**	**$ 3,159**	**$ 97,902**
Total cash inflow	**$23,505**	**$ 14,332**	**$ 2,864**	**$ 2,958**	**$ 3,052**	**$170,812**
Cash outflows						
Repayment of principal	$ 272	$ 273	$ 276	$ 278	$ 281	$ 3,232
A/P decreases	$ 2,075	$ 2,075	$ 2,075	$ 2,075	$ 2,075	$ 24,897
A/R increases	$ 0	$ 0	$ 0	$ 0	$ 0	$ 0
Asset purchases	$ 0	$ 0	$ 0	$ 0	$ 0	$ 32,000
Dividends	$ 0	$ 0	$ 0	$ 0	$51,037	$ 51,037
Total cash outflows	**$ 2,347**	**$ 2,348**	**$ 2,351**	**$ 2,353**	**$53,392**	**$111,166**
Net cash flow	**$21,158**	**$ 11,984**	**$ 513**	**$ 605**	**−$50,340**	**$ 59,646**
Cash balance	**$96,886**	**$108,869**	**$109,383**	**$109,988**	**$59,648**	**$ 59,646**

Cash flow analysis (second year)

Quarter	Q1	2 Q2	Q3	Q4	2
Cash from operations	$18,214	$22,767	$24,588	$25,499	$ 91,068
Cash from receivables	$ 0	$ 0	$ 0	$ 0	$ 0
Operating cash inflow	**$18,214**	**$22,767**	**$24,588**	**$25,499**	**$ 91,068**
Other cash inflows					
Equity investment	$ 0	$ 0	$ 0	$ 0	$ 0
Increased borrowings	$ 0	$ 0	$ 0	$ 0	$ 0
Sales of business assets	$ 0	$ 0	$ 0	$ 0	$ 0
A/P increases	$ 8,717	$10,897	$11,769	$12,204	$ 43,587
Total other cash inflows	**$ 8,717**	**$10,897**	**$11,769**	**$12,204**	**$ 43,587**
Total cash inflow	**$26,931**	**$33,664**	**$36,357**	**$37,704**	**$134,655**
Cash outflows					
Repayment of principal	$ 854	$ 874	$ 893	$ 914	$ 3,535
A/P decreases	$ 5,975	$ 7,469	$ 8,067	$ 8,365	$ 29,876
A/R increases	$ 0	$ 0	$ 0	$ 0	$ 0
Asset purchases	$ 4,553	$ 5,692	$ 6,147	$ 6,375	$ 22,767
Dividends	$12,750	$15,937	$17,212	$17,849	$ 63,748
Total cash outflows	**$24,132**	**$29,971**	**$32,319**	**$33,503**	**$119,926**
Net cash flow	**$ 2,799**	**$ 3,692**	**$ 4,038**	**$ 4,200**	**$ 14,729**
Cash balance	**$62,445**	**$66,138**	**$70,175**	**$74,376**	**$ 74,376**

Cash flow analysis (third year)

Quarter	Q1	Q2	Q3	Q4	3
Cash from operations	$21,898	$27,372	$29,562	$30,657	$109,489
Cash from receivables	$ 0	$ 0	$ 0	$ 0	$ 0
Operating cash inflow	**$21,898**	**$27,372**	**$29,562**	**$30,657**	**$109,489**
Other cash inflows					
Equity investment	$ 0	$ 0	$ 0	$ 0	$ 0
Increased borrowings	$ 0	$ 0	$ 0	$ 0	$ 0
Sales of business assets	$ 0	$ 0	$ 0	$ 0	$ 0
A/P increases	$10,025	$12,531	$13,534	$14,035	$ 50,125
Total other cash inflows	**$10,025**	**$12,531**	**$13,534**	**$14,035**	**$ 50,125**
Total cash inflow	**$31,923**	**$39,904**	**$43,096**	**$44,692**	**$159,615**
Cash outflows					
Repayment of principal	$ 934	$ 956	$ 977	$ 999	$ 3,866
A/P decreases	$ 7,170	$ 8,963	$ 9,680	$10,038	$ 35,852
A/R increases	$ 0	$ 0	$ 0	$ 0	$ 0
Asset purchases	$ 5,474	$ 6,843	$ 7,391	$ 7,664	$ 27,372
Dividends	$15,329	$19,161	$20,693	$21,460	$ 76,643
Total cash outflows	**$28,908**	**$35,922**	**$38,741**	**$40,162**	**$143,733**
Net cash flow	**$ 3,015**	**$ 3,982**	**$ 4,355**	**$ 4,530**	**$ 15,882**
Cash balance	**$77,391**	**$81,373**	**$85,727**	**$90,258**	**$ 90,258**

Church

New Beginnings Ministry

6600 Second St.
Middletown, New York 10940

BizPlanDB.com

The purpose of this business plan is to raise $250,000 for the development of a religious church, New Beginnings Ministry.

1.0 EXECUTIVE SUMMARY

The purpose of this business plan is to raise $250,000 for the development of a religious church while showcasing the expected financials and operations over the next three years. New Beginnings Ministry is a New York based 501(c)(3) corporation that will provide religious services and activities within the target market. New Beginnings Ministry was founded by Mark Sikes.

1.1 New Beginnings Ministry

As stated above, New Beginnings Ministry will render religious services on a daily basis. The business intends to have a congregation of approximately 500 individuals and families within the target market.

New Beginnings Ministry will generate revenues from ongoing donations from its congregation.

The third section of the business plan will further describe the operations offered by New Beginnings Ministry.

1.2 Financing

New Beginnings Ministry intends that the first round of capital will come as a sponsorship grant for $250,000, which will be used to launch New Beginnings Ministry. As the organization is a non-stock corporation, no equity position or distribution of EBITDA income will be distributed to any party that provides capital for New Beginnings Ministry. After immediately receiving the capital infusion, the Foundation will establish its church location and begin to hold religious services and religious tutelage. The initial funds will be used for the following:

- Establishment of the 501(c)(3) entity.

- Financing for the initial capital to develop the facility.

- General working capital for New Beginnings Ministry.

The second section of the business plan will further document the initial uses of the grant/sponsorship funds.

17

1.3 Mission Statement

New Beginnings Ministry's mission is to provide enlightening religious services to the congregation in the target market.

1.4 Management Team

New Beginnings Ministry was founded by Mark Sikes. Mr. Sikes has more than 10 years of experience as a member of the clergy. Through his expertise, he will be able to bring the operations of the business to profitability within its first year of operations.

1.5 Sales Forecasts

Mr. Sikes expects a strong rate of growth at the start of operations. Below are the expected financials over the next three years.

Revenues and income statement (yearly)

Year	1	2	3
Sales	$1,046,304	$1,255,565	$1,469,011
Operating costs	$ 585,689	$ 691,309	$ 750,907
EBITDA	$ 174,335	$ 220,719	$ 316,166
Taxes, interest, and depreciation	$ 5,893	$ 5,893	$ 5,893
Net income	$ 168,442	$ 214,826	$ 310,273

Sales, operating costs, and profit forecast

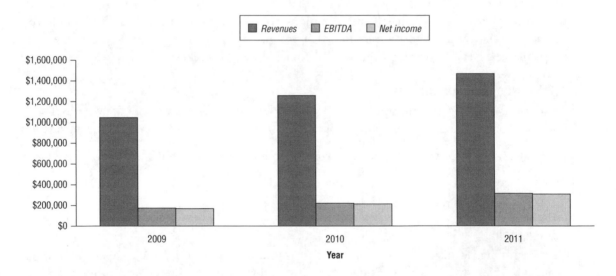

1.6 Expansion Plan

The Founder expects that the business will aggressively expand during the first three years of operation. Mr. Sikes intends to implement marketing campaigns that will effectively target individuals that will become members of the congregation.

2.0 COMPANY AND FINANCING SUMMARY

2.1 Registered Name and Corporate Structure

New Beginnings Ministry is registered as a 501(c)(3) corporation in the State of New York.

2.2 Required Funds

At this time, New Beginnings Ministry requires $250,000 of grant or sponsorship funds. Below is a breakdown of how these funds will be used:

Projected startup costs

Leasehold improvements	$ 35,000
Working capital	$ 65,000
FF&E	$ 15,000
Lease deposits	$ 5,000
Registration fees and licensure	$ 10,000
Initial marketing budget	$ 15,000
Church literature materials	$ 7,500
Initial funds for church operations	$ 92,500
Miscellaneous development costs	$ 5,000
Total startup costs	**$250,000**

Use of funds

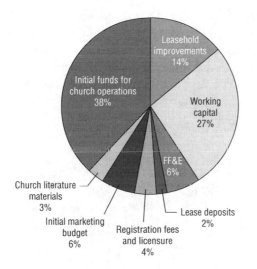

2.3 Investor Equity

Because the business is a non-stock corporation, no formal ownership will be held by donors, Management, or corporate sponsors.

2.4 Management Equity

The non-stock corporation exists as its own entity. Management will retain no formal equity interest in the corporation.

2.5 Exit Strategy

In the event that Church wishes to cease operations, the Management will file the appropriate articles of dissolution, and the assets of the Foundation will be liquidated and granted to other charitable organizations.

3.0 CHURCH SERVICES

As stated in the executive summary, New Beginnings Ministry will provide a broad array of religious services and tutelage to families and individuals that are members of the congregation.

In regards to revenues, New Beginnings Ministry will generate income from the ongoing donations collected from members as well as other forms of revenue, including but not limited to:

- Sales of Bibles

- Banquet Events

- Bake Sales

- Specific Donation Programs

4.0 STRATEGIC AND MARKET ANALYSIS

4.1 Economic Outlook

This section of the analysis will detail the economic climate, the not for profit organization industry (which includes religious organizations), the demographic profile, and the competition that the business will face as it progresses through its business operations.

Presently, the economic market condition in the United States is moderate. The meltdown of the sub prime mortgage market coupled with increasing gas prices has led many people to believe that the US is on the cusp of a potential double dip economic recession. This slowdown in the economy has also greatly impacted real estate sales, which has halted to historical lows. This downturn in the economy may lead to fewer donations and sponsorships for New Beginnings Ministry as consumers and corporations will have less discretionary income and profits for distribution to religious based causes and institutions.

4.2 Industry Analysis

Last year, charitable giving to organized charities totaled more than $245 billion dollars. Charitable giving is a luxury for most people and businesses, and as such, during periods of economic decline, Management expects a severe decrease in the amount of donations made to the Foundation. However, there are tremendous tax benefits that allow charitable giving to have benefits regardless of the overall economic market.

Below are some statistics regarding American charitable organizations:

- The majority of that giving came from individuals, $187.9 billion. Giving by individuals grew by 1.4 percent (when adjusted for inflation).

- Giving by bequest was $19.8 billion, foundations gave $28.8 billion, and corporations donated $12 billion.

- Religious organizations received the most support—$88.3 billion. Much of these contributions can be attributed to people giving to their local place of worship. The next largest sector was education ($33.8 billion). When adjusted for inflation, all but two categories of charities saw increases in contributions. Giving to international affairs groups in 2010 declined by 1.8 percent and giving to human services organizations dropped by 1.1 percent.

4.3 Donor Profile

New Beginnings Ministry expects that the average single donor to the Foundation will be a middle-aged, upper-middle income earning individual that wants to give back to their religious community.

Demographics

- Male or Female

- Aged 35+

• Annual household income exceeding $75,000

• Actively participates in religious activities

4.4 Competition

It is hard to categorize among religious institutions as the nature of competition stems from a congregation's ability to acquire and retain members. There is no true business profit motive among these institutions, but there is a still competition for new congregants. There is a limited supply of the amount of money spent by families and individuals on monthly religious contributions. However, New Beginnings Ministry can use its "competition" to its advantage by seeking to partner with these institutions for sponsorship projects and community events. By co-marketing religious activities, missions, etc, the organization may be able to expose its congregation and church philosophy to other congregations. Additionally, this will assist New Beginnings Ministry in promoting its mission to spread the gospel of Christ.

5.0 MARKETING PLAN

New Beginnings Ministry intends to maintain an extensive marketing campaign that will ensure maximum visibility for the religious services offered in its targeted market. Below is an overview of the marketing strategies and objectives of New Beginnings Ministry.

5.1 Marketing Objectives

• Regularly hold large scale events that will generate publicity and donation revenue for New Beginnings Ministry.

• Establish relationships with not-for-profit organizations within the target market.

5.2 Marketing Strategies

New Beginnings Ministry will solicit donation revenue from multiple sources. New Beginnings Ministry intends to engage a large public relations and marketing firm to raise awareness of the Church's services, tutelage, and not-for-profit activities that seek to benefit the community in a religious sense.

New Beginnings Ministry will conduct several mass mailings several times per year in order to gain continual support from its enrolled congregation in order to expand donation revenues.

Publicity activities will be designed to generate ongoing coverage about New Beginnings Ministry and will be conveyed through an ongoing newsletter that will be drafted by the Church's administration and clergy. This will inform the congregation and the general public of the Church's activities.

5.3 Pricing

As it pertains to pricing for the Church's ongoing activities, the organization will charge flat fees for sales of bibles, sales of memorial pews, and other aspects to the Church's operations. However, donation revenues are subject to the wealth of the individual congregant. The Management of New Beginnings Ministry anticipates gross margins of approximately 73% on each dollar of revenue provided to the organization from its congregants.

6.0 ORGANIZATIONAL PLAN AND PERSONNEL SUMMARY

6.1 Corporate Organization

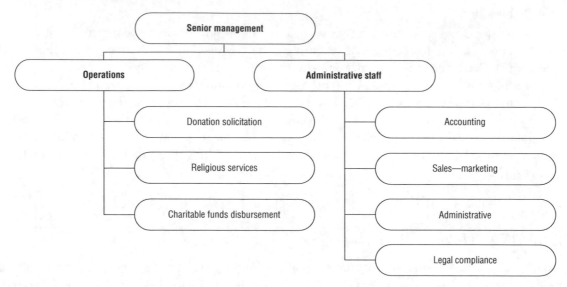

6.2 Organizational Budget

Personnel plan—yearly

Year	1	2	3
Senior management	$ 65,000	$ 66,950	$ 68,959
Clergy	$110,000	$113,300	$116,699
Marketing staff	$ 85,000	$131,325	$135,265
Administrative	$ 84,000	$115,360	$148,526
Accounting	$ 70,000	$ 72,100	$ 74,263
Total	**$414,000**	**$499,035**	**$543,711**

Numbers of personnel

Year	1	2	3
Senior management	1	1	1
Clergy	2	2	2
Marketing staff	2	3	3
Administrative	3	4	5
Accounting	2	2	2
Totals	**10**	**12**	**13**

Personnel expense breakdown

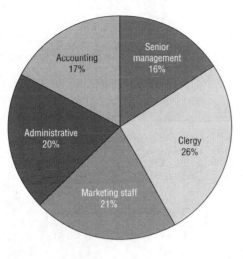

7.0 FINANCIAL PLAN

7.1 Underlying Assumptions

New Beginnings Ministry has based its proforma financial statements on the following:

- New Beginnings Ministry will have an annual revenue growth rate of 14% per year.

- The Foundation will initially be seeded with $250,000 of grant capital.

7.2 Sensitivity Analysis

New Beginnings Ministry's revenues are sensitive to the overall condition of the financial markets. Charitable contributions are a luxury, and as such, during times of economic recession New Beginnings Ministry expects that its incoming contributions will decrease. Management will enact several procedures to ensure that New Beginnings Ministry can survive severe decreases in its charitable revenue.

7.3 Source of Funds

Financing

Equity contributions	
Initial grants	$ 250,000.00
Total equity financing	**$250,000.00**
Banks and lenders	
Total debt financing	**$ 0.00**
Total financing	**$250,000.00**

7.4 General Assumptions

General assumptions

Year	1	2	3
Short term interest rate	9.5%	9.5%	9.5%
Long term interest rate	10.0%	10.0%	10.0%
Federal tax rate	0.0%	0.0%	0.0%
State tax rate	0.0%	0.0%	0.0%
Personnel taxes	15.0%	15.0%	15.0%

7.5 Profit and Loss Statements

Revenues and income statement (yearly)

Year	1	2	3
Revenues	**$1,046,304**	**$1,255,565**	**$1,469,011**
Cost of generating revenues	$ 286,280	$ 343,536	$ 401,938
Gross margin	72.64%	72.64%	72.64%
Operating income	**$ 760,024**	**$ 912,028**	**$1,067,073**
Expenses			
Payroll	$ 414,000	$ 499,035	$ 543,711
General and administrative	$ 25,200	$ 26,208	$ 27,256
Marketing expenses	$ 20,000	$ 21,000	$ 22,050
Professional fees and licensure	$ 8,000	$ 8,240	$ 8,487
Insurance costs	$ 11,987	$ 12,586	$ 13,216
Office expenses	$ 17,596	$ 19,356	$ 21,291
Rent and utilities	$ 14,250	$ 14,963	$ 15,711
Miscellaneous costs	$ 12,556	$ 15,067	$ 17,628
Payroll taxes	$ 62,100	$ 74,855	$ 81,557
Total operating costs	**$ 585,689**	**$ 691,309**	**$ 750,907**
EBITDA	**$ 174,335**	**$ 220,719**	**$ 316,166**
Federal income tax	$ 0	$ 0	$ 0
State income tax	$ 0	$ 0	$ 0
Interest expense	$ 0	$ 0	$ 0
Depreciation expenses	$ 5,893	$ 5,893	$ 5,893
Net income	**$ 168,442**	**$ 214,826**	**$ 310,273**
Net income margin	**16.10%**	**17.11%**	**21.12%**

Sales, operating costs, and profit forecast

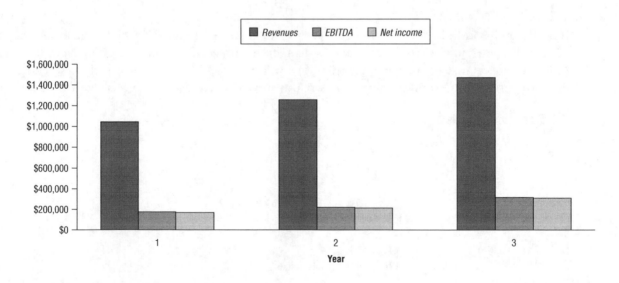

7.6 Cash Flow Analysis

Proforma cash flow analysis—yearly

Year	1	2	3
Cash from operations	$174,335	$220,719	$316,166
Cash from receivables	$ 0	$ 0	$ 0
Operating cash inflow	**$174,335**	**$220,719**	**$316,166**
Other cash inflows			
Equity investment	$250,000	$ 0	$ 0
Increased borrowings	$ 0	$ 0	$ 0
Sales of business assets	$ 0	$ 0	$ 0
A/P increases	$ 37,902	$ 43,587	$ 50,125
Total other cash inflows	**$287,902**	**$ 43,587**	**$ 50,125**
Total cash inflow	**$462,237**	**$264,306**	**$366,291**
Cash outflows			
Repayment of principal	$ 0	$ 0	$ 0
A/P decreases	$ 24,897	$ 29,876	$ 35,852
A/R increases	$ 0	$ 0	$ 0
Asset purchases	$ 82,500	$ 0	$ 0
Charitable disbursements	$132,495	$167,746	$240,286
Total cash outflows	**$239,892**	**$197,623**	**$276,138**
Net cash flow	**$222,345**	**$ 66,683**	**$ 90,154**
Cash balance	**$222,345**	**$289,029**	**$379,182**

Proforma cash flow (yearly)

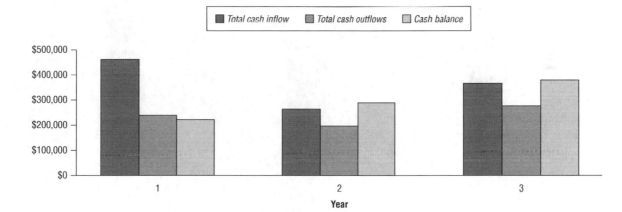

7.7 Balance Sheet

Proforma balance sheet—yearly

Year	1	2	3
Assets			
Cash	$222,345	$289,029	$379,182
Amortized development costs	$ 55,000	$ 55,000	$ 55,000
FF&E	$ 15,000	$ 15,000	$ 15,000
Security deposits	$ 5,000	$ 5,100	$ 5,202
Literature inventory	$ 7,500	$ 7,500	$ 7,500
Accumulated depreciation	($ 5,893)	($ 11,786)	($ 17,679)
Total assets	**$298,953**	**$359,843**	**$444,206**
Liabilities and equity			
Accounts payable	$ 13,005	$ 26,716	$ 40,990
Long term liabilities	$ 0	$ 0	$ 0
Other liabilities	$ 8,200	$ 8,528	$ 8,869
Total liabilities	**$ 21,205**	**$ 35,244**	**$ 49,859**
Net worth	**$277,748**	**$324,599**	**$394,347**
Total liabilities and equity	**$298,953**	**$359,843**	**$444,206**

Proforma balance sheet

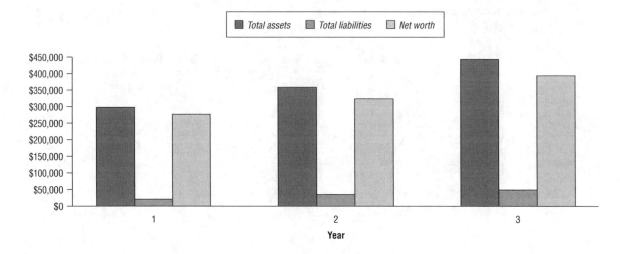

7.8 Breakeven Analysis

Monthly break even analysis

Year	1	2	3
Monthly revenue	$ 67,192	$ 79,309	$ 86,146
Yearly revenue	$806,302	$951,707	$1,033,753

Break even analysis

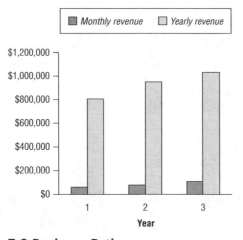

7.9 Business Ratios

Business ratios—yearly

Year	1	2	3
Sales			
Revenue growth	0.00%	20.00%	17.00%
Gross margin	72.60%	72.60%	72.60%
Financials			
Net income margin	16.10%	17.11%	21.12%
Assets to liabilities	14.10	10.21	8.91
Equity to liabilities	13.10	9.21	7.91
Assets to equity	1.08	1.11	1.13
Liquidity			
Acid test	10.49	8.20	7.61
Cash to assets	0.74	0.80	0.85

7.10 Three Year Profit and Loss Statement

Revenues and income statement (first year)

Months	1	2	3	4	5	6	7
Revenues	$86,400	$86,544	$86,688	$86,832	$86,976	$87,120	$87,264
Cost of generating revenues	$23,640	$23,679	$23,719	$23,758	$23,798	$23,837	$23,876
Gross margin	72.6%	72.6%	72.6%	72.6%	72.6%	72.6%	72.6%
Operating income	$62,760	$62,865	$62,969	$63,074	$63,178	$63,283	$63,388
Expenses							
Payroll	$34,500	$34,500	$34,500	$34,500	$34,500	$34,500	$34,500
General and administrative	$ 2,100	$ 2,100	$ 2,100	$ 2,100	$ 2,100	$ 2,100	$ 2,100
Marketing expenses	$ 1,667	$ 1,667	$ 1,667	$ 1,667	$ 1,667	$ 1,667	$ 1,667
Professional fees and licensure	$ 667	$ 667	$ 667	$ 667	$ 667	$ 667	$ 667
Insurance costs	$ 999	$ 999	$ 999	$ 999	$ 999	$ 999	$ 999
Office expenses	$ 1,466	$ 1,466	$ 1,466	$ 1,466	$ 1,466	$ 1,466	$ 1,466
Rent and utilities	$ 1,188	$ 1,188	$ 1,188	$ 1,188	$ 1,188	$ 1,188	$ 1,188
Miscellaneous costs	$ 1,046	$ 1,046	$ 1,046	$ 1,046	$ 1,046	$ 1,046	$ 1,046
Payroll taxes	$ 5,175	$ 5,175	$ 5,175	$ 5,175	$ 5,175	$ 5,175	$ 5,175
Total operating costs	$48,807	$48,807	$48,807	$48,807	$48,807	$48,807	$48,807
EBITDA	$13,953	$14,057	$14,162	$14,266	$14,371	$14,476	$14,580
Federal income tax	$ 0	$ 0	$ 0	$ 0	$ 0	$ 0	$ 0
State income tax	$ 0	$ 0	$ 0	$ 0	$ 0	$ 0	$ 0
Interest expense	$ 0	$ 0	$ 0	$ 0	$ 0	$ 0	$ 0
Depreciation expense	$ 491	$ 491	$ 491	$ 491	$ 491	$ 491	$ 491
Net income	$13,462	$13,566	$13,671	$13,775	$13,880	$13,985	$14,089

Revenues and income statement (first year cont.)

Month	8	9	10	11	12	1
Revenues	**$87,408**	**$87,552**	**$87,696**	**$87,840**	**$87,984**	**$1,046,304**
Cost of generating revenues	$23,916	$23,955	$23,995	$24,034	$24,073	$ 286,280
Gross margin	72.6%	72.6%	72.6%	72.6%	72.6%	72.6%
Operating income	**$63,492**	**$63,597**	**$63,701**	**$63,806**	**$63,911**	**$ 760,024**
Expenses						
Payroll	$34,500	$34,500	$34,500	$34,500	$34,500	$ 414,000
General and administrative	$ 2,100	$ 2,100	$ 2,100	$ 2,100	$ 2,100	$ 25,200
Marketing expenses	$ 1,667	$ 1,667	$ 1,667	$ 1,667	$ 1,667	$ 20,000
Professional fees and licensure	$ 667	$ 667	$ 667	$ 667	$ 667	$ 8,000
Insurance costs	$ 999	$ 999	$ 999	$ 999	$ 999	$ 11,987
Office expenses	$ 1,466	$ 1,466	$ 1,466	$ 1,466	$ 1,466	$ 17,596
Rent and utilities	$ 1,188	$ 1,188	$ 1,188	$ 1,188	$ 1,188	$ 14,250
Miscellaneous costs	$ 1,046	$ 1,046	$ 1,046	$ 1,046	$ 1,046	$ 12,556
Payroll taxes	$ 5,175	$ 5,175	$ 5,175	$ 5,175	$ 5,175	$ 62,100
Total operating costs	**$48,807**	**$48,807**	**$48,807**	**$48,807**	**$48,807**	**$ 585,689**
EBITDA	**$14,685**	**$14,789**	**$14,894**	**$14,999**	**$15,103**	**$ 174,335**
Federal income tax	$ 0	$ 0	$ 0	$ 0	$ 0	$ 0
State income tax	$ 0	$ 0	$ 0	$ 0	$ 0	$ 0
Interest expense	$ 0	$ 0	$ 0	$ 0	$ 0	$ 0
Depreciation expense	$ 491	$ 491	$ 491	$ 491	$ 491	$ 5,893
Net profit	**$14,194**	**$14,298**	**$14,403**	**$14,508**	**$14,612**	**$ 168,442**

Revenues and income statement (second year)

Quarter	Q1	2 Q2	Q3	Q4	2
Revenues	**$251,113**	**$313,891**	**$339,002**	**$351,558**	**$1,255,565**
Cost of generating revenues	$ 68,707	$ 85,884	$ 92,755	$ 96,190	$ 343,536
Gross margin	72.6%	72.6%	72.6%	72.6%	72.6%
Operating income	**$182,406**	**$228,007**	**$246,248**	**$255,368**	**$ 912,028**
Expenses					
Payroll	$ 99,807	$124,759	$134,739	$139,730	$ 499,035
General and administrative	$ 5,242	$ 6,552	$ 7,076	$ 7,338	$ 26,208
Marketing expenses	$ 4,200	$ 5,250	$ 5,670	$ 5,880	$ 21,000
Professional fees and licensure	$ 1,648	$ 2,060	$ 2,225	$ 2,307	$ 8,240
Insurance costs	$ 2,517	$ 3,147	$ 3,398	$ 3,524	$ 12,586
Office expenses	$ 3,871	$ 4,839	$ 5,226	$ 5,420	$ 19,356
Rent and utilities	$ 2,993	$ 3,741	$ 4,040	$ 4,190	$ 14,963
Miscellaneous costs	$ 3,013	$ 3,767	$ 4,068	$ 4,219	$ 15,067
Payroll taxes	$ 14,971	$ 18,714	$ 20,211	$ 20,959	$ 74,855
Total operating costs	**$138,262**	**$172,827**	**$186,654**	**$193,567**	**$ 691,309**
EBITDA	**$ 44,144**	**$ 55,180**	**$ 59,594**	**$ 61,801**	**$ 220,719**
Federal income tax	$ 0	$ 0	$ 0	$ 0	$ 0
State income tax	$ 0	$ 0	$ 0	$ 0	$ 0
Interest expense	$ 0	$ 0	$ 0	$ 0	$ 0
Depreciation expense	$ 1,473	$ 1,473	$ 1,473	$ 1,473	$ 5,893
Net profit	**$ 42,671**	**$ 53,706**	**$ 58,121**	**$ 60,328**	**$ 214,826**

Revenues and income statement (third year)

Quarter	Q1	3 Q2	Q3	Q4	3
Revenues	**$293,802**	**$367,253**	**$396,633**	**$411,323**	**$1,469,011**
Cost of generating revenues	$ 80,388	$100,484	$108,523	$112,543	$ 401,938
Gross margin	72.6%	72.6%	72.6%	72.6%	72.6%
Operating income	**$213,415**	**$266,768**	**$288,110**	**$298,780**	**$1,067,073**
Expenses					
Payroll	$108,742	$135,928	$146,802	$152,239	$ 543,711
General and administrative	$ 5,451	$ 6,814	$ 7,359	$ 7,632	$ 27,256
Marketing expenses	$ 4,410	$ 5,513	$ 5,954	$ 6,174	$ 22,050
Professional fees and licensure	$ 1,697	$ 2,122	$ 2,292	$ 2,376	$ 8,487
Insurance costs	$ 2,643	$ 3,304	$ 3,568	$ 3,700	$ 13,216
Office expenses	$ 4,258	$ 5,323	$ 5,749	$ 5,962	$ 21,291
Rent and utilities	$ 3,142	$ 3,928	$ 4,242	$ 4,399	$ 15,711
Miscellaneous costs	$ 3,526	$ 4,407	$ 4,760	$ 4,936	$ 17,628
Payroll taxes	$ 16,311	$ 20,389	$ 22,020	$ 22,836	$ 81,557
Total operating costs	**$150,181**	**$187,727**	**$202,745**	**$210,254**	**$ 750,907**
EBITDA	**$ 63,233**	**$ 79,042**	**$ 85,365**	**$ 88,527**	**$ 316,166**
Federal income tax	$ 0	$ 0	$ 0	$ 0	$ 0
State income tax	$ 0	$ 0	$ 0	$ 0	$ 0
Interest expense	$ 0	$ 0	$ 0	$ 0	$ 0
Depreciation expense	$ 1,473	$ 1,473	$ 1,473	$ 1,473	$ 5,893
Net profit	**$ 61,760**	**$ 77,568**	**$ 83,892**	**$ 87,053**	**$ 310,273**

7.11 Three Year Cash Flow Analysis

Cash flow analysis (first year)

Month	1	2	3	4	5	6	7
Cash from operations	$ 13,953	$ 14,057	$ 14,162	$ 14,266	$ 14,371	$ 14,476	$ 14,580
Cash from receivables	$ 0	$ 0	$ 0	$ 0	$ 0	$ 0	$ 0
Operating cash inflow	**$ 13,953**	**$ 14,057**	**$ 14,162**	**$ 14,266**	**$ 14,371**	**$ 14,476**	**$ 14,580**
Other cash inflows							
Equity investment	$250,000	$ 0	$ 0	$ 0	$ 0	$ 0	$ 0
Increased borrowings	$ 0	$ 0	$ 0	$ 0	$ 0	$ 0	$ 0
Sales of business assets	$ 0	$ 0	$ 0	$ 0	$ 0	$ 0	$ 0
A/P increases	$ 3,159	$ 3,159	$ 3,159	$ 3,159	$ 3,159	$ 3,159	$ 3,159
Total other cash inflows	**$253,159**	**$ 3,159**	**$ 3,159**	**$ 3,159**	**$ 3,159**	**$ 3,159**	**$ 3,159**
Total cash inflow	**$267,111**	**$ 17,216**	**$ 17,320**	**$ 17,425**	**$ 17,530**	**$ 17,634**	**$ 17,739**
Cash outflows							
Repayment of principal	$ 0	$ 0	$ 0	$ 0	$ 0	$ 0	$ 0
A/P decreases	$ 2,075	$ 2,075	$ 2,075	$ 2,075	$ 2,075	$ 2,075	$ 2,075
A/R increases	$ 0	$ 0	$ 0	$ 0	$ 0	$ 0	$ 0
Asset purchases	$ 82,500	$ 0	$ 0	$ 0	$ 0	$ 0	$ 0
Charitable disbursements	$ 0	$ 0	$ 0	$ 0	$ 0	$ 0	$ 0
Total cash outflows	**$ 84,575**	**$ 2,075**	**$ 2,075**	**$ 2,075**	**$ 2,075**	**$ 2,075**	**$ 2,075**
Net cash flow	**$182,536**	**$ 15,141**	**$ 15,246**	**$ 15,350**	**$ 15,455**	**$ 15,559**	**$ 15,664**
Cash balance	**$182,536**	**$197,677**	**$212,923**	**$228,273**	**$243,728**	**$259,287**	**$274,951**

Cash flow analysis (first year cont.)

Month	8	9	10	11	12	1
Cash from operations	$ 14,685	$ 14,789	$ 14,894	$ 14,999	$ 15,103	$174,335
Cash from receivables	$ 0	$ 0	$ 0	$ 0	$ 0	$ 0
Operating cash inflow	**$ 14,685**	**$ 14,789**	**$ 14,894**	**$ 14,999**	**$ 15,103**	**$174,335**
Other cash inflows						
Equity investment	$ 0	$ 0	$ 0	$ 0	$ 0	$250,000
Increased borrowings	$ 0	$ 0	$ 0	$ 0	$ 0	$ 0
Sales of business assets	$ 0	$ 0	$ 0	$ 0	$ 0	$ 0
A/P increases	$ 3,159	$ 3,159	$ 3,159	$ 3,159	$ 3,159	$ 37,902
Total other cash inflows	**$ 3,159**	**$ 3,159**	**$ 3,159**	**$ 3,159**	**$ 3,159**	**$287,902**
Total cash inflow	**$ 17,843**	**$ 17,948**	**$ 18,053**	**$ 18,157**	**$ 18,262**	**$462,237**
Cash outflows						
Repayment of principal	$ 0	$ 0	$ 0	$ 0	$ 0	$ 0
A/P decreases	$ 2,075	$ 2,075	$ 2,075	$ 2,075	$ 2,075	$ 24,897
A/R increases	$ 0	$ 0	$ 0	$ 0	$ 0	$ 0
Asset purchases	$ 0	$ 0	$ 0	$ 0	$ 0	$ 82,500
Charitable disbursements	$ 0	$ 0	$ 0	$ 0	$132,495	$132,495
Total cash outflows	**$ 2,075**	**$ 2,075**	**$ 2,075**	**$ 2,075**	**$134,570**	**$239,892**
Net cash flow	**$ 15,769**	**$ 15,873**	**$ 15,978**	**$ 16,082**	**$116,308**	**$222,345**
Cash balance	**$290,720**	**$306,593**	**$322,571**	**$338,653**	**$222,345**	**$222,345**

Cash flow analysis (second year)

Quarter	Q1	2 Q2	Q3	Q4	2
Cash from operations	$ 44,144	$ 55,180	$ 59,594	$ 61,801	$220,719
Cash from receivables	$ 0	$ 0	$ 0	$ 0	$ 0
Operating cash inflow	**$ 44,144**	**$ 55,180**	**$ 59,594**	**$ 61,801**	**$220,719**
Other cash inflows						
Equity investment	$ 0	$ 0	$ 0	$ 0	$ 0
Increased borrowings	$ 0	$ 0	$ 0	$ 0	$ 0
Sales of business assets	$ 0	$ 0	$ 0	$ 0	$ 0
A/P increases	$ 8,717	$ 10,897	$ 11,769	$ 12,204	$ 43,587
Total other cash inflows	**$ 8,717**	**$ 10,897**	**$ 11,769**	**$ 12,204**	**$ 43,587**
Total cash inflow	**$ 52,861**	**$ 66,077**	**$ 71,363**	**$ 74,006**	**$264,306**
Cash outflows						
Repayment of principal	$ 0	$ 0	$ 0	$ 0	$ 0
A/P decreases	$ 5,975	$ 7,469	$ 8,067	$ 8,365	$ 29,876
A/R increases	$ 0	$ 0	$ 0	$ 0	$ 0
Asset purchases	$ 0	$ 0	$ 0	$ 0	$ 0
Charitable disbursements	$ 33,549	$ 41,937	$ 45,292	$ 46,969	$167,746
Total cash outflows	**$ 39,525**	**$ 49,406**	**$ 53,358**	**$ 55,334**	**$197,623**
Net cash flow	**$ 13,337**	**$ 16,671**	**$ 18,005**	**$ 18,671**	**$ 66,683**
Cash balance	**$235,682**	**$252,353**	**$270,357**	**$289,029**	**$289,029**

Cash flow analysis (third year)

Quarter	Q1	3 Q2	Q3	Q4	3
Cash from operations	$ 63,233	$ 79,042	$ 85,365	$ 88,527	$316,166
Cash from receivables	$ 0	$ 0	$ 0	$ 0	$0
Operating cash inflow	**$ 63,233**	**$ 79,042**	**$ 85,365**	**$ 88,527**	**$316,166**
Other cash inflows					
Equity investment	$ 0	$ 0	$ 0	$ 0	$ 0
Increased borrowings	$ 0	$ 0	$ 0	$ 0	$ 0
Sales of business assets	$ 0	$ 0	$ 0	$ 0	$ 0
A/P increases	$ 10,025	$ 12,531	$ 13,534	$ 14,035	$ 50,125
Total other cash inflows	**$ 10,025**	**$ 12,531**	**$ 13,534**	**$ 14,035**	**$ 50,125**
Total cash inflow	**$ 73,258**	**$ 91,573**	**$ 98,899**	**$102,562**	**$366,291**
Cash outflows					
Repayment of principal	$ 0	$ 0	$ 0	$ 0	$ 0
A/P decreases	$ 7,170	$ 8,963	$ 9,680	$ 10,038	$ 35,852
A/R increases	$ 0	$ 0	$ 0	$ 0	$ 0
Asset purchases	$ 0	$ 0	$ 0	$ 0	$ 0
Charitable disbursements	$ 48,057	$ 60,072	$ 64,877	$ 67,280	$240,286
Total cash outflows	**$ 55,228**	**$ 69,034**	**$ 74,557**	**$ 77,319**	**$276,138**
Net cash flow	**$ 18,031**	**$ 22,538**	**$ 24,341**	**$ 25,243**	**$ 90,154**
Cash balance	**$307,060**	**$329,598**	**$353,939**	**$379,182**	**$379,182**

Commercial Diving Service

Working Diver & Marine Services

3600 Lake Rd.
Grosse Ile, Michigan 48138

BizPlanDB.com

Working Diver & Marine Services will provide commercial diving services to companies within the Michigan market. These services include ship husbandry, salvage, repairs, and plant removal.

1.0 EXECUTIVE SUMMARY

The purpose of this business plan is to raise $400,000 for the development of a commercial diving business while showcasing the expected financials and operations over the next three years. Working Diver & Marine Services, Inc. is a Michigan-based corporation that will provide a number of commercial diving services. The Company was founded by Mike Cleaver.

1.1 The Services

The business will provide commercial diving services to companies within the Michigan market. These services include ship husbandry, salvage, repairs, and plant removal.

Working Diver & Marine Services will also frequently work with municipal agencies, state agencies, and private contractors as it relates to underwater construction and maintenance of large scale underwater structures.

The third section of the business plan will further describe the services offered by the Working Diver & Marine Services.

1.2 Financing

Mr. Cleaver is seeking to raise $400,000 from a bank loan. The interest rate and loan agreement are to be further discussed during negotiation. This business plan assumes that the business will receive a 10 year loan with a 9% fixed interest rate. The financing will be used for the following:

- Development of the Company's office location.
- Financing for the first six months of operation.
- Capital to purchase FF&E and equipment associated with the Company's operations.

Mr. Cleaver will contribute $100,000 to the venture.

1.3 Mission Statement

Working Diver & Marine Services' mission is to provide a broad range of commercial diving and scuba instruction to the general public as well as businesses.

33

1.4 Management Team

Working Diver & Marine Services was founded by Mike Cleaver. Mr. Cleaver has more than 10 years of experience in the commercial diving industry. Through his expertise, he will be able to bring the operations of the business to profitability within its first year of operations.

1.5 Sales Forecasts

Mr. Cleaver expects a strong rate of growth at the start of operations. Below are the expected financials over the next three years.

Proforma profit and loss (yearly)

Year	1	2	3
Sales	$753,000	$828,300	$911,130
Operating costs	$331,787	$346,822	$362,770
EBITDA	$120,013	$150,158	$183,908
Taxes, interest, and depreciation	$110,841	$107,512	$118,692
Net profit	$ 9,172	$ 42,646	$ 65,216

Sales, operating costs, and profit forecast

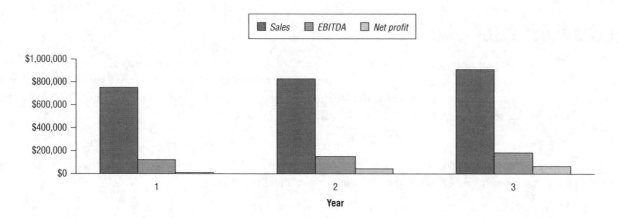

1.6 Expansion Plan

The Founder expects that the business will aggressively expand during the first three years of operation. Mr. Cleaver intends to implement marketing campaigns that will effectively target people and businesses with commercial diving needs within the target market.

2.0 COMPANY AND FINANCING SUMMARY

2.1 Registered Name and Corporate Structure

The Company is registered as a corporation in the State of Michigan.

2.2 Required Funds

At this time, Working Diver & Marine Services, Inc. requires $400,000 of debt funds. Below is a breakdown of how these funds will be used:

Projected startup costs

Land	$150,000
Working capital	$ 40,000
FF&E	$ 50,000
Improvements	$ 15,000
Security deposits	$ 10,000
Insurance	$ 5,000
Diving equipment	$200,000
Marketing budget	$ 20,000
Miscellaneous and unforeseen costs	$ 10,000
Total startup costs	**$500,000**

Use of funds

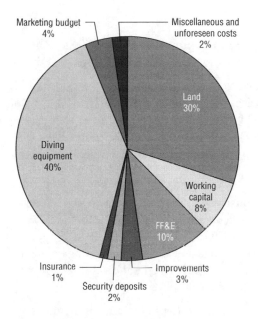

2.3 Investor Equity

Mr. Cleaver is not seeking an investment from a third party at this time.

2.4 Management Equity

Mr. Cleaver owns 100% of Working Diver & Marine Services, Inc.

2.5 Exit Strategy

If the business is very successful, Mr. Cleaver may seek to sell the business to a third party for a significant earnings multiple. Most likely, Working Diver & Marine Services will hire a qualified business broker to sell the business on behalf of Working Diver & Marine Services, Inc. Based on historical numbers, the business could fetch a sales premium of up to 3 to 5 times the previous year's net earnings. The new business owner will need to have the appropriate state licensure in place in order to buy this business from Mr. Cleaver.

3.0 COMMERCIAL DIVING OPERATIONS

Below is an overview of the commercial diving services to be offered by the business:

- Ship Husbandry

- Salvage

- Repairs

- Dredging

- Waterborne Plant Removal

The business, from time to time, will also specialize in providing sheet pile coatings, certified underwater bridge inspection, cathodic protection, underwater steel preservation, sheet pile rehabilitation, heavy underwater construction, and providing certified underwater coating applicators.

Working Diver & Marine Services will charge fees on a per project basis. A discussion pertaining to the Company's pricing will be further discussed in the fifth section of the business plan.

4.0 STRATEGIC AND MARKET ANALYSIS

4.1 Economic Outlook

This section of the analysis will detail the economic climate, the commercial diving industry, the customer profile, and the competition that the business will face as it progresses through its business operations.

Presently the economic market condition in the United States is moderate. The meltdown of the sub prime mortgage market coupled with increasing gas prices has led many people to believe that the US is on the cusp of a double dip economic recession. This slowdown in the economy has also greatly impacted real estate sales, which has halted to historical lows. However, this should have a minimal impact on Working Diver & Marine Services' ability to generate revenues.

4.2 Industry Analysis

In the United States, there are approximately 2,000 businesses that specialize in commercial diving services. Among these businesses, the aggregate revenues generated on a yearly basis exceed $1.8 billion dollars and provides jobs to 20,000 people. Aggregate payrolls for the industry are approximately $200,000,000 per year. The commercial diving industry is a mature business, and Management expects that the continued growth rate of the business will mirror that of the general economy. For each of the last five years, the industry has grown at an average rate of about 2.2%.

Future growth may increase faster than the general economic growth as more individuals purchase boats during their retirement. As such, the business could see significant growth within the next five years as more and more people enter retirement.

4.3 Customer Profile

For businesses and individuals that will require commercial diving, Management has outlined the following demographic:

- Is a Marina or business that requires continuous commercial diving services.

- Annual revenues exceeding $1,000,000 per year.

- Among private boat owners, has an annual household exceeding $250,000.

- Lives or operates within the state of Michigan.

Working Diver & Marine Services may also seek to develop ongoing relationships with municipal agencies that frequently need commercial diving services as it relates to publicly owned underwater constructions. Within the Company's target market, there are at least 10 government agencies that maintain underwater structures or bridges.

4.4 Competition

There are approximately 150 companies within the state of Michigan that provide commercial diving services to marinas, private boat owners, and municipal agencies. Working Diver & Marine Services will need to immediately and aggressively develop direct relationships with private boat owners and marinas so that the business can gain a foothold in this very competitive market. As such, Working Diver & Marine Services should differentiate itself from other competitors by offering cost effective pricing coupled with highly skilled diving services.

5.0 MARKETING PLAN

Working Diver & Marine Services, Inc. intends to maintain an extensive marketing campaign that will ensure maximum visibility for the business in its targeted market. Below is an overview of the marketing strategies and objectives of Working Diver & Marine Services, Inc.

5.1 Marketing Objectives

- Develop ongoing service order relationships with marinas throughout the target market.

- Develop relationships with boat owners and dealers within the targeted Michigan market.

- Develop relationships with municipal agencies that maintain underwater structures.

5.2 Marketing Strategies

Foremost, Management will aggressively develop relationships with boat owners, marinas, and industrial businesses that frequently have a need for commercial diving services. To a certain extent, Management has already developed these relationships with businesses within Michigan.

Management, at the onset of operations, will also seek to develop ongoing relationships with municipal agencies that have frequent needs for commercial diving services. As discussed earlier, due to extremely important maintenance needs, these agencies often provide ongoing service orders to commercial diving service firms.

For large scale construction projects, Mr. Cleaver will frequently bid on contracts that are offered by both government agencies and private contractors. The business will actively work with private contractors in order to ensure that Working Diver & Marine Services is able to generate revenues on a year round basis.

5.3 Pricing

Management expects that Working Diver & Marine Services will charge $75 to $100 per hour for its services. For large projects, such as working on municipal/state owned underwater structures, Management anticipates per project fees of $5,000 to $50,000.

6.0 ORGANIZATIONAL PLAN AND PERSONNEL SUMMARY

6.1 Corporate Organization

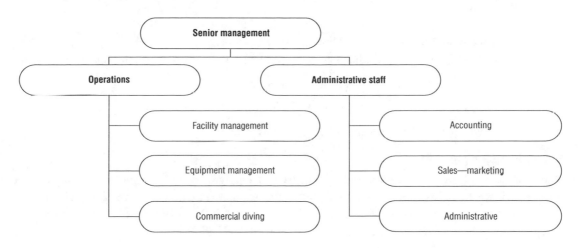

6.2 Organizational Budget

Personnel plan—yearly

Year	1	2	3
Owner	$ 50,000	$ 51,500	$ 53,045
Office manager	$ 35,000	$ 36,050	$ 37,132
Divers	$ 70,000	$ 72,100	$ 74,263
Bookkeeper (P/T)	$ 10,000	$ 10,300	$ 10,609
Administrative	$ 22,500	$ 23,175	$ 23,870
Total	**$187,500**	**$193,125**	**$198,919**

Numbers of personnel

Year	1	2	3
Owner	1	1	1
Office manager	1	1	1
Divers	4	4	4
Bookkeeper (P/T)	1	1	1
Administrative	1	1	1
Totals	**8**	**8**	**8**

Personnel expense breakdown

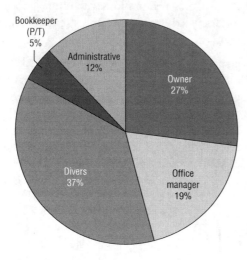

7.0 FINANCIAL PLAN

7.1 Underlying Assumptions

Working Diver & Marine Services has based its proforma financial statements on the following:

- Working Diver & Marine Services, Inc. will have an annual revenue growth rate of 11% per year.

- The Owner will acquire $400,000 of debt funds to develop the business.

- The loan will have a 10 year term with a 9% interest rate.

7.2 Sensitivity Analysis

The Company's revenues are somewhat sensitive to changes in the general economy. The demand among private boat owners for commercial diving services (to maintain their vessels) may decline during an economic recession. However, Working Diver & Marine Services generates strong gross margins which will allow the business to remain profitable and cash flow positive.

7.3 Source of Funds

Financing

Equity contributions

Management Investment	$ 100,000.00
Total equity financing	**$100,000.00**
Banks and lenders	
Banks and lenders	$ 400,000.00
Total debt financing	**$400,000.00**
Total financing	**$500,000.00**

7.4 General Assumptions

General assumptions

Year	1	2	3
Short term interest rate	9.5%	9.5%	9.5%
Long term interest rate	10.0%	10.0%	10.0%
Federal tax rate	33.0%	33.0%	33.0%
State tax rate	5.0%	5.0%	5.0%
Personnel taxes	15.0%	15.0%	15.0%

7.5 Profit and Loss Statements

Proforma profit and loss (yearly)

Year	1	2	3
Sales	**$753,000**	**$828,300**	**$911,130**
Cost of goods sold	$301,200	$331,320	$364,452
Gross margin	60.00%	60.00%	60.00%
Operating income	**$451,800**	**$496,980**	**$546,678**
Expenses			
Payroll	$187,500	$193,125	$198,919
General and administrative	$ 12,500	$ 13,000	$ 13,520
Product distribution expenses	$ 37,650	$ 41,415	$ 45,557
Professional fees and licensure	$ 5,000	$ 5,150	$ 5,305
Insurance costs	$ 14,000	$ 14,700	$ 15,435
Travel and vehicle costs	$ 19,000	$ 20,900	$ 22,990
Utility costs	$ 25,000	$ 26,250	$ 27,563
Miscellaneous costs	$ 3,012	$ 3,313	$ 3,645
Payroll taxes	$ 28,125	$ 28,969	$ 29,838
Total operating costs	**$331,787**	**$346,822**	**$362,770**
EBITDA	**$120,013**	**$150,158**	**$183,908**
Federal income tax	$ 39,604	$ 38,819	$ 50,832
State income tax	$ 6,001	$ 5,882	$ 7,702
Interest expense	$ 34,951	$ 32,526	$ 29,873
Depreciation expenses	$ 30,286	$ 30,286	$ 30,286
Net profit	**$ 9,172**	**$ 42,646**	**$ 65,216**
Profit margin	**1.22%**	**5.15%**	**7.16%**

Sales, operating costs, and profit forecast

Year

7.6 Cash Flow Analysis

Proforma cash flow analysis—yearly

Year	1	2	3
Cash from operations	$ 39,457	$72,932	$ 95,502
Cash from receivables	$ 0	$ 0	$ 0
Operating cash inflow	**$ 39,457**	**$72,932**	**$ 95,502**
Other cash inflows			
Equity investment	$100,000	$ 0	$ 0
Increased borrowings	$400,000	$ 0	$ 0
Sales of business assets	$ 0	$ 0	$ 0
A/P increases	$ 10,000	$11,500	$ 13,225
Total other cash inflows	**$510,000**	**$11,500**	**$ 13,225**
Total cash inflow	**$549,457**	**$84,432**	**$108,727**
Cash outflows			
Repayment of principal	$ 25,854	$28,279	$ 30,932
A/P decreases	$ 9,000	$10,800	$ 12,960
A/R increases	$ 0	$ 0	$ 0
Asset purchases	$471,500	$ 7,293	$ 9,550
Dividends	$ 31,566	$36,466	$ 47,751
Total cash outflows	**$537,919**	**$82,838**	**$101,193**
Net cash flow	**$ 11,538**	**$ 1,594**	**$ 7,534**
Cash balance	**$ 11,538**	**$13,132**	**$ 20,666**

Proforma cash flow (yearly)

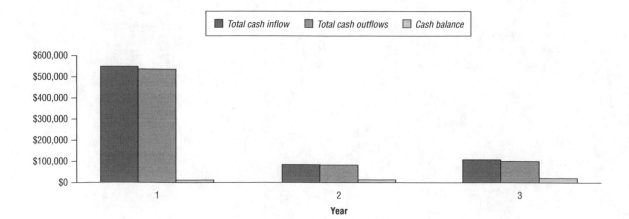

Year

7.7 Balance Sheet

Proforma balance sheet—yearly

Year	1	2	3
Assets			
Cash	$ 11,538	$ 13,132	$ 20,666
Amortized development/expansion costs	$ 40,000	$ 40,729	$ 41,684
Equipment	$175,000	$178,647	$183,422
FF&E	$ 50,000	$ 52,917	$ 56,737
Property	$159,000	$168,540	$178,652
Accumulated depreciation	($ 30,286)	($ 60,571)	($ 90,857)
Total assets	**$405,252**	**$393,394**	**$390,305**
Liabilities and equity			
Accounts payable	$ 1,000	$ 1,700	$ 1,965
Long term liabilities	$374,146	$345,868	$317,589
Other liabilities	$ 0	$ 0	$ 0
Total liabilities	**$375,146**	**$347,568**	**$319,554**
Net worth	**$ 30,106**	**$ 45,826**	**$ 70,751**
Total liabilities and equity	**$405,252**	**$393,394**	**$390,305**

Proforma balance sheet

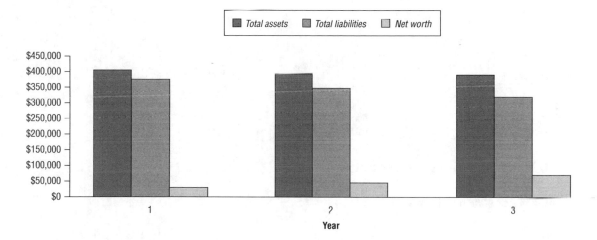

7.8 Breakeven Analysis

Monthly break even analysis

Year	1	2	3
Monthly revenue	$ 46,082	$ 48,170	$ 50,385
Yearly revenue	$552,978	$578,037	$604,616

Break even analysis

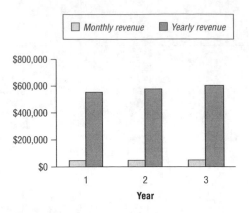

7.9 Business Ratios

Business ratios—yearly

Year	1	2	3
Sales			
Sales growth	0.00%	10.00%	10.00%
Gross margin	60.00%	60.00%	60.00%
Financials			
Profit margin	1.22%	5.15%	7.16%
Assets to liabilities	1.08	1.13	1.22
Equity to liabilities	0.08	0.13	0.22
Assets to equity	13.46	8.58	5.52
Liquidity			
Acid test	0.03	0.04	0.06
Cash to assets	0.03	0.03	0.05

7.10 Three Year Profit and Loss Statement

Profit and loss statement (first year)

Months	1	2	3	4	5	6	7
Sales	**$60,000**	**$60,500**	**$61,000**	**$61,500**	**$62,000**	**$62,500**	**$63,000**
Cost of goods sold	$24,000	$24,200	$24,400	$24,600	$24,800	$25,000	$25,200
Gross margin	60.0%	60.0%	60.0%	60.0%	60.0%	60.0%	60.0%
Operating income	**$36,000**	**$36,300**	**$36,600**	**$36,900**	**$37,200**	**$37,500**	**$37,800**
Expenses							
Payroll	$15,625	$15,625	$15,625	$15,625	$15,625	$15,625	$15,625
General and administrative	$ 1,042	$ 1,042	$ 1,042	$ 1,042	$ 1,042	$ 1,042	$ 1,042
Product distribution expenses	$ 3,138	$ 3,138	$ 3,138	$ 3,138	$ 3,138	$ 3,138	$ 3,138
Professional fees and licensure	$ 417	$ 417	$ 417	$ 417	$ 417	$ 417	$ 417
Insurance costs	$ 1,167	$ 1,167	$ 1,167	$ 1,167	$ 1,167	$ 1,167	$ 1,167
Travel and vehicle costs	$ 1,583	$ 1,583	$ 1,583	$ 1,583	$ 1,583	$ 1,583	$ 1,583
Utility costs	$ 2,083	$ 2,083	$ 2,083	$ 2,083	$ 2,083	$ 2,083	$ 2,083
Miscellaneous costs	$ 251	$ 251	$ 251	$ 251	$ 251	$ 251	$ 251
Payroll taxes	$ 2,344	$ 2,344	$ 2,344	$ 2,344	$ 2,344	$ 2,344	$ 2,344
Total operating costs	**$27,649**	**$27,649**	**$27,649**	**$27,649**	**$27,649**	**$27,649**	**$27,649**
EBITDA	**$ 8,351**	**$ 8,651**	**$ 8,951**	**$ 9,251**	**$ 9,551**	**$ 9,851**	**$10,151**
Federal income tax	$ 3,156	$ 3,182	$ 3,208	$ 3,235	$ 3,261	$ 3,287	$ 3,314
State income tax	$ 478	$ 482	$ 486	$ 490	$ 494	$ 498	$ 502
Interest expense	$ 3,000	$ 2,984	$ 2,969	$ 2,953	$ 2,937	$ 2,921	$ 2,905
Depreciation expense	$ 2,524	$ 2,524	$ 2,524	$ 2,524	$ 2,524	$ 2,524	$ 2,524
Net profit	−$ 807	−$ 521	−$ 236	$ 49	$ 335	$ 621	$ 906

Profit and loss statement (first year cont.)

Month	8	9	10	11	12	1
Sales	$63,500	$64,000	$64,500	$65,000	$65,500	$753,000
Cost of goods sold	$25,400	$25,600	$25,800	$26,000	$26,200	$301,200
Gross margin	60.0%	60.0%	60.0%	60.0%	60.0%	60.0%
Operating income	$38,100	$38,400	$38,700	$39,000	$39,300	$451,800
Expenses						
Payroll	$15,625	$15,625	$15,625	$15,625	$15,625	$187,500
General and administrative	$ 1,042	$ 1,042	$ 1,042	$ 1,042	$ 1,042	$ 12,500
Product distribution expenses	$ 3,138	$ 3,138	$ 3,138	$ 3,138	$ 3,138	$ 37,650
Professional fees and licensure	$ 417	$ 417	$ 417	$ 417	$ 417	$ 5,000
Insurance costs	$ 1,167	$ 1,167	$ 1,167	$ 1,167	$ 1,167	$ 14,000
Travel and vehicle costs	$ 1,583	$ 1,583	$ 1,583	$ 1,583	$ 1,583	$ 19,000
Utility costs	$ 2,083	$ 2,083	$ 2,083	$ 2,083	$ 2,083	$ 25,000
Miscellaneous costs	$ 251	$ 251	$ 251	$ 251	$ 251	$ 3,012
Payroll taxes	$ 2,344	$ 2,344	$ 2,344	$ 2,344	$ 2,344	$ 28,125
Total operating costs	$27,649	$27,649	$27,649	$27,649	$27,649	$331,787
EBITDA	$10,451	$10,751	$11,051	$11,351	$11,651	$120,013
Federal income tax	$ 3,340	$ 3,366	$ 3,392	$ 3,419	$ 3,445	$ 39,604
State income tax	$ 506	$ 510	$ 514	$ 518	$ 522	$ 6,001
Interest expense	$ 2,889	$ 2,873	$ 2,856	$ 2,840	$ 2,823	$ 34,951
Depreciation expense	$ 2,524	$ 2,524	$ 2,524	$ 2,524	$ 2,524	$ 30,286
Net profit	$ 1,192	$ 1,478	$ 1,765	$ 2,051	$ 2,337	$ 9,172

Profit and loss statement (second year)

Quarter	Q1	Q2	Q3	Q4	2
Sales	$165,660	$207,075	$223,641	$231,924	$828,300
Cost of goods sold	$ 66,264	$ 82,830	$ 89,456	$ 92,770	$331,320
Gross margin	60.0%	60.0%	60.0%	60.0%	60.0%
Operating income	$ 99,396	$124,245	$134,185	$139,154	$496,980
Expenses					
Payroll	$ 38,625	$ 48,281	$ 52,144	$ 54,075	$193,125
General and administrative	$ 2,600	$ 3,250	$ 3,510	$ 3,640	$ 13,000
Product distribution expenses	$ 8,283	$ 10,354	$ 11,182	$ 11,596	$ 41,415
Professional fees and licensure	$ 1,030	$ 1,288	$ 1,391	$ 1,442	$ 5,150
Insurance costs	$ 2,940	$ 3,675	$ 3,969	$ 4,116	$ 14,700
Travel and vehicle costs	$ 4,180	$ 5,225	$ 5,643	$ 5,852	$ 20,900
Utility cost	$ 5,250	$ 6,563	$ 7,088	$ 7,350	$ 26,250
Miscellaneous costs	$ 663	$ 828	$ 895	$ 928	$ 3,313
Payroll taxes	$ 5,794	$ 7,242	$ 7,822	$ 8,111	$ 28,969
Total operating costs	$ 69,364	$ 86,705	$ 93,642	$ 97,110	$346,822
EBITDA	$ 30,032	$ 37,540	$ 40,543	$ 42,044	$150,158
Federal income tax	$ 7,764	$ 9,705	$ 10,481	$ 10,869	$ 38,819
State income tax	$ 1,176	$ 1,470	$ 1,588	$ 1,647	$ 5,882
Interest expense	$ 8,367	$ 8,212	$ 8,054	$ 7,892	$ 32,526
Depreciation expense	$ 7,571	$ 7,571	$ 7,571	$ 7,571	$ 30,286
Net profit	$ 5,153	$ 10,581	$ 12,848	$ 14,065	$ 42,646

Profit and loss statement (third year)

Quarter	Q1	3 Q2	Q3	Q4	3
Sales	$182,226	$227,783	$246,005	$255,116	$911,130
Cost of goods sold	$ 72,890	$ 91,113	$ 98,402	$102,047	$364,452
Gross margin	60.0%	60.0%	60.0%	60.0%	60.0%
Operating income	$ 109,336	$136,670	$147,603	$153,070	$546,678
Expenses					
Payroll	$ 39,784	$ 49,730	$ 53,708	$ 55,697	$198,919
General and administrative	$ 2,704	$ 3,380	$ 3,650	$ 3,786	$ 13,520
Product distribution expenses	$ 9,111	$ 11,389	$ 12,300	$ 12,756	$ 45,557
Professional fees and licensure	$ 1,061	$ 1,326	$ 1,432	$ 1,485	$ 5,305
Insurance costs	$ 3,087	$ 3,859	$ 4,167	$ 4,322	$ 15,435
Travel and vehicle costs	$ 4,598	$ 5,748	$ 6,207	$ 6,437	$ 22,990
Utility cost	$ 5,513	$ 6,891	$ 7,442	$ 7,718	$ 27,563
Miscellaneous costs	$ 729	$ 911	$ 984	$ 1,020	$ 3,645
Payroll taxes	$ 5,968	$ 7,459	$ 8,056	$ 8,355	$ 29,838
Total operating costs	$ 72,554	$ 90,692	$ 97,948	$101,575	$346,822
EBITDA	$ 36,782	$ 45,977	$ 49,655	$ 51,494	$183,908
Federal income tax	$ 10,166	$ 12,708	$ 13,725	$ 14,233	$ 50,832
State income tax	$ 1,540	$ 1,925	$ 2,079	$ 2,156	$ 7,702
Interest expense	$ 7,726	$ 7,557	$ 7,384	$ 7,206	$ 29,873
Depreciation expense	$ 7,571	$ 7,571	$ 7,571	$ 7,571	$ 30,286
Net profit	$ 9,777	$ 16,216	$ 18,896	$ 20,327	$ 65,216

7.11 Three Year Cash Flow Analysis

Cash flow analysis (first year)

Month	1	2	3	4	5	6	7
Cash from operations	$ 1,717	$ 2,002	$ 2,288	$ 2,573	$ 2,859	$ 3,144	$ 3,430
Cash from receivables	$ 0	$ 0	$ 0	$ 0	$ 0	$ 0	$ 0
Operating cash inflow	$ 1,717	$ 2,002	$ 2,288	$ 2,573	$ 2,859	$ 3,144	$ 3,430
Other cash inflows							
Equity investment	$100,000	$ 0	$ 0	$ 0	$ 0	$ 0	$ 0
Increased borrowings	$400,000	$ 0	$ 0	$ 0	$ 0	$ 0	$ 0
Sales of business assets	$ 0	$ 0	$ 0	$ 0	$ 0	$ 0	$ 0
A/P increases	$ 833	$ 833	$ 833	$ 833	$ 833	$ 833	$ 833
Total other cash inflows	$500,833	$ 833	$ 833	$ 833	$ 833	$ 833	$ 833
Total cash inflow	$502,551	$ 2,836	$ 3,121	$ 3,407	$ 3,692	$ 3,978	$ 4,264
Cash outflows							
Repayment of principal	$ 2,067	$ 2,083	$ 2,098	$ 2,114	$ 2,130	$ 2,146	$ 2,162
A/P decreases	$ 750	$ 750	$ 750	$ 750	$ 750	$ 750	$ 750
A/R increases	$ 0	$ 0	$ 0	$ 0	$ 0	$ 0	$ 0
Asset purchases	$471,500	$ 0	$ 0	$ 0	$ 0	$ 0	$ 0
Dividends	$ 0	$ 0	$ 0	$ 0	$ 0	$ 0	$ 0
Total cash outflows	$474,317	$ 2,833	$ 2,848	$ 2,864	$ 2,880	$ 2,896	$ 2,912
Net cash flow	$ 28,234	$ 3	$ 273	$ 543	$ 812	$ 1,082	$ 1,352
Cash balance	$ 28,234	$28,237	$28,510	$29,052	$29,865	$30,947	$32,299

Cash flow analysis (first year cont.)

Month	8	9	10	11	12	1
Cash from operations	$ 3,716	$ 4,002	$ 4,288	$ 4,575	$ 4,861	$ 39,457
Cash from receivables	$ 0	$ 0	$ 0	$ 0	$ 0	$ 0
Operating cash inflow	**$ 3,716**	**$ 4,002**	**$ 4,288**	**$ 4,575**	**$ 4,861**	**$ 39,457**
Other cash inflows						
Equity investment	$ 0	$ 0	$ 0	$ 0	$ 0	$100,000
Increased borrowings	$ 0	$ 0	$ 0	$ 0	$ 0	$400,000
Sales of business assets	$ 0	$ 0	$ 0	$ 0	$ 0	$ 0
A/P increases	$ 833	$ 833	$ 833	$ 833	$ 833	$ 10,000
Total other cash inflows	**$ 833**	**$ 833**	**$ 833**	**$ 833**	**$ 833**	**$510,000**
Total cash inflow	**$ 4,550**	**$ 4,836**	**$ 5,122**	**$ 5,408**	**$ 5,695**	**$549,457**
Cash outflows						
Repayment of principal	$ 2,178	$ 2,194	$ 2,211	$ 2,227	$ 2,244	$ 25,854
A/P decreases	$ 750	$ 750	$ 750	$ 750	$ 750	$ 9,000
A/R increases	$ 0	$ 0	$ 0	$ 0	$ 0	$ 0
Asset purchases	$ 0	$ 0	$ 0	$ 0	$ 0	$471,500
Dividends	$ 0	$ 0	$ 0	$ 0	$31,566	$ 31,566
Total cash outflows	**$ 2,928**	**$ 2,944**	**$ 2,961**	**$ 2,977**	**$34,560**	**$537,919**
Net cash flow	**$ 1,622**	**$ 1,891**	**$ 2,161**	**$ 2,431**	**−$28,866**	**$ 11,538**
Cash balance	**$33,920**	**$35,812**	**$37,973**	**$40,403**	**$11,538**	**$ 11,538**

Cash flow analysis (second year)

Quarter	Q1	Q2 (2)	Q3	Q4	2
Cash from operations	$14,586	$18,233	$19,692	$20,421	$72,932
Cash from receivables	$ 0	$ 0	$ 0	$ 0	$ 0
Operating cash inflow	**$14,586**	**$18,233**	**$19,692**	**$20,421**	**$72,932**
Other cash inflows					
Equity investment	$ 0	$ 0	$ 0	$ 0	$ 0
Increased borrowings	$ 0	$ 0	$ 0	$ 0	$ 0
Sales of business assets	$ 0	$ 0	$ 0	$ 0	$ 0
A/P increases	$ 2,300	$ 2,875	$ 3,105	$ 3,220	$11,500
Total other cash inflows	**$ 2,300**	**$ 2,875**	**$ 3,105**	**$ 3,220**	**$11,500**
Total cash inflow	**$16,886**	**$21,108**	**$22,797**	**$23,641**	**$84,432**
Cash outflows					
Repayment of principal	$ 6,834	$ 6,989	$ 7,147	$ 7,309	$28,279
A/P decreases	$ 2,160	$ 2,700	$ 2,916	$ 3,024	$10,800
A/R increases	$ 0	$ 0	$ 0	$ 0	$ 0
Asset purchases	$ 1,459	$ 1,823	$ 1,969	$ 2,042	$ 7,293
Dividends	$ 7,293	$ 9,117	$ 9,846	$10,211	$36,466
Total cash outflows	**$17,746**	**$20,629**	**$21,878**	**$22,586**	**$82,838**
Net cash flow	**−$ 859**	**$ 480**	**$ 919**	**$ 1,055**	**$ 1,594**
Cash balance	**$10,679**	**$11,158**	**$12,077**	**$13,132**	**$13,132**

Cash flow analysis (third year)

Quarter	Q1	Q2	Q3	Q4	3
Cash from operations	$19,100	$23.876	$25,786	$26,741	$ 95,502
Cash from receivables	$ 0	$ 0	$ 0	$ 0	$ 0
Operating cash inflow	**$19,100**	**$28,876**	**$25,786**	**$26,741**	**$ 95,502**
Other cash inflows					
Equity investment	$ 0	$ 0	$ 0	$ 0	$ 0
Increased borrowings	$ 0	$ 0	$ 0	$ 0	$ 0
Sales of business assets	$ 0	$ 0	$ 0	$ 0	$ 0
A/P increases	$ 2,645	$ 3,306	$ 3,571	$ 3,703	$ 13,225
Total other cash inflows	**$ 2,645**	**$ 3,306**	**$ 3,571**	**$ 3,703**	$ 13,225
Total cash inflow	**$21,745**	**$27,182**	**$29,356**	**$30,444**	$108,727
Cash outflows					
Repayment of principal	$ 7,475	$ 7,644	$ 7,818	$ 7,995	$ 30,932
A/P decreases	$ 2,592	$ 3,240	$ 3,499	$ 3,629	$ 12,960
A/R increases	$ 0	$ 0	$ 0	$ 0	$ 0
Asset purchases	$ 1,910	$ 2.388	$ 2,579	$ 2,674	$ 9,550
Dividends	$ 9,550	$ 11,938	$12,893	$13,370	$ 47,751
Total cash outflows	**$21,527**	**$25,210**	**$26,788**	**$27,668**	**$101,193**
Net cash flow	**$ 218**	**$ 1,972**	**$ 2,568**	**$ 2,776**	**$ 7,534**
Cash balance	**$13,350**	**$15,322**	**$17,891**	**$20,666**	**$ 20,666**

Concession Equipment Rental Business

ConcessionMaster Enterprises LLC

24868 N. Price St.
Grand Junction, Colorado 81503

Paul Greenland

ConcessionMaster is a concession equipment rental business that provides popcorn machines, hot dog steamers, cotton candy makers, snow cone machines, and nacho chip and cheese warmers to both individual consumers and organizations for events such as block parties, races, concerts, festivals, birthday parties, picnics, fun fairs, and more.

EXECUTIVE SUMMARY

Business Overview

ConcessionMaster is a concession equipment rental business that provides popcorn machines, hot dog steamers, cotton candy makers, snow cone machines, and nacho chip and cheese warmers to both individual consumers and organizations for events such as block parties, races, concerts, festivals, birthday parties, picnics, fun fairs, and more. Initially beginning as a part-time business, Concession-Master's owners plan to take the operation full-time during its third year.

ConcessionMaster is located in Grand Junction, Colorado, a community of approximately 54,000 people that is located near the towns of Clifton, Montrose, and Delta. It is owned by Bill and Paul Johnson. Bill owns Johnson's Diner, an established eatery in Grand Junction for 15 years. He plans to sell his share of the diner to business partner John Stanfield in three years and is looking for a scalable business he can operate with his son. Paul is a carpenter who is looking for a business to supplement his carpentry income, which has been sporadic during the economic downturn.

Through their involvement with several civic, business, and trade organizations, Bill and Paul are both well known throughout the community. With many years of small business ownership experience, Bill will share his knowledge with Paul and ensure that ConcessionMaster gets off to a strong start. Paul brings energy and enthusiasm to the table. Although family and business sometimes don't mix, Bill and Paul work well together. Before becoming a carpenter, Paul spent many hours working with his father at Johnson's Diner, and the two make an excellent team.

MARKET ANALYSIS

ConcessionMaster will serve consumers and organizations in a 45-mile radius around the community of Grand Junction, Colorado. According to data from DemographicsNow, this area included nearly

185,000 people in 2010, and was projected to grow 13.7 percent by 2015, reaching about 210,250. In addition, this area included 7,800 business establishments in 2010.

Consumers

The average household income in our primary market was $56,973 in 2010. This figure is expected to grow 8.5 percent by 2015, reaching $61,834. ConcessionMaster will target its consumer marketing initiatives toward households with income of $50,000 or more. In 2010 approximately 19.6 percent of households (the largest segment in our market area) had income between $50,000 and $74,999. Next were households with income between $75,000 and $99,999 (10.4%), $100,000 and $149,999 (7.4%), and more than $150,000 (4.4%).

Organizations

Beyond the consumer market, services will be marketed to specific types of organizations. These include, but are not limited to:

- Auto Dealers & Gas Stations (192 establishments)

- Bars (20 establishments)

- Childcare Services (44 establishments)

- Colleges & Universities (11 establishments)

- Entertainment & Recreation Services (128 establishments)

- Hospitals (2 establishments)

- Health & Medical Services (465 establishments)

- Membership Organizations (277 establishments)

- Museums & Zoos (9 establishments)

- Primary & Secondary Education (96 establishments)

- Churches & Religious Organizations (75 establishments)

INDUSTRY ANALYSIS

According to the Moline, Illinois-based American Rental Association (ARA), a trade association for equipment rental businesses, manufacturers, and other industry players, the North American equipment rental industry was valued at nearly $32 billion in 2009.

Established in 1955, the ARA bills itself as "the source for information, government affairs, business development tools, education and training, networking and marketplace opportunities for the rental equipment industry throughout the world." The association counted some 7,500 rental businesses, as well as approximately 900 manufacturers and suppliers, among its membership base in 2011.

The ARA breaks down the equipment rental industry into three sectors:

- Construction and industrial equipment

- General tool and homeowner equipment

- Special event and party equipment

ConcessionMaster falls within the special event and party equipment category.

Although economic conditions were difficult in 2011, businesses like ConcessionMaster are somewhat recession-resistant. This is because, even during difficult times, businesses and organizations need affordable sources of entertainment.

PERSONNEL

Bill and Paul Johnson are lifelong residents of Grand Junction. Through their involvement with several civic, business, and trade organizations, they are especially well known throughout the community.

Bill Johnson

Bill has co-owned and operated Johnson's Diner with partner John Stanfield since 1996. Before that time he worked for Clifton Foods, a supplier to the food service industry throughout Colorado, for 20 years. After spending five years as a salesman, Bill was promoted to regional sales manager. Serving in that role for five years, he was then elevated to the position of sales director. Bill's entrepreneurial spirit, along with a desire to spend more time with his family, prompted him to leave Clifton Foods and establish his own business.

As he approaches retirement age, Bill plans to sell his share of the diner to business partner John Stanfield in three years, and is looking for a scalable business he can operate with his son, Paul Johnson, on a part-time basis. He will share his knowledge with Paul and ensure that ConcessionMaster gets off to a strong start.

Bill is a member of the Kiwanis Club of Grand Junction and the Rotary Club of Grand Junction.

Paul Johnson

A proud member of Carpenters Local Union 222, Paul has worked as a carpenter in the Grand Junction area for 10 years. Before working in the trades, Paul "grew up" working in his father's diner. Although family and business sometimes don't mix, father and son work well together, making an excellent team. Paul is interested in following in his father's entrepreneurial footsteps. In addition, he is seeking a way to supplement his carpentry income, which has been sporadic during the economic downturn of the late 2000s and early 2010s.

Like his father, Paul is a member of the Kiwanis Club of Grand Junction and the Rotary Club of Grand Junction.

Professional and Advisory Support

ConcessionMaster has selected Grand Junction Professional Accounting to provide bookkeeping and tax assistance. A commercial checking account has been established with Academy Bank, which has agreed to provide merchant accounts so that the business can accept credit card and debit card payments. Legal services will be provided by Kurt Lofton, who will develop a basic customer rental agreement for the business.

BUSINESS STRATEGY

ConcessionMaster will begin operations on a small scale. Initially, we will invest in a modest inventory of concession equipment, including:

- Nacho Chip Warmers
- Popcorn Machines
- Snow Cone Machines

- Hot Dog Steamers
- Hot Dog Roller Grills
- Cotton Candy Makers

We will reinvest the majority of profits made during our first year into the business, in order to expand our inventory significantly during the second year. At that time, we will bolster the amount of equipment listed in the above categories.

Bill and Paul will personally deliver, set up, and haul away all rental equipment during the business' first year. This way, they will familiarize themselves with the equipment and experience operations first-hand.

During the second year, Bill will transition into more of an account management/business operations role, while Paul will recruit and supervise a crew of independent contractors (number of staff based on demand) from the campuses of Grand Junction Junior College, Western Colorado Community College, and Colorado State University.

One key business strategy will be the promotion of special package deals, whereby we offer a special discount to customers for renting two or three equipment selections. This allows us to generate additional revenue with little additional effort (e.g., without having to travel to additional customer sites, etc.).

ConcessionMaster will become a full-time enterprise in year three. At that time Bill Johnson will make a personal investment (using partial proceeds from the sale of his share of the diner) in the business, in order to further expand ConcessionMaster's equipment inventory. At that time, we will consider adding additional types of equipment, including:

- Concession Trailer(s)
- Pizza Equipment (e.g., pizza ovens and warmers)
- Pretzel Equipment
- Candy & Caramel Apple Equipment
- Waffle Equipment
- Frost Nut Equipment
- Gasoline Generators
- Propane Patio Heaters
- Tents

SERVICES

Available Equipment & Pricing
- Nacho Chip Warmers: $30
- 4 Ounce Popcorn Machines: $55
- 8 Ounce Popcorn Machines: $55
- 12 Ounce Popcorn Machines: $55
- Snow Cone Machines: $55
- Hot Dog Steamers: $55
- Hot Dog Roller Grills: $55
- Cotton Candy Makers: $55

Delivery, Setup & Teardown

ConcessionMaster will provide delivery, setup, and tear-down services for a $50 charge within our service area.

Supplies

ConcessionMaster will offer a wide range of supplies for all of its rental equipment. A complete price list for the following items is available upon request (prices sometimes will vary slightly depending on suppliers):

- Nacho Chips (2 pound)
- Nacho Chips (6 pound)
- Nacho Cheese (individual portion containers, and bulk quantities)
- Snow Cone Cups Snow Syrup (cherry, grape, raspberry, lemon/lime, strawberry, orange, pineapple, coconut, root beer, sour apple, strawberry, strawberry/kiwi, bubblegum)
- Snow Cone Spoon Straws
- Floss Sugar (blue raspberry, grape, red cherry, bubblegum, mint green, vanilla, orange, lime green, watermelon, yellow piña colada, strawberry, pink vanilla)
- Cotton Candy Floss Cones
- Foil Hot Dog Bags
- King-Size Hot Dog Bags
- Slit Open-Top Hot Dog Bags
- Popcorn Boxes (various sizes)
- Popcorn Bags (various sizes)
- Popping Oil (canola, coconut & sunflower)
- Bulk Popping Corn (35-and 50-pound bags)
- Buttery Topping Oil (1 gallon)

Event Staffing

During year three, we will consider offering on-site equipment operations for customers who wish to have their event staffed by a ConcessionMaster associate.

MARKETING & SALES

A marketing plan has been developed for ConcessionMaster that includes these main tactics:

1. Web Site: ConcessionMaster has developed a basic Web site that lists information about our available equipment and prices, special discounts and packages, or rental policy, details about deliveries, contact information, FAQs, and reservation information.

2. Promotional Fliers: With the help of a local graphic designer, we have developed two four-color fliers. One addresses the consumer market, while another addresses organizations. These fliers can be left behind following sales calls, used in direct mailings, and more.

3. Direct Marketing: Bill and Paul Johnson will initiate a three-wave direct-mail campaign during the first year of operations. A mailing list has been obtained from a local list broker, allowing us to target prospective organizational clients. In addition, working with the local Chamber of Commerce and other community groups, we have compiled a list of recurring annual events and festivals in our market area.

Bill and/or Paul will personally contact the organizers of each event in order to communicate information about ConcessionMaster. A complete listing of events, along with contact information, is available upon request.

4. Advertising: ConcessionMaster will maintain a regular advertising presence in The Chamber Times, a newspaper published by our local Chamber of Commerce, enabling us to stay visible within the business community. In addition, we will run a sizable ad in the Grand Junction Yellow Pages.

5. Sales Presentations/Incentives: Each month, Bill and Paul Johnson will make 3 to 5 sales calls to organizations in the Grand Junction area promoting ConcessionMaster's equipment rental services. Following the presentation, they will distribute certificates that entitle the holder to a 20 percent discount off their first order. A schedule of planned sales calls for our first year of operation is available for review.

We will evaluate our marketing plan on a semi-annual basis during our first three years of operations, and annually thereafter.

OPERATIONS

Hours
ConcessionMaster will accept phone calls and/or e-mails during regular business hours (9 AM-5 PM) via a dedicated mobile phone number. Our policy will be to respond to customer inquiries within one business day.

Payment
ConcessionMaster will require customers to make a 20 percent deposit within 10 days of their reservation. Customers will then be required to pay the entire rental fee on the day of equipment delivery. Credit/debit card payments, checks, and cash will be accepted.

Facility and Location
ConcessionMaster initially will store equipment in an unused garage at Bill Johnson's residence. However, this option only will work for the business's first year, after which time suitable warehouse space will be required. In addition, Bill will utilize dedicated office space within his home for administrative purposes. A business insurance policy, along with a home-office rider, will be obtained.

The Johnsons already own a pickup truck and cargo trailer that can be used for equipment deliveries and other business purposes during the first year.

FINANCIAL ANALYSIS

First-year Start-up Costs
Acquisition of the following equipment will be required for ConcessionMaster's operations during the first year:

- Nacho Chip Warmers (4): $1,200
- 4 Ounce Popcorn Machines (2): $500
- 8 Ounce Popcorn Machines (2): $900
- 12 Ounce Popcorn Machine (2): $1,800
- Snow Cone Machines (3): $1,500

- Hot Dog Steamers (3): $1,500

- Hot Dog Roller Grills (2): $1,500

- Cotton Candy Makers (3): $1,500

- Supplies (initial inventory): $3,500

- Total: $13,900

*A list of projected capital acquisitions for our second year of business is available upon request.

Revenue Projections

Including supplies and delivery charges, the Johnsons estimate that ConcessionMaster will generate revenues of approximately $200 per rental, averaging three rentals per week during year one. Based on this figure, they are estimating revenues of $30,000. Following the addition of more equipment, revenues are expected to reach $45,000 during year two. Finally, the significant equipment expansion planned for year three, along with organic growth, should push revenues to approximately $90,000. Detailed financial statements, prepared in cooperation with Grand Junction Professional Accounting, are available for review.

Cosmetics Manufacturer

Glamour Girl Cosmetics

9300 Park View St.
Los Angeles, California 90001

BizPlanDB.com

Glamour Girl Cosmetics will develop, manufacture, and brand an expansive line of makeup, perfumes, and cosmetic accessories that are popular among female buyers.

1.0 EXECUTIVE SUMMARY

The purpose of this business plan is to raise $125,000 for the development of a cosmetics manufacturer while showcasing the expected financials and operations over the next three years. Glamour Girl Cosmetics ("the Company") is a California-based corporation that will provide a diverse line of brand label perfumes, makeup, and related accessories to customers in its targeted market. The Company was founded by Isabella Gorinski.

1.1 The Products

At stated above, Glamour Girl Cosmetics will develop, manufacture, and brand an expansive line of makeup, perfumes, and cosmetic accessories that are popular among female buyers. Ms. Gorinski is currently sourcing a number of regional and national wholesalers that will acquire inventories of its produced products.

In regards to the manufacturing process, the Company will work with several overseas manufacturing firms to coordinate the production of the Company's proprietary cosmetics products.

The third section of the business plan will further describe the services offered by Glamour Girl Cosmetics.

1.2 Financing

Ms. Gorinski is seeking to raise $125,000 from a bank loan. The interest rate and loan agreement are to be further discussed during negotiation. This business plan assumes that the business will receive a 10 year loan with a 9% fixed interest rate. The financing will be used for the following:

- Development of the Company's office and manufaturing location.

- Financing for the first six months of operation.

- Capital to purchase the initial inventories of proprietary cosmetics.

Ms. Gorinski will contribute $25,000 to the venture.

1.3 Mission Statement

The Company's mission is to become the recognized leader in its targeted market for developing, producing, and branding a diverse line of in demand cosmetics including perfumes, makeup, and other accessories.

1.4 Management Team

The Company was founded by Isabella Gorinski. Ms. Gorinski has more than 10 years of experience in the cosmetics industry. Through her expertise, she will be able to bring the operations of the business to profitability within its first year of operations.

1.5 Sales Forecasts

Ms. Gorinski expects a strong rate of growth at the start of operations. Below are the expected financials over the next three years.

Proforma profit and loss (yearly)

Year	1	2	3
Sales	$864,234	$1,037,081	$1,213,385
Operating costs	$341,823	$ 357,378	$ 373,482
EBITDA	$263,141	$ 368,579	$ 475,887
Taxes, interest, and depreciation	$118,951	$ 154,398	$ 194,661
Net profit	$144,189	$ 214,181	$ 281,227

Sales, operating costs, and profit forecast

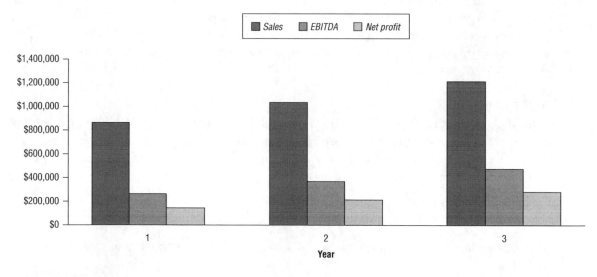

1.6 Expansion Plan

The Founder expects that the business will aggressively expand during the first three years of operation. Ms. Gorinski intends to implement marketing campaigns that will effectively target individuals within the target market.

2.0 COMPANY AND FINANCING SUMMARY

2.1 Registered Name and Corporate Structure

The Company is registered as a corporation in the State of California.

2.2 Required Funds

At this time, Glamour Girl Cosmetics requires $125,000 of debt funds. Below is a breakdown of how these funds will be used:

Projected startup costs

Initial lease payments and deposits	$ 20,000
Working capital	$ 20,000
FF&E	$ 25,000
Leasehold improvements	$ 15,000
Security deposits	$ 7,500
Insurance	$ 5,000
Initial cosmetics inventory	$ 35,000
Marketing budget	$ 17,500
Miscellaneous and unforeseen costs	$ 5,000
Total startup costs	**$150,000**

Use of funds

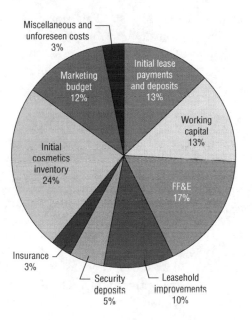

2.3 Investor Equity

Ms. Gorinski is not seeking an investment from a third party at this time.

2.4 Management Equity

Ms. Gorinski owns 100% of Glamour Girl Cosmetics.

2.5 Exit Strategy

If the business is very successful, Ms. Gorinski may seek to sell the business to a third party for a significant earnings multiple. Most likely, the Company will hire a qualified business broker to sell the business on behalf of Glamour Girl Cosmetics. Based on historical numbers, the business could fetch a sales premium of up to 5 times earnings.

3.0 PRODUCTS AND SERVICES

Below is a description of the products offered by Glamour Girl Cosmetics.

3.1 Manufacturing and Distribution of Cosmetics and Accessories

The primary revenue source for the business will come from the direct sale of cosmetics to wholesalers from which the Company will have developed, produced, and marketed.

Ms. Gorinski intends to produce and distribute a number of mid-to high-end brands of perfumes, makeup, accessories, and other goods that are used for health and beauty. Ms. Gorinski intends to source these inventories for regional and national level manufacturers that will coordinate the development of cosmetics and cosmetics packaging with the Management Team.

4.0 STRATEGIC AND MARKET ANALYSIS

4.1 Economic Outlook

This section of the analysis will detail the economic climate, the cosmetics industry, the customer profile, and the competition that the business will face as it progresses through its business operations.

Presently, the economic market condition in the United States is sluggish. This slowdown in the economy has also greatly impacted real estate sales, which has halted to historical lows. Many economists expect that this sluggish will continue for a significant period of time, at which point the economy will begin a prolonged recovery period. However, the Company will earn significant gross margins on each item sold, and despite the current economic climate, the business will be able to maintain profitable and cash flow positive operations.

4.2 Industry Analysis

Within the United States there are approximately 82,000 companies that specialize in the manufacture and sale/distribution of beauty supply goods to the general public. Each year, these businesses aggregately generate more than $125 billion dollars of revenue and provide jobs for almost 1,000,000 Americans. For the last five years, annual payrolls have exceeded $20 billion dollars a year among these individuals.

The industry has experienced solid growth over the last ten years as more people are becoming concerned with their appearance. This growth corresponds to the increase in capital stock and general wealth of the American public. As such, the industry has grown at an average annual rate of 6% per year for each of the last five years. This trend is expected to continue, and then taper off as the market normalizes and the industry becomes consolidated. Currently, this industry has a number of fragmented market agents that will most likely be rolled up as time progresses. However, this expansive growth rate may slow over the next 12 to 18 months as the current economy further depresses consumers' discretionary income.

4.3 Customer Profile

The cosmetics customer will typically be a middle- to upper-middle class woman living in the Company's target market. Common traits among clients will include:

- Annual household income exceeding $50,000
- Will spend $25 to $100 on cosmetics
- Lives within a metropolitan area

Among retailers that will sell the Company's manufactured cosmetics, Management has outlined the demographics:

- Operates 10 or more retail locations.
- Annual revenues exceeding $5,000,000 per year

- Annual EBITDA exceeding $350,000 per year

- Will spend $25,000 to $50,000 with the Company.

4.4 Competition

There are a number of competitors within the beauty supply and health product industry, and the market has become commoditized as all products essentially provide the same end user benefit. The key to maintaining successful operations is to properly market the Company's products to its core demographic of female purchasers. As such, it is imperative that Management use a multifacted marketing strategy that will showcase the premium quality of our products while concurrently showcasing the moderate pricing structure for sales.

Major competitors within the market include Revlon, Cover Girl, L'Oreal, NIVEA, Chanel, Mac, and many others.

5.0 MARKETING PLAN

The Company intends to maintain an extensive marketing campaign that will ensure maximum visibility for the business in its targeted market. Below is an overview of the marketing strategies and objectives of the Company.

5.1 Marketing Objectives

- Develop e-commerce functionality for the Company's website.

- Develop ongoing relationships with cosmetics wholesalers and retailers throughout the United States.

5.2 Marketing Strategies

Ms. Gorinski intends on using a number of marketing strategies that will allow Glamour Girl Cosmetics to easily target retail stores and cosmetics wholesalers within the target market. Primarily, Ms. Gorinski intends to develop an expansive independent sales organization that will directly promote and sell the Company's manufactured cosmetics to these entities in exchange for a commission. Management anticipates that commissions will range from 5% to 15% depending on the ongoing success of the individual salesperson. Management may also develop territories for each independent salesperson so that salespeople do not need to compete within any one specific market.

A marketing firm will be retained to assist Glamour Girl Cosmetics with appropriately branding and marketing its products to the targeted demographics.

As with many businesses these days, Management intends to develop a highly interactive website that showcases the products produced by the business, how to contact the Company for wholesale distribution agreements, and ecommerce functionality among end users that want to purchase cosmetic products directly from the Company. Ecommerce functionality may also be integrated for wholesalers and retailers as well.

5.3 Pricing

As the Company intends to sell its manufactured cosmetics in bulk to wholesalers, Management cannot accurately determine the exact pricing that will be used as discounts will be applied for extremely large purchases. However, Management anticipates gross margins of approximately 70% on each dollar of revenue generated.

6.0 ORGANIZATIONAL PLAN AND PERSONNEL SUMMARY

6.1 Corporate Organization

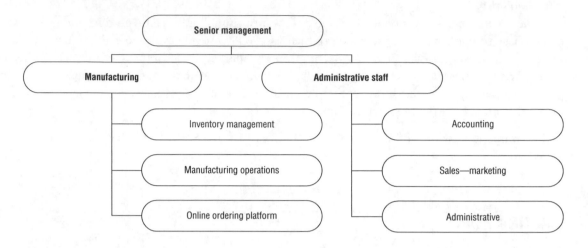

6.2 Organizational Budget

Personnel plan—yearly

Year	1	2	3
Owner	$ 50,000	$ 51,500	$ 53,045
Manufacturing manager	$ 45,000	$ 46,350	$ 47,741
Distribution employees	$ 76,000	$ 78,280	$ 80,628
Bookkeeper (P/T)	$ 13,000	$ 13,390	$ 13,792
Administrative	$ 22,000	$ 22,660	$ 23,340
Total	**$206,000**	**$212,180**	**$218,545**

Numbers of personnel

Year	1	2	3
Owner	1	1	1
Manufacturing manager	1	1	1
Distribution employees	4	4	4
Bookkeeper (P/T)	1	1	1
Administrative	1	1	1
Totals	**8**	**8**	**8**

Personnel expense breakdown

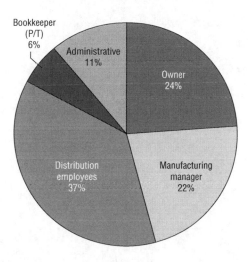

7.0 FINANCIAL PLAN

7.1 Underlying Assumptions

The Company has based its proforma financial statements on the following:

*   Glamour Girl Cosmetics will have an annual revenue growth rate of 15.5% per year.

*   The Owner will acquire $125,000 of debt funds to develop the business.

*   The loan will have a 10 year term with a 9% interest rate.

7.2 Sensitivity Analysis

In the event of an economic downturn, the business may have a decline in its revenues. Cosmetics and related goods are purchased with discretionary income, and during times of economic recession, the business may see a decline in its top line income. However, the business will earn substantial margins from its product sales, and the business will be able to remain profitable and cash flow positive despite moderate declines in revenue.

7.3 Source of Funds

Financing

Equity contributions

Management investment	$ 25,000.00
Total equity financing	**$ 25,000.00**
Banks and lenders	
Banks and lenders	$ 125,000.00
Total debt financing	**$125,000.00**
Total financing	**$150,000.00**

7.4 General Assumptions

General assumptions

Year	1	2	3
Short term interest rate	9.5%	9.5%	9.5%
Long term interest rate	10.0%	10.0%	10.0%
Federal tax rate	33.0%	33.0%	33.0%
State tax rate	5.0%	5.0%	5.0%
Personnel taxes	15.0%	15.0%	15.0%

7.5 Profit and Loss Statements

Proforma profit and loss (yearly)

Year	1	2	3
Sales	**$864,234**	**$1,037,081**	**$1,213,385**
Cost of goods sold	$259,270	$ 311,124	$ 364,015
Gross margin	70.00%	70.00%	70.00%
Operating income	**$604,964**	**$ 725,957**	**$ 849,369**
Expenses			
Payroll	$206,000	$ 212,180	$ 218,545
General and administrative	$ 13,200	$ 13,728	$ 14,277
Marketing expenses	$ 17,285	$ 20,742	$ 24,268
Professional fees and licensure	$ 7,500	$ 7,725	$ 7,957
Insurance costs	$ 12,500	$ 13,125	$ 13,781
Travel and vehicle costs	$ 9,000	$ 9,900	$ 10,890
Rent and utilities	$ 42,500	$ 44,625	$ 46,856
Miscellaneous costs	$ 2,938	$ 3,526	$ 4,126
Payroll taxes	$ 30,900	$ 31,827	$ 32,782
Total operating costs	**$341,823**	**$ 357,378**	**$ 373,482**
EBITDA	**$263,141**	**$ 368,579**	**$ 475,887**
Federal income tax	$ 86,836	$ 118,277	$ 153,962
State income tax	$ 13,157	$ 17,921	$ 23,328
Interest expense	$ 10,922	$ 10,164	$ 9,335
Depreciation expenses	$ 8,036	$ 8,036	$ 8,036
Net profit	**$144,189**	**$ 214,181**	**$ 281,227**
Profit margin	**16.68%**	**20.65%**	**23.18%**

Sales, operating costs, and profit forecast

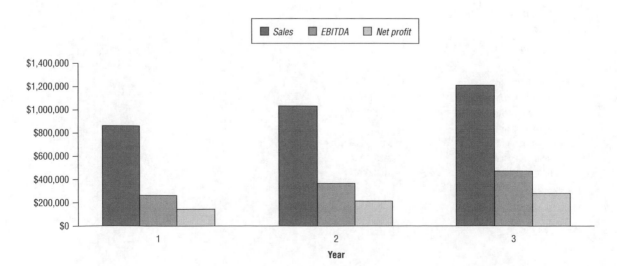

7.6 Cash Flow Analysis

Proforma cash flow analysis—yearly

Year	1	2	3
Cash from operations	$152,225	$222,217	$289,262
Cash from receivables	$ 0	$ 0	$ 0
Operating cash inflow	**$152,225**	**$222,217**	**$289,262**
Other cash inflows			
Equity investment	$ 25,000	$ 0	$ 0
Increased borrowings	$125,000	$ 0	$ 0
Sales of business assets	$ 0	$ 0	$ 0
A/P increases	$ 37,902	$ 43,587	$ 50,125
Total other cash inflows	**$187,902**	**$ 43,587**	**$ 50,125**
Total cash inflow	**$340,127**	**$265,804**	**$339,388**
Cash outflows			
Repayment of principal	$ 8,079	$ 8,837	$ 9,666
A/P decreases	$ 24,897	$ 29,876	$ 35,852
A/R increases	$ 0	$ 0	$ 0
Asset purchases	$112,500	$ 55,554	$ 72,316
Dividends	$106,558	$155,552	$202,484
Total cash outflows	**$252,034**	**$249,820**	**$320,317**
Net cash flow	**$ 88,093**	**$ 15,985**	**$ 19,071**
Cash balance	**$ 88,093**	**$104,078**	**$123,149**

Proforma cash flow (yearly)

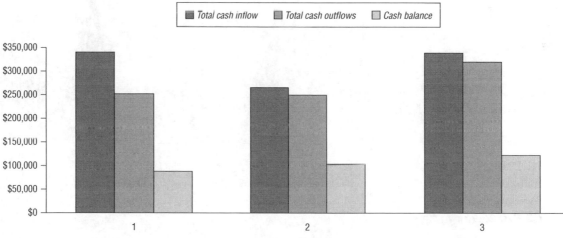

7.7 Balance Sheet

Proforma balance sheet—yearly

Year	1	2	3
Assets			
Cash	$ 88,093	$104,078	$123,149
Amortized development/expansion costs	$ 52,500	$ 58,055	$ 65,287
Inventory	$ 35,000	$ 62,777	$ 98,935
FF&E	$ 25,000	$ 47,222	$ 76,148
Accumulated depreciation	($ 8,036)	($ 16,071)	($ 24,107)
Total assets	**$192,558**	**$256,061**	**$339,411**
Liabilities and equity			
Accounts payable	$ 13,005	$ 26,716	$ 40,990
Long term liabilities	$116,921	$108,084	$ 99,247
Other liabilities	$ 0	$ 0	$ 0
Total liabilities	**$129,926**	**$134,800**	**$140,236**
Net worth	**$ 62,632**	**$121,261**	**$199,175**
Total liabilities and equity	**$192,558**	**$256,061**	**$339,411**

Proforma balance sheet

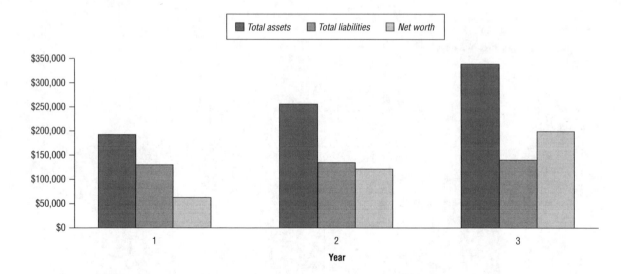

7.8 Breakeven Analysis

Monthly break even analysis

Year	1	2	3
Monthly revenue	$ 40,693	$ 42,545	$ 44,462
Yearly revenue	$488,319	$510,540	$533,545

Break even analysis

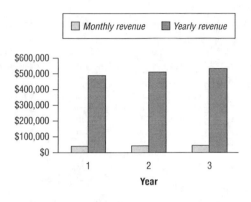

7.9 Business Ratios

Business ratios—yearly

Year	1	2	3
Sales			
Sales growth	0.00%	20.00%	17.00%
Gross margin	70.00%	70.00%	70.00%
Financials			
Profit margin	16.68%	20.65%	23.18%
Assets to liabilities	1.48	1.90	2.42
Equity to liabilities	0.48	0.90	1.42
Assets to equity	3.07	2.11	1.70
Liquidity			
Acid test	0.68	0.77	0.88
Cash to assets	0.46	0.41	0.36

7.10 Three Year Profit and Loss Statement

Profit and loss statement (first year)

Months	1	2	3	4	5	6	7
Sales	$69,825	$70,224	$70,623	$71,022	$71,421	$71,820	$72,219
Cost of goods sold	$20,948	$21,067	$21,187	$21,307	$21,426	$21,546	$21,666
Gross margin	70.0%	70.0%	70.0%	70.0%	70.0%	70.0%	70.0%
Operating income	$48,878	$49,157	$49,436	$49,715	$49,995	$50,274	$50,553
Expenses							
Payroll	$17,167	$17,167	$17,167	$17,167	$17,167	$17,167	$17,167
General and administrative	$ 1,100	$ 1,100	$ 1,100	$ 1,100	$ 1,100	$ 1,100	$ 1,100
Marketing expenses	$ 1,440	$ 1,440	$ 1,440	$ 1,440	$ 1,440	$ 1,440	$ 1,440
Professional fees and licensure	$ 625	$ 625	$ 625	$ 625	$ 625	$ 625	$ 625
Insurance costs	$ 1,042	$ 1,042	$ 1,042	$ 1,042	$ 1,042	$ 1,042	$ 1,042
Travel and vehicle costs	$ 750	$ 750	$ 750	$ 750	$ 750	$ 750	$ 750
Rent and utilities	$ 3,542	$ 3,542	$ 3,542	$ 3,542	$ 3,542	$ 3,542	$ 3,542
Miscellaneous costs	$ 245	$ 245	$ 245	$ 245	$ 245	$ 245	$ 245
Payroll taxes	$ 2,575	$ 2,575	$ 2,575	$ 2,575	$ 2,575	$ 2,575	$ 2,575
Total operating costs	$28,485	$28,485	$28,485	$28,485	$28,485	$28,485	$28,485
EBITDA	$20,392	$20,672	$20,951	$21,230	$21,509	$21,789	$22,068
Federal income tax	$ 7,016	$ 7,056	$ 7,096	$ 7,136	$ 7,176	$ 7,216	$ 7,256
State income tax	$ 1,063	$ 1,069	$ 1,075	$ 1,081	$ 1,087	$ 1,093	$ 1,099
Interest expense	$ 938	$ 933	$ 928	$ 923	$ 918	$ 913	$ 908
Depreciation expenses	$ 670	$ 670	$ 670	$ 670	$ 670	$ 670	$ 670
Net profit	$10,706	$10,944	$11,182	$11,420	$11,658	$11,896	$12,135

Profit and loss statement (first year cont.)

Months	8	9	10	11	12	1
Sales	$72,618	$73,017	$73,416	$73,815	$74,214	$864,234
Cost of goods sold	$21,785	$21,905	$22,025	$22,145	$22,264	$259,270
Gross margin	70.0%	70.0%	70.0%	70.0%	70.0%	70.0%
Operating income	$50,833	$51,112	$51,391	$51,671	$51,950	$604,964
Expenses						
Payroll	$17,167	$17,167	$17,167	$17,167	$17,167	$206,000
General and administrative	$ 1,100	$ 1,100	$ 1,100	$ 1,100	$ 1,100	$ 13,200
Marketing expenses	$ 1,440	$ 1,440	$ 1,440	$ 1,440	$ 1,440	$ 17,285
Professional fees and licensure	$ 625	$ 625	$ 625	$ 625	$ 625	$ 7,500
Insurance costs	$ 1,042	$ 1,042	$ 1,042	$ 1,042	$ 1,042	$ 12,500
Travel and vehicle costs	$ 750	$ 750	$ 750	$ 750	$ 750	$ 9,000
Rent and utilities	$ 3,542	$ 3,542	$ 3,542	$ 3,542	$ 3,542	$ 42,500
Miscellaneous costs	$ 245	$ 245	$ 245	$ 245	$ 245	$ 2,938
Payroll taxes	$ 2,575	$ 2,575	$ 2,575	$ 2,575	$ 2,575	$ 30,900
Total operating costs	$28,485	$28,485	$28,485	$28,485	$28,485	$341,823
EBITDA	$22,347	$22,627	$22,906	$23,185	$23,465	$263,141
Federal income tax	$ 7,297	$ 7,337	$ 7,377	$ 7,417	$ 7,457	$ 86,836
State income tax	$ 1,106	$ 1,112	$ 1,118	$ 1,124	$ 1,130	$ 13,157
Interest expense	$ 903	$ 898	$ 893	$ 887	$ 882	$ 10,922
Depreciation expenses	$ 670	$ 670	$ 670	$ 670	$ 670	$ 8,036
Net profit	$12,373	$12,611	$12,849	$13,088	$13,326	$144,189

Profit and loss statement (second year)

Quarter	Q1	2 Q2	Q3	Q4	2
Sales	$207,416	$259,270	$280,012	$290,383	$1,037,081
Cost of goods sold	$ 62,225	$ 77,781	$ 84,004	$ 87,115	$ 311,124
Gross margin	70.0%	70.0%	70.0%	70.0%	70.0%
Operating income	$145,191	$181,489	$196,008	$203,268	$ 725,957
Expenses					
Payroll	$ 42,436	$ 53,045	$ 57,289	$ 59,410	$ 212,180
General and administrative	$ 2,746	$ 3,432	$ 3,707	$ 3,844	$ 13,728
Marketing expenses	$ 4,148	$ 5,185	$ 5,600	$ 5,808	$ 20,742
Professional fees and licensure	$ 1,545	$ 1,931	$ 2,086	$ 2,163	$ 7,725
Insurance costs	$ 2,625	$ 3,281	$ 3,544	$ 3,675	$ 13,125
Travel and vehicle costs	$ 1,980	$ 2,475	$ 2,673	$ 2,772	$ 9,900
Rent and utilities	$ 8,925	$ 11,156	$ 12,049	$ 12,495	$ 44,625
Miscellaneous costs	$ 705	$ 882	$ 952	$ 987	$ 3,526
Payroll taxes	$ 6,365	$ 7,957	$ 8,593	$ 8,912	$ 31,827
Total operating costs	$ 71,476	$ 89,344	$ 96,492	$100,066	$ 357,378
EBITDA	$ 73,716	$ 92,145	$ 99,516	$103,202	$ 368,579
Federal income tax	$ 23,655	$ 29,569	$ 31,935	$ 33,118	$ 118,277
State income tax	$ 3,584	$ 4,480	$ 4,839	$ 5,018	$ 17,921
Interest expense	$ 2,615	$ 2,566	$ 2,517	$ 2,466	$ 10,164
Depreciation expense	$ 2,009	$ 2,009	$ 2,009	$ 2,009	$ 8,036
Net profit	$ 41,853	$ 53,520	$ 58,217	$ 60,592	$ 214,181

Profit and loss statement (third year)

Quarter	Q1	3 Q2	Q3	Q4	3
Sales	$242,677	$303,346	$327,614	$339,748	$1,213,385
Cost of goods sold	$ 72,803	$ 91,004	$ 98,284	$101,924	$ 364,015
Gross margin	70.0%	70.0%	70.0%	70.0%	70.0%
Operating income	$169,874	$212,342	$229,330	$237,823	$ 849,369
Expenses					
Payroll	$ 43,709	$ 54,636	$ 59,007	$ 61,193	$ 218,545
General and administrative	$ 2,855	$ 3,569	$ 3,855	$ 3,998	$ 14,277
Marketing expenses	$ 4,854	$ 6,067	$ 6,552	$ 6,795	$ 24,268
Professional fees and licensure	$ 1,591	$ 1,989	$ 2,148	$ 2,228	$ 7,957
Insurance costs	$ 2,756	$ 3,445	$ 3,721	$ 3,859	$ 13,781
Travel and vehicle costs	$ 2,178	$ 2,723	$ 2,940	$ 3,049	$ 10,890
Rent and utilities	$ 9,371	$ 11,714	$ 12,651	$ 13,120	$ 46,856
Miscellaneous costs	$ 825	$ 1,031	$ 1,114	$ 1,155	$ 4,126
Payroll taxes	$ 6,556	$ 8,195	$ 8,851	$ 9,179	$ 32,782
Total operating costs	$ 74,696	$ 93,370	$100,840	$104,575	$ 373,482
EBITDA	$ 95,177	$118,972	$128,490	$133,248	$ 475,887
Federal income tax	$ 30,792	$ 38,491	$ 41,570	$ 43,109	$ 153,962
State income tax	$ 4,666	$ 5,832	$ 6,298	$ 6,532	$ 23,328
Interest expense	$ 2,414	$ 2,361	$ 2,307	$ 2,252	$ 9,335
Depreciation expense	$ 2,009	$ 2,009	$ 2,009	$ 2,009	$ 8,036
Net profit	$ 55,296	$ 70,279	$ 76,305	$ 79,346	$ 281,227

7.11 Three Year Cash Flow Analysis

Cash flow analysis (first year)

Month	1	2	3	4	5	6	7	8
Cash from operations	$ 11,376	$11,614	$11,852	$12,090	$12,328	$ 12,566	$ 12,804	$ 13,042
Cash from receivables	$ 0	$ 0	$ 0	$ 0	$ 0	$ 0	$ 0	$ 0
Operating cash inflow	$ 11,376	$11,614	$11,852	$12,090	$12,328	$ 12,566	$ 12,804	$ 13,042
Other cash inflows								
Equity investment	$ 25,000	$ 0	$ 0	$ 0	$ 0	$ 0	$ 0	$ 0
Increased borrowings	$125,000	$ 0	$ 0	$ 0	$ 0	$ 0	$ 0	$ 0
Sales of business assets	$ 0	$ 0	$ 0	$ 0	$ 0	$ 0	$ 0	$ 0
A/P increases	$ 3,159	$ 3,159	$ 3,159	$ 3,159	$ 3,159	$ 3,159	$ 3,159	$ 3,159
Total other cash inflows	$153,159	$ 3,159	$ 3,159	$ 3,159	$ 3,159	$ 3,159	$ 3,159	$ 3,159
Total cash inflow	$164,534	$14,772	$15,010	$15,248	$15,486	$ 15,725	$ 15,963	$ 16,201
Cash outflows								
Repayment of principal	$ 646	$ 651	$ 656	$ 661	$ 666	$ 671	$ 676	$ 681
A/P decreases	$ 2,075	$ 2,075	$ 2,075	$ 2,075	$ 2,075	$ 2,075	$ 2,075	$ 2,075
A/R increases	$ 0	$ 0	$ 0	$ 0	$ 0	$ 0	$ 0	$ 0
Asset purchases	$112,500	$ 0	$ 0	$ 0	$ 0	$ 0	$ 0	$ 0
Dividends	$ 0	$ 0	$ 0	$ 0	$ 0	$ 0	$ 0	$ 0
Total cash outflows	$115,221	$ 2,726	$ 2,730	$ 2,735	$ 2,740	$ 2,745	$ 2,750	$ 2,755
Net cash flow	$ 49,314	$12,047	$12,280	$12,513	$12,746	$ 12,979	$ 13,212	$ 13,446
Cash balance	$ 49,314	$61,360	$73,640	$86,153	$98,900	$111,879	$125,091	$138,537

Cash flow analysis (first year cont.)

Month	9	10	11	12	1
Cash from operations	$ 13,281	$ 13,519	$ 13,757	$ 13,996	$152,225
Cash from receivables	$ 0	$ 0	$ 0	$ 0	$ 0
Operating cash inflow	**$ 13,281**	**$ 13,519**	**$ 13,757**	**$ 13,996**	**$152,225**
Other cash inflows					
Equity investment	$ 0	$ 0	$ 0	$ 0	$ 25,000
Increased borrowings	$ 0	$ 0	$ 0	$ 0	$125,000
Sales of business assets	$ 0	$ 0	$ 0	$ 0	$ 0
A/P increases	$ 3,159	$ 3,159	$ 3,159	$ 3,159	$ 37,902
Total other cash inflows	**$ 3,159**	**$ 3,159**	**$ 3,159**	**$ 3,159**	**$187,902**
Total cash inflow	**$ 16,439**	**$ 16,678**	**$ 16,916**	**$ 17,154**	**$340,127**
Cash outflows					
Repayment of principal	$ 686	$ 691	$ 696	$ 701	$ 8,079
A/P decreases	$ 2,075	$ 2,075	$ 2,075	$ 2,075	$ 24,897
A/R increases	$ 0	$ 0	$ 0	$ 0	$ 0
Asset purchases	$ 0	$ 0	$ 0	$ 0	$112,500
Dividends	$ 0	$ 0	$ 0	$106,558	$106,558
Total cash outflows	**$ 2,760**	**$ 2,766**	**$ 2,771**	**$109,334**	**$252,034**
Net cash flow	**$ 13,679**	**$ 13,912**	**$ 14,145**	**−$ 92,180**	**$ 88,093**
Cash balance	**$152,216**	**$166,128**	**$180,273**	**$ 88,093**	**$ 88,093**

Cash flow analysis (second year)

Quarter	Q1	2 Q2	Q3	Q4	2
Cash from operations	$44,443	$55,554	$59,999	$ 62,221	$222,217
Cash from receivables	$ 0	$ 0	$ 0	$ 0	$ 0
Operating cash inflow	**$44,443**	**$55,554**	**$59,999**	**$ 62,221**	**$222,217**
Other cash inflows					
Equity investment	$ 0	$ 0	$ 0	$ 0	$ 0
Increased borrowings	$ 0	$ 0	$ 0	$ 0	$ 0
Sales of business assets	$ 0	$ 0	$ 0	$ 0	$ 0
A/P increases	$ 8,717	$10,897	$11,769	$ 12,204	$ 43,587
Total other cash inflows	**$ 8,717**	**$10,897**	**$11,769**	**$ 12,204**	**$ 43,587**
Total cash inflow	**$53,161**	**$66,451**	**$71,767**	**$ 74,425**	**$265,804**
Cash outflows					
Repayment of principal	$ 2,136	$ 2,184	$ 2,233	$ 2,284	$ 8,837
A/P decreases	$ 5,975	$ 7,469	$ 8,067	$ 8,365	$ 29,876
A/R increases	$ 0	$ 0	$ 0	$ 0	$ 0
Asset purchases	$11,111	$13,889	$15,000	$ 15,555	$ 55,554
Dividends	$31,110	$38,888	$41,999	$ 43,555	$155,552
Total cash outflows	**$50,332**	**$62,430**	**$67,299**	**$ 69,759**	**$249,820**
Net cash flow	**$ 2,829**	**$ 4,021**	**$ 4,468**	**$ 4,666**	**$ 15,985**
Cash balance	**$90,922**	**$94,944**	**$99,412**	**$104,078**	**$104,078**

Cash flow analysis (third year)

Quarter	Q1	Q2	Q3	Q4	3
Cash from operations	$ 57,852	$ 72,316	$ 78,101	$ 80,993	$289,262
Cash from receivables	$ 0	$ 0	$ 0	$ 0	$ 0
Operating cash inflow	**$ 57,852**	**$ 72,316**	**$ 78,101**	**$ 80,993**	**$289,262**
Other cash inflows					
Equity investment	$ 0	$ 0	$ 0	$ 0	$ 0
Increased borrowings	$ 0	$ 0	$ 0	$ 0	$ 0
Sales of business assets	$ 0	$ 0	$ 0	$ 0	$ 0
A/P increases	$ 10,025	$ 12,531	$ 13,534	$ 14,035	$ 50,125
Total other cash inflows	**$ 10,025**	**$ 12,531**	**$ 13,534**	**$ 14,035**	**$ 50,125**
Total cash inflow	**$ 67,878**	**$ 84,847**	**$ 91,635**	**$ 95,029**	**$339,388**
Cash outflows					
Repayment of principal	$ 2,336	$ 2,389	$ 2,443	$ 2,498	$ 9,666
A/P decreases	$ 7,170	$ 8,963	$ 9,680	$ 10,038	$ 35,852
A/R increases	$ 0	$ 0	$ 0	$ 0	$ 0
Asset purchases	$ 14,463	$ 18,079	$ 19,525	$ 20,248	$ 72,316
Dividends	$ 40,497	$ 50,621	$ 54,671	$ 56,695	$202,484
Total cash outflows	**$ 64,466**	**$ 80,052**	**$ 86,319**	**$ 89,481**	**$320,317**
Net cash flow	**$ 3,411**	**$ 4,795**	**$ 5,316**	**$ 5,548**	**$ 19,071**
Cash balance	**$107,489**	**$112,285**	**$117,601**	**$123,149**	**$123,149**

DVD Kiosk Rental Business

Movies To Go, Inc.

4700 Broad St.
Chicago, Illinois 60601

BizPlanDB.com

Movies To Go, Inc. will provide customers with state-of-the-art DVD kiosk machines and access to a large number of DVDs. The Company will provide location partners with a 30% revenue share for all income derived from each kiosk.

1.0 EXECUTIVE SUMMARY

The purpose of this business plan is to raise $100,000 for the development of a business that manages a network of DVD kiosks while showcasing the expected financials and operations over the next three years. Movies To Go, Inc. is an Illinois-based corporation that will manage several stand alone DVD rental kiosk machines in grocery stores and malls throughout the state. The Company was founded by Ethan Decker.

1.1 The Services

As stated above, the Company's state of the art DVD kiosk machines will provide customers with access to a number of DVDs. The Company will provide location partners with a 30% revenue share for all income derived from each kiosk.

The Founder, prior to the onset of operations, will develop relationships with malls, grocery stores, and property management firms for the distribution of the Company's DVD Kiosks.

The third section of the business plan will further describe the services offered by Movies To Go, Inc.

1.2 Financing

Mr. Decker is seeking to raise $100,000 from a bank loan. The interest rate and loan agreement are to be further discussed during negotiation. This business plan assumes that the business will receive a 10 year loan with a 9% fixed interest rate. The financing will be used for the following:

- Acquisition and distribution of at least 6 DVD kiosks

- Financing for the first six months of operation.

- Capital to purchase the inventory

Mr. Decker will contribute $10,000 to the venture.

1.3 Mission Statement

Mr. Decker's mission is to provide quick access to in-demand DVDs to customers while concurrently ensuring that businesses and organizations that allow the Company's machines on-site are compensated for their rental of space.

1.4 Management Team

The Company was founded by Ethan Decker. Mr. Decker has more than 10 years of experience in the retail industry. Through his expertise, he will be able to bring the operations of the business to profitability within its first year of operations.

1.5 Sales Forecasts

Mr. Decker expects a strong rate of growth at the start of operations. Below are the expected financials over the next three years.

Proforma profit and loss (yearly)

Year	1	2	3
Sales	$378,600	$454,320	$531,554
Operating costs	$188,688	$196,351	$204,301
EBITDA	$ 76,332	$121,673	$167,787
Taxes, interest, and depreciation	$ 43,815	$ 57,348	$ 74,461
Net profit	$ 32,517	$ 64,324	$ 93,326

Sales, operating costs, and profit forecast

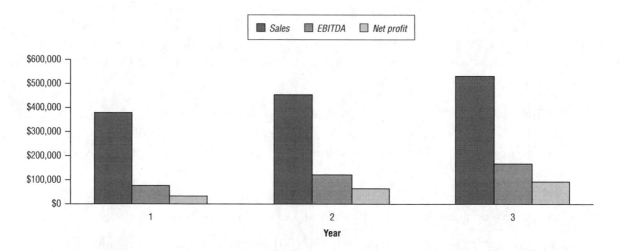

1.6 Expansion Plan

Within the next three years, Mr. Decker intends to reinvest the after tax cash flow of the business into the purchase of new DVD kiosks which will substantially increase the revenues of the business. The Company will continually source new high traffic locations where the business can place additional kiosks.

2.0 COMPANY AND FINANCING SUMMARY

2.1 Registered Name and Corporate Structure

Movies To Go, Inc. is registered as a corporation in the State of Illinois.

2.2 Required Funds

At this time, Movies To Go, Inc. requires $100,000 of debt funds. Below is a breakdown of how these funds will be used:

Projected startup costs

Working capital	$ 35,000
General FF&E	$ 10,000
DVD kiosks	$ 45,000
Inventory	$ 5,000
Insurance	$ 2,500
Distribution budget	$ 7,500
Miscellaneous and unforeseen costs	$ 5,000
Total startup costs	**$110,000**

Use of funds

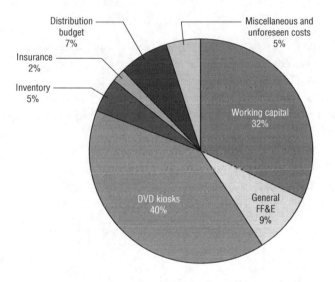

2.3 Investor Equity

Mr. Decker is not seeking an investment from a third party at this time.

2.4 Management Equity

Mr. Decker owns 100% of Movies To Go, Inc.

2.5 Exit Strategy

If the business is very successful, Mr. Decker may seek to sell the business to a third party for a significant earnings multiple. Most likely, the Company will hire a qualified business broker to sell the business on behalf of Movies To Go, Inc. Based on historical numbers, the business could fetch a sales premium of up to 2 times earnings plus the value of the Company's inventory of DVD Kiosks and related furniture, fixtures, and equipment.

3.0 PRODUCTS AND SERVICES

Below is a description of the products offered by Movies To Go, Inc.

3.1 DVD Rental Services

As stated in the executive summary, Movies To Go, Inc. intends to place a number of terminals that can provide rented DVDs to customers. These kiosks will be primarily placed in grocery stores, malls, and other highly trafficked areas.

The DVD kiosk will allow customers to rent a physical DVD after they pay (via cash or electronic card) at the card terminal. The business will charge $1 per night for usage of a DVD.

Please note that the fifth section of the business plan will further discuss the marketing and distribution strategies to be used by the Company.

4.0 STRATEGIC AND MARKET ANALYSIS

4.1 Economic Outlook

The business of DVD kiosk management is a relatively simple business. This section of analysis will detail the overall economic climate, and the interest rate environment, and the industry.

The current economic market in the United States is moderate. The meltdown of the sub prime mortgage market coupled with increasing gas prices has led many people to believe that the US is on the cusp of a double dip economic recession. This slowdown in the economy has also greatly impacted real estate sales, which has halted to historical lows. However, the low pricing point of the Company's DVD rental services will ensure that the Company can remain profitable despite the current issues with the economy.

4.2 Industry Analysis

Within the United States, there are 1,000 companies that maintain DVD standalone terminals. Each year, these businesses aggregately generate more than $500 million dollars of revenue.

This is a mature industry, and future growth is expected to be on par with that of the general economy.

4.3 Customer Profile

The DVD kiosk terminals are used by people from all socioeconomic levels. However, Management will target the following entities for placement of the Company's DVD rental terminals:

- Grocery stores

- Apartment buildings

- Malls

Management anticipates that among grocery stores, annual revenues will be $15 million to $30 million per year. These businesses are expected to currently not have DVD Kiosks on premises.

Among apartment buildings, Management anticipates that these complexes will have at least 150 units and annual rent rolls exceeding $1 million per year.

Within malls, Management anticipates that these will be large scale facilities with at least three department stores and 80 general stores.

4.4 Competition

At this time it is difficult to determine the competition that the Company will face as it progresses through its operations. There are a number of companies that maintain DVD kiosks within grocery stores, apartment buildings, and malls.

5.0 MARKETING PLAN

Below is a description of the marketing plan that Movies To Go, Inc. will use to establish its locations throughout the State of Illinois.

5.1 Marketing Objectives

- Establish relationships with property management firms, grocery stores, and malls.

- Maintain strong relationships with DVD kiosk equipment wholesalers throughout the State of Illinois.

5.2 Marketing Strategies

Marketing for the DVD kiosks will be very limited. The Company's marketing campaigns will be limited to developing relationships with property management firms. Prior to the onset of operations, Mr. Decker will approach these businesses for placing DVD kiosks on their properties.

The Company intends to also develop a website that will showcase the operations of the business, how a potential location can work with Movies To Go, Inc. and relevant contact information. As the economy is currently sluggish, many property management firms and related organizations are looking for ways to establish secondary lines of revenue; namely through the rental of space to DVD kiosk businesses.

Management will also directly approach newly developed properties that are looking to expand their secondary revenue streams as well.

5.3 Pricing

Management anticipates that the nightly rental of a DVD from one of the Company's kiosks will generate $1. Gross profits from sales will be $0.70. The business will need to pay out 30% of its income to the location owner.

6.0 ORGANIZATIONAL PLAN AND PERSONNEL SUMMARY

6.1 Corporate Organization

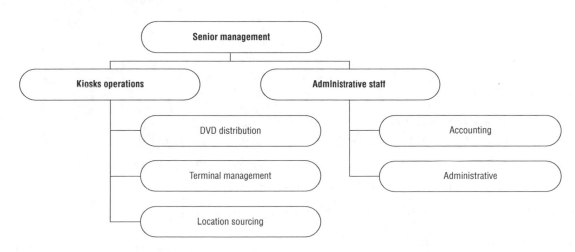

6.2 Organizational Budget

Personnel plan—yearly

Year	1	2	3
Owner	$ 40,000	$ 41,200	$ 42,436
Owner's assistant	$ 35,000	$ 36,050	$ 37,132
Kiosk manager	$ 32,500	$ 33,475	$ 34,479
Accountant (P/T)	$ 12,500	$ 12,875	$ 13,261
Total	**$120,000**	**$123,600**	**$127,308**

Numbers of personnel

Year	1	2	3
Owner	1	1	1
Owner's assistant	1	1	1
Kiosk manager	1	1	1
Accountant (P/T)	1	1	1
Totals	**4**	**4**	**4**

Personnel expense breakdown

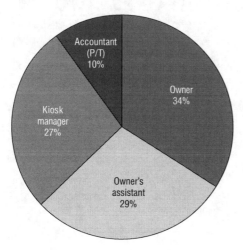

7.0 FINANCIAL PLAN

7.1 Underlying Assumptions

The Company has based its proforma financial statements on the following:

- Movies To Go, Inc. will have an annual revenue growth rate of 12% per year.

- The Owner will acquire $100,000 of debt funds to develop the business.

- The loan will have a 10 year term with a 9% interest rate.

7.2 Sensitivity Analysis

The Company's revenues are not sensitive to changes in the general economy. As the pricing for the DVD rental service, a decline in economic productivity will have a diminutive effect on the Company's ability to generate revenue. As such, Management will be able to continually grow the business despite the external business climate.

7.3 Source of Funds

Financing

Equity contributions

Management investment	$ 10,000.00
Total equity financing	**$ 10,000.00**

Banks and lenders

Banks and lenders	$ 100,000.00
Total debt financing	**$100,000.00**
Total financing	**$110,000.00**

7.4 General Assumptions

General assumptions

Year	1	2	3
Short term interest rate	9.5%	9.5%	9.5%
Long term interest rate	10.0%	10.0%	10.0%
Federal tax rate	33.0%	33.0%	33.0%
State tax rate	5.0%	5.0%	5.0%
Personnel taxes	15.0%	15.0%	15.0%

7.5 Profit and Loss Statements

Proforma profit and loss (yearly)

Year	1	2	3
Sales	**$378,600**	**$454,320**	**$531,554**
Cost of goods sold	$113,580	$136,296	$159,466
Gross margin	70.00%	70.00%	70.00%
Operating income	**$265,020**	**$318,024**	**$372,088**
Expenses			
Payroll	$120,000	$123,600	$127,308
General and administrative	$ 25,200	$ 26,208	$ 27,256
Marketing expenses	$ 1,893	$ 2,272	$ 2,058
Professional fees and licensure	$ 5,219	$ 5,376	$ 5,537
Insurance costs	$ 1,987	$ 2,086	$ 2,191
Travel and vehicle costs	$ 7,596	$ 8,356	$ 9,191
Rent and utilities	$ 4,250	$ 4,463	$ 4,686
Miscellaneous costs	$ 4,543	$ 5,452	$ 6,379
Payroll taxes	$ 18,000	$ 18,540	$ 19,096
Total operating costs	**$188,688**	**$196,351**	**$204,301**
EBITDA	**$ 76,332**	**$121,673**	**$167,787**
Federal income tax	$ 25,189	$ 37,469	$ 52,905
State income tax	$ 3,817	$ 5,677	$ 8,016
Interest expense	$ 8,738	$ 8,131	$ 7,468
Depreciation expenses	$ 6,071	$ 6,071	$ 6,071
Net profit	**$ 32,517**	**$ 64,324**	**$ 93,326**
Profit margin	**8.59%**	**14.16%**	**17.56%**

Sales, operating costs, and profit forecast

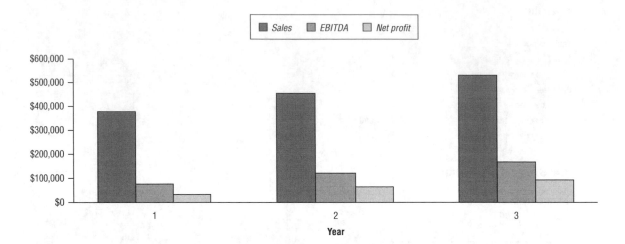

7.6 Cash Flow Analysis

Proforma cash flow analysis—yearly

Year	1	2	3
Cash from operations	$ 38,588	$ 70,396	$ 99,398
Cash from receivables	$ 0	$ 0	$ 0
Operating cash inflow	**$ 38,588**	**$ 70,396**	**$ 99,398**
Other cash inflows			
Equity investment	$ 10,000	$ 0	$ 0
Increased borrowings	$100,000	$ 0	$ 0
Sales of business assets	$ 0	$ 0	$ 0
A/P increases	$ 37,902	$ 43,587	$ 50,125
Total other cash inflows	**$147,902**	**$ 43,587**	**$ 50,125**
Total cash inflow	**$186,490**	**$113,983**	**$149,523**
Cash outflows			
Repayment of principal	$ 6,463	$ 7,070	$ 7,733
A/P decreases	$ 24,897	$ 29,876	$ 35,852
A/R increases	$ 0	$ 0	$ 0
Asset purchases	$ 85,000	$ 17,599	$ 24,849
Dividends	$ 27,012	$ 49,277	$ 69,578
Total cash outflows	**$143,372**	**$103,822**	**$138,012**
Net cash flow	**$ 43,118**	**$ 10,161**	**$ 11,511**
Cash balance	**$ 43,118**	**$ 53,279**	**$ 64,790**

Proforma cash flow (yearly)

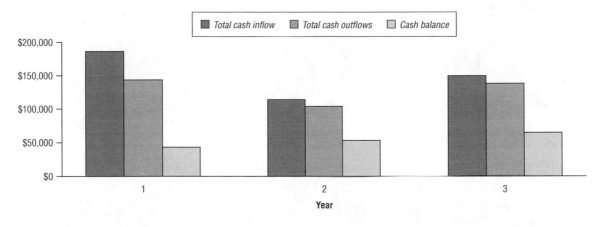

7.7 Balance Sheet

Proforma balance sheet—yearly

Year	1	2	3
Assets			
Cash	$ 43,118	$ 53,279	$ 64,790
Amortized development/expansion costs	$ 30,000	$ 34,400	$ 40,612
FF&E	$ 10,000	$ 10,000	$ 10,000
DVD kiosks	$ 45,000	$ 58,199	$ 76,836
Accumulated depreciation	($ 6,071)	($ 12,143)	($ 18,214)
Total assets	**$122,047**	**$143,735**	**$174,024**
Liabilities and equity			
Accounts payable	$ 13,005	$ 26,716	$ 40,990
Long term liabilities	$ 93,537	$ 86,467	$ 79,397
Other liabilities	$ 0	$ 0	$ 0
Total liabilities	**$106,542**	**$113,183**	**$120,387**
Net worth	**$ 15,505**	**$ 30,552**	**$ 53,637**
Total liabilities and equity	**$122,047**	**$143,735**	**$174,024**

Proforma balance sheet

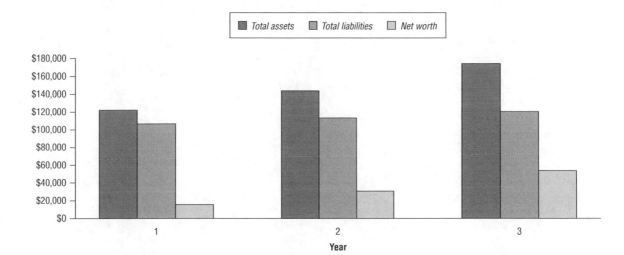

7.8 Breakeven Analysis

Monthly break even analysis

Year	1	2	3
Monthly revenue	$ 22,463	$ 23,375	$ 24,322
Yearly revenue	$269,555	$280,502	$291,859

Break even analysis

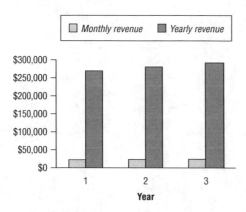

7.9 Business Ratios

Business ratios—yearly

Year	1	2	3
Sales			
Sales growth	0.00%	20.00%	17.00%
Gross margin	70.00%	70.00%	70.00%
Financials			
Profit margin	8.59%	14.16%	17.56%
Assets to liabilities	1.15	1.27	1.45
Equity to liabilities	0.15	0.27	0.45
Assets to equity	7.87	4.70	3.24
Liquidity			
Acid test	0.40	0.47	0.54
Cash to assets	0.35	0.37	0.37

7.10 Three Year Profit and Loss Statement

Profit and loss statement (first year)

Months	1	2	3	4	5	6	7
Sales	$31,000	$31,100	$31,200	$31,300	$31,400	$31,500	$31,600
Cost of goods sold	$ 9,300	$ 9,330	$ 9,360	$ 9,390	$ 9,420	$ 9,450	$ 9,480
Gross margin	70.0%	70.0%	70.0%	70.0%	70.0%	70.0%	70.0%
Operating income	**$21,700**	**$21,770**	**$21,840**	**$21,910**	**$21,980**	**$22,050**	**$22,120**
Expenses							
Payroll	$10,000	$10,000	$10,000	$10,000	$10,000	$10,000	$10,000
General and administrative	$ 2,100	$ 2,100	$ 2,100	$ 2,100	$ 2,100	$ 2,100	$ 2,100
Marketing expenses	$ 158	$ 158	$ 158	$ 158	$ 158	$ 158	$ 158
Professional fees and licensure	$ 435	$ 435	$ 435	$ 435	$ 435	$ 435	$ 435
Insurance costs	$ 166	$ 166	$ 166	$ 166	$ 166	$ 166	$ 166
Travel and vehicle costs	$ 633	$ 633	$ 633	$ 633	$ 633	$ 633	$ 633
Rent and utilities	$ 354	$ 354	$ 354	$ 354	$ 354	$ 354	$ 354
Miscellaneous costs	$ 379	$ 379	$ 379	$ 379	$ 379	$ 379	$ 379
Payroll taxes	$ 1,500	$ 1,500	$ 1,500	$ 1,500	$ 1,500	$ 1,500	$ 1,500
Total operating costs	**$15,724**	**$15,724**	**$15,724**	**$15,724**	**$15,724**	**$15,724**	**$15,724**
EBITDA	**$ 5,976**	**$ 6,046**	**$ 6,116**	**$ 6,186**	**$ 6,256**	**$ 6,326**	**$ 6,396**
Federal income tax	$ 2,063	$ 2,069	$ 2,076	$ 2,082	$ 2,089	$ 2,096	$ 2,102
State income tax	$ 313	$ 314	$ 315	$ 316	$ 317	$ 318	$ 319
Interest expense	$ 750	$ 746	$ 742	$ 738	$ 734	$ 730	$ 726
Depreciation expense	$ 506	$ 506	$ 506	$ 506	$ 506	$ 506	$ 506
Net profit	**$ 2,345**	**$ 2,411**	**$ 2,477**	**$ 2,544**	**$ 2,610**	**$ 2,676**	**$ 2,743**

Profit and loss statement (first year cont.)

Month	8	9	10	11	12	1
Sales	$31,700	$31,800	$31,900	$32,000	$32,100	$378,600
Cost of goods sold	$ 9,510	$ 9,540	$ 9,570	$ 9,600	$ 9,630	$113,580
Gross margin	70.0%	70.0%	70.0%	70.0%	70.0%	70.0%
Operating income	**$22,190**	**$22,260**	**$22,330**	**$22,400**	**$22,470**	**$265,020**
Expenses						
Payroll	$10,000	$10,000	$10,000	$10,000	$10,000	$120,000
General and administrative	$ 2,100	$ 2,100	$ 2,100	$ 2,100	$ 2,100	$ 25,200
Marketing expenses	$ 158	$ 158	$ 158	$ 158	$ 158	$ 1,893
Professional fees and licensure	$ 435	$ 435	$ 435	$ 435	$ 435	$ 5,219
Insurance costs	$ 166	$ 166	$ 166	$ 166	$ 166	$ 1,987
Travel and vehicle costs	$ 633	$ 633	$ 633	$ 633	$ 633	$ 7,596
Rent and utilities	$ 354	$ 354	$ 354	$ 354	$ 354	$ 4,250
Miscellaneous costs	$ 379	$ 379	$ 379	$ 379	$ 379	$ 4,543
Payroll taxes	$ 1,500	$ 1,500	$ 1,500	$ 1,500	$ 1,500	$ 18,000
Total operating costs	**$15,724**	**$15,724**	**$15,724**	**$15,724**	**$15,724**	**$188,688**
EBITDA	**$ 6,466**	**$ 6,536**	**$ 6,606**	**$ 6,676**	**$ 6,746**	**$ 76,332**
Federal income tax	$ 2,109	$ 2,116	$ 2,122	$ 2,129	$ 2,136	$ 25,189
State income tax	$ 320	$ 321	$ 322	$ 323	$ 324	$ 3,817
Interest expense	$ 722	$ 718	$ 714	$ 710	$ 706	$ 8,738
Depreciation expense	$ 506	$ 506	$ 506	$ 506	$ 506	$ 6,071
Net profit	**$ 2,809**	**$ 2,876**	**$ 2,942**	**$ 3,008**	**$ 3,075**	**$ 32,517**

DVD KIOSK RENTAL BUSINESS

Profit and loss statement (second year)

Quarter	Q1	Q2	Q3	Q4	2
Sales	$90,864	$113,580	$122,666	$127,210	$454,320
Cost of goods sold	$27,259	$ 34,074	$ 36,800	$ 38,163	$136,296
Gross margin	70.0%	70.0%	70.0%	70.0%	70.0%
Operating income	$63,605	$ 79,506	$ 85,866	$ 89,047	$318,024
Expenses					
Payroll	$24,720	$ 30,900	$ 33,372	$ 34,608	$123,600
General and administrative	$ 5,242	$ 6,552	$ 7,076	$ 7,338	$ 26,208
Marketing expenses	$ 454	$ 568	$ 613	$ 636	$ 2,272
Professional fees and licensure	$ 1,075	$ 1,344	$ 1,451	$ 1,505	$ 5,376
Insurance costs	$ 417	$ 522	$ 563	$ 584	$ 2,086
Travel and vehicle costs	$ 1,671	$ 2,089	$ 2,256	$ 2,340	$ 8,356
Rent and utilities	$ 893	$ 1,116	$ 1,205	$ 1,250	$ 4,463
Miscellaneous costs	$ 1,090	$ 1,363	$ 1,472	$ 1,527	$ 5,452
Payroll taxes	$ 3,708	$ 4,635	$ 5,006	$ 5,191	$ 18,540
Total operating costs	$39,270	$ 49,088	$ 53,015	$ 54,978	$196,351
EBITDA	$24,335	$ 30,418	$ 32,852	$ 34,068	$121,673
Federal income tax	$ 7,494	$ 9,367	$ 10,117	$ 10,491	$ 37,469
State income tax	$ 1,135	$ 1,419	$ 1,533	$ 1,590	$ 5,677
Interest expense	$ 2,092	$ 2,053	$ 2,013	$ 1,973	$ 8,131
Depreciation expense	$ 1,518	$ 1,518	$ 1,518	$ 1,518	$ 6,071
Net profit	$12,096	$ 16,061	$ 17,671	$ 18,497	$ 64,324

Profit and loss statement (third year)

Quarter	Q1	Q2	Q3	Q4	3
Sales	$106,311	$132,889	$143,520	$148,835	$531,554
Cost of goods sold	$ 31,893	$ 39,867	$ 43,056	$ 44,651	$159,466
Gross margin	70.0%	70.0%	70.0%	70.0%	70.0%
Operating income	$ 74,418	$ 93,022	$100,464	$104,185	$372,088
Expenses					
Payroll	$ 25,462	$ 31,827	$ 34,373	$ 35,646	$127,308
General and administrative	$ 5,451	$ 6,814	$ 7,359	$ 7,632	$ 27,256
Marketing expenses	$ 532	$ 664	$ 718	$ 744	$ 2,658
Professional fees and licensure	$ 1,107	$ 1,384	$ 1,495	$ 1,550	$ 5,537
Insurance costs	$ 438	$ 548	$ 591	$ 613	$ 2,191
Travel and vehicle costs	$ 1,838	$ 2,298	$ 2,482	$ 2,574	$ 9,191
Rent and utilities	$ 937	$ 1,171	$ 1,265	$ 1,312	$ 4,686
Miscellaneous costs	$ 1,276	$ 1,595	$ 1,722	$ 1,786	$ 6,379
Payroll taxes	$ 3,819	$ 4,774	$ 5,156	$ 5,347	$ 19,096
Total operating costs	$ 40,860	$ 51,075	$ 55,161	$ 57,204	$204,301
EBITDA	$ 33,557	$ 41,947	$ 45,302	$ 46,980	$167,787
Federal income tax	$ 10,581	$ 13,226	$ 14,284	$ 14,813	$ 52,905
State income tax	$ 1,603	$ 2,004	$ 2,164	$ 2,244	$ 8,016
Interest expense	$ 1,932	$ 1,889	$ 1,846	$ 1,802	$ 7,468
Depreciation expense	$ 1,518	$ 1,518	$ 1,518	$ 1,518	$ 6,071
Net profit	$ 17,924	$ 23,309	$ 25,490	$ 26,603	$ 93,326

7.11 Three Year Cash Flow Analysis

Cash flow analysis (first year)

Month	1	2	3	4	5	6	7
Cash from operations	$ 2,851	$ 2,917	$ 2,983	$ 3,050	$ 3,116	$ 3,182	$ 3,249
Cash from receivables	$ 0	$ 0	$ 0	$ 0	$ 0	$ 0	$ 0
Operating cash inflow	**$ 2,851**	**$ 2,917**	**$ 2,983**	**$ 3,050**	**$ 3,116**	**$ 3,182**	**$ 3,249**
Other cash inflows							
Equity investment	$ 10,000	$ 0	$ 0	$ 0	$ 0	$ 0	$ 0
Increased borrowings	$100,000	$ 0	$ 0	$ 0	$ 0	$ 0	$ 0
Sales of business assets	$ 0	$ 0	$ 0	$ 0	$ 0	$ 0	$ 0
A/P increases	$ 3,159	$ 3,159	$ 3,159	$ 3,159	$ 3,159	$ 3,159	$ 3,159
Total other cash inflows	**$113,159**	**$ 3,159**	**$ 3,159**	**$ 3,159**	**$ 3,159**	**$ 3,159**	**$ 3,159**
Total cash inflow	**$116,009**	**$ 6,076**	**$ 6,142**	**$ 6,208**	**$ 6,274**	**$ 6,341**	**$ 6,407**
Cash outflows							
Repayment of principal	$ 517	$ 521	$ 525	$ 528	$ 532	$ 536	$ 540
A/P decreases	$ 2,075	$ 2,075	$ 2,075	$ 2,075	$ 2,075	$ 2,075	$ 2,075
A/R increases	$ 0	$ 0	$ 0	$ 0	$ 0	$ 0	$ 0
Asset purchases	$ 85,000	$ 0	$ 0	$ 0	$ 0	$ 0	$ 0
Dividends	$ 0	$ 0	$ 0	$ 0	$ 0	$ 0	$ 0
Total cash outflows	**$ 87,592**	**$ 2,595**	**$ 2,599**	**$ 2,603**	**$ 2,607**	**$ 2,611**	**$ 2,615**
Net cash flow	**$ 28,418**	**$ 3,480**	**$ 3,543**	**$ 3,605**	**$ 3,667**	**$ 3,730**	**$ 3,792**
Cash balance	**$ 28,418**	**$31,898**	**$35,441**	**$39,046**	**$42,713**	**$46,443**	**$50,235**

Cash flow analysis (first year cont.)

Month	8	9	10	11	12	1
Cash from operations	$ 3,315	$ 3,381	$ 3,448	$ 3,514	$ 3,581	$ 38,588
Cash from receivables	$ 0	$ 0	$ 0	$ 0	$ 0	$ 0
Operating cash inflow	**$ 3,315**	**$ 3,381**	**$ 3,448**	**$ 3,514**	**$ 3,581**	**$ 38,588**
Other cash inflows						
Equity investment	$ 0	$ 0	$ 0	$ 0	$ 0	$ 10,000
Increased borrowings	$ 0	$ 0	$ 0	$ 0	$ 0	$100,000
Sales of business assets	$ 0	$ 0	$ 0	$ 0	$ 0	$ 0
A/P increases	$ 3,159	$ 3,159	$ 3,159	$ 3,159	$ 3,159	$ 37,902
Total other cash inflows	**$ 3,159**	**$ 3,159**	**$ 3,159**	**$ 3,159**	**$ 3,159**	**$147,902**
Total cash inflow	**$ 6,474**	**$ 6,540**	**$ 6,606**	**$ 6,673**	**$ 6,739**	**$186,490**
Cash outflows						
Repayment of principal	$ 545	$ 549	$ 553	$ 557	$ 561	$ 6,463
A/P decreases	$ 2,075	$ 2,075	$ 2,075	$ 2,075	$ 2,075	$ 24,897
A/R increases	$ 0	$ 0	$ 0	$ 0	$ 0	$ 0
Asset purchases	$ 0	$ 0	$ 0	$ 0	$ 0	$ 85,000
Dividends	$ 0	$ 0	$ 0	$ 0	$ 27,012	$ 27,012
Total cash outflows	**$ 2,619**	**$ 2,623**	**$ 2,627**	**$ 2,632**	**$ 29,648**	**$143,372**
Net cash flow	**$ 3,854**	**$ 3,917**	**$ 3,979**	**$ 4,041**	**−$ 22,908**	**$ 43,118**
Cash balance	**$54,089**	**$58,006**	**$61,985**	**$66,026**	**$ 43,118**	**$ 43,118**

Cash flow analysis (second year)

Quarter	Q1	2 Q2	Q3	Q4	2
Cash from operations	$14,079	$17,599	$19,007	$19,711	$ 70,396
Cash from receivables	$ 0	$ 0	$ 0	$ 0	$ 0
Operating cash inflow	**$14,079**	**$17,599**	**$19,007**	**$19,711**	**$ 70,396**
Other cash inflows					
Equity investment	$ 0	$ 0	$ 0	$ 0	$ 0
Increased borrowings	$ 0	$ 0	$ 0	$ 0	$ 0
Sales of business assets	$ 0	$ 0	$ 0	$ 0	$ 0
A/P increases	$ 8,717	$10,897	$11,769	$12,204	$ 43,587
Total other cash inflows	**$ 8,717**	**$10,897**	**$11,769**	**$12,204**	**$ 43,587**
Total cash inflow	**$22,797**	**$28,496**	**$30,775**	**$31,915**	**$113,983**
Cash outflows					
Repayment of principal	$ 1,708	$ 1,747	$ 1,787	$ 1,827	$ 7,070
A/P decreases	$ 5,975	$ 7,469	$ 8,067	$ 8,365	$ 29,876
A/R increases	$ 0	$ 0	$ 0	$ 0	$ 0
Asset purchases	$ 3,520	$ 4,400	$ 4,752	$ 4,928	$ 17,599
Dividends	$ 9,855	$12,319	$13,305	$13,798	$ 49,277
Total cash outflows	**$21,059**	**$25,935**	**$27,910**	**$28,918**	**$103,822**
Net cash flow	**$ 1,738**	**$ 2,560**	**$ 2,865**	**$ 2,997**	**$ 10,161**
Cash balance	**$44,856**	**$47,416**	**$50,282**	**$53,279**	**$ 53,279**

Cash flow analysis (third year)

Quarter	Q1	3 Q2	Q3	Q4	3
Cash from operations	$19,880	$24,849	$26,837	$27,831	$ 99,398
Cash from receivables	$ 0	$ 0	$ 0	$ 0	$ 0
Operating cash inflow	**$19,880**	**$24,849**	**$26,837**	**$27,831**	**$ 99,398**
Other cash inflows					
Equity investment	$ 0	$ 0	$ 0	$ 0	$ 0
Increased borrowings	$ 0	$ 0	$ 0	$ 0	$ 0
Sales of business assets	$ 0	$ 0	$ 0	$ 0	$ 0
A/P increases	$10,025	$12,531	$13,534	$14,035	$ 50,125
Total other cash inflows	**$10,025**	**$12,531**	**$13,534**	**$14,035**	**$ 50,125**
Total cash inflow	**$29,905**	**$37,381**	**$40,371**	**$41,866**	**$149,523**
Cash outflows					
Repayment of principal	$ 1,869	$ 1,911	$ 1,954	$ 1,999	$ 7,733
A/P decreases	$ 7,170	$ 8,963	$ 9,680	$10,038	$ 35,852
A/R increases	$ 0	$ 0	$ 0	$ 0	$ 0
Asset purchases	$ 4,970	$ 6,212	$ 6,709	$ 6,958	$ 24,849
Dividends	$13,916	$17,395	$18,786	$19,482	$ 69,578
Total cash outflows	**$27,925**	**$34,481**	**$37,130**	**$38,477**	**$138,012**
Net cash flow	**$ 1,980**	**$ 2,900**	**$ 3,241**	**$ 3,390**	**$ 11,511**
Cash balance	**$55,259**	**$58,159**	**$61,400**	**$64,790**	**$ 64,790**

Grant Writer

Landon Consulting

8800 15th St.
Washington, DC 20001

BizPlanDB.com

Landon Consulting will specialize in providing searches and grant writing for business and personal grants to the general public within the Washington, DC, metropolitan area. The business will generate revenues, on a per hour basis, for the development of grant applications and documentation related to acquiring business grants and personal grants.

1.0 EXECUTIVE SUMMARY

The purpose of this business plan is to raise $50,000 for the development of a grant writing and grant search company while showcasing the expected financials and operations over the next three years. Landon Consulting is a Washington, DC-based corporation that will provide grant searches and grant writing to small- and medium-sized businesses in its targeted market. The Company was founded by Cliff Landon.

1.1 The Services

Landon Consulting will specialize in providing searches and grant writing for business and personal grants to the general public within the Washington, DC, metropolitan area. The business will generate revenues, on a per hour basis, for the development of grant applications and documentation related to acquiring business grants and personal grants.

The Company will generate revenues on a secondary basis from the success fees from acquiring grants on behalf of individuals and businesses. The average success fee will be equal to 5% of the total amount of the secured grant.

The third section of the business plan will further describe the services offered by Landon Consulting.

1.2 Financing

Mr. Landon is seeking to raise $50,000 from a bank loan. The interest rate and loan agreement are to be further discussed during negotiation. This business plan assumes that the business will receive a 10 year loan with a 9% fixed interest rate. The financing will be used for the following:

• Development of the Company's office location.

• Financing for the first six months of operation.

• Capital to purchase computer and technology equipment.

Mr. Landon will contribute $10,000 to the venture.

1.3 Mission Statement

Landon Consulting's mission is to become the recognized leader in its targeted market for grant writing and grant search services.

1.4 Management Team

The Company was founded by Cliff Landon. Mr. Landon has more than 10 years of experience in the grant industry. Through his expertise, he will be able to bring the operations of the business to profitability within its first year of operations.

1.5 Sales Forecasts

Mr. Landon expects a strong rate of growth at the start of operations. Below are the expected financials over the next three years.

Proforma profit and loss (yearly)

Year	1	2	3
Sales	$549,000	$658,800	$770,796
Operating costs	$496,639	$548,981	$573,655
EBITDA	$ 24,911	$ 76,879	$158,601
Taxes, interest, and depreciation	$ 16,692	$ 34,592	$ 65,441
Net profit	$ 8,219	$ 42,287	$ 93,160

Sales, operating costs, and profit forecast

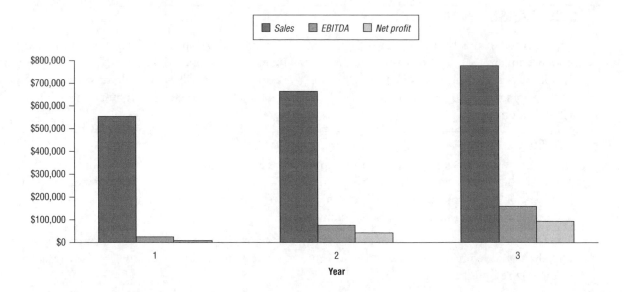

1.6 Expansion Plan

The Founder expects that the business will aggressively expand during the first three years of operation. Mr. Landon intends to implement marketing campaigns that will effectively target small and medium sized businesses as well as individuals within the target market that are in need of small business grants.

2.0 COMPANY AND FINANCING SUMMARY

2.1 Registered Name and Corporate Structure

Landon Consulting is registered as a corporation in Washington, DC.

2.2 Required Funds

At this time, Landon Consulting requires $50,000 of debt funds. Below is a breakdown of how these funds will be used:

Projected startup costs

Initial lease payments and deposits	$ 5,000
Working capital	$10,000
FF&E	$15,000
Leasehold improvements	$ 2,500
Security deposits	$ 2,500
Insurance	$ 2,500
Computer and technology equipment	$15,000
Marketing budget	$ 5,000
Miscellaneous and unforeseen costs	$ 2,500
Total startup costs	**$60,000**

Use of funds

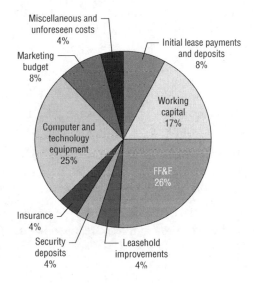

2.3 Investor Equity

Mr. Landon is not seeking an investment from a third party at this time.

2.4 Management Equity

Mr. Landon owns 100% of the Landon Consulting

2.5 Exit Strategy

If the business is very successful, Mr. Landon may seek to sell the business to a third party for a significant earnings multiple. Most likely, Landon Consulting will hire a qualified business broker to sell the business on behalf of Landon Consulting. Based on historical numbers, the business could fetch a sales premium of up to 5 times earnings.

3.0 GRANT SEARCH SERVICES

Following is a description of the services offered by Landon Consulting.

3.2 Grant Writing Services

The Company will generate its primary streams of revenue through the ongoing preparation of documents as it relates to grant searches. Landon Consulting will charge $50 to $100 per hour for these services.

3.3 Grant Search Services

A secondary revenue center for the business will come from grant searches and grant placement. For each successfully placed grant, the business will receive a fee of approximately 5% of the total funds secured.

4.0 STRATEGIC AND MARKET ANALYSIS

4.1 Economic Outlook

This section of the analysis will detail the economic climate, the grant writing and grant search consulting industry, the customer profile, and the competition that the business will face as it progresses through its business operations.

Currently, the economic market condition in the United States is moderate. The meltdown of the sub prime mortgage market coupled with increasing gas prices has led many people to believe that the US is on the cusp of a double dip economic recession. This slowdown in the economy has also greatly impacted real estate sales, which has halted to historical lows.

4.2 Industry Analysis

The grant search, grant writing, and consulting industry is a highly fragmented group of individual practitioners, small firms, and large auditing institutions. There are over 621,000 consulting in the United States. The industry generates over $38 billion dollars a year, and employs over 390,000 Americans.

Specific to companies that write grants and perform grant searches, there are approximately 15,000 market agents that provide this service for individuals, small businesses, and large companies that have specialized grant needs. Each year, these firms aggregately generate approximately $1.3 billion of revenues.

The demand for grant search and related services is expected to increase as the demand among individuals for federal, state, and private agency grants will expand as Congress creates new programs to develop the struggling US economy.

4.3 Customer Profile

By acting in a multifaceted grant search and grant writing capacity, Landon Consulting will be able to instruct and guide small businesses and corporate clients based on their specific grant needs. Below is a demographic profile of the businesses that Management will continue to target as potential clientele:

- Privately owned business

- Has less than $1,000,000 per year of revenue

- Has EBITDA of $50,000 to $250,000 per year.

4.4 Competition

Grant writing has become somewhat of a commoditized business. With the advent of the Internet, many firms can now reach potentially millions of individuals and businesses that are seeking to capitalize on federal, state, and municipal grants for their specific projects. This is especially true among businesses that are owned by minorities and women. Landon Consulting intends to maintain an expansive competitive advantage by coupling its grant writing services with grant search services. Over time, and as the business is able to secure grants on behalf of its clients, Landon Consulting will be able to capitalize on the success of the Company's operations as part of its overall marketing infrastructure.

5.0 MARKETING PLAN

Landon Consulting intends to maintain an extensive marketing campaign that will ensure maximum visibility for the business in its targeted market. Below is an overview of the marketing strategies and objectives of Landon Consulting.

5.1 Marketing Objectives

- Establish relationships with other business consultants within the targeted market.

- Establish ongoing referral relationships with accountants that have clients that are seeking specific types of grants.

- Develop strong relationships with grant program directors so that proposals can be quickly submitted on behalf of clients.

5.2 Marketing Strategies

Mr. Landon intends on using a number of marketing strategies that will allow Landon Consulting to easily target small and medium sized businesses (as well as individuals) within the market. To that end, Management intends to use both traditional advertising methods as well as internet marketing strategies.

Landon Consulting will frequently take out advertisements in magazines and publications that focus on entrepreneurship and green energy developments (there are a number of grants for green energy businesses and initiatives). These advertisements will clearly showcase the Company's operations, its services offered, previous successes with grant applications, and preliminary fee structures.

Landon Consulting will also harness the power of the Internet in order to have potential grant applicants use the Company's services. This website will feature much of the same information that is found in the Company's traditional print advertisements. The website may also feature samples of previous written grants while concurrently showcasing the success rate of the business.

Additionally, and as stated above, Landon Consulting will develop strong connections with business consultants and accountants that have clients that are seeking to obtain grants. In time, this will become an invaluable source of marketing for the business. Management must develop an outstanding track record in order to develop a stable of referring partners.

5.3 Pricing

Management intends to charge $50 to $100 per hour for the writing of grant proposals for individuals and business clients. Additionally, in regards to the Company's grant search/placement services the business will receive a fee equal to 5% of the face value of the disbursed grant.

6.0 ORGANIZATIONAL PLAN AND PERSONNEL SUMMARY

6.1 Corporate Organization

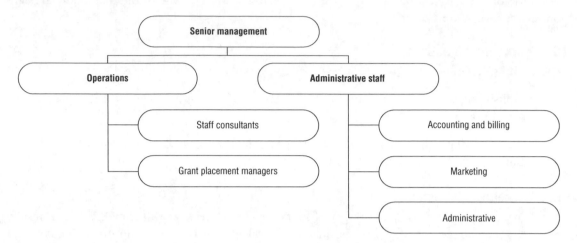

6.2 Organizational Budget

Personnel plan—yearly

Year	1	2	3
Senior management	$ 75,000	$ 77,250	$ 79,568
Business advisors and consultants	$110,000	$113,300	$116,699
Project managers	$ 90,000	$ 92,700	$ 95,481
Accountant	$ 32,500	$ 33,475	$ 34,479
Administrative	$ 25,000	$ 51,500	$ 53,045
Total	**$332,500**	**$368,225**	**$379,272**

Numbers of personnel

Year	1	2	3
Senior management	1	1	1
Business advisors and consultants	2	2	2
Project managers	2	2	2
Accountant	1	1	1
Administrative	1	2	2
Totals	**7**	**8**	**8**

Personnel expense breakdown

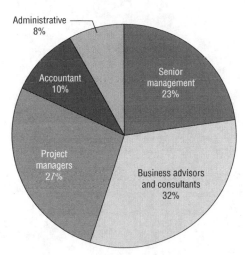

7.0 FINANCIAL PLAN

7.1 Underlying Assumptions

The proforma financial statements are based on the following:

- Landon Consulting will have an annual revenue growth rate of 13.7% per year.

- The Owner will acquire $50,000 of debt funds to develop the business.

- The loan will have a 10 year term with a 9% interest rate.

7.2 Sensitivity Analysis

In the event of an economic downturn, the business may have a decline in its revenues. However, specialized grant writing and related consulting services are typically in demand despite difficult economic climates as small and medium sized businesses seek grants. Additionally, the very high margin revenues generated from per hour fees and grant placement fees will ensure that the business can continually satisfy its debt obligations despite declines in top line income.

7.3 Source of Funds

Financing

Equity contributions	
Investor(s)	$ 10,000.00
Total equity financing	**$10,000.00**
Banks and lenders	
Banks and lenders	$ 50,000.00
Total debt financing	**$50,000.00**
Total financing	**$60,000.00**

7.4 General Assumptions

General assumptions

Year	1	2	3
Short term interest rate	9.5%	9.5%	9.5%
Long term interest rate	10.0%	10.0%	10.0%
Federal tax rate	33.0%	33.0%	33.0%
State tax rate	5.0%	5.0%	5.0%
Personnel taxes	15.0%	15.0%	15.0%

7.5 Profit and Loss Statements

Proforma profit and loss (yearly)

Year	1	2	3
Sales	**$549,000**	**$658,800**	**$770,796**
Cost of goods sold	$ 27,450	$ 32,940	$ 38,540
Gross margin	95.00%	95.00%	95.00%
Operating income	**$521,550**	**$625,860**	**$732,256**
Expenses			
Payroll	$332,500	$368,225	$379,272
General and administrative	$ 12,000	$ 12,480	$ 12,979
Marketing expenses	$ 13,176	$ 15,811	$ 18,499
Professional fees and licensure	$ 2,500	$ 2,575	$ 2,652
Insurance costs	$ 10,000	$ 10,500	$ 11,025
Travel and vehicle costs	$ 55,000	$ 60,500	$ 66,550
Rent and utilities	$ 15,000	$ 15,750	$ 16,538
Miscellaneous costs	$ 6,588	$ 7,906	$ 9,250
Payroll taxes	$ 49,875	$ 55,234	$ 56,891
Total operating costs	**$496,639**	**$548,981**	**$573,655**
EBITDA	**$ 24,911**	**$ 76,879**	**$158,601**
Federal income tax	$ 8,221	$ 24,029	$ 51,106
State income tax	$ 1,246	$ 3,641	$ 7,743
Interest expense	$ 4,369	$ 4,066	$ 3,734
Depreciation expenses	$ 2,857	$ 2,857	$ 2,857
Net profit	**$ 8,219**	**$ 42,287**	**$ 93,160**
Profit margin	**1.50%**	**6.42%**	**12.09%**

Sales, operating costs, and profit forecast

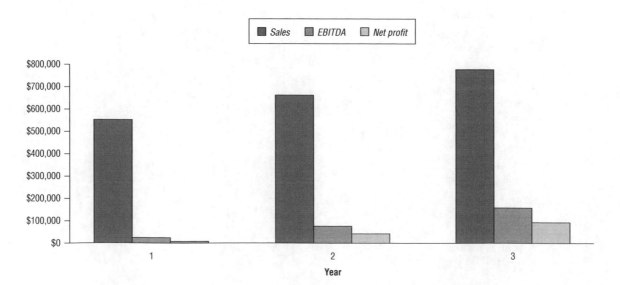

7.6 Cash Flow Analysis

Proforma cash flow analysis—yearly

Year	1	2	3
Cash from operations	$11,076	$45,145	$ 96,018
Cash from receivables	$ 0	$ 0	$ 0
Operating cash inflow	**$11,076**	**$45,145**	**$ 96,018**
Other cash inflows			
Equity investment	$10,000	$ 0	$ 0
Increased borrowings	$50,000	$ 0	$ 0
Sales of business assets	$ 0	$ 0	$ 0
A/P increases	$ 7,500	$ 8,625	$ 9,919
Total other cash inflows	**$67,500**	**$ 8,625**	**$ 9,919**
Total cash inflow	**$78,576**	**$53,770**	**$105,936**
Cash outflows			
Repayment of principal	$ 3,232	$ 3,535	$ 3,866
A/P decreases	$ 6,000	$ 7,200	$ 8,640
A/R increases	$ 0	$ 0	$ 0
Asset purchases	$40,000	$11,286	$ 24,004
Dividends	$ 7,753	$31,601	$ 67,212
Total cash outflows	**$56,985**	**$53,622**	**$103,723**
Net cash flow	**$21,591**	**$ 147**	**$ 2,213**
Cash balance	**$21,591**	**$21,738**	**$ 23,952**

Proforma cash flow (yearly)

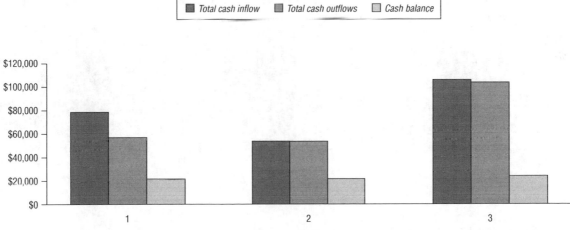

7.7 Balance Sheet

Proforma balance sheet—yearly

Year	1	2	3
Assets			
Cash	$21,591	$21,738	$23,952
Amortized expansion costs	$10,000	$11,129	$13,529
Computer and technology assets	$15,000	$23,465	$41,468
FF&E	$15,000	$16,693	$20,294
Accumulated depreciation	($ 2,857)	($ 5,714)	($ 8,571)
Total assets	**$58,734**	**$67,310**	**$90,671**
Liabilities and equity			
Accounts payable	$ 1,500	$ 2,925	$ 4,204
Long term liabilities	$46,768	$43,233	$39,699
Other liabilities	$ 0	$ 0	$ 0
Total liabilities	**$48,268**	**$46,158**	**$43,902**
Net worth	**$10,466**	**$21,152**	**$46,768**
Total liabilities and equity	**$58,734**	**$67,310**	**$90,671**

Proforma balance sheet

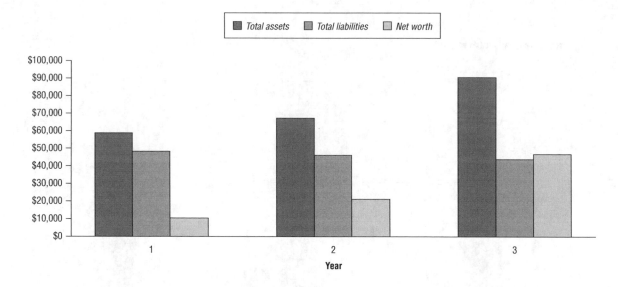

7.8 Breakeven Analysis

Monthly break even analysis

Year	1	2	3
Monthly revenue	$ 43,565	$ 48,156	$ 50,321
Yearly revenue	$522,778	$577,874	$603,847

Break even analysis

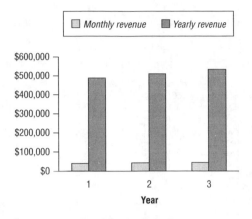

| | Monthly revenue | Yearly revenue |

7.9 Business Ratios

Business ratios—yearly

Year	1	2	3
Sales			
Sales growth	0.00%	20.00%	17.00%
Gross margin	95.00%	95.00%	95.00%
Financials			
Profit margin	1.50%	6.42%	12.09%
Assets to liabilities	1.22	1.46	2.07
Equity to liabilities	0.22	0.46	1.07
Assets to equity	5.61	3.18	1.94
Liquidity			
Acid test	0.45	0.47	0.55
Cash to assets	0.37	0.32	0.26

7.10 Three Year Profit and Loss Statement

Profit and loss statement (first year)

Months	1	2	3	4	5	6	7
Sales	$37,500	$39,000	$40,500	$42,000	$43,500	$45,000	$46,500
Cost of goods sold	$ 1,875	$ 1,950	$ 2,025	$ 2,100	$ 2,175	$ 2,025	$ 2,325
Gross margin	95.0%	95.0%	95.0%	95.0%	95.0%	95.0%	95.0%
Operating income	$35,625	$37,050	$38,475	$39,900	$41,325	$42,750	$44,175
Expenses							
Payroll	$27,708	$27,708	$27,708	$27,708	$27,708	$27,708	$27,708
General and administrative	$ 1,000	$ 1,000	$ 1,000	$ 1,000	$ 1,000	$ 1,000	$ 1,000
Marketing expenses	$ 1,098	$ 1,098	$ 1,098	$ 1,098	$ 1,098	$ 1,098	$ 1,098
Professional fees and licensure	$ 208	$ 208	$ 208	$ 208	$ 208	$ 208	$ 208
Insurance costs	$ 833	$ 833	$ 833	$ 833	$ 833	$ 833	$ 833
Travel and vehicle costs	$ 4,583	$ 4,583	$ 4,583	$ 4,583	$ 4,583	$ 4,583	$ 4,583
Rent and utilities	$ 1,250	$ 1,250	$ 1,250	$ 1,250	$ 1,250	$ 1,250	$ 1,250
Miscellaneous costs	$ 549	$ 549	$ 549	$ 549	$ 549	$ 549	$ 549
Payroll taxes	$ 4,156	$ 4,156	$ 4,156	$ 4,156	$ 4,156	$ 4,156	$ 4,156
Total operating costs	$41,387	$41,387	$41,387	$41,387	$41,387	$41,387	$41,387
EBITDA	−$ 5,762	−$ 4,337	−$ 2,912	−$ 1,487	−$ 62	$ 1,363	$ 2,788
Federal income tax	$ 562	$ 584	$ 606	$ 629	$ 651	$ 674	$ 696
State income tax	$ 85	$ 88	$ 92	$ 95	$ 99	$ 102	$ 105
Interest expense	$ 375	$ 373	$ 371	$ 369	$ 367	$ 365	$ 363
Depreciation expenses	$ 238	$ 238	$ 238	$ 238	$ 238	$ 238	$ 238
Net profit	−$ 7,021	−$ 5,620	−$ 4,219	−$ 2,818	−$ 1,417	−$ 16	$ 1,385

Profit and loss statement (first year cont.)

Month	8	9	10	11	12	1
Sales	$48,000	$49,500	$51,000	$52,500	$54,000	$549,000
Cost of goods sold	$ 2,400	$ 2,475	$ 2,550	$ 2,625	$ 2,700	$ 27,450
Gross margin	95.0%	95.0%	95.0%	95.0%	95.0%	95.0%
Operating income	$45,600	$47,025	$48,450	$49,875	$51,300	$521,550
Expenses						
Payroll	$27,708	$27,708	$27,708	$27,708	$27,708	$332,500
General and administrative	$ 1,000	$ 1,000	$ 1,000	$ 1,000	$ 1,000	$ 12,000
Marketing expenses	$ 1,098	$ 1,098	$ 1,098	$ 1,098	$ 1,098	$ 13,176
Professional fees and licensure	$ 208	$ 208	$ 208	$ 208	$ 208	$ 2,500
Insurance costs	$ 833	$ 833	$ 833	$ 833	$ 833	$ 10,000
Travel and vehicle costs	$ 4,583	$ 4,583	$ 4,583	$ 4,583	$ 4,583	$ 55,000
Rent and utilities	$ 1,250	$ 1,250	$ 1,250	$ 1,250	$ 1,250	$ 15,000
Miscellaneous costs	$ 549	$ 549	$ 549	$ 549	$ 549	$ 6,588
Payroll taxes	$ 4,156	$ 4,156	$ 4,156	$ 4,156	$ 4,156	$ 49,875
Total operating costs	$41,387	$41,387	$41,387	$41,387	$41,387	$496,639
EBITDA	$ 4,213	$ 5,638	$ 7,063	$ 8,488	$ 9,913	$ 24,911
Federal income tax	$ 719	$ 741	$ 764	$ 786	$ 809	$ 8,221
State income tax	$ 109	$ 112	$ 116	$ 119	$ 123	$ 1,246
Interest expense	$ 361	$ 359	$ 357	$ 355	$ 353	$ 4,369
Depreciation expenses	$ 238	$ 238	$ 238	$ 238	$ 238	$ 2,857
Net profit	$ 2,787	$ 4,188	$ 5,589	$ 6,990	$ 8,391	$ 8,219

Profit and loss statement (second year)

Quarter	Q1	2			
		Q2	Q3	Q4	2
Sales	$131,760	$164,700	$177,876	$184,464	$658,800
Cost of goods sold	$ 6,588	$ 8,235	$ 8,894	$ 9,223	$ 32,940
Gross margin	95.0%	95.0%	95.0%	95.0%	95.0%
Operating income	$125,172	$156,465	$168,982	$175,241	$625,860
Expenses					
Payroll	$ 73,645	$ 92,056	$ 99,421	$103,103	$368,225
General and administrative	$ 2,496	$ 3,120	$ 3,370	$ 3,494	$ 12,480
Marketing expenses	$ 3,162	$ 3,953	$ 4,269	$ 4,427	$ 15,811
Professional fees and licensure	$ 515	$ 644	$ 695	$ 721	$ 2,575
Insurance costs	$ 2,100	$ 2,625	$ 2,835	$ 2,940	$ 10,500
Travel and vehicle costs	$ 12,100	$ 15,125	$ 16,335	$ 16,940	$ 60,500
Rent and utilities	$ 3,150	$ 3,938	$ 4,253	$ 4,410	$ 15,750
Miscellaneous costs	$ 1,581	$ 1,976	$ 2,135	$ 2,214	$ 7,906
Payroll taxes	$ 11,047	$ 13,808	$ 14,913	$ 15,465	$ 55,234
Total operating costs	$109,796	$137,245	$148,225	$153,715	$548,981
EBITDA	$ 15,376	$ 19,220	$ 20,757	$ 21,526	$ 76,879
Federal income tax	$ 4,806	$ 6,007	$ 6,488	$ 6,728	$ 24,029
State income tax	$ 728	$ 910	$ 983	$ 1,019	$ 3,641
Interest expense	$ 1,046	$ 1,027	$ 1,007	$ 986	$ 4,066
Depreciation expenses	$ 714	$ 714	$ 714	$ 714	$ 2,857
Net profit	$ 8,082	$ 10,562	$ 11,566	$ 12,078	$ 42,287

Profit and loss statement (third year)

Quarter	Q1	3 Q2	Q3	Q4	3
Sales	**$154,159**	**$192,699**	**$208,115**	**$215,823**	**$770,796**
Cost of goods sold	$ 7,708	$ 9,635	$ 10,406	$ 10,791	$ 38,540
Gross margin	95.0%	95.0%	95.0%	95.0%	95.0%
Operating income	**$146,451**	**$183,064**	**$197,709**	**$205,032**	**$732,256**
Expenses					
Payroll	$ 75,854	$ 94,818	$102,403	$106,196	$379,272
General and administrative	$ 2,596	$ 3,245	$ 3,504	$ 3,634	$ 12,979
Marketing expenses	$ 3,700	$ 4,625	$ 4,995	$ 5,180	$ 18,499
Professional fees and licensure	$ 530	$ 663	$ 716	$ 743	$ 2,652
Insurance costs	$ 2,205	$ 2,756	$ 2,977	$ 3,087	$ 11,025
Travel and vehicle costs	$ 13,310	$ 16,638	$ 17,969	$ 18,634	$ 66,550
Rent and utilities	$ 3,308	$ 4,134	$ 4,465	$ 4,631	$ 16,538
Miscellaneous costs	$ 1,850	$ 2,312	$ 2,497	$ 2,590	$ 9,250
Payroll taxes	$ 11,378	$ 14,223	$ 15,361	$ 15,929	$ 56,891
Total operating costs	**$114,731**	**$143,414**	**$154,887**	**$160,623**	**$573,655**
EBITDA	**$ 31,720**	**$ 39,650**	**$ 42,822**	**$ 44,408**	**$158,601**
Federal income tax	$ 10,221	$ 12,777	$ 13,799	$ 14,310	$ 51,106
State income tax	$ 1,549	$ 1,936	$ 2,091	$ 2,168	$ 7,743
Interest expense	$ 966	$ 945	$ 923	$ 901	$ 3,734
Depreciation expenses	$ 714	$ 714	$ 714	$ 714	$ 2,857
Net profit	**$ 18,270**	**$ 23,279**	**$ 25,296**	**$ 26,315**	**$ 93,160**

7.11 Three Year Cash Flow Analysis

Cash flow analysis (first year)

Month	1	2	3	4	5	6	7
Cash from operations	−$ 6,783	−$ 5,382	−$ 3,981	−$ 2,580	−$1,179	$ 222	$ 1,623
Cash from receivables	$ 0	$ 0	$ 0	$ 0	$ 0	$ 0	$ 0
Operating cash inflow	**−$ 6,783**	**−$ 5,382**	**−$ 3,981**	**−$ 2,580**	**−$1,179**	**$ 222**	**$ 1,623**
Other cash inflows							
Equity investment	$10,000	$ 0	$ 0	$ 0	$ 0	$ 0	$ 0
Increased borrowings	$50,000	$ 0	$ 0	$ 0	$ 0	$ 0	$ 0
Sales of business assets	$ 0	$ 0	$ 0	$ 0	$ 0	$ 0	$ 0
A/P increases	$ 625	$ 625	$ 625	$ 625	$ 625	$ 625	$ 625
Total other cash inflows	**$60,625**	**$ 625**	**$ 625**	**$ 625**	**$ 625**	**$ 625**	**$ 625**
Total cash inflow	**$53,842**	**−$ 4,757**	**−$ 3,356**	**−$ 1,955**	**−$ 554**	**$ 847**	**$ 2,248**
Cash outflows							
Repayment of principal	$ 258	$ 260	$ 262	$ 264	$ 266	$ 268	$ 270
A/P decreases	$ 500	$ 500	$ 500	$ 500	$ 500	$ 500	$ 500
A/R increases	$ 0	$ 0	$ 0	$ 0	$ 0	$ 0	$ 0
Asset purchases	$30,000	$ 0	$ 0	$ 0	$ 0	$ 0	$ 0
Dividends	$ 0	$ 0	$ 0	$ 0	$ 0	$ 0	$ 0
Total cash outflows	**$30,758**	**$ 760**	**$ 762**	**$ 764**	**$ 766**	**$ 768**	**$ 770**
Net cash flow	**$23,083**	**−$ 5,517**	**−$ 4,118**	**−$ 2,719**	**−$1,320**	**$ 79**	**$ 1,478**
Cash balance	**$23,083**	**$17,566**	**$13,448**	**$10,729**	**$9,409**	**$9,488**	**$10,966**

Cash flow analysis (first year cont.)

Month	8	9	10	11	12	1
Cash from operations	$ 3,025	$ 4,426	$ 5,827	$ 7,228	$ 8,629	$11,076
Cash from receivables	$ 0	$ 0	$ 0	$ 0	$ 0	$ 0
Operating cash inflow	**$ 3,025**	**$ 4,426**	**$ 5,827**	**$ 7,228**	**$ 8,629**	**$11,076**
Other cash inflows						
Equity investment	$ 0	$ 0	$ 0	$ 0	$ 0	$10,000
Increased borrowings	$ 0	$ 0	$ 0	$ 0	$ 0	$50,000
Sales of business assets	$ 0	$ 0	$ 0	$ 0	$ 0	$ 0
A/P increases	$ 625	$ 625	$ 625	$ 625	$ 625	$ 7,500
Total other cash Inflows	**$ 625**	**$ 625**	**$ 625**	**$ 625**	**$ 625**	**$67,500**
Total cash inflow						
Cash outflows	**$ 3,650**	**$ 5,051**	**$ 6,452**	**$ 7,853**	**$ 9,254**	**$78,576**
Repayment of principal	$ 272	$ 274	$ 276	$ 278	$ 281	$ 3,232
A/P decreases	$ 500	$ 500	$ 500	$ 500	$ 500	$ 6,000
A/R increases	$ 0	$ 0	$ 0	$ 0	$ 0	$ 0
Asset purchases	$ 0	$ 0	$ 5,000	$ 0	$ 5,000	$40,000
Dividends	$ 0	$ 0	$ 0	$ 0	$ 7,753	$ 7,753
Total cash outflows	**$ 772**	**$ 774**	**$ 5,776**	**$ 778**	**$13,534**	**$56,985**
Net cash flow	**$ 2,877**	**$ 4,277**	**$ 676**	**$ 7,075**	**−$ 4,279**	**$21,591**
Cash balance	**$13,843**	**$18,120**	**$18,796**	**$25,870**	**$21,591**	**$21,591**

Cash flow analysis (second year)

Quarter	Q1	2 Q2	Q3	Q4	2
Cash from operations	$ 9,029	$11,286	$12,189	$12,640	$45,145
Cash from receivables	$ 0	$ 0	$ 0	$ 0	$ 0
Operating cash inflow	**$ 9,029**	**$11,286**	**$12,189**	**$12,640**	**$45,145**
Other cash inflows					
Equity investment	$ 0	$ 0	$ 0	$ 0	$ 0
Increased borrowings	$ 0	$ 0	$ 0	$ 0	$ 0
Sales of business assets	$ 0	$ 0	$ 0	$ 0	$ 0
A/P increases	$ 1,725	$ 2,156	$ 329	$ 2,415	$ 8,625
Total other cash inflows	**$ 1,725**	**$ 2,156**	**$ 2,329**	**$ 2,415**	**$ 8,625**
Total cash inflow	**$10,754**	**$13,442**	**$14,518**	**$15,055**	**$53,770**
Cash outflows					
Repayment of principal	$ 854	$ 874	$ 893	$ 914	$ 3,535
A/P decreases	$ 1,440	$ 1,800	$ 1,944	$ 2,016	$ 7,200
A/R increases	$ 0	$ 0	$ 0	$ 0	$ 0
Asset purchases	$ 2,257	$ 2,822	$ 3,047	$ 3,160	$11,286
Dividends	$ 6,320	$ 7,900	$ 8,532	$ 8,848	$31,601
Total cash outflows	**$10,872**	**$13,395**	**$14,417**	**$14,938**	**$53,622**
Net cash flow	**−$ 118**	**$ 47**	**$ 101**	**$ 117**	**$ 147**
Cash balance	**$21,473**	**$21,520**	**$21,621**	**$21,738**	**$21,738**

Cash flow analysis (third year)

Quarter	Q1	Q2	Q3	Q4	3
		3			
Cash from operations	$19,204	$24,004	$25,925	$26,885	$ 96,018
Cash from receivables	$ 0	$ 0	$ 0	$ 0	$ 0
Operating cash inflow	**$19,204**	**$24,004**	**$25,925**	**$26,885**	**$ 96,018**
Other cash inflows					
Equity investment	$ 0	$ 0	$ 0	$ 0	$ 0
Increased borrowings	$ 0	$ 0	$ 0	$ 0	$ 0
Sales of business assets	$ 0	$ 0	$ 0	$ 0	$ 0
A/P increases	$ 1,984	$ 2,480	$ 2,678	$ 2,777	$ 9,919
Total other cash inflows	**$ 1,984**	**$ 2,480**	**$ 2,678**	**$ 2,777**	**$ 9,919**
Total cash inflow	**$21,187**	**$26,484**	**$28,603**	**$29,662**	**$105,936**
Cash outflows					
Repayment of principal	$ 934	$ 956	$ 977	$ 999	$ 3,866
A/P decreases	$ 1,728	$ 2,160	$ 2,333	$ 2,419	$ 8,640
A/R increases	$ 0	$ 0	$ 0	$ 0	$ 0
Asset purchases	$ 4,801	$ 6,001	$ 6,481	$ 6,721	$ 24,004
Dividends	$13,442	$16,803	$18,147	$18,819	$ 67,212
Total cash outflows	**$20,906**	**$25,920**	**$27,938**	**$28,959**	**$103,723**
Net cash flow	**$ 282**	**$ 564**	**$ 664**	**$ 703**	**$ 2,213**
Cash balance	**$22,020**	**$22,584**	**$23,249**	**$23,952**	**$ 23,952**

Inflatable Amusement Rental Business

FunGiant Enterprises Inc.

9627 McIntosh Road
Worthington, WI 54912

Paul Greenland

FunGiant is an inflatable amusement rental business, providing bounce houses, slides, obstacle courses, and similar attractions to both individual consumers and organizations for events such as birthday parties, picnics, fun fairs, and barbecues.

EXECUTIVE SUMMARY

Business Overview

FunGiant is an inflatable amusement rental business, providing bounce houses, slides, obstacle courses, and similar attractions to both individual consumers and organizations for events such as birthday parties, picnics, fun fairs, and barbecues. This part-time business with full-time potential is located in Worthington, Wisconsin, a small town situated between the larger communities of Stevens Point and Appleton.

FunGiant is owned by Stan Peters, an elementary school teacher in Appleton, and his wife, Sarah. Because the business is largely seasonal, it complements Stan's teaching career nicely. During the off-season (e.g., colder months), requests for inflatable rentals are limited mainly to organizations (e.g., churches, schools, etc.) with large indoor spaces such as gymnasiums. Such rentals typically are for weekend events, which is manageable for Stan and Sarah.

MARKET ANALYSIS

FunGiant is located in the small town of Worthington, Wisconsin. However, the business serves a primary market area that consists of the larger communities of Appleton and Stevens Point. The target market for our attractions is children under the age of 14.

Appleton

According to market data from DemographicsNow the community of Appleton was home to 71,385 people in 2010. This figure essentially was expected to remain steady through 2015, with nominal growth projected. In 2010 nearly 20 percent of the population was under the age of 14. Individuals aged 0 to 4 accounted for 6.5 percent of the population, while those in the 5 to 14 age category accounted for 13 percent.

FunGiant will target its marketing initiatives toward households with income of $40,000 or more. In 2010 approximately 15 percent of households had income between $35,000 and $49,999. The largest household income segment (19.6%) was the $50,000 to $74,999 category. Next were households with income between $75,000 and $99,999 (15.3%), $100,000 to $149,999 (12.7%), and more than $150,000 (6%).

Beyond the consumer market, services will be marketed to specific types of organizations. These include, but are not limited to:

- Childcare Services (25 establishments)

- Entertainment & Recreation Services (50 establishments)

- Hospitals (5 establishments)

- Membership Organizations (106 establishments)

- Appleton Area School District

- Churches & Religious Organizations (150 establishments)

Stevens Point

DemographicsNow reveals that the community of Stevens Point was home to 24,511 people in 2010. This figure essentially was expected to remain steady through 2015, with nominal growth projected. In 2010 about 15 percent of the population was under the age of 14. Individuals aged 0 to 4 accounted for 6 percent of the population, while those in the 5 to 14 age category accounted for 9.3 percent.

In 2010 approximately 15 percent of households had income between $35,000 and $49,999. The largest household income segment (16.5%) was the $50,000 to $74,999 category. Next were households with income between $75,000 and $99,999 (10.5%), $100,000 to $149,999 (8.3%), and more than $150,000 (3.8%).

Organizational prospects include:

- Childcare Services (13 establishments)

- Entertainment & Recreation Services (28 establishments)

- Hospitals (3 establishments)

- Membership Organizations (45 establishments)

- Stevens Point Area School District

- Churches & Religious Organizations (115 establishments)

INDUSTRY ANALYSIS

According to the Moline, Illinois-based American Rental Association (ARA), a trade association for equipment rental businesses, manufacturers, and other industry players, the North American equipment rental industry was valued at nearly $32 billion in 2009.

Established in 1955, the ARA bills itself as "the source for information, government affairs, business development tools, education and training, networking and marketplace opportunities for the rental equipment industry throughout the world." The association counted some 7,500 rental businesses, as well as approximately 900 manufacturers and suppliers, among its membership base in 2011.

The ARA breaks down the equipment rental industry into three sectors:

- Construction and industrial equipment
- General tool and homeowner equipment
- Special event and party equipment

FunGiant falls within the special event and party equipment category.

Although economic conditions were difficult in 2011, businesses like FunGiant are somewhat recession-resistant. This is because, even during difficult times, businesses and organizations need affordable sources of entertainment.

PERSONNEL

FunGiant is owned by Stan Peters, who works as an elementary school teacher in Appleton, and his wife, Sarah. Because the business is largely seasonal, it complements Stan's teaching career nicely. During the off-season (e.g., colder months), requests for inflatable rentals are limited mainly to organizations (e.g., churches, schools, etc.) with large indoor spaces such as gymnasiums. Such rentals typically are for weekend events, which is manageable for Stan and Sarah.

Stan's background as a teacher will come in useful at FunGiant. He is adept at working with both parents and children. In addition, Sarah brings valuable business and logistical experience to the table. She currently helps manage the office of a local photographer, where her experience involves functions such as invoicing, accounts payable, and scheduling. Sarah holds an associate's degree in business management from Smithfield Community College.

Professional and Advisory Support

FunGiant has retained Action Accounting Inc., an accounting firm in Stevens Point, to assist us with bookkeeping and tax responsibilities. A commercial checking account has been established with Appleton Community Bank, which has agreed to provide merchant accounts so that the business can accept credit card and debit card payments. Legal services will be provided by the area firm of Beecher & Wellington, which has helped us to develop a basic customer rental agreement for the business.

BUSINESS STRATEGY

FunGiant will commence operations with the following attractions:

- Backyard Obstacle Challenge
- Double Lane Slide
- Bounce and Slide Castle

In addition, we will purchase five low-cost SkyDancers (used to attract attention for special events and advertising/promotions), which can be used by both consumers and organizations.

Acknowledging that the introduction of new selections will be important for our continued growth, we will purchase the following deluxe attractions during our second and third years of operation, respectively (detailed pricing information is available upon request):

- Jump'n Dodgeball Game Commercial Bounce House.
- Cyclone Double Waterpark (includes two waterslides that curve, landing in a pool of water and a "lazy river" feature.)

Additional SkyDancers also will be purchased during years two and three, based on customer response during our first year.

During years two and three we will emphasize the promotion of special packages, whereby customers receive a discount for renting two or three attractions at the same time. This allows us to generate additional revenue with minimal effort (e.g., without having to travel to additional customer sites, etc.).

After year three, the acquisition of additional attractions will likely be limited to replacements, because the business will then be at a size that is manageable for the owners. In the event of especially strong demand, the owners will consider the option of a significant expansion initiative, which will involve hiring additional employees.

SERVICES

Inflatable Amusements

Our business will begin by offering the following inflatable amusement selections:

- Backyard Obstacle Challenge

- Double Lane Slide

- Bounce and Slide Castle

- SkyDancers (used to attract attention for special events and advertising/promotions)

Each unit is equipped with a dedicated blower for inflation purposes.

Delivery, Setup & Teardown

Delivery, setup, and teardown are provided as part of the rental agreement to locations within a 20-mile radius of Worthington, Wisconsin. Additional charges apply beyond this radius (see below).

Additional Equipment

We provide generators for customers in need of a power source.

Event Staffing

We offer on-site supervision to customers who wish to have their event staffed by a FunGiant associate.

MARKETING & SALES

A marketing plan has been developed for FunGiant that includes these main tactics:

1. *Web Site:* FunGiant has developed a basic Web site that lists information about our inflatable attractions, equipment, special discount and/or party packages, prices, policies, delivering information, contact information, FAQs, and information about placing online reservations.

2. *Promotional Flier:* A four-color flier, targeted toward parents of young children and organizations interested in entertainment options for various functions, has been developed. This printed piece can be used for direct mailings, left behind, or posted at various public places. A local printer with a digital press can produce these for us in small quantities as needed, enabling us to avoid the large print runs associated with a traditional offset press.

3. *Advertising:* A regular classified advertising presence will be established in **The Portage County Gazette,** the only locally owned and operated newspaper in the county, which offers more affordable advertising rates than either the **Appleton Post Crescent** or the **Stevens Point Journal.**

In addition, we will explore the use of interactive advertising on Facebook, which is highly targeted and allows keyword-advertising.

4. ***Sales Presentations/Incentives:*** Each month, Stan and Sarah Peters will make presentations to local community groups and organizations promoting FunGiant. Following the presentation, they will distribute certificates that entitle the holder to a 15 percent discount off their first order. A schedule of planned presentations during the first year is available upon request.

5. ***Word-of-Mouth Marketing:*** FunGiant will rely heavily upon word-of-mouth to promote the business. To encourage referrals among family and friends, Stan and Sarah Peters will present the aforementioned 15 percent discount certificates to each new customer, entitling them to a discount off their next booking if they make a successful referral. In addition, the discount will apply to the referred customer as well.

We will evaluate our marketing plan on a semi-annual basis during our first year of operations, and annually thereafter.

OPERATIONS

Hours
FunGiant will accept phone calls and/or e-mails during regular business hours (9 AM-5 PM) via a dedicated mobile phone number. Our policy will be to respond to customer inquiries within one business day.

Rates
Although we will offer discounts to customers who wish to rent more than one attraction at a time, our rates typically will adhere to the following structure:

- Double Lane Slide ($275/4 hours)
- Backyard Obstacle Challenge ($250/4 hours)
- Bounce and Slide Castle ($225/4 hours)
- SkyDancers ($25/4 hours; $45/day)
- Generators ($40/day)
- On-site associate ($85/4 hours, $150/8 hours)

*Delivery is provided as part of the rental fee within a 20-mile radius of Worthington, Wisconsin. We will charge customers a $20 fee for deliveries outside of this service area, and will not provide rental services beyond a 50-mile radius of Worthington.

Payment
FunGiant will require customers to make a $35 deposit within seven days of their reservation. Customers will then be required to pay the entire rental fee on the day of the event, prior to set-up. In addition to cash, we will accept debit/credit card payments and money orders. Payments can be made via our Web site, by phone, or on-site.

Facility and Location
FunGiant will begin operations as a home-based business. Stan and Sarah Peters live on a five-acre lot, which includes an outbuilding suitable for storing inflatable attractions, related equipment, and the trailer they will use for transporting attractions to and from customer locations. In addition, they will

utilize a dedicated space within their home as a home office. A separate insurance policy will be obtained for the outbuilding, along with a home-office rider for the home-based office space.

FINANCIAL ANALYSIS

Start-up Costs

FunGiant will need to purchase the following attractions prior to start-up:

18' Double Lane Slide ($5,000)

Backyard Obstacle Challenge ($1,895)

Bounce and Slide Castle ($1,895)

5 SkyDancers ($1,250)

3 Generac GP3250 3750 Watt 205cc OHV Portable Gas Powered Generators ($1,200)

6 x 14 x 6 Cargo Trailer ($2,500)

The owners already have a 2008 Dodge Ram 1500 Truck that they will utilize for business purposes.

Total: $13,740

Three-year income statement

	2012	2013	2014
Sales	$31,660	$39,460	$47,260
Expenses			
Marketing & advertising	$ 5,000	$ 3,500	$ 3,500
General/administrative	$ 500	$ 500	$ 500
Accounting/legal	$ 1,100	$ 750	$ 750
Office supplies	$ 350	$ 350	$ 350
Inflatable attractions	$ 0	$ 5,000	$ 5,000
Computer/technology	$ 750	$ 0	$ 0
Insurance	$ 1,250	$ 1,350	$ 1,450
Payroll	$12,000	$15,000	$18,000
Payroll taxes	$ 1,440	$ 1,800	$ 2,160
Postage	$ 750	$ 750	$ 750
Utilities	$ 450	$ 500	$ 550
Fuel	$ 1,000	$ 1,250	$ 1,500
Maintenance & repairs	$ 1,000	$ 1,250	$ 1,500
Telecommunications	$ 750	$ 750	$ 750
Total expenses	$26,340	$32,750	$36,760
Net income	$ 5,320	$ 6,710	$10,500

The owners will provide the funds needed to cover start-up costs and ongoing operations from their personal savings. Net income from the business will be used to recoup their investment, which should be achieved by the early part of 2014.

Infusion Therapy

Pharma Infusion Services, Inc.

2700 West Elm St.
Bowling Green, New York 10004

BizPlanDB.com

The purpose of this business plan is to raise $160,000 for the development of an infusion therapy focused pharmacy. The business will receive a majority of its income from co-payments, insurance payments, and from publicly funded health sources such as Medicare and Medicaid.

1.0 EXECUTIVE SUMMARY

The purpose of this business plan is to raise $160,000 for the development of an infusion therapy focused pharmacy while showcasing the expected financials and operations over the next three years. Pharma Infusion Services, Inc. ("the Company") is a New York-based corporation that will provide prescription drugs that are delivered intravenously to patients that have severe disorders. The Company was founded by Donna Gorrell.

1.1 The Products and Services

The primary revenue source for the business is the ongoing sale of drugs and products that are related to prescription infusion therapy. Specifically, infusion therapy is used among patients that cannot take drugs orally. As such, additional special attention must be paid to the specific needs of the patient.

The business will receive a majority of its income from co-payments, insurance payments, and from publicly funded health sources such as Medicare and Medicaid.

The third section of the business plan will further describe the services offered by Pharma Infusion Services, Inc.

1.2 Financing

Ms. Gorrell is seeking to raise $160,000 from a bank loan. The interest rate and loan agreement are to be further discussed during negotiation. This business plan assumes that the business will receive a 10 year loan with a 9% fixed interest rate. The financing will be used for the following:

- Development of the office location.

- Financing for the first six months of operation.

- Capital to purchase the Company's inventory of infusion pharmaceuticals.

Ms. Gorrell will contribute $10,000 to the venture.

1.3 Mission Statement

Pharma Infusion Services, Inc.'s mission is to provide an extensive line of drugs that can be delivered intravenously to patients within the Company's target market. The business will also provide delivery services to patients that cannot come directly to Pharma Infusion Services, Inc.

1.4 Management Team

The Company was founded by Donna Gorrell. Ms. Gorrell has more than 10 years of experience in the pharmaceutical industry. Through her expertise, she will be able to bring the operations of the business to profitability within its first year of operations.

1.5 Sales Forecasts

Ms. Gorrell expects a strong rate of growth at the start of operations. Below are the expected financials over the next three years.

Proforma profit and loss (yearly)

Year	1	2	3
Sales	$1,749,570	$2,099,484	$2,456,396
Operating costs	$ 388,745	$ 406,572	$ 424,954
EBITDA	$ 178,357	$ 273,951	$ 371,258
Taxes, interest, and depreciation	$ 90,685	$ 121,096	$ 157,415
Net profit	$ 87,673	$ 152,854	$ 213,843

Sales, operating costs, and profit forecast

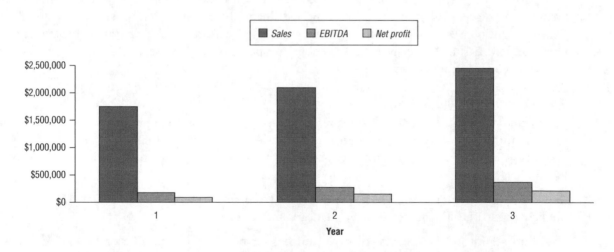

1.6 Expansion Plan

The Founder expects that the business will aggressively expand during the first three years of operation. Ms. Gorrell intends to implement marketing campaigns that will effectively target individuals, nursing homes, and assisted living facilities within the target market.

2.0 COMPANY AND FINANCING SUMMARY

2.1 Registered Name and Corporate Structure

The Company is registered as a corporation in the State of New York.

2.2 Required Funds

At this time, Pharma Infusion Services, Inc. requires $160,000 of debt funds. Below is a breakdown of how these funds will be used:

Projected startup costs

Initial lease payments and deposits	$ 10,000
Working capital	$ 35,000
FF&E	$ 25,000
Leasehold improvements	$ 5,000
Security deposits	$ 5,000
Insurance	$ 2,500
Pharmaceutical inventories	$ 75,000
Marketing budget	$ 7,500
Miscellaneous and unforeseen costs	$ 5,000
Total startup costs	**$170,000**

Use of funds

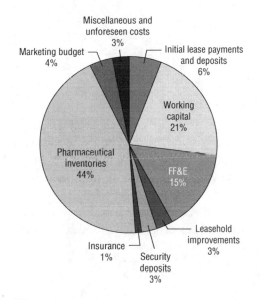

2.3 Investor Equity

Ms. Gorrell is not seeking an investment from a third party at this time.

2.4 Management Equity

Ms. Gorrell owns 100% of Pharma Infusion Services, Inc.

2.5 Exit Strategy

If the business is very successful, Ms. Gorrell may seek to sell the business to a third party for a significant earnings multiple. Most likely, the Company will hire a qualified business broker to sell the business on behalf of Pharma Infusion Services, Inc. Based on historical numbers, the business could fetch a sales premium of up to 8 times earnings.

3.0 PRODUCTS AND SERVICES

Below is a description of the products offered by Pharma Infusion Services, Inc.

3.1 Sales of Infusion Therapy Drugs

As stated in the executive summary, the business will specialize in the ongoing distribution of infusion therapy focused drugs for highly ill individuals. The business' entire line of medications will be drugs that can be introduced into the body via a catheter or an IV needle.

Ms. Gorrell is currently obtaining the proper licensure so that the business can distribute prescription medication from its retail location.

3.2 Delivery of Medication

As a value-added benefit for its patients, the Company will provide delivery services to large scale facilities such as nursing homes, assisted living facilities, and hospitals. Approximately 10% of the Company's revenues will come from this value-added service.

4.0 STRATEGIC AND MARKET ANALYSIS

4.1 Economic Outlook

This section of the analysis will detail the economic climate, the infusion therapy pharmacy industry, the customer profile, and the competition that the business will face as it progresses through its business operations.

The current economic market conditions in the United States are moderate. The meltdown of the sub prime mortgage market coupled with increasing gas prices has led many people to believe that the US is on the cusp of a double dip economic recession. This slowdown in the economy has also greatly impacted real estate sales, which has halted to historical lows. However, infusion therapy businesses operate with great economic stability as people will continue to require medications despite drawbacks in the general economy. Additionally, and as stated earlier, many people have health insurance that covers these drug costs.

4.2 Industry Analysis

The retail distribution of pharmaceutical products is one the United States' largest industries. Each year, the 45,000 retail pharmacy companies in the country aggregately generate more than $185 billion dollars of revenue. The industry employs more than 800,000 people and provides payrolls in excess of $25 billion dollars per year.

The industry is expected to grow significantly over the next fifteen years as more people in the "Baby Boomer" generation move into their senior years. As such, they will require greater use of prescription medication including infusion therapy-based medications. Based on information from the US federal government, the industry is expected to have an annual average growth rate of 6% per year during the next fifteen years.

4.3 Customer Profile

The average client will be a middle- to upper-middle class man or woman living in the Company's target market. Common traits among clients will include:

- Annual household income exceeding $50,000

- Lives or works no more than 15 miles from the Company's location.

- Will spend $250 per visit to Pharma Infusion Services, Inc.

Within the Company's New York metropolitan area market, there are approximately 200,000 people that have an ongoing demand for drugs that need to be administered via infusion therapy. As such, Management feels that this area is an excellent location to launch the business' operations.

4.4 Competition

The major competitive advantage that the business will maintain over other pharmacies is that the business will specialize specifically in the distribution of infusion therapy drugs. Additionally, Ms. Gorrell will hire pharmacists and pharmacy assistants that have experience working with these specific drugs. The additional competitive advantage the Company will maintain is the Company's delivery services which will allow patients that cannot travel to receive their drugs quickly and cost effectively.

5.0 MARKETING PLAN

Pharma Infusion Services, Inc. intends to maintain an extensive marketing campaign that will ensure maximum visibility for the business in its targeted market. Below is an overview of the marketing strategies and objectives of Pharma Infusion Services, Inc.

5.1 Marketing Objectives

- Establish relationships with nursing homes, assisted living facilities, and hospitals.

- Maintain strong relationships with private health insurance companies that may refer patients seeking authorization for drugs Pharma Infusion Services, Inc.

5.2 Marketing Strategies

Foremost, Ms. Gorrell will also develop a number of contractual relationships with nursing homes, assisted living facilities, hospitals, and doctors that regularly need to provide their patients with IV, injection, and catheter based drugs. These contractual relationships will allow the business to generate highly predictable streams of revenue from the ongoing preparation and distribution of infusion therapy drugs.

Second, Management intends to develop a number of press releases and advertisements that will be placed in medical journals, industry publications, and other periodicals that focus on the New York medical and healthcare community. This will make the local medical industry more aware of the Company's brand name, the services offered, and how to contact the business.

Finally, Management will develop a website that showcases the Company's line of infusion therapy drugs, the delivery services offered by the business, types of insurance accepted, and other important information as it relates to infusion therapy services. In the future, Management may expand this website to have functionality where users can see billing information and histories of prescriptions via specialized login functions.

5.3 Pricing

Management anticipates that each patient will generate $1,000 to $3,000 per month for the business from the ongoing prescription of infusion therapy-based drugs. Management anticipates that 85% of this income will come from private insurance companies, Medicare, and Medicaid. The remaining payments will come from copayments and direct patient payments.

6.0 ORGANIZATIONAL PLAN AND PERSONNEL SUMMARY

6.1 Corporate Organization

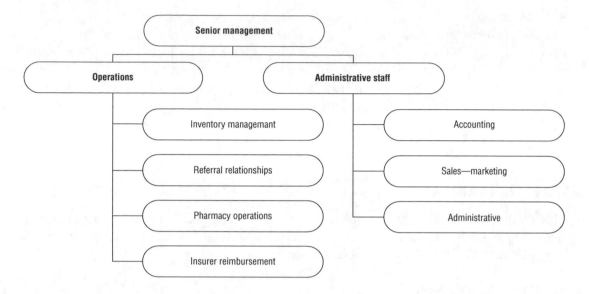

6.2 Organizational Budget

Personnel plan—yearly

Year	1	2	3
Owner	$ 80,000	$ 82,400	$ 84,872
Pharmacist	$ 75,000	$ 77,250	$ 79,568
Pharmacy employees	$ 63,000	$ 64,890	$ 66,837
Bookkeeper	$ 24,000	$ 24,720	$ 25,462
Administrative	$ 23,000	$ 23,690	$ 24,401
Total	**$265,000**	**$272,950**	**$281,139**

Numbers of personnel

Year	1	2	3
Owner	1	1	1
Pharmacist	1	1	1
Pharmacy employees	3	3	3
Bookkeeper	1	1	1
Administrative	1	1	1
Totals	**7**	**7**	**7**

Personnel expense breakdown

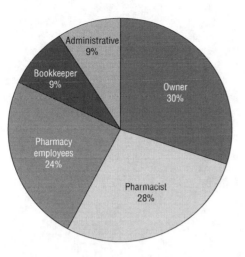

7.0 FINANCIAL PLAN

7.1 Underlying Assumptions

The Company has based its proforma financial statements on the following:

- Pharma Infusion Services, Inc. will have an annual revenue growth rate of 17% per year.

- The Owner will acquire $160,000 of debt funds to develop the business.

- The loan will have a 10 year term with a 9% interest rate.

7.2 Sensitivity Analysis

The Company's revenues are not sensitive to changes in the general economy. As discussed earlier, the business provides life critical infusion therapy-based medications to its customers and as such, the business will not suffer any major declines in revenues despite deleterious changes in the economy. As such, Pharma Infusion Services, Inc. will be able to remain profitable and cash flow positive at all times.

7.3 Source of Funds

Financing

Equity contributions	
Management investment	$ 10,000.00
Total equity financing	**$ 10,000.00**
Banks and lenders	
Banks and lenders	$ 160,000.00
Total debt financing	**$160,000.00**
Total financing	**$170,000.00**

7.4 General Assumptions

General assumptions

Year	1	2	3
Short term interest rate	9.5%	9.5%	9.5%
Long term interest rate	10.0%	10.0%	10.0%
Federal tax rate	33.0%	33.0%	33.0%
State tax rate	5.0%	5.0%	5.0%
Personnel taxes	15.0%	15.0%	15.0%

7.5 Profit and Loss Statements

Proforma profit and loss (yearly)

Year	1	2	3
Sales	$1,749,570	$2,099,484	$2,456,396
Cost of goods sold	$1,182,468	$1,418,962	$1,660,185
Gross margin	32.41%	32.41%	32.41%
Operating income	$ 567,102	$ 680,522	$ 796,211
Expenses			
Payroll	$ 265,000	$ 272,950	$ 281,139
General and administrative	$ 25,200	$ 26,208	$ 27,256
Marketing expenses	$ 8,748	$ 10,497	$ 12,282
Professional fees and licensure	$ 5,219	$ 5,376	$ 5,537
Insurance costs	$ 1,987	$ 2,086	$ 2,191
Drug sourcing costs	$ 7,596	$ 8,356	$ 9,191
Rent and utilities	$ 14,250	$ 14,963	$ 15,711
Miscellaneous costs	$ 20,995	$ 25,194	$ 29,477
Payroll taxes	$ 39,750	$ 40,943	$ 42,171
Total operating costs	$ 388,745	$ 406,572	$ 424,954
EBITDA	$ 178,357	$ 273,951	$ 371,258
Federal income tax	$ 58,858	$ 86,110	$ 118,572
State income tax	$ 8,918	$ 13,047	$ 17,965
Interest expense	$ 13,980	$ 13,010	$ 11,949
Depreciation expenses	$ 8,929	$ 8,929	$ 8,929
Net profit	$ 87,673	$ 152,854	$ 213,843
Profit margin	5.01%	7.28%	8.71%

Sales, operating costs, and profit forecast

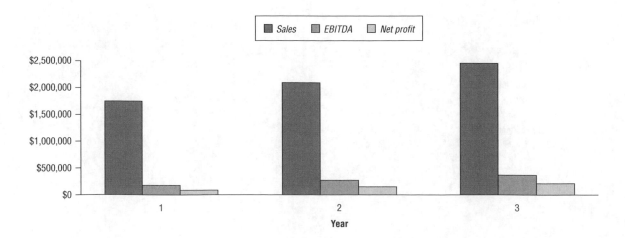

7.6 Cash Flow Analysis

Proforma cash flow analysis—yearly

Year	1	2	3
Cash from operations	$ 96,601	$161,783	$222,771
Cash from receivables	$ 0	$ 0	$ 0
Operating cash inflow	**$ 96,601**	**$161,783**	**$222,771**
Other cash inflows			
Equity investment	$ 10,000	$ 0	$ 0
Increased borrowings	$160,000	$ 0	$ 0
Sales of business assets	$ 0	$ 0	$ 0
A/P increases	$ 37,902	$ 43,587	$ 50,125
Total other cash inflows	**$207,902**	**$ 43,587**	**$ 50,125**
Total cash inflow	**$304,503**	**$205,370**	**$272,897**
Cash outflows			
Repayment of principal	$ 10,341	$ 11,312	$ 12,373
A/P decreases	$ 24,897	$ 29,876	$ 35,852
A/R increases	$ 0	$ 0	$ 0
Asset purchases	$125,000	$ 40,446	$ 55,693
Dividends	$ 86,941	$113,248	$155,940
Total cash outflows	**$247,180**	**$194,882**	**$259,857**
Net cash flow	**$ 57,324**	**$ 10,489**	**$ 13,040**
Cash balance	**$ 57,324**	**$ 67,812**	**$ 80,852**

Proforma cash flow (yearly)

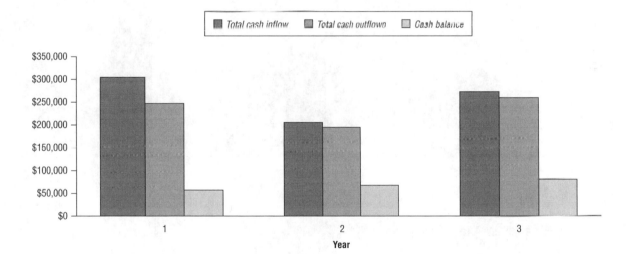

7.7 Balance Sheet

Proforma balance sheet—yearly

Year	1	2	3
Assets			
Cash	$ 57,324	$ 67,812	$ 80,852
Amortized development costs	$ 25,000	$ 29,045	$ 34,614
Inventories	$ 75,000	$105,334	$147,104
FF&E	$ 25,000	$ 31,067	$ 39,421
Accumulated depreciation	($ 8,929)	($ 17,857)	($ 26,786)
Total assets	**$173,395**	**$215,401**	**$275,205**
Liabilities and equity			
Accounts payable	$ 13,005	$ 26,716	$ 40,990
Long term liabilities	$149,659	$138,347	$127,036
Other liabilities	$ 0	$ 0	$ 0
Total liabilities	**$162,664**	**$165,063**	**$168,025**
Net worth	**$ 10,732**	**$ 50,338**	**$107,180**
Total liabilities and equity	**$173,395**	**$215,401**	**$275,205**

Proforma balance sheet

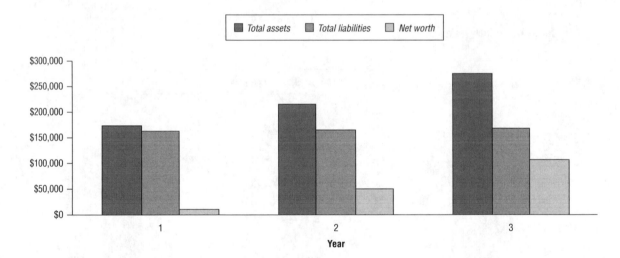

7.8 Breakeven Analysis

Monthly break even analysis

Year	1	2	3
Monthly revenue	$ 99,943	$ 104,526	$ 109,252
Yearly revenue	$1,199,319	$1,254,317	$1,311,027

Break even analysis

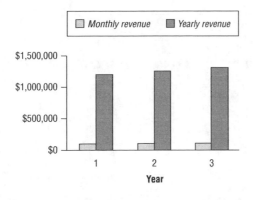

7.9 Business Ratios

Business ratios—yearly

Year	1	2	3
Sales			
Sales growth	0.00%	20.00%	17.00%
Gross margin	32.40%	32.40%	32.40%
Financials			
Profit margin	5.01%	7.28%	8.71%
Assets to liabilities	1.07	1.30	1.64
Equity to liabilities	0.07	0.30	0.64
Assets to equity	16.16	4.28	2.57
Liquidity			
Acid test	0.35	0.41	0.48
Cash to assets	0.33	0.31	0.29

7.10 Three Year Profit and Loss Statement

Profit and loss statement (first year)

Months	1	2	3	4	5	6	7
Sales	$145,000	$145,145	$145,290	$145,435	$145,580	$145,725	$145,870
Cost of goods sold	$ 98,000	$ 98,098	$ 98,196	$ 98,294	$ 98,392	$ 98,490	$ 98,588
Gross margin	32.4%	32.4%	32.4%	32.4%	32.4%	32.4%	32.4%
Operating income	$ 47,000	$ 47,047	$ 47,094	$ 47,141	$ 47,188	$ 47,235	$ 47,282
Expenses							
Payroll	$ 22,083	$ 22,083	$ 22,083	$ 22,083	$ 22,083	$ 22,083	$ 22,083
General and administrative	$ 2,100	$ 2,100	$ 2,100	$ 2,100	$ 2,100	$ 2,100	$ 2,100
Marketing expenses	$ 729	$ 729	$ 729	$ 729	$ 729	$ 729	$ 729
Professional fees and licensure	$ 435	$ 435	$ 435	$ 435	$ 435	$ 435	$ 435
Insurance costs	$ 166	$ 166	$ 166	$ 166	$ 166	$ 166	$ 166
Drug sourcing costs	$ 633	$ 633	$ 633	$ 633	$ 633	$ 633	$ 633
Rent and utilities	$ 1,188	$ 1,188	$ 1,188	$ 1,188	$ 1,188	$ 1,188	$ 1,188
Miscellaneous costs	$ 1,750	$ 1,750	$ 1,750	$ 1,750	$ 1,750	$ 1,750	$ 1,750
Payroll taxes	$ 3,313	$ 3,313	$ 3,313	$ 3,313	$ 3,313	$ 3,313	$ 3,313
Total operating costs	$ 32,395	$ 32,395	$ 32,395	$ 32,395	$ 32,395	$ 32,395	$ 32,395
EBITDA	$ 14,605	$ 14,652	$ 14,699	$ 14,746	$ 14,793	$ 14,840	$ 14,887
Federal income tax	$ 4,878	$ 4,883	$ 4,888	$ 4,093	$ 4,898	$ 4,902	$ 4,907
State income tax	$ 739	$ 740	$ 741	$ 741	$ 742	$ 743	$ 744
Interest expense	$ 1,200	$ 1,194	$ 1,188	$ 1,181	$ 1,175	$ 1,169	$ 1,162
Depreciation expense	$ 744	$ 744	$ 744	$ 744	$ 744	$ 744	$ 744
Net profit	$ 7,043	$ 7,091	$ 7,139	$ 7,186	$ 7,234	$ 7,282	$ 7,330

Profit and loss statement (first year cont.)

Month	8	9	10	11	12	1
Sales	$146,015	$146,160	$146,305	$146,450	$146,595	$1,749,570
Cost of goods sold	$ 98,686	$ 98,784	$ 98,882	$ 98,980	$ 99,078	$1,182,468
Gross margin	32.4%	32.4%	32.4%	32.4%	32.4%	32.4%
Operating income	$ 47,329	$ 47,376	$ 47,423	$ 47,470	$ 47,517	$ 567,102
Expenses						
Payroll	$ 22,083	$ 22,083	$ 22,083	$ 22,083	$ 22,083	$ 265,000
General and administrative	$ 2,100	$ 2,100	$ 2,100	$ 2,100	$ 2,100	$ 25,200
Marketing expenses	$ 729	$ 729	$ 729	$ 729	$ 729	$ 8,748
Professional fees and licensure	$ 435	$ 435	$ 435	$ 435	$ 435	$ 5,219
Insurance costs	$ 166	$ 166	$ 166	$ 166	$ 166	$ 1,987
Drug sourcing costs	$ 633	$ 633	$ 633	$ 633	$ 633	$ 7,596
Rent and utilities	$ 1,188	$ 1,188	$ 1,188	$ 1,188	$ 1,188	$ 14,250
Miscellaneous costs	$ 1,750	$ 1,750	$ 1,750	$ 1,750	$ 1,750	$ 20,995
Payroll taxes	$ 3,313	$ 3,313	$ 3,313	$ 3,313	$ 3,313	$ 39,750
Total operating costs	$ 32,395	$ 32,395	$ 32,395	$ 32,395	$ 32,395	$ 388,745
EBITDA	$ 14,934	$ 14,981	$ 15,028	$ 15,075	$ 15,122	$ 178,357
Federal income tax	$ 4,912	$ 4,917	$ 4,922	$ 4,927	$ 4,932	$ 58,858
State income tax	$ 744	$ 745	$ 746	$ 746	$ 747	$ 8,918
Interest expense	$ 1,156	$ 1,149	$ 1,142	$ 1,136	$ 1,129	$ 13,980
Depreciation expense	$ 744	$ 744	$ 744	$ 744	$ 744	$ 8,929
Net profit	$ 7,378	$ 7,425	$ 7,473	$ 7,521	$ 7,570	$ 87,673

Profit and loss statement (second year)

Quarter	Q1	2 Q2	Q3	Q4	2
Sales	$419,897	$524,871	$566,861	$587,856	$2,099,484
Cost of goods sold	$283,792	$354,740	$383,120	$397,309	$1,418,962
Gross margin	32.4%	32.4%	32.4%	32.4%	32.4%
Operating income	$136,104	$170,131	$183,741	$190,546	$ 680,522
Expenses					
Payroll	$ 54,590	$ 68,238	$ 73,697	$ 76,426	$ 272,950
General and administrative	$ 5,242	$ 6,552	$ 7,076	$ 7,338	$ 26,208
Marketing expenses	$ 2,099	$ 2,624	$ 2,834	$ 2,939	$ 10,497
Professional fees and licensure	$ 1,075	$ 1,344	$ 1,451	$ 1,505	$ 5,376
Insurance costs	$ 417	$ 522	$ 563	$ 584	$ 2,086
Drug sourcing costs	$ 1,671	$ 2,089	$ 2,256	$ · 2,340	$ 8,356
Rent and utilities	$ 2,993	$ 3,741	$ 4,040	$ 4,190	$ 14,963
Miscellaneous costs	$ 5,039	$ 6,298	$ 6,802	$ 7,054	$ 25,194
Payroll taxes	$ 8,189	$ 10,236	$ 11,054	$ 11,464	$ 40,943
Total operating costs	$ 81,314	$101,643	$109,774	$113,840	$ 406,572
EBITDA	$ 54,790	$ 68,488	$ 73,967	$ 76,706	$ 273,951
Federal income tax	$ 17,222	$ 21,528	$ 23,250	$ 24,111	$ 86,110
State income tax	$ 2,609	$ 3,262	$ 3,523	$ 3,653	$ 13,047
Interest expense	$ 3,347	$ 3,285	$ 3,222	$ 3,157	$ 13,010
Depreciation expense	$ 2,232	$ 2,232	$ 2,232	$ 2,232	$ 8,929
Net profit	$ 29,380	$ 38,181	$ 41,740	$ 43,553	$ 152,854

Profit and loss statement (third year)

Quarter	Q1	3 Q2	Q3	Q4	3
Sales	$491,279	$614,099	$663,227	$687,791	$2,456,396
Cost of goods sold	$332,037	$415,046	$448,250	$464,852	$1,660,185
Gross margin	32.4%	32.4%	32.4%	32.4%	32.4%
Operating income	$159,242	$199,053	$214,977	$222,939	$ 796,211
Expenses					
Payroll	$ 56,228	$ 70,285	$ 75,907	$ 78,719	$ 281,139
General and administrative	$ 5,451	$ 6,814	$ 7,359	$ 7,632	$ 27,256
Marketing expenses	$ 2,456	$ 3,070	$ 3,316	$ 3,439	$ 12,282
Professional fees and licensure	$ 1,107	$ 1,384	$ 1,495	$ 1,550	$ 5,537
Insurance costs	$ 438	$ 548	$ 591	$ 613	$ 2,191
Drug sourcing costs	$ 1,838	$ 2,298	$ 2,482	$ 2,574	$ 9,191
Rent and utilities	$ 3,142	$ 3,928	$ 4,242	$ 4,399	$ 15,711
Miscellaneous costs	$ 5,895	$ 7,369	$ 7,959	$ 8,253	$ 29,477
Payroll taxes	$ 8,434	$ 10,543	$ 11,386	$ 11,808	$ 42,171
Total operating costs	$ 84,991	$106,238	$114,737	$118,987	$ 424,954
EBITDA	$ 74,252	$ 92,814	$100,240	$103,952	$ 371,258
Federal income tax	$ 23,714	$ 29,643	$ 32,014	$ 33,200	$ 118,572
State income tax	$ 3,593	$ 4,491	$ 4,851	$ 5,030	$ 17,965
Interest expense	$ 3,090	$ 3,023	$ 2,953	$ 2,883	$ 11,949
Depreciation expense	$ 2,232	$ 2,232	$ 2,232	$ 2,232	$ 8,929
Net profit	$ 41,621	$ 53,425	$ 58,189	$ 60,607	$ 213,843

7.11 Three Year Cash Flow Analysis

Cash flow analysis (first year)

Month	1	2	3	4	5	6	7
Cash from operations	$ 7,788	$ 7,835	$ 7,883	$ 7,930	$ 7,978	$ 8,026	$ 8,074
Cash from receivables	$ 0	$ 0	$ 0	$ 0	$ 0	$ 0	$ 0
Operating cash inflow	$ 7,788	$ 7,835	$ 7,883	$ 7,930	$ 7,978	$ 8,026	$ 8,074
Other cash inflows							
Equity investment	$ 10,000	$ 0	$ 0	$ 0	$ 0	$ 0	$ 0
Increased borrowings	$160,000	$ 0	$ 0	$ 0	$ 0	$ 0	$ 0
Sales of business assets	$ 0	$ 0	$ 0	$ 0	$ 0	$ 0	$ 0
A/P increases	$ 3,159	$ 3,159	$ 3,159	$ 3,159	$ 3,159	$ 3,159	$ 3,159
Total other cash inflows	$173,159	$ 3,159	$ 3,159	$ 3,159	$ 3,159	$ 3,159	$ 3,159
Total cash inflow	$180,946	$10,994	$11,041	$11,089	$11,137	$11,184	$ 11,232
Cash outflows							
Repayment of principal	$ 827	$ 833	$ 839	$ 846	$ 852	$ 858	$ 865
A/P decreases	$ 2,075	$ 2,075	$ 2,075	$ 2,075	$ 2,075	$ 2,075	$ 2,075
A/R increases	$ 0	$ 0	$ 0	$ 0	$ 0	$ 0	$ 0
Asset purchases	$125,000	$ 0	$ 0	$ 0	$ 0	$ 0	$ 0
Dividends	$ 0	$ 0	$ 0	$ 0	$ 0	$ 0	$ 0
Total cash outflows	$127,902	$ 2,908	$ 2,914	$ 2,920	$ 2,927	$ 2,933	$ 2,939
Net cash flow	$ 53,044	$ 8,086	$ 8,127	$ 8,169	$ 8,210	$ 8,251	$ 8,293
Cash balance	$ 53,044	$61,130	$69,258	$77,426	$85,636	$93,887	$102,180

Cash flow analysis (first year cont.)

Month	8	9	10	11	12	1
Cash from operations	$ 8,122	$ 8,170	$ 8,217	$ 8,265	$ 8,314	$ 96,601
Cash from receivables	$ 0	$ 0	$ 0	$ 0	$ 0	$ 0
Operating cash inflow	**$ 8,122**	**$ 8,170**	**$ 8,217**	**$ 8,265**	**$ 8,314**	**$ 96,601**
Other cash inflows						
Equity investment	$ 0	$ 0	$ 0	$ 0	$ 0	$ 10,000
Increased borrowings	$ 0	$ 0	$ 0	$ 0	$ 0	$160,000
Sales of business assets	$ 0	$ 0	$ 0	$ 0	$ 0	$ 0
A/P increases	$ 3,159	$ 3,159	$ 3,159	$ 3,159	$ 3,159	$ 37,902
Total other cash inflows	**$ 3,159**	**$ 3,159**	**$ 3,159**	**$ 3,159**	**$ 3,159**	**$207,902**
Total cash inflow	**$ 11,280**	**$ 11,328**	**$ 11,376**	**$ 11,424**	**$11,472**	**$304,503**
Cash outflows						
Repayment of principal	$ 871	$ 878	$ 884	$ 891	$ 898	$ 10,341
A/P decreases	$ 2,075	$ 2,075	$ 2,075	$ 2,075	$ 2,075	$ 24,897
A/R increases	$ 0	$ 0	$ 0	$ 0	$ 0	$ 0
Asset purchases	$ 0	$ 0	$ 0	$ 0	$ 0	$125,000
Dividends	$ 0	$ 0	$ 0	$ 0	$86,941	$ 86,941
Total cash outflows	**$ 2,946**	**$ 2,952**	**$ 2,959**	**$ 2,966**	**$89,913**	**$247,180**
Net cash flow	**$ 8,334**	**$ 8,376**	**$ 8,417**	**$ 8,458**	**−$78,441**	**$ 57,324**
Cash balance	**$110,514**	**$118,890**	**$127,307**	**$135,765**	**$57,324**	**$ 57,324**

Cash flow analysis (second year)

Quarter	Q1	2 Q2	Q3	Q4	2
Cash from operations	$32,357	$40,446	$43,681	$45,299	$161,783
Cash from receivables	$ 0	$ 0	$ 0	$ 0	$ 0
Operating cash inflow	**$32,357**	**$40,446**	**$43,681**	**$45,299**	**$161,783**
Other cash inflows					
Equity investment	$ 0	$ 0	$ 0	$ 0	$ 0
Increased borrowings	$ 0	$ 0	$ 0	$ 0	$ 0
Sales of business assets	$ 0	$ 0	$ 0	$ 0	$ 0
A/P increases	$ 8,717	$10,897	$11,769	$12,204	$ 43,587
Total other cash inflows	**$ 8,717**	**$10,897**	**$11,769**	**$12,204**	**$ 43,587**
Total cash inflow	**$41,074**	**$51,343**	**$55,450**	**$57,504**	**$205,370**
Cash outflows					
Repayment of principal	$ 2,734	$ 2,795	$ 2,859	$ 2,924	$ 11,312
A/P decreases	$ 5,975	$ 7,469	$ 8,067	$ 8,365	$ 29,876
A/R increases	$ 0	$ 0	$ 0	$ 0	$ 0
Asset purchases	$ 8,089	$10,111	$10,920	$11,325	$ 40,446
Dividends	$22,650	$28,312	$30,577	$31,709	$113,248
Total cash outflows	**$39,448**	**$48,688**	**$52,423**	**$54,323**	**$194,882**
Net cash flow	**$ 1,626**	**$ 2,655**	**$ 3,027**	**$ 3,180**	**$ 10,489**
Cash balance	**$58,950**	**$61,605**	**$64,632**	**$67,812**	**$ 67,812**

Cash flow analysis (third year)

Quarter	Q1	3 Q2	Q3	Q4	3
Cash from operations	$44,554	$55,693	$60,148	$62,376	$222,771
Cash from receivables	$ 0	$ 0	$ 0	$ 0	$ 0
Operating cash inflow	**$44,554**	**$55,693**	**$60,148**	**$62,376**	**$222,771**
Other cash inflows					
Equity investment	$ 0	$ 0	$ 0	$ 0	$ 0
Increased borrowings	$ 0	$ 0	$ 0	$ 0	$ 0
Sales of business assets	$ 0	$ 0	$ 0	$ 0	$ 0
A/P increases	$10,025	$12,531	$13,534	$14,035	$ 50,125
Total other cash inflows	**$10,025**	**$12,531**	**$13,534**	**$14,035**	**$ 50,125**
Total cash inflow	**$54,579**	**$68,224**	**$73,682**	**$76,411**	**$272,897**
Cash outflows					
Repayment of principal	$ 2,990	$ 3,058	$ 3,127	$ 3,198	$ 12,373
A/P decreases	$ 7,170	$ 8,963	$ 9,680	$10,038	$ 35,852
A/R increases	$ 0	$ 0	$ 0	$ 0	$ 0
Asset purchases	$11,139	$13,923	$15,037	$15,594	$ 55,693
Dividends	$31,188	$38,985	$42,104	$43,663	$155,940
Total cash outflows	**$52,487**	**$64,929**	**$69,948**	**$72,494**	**$259,857**
Net cash flow	**$ 2,093**	**$ 3,295**	**$ 3,734**	**$ 3,918**	**$ 13,040**
Cash balance	**$69,905**	**$73,200**	**$76,934**	**$80,852**	**$ 80,852**

iPhone App Developer

AppStar

5300 Ninth St.
New York, New York 10001

BizPlanDB.com

AppStar will sell applications specific for the Apple iPhone, iPad, and iPod Touch.

1.0 EXECUTIVE SUMMARY

The purpose of this business plan is to raise $150,000 for the development of an iPhone app development company that will sell applications specific for the Apple iPhone, iPad, and iPod Touch. This business plan will also showcase the expected financials and operations over the next three years. AppStar ("the Company") is a New York based corporation that will generate revenues through the sale of applications via the Apple App Store. The Company was founded by Jeff Martin.

1.1 The Applications

The primary revenue center for the business will come from the ongoing development of applications for the iPhone (as well as the iPad and iPod Touch) that will be sold through the Apple App Store.

The business will also generate revenues from developing applications on an outsourced basis on behalf of third parties.

The third section of the business plan will further discuss the operations of AppStar.

1.2 Financing

Mr. Martin is seeking to raise $150,000 from a bank loan. The interest rate and loan agreement are to be further discussed during negotiation. This business plan assumes that the business will receive a 10 year loan with a 9% fixed interest rate. The financing will be used for the following:

- Development of the Company's application development platform.

- Financing for the first six months of operation.

- Capital to purchase servers, computers, and related technology

Mr. Martin will contribute $25,000 to the venture.

1.3 Mission Statement

AppStar's mission is to develop high quality applications for Apple-based consumer electronic devices.

1.4 Management Team

The Company was founded by Jeff Martin. Mr. Martin has more than 8 years of experience in the software programming industry. Through his expertise, he will be able to bring the operations of the business to profitability within its first year of operations.

1.5 Sales Forecasts

Mr. Martin expects a strong rate of growth at the start of operations. Below are the expected financials over the next three years.

Proforma profit and loss (yearly)

Year	1	2	3
Sales	$990,450	$1,436,153	$1,938,806
Operating costs	$429,373	$ 480,774	$ 536,571
EBITDA	$462,033	$ 811,763	$1,208,354
Taxes, interest, and depreciation	$197,607	$ 324,961	$ 475,048
Net profit	$264,425	$ 486,802	$ 733,305

Sales, operating costs, and profit forecast

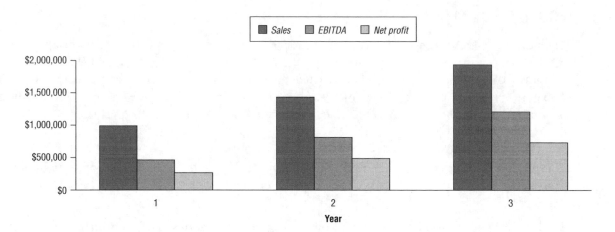

1.6 Expansion Plan

The Founder expects that the business will aggressively expand during the first three years of operation. Mr. Martin intends to implement marketing campaigns that will effectively target individuals and businesses that want in demand iPhone and iPad applications. The business will work closely with Apple, Inc. (via its application store) as well as through proprietary marketing channels to promote sales of its developed applications.

2.0 COMPANY AND FINANCING SUMMARY

2.1 Registered Name and Corporate Structure

AppStar is registered as a corporation in the State of New York.

2.2 Required Funds

At this time, AppStar requires $150,000 of debt funds. Below is a breakdown of how these funds will be used:

Projected startup costs

Initial lease payments and deposits	$ 15,000
Working capital	$ 25,000
FF&E	$ 30,000
Website development	$ 42,500
Security deposits	$ 5,000
Insurance	$ 2,500
Servers and technology equipment	$ 25,000
Marketing budget	$ 25,000
Miscellaneous and unforeseen costs	$ 5,000
Total startup costs	**$175,000**

Use of funds

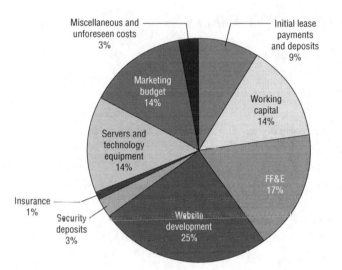

2.3 Investor Equity

Mr. Martin is not seeking an investment from a third party at this time.

2.4 Management Equity

Mr. Martin owns 100% of AppStar.

2.5 Exit Strategy

If the business is very successful, Mr. Martin may seek to sell the business to a third party for a significant earnings multiple. Most likely, the Company will hire a qualified business broker to sell the business on behalf of AppStar. Based on historical numbers, the business could fetch a sales premium of up to 10 times earnings.

3.0 PRODUCTS AND SERVICES

Below is a description of the services offered by AppStar.

3.1 iPhone Application Sales and Development

As stated in the executive summary, the business will specialize in developing unique entertainment and business applications for the following Apple devices:

- iPhone

- iPad

- iPod Touch

The business will generate a substantial amount of secondary revenues from the ongoing third party programming and development of iPhone, iPod, and iPad applications. The business will not earn ongoing royalties from the ongoing sale of these programs.

The Company's two pronged approach in developing applications that are sold on a proprietary basis as well as for the development of applications for third parties will ensure that AppStar is able to generate substantial and ongoing revenues from its services.

4.0 STRATEGIC AND MARKET ANALYSIS

4.1 Economic Outlook

This section of the analysis will detail the economic climate, the software development industry, the customer profile, and the competition that the business will face as it progresses through its business operations.

Currently, the economic market condition in the United States is sluggish. This slowdown in the economy has also greatly impacted real estate sales, which has halted to historical lows. Many economists expect that this sluggish will continue for a significant period of time, at which point the economy will begin a prolonged recovery period.

4.2 Industry Analysis

Below is an overview of the industries that AppStar will operate within:

E-Commerce Transactions
Online retailers are expected to generate $115 billion dollars this year. The United States Economic Census indicates that over the next five years, 60% of the businesses in the United States will have an internet presence. In early 2008, industry reports estimate that 210 million people will have access to the internet with approximately 65% of these people having direct high speed internet access. Management expects that the e-commerce industry will grow steadily as more people obtain high speed internet access. By 2010, e-commerce transactions will reach $250 billion.

Application Services
Currently, there are approximately 200,000 applications that are available through the Apple App Store. Many industry experts anticipate that there will be more than 1 million applications available by the end of 2012. The average sales price of an application is $5.50.

4.3 Customer Profile

AppStar's average client will be young middle- to upper-middle class males or females or businesses that own an Apple consumer product. Common traits among end users will include:

- Annual household income exceeding $50,000

- Between the ages of 25 to 50

- Has high speed internet access

- Owns an iPhone, iPod Touch, or iPad.

There are more than 300,000,000 worldwide users of iPods, iPads, and iPhones. Each of these devices allows individuals to purchase specific applications for a variety of functions. As such, the market for the Company's proprietarily produced applications and third party applications have a tremendous market from which the Company can market its software products. This market is expected to grow at an annualized rate of 20% per year during the next five years.

4.4 Competition

Competition in the iPhone, iPad, iPod, and other Apple based consumer market is substantial. This is primarily due to the fact that there has become an extremely high demand among consumers for unique applications that focus on both productivity and entertainment. However, Management feels that the business will be in an excellent position to capitalize on this broad market by developing unique applications that it will sell for its own account while also selling developed applications for third parties.

5.0 MARKETING PLAN

AppStar intends to maintain an extensive marketing campaign that will ensure maximum visibility for the business in its targeted market. Below is an overview of the marketing strategies and objectives of AppStar.

5.1 Marketing Objectives

- Develop an expansive online presence through the use of pay per click marketing and search engine optimization.

- Establish relationships with software professionals that need outsourced iPhone app development services.

- Develop a high impact marketing campaign to inform businesses regarding the Company's newly developed applications.

5.2 Marketing Strategies

Mr. Martin intends to use a high impact marketing campaign that will generate a substantial amount of traffic to the website that will feature descriptions showcasing the Company's produced iPhone, iPod, and iPad applications. Of course, all sales will be made through the Apple App Store. These strategies include the use of search engine optimization and pay per click marketing to drive traffic to the Company's website.

The Company's web development firm will place large amounts of linking text on the Company's website. For instance, when a person does a Google search for a specialized type of iPhone applications, the Company will appear on the first page of the search. This strategy is technically complicated, and AppStar will use a search engine optimization firm to develop the Company's visibility on a non-paid basis. Management expects that a SEO firm will place large amounts of linking data and text specific keywords into the business's website, which will allow the Company to appear more frequently among search engines.

Additionally, AppStar will develop ongoing relationships with software development companies that will outsource the development of applications to the Company in exchange for per project and per hour fees relating to the development of the applications.

5.3 Pricing

Most applications typically sell for approximately $1.99 to $12.99 depending on the nature and usage of the iPhone, iPad, or iPod application. Management anticipates that the business will generate approximately $5 of revenue per application sold. Applications developed on a third party basis are expected to generate $5,000 to $10,000 for the business as the Company will only act in a developmental capacity for these third party businesses.

6.0 ORGANIZATIONAL PLAN AND PERSONNEL SUMMARY

6.1 Corporate Organization

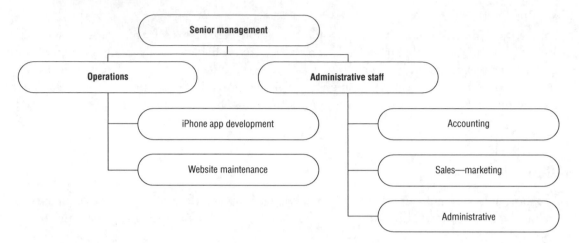

6.2 Organizational Budget

Personnel plan—yearly

Year	1	2	3
Owners	$ 80,000	$ 82,400	$ 84,872
Sales manager	$ 35,000	$ 36,050	$ 37,132
Assistant	$ 32,500	$ 33,475	$ 34,479
App developers	$ 37,500	$ 51,500	$ 66,306
Administrative	$ 44,000	$ 45,320	$ 46,680
Total	**$229,000**	**$248,745**	**$269,469**

Numbers of personnel

Year	1	2	3
Owners	2	2	2
Sales manager	1	1	1
Assistant	1	1	1
App developers	3	4	5
Administrative	2	2	2
Totals	**9**	**10**	**11**

Personnel expense breakdown

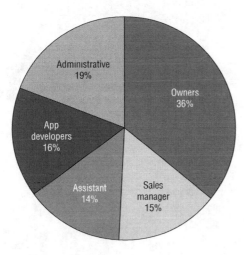

7.0 FINANCIAL PLAN

7.1 Underlying Assumptions

The Company has based its proforma financial statements on the following:

- AppStar will have an annual revenue growth rate of 31% per year.
- The Owner will acquire $150,000 of debt funds to develop the business.
- The loan will have a 10 year term with a 9% interest rate.

7.2 Sensitivity Analysis

In the event of a severe economic decline, the revenues of AppStar should not decrease as the business will continue to generate revenues on a monthly basis from the Company's sales of applications. This is primarily due to the fact that the costs related to these applications are relatively low.

7.3 Source of Funds

Financing

Equity contributions	
Management investment	$ 25,000.00
Total equity financing	**$ 25,000.00**
Banks and lenders	
Banks and lenders	$ 150,000.00
Total debt financing	**$150,000.00**
Total financing	**$175,000.00**

7.4 General Assumptions

General assumptions

Year	1	2	3
Short term interest rate	9.5%	9.5%	9.5%
Long term interest rate	10.0%	10.0%	10.0%
Federal tax rate	33.0%	33.0%	33.0%
State tax rate	5.0%	5.0%	5.0%
Personnel taxes	15.0%	15.0%	15.0%

7.5 Profit and Loss Statements

Proforma profit and loss (yearly)

Year	1	2	3
Sales	**$990,450**	**$1,436,153**	**$1,938,806**
Cost of goods sold	$ 99,045	$ 143,615	$ 193,881
Gross margin	90.00%	90.00%	90.00%
Operating income	**$891,405**	**$1,292,537**	**$1,744,925**
Expenses			
Payroll	$229,000	$ 248,745	$ 269,469
General and administrative	$ 32,500	$ 33,800	$ 35,152
Marketing expenses	$ 39,618	$ 57,446	$ 77,552
Professional fees and licensure	$ 17,000	$ 17,510	$ 18,035
Insurance costs	$ 12,000	$ 12,600	$ 13,230
Server and technology costs	$ 25,000	$ 27,500	$ 30,250
Rent and utilities	$ 30,000	$ 31,500	$ 33,075
Miscellaneous costs	$ 9,905	$ 14,362	$ 19,388
Payroll taxes	$ 34,350	$ 37,312	$ 40,420
Total operating costs	**$429,373**	**$ 480,774**	**$ 536,571**
EBITDA	**$462,033**	**$ 811,763**	**$1,208,354**
Federal income tax	$152,471	$ 263,857	$ 395,060
State income tax	$ 23,102	$ 39,978	$ 59,858
Interest expense	$ 13,107	$ 12,197	$ 11,202
Depreciation expenses	$ 8,929	$ 8,929	$ 8,929
Net profit	**$264,425**	**$ 486,802**	**$ 733,305**
Profit margin	**26.70%**	**33.90%**	**37.82%**

Sales, operating costs, and profit forecast

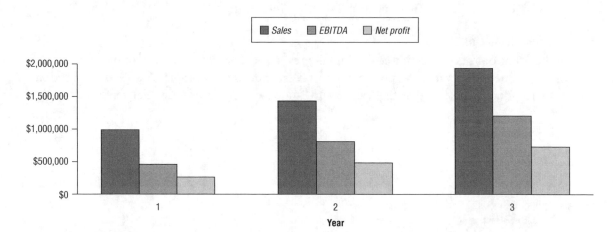

7.6 Cash Flow Analysis

Proforma cash flow analysis—yearly

Year	1	2	3
Cash from operations	$273,354	$495,731	$742,234
Cash from receivables	$ 0	$ 0	$ 0
Operating cash inflow	**$273,354**	**$495,731**	**$742,234**
Other cash inflows			
Equity investment	$ 25,000	$ 0	$ 0
Increased borrowings	$150,000	$ 0	$ 0
Sales of business assets	$ 0	$ 0	$ 0
A/P increases	$ 37,902	$ 43,587	$ 50,125
Total other cash inflows	**$212,902**	**$ 43,587**	**$ 50,125**
Total cash inflow	**$486,256**	**$539,318**	**$792,359**
Cash outflows			
Repayment of principal	$ 9,695	$ 10,605	$ 11,599
A/P decreases	$ 24,897	$ 29,876	$ 35,852
A/R increases	$ 0	$ 0	$ 0
Asset purchases	$125,000	$123,933	$185,558
Dividends	$191,348	$347,012	$519,564
Total cash outflows	**$350,940**	**$511,425**	**$752,573**
Net cash flow	**$135,316**	**$ 27,893**	**$ 39,786**
Cash balance	**$135,316**	**$163,209**	**$202,995**

Proforma cash flow (yearly)

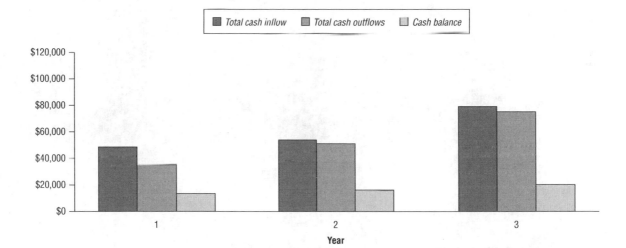

7.7 Balance Sheet

Proforma balance sheet—yearly

Year	1	2	3
Assets			
Cash	$ 135,316	$163,209	$ 202,995
Amortized development costs	$ 70,000	$ 82,393	$ 100,949
Servers and technology equipment	$ 25,000	$117,950	$ 257,118
FF&E	$ 30,000	$ 48,590	$ 76,424
Accumulated depreciation	($ 8,929)	($ 17,857)	($ 26,786)
Total assets	**$251,387**	**$394,284**	**$610,700**
Liabilities and equity			
Accounts payable	$ 13,005	$ 26,716	$ 40,990
Long term liabilities	$140,305	$129,700	$ 119,096
Other liabilities	$ 0	$ 0	$ 0
Total liabilities	**$153,310**	**$156,416**	**$160,085**
Net worth	**$ 98,078**	**$237,868**	**$450,615**
Total liabilities and equity	**$251,387**	**$394,284**	**$610,700**

Proforma balance sheet

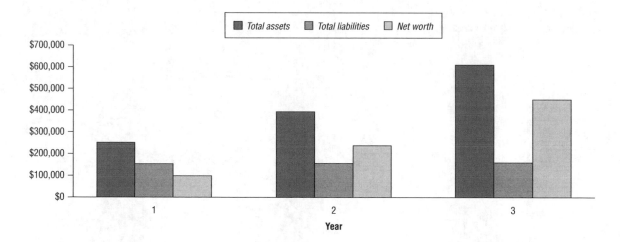

7.8 Breakeven Analysis

Monthly break even analysis

Year	1	2	3
Monthly revenue	$ 39,757	$ 44,516	$ 49,683
Yearly revenue	$477,081	$534,194	$596,191

Break even analysis

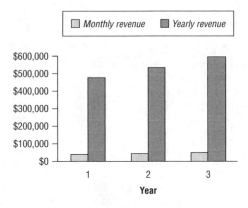

7.9 Business Ratios

Business ratios—yearly

Year	1	2	3
Sales			
Sales growth	0.00%	45.00%	35.00%
Gross margin	90.00%	90.00%	90.00%
Financials			
Profit margin	26.70%	33.90%	37.82%
Assets to liabilities	1.64	2.52	3.81
Equity to liabilities	0.64	1.52	2.81
Assets to equity	2.56	1.66	1.36
Liquidity			
Acid test	0.88	1.04	1.27
Cash to assets	0.54	0.41	0.33

7.10 Three Year Profit and Loss Statement

Profit and loss statement (first year)

Months	1	2	3	4	5	6	7
Sales	$69,750	$72,075	$74,400	$76,725	$79,050	$81,375	$83,700
Cost of goods sold	$ 6,975	$ 7,208	$ 7,440	$ 7,673	$ 7,905	$ 8,138	$ 8,370
Gross margin	90.0%	90.0%	90.0%	90.0%	90.0%	90.0%	90.0%
Operating income	$62,775	$64,868	$66,960	$69,053	$71,145	$73,238	$75,330
Expenses							
Payroll	$19,083	$19,083	$19,083	$19,083	$19,083	$19,083	$19,083
General and administrative	$ 2,708	$ 2,708	$ 2,708	$ 2,708	$ 2,708	$ 2,708	$ 2,708
Marketing expenses	$ 3,302	$ 3,302	$ 3,302	$ 3,302	$ 3,302	$ 3,302	$ 3,302
Professional fees and licensure	$ 1,417	$ 1,417	$ 1,417	$ 1,417	$ 1,417	$ 1,417	$ 1,417
Insurance costs	$ 1,000	$ 1,000	$ 1,000	$ 1,000	$ 1,000	$ 1,000	$ 1,000
Server and technology costs	$ 2,083	$ 2,083	$ 2,083	$ 2,083	$ 2,083	$ 2,083	$ 2,083
Rent and utilities	$ 2,500	$ 2,500	$ 2,500	$ 2,500	$ 2,500	$ 2,500	$ 2,500
Miscellaneous costs	$ 825	$ 825	$ 825	$ 825	$ 825	$ 825	$ 825
Payroll taxes	$ 2,863	$ 2,863	$ 2,863	$ 2,863	$ 2,863	$ 2,863	$ 2,863
Total operating costs	$35,781	$35,781	$35,781	$35,781	$35,781	$35,781	$35,781
EBITDA	$26,994	$29,086	$31,179	$33,271	$35,364	$37,456	$39,549
Federal income tax	$10,737	$11,095	$11,453	$11,811	$12,169	$12,527	$12,885
State income tax	$ 1,627	$ 1,681	$ 1,735	$ 1,790	$ 1,844	$ 1,898	$ 1,952
Interest expense	$ 1,125	$ 1,119	$ 1,113	$ 1,107	$ 1,101	$ 1,095	$ 1,089
Depreciation expense	$ 744	$ 744	$ 744	$ 744	$ 744	$ 744	$ 744
Net profit	$12,761	$14,447	$16,133	$17,819	$19,506	$21,192	$22,878

Profit and loss statement (first year cont.)

Month	8	9	10	11	12	1
Sales	$86,025	$88,350	$90,675	$93,000	$95,325	$990,450
Cost of goods sold	$ 8,603	$ 8,835	$ 9,068	$ 9,300	$ 9,533	$ 99,045
Gross margin	90.0%	90.0%	90.0%	90.0%	90.0%	90.0%
Operating income	$77,423	$79,515	$81,608	$83,700	$85,793	$891,405
Expenses						
Payroll	$19,083	$19,083	$19,083	$19,083	$19,083	$229,000
General and administrative	$ 2,708	$ 2,708	$ 2,708	$ 2,708	$ 2,708	$ 32,500
Marketing expenses	$ 3,302	$ 3,302	$ 3,302	$ 3,302	$ 3,302	$ 39,618
Professional fees and licensure	$ 1,417	$ 1,417	$ 1,417	$ 1,417	$ 1,417	$ 17,000
Insurance costs	$ 1,000	$ 1,000	$ 1,000	$ 1,000	$ 1,000	$ 12,000
Server and technology costs	$ 2,083	$ 2,083	$ 2,083	$ 2,083	$ 2,083	$ 25,000
Rent and utilities	$ 2,500	$ 2,500	$ 2,500	$ 2,500	$ 2,500	$ 30,000
Miscellaneous costs	$ 825	$ 825	$ 825	$ 825	$ 825	$ 9,905
Payroll taxes	$ 2,863	$ 2,863	$ 2,863	$ 2,863	$ 2,863	$ 34,350
Total operating costs	$35,781	$35,781	$35,781	$35,781	$35,781	$429,373
EBITDA	$41,641	$43,734	$45,826	$47,919	$50,011	$462,033
Federal income tax	$13,243	$13,601	$13,959	$14,317	$14,674	$152,471
State income tax	$ 2,006	$ 2,061	$ 2,115	$ 2,169	$ 2,223	$ 23,102
Interest expense	$ 1,083	$ 1,077	$ 1,071	$ 1,065	$ 1,059	$ 13,107
Depreciation expense	$ 744	$ 744	$ 744	$ 744	$ 744	$ 8,929
Net profit	$24,565	$26,251	$27,938	$29,624	$31,311	$264,425

Profit and loss statement (second year)

Quarter	Q1	2 Q2	Q3	Q4	2
Sales	$287,231	$359,038	$387,761	$402,123	$1,436,153
Cost of goods sold	$ 28,723	$ 35,904	$ 38,776	$ 40,212	$ 143,615
Gross margin	90.0%	90.0%	90.0%	90.0%	90.0%
Operating income	$258,507	$323,134	$348,985	$361,910	$1,292,537
Expenses					
Payroll	$ 49,749	$ 62,186	$ 67,161	$ 69,649	$ 248,745
General and administrative	$ 6,760	$ 8,450	$ 9,126	$ 9,464	$ 33,800
Marketing expenses	$ 11,489	$ 14,362	$ 15,510	$ 16,085	$ 57,446
Professional fees and licensure	$ 3,502	$ 4,378	$ 4,728	$ 4,903	$ 17,510
Insurance costs	$ 2,520	$ 3,150	$ 3,402	$ 3,528	$ 12,600
Server and technology costs	$ 5,500	$ 6,875	$ 7,425	$ 7,700	$ 27,500
Rent and utilities	$ 6,300	$ 7,875	$ 8,505	$ 8,820	$ 31,500
Miscellaneous costs	$ 2,872	$ 3,590	$ 3,878	$ 4,021	$ 14,362
Payroll taxes	$ 7,462	$ 9,328	$ 10,074	$ 10,447	$ 37,312
Total operating costs	$ 96,155	$120,194	$129,809	$134,617	$ 480,774
EBITDA	$162,353	$202,941	$219,176	$227,294	$ 811,763
Federal income tax	$ 52,771	$ 65,964	$ 71,241	$ 73,880	$ 263,857
State income tax	$ 7,996	$ 9,995	$ 10,794	$ 11,194	$ 39,978
Interest expense	$ 3,138	$ 3,080	$ 3,020	$ 2,959	$ 12,197
Depreciation expense	$ 2,232	$ 2,232	$ 2,232	$ 2,232	$ 8,929
Net profit	$ 96,216	$121,670	$131,888	$137,028	$ 486,802

Profit and loss statement (third year)

Quarter	Q1	3 Q2	Q3	Q4	3
Sales	$387,761	$484,701	$523,478	$542,866	$1,938,806
Cost of goods sold	$ 38,776	$ 48,470	$ 52,348	$ 54,287	$ 193,881
Gross margin	90.0%	90.0%	90.0%	90.0%	90.0%
Operating income	$348,985	$436,231	$471,130	$488,579	$1,744,925
Expenses					
Payroll	$ 53,894	$ 67,367	$ 72,757	$ 75,451	$ 269,469
General and administrative	$ 7,030	$ 8,788	$ 9,491	$ 9,843	$ 35,152
Marketing expenses	$ 15,510	$ 19,388	$ 20,939	$ 21,715	$ 77,552
Professional fees and licensure	$ 3,607	$ 4,509	$ 4,870	$ 5,050	$ 18,035
Insurance costs	$ 2,646	$ 3,308	$ 3,572	$ 3,704	$ 13,230
Server and technology costs	$ 6,050	$ 7,563	$ 8,168	$ 8,470	$ 30,250
Rent and utilities	$ 6,615	$ 8,269	$ 8,930	$ 9,261	$ 33,075
Miscellaneous costs	$ 3,878	$ 4,847	$ 5,235	$ 5,429	$ 19,388
Payroll taxes	$ 8,084	$ 10,105	$ 10,913	$ 11,318	$ 40,420
Total operating costs	$107,314	$134,143	$144,874	$150,240	$ 536,571
EBITDA	$241,671	$302,088	$326,256	$338,339	$1,208,354
Federal income tax	$ 79,012	$ 98,765	$106,666	$110,617	$ 395,060
State income tax	$ 11,972	$ 14,964	$ 16,162	$ 16,760	$ 59,858
Interest expense	$ 2,897	$ 2,834	$ 2,769	$ 2,702	$ 11,202
Depreciation expense	$ 2,232	$ 2,232	$ 2,232	$ 2,232	$ 8,929
Net profit	$145,558	$183,293	$198,427	$206,028	$ 733,305

7.11 Three Year Cash Flow Analysis

Cash flow analysis (first year)

Month	1	2	3	4	5	6	7
Cash from operations	$ 13,505	$15,191	$16,877	$ 18,563	$ 20,250	$ 21,936	$ 23,622
Cash from receivables	$ 0	$ 0	$ 0	$ 0	$ 0	$ 0	$ 0
Operating cash inflow	$ 13,505	$15,191	$16,877	$ 18,563	$ 20,250	$ 21,936	$ 23,622
Other cash inflows							
Equity investment	$ 25,000	$ 0	$ 0	$ 0	$ 0	$ 0	$ 0
Increased borrowings	$150,000	$ 0	$ 0	$ 0	$ 0	$ 0	$ 0
Sales of business assets	$ 0	$ 0	$ 0	$ 0	$ 0	$ 0	$ 0
A/P increases	$ 3,150	$ 3,159	$ 3,159	$ 3,159	$ 3,159	$ 3,159	$ 3,159
Total other cash inflows	$178,159	$ 3,159	$ 3,159	$ 3,159	$ 3,159	$ 3,159	$ 3,159
Total cash inflow	$191,663	$18,349	$20,036	$ 21,722	$ 23,408	$ 25,095	$ 26,781
Cash outflows							
Repayment of principal	$ 775	$ 781	$ 787	$ 793	$ 799	$ 805	$ 811
A/P decreases	$ 2,075	$ 2,075	$ 2,075	$ 2,075	$ 2,075	$ 2,075	$ 2,075
A/R increases	$ 0	$ 0	$ 0	$ 0	$ 0	$ 0	$ 0
Asset purchases	$125,000	$ 0	$ 0	$ 0	$ 0	$ 0	$ 0
Dividends	$ 0	$ 0	$ 0	$ 0	$ 0	$ 0	$ 0
Total cash outflows	$127,850	$ 2,856	$ 2,862	$ 2,867	$ 2,873	$ 2,879	$ 2,885
Net cash flow	$ 63,813	$15,494	$17,174	$ 18,854	$ 20,535	$ 22,215	$ 23,895
Cash balance	$ 63,813	$79,307	$96,481	$115,335	$135,870	$158,085	$181,981

Cash flow analysis (first year cont.)

Month	8	9	10	11	12	1
Cash from operations	$ 25,309	$ 26,995	$ 28,682	$ 30,368	$ 32,055	$273,354
Cash from receivables	$ 0	$ 0	$ 0	$ 0	$ 0	$ 0
Operating cash inflow	**$ 25,309**	**$ 26,995**	**$ 28,682**	**$ 30,368**	**$ 32,055**	**$273,354**
Other cash inflows						
Equity investment	$ 0	$ 0	$ 0	$ 0	$ 0	$ 25,000
Increased borrowings	$ 0	$ 0	$ 0	$ 0	$ 0	$150,000
Sales of business assets	$ 0	$ 0	$ 0	$ 0	$ 0	$ 0
A/P increases	$ 3,159	$ 3,159	$ 3,159	$ 3,159	$ 3,159	$ 37,902
Total other cash inflows	**$ 3,159**	**$ 3,159**	**$ 3,159**	**$ 3,159**	**$ 3,159**	**$212,902**
Total cash inflow	**$ 28,467**	**$ 30,154**	**$ 31,840**	**$ 33,527**	**$ 35,214**	**$486,256**
Cash outflows						
Repayment of principal	$ 817	$ 823	$ 829	$ 835	$ 842	$ 9,695
A/P decreases	$ 2,075	$ 2,075	$ 2,075	$ 2,075	$ 2,075	$ 24,897
A/R increases	$ 0	$ 0	$ 0	$ 0	$ 0	$ 0
Asset purchases	$ 0	$ 0	$ 0	$ 0	$ 0	$125,000
Dividends	$ 0	$ 0	$ 0	$ 0	$191,348	$191,348
Total cash outflows	**$ 2,892**	**$ 2,898**	**$ 2,904**	**$ 2,910**	**$194,264**	**$350,940**
Net cash flow	**$ 25,576**	**$ 27,256**	**$ 28,937**	**$ 30,617**	**−$159,051**	**$135,316**
Cash balance	**$207,557**	**$234,813**	**$263,749**	**$294,366**	**$135,316**	**$135,316**

Cash flow analysis (second year)

Quarter	Q1	2 Q2	Q3	Q4	2
Cash from operations	$ 99,146	$123,933	$133,847	$138,805	$495,731
Cash from receivables	$ 0	$ 0	$ 0	$ 0	$ 0
Operating cash inflow	**$ 99,146**	**$123,933**	**$133,847**	**$138,805**	**$495,731**
Other cash inflows					
Equity investment	$ 0	$ 0	$ 0	$ 0	$ 0
Increased borrowings	$ 0	$ 0	$ 0	$ 0	$ 0
Sales of business assets	$ 0	$ 0	$ 0	$ 0	$ 0
A/P increases	$ 8,717	$ 10,897	$ 11,769	$ 12,204	$ 43,587
Total other cash inflows	**$ 8,717**	**$ 10,897**	**$ 11,769**	**$ 12,204**	**$ 43,587**
Total cash inflow	**$107,864**	**$134,830**	**$145,616**	**$151,009**	**$539,318**
Cash outflows					
Repayment of principal	$ 2,563	$ 2,621	$ 2,680	$ 2,741	$ 10,605
A/P decreases	$ 5,975	$ 7,469	$ 8,067	$ 8,365	$ 29,876
A/R increases	$ 0	$ 0	$ 0	$ 0	$ 0
Asset purchases	$ 24,787	$ 30,983	$ 33,462	$ 34,701	$123,933
Dividends	$ 69,402	$ 86,753	$ 93,693	$ 97,163	$347,012
Total cash outflows	**$102,727**	**$127,826**	**$137,902**	**$142,971**	**$511,425**
Net cash flow	**$ 5,137**	**$ 7,004**	**$ 7,714**	**$ 8,038**	**$ 27,893**
Cash balance	**$140,453**	**$147,456**	**$155,171**	**$163,209**	**$163,209**

Cash flow analysis (third year)

Quarter	Q1	3 Q2	Q3	Q4	3
Cash from operations	$148,447	$185,558	$200,403	$207,826	$742,234
Cash from receivables	$ 0	$ 0	$ 0	$ 0	$ 0
Operating cash inflow	**$148,447**	**$185,558**	**$200,403**	**$207,826**	**$742,234**
Other cash inflows					
Equity investment	$ 0	$ 0	$ 0	$ 0	$ 0
Increased borrowings	$ 0	$ 0	$ 0	$ 0	$ 0
Sales of business assets	$ 0	$ 0	$ 0	$ 0	$ 0
A/P increases	$ 10,025	$ 12,531	$ 13,534	$ 14,035	$ 50,125
Total other cash inflows	**$ 10,025**	**$ 12,531**	**$ 13,534**	**$ 14,035**	**$ 50,125**
Total cash inflow	**$158,472**	**$198,090**	**$213,937**	**$221,861**	**$792,359**
Cash outflows					
Repayment of principal	$ 2,803	$ 2,867	$ 2,932	$ 2,998	$ 11,599
A/P decreases	$ 7,170	$ 8,963	$ 9,680	$ 10,038	$ 35,852
A/R increases	$ 0	$ 0	$ 0	$ 0	$ 0
Asset purchases	$ 37,112	$ 46,390	$ 50,101	$ 51,956	$185,558
Dividends	$103,913	$129,891	$140,282	$145,478	$519,564
Total cash outflows	**$150,998**	**$188,110**	**$202,995**	**$210,471**	**$752,573**
Net cash flow	**$ 7,474**	**$ 9,980**	**$ 10,942**	**$ 11,390**	**$ 39,786**
Cash balance	**$170,683**	**$180,663**	**$191,605**	**$202,995**	**$202,995**

IT Network Installer

Misch Computer Network Services

4400 Elm St.
Boulder, Colorado 80309

BizPlanDB.com

Misch Computer Network Services will provide its clients with advice and service regarding the purchase, installation, and maintenance of information technology products. The Company intends to develop ongoing relationships with businesses that will be billed on a monthly basis.

1.0 EXECUTIVE SUMMARY

The purpose of this business plan is to raise $100,000 for the development of an IT network installation company while showcasing the expected financials and operations over the next three years. Misch Computer Network Services, Inc. is a Colorado-based corporation that will provide an expansive array of IT installation and product sales to customers in its targeted market. The Company was founded by Peter Misch.

1.1 The Services

Misch Computer Network Services will provide its clients with advice and service regarding the purchase, installation, and maintenance of information technology products. The Company intends to develop ongoing relationships with businesses that will be billed on a monthly basis.

From time to time, the Company will also make product sales from the Company's vendors to the business' clients. This is a very important secondary stream of revenue for the business.

The third section of the business plan will further describe the services offered by Misch Computer Network Services.

1.2 Financing

Mr. Misch is seeking to raise $100,000 from a bank loan. The interest rate and loan agreement are to be further discussed during negotiation. This business plan assumes that the business will receive a 10 year loan with a 9% fixed interest rate. The financing will be used for the following:

- Development of the Company's office location.

- Financing for the first six months of operation.

- Capital to purchase initial inventories of IT related hardware and software.

Mr. Misch will contribute $10,000 to the venture.

1.3 Mission Statement

Misch Computer Network Services' mission is to become the recognized leader in its targeted market for IT installation and maintenance services.

1.4 Management Team

The Company was founded by Peter Misch. Mr. Misch has more than 10 years of experience in the IT industry. Through his expertise, he will be able to bring the operations of the business to profitability within its first year of operations.

1.5 Sales Forecasts

Mr. Misch expects a strong rate of growth at the start of operations. Below are the expected financials over the next three years.

Proforma profit and loss (yearly)

Year	1	2	3
Sales	$940,230	$1,128,276	$1,320,083
Operating costs	$323,586	$ 351,725	$ 381,191
EBITDA	$469,240	$ 599,666	$ 731,937
Taxes, interest, and depreciation	$191,156	$ 237,022	$ 286,874
Net profit	$278,084	$ 362,644	$ 445,064

Sales, operating costs, and profit forecast

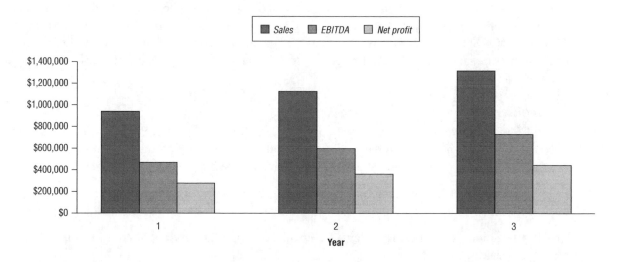

1.6 Expansion Plan

The Founder expects that the business will aggressively expand during the first three years of operation. Mr. Misch intends to implement marketing campaigns that will effectively target small businesses and individuals within the target market.

2.0 COMPANY AND FINANCING SUMMARY

2.1 Registered Name and Corporate Structure

Misch Computer Network Services is registered as a corporation in the State of Colorado.

2.2 Required Funds

At this time, Misch Computer Network Services requires $100,000 of debt funds. Below is a breakdown of how these funds will be used:

Projected startup costs

Initial lease payments and deposits	$ 10,000
Working capital	$ 35,000
FF&E	$ 23,000
Leasehold improvements	$ 5,000
Security deposits	$ 5,000
Insurance	$ 2,500
IT hardware inventories	$ 17,000
Marketing budget	$ 7,500
Miscellaneous and unforeseen costs	$ 5,000
Total startup costs	**$110,000**

Use of funds

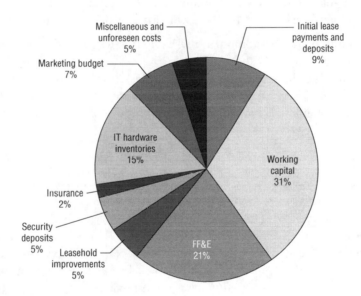

2.3 Investor Equity

Mr. Misch is not seeking an investment from a third party at this time.

2.4 Management Equity

Mr. Misch owns 100% of Misch Computer Network Services, Inc.

2.5 Exit Strategy

If the business is very successful, Mr. Misch may seek to sell the business to a third party for a significant earnings multiple. Most likely, the Company will hire a qualified business broker to sell the business on behalf of Misch Computer Network Services. Based on historical numbers, the business could fetch a sales premium of up to 3 times earnings.

3.0 PRODUCTS AND SERVICES

3.1 IT Network Services

The business, through its employed personnel, will provide IT consulting, networking, data storage and management, computer consulting, software development, and enterprise computing solutions. Each client of Misch Computer Network Services will receive only the highest level of professional computing services. Each IT professional or consultant is certified in each of the segments from which their expertise stems.

3.2 IT Product Sales

Misch Computer Network Services may also offer all of the products that a person could purchase at a regular computer store through moderate inventory holdings. Unlike these companies, our Company's services come before the products. The Company's hardware, software, and periphery sales would be rendered directly on site. The margins derived from combining the products complimentary to our services are much higher than the industry standard.

4.0 STRATEGIC AND MARKET ANALYSIS

4.1 Economic Outlook

This section of the analysis will detail the economic climate, the computer/IT industry, the customer profile, and the competition that the business will face as it progresses through its business operations.

The current economic market condition in the United States is moderate. The meltdown of the sub prime mortgage market coupled with increasing gas prices has led many people to believe that the US is on the cusp of a double dip economic recession. This slowdown in the economy has also greatly impacted real estate sales, which has halted to historical lows. However, IT network installers operate with great economic stability as businesses will continue to require IT services despite deleterious changes in the general economy.

4.2 Industry Analysis

The computer technical consulting industry has mushroomed in size over the last five years. Rapid increases and developments in computer technology has caused the average user to rely on computer professionals to handle their computing repair and consulting needs. In the United States, the market for computer repair services is immense. Last year $300 billion dollars was spent nationwide on computer and computer related services. Approximately 55% of this revenue was generated specifically from the management of computer systems, network installation and consulting. This growth has caused a number of businesses to develop and expand franchise-based computer consulting and repair businesses. The United States Economic Census estimates that there are more than 200,000 businesses that provide services similar or identical to that of the Company.

As time progresses, Mr. Misch expects that the number of businesses operating within this market will continue to grow. One of the primary attractive elements to this market is that the demand for computer and networking services is insulated from changes in the general economy. Computers will not work properly regardless of the prosperity or recession of the economic market. Management also expects that as the number of agents entering the market increases, the aggregate fees generated per firm will decrease as price competition becomes the primary differential among service providers.

4.3 Customer Profile

Misch Computer Network Services' average client will be small- or medium-sized businesses in the Company's target market. Common traits among business clients will include:

* Annual revenues of approximately $250,000 per year.

* Operates no more than 15 miles from the Company's location.

* Will spend $500 to $2,500 with the business on a yearly basis.

Among residential clients, Management has developed the following demographic profile:

- Annual household income of $75,000 per year.

- Is seeking to integrate a household network for their Internet connectivity and content sharing within their residence.

- Will spend $500 for this service on a one-time basis.

4.4 Competition

As stated above, there are more than 200,000 businesses within the United States that are able to provide information technology capabilities to residences and businesses domestically. Within the Company's targeted market of the Boulder, Colorado metropolitan area, there are approximately 10,000 businesses that are able to offer this service. Management intends to maintain a significant competitive advantage by being able to provide comprehensive business and home networking installations at a cost that is 30% less expensive among related competitors.

5.0 MARKETING PLAN

Misch Computer Network Services intends to maintain an extensive marketing campaign that will ensure maximum visibility for the business in its targeted market. Below is an overview of the marketing strategies and objectives of Misch Computer Network Services.

5.1 Marketing Objectives

- Develop an online presence by developing a website and placing the Company's name and contact information with online directories that specifically focus on the IT industry.

- Establish relationships with other IT firms within the targeted market.

5.2 Marketing Strategies

Mr. Misch intends on using a number of marketing strategies that will allow Misch Computer Network Services to easily target small- and medium-sized businesses within the target market. These strategies include traditional print advertisements and ads placed on search engines on the Internet. Below is a description of how the business intends to market its services to the general public.

Management intends to maintain a broad website that showcases the operations of the business, the preliminary costs associated with developing a business/in-home IT network, the Company's Management Team and their expertise, and how to contact the Company in regards to their specific information technology needs. The Company will use a number of search engine optimization and pay per click marketing strategies that will be managed by a third party in order to drive traffic to this highly informative website.

The Company will maintain a sizable amount of print advertising methods within local markets to promote the IT installation and product sales that the Company is offering. These traditional print campaigns will include advertisements in local trade journals, local newspapers, and other publications that are frequently distributed to the Boulder, Colorado, metropolitan area residents.

5.3 Pricing

For each business customer, Management, again, anticipates that they will spend $500 to $2,000 on a per annum basis on the IT infrastructure costs. For residential users that have unique IT needs, Management anticipates one time installation and set up fees of $500 per client.

6.0 ORGANIZATIONAL PLAN AND PERSONNEL SUMMARY

6.1 Corporate Organization

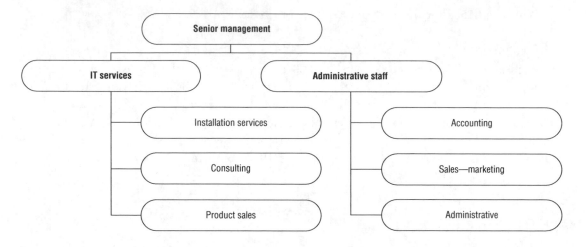

6.2 Organizational Budget

Personnel plan—yearly

Year	1	2	3
Owners	$ 80,000	$ 82,400	$ 84,872
IT manager	$ 35,000	$ 36,050	$ 37,132
Owners' assistant	$ 32,500	$ 33,475	$ 34,479
IT personnel	$ 37,500	$ 51,500	$ 66,306
Receptionist	$ 44,000	$ 45,320	$ 46,680
Totals	**$229,000**	**$248,745**	**$269,469**

Numbers of personnel

Year	1	2	3
Owners	2	2	2
IT manager	1	1	1
Owners' assistant	1	1	1
IT personnel	3	4	5
Receptionist	2	2	2
Totals	**9**	**10**	**11**

Personnel expense breakdown

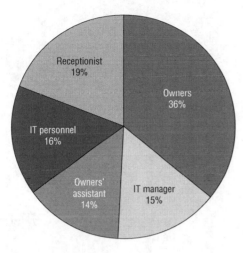

7.0 FINANCIAL PLAN

7.1 Underlying Assumptions

The Company has based its proforma financial statements on the following:

• The IT Consulting Firm will have an annual revenue growth rate of 16% per year.

• The Owner will acquire $100,000 of debt funds to develop the business.

• The loan will have a 10 year term with a 9% interest rate.

7.2 Sensitivity Analysis

In the event of an economic downturn, the business may have a decline in its revenues. However, IT consulting and computer services are demanded regardless of the general economy, and only a trained IT professional can manage large scale networks for small- and medium-sized businesses. As such, only a severe economic downturn would result in a decline in revenues.

7.3 Source of Funds

Financing

Equity contributions	
Management investment	$ 10,000.00
Total equity financing	**$ 10,000.00**
Banks and lenders	
Banks and lenders	$ 100,000.00
Total debt financing	**$100,000.00**
Total financing	**$110,000.00**

7.4 General Assumptions

General assumptions

Year	1	2	3
Short term interest rate	9.5%	9.5%	9.5%
Long term interest rate	10.0%	10.0%	10.0%
Federal tax rate	33.0%	33.0%	33.0%
State tax rate	5.0%	5.0%	5.0%
Personnel taxes	15.0%	15.0%	15.0%

7.5 Profit and Loss Statements

Proforma profit and loss (yearly)

Year	1	2	3
Sales	**$940,230**	**$1,128,276**	**$1,320,083**
Cost of goods sold	$147,404	$ 176,885	$ 206,955
Gross margin	84.32%	84.32%	84.32%
Operating income	**$792,826**	**$ 951,391**	**$1,113,128**
Expenses			
Payroll	$229,000	$ 248,745	$ 269,469
General and administrative	$ 25,200	$ 26,208	$ 27,256
Marketing expenses	$ 4,701	$ 5,641	$ 6,600
Professional fees and licensure	$ 5,219	$ 5,376	$ 5,537
Insurance costs	$ 1,987	$ 2,086	$ 2,191
Travel and vehicle costs	$ 7,596	$ 8,356	$ 9,191
Rent and utilities	$ 4,250	$ 4,463	$ 4,686
Miscellaneous costs	$ 11,283	$ 13,539	$ 15,841
Payroll taxes	$ 34,350	$ 37,312	$ 40,420
Total operating costs	**$323,586**	**$ 351,725**	**$ 381,191**
EBITDA	**$469,240**	**$ 599,666**	**$ 731,937**
Federal income tax	$154,849	$ 195,206	$ 239,075
State income tax	$ 23,462	$ 29,577	$ 36,223
Interest expense	$ 8,738	$ 8,131	$ 7,468
Depreciation expense	$ 4,107	$ 4,107	$ 4,107
Net profit	**$278,084**	**$ 362,644**	**$ 445,064**
Profit margin	**29.58%**	**32.14%**	**33.71%**

Sales, operating costs, and profit forecast

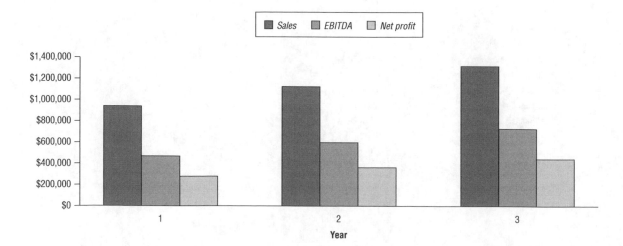

7.6 Cash Flow Analysis

Proforma cash flow analysis—yearly

Year	1	2	3
Cash from operations	$282,191	$366,751	$449,171
Cash from receivables	$ 0	$ 0	$ 0
Operating cash inflow	**$282,191**	**$366,751**	**$449,171**
Other cash inflows			
Equity investment	$ 10,000	$ 0	$ 0
Increased borrowings	$100,000	$ 0	$ 0
Sales of business assets	$ 0	$ 0	$ 0
A/P increases	$ 37,902	$ 43,587	$ 50,125
Total other cash inflows	**$147,902**	**$ 43,587**	**$ 50,125**
Total cash inflow	**$430,093**	**$410,339**	**$499,296**
Cash outflows			
Repayment of principal	$ 6,463	$ 7,070	$ 7,733
A/P decreases	$ 24,897	$ 29,876	$ 35,852
A/R increases	$ 0	$ 0	$ 0
Asset purchases	$ 57,500	$ 91,688	$112,293
Dividends	$197,534	$256,726	$314,419
Total cash outflows	**$286,394**	**$385,360**	**$470,297**
Net cash flow	**$143,699**	**$ 24,979**	**$ 28,999**
Cash balance	**$143,699**	**$168,678**	**$197,677**

Proforma cash flow (yearly)

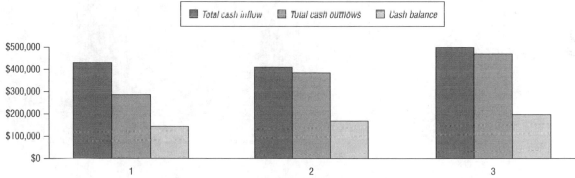

7.7 Balance Sheet

Proforma balance sheet—yearly

Year	1	2	3
Assets			
Cash	$143,699	$168,678	$197,677
Amortized expansion costs	$ 17,500	$ 26,669	$ 37,898
It hardware inventories	$ 17,000	$ 85,766	$169,985
FF&E	$ 23,000	$ 36,753	$ 53,597
Accumulated depreciation	($ 4,107)	($ 8,214)	($ 12,321)
Total assets	**$197,092**	**$309,651**	**$446,836**
Liabilities and equity			
Accounts payable	$ 13,005	$ 26,716	$ 40,990
Long term liabilities	$ 93,537	$ 86,467	$ 79,397
Other liabilities	$ 0	$ 0	$ 0
Total liabilities	**$106,542**	**$113,183**	**$120,387**
Net worth	**$ 90,550**	**$196,469**	**$326,449**
Total liabilities and equity	**$197,092**	**$309,651**	**$446,836**

Proforma balance sheet

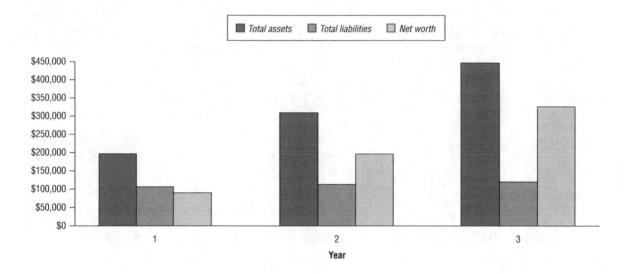

7.8 Breakeven Analysis

Monthly break even analysis

Year	1	2	3
Monthly revenue	$ 31,979	$ 34,760	$ 37,672
Yearly revenue	$383,748	$417,119	$452,063

Break even analysis

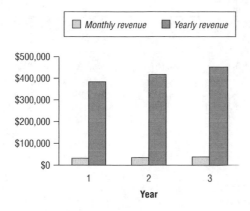

7.9 Business Ratios

Business ratios—yearly

Year	1	2	3
Sales			
Sales growth	0.00%	20.00%	17.00%
Gross margin	84.30%	84.30%	84.30%
Financials			
Profit margin	29.58%	32.14%	33.71%
Assets to liabilities	1.85	2.74	3.71
Equity to liabilities	0.85	1.74	2.71
Assets to equity	2.18	1.58	1.37
Liquidity			
Acid test	1.35	1.49	1.64
Cash to assets	0.73	0.54	0.44

7.10 Three Year Profit and Loss Statement

Profit and loss statement (first year)

Months	1	2	3	4	5	6	7
Sales	$77,500	$77,655	$77,810	$77,965	$78,120	$78,275	$78,430
Cost of goods sold	$12,150	$12,174	$12,199	$12,223	$12,247	$12,272	$12,296
Gross margin	84.3%	84.3%	84.3%	84.3%	84.3%	84.3%	84.3%
Operating income	$65,350	$65,481	$65,611	$65,742	$65,873	$66,004	$66,134
Expenses							
Payroll	$19,083	$19,083	$19,083	$19,083	$19,083	$19,083	$19,083
General and administrative	$ 2,100	$ 2,100	$ 2,100	$ 2,100	$ 2,100	$ 2,100	$ 2,100
Marketing expenses	$ 392	$ 392	$ 392	$ 392	$ 392	$ 392	$ 392
Professional fees and licensure	$ 435	$ 435	$ 435	$ 435	$ 435	$ 435	$ 435
Insurance costs	$ 166	$ 166	$ 166	$ 166	$ 166	$ 166	$ 166
Travel and vehicle costs	$ 633	$ 633	$ 633	$ 633	$ 633	$ 633	$ 633
Rent and utilities	$ 354	$ 354	$ 354	$ 354	$ 354	$ 354	$ 354
Miscellaneous costs	$ 940	$ 940	$ 940	$ 940	$ 940	$ 940	$ 940
Payroll taxes	$ 2,863	$ 2,863	$ 2,863	$ 2,863	$ 2,863	$ 2,863	$ 2,863
Total operating costs	$26,965	$26,965	$26,965	$26,965	$26,965	$26,965	$26,965
EBITDA	$38,385	$38,515	$38,646	$38,777	$38,907	$39,038	$39,169
Federal income tax	$12,764	$12,789	$12,815	$12,840	$12,866	$12,891	$12,917
State income tax	$ 1,934	$ 1,938	$ 1,942	$ 1,945	$ 1,949	$ 1,953	$ 1,957
Interest expense	$ 750	$ 746	$ 742	$ 738	$ 734	$ 730	$ 726
Depreciation expense	$ 342	$ 342	$ 342	$ 342	$ 342	$ 342	$ 342
Net profit	$22,595	$22,700	$22,805	$22,910	$23,016	$23,121	$23,226

Profit and loss statement (first year cont.)

Month	8	9	10	11	12	1
Sales	$78,585	$78,740	$78,895	$79,050	$79,205	$940,230
Cost of goods sold	$12,320	$12,344	$12,369	$12,393	$12,417	$147,404
Gross margin	84.3%	84.3%	84.3%	84.3%	84.3%	84.3%
Operating income	**$66,265**	**$66,396**	**$66,526**	**$66,657**	**$66,788**	**$792,826**
Expenses						
Payroll	$19,083	$19,083	$19,083	$19,083	$19,083	$229,000
General and administrative	$ 2,100	$ 2,100	$ 2,100	$ 2,100	$ 2,100	$ 25,200
Marketing expenses	$ 392	$ 392	$ 392	$ 392	$ 392	$ 4,701
Professional fees and licensure	$ 435	$ 435	$ 435	$ 435	$ 435	$ 5,219
Insurance costs	$ 166	$ 166	$ 166	$ 166	$ 166	$ 1,987
Travel and vehicle costs	$ 633	$ 633	$ 633	$ 633	$ 633	$ 7,596
Rent and utilities	$ 354	$ 354	$ 354	$ 354	$ 354	$ 4,250
Miscellaneous costs	$ 940	$ 940	$ 940	$ 940	$ 940	$ 11,283
Payroll taxes	$ 2,863	$ 2,863	$ 2,863	$ 2,863	$ 2,863	$ 34,350
Total operating costs	**$26,965**	**$26,965**	**$26,965**	**$26,965**	**$26,965**	**$323,586**
EBITDA	**$39,299**	**$39,430**	**$39,561**	**$39,692**	**$39,822**	**$469,240**
Federal income tax	$12,942	$12,968	$12,993	$13,019	$13,045	$154,849
State income tax	$ 1,961	$ 1,965	$ 1,969	$ 1,973	$ 1,976	$ 23,462
Interest expense	$ 722	$ 718	$ 714	$ 710	$ 706	$ 8,738
Depreciation expense	$ 342	$ 342	$ 342	$ 342	$ 342	$ 4,107
Net profit	**$23,332**	**$23,437**	**$23,542**	**$23,648**	**$23,753**	**$278,084**

Profit and loss statement (second year)

Quarter	Q1	2 Q2	Q3	Q4	2
Sales	$225,655	$282,069	$304,635	$315,917	$1,128,276
Cost of goods sold	$ 35,377	$ 44,221	$ 47,759	$ 49,528	$ 176,885
Gross margin	84.3%	84.3%	84.3%	84.3%	84.3%
Operating income	**$190,278**	**$237,848**	**$256,876**	**$266,390**	**$ 951,391**
Expenses					
Payroll	$ 49,749	$ 62,186	$ 67,161	$ 69,649	$ 248,745
General and administrative	$ 5,242	$ 6,552	$ 7,076	$ 7,338	$ 26,208
Marketing expenses	$ 1,128	$ 1,410	$ 1,523	$ 1,580	$ 5,641
Professional fees and licensure	$ 1,075	$ 1,344	$ 1,451	$ 1,505	$ 5,376
Insurance costs	$ 417	$ 522	$ 563	$ 584	$ 2,086
Travel and vehicle costs	$ 1,671	$ 2,089	$ 2,256	$ 2,340	$ 8,356
Rent and utilities	$ 893	$ 1,116	$ 1,205	$ 1,250	$ 4,463
Miscellaneous costs	$ 2,708	$ 3,385	$ 3,656	$ 3,791	$ 13,539
Payroll taxes	$ 7,462	$ 9,328	$ 10,074	$ 10,447	$ 37,312
Total operating costs	**$ 70,345**	**$ 87,931**	**$ 94,966**	**$ 98,483**	**$ 351,725**
EBITDA	**$119,933**	**$149,916**	**$161,910**	**$167,906**	**$ 599,666**
Federal income tax	$ 39,041	$ 48,802	$ 52,706	$ 54,658	$ 195,206
State income tax	$ 5,915	$ 7,394	$ 7,986	$ 8,281	$ 29,577
Interest expense	$ 2,092	$ 2,053	$ 2,013	$ 1,973	$ 8,131
Depreciation expense	$ 1,027	$ 1,027	$ 1,027	$ 1,027	$ 4,107
Net profit	**$ 71,858**	**$ 90,641**	**$ 98,178**	**$101,967**	**$ 362,644**

Profit and loss statement (third year)

Quarter	Q1	3 Q2	Q3	Q4	3
Sales	$264,017	$330,021	$356,422	$369,623	$1,320,083
Cost of goods sold	$ 41,391	$ 51,739	$ 55,878	$ 57,947	$ 206,955
Gross margin	84.3%	84.3%	84.3%	84.3%	84.3%
Operating income	$222,626	$278,282	$300,545	$311,676	$1,113,128
Expenses					
Payroll	$ 53,894	$ 67,367	$ 72,757	$ 75,451	$ 269,469
General and administrative	$ 5,451	$ 6,814	$ 7,359	$ 7,632	$ 27,256
Marketing expenses	$ 1,320	$ 1,650	$ 1,782	$ 1,848	$ 6,600
Professional fees and licensure	$ 1,107	$ 1,384	$ 1,495	$ 1,550	$ 5,537
Insurance costs	$ 438	$ 548	$ 591	$ 613	$ 2,191
Travel and vehicle costs	$ 1,838	$ 2,298	$ 2,482	$ 2,574	$ 9,191
Rent and utilities	$ 937	$ 1,171	$ 1,265	$ 1,312	$ 4,686
Miscellaneous costs	$ 3,168	$ 3,960	$ 4,277	$ 4,435	$ 15,841
Payroll taxes	$ 8,084	$ 10,105	$ 10,913	$ 11,318	$ 40,420
Total operating costs	$ 76,238	$ 95,298	$102,922	$106,733	$ 381,191
EBITDA	$146,387	$182,984	$197,623	$204,942	$ 731,937
Federal income tax	$ 47,815	$ 59,769	$ 64,550	$ 66,941	$ 239,075
State income tax	$ 7,245	$ 9,056	$ 9,780	$ 10,143	$ 36,223
Interest expense	$ 1,932	$ 1,889	$ 1,846	$ 1,802	$ 7,468
Depreciation expense	$ 1,027	$ 1,027	$ 1,027	$ 1,027	$ 4,107
Net profit	$ 88,369	$111,244	$120,420	$125,031	$ 445,064

7.11 Three Year Cash Flow Analysis

Cash flow analysis (first year)

Month	1	2	3	4	5	6	7
Cash from operations	$ 22,937	$23,042	$ 23,147	$ 23,253	$ 23,358	$ 23,463	$ 23,568
Cash from receivables	$ 0	$ 0	$ 0	$ 0	$ 0	$ 0	$ 0
Operating cash inflow	$ 22,937	$23,042	$ 23,147	$ 23,253	$ 23,358	$ 23,463	$ 23,568
Other cash inflows							
Equity investment	$ 10,000	$ 0	$ 0	$ 0	$ 0	$ 0	$ 0
Increased borrowings	$100,000	$ 0	$ 0	$ 0	$ 0	$ 0	$ 0
Sales of business assets	$ 0	$ 0	$ 0	$ 0	$ 0	$ 0	$ 0
A/P increases	$ 3,159	$ 3,159	$ 3,159	$ 3,159	$ 3,159	$ 3,159	$ 3,159
Total other cash inflows	$113,159	$ 3,159	$ 3,159	$ 3,159	$ 3,159	$ 3,159	$ 3,159
Total cash inflow	$136,095	$26,201	$ 26,306	$ 26,411	$ 26,516	$ 26,622	$ 26,727
Cash outflows							
Repayment of principal	$ 517	$ 521	$ 525	$ 528	$ 532	$ 536	$ 540
A/P decreases	$ 2,075	$ 2,075	$ 2,075	$ 2,075	$ 2,075	$ 2,075	$ 2,075
A/R increases	$ 0	$ 0	$ 0	$ 0	$ 0	$ 0	$ 0
Asset purchases	$ 57,500	$ 0	$ 0	$ 0	$ 0	$ 0	$ 0
Dividends	$ 0	$ 0	$ 0	$ 0	$ 0	$ 0	$ 0
Total cash outflows	$ 60,092	$ 2,595	$ 2,599	$ 2,603	$ 2,607	$ 2,611	$ 2,615
Net cash flow	$ 76,004	$23,605	$ 23,707	$ 23,808	$ 23,909	$ 24,010	$ 24,112
Cash balance	$ 76,004	$99,609	$123,316	$147,123	$171,033	$195,043	$219,155

Cash flow analysis (first year cont.)

Month	8	9	10	11	12	1
Cash from operations	$ 23,674	$ 23,779	$ 23,885	$ 23,990	$ 24,096	$282,191
Cash from receivables	$ 0	$ 0	$ 0	$ 0	$ 0	$ 0
Operating cash inflow	**$ 23,674**	**$ 23,779**	**$ 23,885**	**$ 23,990**	**$ 24,096**	**$282,191**
Other cash inflows						
Equity investment	$ 0	$ 0	$ 0	$ 0	$ 0	$ 10,000
Increased borrowings	$ 0	$ 0	$ 0	$ 0	$ 0	$100,000
Sales of business assets	$ 0	$ 0	$ 0	$ 0	$ 0	$ 0
A/P increases	$ 3,159	$ 3,159	$ 3,159	$ 3,159	$ 3,159	$ 37,902
Total other cash inflows	**$ 3,159**	**$ 3,159**	**$ 3,159**	**$ 3,159**	**$ 3,159**	**$147,902**
Total cash inflow	**$ 26,832**	**$ 26,938**	**$ 27,043**	**$ 27,149**	**$ 27,254**	**$430,093**
Cash outflows						
Repayment of principal	$ 545	$ 549	$ 553	$ 557	$ 561	$ 6,463
A/P decreases	$ 2,075	$ 2,075	$ 2,075	$ 2,075	$ 2,075	$ 24,897
A/R increases	$ 0	$ 0	$ 0	$ 0	$ 0	$0
Asset purchases	$ 0	$ 0	$ 0	$ 0	$ 0	$ 57,500
Dividends	$ 0	$ 0	$ 0	$ 0	$197,534	$197,534
Total cash outflows	**$ 2,619**	**$ 2,623**	**$ 2,627**	**$ 2,632**	**$200,170**	**$286,394**
Net cash flow	**$ 24,213**	**$ 24,314**	**$ 24,416**	**$ 24,517**	**−$172,916**	**$143,699**
Cash balance	**$243,368**	**$267,682**	**$292,098**	**$316,615**	**$143,699**	**$143,699**

Cash flow analysis (second year)

Quarter	Q1	2 Q2	Q3	Q4	2
Cash from operations	$ 73,350	$ 91,688	$ 99,023	$102,690	$366,751
Cash from receivables	$ 0	$ 0	$ 0	$ 0	$ 0
Operating cash inflow	**$ 73,350**	**$ 91,688**	**$ 99,023**	**$102,690**	**$366,751**
Other cash inflows					
Equity investment	$ 0	$ 0	$ 0	$ 0	$ 0
Increased borrowings	$ 0	$ 0	$ 0	$ 0	$ 0
Sales of business assets	$ 0	$ 0	$ 0	$ 0	$ 0
A/P increases	$ 8,717	$ 10,897	$ 11,769	$ 12,204	$ 43,587
Total other cash inflows	**$ 8,717**	**$ 10,897**	**$ 11,769**	**$ 12,204**	**$ 43,587**
Total cash inflow	**$ 82,068**	**$102,585**	**$110,791**	**$114,895**	**$410,339**
Cash outflows					
Repayment of principal	$ 1,708	$ 1,747	$ 1,787	$ 1,827	$ 7,070
A/P decreases	$ 5,975	$ 7,469	$ 8,067	$ 8,365	$ 29,876
A/R increases	$ 0	$ 0	$ 0	$ 0	$ 0
Asset purchases	$ 18,338	$ 22,922	$ 24,756	$ 25,673	$ 91,688
Dividends	$ 51,345	$ 64,182	$ 69,316	$ 71,883	$256,726
Total cash outflows	**$ 77,367**	**$ 96,320**	**$103,925**	**$107,749**	**$385,360**
Net cash flow	**$ 4,701**	**$ 6,265**	**$ 6,866**	**$ 7,146**	**$ 24,979**
Cash balance	**$148,400**	**$154,665**	**$161,531**	**$168,678**	**$168,678**

Cash flow analysis (third year)

Quarter	Q1	3 Q2	Q3	Q4	3
Cash from operations	$ 89,834	$112,293	$121,276	$125,768	$449,171
Cash from receivables	$ 0	$ 0	$ 0	$ 0	$ 0
Operating cash inflow	**$ 89,834**	**$112,293**	**$121,276**	**$125,768**	**$449,171**
Other cash inflows					
Equity investment	$ 0	$ 0	$ 0	$ 0	$ 0
Increased borrowings	$ 0	$ 0	$ 0	$ 0	$ 0
Sales of business assets	$ 0	$ 0	$ 0	$ 0	$ 0
A/P increases	$ 10,025	$ 12,531	$ 13,534	$ 14,035	$ 50,125
Total other cash inflows	**$ 10,025**	**$ 12,531**	**$ 13,534**	**$ 14,035**	**$ 50,125**
Total cash inflow	**$ 99,859**	**$124,824**	**$134,810**	**$139,803**	**$499,296**
Cash outflows					
Repayment of principal	$ 1,869	$ 1,911	$ 1,954	$ 1,999	$ 7,733
A/P decreases	$ 7,170	$ 8,963	$ 9,680	$ 10,038	$ 35,852
A/R increases	$ 0	$ 0	$ 0	$ 0	$ 0
Asset purchases	$ 22,459	$ 28,073	$ 30,319	$ 31,442	$112,293
Dividends	$ 62,884	$ 78,605	$ 84,893	$ 88,037	$314,419
Total cash outflows	**$ 94,381**	**$117,552**	**$126,847**	**$131,517**	**$470,297**
Net cash flow	**$ 5,478**	**$ 7,272**	**$ 7,963**	**$ 8,286**	**$ 28,999**
Cash balance	**$174,155**	**$181,427**	**$189,391**	**$197,677**	**$197,677**

Medical Practice

North Oakland Medical Associates

3500 Cedar Ave.
Newark, New Jersey 07029

BizPlanDB.com

The physicians of this group medical practice will render family medicine services to adults and children within the greater Newark, New Jersey, area. These services include examination, blood work, general medical counseling/advice, referrals to other physicians, and other family medicine services.

1.0 EXECUTIVE SUMMARY

The purpose of this business plan is to raise $250,000 for the development of a group-based medical practice while showcasing the expected financials and operations over the next three years. North Oakland Medical Associates is a New Jersey based corporation that will provide general medical care to customers in its targeted market. The Company was founded by Dr. Anthony Ronan, Dr. Alex Angbrandt, and Dr. Joseph Ahmann.

1.1 The Services

The physicians of this group medical practice will render family medicine services to adults and children within the greater Newark community. These services include examination, blood work, general medical counseling/advice, referrals to other physicians, and other family medicine services. It should be noted that Management intends to aggressively expand the group medical practice by hiring associate physicians on a general contractor basis in order to render specialized medical services on site to the Company's patients.

The Company will also recognize revenues from the sale of medical appliances prescribed by the physicians. A majority of revenues will come from reimbursements from insurance companies.

The third section of the business plan will further describe the services offered by North Oakland Medical Associates.

1.2 Financing

Mr. Ronan is seeking to raise $250,000 from a bank loan. The interest rate and loan agreement are to be further discussed during negotiation. This business plan assumes that the business will receive a 10 year loan with a 9% fixed interest rate. The financing will be used for the following:

- Development of the medical facility.

- Financing for the first six months of operation.

- Capital to purchase medical equipment.

The Physician-Owners will contribute $50,000 towards the development of North Oakland Medical Associates.

1.3 Mission Statement

The mission is to become the recognized leader in its targeted market for general medical services in a group setting where they can have access to specialized physicians as well.

1.4 Management Team

The Company was founded by Dr. Anthony Ronan, Dr. Alex Angbrandt, and Dr. Joseph Ahmann. All three physicians have more than 10 years of experience as practicing physicians. Through their expertise, they will be able to bring the operations of the business to profitability within its first year of operations.

1.5 Sales Forecasts

The Company expects a strong rate of growth at the start of operations. Below are the expected financials over the next three years.

Proforma profit and loss (yearly)

Year	1	2	3
Sales	$2,243,178	$2,467,496	$2,714,245
Operating costs	$1,176,995	$1,219,051	$1,262,981
EBITDA	$ 814,879	$ 972,011	$1,147,187
Taxes, interest, and depreciation	$ 343,284	$ 393,754	$ 459,293
Net profit	$ 471,595	$ 578,258	$ 687,895

Sales, operating costs, and profit forecast

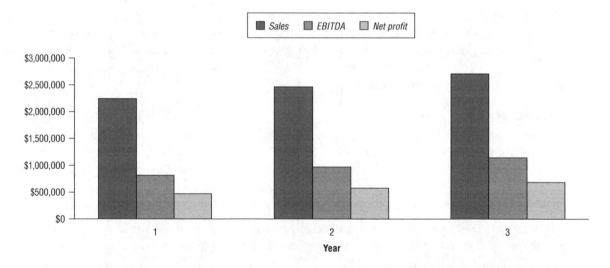

1.6 Expansion Plan

The Founders expect that the business will aggressively expand during the first three years of operation. Management intends to implement marketing campaigns that will effectively target individuals and families within the target market while concurrently developing relationships with specialty physicians that will work within the Company's group practice setting.

2.0 COMPANY AND FINANCING SUMMARY

2.1 Registered Name and Corporate Structure

The Company is registered as a corporation in the State of New Jersey.

2.2 Required Funds

At this time, North Oakland Medical Associates requires $250,000 of debt funds. Below is a breakdown of how these funds will be used:

Projected startup costs

Initial lease payments and deposits	$ 35,000
Working capital	$ 75,000
FF&E	$ 30,000
Leasehold improvements	$ 15,000
Security deposits	$ 7,500
Insurance	$ 5,000
Medical equipment	$ 65,000
Marketing budget	$ 10,000
Miscellaneous and unforeseen costs	$ 7,500
Total startup costs	**$250,000**

Use of funds

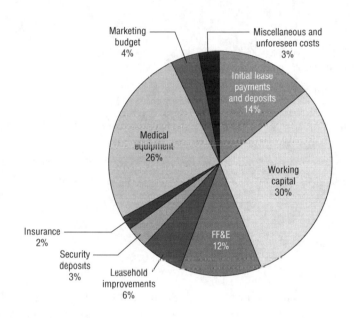

2.3 Investor Equity

The company is not seeking an investment from a third party at this time.

2.4 Management Equity

The three Physician-Owners will retain an equal 1/3 ownership interest in the practice.

2.5 Exit Strategy

If the business is very successful, Management may seek to sell the practice to a third party for a significant earnings multiple. Most likely, the Company will hire a qualified business broker to sell the business on behalf of North Oakland Medical Associates. Based on historical numbers, the business could fetch a sales premium of up to 2 to 3 times earnings.

3.0 GROUP MEDICAL SERVICES

Below is a description of the medical services offered by North Oakland Medical Associates.

3.1 Group Medical Services

The primary source of revenue for the business will be the medical services provided by the three Physician-Owners. The Company will offer treatment of medial issues including high blood pressure, cholesterol, and diabetes. This part of the business will also provide work physicals, cancer screenings, heart disease screenings, and other tests normally associated with the practice of a general physician.

As stated earlier, North Oakland Medical Associates may expand to include doctors that have the following specialties:

- Cardiology

- Radiology

- Rheumatology

- Pediatric Medicine

- Ophthalmology

- Otorhinolaryngology

- General Surgery

- Colon Rectal Surgeries and Examinations

3.2 Medical Appliances

The Company will also generate secondary revenues from the sale of medical appliances, prescribed by the Physician-Owners to their patients. This is a very important revenue center for the business as the Company will generate substantial gross margins from each product sold.

4.0 STRATEGIC AND MARKET ANALYSIS

4.1 Economic Outlook

This section of the analysis will detail the economic climate, the medical industry, the customer profile, and the competition that the business will face as it progresses through its business operations.

Presently the economic market condition in the United States is in a state of sluggish growth. This slowdown in the economy has also greatly impacted real estate sales, which has halted to historical lows. Many economists expect that this sluggish growth will continue for a significant period of time, at which point the economy will begin a prolonged recovery period. However, this should have a minimal impact on the Company's ability to generate income.

4.2 Industry Analysis

In the United States there are approximately 200,000 medical practices (excluding mental health practices) that comprise of one or more doctors that act in a private practice capacity. Each year, these practices generate more than $190 billion dollars of revenue and employ more than 1.8 million people (including the doctors). The growth of this industry has remained in lockstep with the growth of the general population. Approximately 5% of these doctors retire each year. Approximately 16,000 doctors enter private practice each year.

Approximately 25% of the private medical practices in the United States operate in a group capacity.

4.3 Customer Profile

North Oakland Medical Associates' average client will be a middle-class man or woman living in the Company's target market. Common traits among clients will include:

- Annual household income exceeding $50,000

- Lives or works no more than 20 miles from the office.

- Has medical insurance or access to publicly funded health systems.

In the Company's targeted market, there are approximately 5,000 other physicians and physician's groups that operate in a similar or substantially similar capacity to North Oakland Medical Associates. However, as the business has access to more than 280,000 potential patients, North Oakland Medical Associates is in an excellent position to capitalize on the strong demand for a medical practice where they can receive all of their requisite medical care due to the highly specialized staff of the business.

4.4 Competition

In the Company's targeted market, there are a number of physicians that operate in a group medical practice setting. However, North Oakland Medical Associates will maintain a substantial competition advantage over other market agents due to the fact that the practice is able to seamlessly discuss ongoing medical issues for specific patients among the number of specialized physicians working at the practice. This, coupled with the ongoing payments from private insurance companies, Medicare, and Medicaid will ensure that the business is able to remain profitable and cash flow positive at all times.

5.0 MARKETING PLAN

North Oakland Medical Associates intends to maintain an extensive marketing campaign that will ensure maximum visibility for the business in its targeted market. Below is an overview of the marketing strategies and objectives of North Oakland Medical Associates.

5.1 Marketing Objectives

- Develop an online presence by developing a website and placing the Company's name and contact information with online directories.

- Implement a local campaign with the Company's targeted market via the use of flyers, local newspaper advertisements, and word of mouth.

- Establish relationships with other doctors (primarily specialists) within the targeted market.

5.2 Marketing Strategies

The Company intends on using a number of marketing strategies that will allow North Oakland Medical Associates to easily target men, women, and families within the target market. These strategies include traditional print advertisements and ads placed on search engines on the Internet. Below is a description of how the business intends to market its services to the general public.

North Oakland Medical Associates will also use an internet based strategy. This is very important as many people seeking local services, such as doctors, now the Internet to conduct their preliminary searches. North Oakland Medical Associates' manager will register the Practice with online portals so that potential customers can easily reach the business. The Company will also develop its own online website that showcases the profiles of the doctors, insurances accepted, medical services rendered, and hours of operation.

The Company will maintain a sizable amount of print and traditional advertising methods within local markets to promote the general and specialty medical services that the Company is selling.

North Oakland Medical Associates will also ensure that each individual physician maintains hospital privileges at local emergency rooms so that patients can see their physician at anytime if there is a medical emergency.

5.3 Pricing

Each medical case will render a different financial result for the business; it is difficult to determine the exact amount of revenue that will be generated by each patient. However, on average, Management anticipates that each patient will generate $200 per visit (or hospital visit).

6.0 ORGANIZATIONAL PLAN AND PERSONNEL SUMMARY

6.1 Corporate Organization

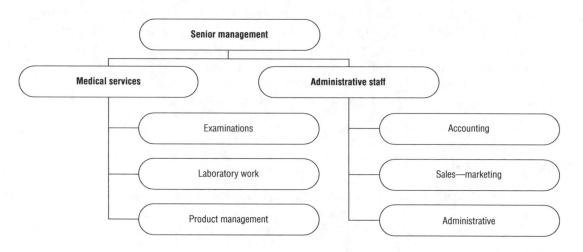

6.2 Organizational Budget

Personnel plan—yearly

Year	1	2	3
Physician owners	$375,000	$386,250	$397,838
Practice manager	$110,000	$113,300	$116,699
Nurses	$234,000	$241,020	$248,251
Assistants	$ 98,000	$100,940	$103,968
Receptionist	$ 66,000	$ 67,980	$ 70,019
Total	**$883,000**	**$909,490**	**$936,775**

Numbers of personnel

Year	1	2	3
Physician owners	3	3	3
Practice manager	2	2	2
Nurses	6	6	6
Assistants	4	4	4
Receptionist	3	3	3
Totals	**18**	**18**	**18**

Personnel expense breakdown

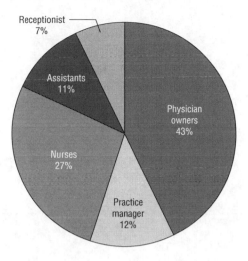

7.0 FINANCIAL PLAN

7.1 Underlying Assumptions

The Company has based its proforma financial statements on the following:

• North Oakland Medical Associates will have an annual revenue growth rate of 10% per year.

• The Founders will acquire $250,000 of debt funds to develop the business.

• The loan will have a 10 year term with a 9% interest rate.

7.2 Sensitivity Analysis

In the event of an economic downturn, the Company will not see a major decline in revenues. Medical services are in demand regardless of the general economic climate as they are an essential service for health.

7.3 Source of Funds

Financing

Equity contributions

Management investment	$ 25,000.00
Total equity financing	**$ 25,000.00**
Banks and lenders	
Banks and lenders	$ 150,000.00
Total debt financing	**$150,000.00**
Total financing	**$175,000.00**

7.4 General Assumptions

General assumptions

Year	1	2	3
Short term interest rate	9.5%	9.5%	9.5%
Long term interest rate	10.0%	10.0%	10.0%
Federal tax rate	33.0%	33.0%	33.0%
State tax rate	5.0%	5.0%	5.0%
Personnel taxes	15.0%	15.0%	15.0%

7.5 Profit and Loss Statements

Proforma profit and loss (yearly)

Year	1	2	3
Sales	$2,243,178	$2,467,496	$2,714,245
Cost of goods sold	$ 251,303	$ 276,434	$ 304,077
Gross margin	88.80%	88.80%	88.80%
Operating income	$1,991,875	$2,191,062	$2,410,168
Expenses			
Payroll	$ 883,000	$ 909,490	$ 936,775
General and administrative	$ 37,500	$ 39,000	$ 40,560
Marketing expenses	$ 44,864	$ 49,350	$ 54,285
Professional fees and licensure	$ 5,000	$ 5,150	$ 5,305
Insurance costs	$ 15,000	$ 15,750	$ 16,538
Equipment costs	$ 12,500	$ 13,750	$ 15,125
Rent and utilities	$ 24,250	$ 25,463	$ 26,736
Miscellaneous costs	$ 22,432	$ 24,675	$ 27,142
Payroll taxes	$ 132,450	$ 136,424	$ 140,516
Total operating costs	$1,176,995	$1,219,051	$1,262,981
EBITDA	$ 814,879	$ 972,011	$1,147,187
Federal income tax	$ 268,910	$ 314,055	$ 372,411
State income tax	$ 40,744	$ 47,584	$ 56,426
Interest expense	$ 21,844	$ 20,328	$ 18,671
Depreciation expenses	$ 11,786	$ 11,786	$ 11,786
Net profit	$ 471,595	$ 578,258	$ 687,895
Profit margin	21.02%	23.43%	25.34%

Sales, operating costs, and profit forecast

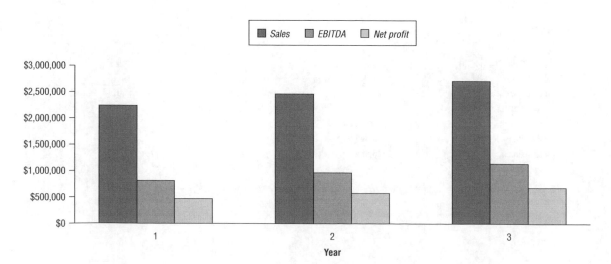

7.6 Cash Flow Analysis

Proforma cash flow analysis—yearly

Year	1	2	3
Cash from operations	$483,381	$590,043	$699,680
Cash from receivables	$ 0	$ 0	$ 0
Operating cash inflow	**$483,381**	**$590,043**	**$699,680**
Other cash inflows			
Equity investment	$ 50,000	$ 0	$ 0
Increased borrowings	$250,000	$ 0	$ 0
Sales of business assets	$ 0	$ 0	$ 0
A/P increases	$ 3,790	$ 4,359	$ 5,012
Total other cash inflows	**$303,790**	**$ 4,359**	**$ 5,012**
Total cash inflow	**$787,171**	**$594,402**	**$704,693**
Cash outflows			
Repayment of principal	$ 16,158	$ 17,674	$ 19,332
A/P decreases	$ 2,487	$ 2,984	$ 3,581
A/R increases	$ 0	$ 0	$ 0
Asset purchases	$165,000	$ 94,407	$111,949
Dividends	$459,212	$442,532	$524,760
Total cash outflows	**$642,857**	**$557,598**	**$659,623**
Net cash flow	**$144,314**	**$ 36,804**	**$ 45,070**
Cash balance	**$144,314**	**$181,117**	**$226,187**

Proforma cash flow (yearly)

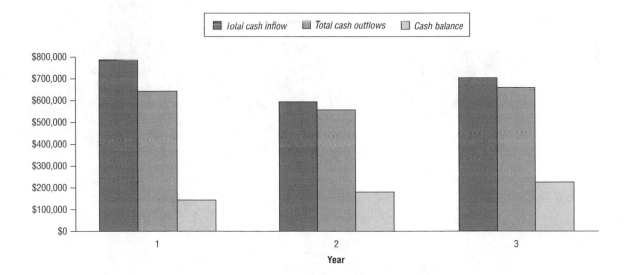

7.7 Balance Sheet

Proforma balance sheet—yearly

Year	1	2	3
Assets			
Cash	$144,314	$181,117	$226,187
Amortized expansion costs	$ 70,000	$ 79,441	$ 90,636
Medical equipment	$ 65,000	$135,805	$219,767
FF&E	$ 30,000	$ 44,161	$ 60,953
Accumulated depreciation	($ 11,786)	($ 23,571)	($ 35,357)
Total assets	**$297,528**	**$416,953**	**$562,186**
Liabilities and equity			
Accounts payable	$ 1,303	$ 2,677	$ 4,108
Long term liabilities	$233,842	$216,167	$198,493
Other liabilities	$ 0	$ 0	$ 0
Total liabilities	**$235,145**	**$218,844**	**$202,601**
Net worth	**$ 62,383**	**$198,108**	**$359,585**
Total liabilities and equity	**$297,528**	**$416,953**	**$562,186**

Proforma balance sheet

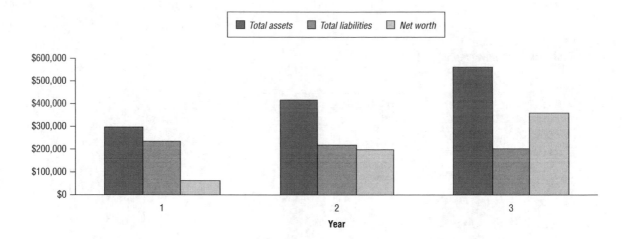

7.8 Breakeven Analysis

Monthly break even analysis

Year	1	2	3
Monthly revenue	$ 110,458	$ 114,404	$ 118,527
Yearly revenue	$1,325,490	$1,372,852	$1,422,324

Break even analysis

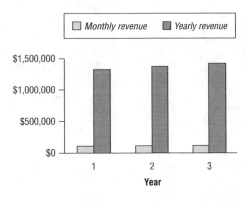

7.9 Business Ratios

Business ratios—yearly

Year	1	2	3
Sales			
Sales growth	0.00%	10.00%	10.00%
Gross margin	88.80%	88.80%	88.80%
Financials			
Profit margin	21.02%	23.43%	25.34%
Assets to liabilities	1.27	1.91	2.77
Equity to liabilities	0.27	0.91	1.77
Assets to equity	4.77	2.10	1.56
Liquidity			
Acid test	0.61	0.83	1.12
Cash to assets	0.49	0.43	0.40

7.10 Three Year Profit and Loss Statement

Profit and loss statement (first year)

Months	1	2	3	4	5	6	7
Sales	$186,200	$186,333	$186,466	$186,599	$186,732	$186,865	$186,998
Cost of goods sold	$ 20,860	$ 20,875	$ 20,890	$ 20,905	$ 20,920	$ 20,935	$ 20,949
Gross margin	88.8%	88.8%	88.8%	88.8%	88.8%	88.8%	88.8%
Operating income	$165,340	$165,458	$165,576	$165,694	$165,812	$165,931	$166,049
Expenses							
Payroll	$ 73,583	$ 73,583	$ 73,583	$ 73,583	$ 73,583	$ 73,583	$ 73,583
General and administrative	$ 3,125	$ 3,125	$ 3,125	$ 3,125	$ 3,125	$ 3,125	$ 3,125
Marketing expenses	$ 3,739	$ 3,739	$ 3,739	$ 3,739	$ 3,739	$ 3,739	$ 3,739
Professional fees and licensure	$ 417	$ 417	$ 417	$ 417	$ 417	$ 417	$ 417
Insurance costs	$ 1,250	$ 1,250	$ 1,250	$ 1,250	$ 1,250	$ 1,250	$ 1,250
Equipment costs	$ 1,042	$ 1,042	$ 1,042	$ 1,042	$ 1,042	$ 1,042	$ 1,042
Rent and utilities	$ 2,021	$ 2,021	$ 2,021	$ 2,021	$ 2,021	$ 2,021	$ 2,021
Miscellaneous costs	$ 1,869	$ 1,869	$ 1,869	$ 1,869	$ 1,869	$ 1,869	$ 1,869
Payroll taxes	$ 11,038	$ 11,038	$ 11,038	$ 11,038	$ 11,038	$ 11,038	$ 11,038
Total operating costs	$ 98,083	$ 98,083	$ 98,083	$ 98,083	$ 98,083	$ 98,083	$ 98,083
EBITDA	$ 67,257	$ 67,375	$ 67,493	$ 67,611	$ 67,729	$ 67,848	$ 67,966
Federal income tax	$ 22,321	$ 22,337	$ 22,353	$ 22,369	$ 22,385	$ 22,401	$ 22,417
State income tax	$ 3,382	$ 3,384	$ 3,387	$ 3,389	$ 3,392	$ 3,394	$ 3,397
Interest expense	$ 1,875	$ 1,865	$ 1,856	$ 1,846	$ 1,836	$ 1,826	$ 1,816
Depreciation expense	$ 982	$ 982	$ 982	$ 982	$ 982	$ 982	$ 982
Net profit	$ 38,696	$ 38,806	$ 38,915	$ 39,025	$ 39,135	$ 39,244	$ 39,354

Profit and loss statement (first year cont.)

Months	8	9	10	11	12	1
Sales	$187,131	$187,264	$187,397	$187,530	$187,663	$2,243,178
Cost of goods sold	$ 20,964	$ 20,979	$ 20,994	$ 21,009	$ 21,024	$ 251,303
Gross margin	88.8%	88.8%	88.8%	88.8%	88.8%	88.8%
Operating income	$166,167	$166,285	$166,403	$166,521	$166,639	$1,991,875
Expenses						
Payroll	$ 73,583	$ 73,583	$ 73,583	$ 73,583	$ 73,583	$ 883,000
General and administrative	$ 3,125	$ 3,125	$ 3,125	$ 3,125	$ 3,125	$ 37,500
Marketing expenses	$ 3,739	$ 3,739	$ 3,739	$ 3,739	$ 3,739	$ 44,864
Professional fees and licensure	$ 417	$ 417	$ 417	$ 417	$ 417	$ 5,000
Insurance costs	$ 1,250	$ 1,250	$ 1,250	$ 1,250	$ 1,250	$ 15,000
Equipment costs	$ 1,042	$ 1,042	$ 1,042	$ 1,042	$ 1,042	$ 12,500
Rent and utilities	$ 2,021	$ 2,021	$ 2,021	$ 2,021	$ 2,021	$ 24,250
Miscellaneous costs	$ 1,869	$ 1,869	$ 1,869	$ 1,869	$ 1,869	$ 22,432
Payroll taxes	$ 11,038	$ 11,038	$ 11,038	$ 11,038	$ 11,038	$ 132,450
Total operating costs	$ 98,083	$ 98,083	$ 98,083	$ 98,083	$ 98,083	$1,176,995
EBITDA	$ 68,084	$ 68,202	$ 68,320	$ 68,438	$ 68,556	$ 814,879
Federal income tax	$ 22,433	$ 22,449	$ 22,465	$ 22,481	$ 22,497	$ 268,910
State income tax	$ 3,399	$ 3,401	$ 3,404	$ 3,406	$ 3,409	$ 40,744
Interest expense	$ 1,806	$ 1,795	$ 1,785	$ 1,775	$ 1,764	$ 21,844
Depreciation expense	$ 982	$ 982	$ 982	$ 982	$ 982	$ 11,786
Net profit	$ 39,464	$ 39,574	$ 39,684	$ 39,794	$ 39,904	$ 471,595

Profit and loss statement (second year)

Quarter	Q1	2 Q2	Q3	Q4	2
Sales	$493,499	$616,874	$666,224	$690,899	$2,467,496
Cost of goods sold	$ 55,287	$ 69,108	$ 74,637	$ 77,401	$ 276,434
Gross margin	88.8%	88.8%	88.8%	88.8%	88.8%
Operating income	$438,212	$547,766	$591,587	$613,497	$2,191,062
Expenses					
Payroll	$181,898	$227,373	$245,562	$254,657	$ 909,490
General and administrative	$ 7,800	$ 9,750	$ 10,530	$ 10,920	$ 39,000
Marketing expenses	$ 9,870	$ 12,337	$ 13,324	$ 13,818	$ 49,350
Professional fees and licensure	$ 1,030	$ 1,288	$ 1,391	$ 1,442	$ 5,150
Insurance costs	$ 3,150	$ 3,938	$ 4,253	$ 4,410	$ 15,750
Equipment costs	$ 2,750	$ 3,438	$ 3,713	$ 3,850	$ 13,750
Rent and utilities	$ 5,093	$ 6,366	$ 6,875	$ 7,130	$ 25,463
Miscellaneous costs	$ 4,935	$ 6,169	$ 6,662	$ 6,909	$ 24,675
Payroll taxes	$ 27,285	$ 34,106	$ 36,834	$ 38,199	$ 136,424
Total operating costs	$243,810	$304,763	$329,144	$341,334	$1,219,051
EBITDA	$194,402	$243,003	$262,443	$272,163	$ 972,011
Federal income tax	$ 62,811	$ 78,514	$ 84,795	$ 87,935	$ 314,055
State income tax	$ 9,517	$ 11,896	$ 12,848	$ 13,324	$ 47,584
Interest expense	$ 5,230	$ 5,133	$ 5,034	$ 4,932	$ 20,328
Depreciation expense	$ 2,946	$ 2,946	$ 2,946	$ 2,946	$ 11,786
Net profit	$113,898	$144,514	$156,820	$163,025	$ 578,258

Profit and loss statement (third year)

Quarter	Q1	3 Q2	Q3	Q4	3
Sales	$542,849	$678,561	$732,846	$759,989	$2,714,245
Cost of goods sold	$ 60,815	$ 76,019	$ 82,101	$ 85,142	$ 304,077
Gross margin	88.8%	88.8%	88.8%	88.8%	88.8%
Operating income	$482,034	$602,542	$650,745	$674,847	$2,410,168
Expenses					
Payroll	$187,355	$234,194	$252,929	$262,297	$ 936,775
General and administrative	$ 8,112	$ 10,140	$ 10,951	$ 11,357	$ 40,560
Marketing expenses	$ 10,857	$ 13,571	$ 14,657	$ 15,200	$ 54,285
Professional fees and licensure	$ 1,061	$ 1,326	$ 1,432	$ 1,485	$ 5,305
Insurance costs	$ 3,308	$ 4,134	$ 4,465	$ 4,631	$ 16,538
Equipment costs	$ 3,025	$ 3,781	$ 4,084	$ 4,235	$ 15,125
Rent and utilities	$ 5,347	$ 6,684	$ 7,219	$ 7,486	$ 26,736
Miscellaneous costs	$ 5,428	$ 6,786	$ 7,328	$ 7,600	$ 27,142
Payroll taxes	$ 28,103	$ 35,129	$ 37,939	$ 39,345	$ 140,516
Total operating costs	$252,596	$315,745	$341,005	$353,635	$1,262,981
EBITDA	$229,437	$286,797	$309,741	$321,212	$1,147,187
Federal income tax	$ 74,482	$ 93,103	$100,551	$104,275	$ 372,411
State income tax	$ 11,285	$ 14,106	$ 15,235	$ 15,799	$ 56,426
Interest expense	$ 4,829	$ 4,723	$ 4,615	$ 4,504	$ 18,671
Depreciation expense	$ 2,946	$ 2,946	$ 2,946	$ 2,946	$ 11,786
Net profit	$135,895	$171,918	$186,394	$193,688	$ 687,895

7.11 Three Year Cash Flow Analysis

Cash flow analysis (first year)

Month	1	2	3	4	5	6	7
Cash from operations	$ 39,679	$ 39,788	$ 39,897	$ 40,007	$ 40,117	$ 40,226	$ 40,336
Cash from receivables	$ 0	$ 0	$ 0	$ 0	$ 0	$ 0	$ 0
Operating cash inflow	$ 39,679	$ 39,788	$ 39,897	$ 40,007	$ 40,117	$ 40,226	$ 40,336
Other cash inflows							
Equity investment	$ 50,000	$ 0	$ 0	$ 0	$ 0	$ 0	$ 0
Increased borrowings	$250,000	$ 0	$ 0	$ 0	$ 0	$ 0	$ 0
Sales of business assets	$ 0	$ 0	$ 0	$ 0	$ 0	$ 0	$ 0
A/P increases	$ 316	$ 316	$ 316	$ 316	$ 316	$ 316	$ 316
Total other cash inflows	$300,316	$ 316	$ 316	$ 316	$ 316	$ 316	$ 316
Total cash inflow	$339,994	$ 40,104	$ 40,213	$ 40,323	$ 40,433	$ 40,542	$ 40,652
Cash outflows							
Repayment of principal	$ 1,292	$ 1,302	$ 1,311	$ 1,321	$ 1,331	$ 1,341	$ 1,351
A/P decreases	$ 207	$ 207	$ 207	$ 207	$ 207	$ 207	$ 207
A/R increases	$ 0	$ 0	$ 0	$ 0	$ 0	$ 0	$ 0
Asset purchases	$165,000	$ 0	$ 0	$ 0	$ 0	$ 0	$ 0
Dividends	$ 0	$ 0	$ 0	$ 0	$ 0	$ 0	$ 0
Total cash outflows	$166,499	$ 1,509	$ 1,519	$ 1,528	$ 1,538	$ 1,548	$ 1,558
Net cash flow	$173,495	$ 38,595	$ 38,695	$ 38,794	$ 38,894	$ 38,994	$ 39,094
Cash balance	$173,495	$212,090	$250,785	$289,579	$328,473	$367,467	$406,561

Cash flow analysis (first year cont.)

Month	8	9	10	11	12	1
Cash from operations	$ 40,446	$ 40,556	$ 40,666	$ 40,776	$ 40,886	$483,381
Cash from receivables	$ 0	$ 0	$ 0	$ 0	$ 0	$ 0
Operating cash inflow	**$ 40,446**	**$ 40,556**	**$ 40,666**	**$ 40,776**	**$ 40,886**	**$483,381**
Other cash inflows						
Equity investment	$ 0	$ 0	$ 0	$ 0	$ 0	$ 50,000
Increased borrowings	$ 0	$ 0	$ 0	$ 0	$ 0	$250,000
Sales of business assets	$ 0	$ 0	$ 0	$ 0	$ 0	$ 0
A/P increases	$ 316	$ 316	$ 316	$ 316	$ 316	$ 3,790
Total other cash inflows	**$ 316**	**$ 316**	**$ 316**	**$ 316**	**$ 316**	**$303,790**
Total cash inflow	**$ 40,762**	**$ 40,872**	**$ 40,982**	**$ 41,092**	**$ 41,202**	**$787,171**
Cash outflows						
Repayment of principal	$ 1,361	$ 1,370	$ 1,382	$ 1,392	$ 1,403	$ 16,158
A/P decreases	$ 207	$ 207	$ 207	$ 207	$ 207	$ 2,487
A/R increases	$ 0	$ 0	$ 0	$ 0	$ 0	$ 0
Asset purchases	$ 0	$ 0	$ 0	$ 0	$ 0	$165,000
Dividends	$ 0	$ 0	$ 0	$ 0	$459,212	$459,212
Total cash outflows	**$ 1,569**	**$ 1,578**	**$ 1,589**	**$ 1,599**	**$460,822**	**$642,857**
Net cash flow	**$ 39,193**	**$ 39,294**	**$ 39,393**	**$ 39,493**	**−$419,620**	**$144,314**
Cash balance	**$445,754**	**$485,049**	**$524,441**	**$563,934**	**$144,314**	**$144,314**

Cash flow analysis (second year)

Quarter	Q1	2 Q2	Q3	Q4	2
Cash from operations	$118,009	$147,511	$159,312	$165,212	$590,043
Cash from receivables	$ 0	$ 0	$ 0	$ 0	$ 0
Operating cash inflow	**$118,009**	**$147,511**	**$159,312**	**$165,212**	**$590,043**
Other cash inflows					
Equity investment	$ 0	$ 0	$ 0	$ 0	$ 0
Increased borrowings	$ 0	$ 0	$ 0	$ 0	$ 0
Sales of business assets	$ 0	$ 0	$ 0	$ 0	$ 0
A/P increases	$ 872	$ 1,090	$ 1,177	$ 1,220	$ 4,359
Total other cash inflows	**$ 872**	**$ 1,090**	**$ 1,177**	**$ 1,220**	**$ 4,359**
Total cash inflow	**$118,880**	**$148,600**	**$160,488**	**$166,432**	**$594,402**
Cash outflows					
Repayment of principal	$ 4,271	$ 4,368	$ 4,467	$ 4,568	$ 17,674
A/P decreases	$ 597	$ 746	$ 806	$ 836	$ 2,984
A/R increases	$ 0	$ 0	$ 0	$ 0	$ 0
Asset purchases	$ 18,881	$ 23,602	$ 25,490	$ 26,434	$ 94,407
Dividends	$ 88,506	$110,633	$119,484	$123,909	$442,532
Total cash outflows	**$112,256**	**$139,349**	**$150,246**	**$155,747**	**$557,598**
Net cash flow	**$ 6,624**	**$ 9,252**	**$ 10,242**	**$ 10,686**	**$ 36,804**
Cash balance	**$150,938**	**$160,190**	**$170,432**	**$181,117**	**$181,117**

Cash flow analysis (third year)

Quarter	Q1	3 Q2	Q3	Q4	3
Cash from operations	$139,936	$174,920	$188,914	$195,911	$699,680
Cash from receivables	$ 0	$ 0	$ 0	$ 0	$ 0
Operating cash inflow	**$139,936**	**$174,920**	**$188,914**	**$195,911**	**$699,680**
Other cash inflows					
Equity investment	$ 0	$ 0	$ 0	$ 0	$ 0
Increased borrowings	$ 0	$ 0	$ 0	$ 0	$ 0
Sales of business assets	$ 0	$ 0	$ 0	$ 0	$ 0
A/P increases	$ 1,002	$ 1,253	$ 1,353	$ 1,403	$ 5,012
Total other cash inflows	**$ 1,002**	**$ 1,253**	**$ 1,353**	**$ 1,403**	**$ 5,012**
Total cash inflow	**$140,939**	**$176,173**	**$190,267**	**$197,314**	**$704,693**
Cash outflows					
Repayment of principal	$ 4,672	$ 4,778	$ 4,886	$ 4,997	$ 19,332
A/P decreases	$ 716	$ 895	$ 967	$ 1,003	$ 3,581
A/R increases	$ 0	$ 0	$ 0	$ 0	$ 0
Asset purchases	$ 22,390	$ 27,987	$ 30,226	$ 31,346	$111,949
Dividends	$104,952	$131,190	$141,685	$146,933	$524,760
Total cash outflows	**$132,730**	**$164,850**	**$177,764**	**$184,278**	**$659,623**
Net cash flow	**$ 8,209**	**$ 11,323**	**$ 12,503**	**$ 13,036**	**$ 45,070**
Cash balance	**$189,326**	**$200,649**	**$213,151**	**$226,187**	**$226,187**

Mobile Oil Change Business

LocationLube Inc.

123 Centerview Rd.
University City, Michigan 48100

Paul Greenland

LocationLube is a mobile oil change business in University City, Michigan.

EXECUTIVE SUMMARY

Business Overview

After working for Lube King, a national oil change franchise, James Moore has decided to establish LocationLube, his own mobile oil change business in University City, Michigan.

Moore is positioned for success because of his unique blend of skills and experience. In addition to first-hand experience changing oil and performing other automotive maintenance services on a wide range of vehicles, he knows what it takes to run a successful oil change business, having served as store manager of three Lube King locations for the last four years. He also has an intimate understanding of the local market.

Unhindered by a non-compete agreement, Moore is free to pursue his dream of business ownership and take advantage of a perfect turn-key opportunity that has presented itself. Larry Hansen, owner of an existing mobile oil change business, has decided to retire and put his business up for sale. Because Hansen has long respected Moore as a worthy competitor, he has approached him regarding a potential sale.

MARKET ANALYSIS

LocationLube will target the busy working professionals who account for nearly 70 percent of the local workforce in University City, Michigan. Specifically, our business will concentrate its marketing efforts on those employed by institutions of higher learning (e.g., professors and other faculty) and healthcare organizations (e.g., busy doctors, nurses, and technicians).

As the community's name suggests, it is home to several colleges and universities. While the largest employer in the city is Central University, there also are 27 other institutions that fall within the colleges & universities category in our local market. In all, more than 28,000 people are employed by area colleges and universities, accounting for nearly 45 percent of all service employees.

In addition, University City also is known as a regional destination for healthcare services. Specifically, 82 organizations are categorized as hospitals in LocationLube's market area. In addition, there are approximately 2,300 facilities categorized under health & medical services (including immediate care clinics, family medicine clinics, and specialty care centers). In all, healthcare workers account for 19.5 percent of all service employees in University City.

PERSONNEL

James Moore has always been known as a "grease monkey." He learned the fundamentals of auto repair at a young age by hanging out in his father's service station. After graduating from high school Moore secured a position with Lube King, a national oil change franchise. After working hard in an entry-level role for only one year, he was promoted to lead technician. Two years later Lube King Promoted James to the role of store manager. After managing one location for nine months, Moore's scope of responsibility quickly increased, and he soon was managing three locations.

James has decided to establish LocationLube, his own mobile oil change business in University City, Michigan. He is positioned for success because of his unique blend of skills and experience. In addition to first-hand experience changing oil and performing other automotive maintenance services on a wide range of vehicles, he knows what it takes to run a successful oil change business, thanks to his management experience with Lube King. He also has an intimate understanding of the local market.

Professional & Advisory Support

LocationLube has established a business banking account with University City Bank, as well as a merchant account for accepting credit card payments. Cindy Gentry, a local accountant, will provide accounting and tax advisory services. James Moore has utilized a popular online legal document service to prepare the paperwork necessary for incorporation.

GROWTH STRATEGY

LocationLube has developed a formal strategy for growing the business during its first few years.

- Year One: Become acquainted with the existing customer base developed by Larry Hansen. Reinforce LocationLube's commitment to quality and service and put to rest any possible concerns customers may have about new ownership.

- Year Two: Increase LocationLube's gross revenues by 15 percent via the expansion of the company's traditional consumer oil change business. Begin networking with area fleet managers and conducting research on the potential for servicing small to mid-sized commercial fleet accounts.

- Year Three: Expand the business by adding a second mobile oil change unit/truck and an additional full-time employee. Increase LocationLube's consumer oil change revenues by 25 percent and begin servicing three to five commercial fleet accounts.

James Moore believes that there is tremendous potential within the local commercial fleet market. He is confident that LocationLube can offer convenience, efficiency, and cost savings to local fleet operators who need routine vehicle maintenance performed quickly. If growth occurs as expected during year three, the business will concentrate its growth efforts on expanding within the commercial sector during years four and five. This likely will involve the addition of a third mobile oil change unit/truck.

SERVICES

LocationLube will perform the following services for its customers:

- Oil Changes (gasoline & diesel engines)
- Battery Replacement
- Tire Rotations

- Fuel Filters
- Air Filters

MARKETING & SALES

A marketing plan has been developed for LocationLube that includes the following primary tactics:

1. Web Site: LocationLube will develop a Web site that lists basic information about our business (e.g., the services we offer, how our business operates, information about owner James Moore, pricing information, coupons/discounts, an online appointment request form, etc.). The previous ownership did not have a Web site.

2. Vehicle Graphics: James Moore will have his pickup truck and mobile oil change trailer wrapped with eye-catching vinyl graphics. Serving as a "mobile billboard," the graphics will display LocationLube's aforementioned Web site address, phone number, and several key thematics (e.g., convenience, quality service, etc.).

3. Consumer Direct Marketing: LocationLube will develop an inexpensive, four-color postcard, which will be mailed to households meeting pre-determined requirements related to geography, income, and number of vehicles in the home. Mailing lists will be obtained from Midwest MailPro LLC, a list broker in University City. In addition, Jefferson Letter Service, a local mail house, will handle mailings for us on a monthly basis.

4. Business-to-Business Marketing: James Moore will promote LocationLube to the human resources and employee concierge departments of local companies, chapters of national professional organizations, service clubs, and the University City Chamber of Commerce. Initially, an introductory letter will be mailed to prospects in the above categories (list available upon request). James will then follow up with prospects by phone two weeks after the mailing. A second letter will be mailed to all non-respondents 90 days after the first mailing, and James will once again follow-up by phone two weeks after the second letter mails.

5. Advertising: LocationLube will maintain a regular advertising presence in The University City Times, the primary local newspaper in our market, in the form of a 15 percent discount coupon. In addition, we will run a large ad in the Yellow Pages in the Auto Oil & Lubrication Services category. Finally, LocationLube will purchase an insert in DiscountPak, a local coupon distributor that mails a coupon packet to area homes on a monthly basis.

James Moore will evaluate LocationLube's marketing plan on a semi-annual basis during the first three years of operations, and annually thereafter.

OPERATIONS

Equipment

LocationLube will operate from a 6 x 12 cargo trailer, which is included in the sale of the business. In addition, the following equipment is included in the purchase price:

- 1200 W generator
- 5.5 hp gas-powered air compressor (175 PSI)
- 3.5 ton hydraulic floor jack
- 3 37-gallon oil storage tanks
- 1 50-gallon oil tank

- 1 50-gallon windshield washer fluid tank
- 1 fresh oil pump
- 1 used oil transfer pump
- 1 windshield washer fluid pump
- 4 40-foot hose reels (air, grease, oil, windshield washer fluid)
- 1 oil removal system (operates through dipstick tube)
- 1 toolbox

Tools
- filter sockets (assorted)
- filter wrenches (assorted)
- strap wrenches (assorted)
- 6-inch adjustable wrench
- 8-inch adjustable wrench
- 10-inch adjustable wrench
- 12-inch adjustable wrench
- 2 channel locks
- 2 pliers
- 2 needle nose pliers
- 2 vice grips
- 1 screwdriver set
- 1/4 inch ratchet
- 3/8 inch ratchet
- 1/2 inch ratchet
- 1/4 inch breaker bar
- 1/2 inch breaker bar
- 3/4 inch breaker bar
- SAE socket set
- metric socket set
- pry bars (assorted)
- Allen wrenches (assorted)
- 1 torch wrench
- 1 air gun
- 1 air drill

Pricing
- *Gasoline Engine: $39.95
- *Diesel Engine: $85.95

- Tire Rotations: $44.95

- Battery Replacement (variable)

- Fuel Filters (variable)

- Air Filters (variable)

*pricing for synthetic oil and some imported vehicles extra

FINANCIAL ANALYSIS

Larry Hansen has agreed to sell his mobile oil change business to James Moore for $12,500. In addition, James Moore has agreed to purchase Hansen's existing inventory of supplies and materials for $9,000, for a total purchase price of $21,500. Moore will contribute $15,000 of his own money to the business, from personal savings, and is seeking a small business loan of $20,000 for initial operations.

According to Hansen, over the past three years the business has generated gross revenues of approximately $80,000 per year. As the new owner, James Moore is confident that he can maintain the business's current volume during year one. Therefore, he is estimating that revenues will remain at about $80,000. Based on the projections outlined in the Growth Strategy section of this plan, Moore estimates that LocationLube's revenues will reach $92,000 during year two. This figure is expected to reach $140,000 during year three, when the company begins servicing small and mid-sized commercial vehicle fleets.

Detailed financial projections have been prepared with assistance from our accountant, Cindy Gentry, and are available upon request.

Nonprofit Concession Stand Business

RGFA Concession Stand

PO Box 67
Richmond, Michigan 48062

Paul Greenland

The purpose of this business plan is to outline the use of a concession stand to be operated during the summer softball season to raise money to help offset the costs of uniforms, equipment, field maintenance, and the like.

PURPOSE

The purpose of this business plan is to outline the use of a concession stand to be operated during the summer softball season for the Richmond Girls Fastpitch Association. The Association consists of 12 teams in three divisions separated by age, with 151 girls ranging from 5-14 playing in the league. The league incurs costs for uniforms, player's equipment, field maintenance, chalk, umpires, port-a-johns, trophies, bleachers, and the like. In an effort to keep costs minimal for players and their families, we have undertaken many efforts to offset these costs. One method of raising the money needed to pay for the basic costs of running the league is to operate a concession stand on the premises during all games.

BUILDING

The concession stand building is located on land owned by Richmond Community Schools, but it was built by the league and is used and maintained exclusively by the league. The structure itself is roughly 20' x 20' cinderblock and has one door and two selling windows. Both selling windows are protected from the elements from a roof overhang. The building sits on a concrete pad and is located near the parking lot close to all of the 6 playing fields.

The building is wired for electricity, but does not have heat or running water. The electricity is connected to the school, so we do not incur electricity costs.

SECURITY

Building Access
One item of concern is the number of people who have access to the building. Over the course of time there have been many board members, concession managers, and other volunteers who held keys to the building. No one can remember the last time the locks were changed, so there is no way to tell exactly how many people are able to access the building.

This has proven to be detrimental in the past, as people have entered the building on non-game days and taken food items and/or used the appliances. Several times the appliances were returned in disrepair and required cash and experienced experts to fix.

To address this issue, the locks have been changed and a limited number of keys have been issued. There should no further unauthorized entrance to the building, and stealing should be at an end.

Inventory

Another way to ensure that no items are taken inappropriately is to perform twice nightly inventories, once at the opening of the building and again at its close. Records will be kept to make sure that the closing inventory of one day matches the opening inventory of the next day.

In addition, the opening and closing inventories can be used as a check that the money collected during the day is correct. While we don't anticipate 100% accuracy, the cash collected should at least cover the cost of the items sold.

Hidden camera

In the event that inventories are off or the cash collected is incorrect, we may decide to install a hidden camera. The cost of this camera is significant ($100 to $200), so the need to install it will be weighed against the cost of the missing items and the extent to which the problem occurs.

WORKFORCE

Volunteers

Our primary workforce consists of volunteers. In addition to the concession manager who coordinates food purchases and oversees the schedule, there are three "key holders" who have volunteered their time to be responsible for opening and closing each day. Key holders are assigned certain days of the week and show up to open the building, perform inventory, and start the machines. They also check the schedule to see who else has signed up to volunteer and make sure they have shown up as scheduled.

The primary workers consist of league parents. It is the responsibility of all parents in the league to cover one shift (approximately 3 hours) at the concession stand for every child playing in the league. During registration, each child must pay the regular registration fee as well as provide a check for a $30 volunteer fee. If the parents fail to sign up for a shift or fail to show up for the shift they signed up for at the concession stand, we will cash their volunteer check and use the money to offset the costs of paying teenage workers to cover their shift. When the parents complete their volunteer requirement, the league secretary returns their volunteer check to them.

Teenagers

We maintain a list of approximately 4 teenagers in the area who are available on short notice to come to the concession stand to work. In the event that parents scheduled to work fail to show up, the concession stand manager calls one of the teenagers to substitute. The teenagers cover the entire shift from 6:00 pm until closing after the last game, or approximately 9:00 pm. Each worker is paid $15 for the shift, payable at the end of each week via check. They are required to fill out a timesheet to get this money.

Training

The concession manager trains the teenage workers and key holders to work in the concession stand. Policies and procedures will be gone over, and emphasis will be made on the importance of inventory control and cash safeguarding. Because the profits will be used to offset the costs of running the league, it is imperative that we maintain meticulous records and guarantee that no food is consumed or given away without proper payment. These rules will be emphasized during training.

CUSTOMER BASE

There are 151 kids in league, with 50 to 75 girls playing each night, four nights per week. Parents, siblings, extended family, and friends of the players also use the concession stand before, during, and after the game.

There is a tradition and unspoken rule that all teams go to the concession stand at the end of their games to purchase snacks. Parents take turns purchasing food for all of the girls on their child's team. Usually a parent will prepay a set amount per child, such as $2.00. When the parent pays, the concession stand workers note the amount per child on the team. When that team arrives at the concession stand at the end of their game, they are told how much they have been given. This reliable stream of income ensures that we bring in at least $100 to $150 a night, before costs.

The games begin at 6:30 pm, with teams meeting at 6:00 pm to warm up on the field. With work schedules and other competing obligations, many people purchase dinner at the concession stand prior to the game out of convenience and necessity. Pizza and hot dogs are common choices for dinner and are easy to prepare. We anticipate at least another $50 in sales will be made nightly through these means.

ITEMS FOR SALE

Food & Drinks

The menu available has been gleaned through several years' experience on what "sells." These items include:

- Candy
- Chips
- Pizza
- Hot dogs
- Pretzels
- Ice cream
- Nachos & cheese
- Popcorn

Drinks for sale include:

- Coke
- Diet Coke
- Sprite
- Bottled water
- Power Aid
- Coffee
- Tea
- Hot chocolate

Items that have been sold in the past but were not as popular have been deleted from the menu. These items include sunflower seeds, fruit snacks, and beef jerky.

OTHER ITEMS NEEDED

In addition to the items we sell, there are many additional items we need to purchase to run the concession stand properly and ensure customers are happy and the stand is sanitary. These items include:

Condiments and related items—ketchup, mustard, cream, sugar, stirrers, foil, cups and lids, napkins, nacho trays, popcorn bags, oil, salt, seasoning, water

Cleaning supplies—Clorox wipes, paper towels, spray cleaner, garbage bags

Food handling items—hand sanitizer, gloves, aprons

Toilet paper—for use in the port-a-johns

PROCUREMENT

All items will be purchased at pre-determined establishments, including Sam's Club, GFS, and Acme Distributing.

Sam's Club

The majority of all food will be purchased at Sam's Club. Membership costs $35 per year. There are 2 locations within a 30-minute drive, and they offer the best prices on the items we offer, even taking the cost of membership into consideration. Because of the drive time and fuel costs, trips are planned no more than once per week or, preferably, once every two weeks. Close attention to inventory must be made to ensure we purchase enough food and supplies to last this time period.

GFS

GFS is located within a 15-minute drive, but charges more for the items we sell. One exception to this is the cheese we use for the liquid cheese warmer/pump; GFS is the only retailer that sells the kind of cheese we need to operate the machine.

Acme Distributing

Acme Distributing is our source for soft drinks, water, and Power Aid. As long as we order a minimum of $500 per season, we are able to keep and use their cooler in our facility. They also provide us with boxes to collect returnable bottles. We place orders on Friday, and the product is delivered on Tuesday afternoon.

APPLIANCES

To prepare the foods, several small appliances are owned and operated in the concession stand. The appliances include:

- Popcorn machine
- George Forman grill (for cooking the hot dogs)
- Pretzel machine
- Keurig coffee machine
- Food warmer
- Freezer

- Cooler
- Grill
- Liquid cheese warmer/pump

OTHER COSTS

Other costs associated with the concession stand that must be taken into account include building maintenance and repairs as well as the upkeep and replacement of the two picnic tables and seven garbage cans that are arranged throughout the fields.

The roof is currently leaking and requires a complete tear-off. Estimates have been obtained, and the league has approved the work at a cost of $2,400. This is being paid using funds previously on hand, and the roof should be in good repair for the foreseeable future. However, this type of cost must be factored into the profit we make at the concession stand. We must set aside some of the profits we make so that we will be able to pay for repairs and maintenance costs in the future, both to the building and the appliances.

PROFIT AND LOSS

Pricing

While we are trying to make a profit on the items we sell so that we offset the costs for running the league as well as set some aside for future maintenance and repairs, we do not have the costs associated with a normal business such as rent, electricity, and employees. However, we also do not enjoy the benefits of buying inventory at wholesale prices, so we pay more for the items we do sell than the typical business. At a typical retail store, items we sell would generally be marked up by 100-200% or more. We intend to mark up items at roughly 75-100%.

A thorough review of the actual cost of each item, including applicable taxes and periphery items, has been done to capture the complete cost of each item sold. Based on this cost, each item was marked up approximately 75-100% into round numbers that will be easy to calculate quickly. In many cases, it was discovered that prices we charged in the past were insufficient to cover the actual, true cost of the item. These prices were adjusted accordingly. Please see the breakdown at the end of this plan for further details.

This markup will allow us to maximize profits while still maintaining prices equal to our competitors such as local convenience stores and gas stations. Although we have a dedicated clientele with little options so close to the fields, we are not out to take advantage of our customers. We simply want to make a decent profit on the items we sell so that we may keep registration costs as low as possible.

Cash Flow and Tracking

Our business deals primarily in cash with some customers choosing to pay via check, especially when they are covering the costs of an entire team. Having a large amount of cash on hand lends itself to thievery.

To ward off attempts at thievery, we will make nightly bank deposits of all cash collected during the day, with the exception of $50 in start-up change. We should maintain $20 in quarters, $20 in ones and two $5 bills at the end of each day to use for change for the next day.

The change will be kept in a locked cash box and brought out by the concession manager or key holder at the beginning of each opening. The same cash will be left in the cash box at the end of each night so that it is available for the next day's sales. All other cash and checks will be deposited nightly into the night deposit box at our local bank.

In addition to this, a once nightly inventory will be done to confirm that the cash collected equals the inventory sold. Any discrepancies will be noted and reviewed, and results will be placed on file for future reference.

No cash payments will be made for services such as field maintenance and umpires from the cash box. These services will be paid for via check at the end of each week so that we can control and track the disbursement of funds.

Receipts will be required for all food and related purchases, and inventory will be done at delivery to make sure all items are accounted for.

Other Income

To bolster our income, we have decided to obtain 2 boxes to collect empty pop cans which can be redeemed for $0.10 each at the local grocery store. No attempts have been made to collect and return these in the past, and most were simply thrown away. By collecting the empty cans that we have sold, we can increase the profit margin on each pop sold to $0.60 instead of merely $0.50.

Issues

If at any time it is discovered that parent volunteers are doing anything inappropriate such as taking food or giving food away, their $30 volunteer fee will be cashed to cover the expenses. If at any time it is discovered that a teenage paid worker is giving away food, taking food, or taking cash, he or she will be immediately terminated and restitution will be sought. If the problem persists and the concession stand is in danger of actually losing money instead of making a profit, the concession stand will be permanently closed.

SWOT ANALYSIS

Strengths: We have a captive audience with a tradition of buying snacks for the teams after the games. We pay no rent or electricity costs and have no overall employee costs. New inventory process, payment process, and nightly deposits will help control cash flow and tracking.

Weaknesses: Prices on several items have been raised from last year to ensure a profit is being made. Customers may not like the price increase. Some items have been taken off the menu.

Opportunities: We have a new Keurig coffee machine and a George Foreman grill. Both appliances should yield superior quality food while maintaining similar costs.

Threats: Unauthorized usage of building or taking/giving away food and illicit money handling are our biggest threats. Attempts have been made to negate or diminish these threats.

Profit margins

Items	Description (incl tax)	Cost	Sales price	Profit	Profit margin
Candy					
Baby Bottle Pops	Assortment—20/0.85 oz. for $10.47	$0.52 each	$1.00	$0.48	48%
Big League Chew	12 ct. for $10.59	$0.88 each	$1.50	$0.62	41%
Licorice Ropes	Red Licorice Super Ropes—30 ct. for $11.64	$0.39 each	$1.00	$0.61	61%
M&Ms	Milk Chocolate—48/1.69 oz. pk. for $25.16	$0.52 each	$1.00	$0.48	48%
Nerds Rope	Wonka® Nerds® Rope—24 ct. for $12.44	$0.52 each	$1.00	$0.48	48%
Push Pops	Assorted Flavors—24 ct. for $10.47	$0.44 each	$1.00	$0.56	56%
Skittles/Starburst	Variety Pack—30 ct. for $13.61	$0.45 each	$1.00	$0.55	55%
Sour Punch Straws	Strawberry—24/2 oz. for $10.26	$0.43 each	$1.00	$0.57	57%
Chips					
Fritos, Classic Potato Chips, BBQ Chips, Sour Cream & Onion Chips, Cool Ranch Doritos, Nacho Cheese Doritos, Cheetos	Frito Lay® Big Grab® Variety Pack—30 for $10.58	$0.35 each	$1.00	$0.65	65%
Pizza	$5 for 8 slices				
Hot dogs (buns and hot dogs)	Hot dog—$0.29	$0.63 each	$1.00	$0.37	37%
	Bun—$0.12	$0.43 each	$1.00	$0.57	57%
	Foil—$0.02				
Pretzels (pretzels and salt)	Box of 60 pretzels for $35.11	$0.59 each	$1.00	$0.41	41%
Ice cream					
Nestle Drum Stick	Variety Cone—16 ct. for $9.31	$0.58 each	$1.00	$0.42	42%
Minute Maid (Cherry, Lemonade, and Strawberry Lemonade)	Soft Frozen Variety Pack—24/4 oz. for $10.58	$0.44 each	$1.00	$0.56	56%
ICEE® Freeze Squeeze Up	Variety—30 ct. for $9.20	$0.31	$1.00	$0.69	69%
Twix® Ice Cream Bars	24 ct. for $10.58	$0.44	$1.00	$0.56	56%
Nachos (chips and cheese)	Chips— $0.27	$0.62	$1.50	$0.88	59%
	Cheese—$0.30 each				
	Tray—$0.05 each				
Popcorn (kernels, salt, oil)	Kernels—$0.12	$0.37	$1.00	$0.63	63%
	Salt—$0.12				
	Oil—$0.13				
Soft drinks—Coke, Diet Coke, Sprite	24–12 ounce cans for $12.10	$0.50 each	$1.00	$0.50	50%
Coffee (coffee, cup, lid, sugar, cream, stirrer)	K-cups—$0.52 each	$0.70 each	$1.00	$0.30	30%
	Cup/lid—$0.10 each				
	Sugar—$0.03 each				
	Cream—$0.03 each				
	Stirrer—$0.02 each				
Tea (tea, cup, lid, sugar, cream, stirrer)	K-cups—$0.10 each	$0.28 each	$1.00	$0.72	72%
	Cup/lid—$0.10 each				
	Sugar—$0.03 each				
	Cream—$0.03 each				
	Stirrer—$0.02 each				
Hot chocolate (hot chocolate, cup and lid)	K-cups—$0.55 each	$0.65 each	$1.00	$0.35	35%
	Cup/lid—$0.10 each				
PowerAid	24–20 ounce bottles for $23.20	$0.97 each	$2.00	$1.03	52%
Water	24–20 ounce bottles for $13.55	$0.56 each	$1.00	$0.44	44%

Profit analysis—nightly

	Mondays	Tuesdays	Wednesdays	Thursdays	Weekly
Sales	$150	$200	$150	$200	$700
Cost of goods sold (50%)	($ 75)	($100)	($ 75)	($100)	($350)
Profit	$ 75	$100	$ 75	$100	$350

Revenue—season

Profit ($350 weekly × 8 weeks)	$2,800
Bottle returns	$ 100
Volunteer fees (minus fees paid to teenage workers)	$ 300
Total	**$3,200**

Online Job Service

CareerConnections LLC

3614 Western Highway
Cleveland, Ohio 44113

Our passion for developing recruiting innovations creates a world of ideas without boundaries. At CareerConnections we help companies merge the immediacy of mobile technology and social media with traditional tactics such as focused print and radio advertising to connect with qualified candidates.

This plan originally appeared in Business Plans Handbook, Volume 8. It has been updated for this edition.

WHO WE ARE

CareerConnections is in the business of helping employment professionals find qualified candidates and successfully fill openings. We are experts in pioneering high-tech and nontraditional recruiting solutions. Our Virtual Job Fairs provide a low-cost, high-impact means of reaching the best prospects. We accomplish this in multiple ways. Examples include targeted campaigns in specific geographic markets, and also the enhancement of clients' existing recruitment efforts with the latest technology.

HOW WE WORK

CareerConnections' Virtual Job Fairs merge the immediacy of mobile technology and social media with traditional tactics such as focused print and radio advertising to connect with qualified candidates. Through the strategic combination of these emerging and established techniques, we are able to mobilize the attention of employed, experienced candidates and ignite the interest of passive job seekers.

Mobile Technology

According to a survey conducted by CTIA-the Wireless Association, at the end of 2010 wireless penetration in United States had reached 96 percent. Wireless users sent and received 2.052 trillion SMS text messages, compared to 1.563 trillion in 2009 (a 231% increase). Smartphone users increased from 49.8 million in 2009 to 78.2 million in 2010 (a 57% increase). In addition, the number of wireless-enabled devices (e.g., tablets, laptops, modems, etc.) was rising at a strong pace.

CareerConnections helps recruiters leverage the power, convenience and immediacy of mobile technologies. We accomplish this by developing text messaging (SMS or "short messaging service") campaigns. In recruitment campaigns and materials, employers encourage prospective job candidates to send a text message to a pre-defined "short code," such as ENGINEERINGJOBS. Once prospective candidates opt in, employers are able to send relevant text messages (which have a much higher read rate than traditional e-mail) to their mobile phones.

Our in-house developers also can assist companies to create their own mobile apps for devices such as Apple's popular iPhone, enabling candidates to stay on top of, and submit applications for, jobs that are of interest to them. In addition, we work in a consulting capacity to help recruiters identify and use recruitment-oriented mobile apps that have been developed by other parties.

Another service we offer is the optimization of existing Web sites for mobile users. This typically involves streamlining or simplifying existing Web content and implementing an "auto detection" function that serves up the proper site version to visitors.

Social Media

CareerConnections helps companies leverage the emerging power of various social media channels. For example, LinkedIn offers an advertising option called LinkedIn Ads, in which advertisements can be purchased based on options such as a user's age, industry, job title, gender, job function, and job title. In turn, these ads drive prospective candidates to a Web site or encourage them to respond to a text messaging campaign and view available job opportunities. Twitter is another channel to reach prospective jobseekers, by utilizing options such as TwitHire.

Sharp Focus

CareerConnections concentrates its efforts on industry sectors with the greatest growth potential, as well as jobs that are the hardest to recruit for (e.g., those with very specific skill requirements). For example, according to the U.S. Bureau of Labor Statistics, the three industry sectors with the strongest projected growth between 2009 and 2018 are: educational services, private; health care and social assistance; and professional and business services.

A Trusted Partner

As partners to the human resources team, we are committed to helping employers raise their corporate profiles and communicate their unique identities. We also dedicate ourselves to the serious task of attracting and maintaining a diverse workforce.

Human resources professionals applaud us for the muscle we add to their recruiting efforts. Candidates appreciate us for our quick and convenient access to a wide range of companies and their openings.

Our Vision

Our passion for developing recruiting innovations creates a world of ideas without boundaries. By aspiring to the highest standards of quality in everything we do, we will become a business without competition.

Our Mission

At CareerConnections we are in the business of helping employers find a diverse group of qualified candidates to make successful hiring decisions. Our search strategies are creative, cost-effective, and dynamic.

- We build trusting relationships with clients through hard work and integrity.

- We value innovation and continually strive to develop better ways to support our clients.

- We keep our promises, respect one another, share rewards, and make time to have fun.

- We view our clients and shareholder as partners. When our partners succeed, so do we.

- We are tenacious.

CareerConnections's vision, mission, and principles are the cornerstone of our culture.

EXECUTIVE SUMMARY

Employee Recruiting Market

- Companies seeking to leverage the latest emerging technologies to fill positions that are in demand/ hard to recruit for.

- Candidates identified effectively and cost efficiently without expensive recruiters.

- A cost-effective way to reach the best prospects during one of the most challenging periods in economic history.

CareerConnections' Virtual Job Fairs Represent Attractive New Channel for Reaching Passive Job Seekers

- Recruiting employed, experienced candidates is a key objective for every employer.

- Opportunity to leverage the power of social media and mobile technology with traditional tactics.

- Clearly the largest untapped recruiting approach for employers.

We've Gotten Started, but Must Increase Resources to Capture Market Share Quickly

- Market penetration dependent on investment in telemarketing, advertising, and technology capability

- Reduce expenses and increase control by bringing systems development and sales functions in-house

- Explore strategic acquisition of a business-to-business telemarketing company to shorten growth cycle

- Enhance our image as a technology company and establish Boston corporate office by September 30, 2012

CareerConnections's Pro Forma Looks Solid and Has A Phased Approach to Growth

- Forecasting $315,000 revenues in 2011 growing to $11.25 million by 2014

CareerConnections strategically merges the immediacy of mobile technology and social media with traditional tactics such as focused print and radio advertising to connect with employed, experienced candidates conveniently and affordably.

BIOGRAPHIES

Management

Gerald Simons—President & Chief Executive Officer

Gerry Simons has over twenty years of experience in the financial services industry. Mr. Simons has held various senior leadership positions with GM Credit, Nissan Financial Services, Citibank Capital Corporation, and Lear Credit. He has had P/L management responsibility for businesses in excess of $200 million and responsibility for sales budgets in excess of $400 million. His expertise includes development of Internet strategies within the equipment leasing industry. Mr. Simons holds his Bachelor of Arts degree in business administration from Ohio State University.

Jill Monroe—Vice President Product Development

Jill Monroe is the author of *Job Hunters' Sourcebook: Where to Find Employment Leads and Other Job Search Resources* (Gale Research Inc.). Under her authorship, *Job Hunters' Sourcebook* was the recipient of two prominent publishing awards. Ms. Monroe has over twenty years of broad human resources management experience, with specialized knowledge in staffing, compensation, benefits, and employee relations. She has held senior human resources positions with Bonior Consulting Group and Ogilvy & Mather. Ms. Monroe holds her Bachelor of Communications degree from Ohio State University. Ms. Monroe is also a former board member of the Human Resources Association of Greater Cleveland.

Frederick Paul—Vice President Operations

Fred Paul has thirteen years of sales, managerial, and entrepreneurial experience. Mr. Paul was National Sales Manager for Mercury Interactions, a subsidiary of ABC Broadcasting. He was responsible for managing all national sales programs associated with ABC's national recruitment Web site. Mr. Paul began his career with Standard & Poors, where he was named Broker of the Year for three consecutive years. He started his own company, Creative Auto Detailing, and successfully built it into three locations before selling the company in 1996. Mr. Paul has a Bachelor of Arts degree in business administration from Northwestern University.

Suzanne Rintimacki—Vice President Business Development

Suzanne Rintimacki has three years of successful sales and business development experience with ABC Broadcasting. Ms. Rintimacki was National Director of Sales and Business Development, and was responsible for creating and implementing nationally ABC's Wonder Job Fair product. She successfully executed nine events, generating over $500,000 in revenue.

Advisory Board

Troy Bennett—Dunston & Ray PLC

Troy Bennett has been a practicing attorney with Dunston & Ray for twelve years and is a partner specializing in Commercial and Product Liability, Commercial Landlord-Tenant, and Securities Litigation. Mr. Bennett is a member of the Litigation Section of the American Bar, State Bar of Ohio, and Cleveland Bar Association. He holds his Juris Doctorate Law degree from Columbia College Law School and his Bachelor of Arts degree from College of the Holy Cross. CareerConnections has engaged Dunston & Ray as its law firm.

Jonathon Williams—Morgan & Reilly, LLP

Jonathon Williams has been a practicing Certified Public Accountant with Morgan & Reilly for seventeen years and is a partner specializing in tax and consulting services to corporations. Mr. Williams is a member of the American Institute of Certified Public Accountants and the Ohio Association of Certified Public Accountants. He holds his Master of Science degree from Ohio State University and his Bachelor of Business Administration, Accounting degree from Ohio University. CareerConnections has engaged Morgan & Reilly as its accounting firm.

Phillip Owens—Citibank

Phillip Owens is Vice President and Deposit Relationship Manager for Citibank. Mr. Owens has over eleven years of banking relationship management experience. He holds his Juris Doctorate Law degree from Ohio College of Law and his Bachelor of Science degree from Ohio University. CareerConnections has engaged Citibank as its primary deposit bank.

Yoko Una—The Smith Group

Yoko Una has over twenty-five years of broad human resources management experience. Ms. Una has held senior human resources leadership positions with Macmillan, General Motors, and the University of Ohio. She is an active member and former officer and board member of the Society for Human Resources Management, Human Resources Association of Greater Cleveland, and Academy for Academic Personnel Administration. She is also a former board member of the College and University Personnel Association and Metro Cleveland Equal Opportunity Forum. Ms. Una holds her Master in Public Administration degree from the University of Virginia and her Bachelor of Arts degree from University of Arkansas.

Sydney Atwater—Atwater Communications, Inc.

Syd Atwater enjoyed a successful 15-year career as a broadcast executive before establishing his own interactive marketing consultancy. His unique blend of experience, which includes mobile marketing campaigns, makes him a tremendous asset to our company's advisory board. Mr. Atwater is an active member and former officer and board member of the Ohio Association of Broadcasters and the Pittsburg Area Radio Broadcasters Association. Mr. Atwater holds his MBA from the University of Michigan.

Miguel Lopez—Vision Information Technologies
Miguel Lopez is the President and CEO of Vision Information Technologies, which he founded in 2007. His firm specializes in interactive marketing campaigns and Web development. Mr. Lopez developed and patented VisionPro, a content management system that allows companies to self-manage their Web sites without technical expertise. His company has over 60 clients including GM Sales, Highland Brands, Michigan State University, and Monroe County. Mr. Lopez is a board member of the Hispanic Business Alliance, University of Ohio Computer & Information Science Professional Advisory Board, Economic Club of Cleveland, and Society of Hispanic Professional Engineers. He holds his Bachelor of Science degree in Computer Science from the University of Ohio.

RECRUITING MARKET OVERVIEW

By 2011 unemployment levels in the United States remained extremely high. Nevertheless, employers were having a difficult time filling certain types of jobs with high skill requirements. With cost consciousness at an all-time high, recruiters were challenged to find candidates at the lowest possible price. Mobile marketing and social media campaigns were a cost-effective way to bolster traditional advertising efforts, and were an affordable alternative to online job boards.

According to results of the 2010 Social Recruiting Survey, conducted by Jobvite and published *HR Magazine's HR Trendbook 2011*, a majority (73%) of recruiters and HR professionals utilized social media or social networks as part of their recruitment efforts in 2010. In addition, another 9 percent of professionals were preparing to do so. At 78.3 percent, LinkedIn was the most highly utilized channel, followed by Facebook (54.6%), Twitter (44.8%), blogs (18.7%), YouTube (13.7%), and MySpace (5.4%).

By 2011 mobile recruiting was still catching on with many employers. Those companies that were taking advantage of mobile recruitment had a significant strategic advantage over their competitors. Tremendous opportunity exists for firms like CareerConnections, which are positioned to help industry leaders take advantage of this new approach to recruitment. By blending mobile marketing, social media, and traditional tactics together with sound strategic advice, we believe that we are somewhat unique in the marketplace.

OUR CLIENTS

What Our Clients Say

Aloha Cottage Health Services
"This was our first Virtual Job Fair. It was so informative and we got a great response. We're already planning for the next event!"

> Joanne Clarkston
>
> Aloha Cottage Health Services
>
> Human Resources Manager

SelectCare
"Of all the Internet recruiting we are currently doing, the Virtual Job Fair made it possible for us to target specific demographics and get results!"

Lori Collins

SelectCare Individual Financial Services

Human Resources Specialist

Greyhound Transportation International

"The CareerConnections Virtual Job Fair got us results! We will be participating in another Virtual Job Fairs in 2012."

Julie Jones

Greyhound Transportation International

Human Resources

Macmillan

"It was a pleasure working with you on the Virtual Job Fair. We were extremely pleased with the results, ease of use, and the excellent customer service."

John Reynolds

Macmillan

Human Resources Manager

Our Clients (June 2011)

1. Little Caesars' Pizza

2. Ameritech

3. Macmillan

4. Valvoline

5. Firestone Tire & Service Centers

6. Citibank

7. IBM

8. Overland Park

9. SelectCare

10. CCX

11. Comerica

12. Olympia Entertainment

13. Kelly Services

14. CTS

15. Alcoa

16. Steak 'n Shake

17. Parklane Chevrolet

18. Sports & Entertainment Dome

19. Compuware

20. Ohio Bank

21. ICA

22. Vision Information Technologies

23. IKON

24. Morgan & Reilly L.L.P.

25. BT Boulevard Retirement Community

26. Enterprise Rent-a-Car

27. ACSIA

28. Parkedale Pharmaceuticals

29. TEK systems

30. Carhartt

31. Army

32. Aloha Cottags Health Services

33. Verizon Wireless

MARKETING STRATEGY

To take Internet recruiting beyond job boards to integrated solutions.

How it works.

1. Build relationships with human resources professional on a personal level and sell them on the merits of utilizing mobile and social media technologies in their recruiting campaigns.

- Become actively involved in the Society for Human Resource Management (SHRM).

- Target 575 local chapters nationally with over 250,000 members.

- Utilize SHRM member directories and other strategic human resources lists to reach decision makers.

2. Implement a pro-active database management sales plan to maximize our sales results.

- Use customized database software to segment the market and achieve a competitive sales advantage.

- Develop qualified leads through a focused lead generation program involving traditional telemarketing and interactive advertising on business-focused social media sites like LinkedIn.

- Augment our database sales effort by high impact marketing techniques through e-mail, social media, interactive advertising, etc.

3. Use the power of mobile technology, social media, and radio to create awareness with human resources professionals and passive job seekers.

- Reach human resources decision makers via telemarketing and direct marketing campaigns.

- Promote Virtual Job Fairs with intensive advertising on social media sites (e.g., LinkedIn) and/or radio (depending on recruitment objectives) to link with passive job seekers.

CareerConnections's marketing strategy is aggressive, disciplined, and efficient.

FINANCIAL OVERVIEW

Detailed financial statements (available upon request) have been prepared for CareerConnections. Following are some key figures:

Number of virtual job fairs

2011	24
2012	48
2013	96
2014	150

Projected revenue (thousands)

2011	$ 315
2012	$ 3,025
2013	$ 6,624
2014	$11,250

CRITICAL SUCCESS FACTORS

To compete and succeed, a minimum $700,000 in additional capitalization is needed.

How the money will be invested

Computers, software, network servers	$ 25,000

Key staff additions

1. National account relationship manager	$ 90,000
2. Inside sales manager	$ 70,000
3. Five inside salespeople	$200,000
4. Two customer service people	$ 90,000
Total	**$450,000**

Working capital

1. Boston corporate office
2. Advertisement and promotion
3. Establish benefit plan
4. Miscellaneous operating expenses

Total	**$250,000**

Personal Loan Company

Marshall Personal Loan Services

6800 7th St.
Manhattan, New York 10002

BizPlanDB.com

Marshall Personal Loan Services will provide short term loans to people who are living within the Company's target market area. The market for these products is immensely large among lower-income borrowers and the unbanked. Personal loans are primarily designed as an emergency line of credit for limited usage based on the income of the borrower and the equity that they hold in their vehicles.

1.0 EXECUTIVE SUMMARY

The purpose of this business plan is to raise $125,000 for the development of a personal loan lender while showcasing the expected financials and operations over the next three years. Marshall Personal Loan Services is a New York based corporation that will provide short term loans to customers in its targeted market based on their credit score and income. The Company was founded in Andrew Ball.

1.1 The Services

Marshall Personal Loan Services will provide short term loans to people who are living within the Company's target market, and which it is authorized to do business based on the income and credit score of customers.

The market for these products is immensely large among lower-income borrowers and the unbanked. Personal loans are primarily designed as an emergency credit vehicle for limited usage based on the income of the borrower and the equity that they hold in their vehicles. The Company will use several credit procedural methods to ensure that the interest rates loans are provided in the ethical manner consistent with all state usury, lending and credit laws. The loans will be secured by the borrower's income and personal credit.

The third section of the business plan will further describe the services offered by Marshall Personal Loan Services.

1.2 Financing

Mr. Ball is seeking to raise $125,000 from a bank loan. The interest rate and loan agreement are to be further discussed during negotiation. This business plan assumes that the business will receive a 10 year loan with a 9% fixed interest rate. The financing will be used for the following:

- Development of the Company's retail location.

- Financing for the first six months of operation.

- Capital to finance the Company's short term loans.

Mr. Ball will contribute $25,000 to the venture.

193

1.3 Mission Statement

The mission of Marshall Personal Loan Services is to become the recognized leader in its targeted market for providing short term loans and lending services based on the customer's income and credit quality.

1.4 Management Team

The Company was founded by Andrew Ball. Mr. Ball has more than 15 years of experience in the lending and retail management industry. Through his expertise, he will be able to bring the operations of the business to profitability within its first year of operations.

1.5 Sales Forecasts

Mr. Ball expects a strong rate of growth at the start of operations. Below are the expected financials over the next three years.

Proforma profit and loss (yearly)

Year	1	2	3
Sales	$555,000	$643,800	$733,932
Operating costs	$378,375	$395,064	$412,302
EBITDA	$ 98,925	$158,604	$218,880
Taxes, interest, and depreciation	$ 55,478	$ 73,536	$ 95,927
Net profit	$ 43,447	$ 85,069	$122,953

Sales, operating costs, and profit forecast

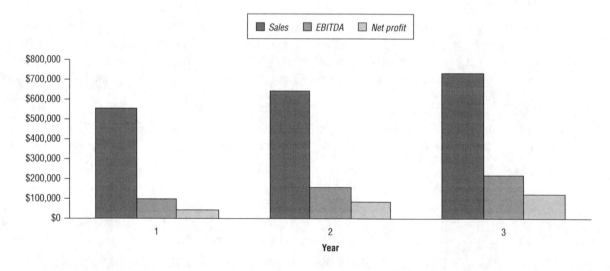

1.6 Expansion Plan

The Founder expects that the business will aggressively expand during the first three years of operation. Mr. Ball intends to implement marketing campaigns that will effectively target lower income individuals.

2.0 COMPANY AND FINANCING SUMMARY

2.1 Registered Name and Corporate Structure

Marshall Personal Loan Services is registered as a corporation in the State of New York.

2.2 Required Funds

At this time, Marshall Personal Loan Services requires $125,000 of debt funds. Below is a breakdown of how these funds will be used:

Projected startup costs

Initial lease payments and deposits	$ 10,000
Working capital	$ 35,000
FF&E	$ 20,000
Leasehold improvements	$ 5,000
Security deposits	$ 5,000
Insurance	$ 2,500
Capital for personal loans	$ 60,000
Marketing budget	$ 7,500
Miscellaneous and unforeseen costs	$ 5,000
Total startup costs	**$150,000**

Use of funds

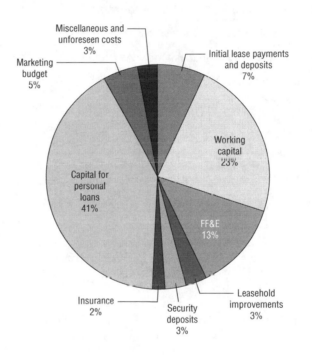

2.3 Investor Equity

Mr. Ball is not seeking an investment from a third party at this time.

2.4 Management Equity

Mr. Ball owns 100% of Marshall Personal Loan Services.

2.5 Exit Strategy

If the business is very successful, Mr. Ball may seek to sell the business to a third party for a significant earnings multiple. Most likely, the Company will hire a qualified business broker to sell the business on behalf of Marshall Personal Loan Services. Based on historical numbers, the business could fetch a sales premium of up to 5 to 7 times earnings.

3.0 PERSONAL LOAN SERVICES

Short term personal loans are made for people that need fast access to capital. These loans are secured by the equity of the individual's income and credit quality. The Company allows borrowers that have employment for three months at the same location and have an active checking to obtain small two-week credit loans. Marshall Personal Loan Services will use the automated clearing house system (or ACH) to ensure that on the date that the loan is due, the business can immediately withdraw funds on the date that the customer is paid. This will ensure that the client does not default on their loan. Customers will not be able to rollover their loans as this creates a tremendous amount of risk for Marshall Personal Loan Services. By not allowing customers to roll over on loans, the Company will promote responsible usage of emergency credit lines for customers as it relates to their income and credit score. Fees for a two-week loan will equal 15% to 25% of the borrowed amount. The minimum loan will be $500 and the maximum loan offered by the business will be $1,500.

Management has developed the following requirements for a loan from Marshall Personal Loan Services:

- Direct Deposit via an active bank accounting
- A job that they have held for at least three months
- Ownership of a vehicle that has no other liens
- Income of at least $1,000 per month

The Company will require the following documentation for a loan:

- Voided Check
- Recent Bank Statement
- Pay Stub
- State Issued Identification

4.0 STRATEGIC AND MARKET ANALYSIS

4.1 Economic Outlook

This section of the analysis will detail the economic climate, the personal loan industry, the customer profile, and the competition that the business will face as it progresses through its business operations.

Current economic market conditions in the United States are moderate. The meltdown of the sub prime mortgage market coupled with increasing gas prices has led many people to believe that the US is on the cusp of a double dip economic recession. This slowdown in the economy has also greatly impacted real estate sales, which has halted to historical lows.

There are several pieces of legislation that are being considered on both the federal and state level that will sufficiently limit the interest rates charged to low-income borrowers for emergency credit services. The payday, title, and personal loan industry generates interest rates of 100% to 600% (on an annual rate) to its customers. These businesses are able to charge these rates of interest as many states do not have upper limits on the interest rates charged on small loans.

4.2 Industry Analysis

Within the United States there are over 60,000 businesses that operate as non-depository credit institutions. Among these businesses, an aggregates receipt over each of the last five years has been in excess of $229 billion dollars of interest revenue. These businesses employ over 500,000 people and provide gross annual payrolls in excess of $22 billion dollars. Approximately 5,000 of these businesses operate within a similar capacity as that of the Company.

The industry has recently undergone a revolution with the advent of the Internet. With instant access to customer verification, people can seamlessly borrow capital from banks that conduct business on the Internet. This aspect of the industry is expected to grow at a rate of 10% per year for the next five years. The Company intends to capitalize on this trend.

4.3 Customer Profile
The Company will cater to a large audience of lower-income people who have limited access to banking services and/or credit. The primary demographics of the people who the Company is targeting include, but are not limited to the following:

- Earns less than $30,000 per year

- Speaks English or Spanish

- Has a bank account (for personal loans)

- Is employed at the same business for the last six months (for loans)

Marshall Personal Loan Services is quickly developing its credit manual to develop guidelines regarding its personal loan business. The business has already employed several techniques to ensure that credit default is kept to an absolute minimum as it relates to personal loans that are granted. In regards to the Company's lending services, the business will require authorization to debit the customer's account on the day that the loan becomes due on a biweekly basis or other basis which has been established with the customer prior to them engaging the business for a personal loan.

4.4 Competition
As stated above, there are approximately 5,000 companies within the United States that provide short term loans (in a high interest rate capacity). Within the Company's targeted market of the New York metropolitan area, there are approximately 500 lenders that provide the loans that were discussed in the third section of the business plan. Management intends to differentiate Marshall Personal Loan Services from other competitors within the industry by providing its short term capital at annual percentage rates that are significantly lower than competitors. Additionally, the business intends to operate in an online capacity so that the business can provide its capital to anyone within the United States that meets the Company's lending qualifications.

5.0 MARKETING PLAN

Marshall Personal Loan Services intends to maintain an extensive marketing campaign that will ensure maximum visibility for the business in its targeted market. Below is an overview of the marketing strategies and objectives of the Company.

5.1 Marketing Objectives
- Develop an online presence by developing a website and placing the Company's name and contact information with online directories.

- Implement a local campaign with the Company's targeted market via the use of flyers, local newspaper advertisements, and word of mouth advertising.

- Establish relationships with check cashing locations that do not offer personal loan services within the targeted market.

5.2 Marketing Strategies

Mr. Ball intends on using a number of marketing strategies that will allow Marshall Personal Loan Services to easily target men and women among the demographics specified in the previous section of the business plan. Marshall Personal Loan Services will use print marketing, radio advertising, billboards, and listings in community circulars in order to drive traffic to the Company's retail location.

Marshall Personal Loan Services will also use an online based marketing strategy. This website will showcase the services offered by Marshall Personal Loan Services, the costs associated with acquiring a personal loan from the business, the Company's location, appropriate documentation disclosures, and other pertinent information. The Company will also integrate ecommerce functionality into the website so that the business can provide loans to any individual within the United States.

The business will also maintain close connections with traditional lending institutions that will refer their customers to Marshall Personal Loan Services for loans that do not meet their criteria as it pertains to acquiring short terms loans on an ongoing or emergency basis. By developing these relationships with traditional loan sources, Marshall Personal Loan Services will be able to generate a substantial amount of additional income through referral leads among small banks and nationally recognized banks that operate within the Company's target market. Mr. Ball will aggressively pursue these relationships from the onset of business operations.

5.3 Pricing

For each personal loan made by the business, Management intends to charge an average interest rate equal to 150% to 200% (on a per annum basis). This translates into approximately $10 of interest every two weeks on a $100 short term personal loan.

6.0 ORGANIZATIONAL PLAN AND PERSONNEL SUMMARY

6.1 Corporate Organization

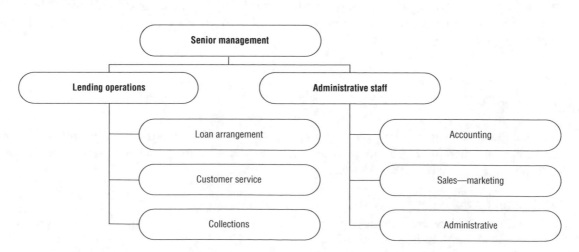

6.2 Organizational Budget

Personnel plan—yearly

Year	1	2	3
Owner	$ 40,000	$ 41,200	$ 42,436
Retail location manager	$ 35,000	$ 36,050	$ 37,132
Customer service employees	$ 96,000	$ 98,880	$101,846
Bookkeeper (P/T)	$ 12,500	$ 12,875	$ 13,261
Administrative	$ 44,000	$ 45,320	$ 46,680
Total	**$227,500**	**$234,325**	**$241,355**

Numbers of personnel

Year	1	2	3
Owner	1	1	1
Retail location manager	1	1	1
Customer service employees	4	4	4
Bookkeeper (P/T)	1	1	1
Administrative	2	2	2
Totals	**9**	**9**	**9**

Personnel expense breakdown

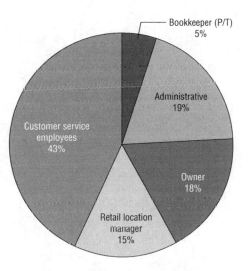

7.0 FINANCIAL PLAN

7.1 Underlying Assumptions

The Company has based its proforma financial statements on the following:

- Marshall Personal Loan Services will have an annual revenue growth rate of 13% per year.

- The Owner will acquire $125,000 of debt funds to develop the business.

- The loan will have a 10 year term with a 9% interest rate.

7.2 Sensitivity Analysis

The business' revenues are not sensitive to the overall change in the general economic market. Personal loans are primarily used as emergency lending vehicles as it relates to income and credit quality among the Company's targeted market, and as such, the people obtaining these loans are in a serious financial situation. As such, as the economy recesses the business may actually notice a marked increase in the lending portfolios generated by the Company. However, severe turns in economic stability may increase the defaults experienced by the business as it relates to providing personal loans to the general public. Management would compensate this higher risk by increasing the fees associated with each personal loan.

7.3 Source of Funds

Financing

Equity contributions	
Management investment	$ 25,000.00
Total equity financing	**$ 25,000.00**
Banks and lenders	
Banks and lenders	$ 125,000.00
Total debt financing	**$ 125,000.00**
Total financing	**$ 150,000.00**

7.4 General Assumptions

General assumptions

Year	1	2	3
Short term interest rate	9.5%	9.5%	9.5%
Long term interest rate	10.0%	10.0%	10.0%
Federal tax rate	33.0%	33.0%	33.0%
State tax rate	5.0%	5.0%	5.0%
Personnel taxes	15.0%	15.0%	15.0%

7.5 Profit and Loss Statements

Proforma profit and loss (yearly)

Year	1	2	3
Sales	**$555,000**	**$643,800**	**$733,932**
Cost of goods sold	$ 77,700	$ 90,132	$102,750
Gross margin	86.00%	86.00%	86.00%
Operating income	**$477,300**	**$553,668**	**$631,182**
Expenses			
Payroll	$227,500	$234,325	$241,355
General and administrative	$ 30,000	$ 31,200	$ 32,448
Marketing expenses	$ 22,200	$ 25,752	$ 29,357
Professional fees and licensure	$ 10,000	$ 10,300	$ 10,609
Insurance costs	$ 15,000	$ 15,750	$ 16,538
Travel and vehicle costs	$ 9,000	$ 9,900	$ 10,890
Rent and utilities	$ 25,000	$ 26,250	$ 27,563
Miscellaneous costs	$ 5,550	$ 6,438	$ 7,339
Payroll taxes	$ 34,125	$ 35,149	$ 36,203
Total operating costs	**$378,375**	**$395,064**	**$412,302**
EBITDA	**$ 98,925**	**$158,604**	**$218,880**
Federal income tax	$ 32,645	$ 48,985	$ 69,150
State income tax	$ 4,946	$ 7,422	$ 10,477
Interest expense	$ 10,922	$ 10,164	$ 9,335
Depreciation expenses	$ 6,964	$ 6,964	$ 6,964
Net profit	**$ 43,447**	**$ 85,069**	**$122,953**
Profit margin	**7.83%**	**13.21%**	**16.75%**

Sales, operating costs, and profit forecast

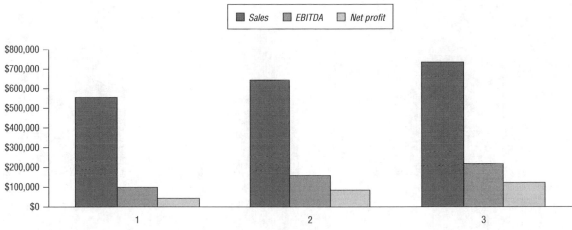

7.6 Cash Flow Analysis

Proforma cash flow analysis—yearly

Year	1	2	3
Cash from operations	$ 50,411	$ 92,033	$129,918
Cash from receivables	$ 0	$ 0	$ 0
Operating cash inflow	**$ 50,411**	**$ 92,033**	**$129,918**
Other cash inflows			
Equity investment	$ 25,000	$ 0	$ 0
Increased borrowings	$125,000	$ 0	$ 0
Sales of business assets	$ 0	$ 0	$ 0
A/P increases	$ 37,902	$ 43,587	$ 50,125
Total other cash inflows	**$187,902**	**$ 43,587**	**$ 50,125**
Total cash inflow	**$238,313**	**$135,620**	**$180,043**
Cash outflows			
Repayment of principal	$ 8,079	$ 8,837	$ 9,666
A/P decreases	$ 24,897	$ 29,876	$ 35,852
A/R increases	$ 0	$ 0	$ 0
Asset purchases	$ 97,500	$ 23,008	$ 32,479
Dividends	$ 35,288	$ 64,423	$ 90,942
Total cash outflows	**$165,764**	**$126,145**	**$168,940**
Net cash flow	**$ 72,549**	**$ 9,475**	**$ 11,103**
Cash balance	**$ 72,549**	**$ 82,025**	**$ 93,128**

Proforma cash flow (yearly)

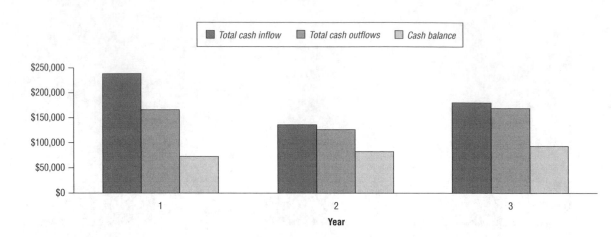

7.7 Balance Sheet

Proforma balance sheet—yearly

Year	1	2	3
Assets			
Cash	$ 72,549	$ 82,025	$ 93,128
Amortized development/expansion costs	$ 17,500	$ 19,801	$ 23,049
Personal loan portfolio	$ 60,000	$ 76,106	$ 98,841
FF&E	$ 20,000	$ 24,602	$ 31,098
Accumulated depreciation	($ 6,964)	($ 13,929)	($ 20,893)
Total assets	**$163,085**	**$188,604**	**$225,223**
Liabilities and equity			
Accounts payable	$ 13,005	$ 26,716	$ 40,990
Long term liabilities	$116,921	$108,084	$ 99,247
Other liabilities	$ 0	$ 0	$ 0
Total liabilities	**$129,926**	**$134,800**	**$140,236**
Net worth	**$ 33,159**	**$ 53,805**	**$ 84,987**
Total liabilities and equity	**$163,085**	**$188,604**	**$225,223**

Proforma balance sheet

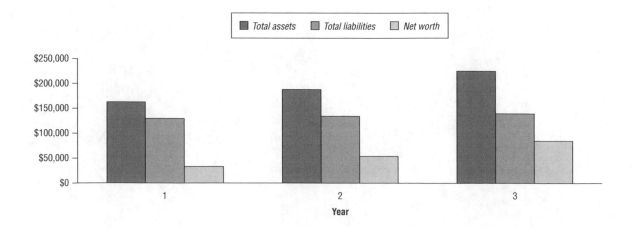

7.8 Breakeven Analysis

Monthly break even analysis

Year	1	2	3
Monthly revenue	$ 36,664	$ 38,281	$ 39,952
Yearly revenue	$439,971	$459,376	$479,420

Break even analysis

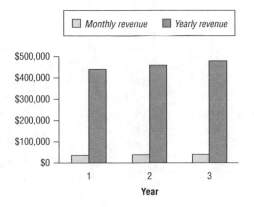

7.9 Business Ratios

Business ratios—yearly

Year	1	2	3
Sales			
Sales growth	0.00%	16.00%	14.00%
Gross margin	86.00%	86.00%	86.00%
Financials			
Profit margin	7.83%	13.21%	16.75%
Assets to liabilities	1.26	1.40	1.61
Equity to liabilities	0.26	0.40	0.61
Assets to equity	4.92	3.51	2.65
Liquidity			
Acid test	0.56	0.61	0.66
Cash to assets	0.44	0.43	0.41

7.10 Three Year Profit and Loss Statement

Profit and loss statement (first year)

Months	1	2	3	4	5	6	7
Sales	$39,375	$40,625	$41,875	$43,125	$44,375	$45,625	$46,875
Cost of goods sold	$ 5,513	$ 5,688	$ 5,863	$ 6,038	$ 6,213	$ 6,388	$ 6,563
Gross margin	86.0%	86.0%	86.0%	86.0%	86.0%	86.0%	86.0%
Operating income	**$33,863**	**$34,938**	**$36,013**	**$37,088**	**$38,163**	**$39,238**	**$40,313**
Expenses							
Payroll	$18,958	$18,958	$18,958	$18,958	$18,958	$18,958	$18,958
General and administrative	$ 2,500	$ 2,500	$ 2,500	$ 2,500	$ 2,500	$ 2,500	$ 2,500
Marketing expenses	$ 1,850	$ 1,850	$ 1,850	$ 1,850	$ 1,850	$ 1,850	$ 1,850
Professional fees and licensure	$ 833	$ 833	$ 833	$ 833	$ 833	$ 833	$ 833
Insurance costs	$ 1,250	$ 1,250	$ 1,250	$ 1,250	$ 1,250	$ 1,250	$ 1,250
Travel and vehicle costs	$ 750	$ 750	$ 750	$ 750	$ 750	$ 750	$ 750
Rent and utilities	$ 2,083	$ 2,083	$ 2,083	$ 2,083	$ 2,083	$ 2,083	$ 2,083
Miscellaneous costs	$ 463	$ 463	$ 463	$ 463	$ 463	$ 463	$ 463
Payroll taxes	$ 2,844	$ 2,844	$ 2,844	$ 2,844	$ 2,844	$ 2,844	$ 2,844
Total operating costs	**$31,531**	**$31,531**	**$31,531**	**$31,531**	**$31,531**	**$31,531**	**$31,531**
EBITDA	**$ 2,331**	**$ 3,406**	**$ 4,481**	**$ 5,556**	**$ 6,631**	**$ 7,706**	**$ 8,781**
Federal income tax	$ 2,316	$ 2,390	$ 2,463	$ 2,537	$ 2,610	$ 2,684	$ 2,757
State income tax	$ 351	$ 362	$ 373	$ 384	$ 395	$ 407	$ 418
Interest expense	$ 938	$ 933	$ 928	$ 923	$ 918	$ 913	$ 908
Depreciation expense	$ 580	$ 580	$ 580	$ 580	$ 580	$ 580	$ 580
Net profit	**−$ 1,854**	**−$ 858**	**$ 137**	**$ 1,132**	**$ 2,127**	**$ 3,123**	**$ 4,118**

Profit and loss statement (first year cont.)

Month	8	9	10	11	12	1
Sales	$48,125	$49,375	$50,625	$51,875	$53,125	$555,000
Cost of goods sold	$ 6,738	$ 6,913	$ 7,088	$ 7,263	$ 7,438	$ 77,700
Gross margin	86.0%	86.0%	86.0%	86.0%	86.0%	86.0%
Operating income	**$41,388**	**$42,463**	**$43,538**	**$44,613**	**$45,688**	**$477,300**
Expenses						
Payroll	$18,958	$18,958	$18,958	$18,958	$18,958	$227,500
General and administrative	$ 2,500	$ 2,500	$ 2,500	$ 2,500	$ 2,500	$ 30,000
Marketing expenses	$ 1,850	$ 1,850	$ 1,850	$ 1,850	$ 1,850	$ 22,200
Professional fees and licensure	$ 833	$ 833	$ 833	$ 833	$ 833	$ 10,000
Insurance costs	$ 1,250	$ 1,250	$ 1,250	$ 1,250	$ 1,250	$ 15,000
Travel and vehicle costs	$ 750	$ 750	$ 750	$ 750	$ 750	$ 9,000
Rent and utilities	$ 2,083	$ 2,083	$ 2,083	$ 2,083	$ 2,083	$ 25,000
Miscellaneous costs	$ 463	$ 463	$ 463	$ 463	$ 463	$ 5,550
Payroll taxes	$ 2,844	$ 2,844	$ 2,844	$ 2,844	$ 2,844	$ 34,125
Total operating costs	**$31,531**	**$31,531**	**$31,531**	**$31,531**	**$31,531**	**$378,375**
EBITDA	**$ 9,856**	**$10,931**	**$12,006**	**$13,081**	**$14,156**	**$ 98,925**
Federal income tax	$ 2,831	$ 2,904	$ 2,978	$ 3,051	$ 3,125	$ 32,645
State income tax	$ 429	$ 440	$ 451	$ 462	$ 473	$ 4,946
Interest expense	$ 903	$ 898	$ 893	$ 887	$ 882	$ 10,922
Depreciation expense	$ 580	$ 580	$ 580	$ 580	$ 580	$ 6,964
Net profit	**$ 5,113**	**$ 6,109**	**$ 7,104**	**$ 8,100**	**$ 9,095**	**$ 43,447**

Profit and loss statement (second year)

Quarter	Q1	2 Q2	Q3	Q4	2
Sales	**$128,760**	**$160,950**	**$173,826**	**$180,264**	**$643,800**
Cost of goods sold	$ 18,026	$ 22,533	$ 24,336	$ 25,237	$ 90,132
Gross margin	86.0%	86.0%	86.0%	86.0%	86.0%
Operating income	**$110,734**	**$138,417**	**$149,490**	**$155,027**	**$553,668**
Expenses					
Payroll	$ 46,865	$ 58,581	$ 63,268	$ 65,611	$234,325
General and administrative	$ 6,240	$ 7,800	$ 8,424	$ 8,736	$ 31,200
Marketing expenses	$ 5,150	$ 6,438	$ 6,953	$ 7,211	$ 25,752
Professional fees and licensure	$ 2,060	$ 2,575	$ 2,781	$ 2,884	$ 10,300
Insurance costs	$ 3,150	$ 3,938	$ 4,253	$ 4,410	$ 15,750
Travel and vehicle costs	$ 1,980	$ 2,475	$ 2,673	$ 2,772	$ 9,900
Rent and utilities	$ 5,250	$ 6,563	$ 7,088	$ 7,350	$ 26,250
Miscellaneous costs	$ 1,288	$ 1,610	$ 1,738	$ 1,803	$ 6,438
Payroll taxes	$ 7,030	$ 8,787	$ 9,490	$ 9,842	$ 35,149
Total operating costs	**$ 79,013**	**$ 98,766**	**$106,667**	**$110,618**	**$395,064**
EBITDA	**$ 31,721**	**$ 39,651**	**$ 42,823**	**$ 44,409**	**$158,604**
Federal income tax	$ 9,797	$ 12,246	$ 13,226	$ 13,716	$ 48,985
State income tax	$ 1,484	$ 1,856	$ 2,004	$ 2,078	$ 7,422
Interest expense	$ 2,615	$ 2,566	$ 2,517	$ 2,466	$ 10,164
Depreciation expense	$ 1,741	$ 1,741	$ 1,741	$ 1,741	$ 6,964
Net profit	**$ 16,084**	**$ 21,242**	**$ 23,335**	**$ 24,408**	**$ 85,069**

Profit and loss statement (third year)

Quarter	Q1	3 Q2	Q3	Q4	3
Sales	**$146,786**	**$183,483**	**$198,162**	**$205,501**	**$733,932**
Cost of goods sold	$ 20,550	$ 25,688	$ 27,743	$ 28,770	$102,750
Gross margin	86.0%	86.0%	86.0%	86.0%	86.0%
Operating income	**$126,236**	**$157,795**	**$170,419**	**$176,731**	**$631,182**
Expenses					
Payroll	$ 48,271	$ 60,339	$ 65,166	$ 67,579	$241,355
General and administrative	$ 6,490	$ 8,112	$ 8,761	$ 9,085	$ 32,448
Marketing expenses	$ 5,871	$ 7,339	$ 7,926	$ 8,220	$ 29,357
Professional fees and licensure	$ 2,122	$ 2,652	$ 2,864	$ 2,971	$ 10,609
Insurance costs	$ 3,308	$ 4,134	$ 4,465	$ 4,631	$ 16,538
Travel and vehicle costs	$ 2,178	$ 2,723	$ 2,940	$ 3,049	$ 10,890
Rent and utilities	$ 5,513	$ 6,891	$ 7,442	$ 7,718	$ 27,563
Miscellaneous costs	$ 1,468	$ 1,835	$ 1,982	$ 2,055	$ 7,339
Payroll taxes	$ 7,241	$ 9,051	$ 9,775	$ 10,137	$ 36,203
Total operating costs	**$ 82,460**	**$103,075**	**$111,321**	**$115,444**	**$412,302**
EBITDA	**$ 43,776**	**$ 54,720**	**$ 59,098**	**$ 61,286**	**$218,880**
Federal income tax	$ 13,830	$ 17,287	$ 18,670	$ 19,362	$ 69,150
State income tax	$ 2,095	$ 2,619	$ 2,829	$ 2,934	$ 10,477
Interest expense	$ 2,414	$ 2,361	$ 2,307	$ 2,252	$ 9,335
Depreciation expense	$ 1,741	$ 1,741	$ 1,741	$ 1,741	$ 6,964
Net profit	**$ 23,695**	**$ 30,711**	**$ 33,550**	**$ 34,998**	**$122,953**

7.11 Three Year Cash Flow Analysis

Cash flow analysis (first year)

Month	1	2	3	4	5	6	7
Cash from operations	−$ 1,273	−$ 278	$ 717	$ 1,712	$ 2,708	$ 3,703	$ 4,698
Cash from receivables	$ 0	$ 0	$ 0	$ 0	$ 0	$ 0	$ 0
Operating cash inflow	**−$ 1,273**	**−$ 278**	**$ 717**	**$ 1,712**	**$ 2,708**	**$ 3,703**	**$ 4,698**
Other cash inflows							
Equity investment	$ 25,000	$ 0	$ 0	$ 0	$ 0	$ 0	$ 0
Increased borrowings	$125,000	$ 0	$ 0	$ 0	$ 0	$ 0	$ 0
Sales of business assets	$ 0	$ 0	$ 0	$ 0	$ 0	$ 0	$ 0
A/P increases	$ 3,159	$ 3,159	$ 3,159	$ 3,159	$ 3,159	$ 3,159	$ 3,159
Total other cash inflows	**$153,159**	**$ 3,159**	**$ 3,159**	**$ 3,159**	**$ 3,159**	**$ 3,159**	**$ 3,159**
Total cash inflow	**$151,885**	**$ 2,880**	**$ 3,876**	**$ 4,871**	**$ 5,866**	**$ 6,862**	**$ 7,857**
Cash outflows							
Repayment of principal	$ 646	$ 651	$ 656	$ 661	$ 666	$ 671	$ 676
A/P decreases	$ 2,075	$ 2,075	$ 2,075	$ 2,075	$ 2,075	$ 2,075	$ 2,075
A/R increases	$ 0	$ 0	$ 0	$ 0	$ 0	$ 0	$ 0
Asset purchases	$ 97,500	$ 0	$ 0	$ 0	$ 0	$ 0	$ 0
Dividends	$ 0	$ 0	$ 0	$ 0	$ 0	$ 0	$ 0
Total cash outflows	**$100,221**	**$ 2,726**	**$ 2,730**	**$ 2,735**	**$ 2,740**	**$ 2,745**	**$ 2,750**
Net cash flow	**$ 51,665**	**$ 155**	**$ 1,145**	**$ 2,136**	**$ 3,126**	**$ 4,116**	**$ 5,107**
Cash balance	**$ 51,665**	**$51,820**	**$52,965**	**$55,100**	**$58,226**	**$62,343**	**$67,449**

Cash flow analysis (first year cont.)

Month	8	9	10	11	12	1
Cash from operations	$ 5,694	$ 6,689	$ 7,685	$ 8,680	$ 9,676	$ 50,411
Cash from receivables	$ 0	$ 0	$ 0	$ 0	$ 0	$ 0
Operating cash inflow	**$ 5,694**	**$ 6,689**	**$ 7,685**	**$ 8,680**	**$ 9,676**	**$ 50,411**
Other cash inflows						
Equity investment	$ 0	$ 0	$ 0	$ 0	$ 0	$ 25,000
Increased borrowings	$ 0	$ 0	$ 0	$ 0	$ 0	$125,000
Sales of business assets	$ 0	$ 0	$ 0	$ 0	$ 0	$ 0
A/P increases	$ 3,159	$ 3,159	$ 3,159	$ 3,159	$ 3,159	$ 37,902
Total other cash inflows	**$ 3,159**	**$ 3,159**	**$ 3,159**	**$ 3,159**	**$ 3,159**	**$187,902**
Total cash inflow	**$ 8,852**	**$ 9,848**	**$10,843**	**$11,839**	**$12,834**	**$238,313**
Cash outflows						
Repayment of principal	$ 681	$ 686	$ 691	$ 696	$ 701	$ 8,079
A/P decreases	$ 2,075	$ 2,075	$ 2,075	$ 2,075	$ 2,075	$ 24,897
A/R increases	$ 0	$ 0	$ 0	$ 0	$ 0	$ 0
Asset purchases	$ 0	$ 0	$ 0	$ 0	$ 0	$ 97,500
Dividends	$ 0	$ 0	$ 0	$ 0	$35,288	$ 35,288
Total cash outflows	**$ 2,755**	**$ 2,760**	**$ 2,766**	**$ 2,771**	**$38,064**	**$165,764**
Net cash flow	**$ 6,097**	**$ 7,087**	**$ 8,078**	**$ 9,068**	**−$25,230**	**$ 72,549**
Cash balance	**$73,546**	**$80,633**	**$88,711**	**$97,779**	**$72,549**	**$ 72,549**

Cash flow analysis (second year)

Quarter	Q1	2 Q2	Q3	Q4	2
Cash from operations	$18,407	$23,008	$24,849	$25,769	$ 92,033
Cash from receivables	$ 0	$ 0	$ 0	$ 0	$ 0
Operating cash inflow	**$18,407**	**$23,008**	**$24,849**	**$25,769**	**$ 92,033**
Other cash inflows					
Equity investment	$ 0	$ 0	$ 0	$ 0	$ 0
Increased borrowings	$ 0	$ 0	$ 0	$ 0	$ 0
Sales of business assets	$ 0	$ 0	$ 0	$ 0	$ 0
A/P increases	$ 8,717	$10,897	$11,769	$12,204	$ 43,587
Total other cash inflows	**$ 8,717**	**$10,897**	**$11,769**	**$12,204**	**$ 43,587**
Total cash inflow	**$27,124**	**$33,905**	**$36,617**	**$37,974**	**$135,620**
Cash outflows					
Repayment of principal	$ 2,136	$ 2,184	$ 2,233	$ 2,284	$ 8,837
A/P decreases	$ 5,975	$ 7,469	$ 8,067	$ 8,365	$ 29,876
A/R increases	$ 0	$ 0	$ 0	$ 0	$ 0
Asset purchases	$ 4,602	$ 5,752	$ 6,212	$ 6,442	$ 23,008
Dividends	$12,885	$16,106	$17,394	$18,038	$ 64,423
Total cash outflows	**$25,597**	**$31,511**	**$33,907**	**$35,130**	**$126,145**
Net cash flow	**$ 1,527**	**$ 2,394**	**$ 2,711**	**$ 2,843**	**$ 9,475**
Cash balance	**$74,076**	**$76,470**	**$79,181**	**$82,025**	**$ 82,025**

Cash flow analysis (third year)

Quarter	Q1	3 Q2	Q3	Q4	3
Cash from operations	$25,984	$32,479	$35,078	$36,377	$129,918
Cash from receivables	$ 0	$ 0	$ 0	$ 0	$ 0
Operating cash inflow	**$25,984**	**$32,479**	**$35,078**	**$36,377**	**$129,918**
Other cash inflows					
Equity investment	$ 0	$ 0	$ 0	$ 0	$ 0
Increased borrowings	$ 0	$ 0	$ 0	$ 0	$ 0
Sales of business assets	$ 0	$ 0	$ 0	$ 0	$ 0
A/P increases	$10,025	$12,531	$13,534	$14,035	$ 50,125
Total other cash inflows	**$10,025**	**$12,531**	**$13,534**	**$14,035**	**$ 50,125**
Total cash inflow	**$36,009**	**$45,011**	**$40,612**	**$50,412**	**$180,043**
Cash outflows					
Repayment of principal	$ 2,336	$ 2,389	$ 2,443	$ 2,498	$ 9,666
A/P decreases	$ 7,170	$ 8,963	$ 9,680	$10,038	$ 35,852
A/R increases	$ 0	$ 0	$ 0	$ 0	$ 0
Asset purchases	$ 6,496	$ 8,120	$ 8,769	$ 9,094	$ 32,479
Dividends	$18,188	$22,736	$24,554	$25,464	$ 90,942
Total cash outflows	**$34,191**	**$42,207**	**$45,447**	**$47,095**	**$168,940**
Net cash flow	**$ 1,818**	**$ 2,804**	**$ 3,165**	**$ 3,317**	**$ 11,103**
Cash balance	**$83,843**	**$86,646**	**$89,811**	**$93,128**	**$ 93,128**

Pressure Washing Business

ABC PressureClean Inc.

47 Rogers Rd.
Indianapolis, Indiana 46208

Paul Greenland

ABC PressureClean Inc. is a mobile pressure washing business in Indianapolis, Indiana, serving both residential and commercial clients.

EXECUTIVE SUMMARY

It's no accident that Sam Sheldon's friends gave him the nickname "Mr. Clean." After starting out as a janitor for Central School District, he was soon promoted to the position of floor finisher. Between these two jobs, Sheldon has seen it all. For the last eight years he has cleaned up just about every kind of mess that elementary, middle school, and high school students can make. Along the way he has learned many "tricks of the trade," and has received formal training in the use of various cleaning agents and equipment.

Two years ago Sheldon invested in a commercial-grade power washer and began doing side jobs for friends and family, cleaning the exteriors of their homes, along with driveways, decks, gutters, awnings, and more. Although residential jobs are more plentiful, he quickly learned that commercial assignments are more lucrative. This came into focus when the owner of a local trucking company, which made deliveries to the school where Sheldon worked, hired him to clean his truck fleet after hours.

Facing a budget deficit and reduced reimbursement from the state, Central School District is streamlining its workforce. Although he did not lose his job, Sheldon has been moved to a part-time position. This situation has presented him with an opportunity to formally establish a part-time power washing business that has full-time potential. Conditions are especially favorable because he already has invested in most of the equipment he will need in a business that already requires a low entry-level investment.

MARKET ANALYSIS

Although ABC PressureClean Inc. will serve both commercial and residential customers, the company will concentrate its marketing efforts on the commercial sector in order to secure more lucrative, recurring contracts.

Commercial Markets

- Arenas
- Banks

- Car Dealers
- Contractors
- Farmers/Ranchers
- Fleet Vehicle Departments
- Grocery Stores
- Manufacturing Companies
- Marinas
- Municipal Governments
- Passenger Transportation Companies
- Property Management Companies
- Residential
- Restaurants
- School Districts
- Trucking Companies

A list of specific prospects (available upon request) has been developed, and will be used for direct marketing efforts. However, according to research from DemographicsNow, in the spring of 2010 prospects in our local market were categorized as follows:

- Construction (1,760 establishments)
- Retail Trade (6,388 establishments)
- Auto Dealers & Gas Stations (812 establishments)
- Convenience Stores (94 establishments)
- Food Markets (180 establishments)
- Restaurants (1,271 establishments)
- Auto Repair/Services (820 establishments)
- Entertainment & Recreation Services (464 establishments)
- Hotels & Lodging (213 establishments)
- Primary & Secondary Education (359 establishments)

Residential Market

ABC PressureClean will focus its residential marketing efforts on households with income of $75,000 or more. In 2010, 36,635 households had income between $75,000 and $99,999. In addition, 30,637 households had income between $100,000 and $149,999. Finally, 16,227 households had income of $150,000 or more. Each of these segments was projected to achieve meaningful growth through 2015, increasing 11.8 percent, 10.4 percent, and 5.4 percent, respectively.

PERSONNEL

After starting out as a janitor for Central School District, Sam Sheldon was promoted to the position of floor finisher within two years. Between these two jobs he has seen it all. For the last eight years Sheldon has cleaned up just about every kind of mess that elementary, middle school, and high school students can make. Along the way he has learned many "tricks of the trade," and has received formal training in the use of various cleaning agents and equipment.

In addition to the hands-on training that Sheldon has received on the job, he also has pursued small business management courses through Indianapolis Community College and the Small Business Administration. By doing this he has acquired knowledge and skills in the areas of record-keeping, estimation/pricing, sales, marketing, finance, and other areas of business administration.

Professional & Advisory Support

ABC PressureClean has established a business banking account with Indianapolis National Bank, as well as a merchant account for accepting credit card payments. Professional Accounting Services, a local accounting firm, will provide the business with accounting and tax advisory services. Sam Sheldon has utilized a popular online legal document service to cost-effectively prepare the paperwork necessary for incorporating his new business.

GROWTH STRATEGY

ABC PressureClean has developed a formal strategy for growing the business during its first few years.

- *Year One:* Build on Sam Sheldon's existing small base of residential customers, and ensure total satisfaction for the company's first commercial client. Increase commercial business to include 3 to 5 clients by the year's end.

- *Year Two:* Operate ABC PressureClean on a full-time basis. Continue to pursue high-income residential clients, and aggressively market to commercial prospects. Increase the company's base of commercial clients by at least 75 percent (8-10 clients total) by the year's end.

- *Year Three:* Expand the business by adding a full-time employee and a second mobile power washing unit (truck/trailer). Continue aggressive marketing efforts to commercial prospects, with a goal of having at least 15 commercial customers by the year's end.

SERVICES

ABC PressureClean Inc.'s cleaning services for residential and commercial customers will include, but are not limited to, the following:

Residential Services

- Awnings
- Decks
- Driveways
- Fencing
- Gutters
- Houses
- Mobile Homes
- Paint Stripping
- Porches
- Roofs
- Sidewalks

Commercial Services

- Awnings
- Basic Surface Cleanup
- Drive-throughs
- Dumpsters
- Entryways
- Fleet Vehicle Services
- Garage Floors
- Graffiti Removal
- Grease/Dumpster Pads
- Grocery Carts
- Heavy Equipment
- Mortar Tag Removal
- Paint Stripping
- Parking Lots
- Parking Spaces (oil/grease, trouble areas)
- Trash Can Stalls
- Ventilation Hoods

MARKETING & SALES

A marketing plan has been developed for ABC PressureClean that includes the following primary tactics:

Web Site: ABC PressureClean will develop a Web site that lists basic information about the pressure cleaning services that we offer for both residential and commercial customers. In addition, the site will include a simple quote request form, which will relay information directly to Sam Sheldon via his mobile phone.

Seasonal Consumer Direct Marketing: ABC PressureClean will develop an inexpensive, four-color postcard that will be mailed on a seasonal basis (April-September) to households meeting the income requirements mentioned earlier in this plan. Mailing lists will be obtained from Indiana MailStar Inc., a list broker in Indianapolis that also will prepare and send the mailings. Quantities will be based on an average industry response rate of 2 percent and will be adjusted based on Sam Sheldon's capacity/availability.

Business-to-Business Marketing: On a continuous basis, Sam Sheldon will promote ABC PressureClean to area companies in the categories listed in the Market section of this business plan. He will begin by sending an introductory letter to his top prospects. Sheldon will follow up by telephone two weeks after the mailing. Based on the initial response, a second letter may be mailed to all non-respondents 90 days after the first mailing, and Sheldon will once again follow-up by phone two weeks after the second letter mails.

Yellow Pages Advertising: We will run a small ad in the Yellow Pages within several categories, concentrating on commercial prospects:

- Building Cleaning-Exterior
- Steam Cleaning-Automotive
- Steam Cleaning-Industrial
- Power & Pressure Washing

Sam Sheldon will evaluate ABC PressureClean's marketing plan on a semi-annual basis during the first three years of operations, and annually thereafter.

OPERATIONS

Equipment

ABC PressureClean is fortunate to begin operations with much of the equipment needed for initial operations, including:

- Hot & Cold Water Pressure Washer (18 hp V-twin Motor, 3,500 PSI)
- Chemicals & Surface Cleaners
- Spray Guns & Wands
- Hoses & Hose Fittings
- Filters & Nozzles
- Extension Ladder
- 14 x 6 Trailer with Ladder Rack

*Sam Sheldon will purchase an additional pressure sprayer unit to ensure the continuity of operations in the event of an equipment malfunction. In addition, he will purchase additional hoses, spray guns and chemicals. The total cost for this investment will be approximately $1,875.

Pricing

Following are average price ranges for many of the services we offer to both residential and commercial customers. Due to the number of unique variables involved in every project, each job will be quoted individually. ABC PressureClean will always secure payment details up front (before beginning any job). A 5 percent discount will be offered for accounts paid in 15 days or less.

Residential Pricing

Awnings ($2.00/linear foot)

Boats ($5.00-$10.00/linear foot)

Decks ($1.35-$1.85/square foot)

Driveways ($.07-$.20/square foot)

Fencing ($1.00-$1.35 per square foot)

Gutters ($50-$150)

Houses ($150-$250)

Mobile Homes ($50-$100)

Porches ($.07-$.20/square foot)

Roofs (composition roofs $.12-$.35/square foot; cedar shake roofs $.50-$.85/square foot)

Sidewalks ($.07-$.20/square foot)

Commercial Pricing

Awnings ($15-$35/each)

Basic Surface Cleanup ($.05 per square foot)

Drive-throughs ($10-$25/lane)

Dumpsters ($75-$225)

Engines ($50-$100)

Entryways ($10-$25/each)

Garage Floors ($.05-$.20/square foot)

Graffiti Removal ($4.50/square foot)

Grease/Dumpster Pads (variable)

Grocery Carts ($1.25/cart)

Heavy Equipment (variable)

Paint Stripping ($1.00-$2.00/square foot)

Parking Lots ($.05-$.20/square foot)

Parking Spaces ($5.00-$20.00/each)

Trash Can Stalls ($.10-$.25/square foot)

Vehicles (Auto Dealers/Fleet Services) ($2/car)

Ventilation Hoods ($115-$275)

Liability

ABC PressureClean will secure a $1 million insurance policy from Stronghold Insurance Associates. In addition, we have secured a standard customer liability waiver form from a legal document service, which we will utilize for all jobs. Work will not be performed until the customer signs a damage waiver. Our business will comply with all local, state, and federal (EPA) laws, regulations, and standards.

Location

Sam Sheldon initially will operate ABC PressureClean from his home, where he has a separate garage that will be dedicated for business use (e.g., the storage of his trailer, hoses, and other equipment). In addition, a small bedroom will be utilized as an office. Sheldon will secure a home office insurance rider through his insurance agent, Brian Thomas.

Hours of Operation

Because Sam Sheldon continues to work as a custodian for the school district, ABC PressureClean's hours will be variable. He will utilize his existing mobile phone for communication with prospective and existing customers. Jobs will be scheduled based upon his availability.

FINANCIAL ANALYSIS

After speaking with the owners of pressure washing companies in several other (similar) markets, Sam Sheldon has prepared conservative gross revenue projections for the first three years of operations. While operating the business part-time during year one, he anticipates revenues of $15,000. After securing a strong base of recurring commercial customers and taking the business full-time, he anticipates revenues of $50,000 during year two. By adding an additional mobile power washing unit and one full-time employee during year three, and further expanding the company's commercial customer base, Sam Sheldon anticipates that ABC PressureClean's gross revenues will reach $85,000.

Income Statement

Following is a projected three-year income statement for ABC PressureClean. Sam Sheldon anticipates a net loss of $9,765 during year one, mainly due to modest sales and the need for investments in both new equipment and marketing/advertising. However, net income is expected during years two and three.

	2012	2013	2014
Sales	**$15,000**	**$50,000**	**$85,000**
Expenses			
Marketing & advertising	$ 5,000	$ 3,500	$ 5,000
General/administrative	$ 250	$ 250	$ 250
Accounting/legal	$ 1,100	$ 750	$ 1,200
Office supplies	$ 200	$ 200	$ 200
Cleaning supplies	$ 375	$ 500	$ 750
Equipment	$ 1,500	$ 500	$ 8,500
Insurance	$ 650	$ 650	$ 1,300
Payroll	$ 12,000	$ 25,000	$ 50,000
Payroll taxes	$ 1,440	$ 3,000	$ 6,000
Health insurance	$ 0	$ 875	$ 1,750
Postage	$ 150	$ 150	$ 150
Fuel	$ 1,250	$ 1,500	$ 2,500
Maintenance & repairs	$ 300	$ 400	$ 600
Telecommunications	$ 550	$ 550	$ 550
Total expenses	**$24,765**	**$37,825**	**$78,750**
Net income	**($ 9,765)**	**$12,175**	**$ 6,250**

Detailed monthly financial projections (available upon request) also have been prepared with assistance from Tom Kwiatkowski, our accountant at Professional Accounting Services.

Financing

Sam Sheldon will contribute $10,500 of his own money to the business, from personal savings, and is seeking a small business loan of $15,000 for initial operations.

Record Company

Stone Records

500 West 47th St.
New York, New York 10117

BizPlanDB.com

Stone Records is multifaceted entertainment company that is currently developing its musical production capabilities so that the business can promote the music of its signed artists from the onset of operations. Most services related to the mixing, engineering, and recording of music will be kept in-house, which allows the business to have maximum efficiency of its capital.

1.0 EXECUTIVE SUMMARY

The purpose of this business plan is to raise $125,000 for the development of a record production company while showcasing the expected financials and operations over the next three years. Stone Records, Inc. ("the Company") is a New York based corporation that will acquire and develop musical intellectual properties with the intent to distribute albums within its targeted market. The Company was founded by Scott Stone.

1.1 The Services

Stone Records is multifaceted entertainment company that is currently developing its musical production capabilities so that the business can promote the music of its signed artists from the onset of operations. The business produces artist tracks and downloadable media for each production completed by the business. Most services related to the mixing, engineering, and recording of music will be kept in-house, which allows the business to have maximum efficiency of its capital.

To achieve these goals, Stone Records will engage an expansive traditional and online marketing campaign to promote album sales, online sales of downloadable music, and of the artists themselves. The Company will also hold a number of promotional events by renting out large bars/clubs that will concurrently promote Stone Records artists while generating a large stream of revenue for the business.

The third section of the business plan will further describe the services offered by Stone Records.

1.2 Financing

Scott Stone is seeking to raise $125,000 from a bank loan. The interest rate and loan agreement are to be further discussed during negotiation. This business plan assumes that the business will receive a 10 year loan with a 9% fixed interest rate. The financing will be used for the following:

- Development of the Company's office/recording location.

- Financing for the first six months of operation.

- Capital to purchase inventories of produced albums.

Mr. Stone will contribute $25,000 to the venture.

1.3 Mission Statement

It is the mission of Stone Records to bring new and innovative artist's music to the mainstream via a comprehensive partnership of music production companies, promotional firms, and the artists themselves. Management will continually strive to supply the market with music that is in style and popular among its targeted demographics.

1.4 Management Team

The Company was founded by Scott Stone. Mr. Stone has more than 17 years of experience in the recording industry. Through his expertise, he will be able to bring the operations of the business to profitability within its first year of operations.

1.5 Sales Forecasts

Mr. Stone expects a strong rate of growth at the start of operations. Below are the expected financials over the next three years.

Proforma profit and loss (yearly)

Year	1	2	3
Sales	$955,500	$1,194,375	$1,433,250
Operating costs	$389,569	$ 429,002	$ 469,848
EBITDA	$361,181	$ 509,436	$ 656,277
Taxes, interest, and depreciation	$155,135	$ 206,852	$ 262,137
Net profit	$206,046	$ 309,548	$ 401,104

Sales, operating costs, and profit forecast

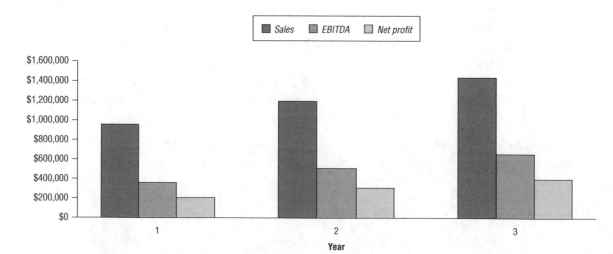

1.6 Expansion Plan

The Founder expects that the business will aggressively expand during the first three years of operation. Mr. Stone intends to implement marketing campaigns that will effectively target individuals, specific to the Company's listening demographics, within the target market.

2.0 COMPANY AND FINANCING SUMMARY

2.1 Registered Name and Corporate Structure

The Company is registered as a corporation in the State of New York.

2.2 Required Funds

At this time, Stone Records requires $125,000 of debt funds. Below is a breakdown of how these funds will be used:

Projected startup costs

Initial lease payments and deposits	$ 15,000
Working capital	$ 45,000
FF&E	$ 20,000
Leasehold improvements	$ 15,000
Security deposits	$ 7,500
Insurance	$ 5,000
Initial album inventories	$ 30,000
Marketing budget	$ 7,500
Miscellaneous and unforeseen costs	$ 5,000
Total startup costs	**$150,000**

Use of funds

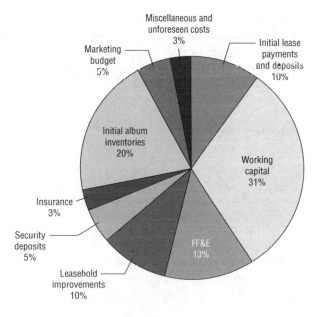

2.3 Investor Equity

Mr. Stone is not seeking an investment from a third party at this time.

2.4 Management Equity

Mr. Stone owns 100% of Stone Records, Inc.

2.5 Exit Strategy

If the business is very successful, Mr. Stone may seek to sell the business to a third party for a significant earnings multiple. Most likely, the Company will hire a qualified business broker to sell the business on behalf of Stone Records. Based on historical numbers, the business could fetch a sales premium of up to 3 to 7 times the previous year's earnings.

3.0 PRODUCTS AND SERVICES

Below is a description of the recording and distribution services offered by Stone Records.

3.1 Record Production and Distribution

The primary function of the business is to find, recruit, record, and promote music from new artists within the United States. The business intends to provide all of the services needed to record, master, and distribute its proprietary music library.

When a new artist or music group is found, the business will actively begin the production of an album and a music video. The most economically viable single(s) on the album will be released for immediate distribution among iTunes, radio stations, You Tube (for videos), and for release among prominent industry executives.

As time progresses and Stone Records' artists become popular, the business may also release DVD compilations featuring music videos, music tracks, and recordings/videos of live performances.

The Company's marketing campaigns will include the use of print, media, and outdoor advertising campaigns to not only promote the artist themselves but the content that they will be introducing to the public at large. Stone Records will also use outdoor street teams as a guerilla marketing tactic. This strategy has been very popular in the music industry and has been met with tremendous success.

4.0 STRATEGIC AND MARKET ANALYSIS

4.1 Economic Outlook

This section of the analysis will detail the economic climate, the recording industry, the customer profile, and the competition that the business will face as it progresses through its business operations.

The economic market condition in the United States is moderate. The meltdown of the sub prime mortgage market coupled with increasing gas prices has led many people to believe that the US is on the cusp of a double dip economic recession. This slowdown in the economy has also greatly impacted real estate sales, which has halted to historical lows. However, Stone Records will operate with great economic stability as people will continue to purchase music despite deleterious changes in the economy.

4.2 Industry Analysis

Sales within the record producing and music publishing industry generate more than $16 billion per year. Additionally, aggregate payrolls for the industry have exceeded $2.2 billion in each of the last five years. There are approximately 38,800 people employed by the industry. The industry has had some pullbacks in recent years with the advent of high speed communications, which has substantially increased the piracy of music on a worldwide basis.

The advent of high speed communications has been both a positive and negative for the industry as record labels can now distribute its products much more quickly, but they are now susceptible to music piracy. However, many companies have developed new technologies that seek to stymie the illegal distribution of recorded music.

4.3 Customer Profile

Stone Records' average end users will be a middle- to upper-middle class man or woman that enjoys several genres of music. Common traits among clients that will purchase the Company's produced albums will include, but are not limited to:

- Annual household income exceeding $50,000

- Enjoys multiple genres of music

- Lives within 50 miles of a major metropolitan area

With each record produced by the business, Management will undertake a substantial analysis of the targeted demographics that will be targeted through the Company's marketing campaigns. Management may also hire a third party marketing firm to assist with this undertaking as the business expands and offers albums among a number of genres.

4.4 Competition

There is a significant amount of competition in the record production industry. This is primarily due to the fact that there are low barriers to entry for this business. Additionally, with the advent of computers, it is now far easier to open and maintain sound recording and record distribution operations. Small studios and labels can now be financed with under $10,000. As such, the market place for music and musical production has become highly fragmented among small and medium sized market agents. Management estimates there are approximately 30,000 independent labels that have their own production and distribution capabilities.

5.0 MARKETING PLAN

Stone Records intends to maintain an extensive marketing campaign that will ensure maximum visibility for the business in its targeted music markets. Below is an overview of the marketing strategies and objectives of Stone Records.

5.1 Marketing Objectives

- Develop an online presence by developing a website and placing the Company's name and contact information with online directories.

- Establish relationships with music distributors within the targeted market.

5.2 Marketing Strategies

The Company intends to use a qualified advertising and marketing firm to help the business reach its intended musician audience. This campaign will include the use of traditional print and media advertising as well as the Internet. Direct advertising campaigns will be of significant importance to the Company as Stone Records is offering our programs a wide variety of musicians and sound artists. The Company's CEO will act as the initial artist and repertoire manager for the initial years of the business.

In regards to promoting artists' materials and music productions, the Company will use many forms of promotion and distribution to generate an audience for its independent genres. The business will produce tracks and music videos simultaneously so that the business can generate as much exposure as possible for each artist.

The true goal of the business is to develop an ongoing distribution with a major record distributor so that the business can shift its distribution capital risk to a third party. While this will decrease the revenues in the business in the long run, Management feels that shifting the capital risk from distribution to a third party outweighs the potential profit benefits in the future. In order to accomplish this, the business must continually develop its track record for the next two to four years.

5.3 Pricing

We anticipate that each album sold will generate approximately $10 of revenue for the business. Among online sales channels (such as through the Apple iTunes store), Management anticipates revenues of $6 per album sold.

6.0 ORGANIZATIONAL PLAN AND PERSONNEL SUMMARY

6.1 Corporate Organization

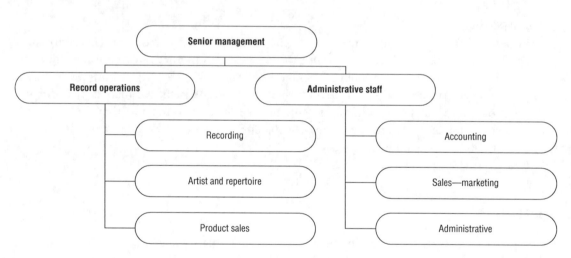

6.2 Organizational Budget

Personnel plan—yearly

Year	1	2	3
Owners	$ 80,000	$ 82,400	$ 84,872
A&R manager	$ 35,000	$ 36,050	$ 37,132
Recording engineer	$ 32,500	$ 33,475	$ 34,479
Studio assistants	$ 37,500	$ 51,500	$ 66,306
Accounting and administrative	$ 44,000	$ 45,320	$ 46,680
Total	**$229,000**	**$248,745**	**$269,469**

Numbers of personnel

Year	1	2	3
Owners	2	2	2
A&R manager	1	1	1
Recording engineer	1	1	1
Studio assistants	3	4	5
Accounting and administrative	2	2	2
Totals	9	10	11

Personnel expense breakdown

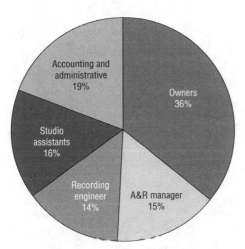

7.0 FINANCIAL PLAN

7.1 Underlying Assumptions

The Company has based its proforma financial statements on the following:

- Stone Records will have an annual revenue growth rate of 18% per year.

- The Owner will acquire $125,000 of debt funds to develop the business.

- The loan will have a 10 year term with a 9% interest rate.

7.2 Sensitivity Analysis

The Company's revenues are sensitive to the overall condition of the economic markets. As stated before, a sudden and dramatic increase in the rate of inflation or real interest rates can have a significant impact on the overall revenue of the business. However, should the economic environment remain stable then Management does not foresee that the Company should have issues regarding top line income. Musical entertainment is demanded in all economic climates, and only severe recessions are expected to decrease the revenues of the business.

7.3 Source of Funds

Financing

Equity contributions

Management investment	$ 25,000.00
Total equity financing	**$ 25,000.00**
Banks and lenders	
Banks and lenders	$ 125,000.00
Total debt financing	**$125,000.00**
Total financing	**$150,000.00**

7.4 General Assumptions

General assumptions

Year	1	2	3
Short term interest rate	9.5%	9.5%	9.5%
Long term interest rate	10.0%	10.0%	10.0%
Federal tax rate	33.0%	33.0%	33.0%
State tax rate	5.0%	5.0%	5.0%
Personnel taxes	15.0%	15.0%	15.0%

7.5 Profit and Loss Statements

Proforma profit and loss (yearly)

Year	1	2	3
Sales	**$955,500**	**$1,194,375**	**$1,433,250**
Cost of goods sold	$204,750	$ 255,938	$ 307,125
Gross margin	78.57%	78.57%	78.57%
Operating income	**$750,750**	**$ 938,438**	**$1,126,125**
Expenses			
Payroll	$229,000	$ 248,745	$ 269,469
General and administrative	$ 25,200	$ 26,208	$ 27,256
Marketing expenses	$ 38,220	$ 47,775	$ 57,330
Professional fees and licensure	$ 7,500	$ 7,725	$ 7,957
Insurance costs	$ 11,987	$ 12,586	$ 13,216
Equipment costs	$ 17,596	$ 19,356	$ 21,291
Rent and utilities	$ 14,250	$ 14,963	$ 15,711
Miscellaneous costs	$ 11,466	$ 14,333	$ 17,199
Payroll taxes	$ 34,350	$ 37,312	$ 40,420
Total operating costs	**$389,569**	**$ 429,002**	**$ 469,848**
EBITDA	**$361,181**	**$ 509,436**	**$ 656,277**
Federal income tax	$119,190	$ 164,760	$ 213,491
State income tax	$ 18,059	$ 24,964	$ 32,347
Interest expense	$ 10,922	$ 10,164	$ 9,335
Depreciation expenses	$ 6,964	$ 6,964	$ 6,964
Net profit	**$206,046**	**$ 309,548**	**$ 401,104**
Profit margin	**21.56%**	**25.92%**	**27.99%**

Sales, operating costs, and profit forecast

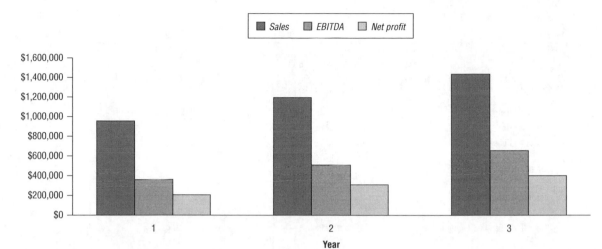

7.6 Cash Flow Analysis

Proforma cash flow analysis—yearly

Year	1	2	3
Cash from operations	$213,010	$316,513	$408,068
Cash from receivables	$ 0	$ 0	$ 0
Operating cash inflow	**$213,010**	**$316,513**	**$408,068**
Other cash inflows			
Equity investment	$ 25,000	$ 0	$ 0
Increased borrowings	$125,000	$ 0	$ 0
Sales of business assets	$ 0	$ 0	$ 0
A/P increases	$ 37,902	$ 43,587	$ 50,125
Total other cash inflows	**$187,902**	**$ 43,587**	**$ 50,125**
Total cash inflow	**$400,912**	**$360,100**	**$458,193**
Cash outflows			
Repayment of principal	$ 8,079	$ 8,837	$ 9,666
A/P decreases	$ 24,897	$ 29,876	$ 35,852
A/R increases	$ 0	$ 0	$ 0
Asset purchases	$ 97,500	$ 70,128	$102,017
Dividends	$149,107	$221,559	$285,648
Total cash outflows	**$279,583**	**$339,401**	**$433,182**
Net cash flow	**$121,329**	**$ 20,699**	**$ 25,011**
Cash balance	**$121,329**	**$142,028**	**$167,039**

Proforma cash flow (yearly)

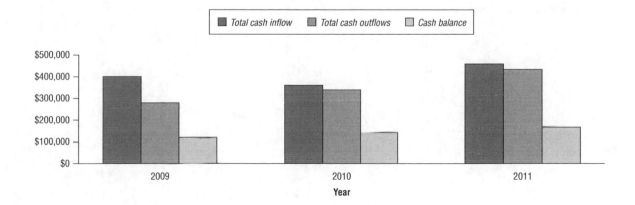

7.7 Balance Sheet

Proforma balance sheet—yearly

Year	1	2	3
Assets			
Cash	$121,329	$142,028	$167,039
Amortized expansion costs	$ 47,500	$ 55,413	$ 65,615
Album inventory	$ 30,000	$ 89,346	$165,859
FF&E	$ 20,000	$ 31,869	$ 47,172
Accumulated depreciation	($ 6,964)	($ 13,929)	($ 20,893)
Total assets	**$211,865**	**$304,728**	**$424,791**
Liabilities and equity			
Accounts payable	$ 13,005	$ 26,716	$ 40,990
Long term liabilities	$116,921	$108,084	$ 99,247
Other liabilities	$ 0	$ 0	$ 0
Total liabilities	**$129,926**	**$134,800**	**$140,236**
Net worth	**$ 81,939**	**$169,928**	**$284,555**
Total liabilities and equity	**$211,865**	**$304,728**	**$424,791**

Proforma balance sheet

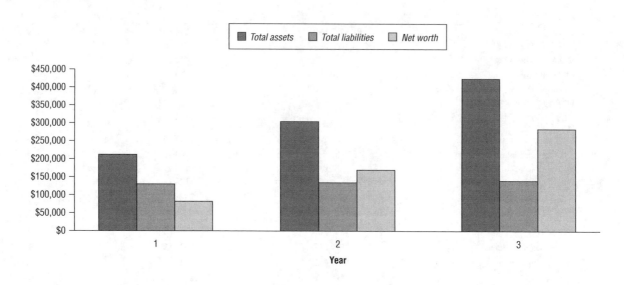

7.8 Breakeven Analysis

Monthly break even analysis

Year	1	2	3
Monthly revenue	$ 41,318	$ 45,500	$ 49,832
Yearly revenue	$ 495,815	$546,002	$597,989

Break even analysis

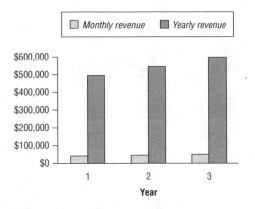

7.9 Business Ratios

Business ratios—yearly

Year	1	2	3
Sales			
Sales growth	0.00%	25.00%	20.00%
Gross margin	78.60%	78.60%	78.60%
Financials			
Profit margin	21.56%	25.92%	27.99%
Assets to liabilities	1.63	2.26	3.03
Equity to liabilities	0.63	1.26	2.03
Assets to equity	2.59	1.79	1.49
Liquidity			
Acid test	0.93	1.05	1.19
Cash to assets	0.57	0.47	0.39

7.10 Three Year Profit and Loss Statement

Profit and loss statement (first year)

Months	1	2	3	4	5	6	7
Sales	**$70,000**	**$71,750**	**$73,500**	**$75,250**	**$77,000**	**$78,750**	**$80,500**
Cost of goods sold	$15,000	$15,375	$15,750	$16,125	$16,500	$16,875	$17,250
Gross margin	78.6%	78.6%	78.6%	78.6%	78.6%	78.6%	78.6%
Operating income	**$55,000**	**$56,375**	**$57,750**	**$59,125**	**$60,500**	**$61,875**	**$63,250**
Expenses							
Payroll	$19,083	$19,083	$19,083	$19,083	$19,083	$19,083	$19,083
General and administrative	$ 2,100	$ 2,100	$ 2,100	$ 2,100	$ 2,100	$ 2,100	$ 2,100
Marketing expenses	$ 3,185	$ 3,185	$ 3,185	$ 3,185	$ 3,185	$ 3,185	$ 3,185
Professional fees and licensure	$ 625	$ 625	$ 625	$ 625	$ 625	$ 625	$ 625
Insurance costs	$ 999	$ 999	$ 999	$ 999	$ 999	$ 999	$ 999
Equipment costs	$ 1,466	$ 1,466	$ 1,466	$ 1,466	$ 1,466	$ 1,466	$ 1,466
Rent and utilities	$ 1,188	$ 1,188	$ 1,188	$ 1,188	$ 1,188	$ 1,188	$ 1,188
Miscellaneous costs	$ 956	$ 956	$ 956	$ 956	$ 956	$ 956	$ 956
Payroll taxes	$ 2,863	$ 2,863	$ 2,863	$ 2,863	$ 2,863	$ 2,863	$ 2,863
Total operating costs	**$32,464**	**$32,464**	**$32,464**	**$32,464**	**$32,464**	**$32,464**	**$32,464**
EBITDA	**$22,536**	**$23,911**	**$25,286**	**$26,661**	**$28,036**	**$29,411**	**$30,786**
Federal income tax	$ 8,732	$ 8,950	$ 9,168	$ 9,387	$ 9,605	$ 9,823	$10,042
State income tax	$ 1,323	$ 1,356	$ 1,389	$ 1,422	$ 1,455	$ 1,488	$ 1,521
Interest expense	$ 938	$ 933	$ 928	$ 923	$ 918	$ 913	$ 908
Depreciation expense	$ 580	$ 580	$ 580	$ 580	$ 580	$ 580	$ 580
Net profit	**$10,963**	**$12,092**	**$13,220**	**$14,349**	**$15,477**	**$16,606**	**$17,735**

Profit and loss statement (first year cont.)

Month	8	9	10	11	12	1
Sales	$82,250	$84,000	$85,750	$87,500	$89,250	$955,500
Cost of goods sold	$17,625	$18,000	$18,375	$18,750	$19,125	$204,750
Gross margin	78.6%	78.6%	78.6%	78.6%	78.6%	78.6%
Operating income	$64,625	$66,000	$67,375	$68,750	$70,125	$750,750
Expenses						
Payroll	$19,083	$19,083	$19,083	$19,083	$19,083	$229,000
General and administrative	$ 2,100	$ 2,100	$ 2,100	$ 2,100	$ 2,100	$ 25,200
Marketing expenses	$ 3,185	$ 3,185	$ 3,185	$ 3,185	$ 3,185	$ 38,220
Professional fees and licensure	$ 625	$ 625	$ 625	$ 625	$ 625	$ 7,500
Insurance costs	$ 999	$ 999	$ 999	$ 999	$ 999	$ 11,987
Equipment costs	$ 1,466	$ 1,466	$ 1,466	$ 1,466	$ 1,466	$ 17,596
Rent and utilities	$ 1,188	$ 1,188	$ 1,188	$ 1,188	$ 1,188	$ 14,250
Miscellaneous costs	$ 956	$ 956	$ 956	$ 956	$ 956	$ 11,466
Payroll taxes	$ 2,863	$ 2,863	$ 2,863	$ 2,863	$ 2,863	$ 34,350
Total operating costs	$32,464	$32,464	$32,464	$32,464	$32,464	$389,569
EBITDA	$32,161	$33,536	$34,911	$36,286	$37,661	$361,181
Federal income tax	$10,260	$10,478	$10,697	$10,915	$11,133	$119,190
State income tax	$ 1,555	$ 1,588	$ 1,621	$ 1,654	$ 1,687	$ 18,059
Interest expense	$ 903	$ 898	$ 893	$ 887	$ 882	$ 10,922
Depreciation expense	$ 580	$ 580	$ 580	$ 580	$ 580	$ 6,964
Net profit	$18,863	$19,992	$21,121	$22,250	$23,378	$206,046

Profit and loss statement (second year)

Quarter	Q1	2 Q2	Q3	Q4	2
Sales	$238,875	$298,594	$322,481	$334,425	$1,194,375
Cost of goods sold	$ 51,188	$ 63,984	$ 69,103	$ 71,663	$ 255,938
Gross margin	78.6%	78.6%	78.6%	78.6%	78.6%
Operating income	$187,688	$234,609	$253,378	$262,763	$ 938,438
Expenses					
Payroll	$ 49,749	$ 62,186	$ 67,161	$ 69,649	$ 248,745
General and administrative	$ 5,242	$ 6,552	$ 7,076	$ 7,338	$ 26,208
Marketing expenses	$ 9,555	$ 11,944	$ 12,899	$ 13,377	$ 47,775
Professional fees and licensure	$ 1,545	$ 1,931	$ 2,086	$ 2,163	$ 7,725
Insurance costs	$ 2,517	$ 3,147	$ 3,398	$ 3,524	$ 12,586
Equipment costs	$ 3,871	$ 4,839	$ 5,226	$ 5,420	$ 19,356
Rent and utilities	$ 2,993	$ 3,741	$ 4,040	$ 4,190	$ 14,963
Miscellaneous costs	$ 2,867	$ 3,583	$ 3,870	$ 4,013	$ 14,333
Payroll taxes	$ 7,462	$ 9,328	$ 10,074	$ 10,447	$ 37,312
Total operating costs	$ 85,800	$107,250	$115,830	$120,120	$ 429,002
EBITDA	$101,887	$127,359	$137,548	$142,642	$ 509,436
Federal income tax	$ 32,952	$ 41,190	$ 44,485	$ 46,133	$ 164,760
State income tax	$ 4,993	$ 6,241	$ 6,740	$ 6,990	$ 24,964
Interest expense	$ 2,615	$ 2,566	$ 2,517	$ 2,466	$ 10,164
Depreciation expense	$ 1,741	$ 1,741	$ 1,741	$ 1,741	$ 6,964
Net profit	$ 59,587	$ 75,621	$ 82,064	$ 85,312	$ 302,584

Profit and loss statement (third year)

Quarter	Q1	3 Q2	Q3	Q4	3
Sales	$286,650	$358,313	$386,978	$401,310	$1,433,250
Cost of goods sold	$ 61,425	$ 76,781	$ 82,924	$ 85,995	$ 307,125
Gross margin	0.0%	0.0%	0.0%	0.0%	0.0%
Operating income	$225,225	$281,531	$304,054	$315,315	$1,126,125
Expenses					
Payroll	$ 53,894	$ 67,367	$ 72,757	$ 75,451	$ 269,469
General and administrative	$ 5,451	$ 6,814	$ 7,359	$ 7,632	$ 27,256
Marketing expenses	$ 11,466	$ 14,333	$ 15,479	$ 16,052	$ 57,330
Professional fees and licensure	$ 1,591	$ 1,989	$ 2,148	$ 2,228	$ 7,957
Insurance costs	$ 2,643	$ 3,304	$ 3,568	$ 3,700	$ 13,216
Equipment costs	$ 4,258	$ 5,323	$ 5,749	$ 5,962	$ 21,291
Rent and utilities	$ 3,142	$ 3,928	$ 4,242	$ 4,399	$ 15,711
Miscellaneous costs	$ 3,440	$ 4,300	$ 4,644	$ 4,816	$ 17,199
Payroll taxes	$ 8,084	$ 10,105	$ 10,913	$ 11,318	$ 40,420
Total operating costs	$ 93,970	$117,462	$126,859	$131,558	$ 469,848
EBITDA	$131,255	$164,069	$177,195	$183,757	$ 656,277
Federal income tax	$ 42,698	$ 53,373	$ 57,642	$ 59,777	$ 213,491
State income tax	$ 6,469	$ 8,087	$ 8,734	$ 9,057	$ 32,347
Interest expense	$ 2,414	$ 2,361	$ 2,307	$ 2,252	$ 9,335
Depreciation expense	$ 1,741	$ 1,741	$ 1,741	$ 1,741	$ 6,964
Net profit	$ 77,932	$ 98,507	$106,770	$110,930	$ 394,139

7.11 Three Year Cash Flow Analysis

Cash flow analysis (first year)

Month	1	2	3	4	5	6	7
Cash from operations	$ 11,544	$12,672	$13,801	$ 14,929	$ 16,058	$ 17,186	$ 18,315
Cash from receivables	$ 0	$ 0	$ 0	$ 0	$ 0	$ 0	$ 0
Operating cash inflow	$ 11,544	$12,672	$13,801	$ 14,929	$ 16,058	$ 17,186	$ 18,315
Other cash inflows							
Equity investment	$ 25,000	$ 0	$ 0	$ 0	$ 0	$ 0	$ 0
Increased borrowings	$125,000	$ 0	$ 0	$ 0	$ 0	$ 0	$ 0
Sales of business assets	$ 0	$ 0	$ 0	$ 0	$ 0	$ 0	$ 0
A/P increases	$ 3,159	$ 3,159	$ 3,159	$ 3,159	$ 3,159	$ 3,159	$ 3,159
Total other cash inflows	$153,159	$ 3,159	$ 3,159	$ 3,159	$ 3,159	$ 3,159	$ 3,159
Total cash inflow	$164,702	$15,831	$16,959	$ 18,088	$ 19,216	$ 20,345	$ 21,473
Cash outflows							
Repayment of principal	$ 646	$ 651	$ 656	$ 661	$ 666	$ 671	$ 676
A/P decreases	$ 2,075	$ 2,075	$ 2,075	$ 2,075	$ 2,075	$ 2,075	$ 2,075
A/R increases	$ 0	$ 0	$ 0	$ 0	$ 0	$ 0	$ 0
Asset purchases	$ 97,500	$ 0	$ 0	$ 0	$ 0	$ 0	$ 0
Dividends	$ 0	$ 0	$ 0	$ 0	$ 0	$ 0	$ 0
Total cash outflows	$100,221	$ 2,726	$ 2,730	$ 2,735	$ 2,740	$ 2,745	$ 2,750
Net cash flow	$ 64,481	$13,105	$14,229	$ 15,352	$ 16,476	$ 17,600	$ 18,723
Cash balance	$ 64,481	$77,586	$91,815	$107,167	$123,643	$141,243	$159,966

Cash flow analysis (first year cont.)

Month	8	9	10	11	12	1
Cash from operations	$ 19,444	$ 20,572	$ 21,701	$ 22,830	$ 23,959	$213,010
Cash from receivables	$ 0	$ 0	$ 0	$ 0	$ 0	$ 0
Operating cash inflow	**$ 19,444**	**$ 20,572**	**$ 21,701**	**$ 22,830**	**$ 23,959**	**$213,010**
Other cash inflows						
Equity investment	$ 0	$ 0	$ 0	$ 0	$ 0	$ 25,000
Increased borrowings	$ 0	$ 0	$ 0	$ 0	$ 0	$125,000
Sales of business assets	$ 0	$ 0	$ 0	$ 0	$ 0	$ 0
A/P increases	$ 3,159	$ 3,159	$ 3,159	$ 3,159	$ 3,159	$ 37,902
Total other cash inflows	**$ 3,159**	**$ 3,159**	**$ 3,159**	**$ 3,159**	**$ 3,159**	**$187,902**
Total cash inflow	**$ 22,602**	**$ 23,731**	**$ 24,860**	**$ 25,988**	**$ 27,117**	**$400,912**
Cash outflows						
Repayment of principal	$ 681	$ 686	$ 691	$ 696	$ 701	$ 8,079
A/P decreases	$ 2,075	$ 2,075	$ 2,075	$ 2,075	$ 2,075	$ 24,897
A/R increases	$ 0	$ 0	$ 0	$ 0	$ 0	$ 0
Asset purchases	$ 0	$ 0	$ 0	$ 0	$ 0	$ 97,500
Dividends	$ 0	$ 0	$ 0	$ 0	$149,107	$149,107
Total cash outflows	**$ 2,755**	**$ 2,760**	**$ 2,766**	**$ 2,771**	**$151,883**	**$279,583**
Net cash flow	**$ 19,847**	**$ 20,970**	**$ 22,094**	**$ 23,218**	**−$124,766**	**$121,329**
Cash balance	**$179,813**	**$200,783**	**$222,877**	**$246,095**	**$121,329**	**$121,329**

Cash flow analysis (second year)

Quarter	Q1	2 Q2	Q3	Q4	2
Cash from operations	$ 63,303	$ 79,128	$ 85,458	$ 88,624	$316,513
Cash from receivables	$ 0	$ 0	$ 0	$ 0	$ 0
Operating cash inflow	**$ 63,303**	**$ 79,128**	**$ 85,458**	**$ 88,624**	**$316,513**
Other cash inflows					
Equity investment	$ 0	$ 0	$ 0	$ 0	$ 0
Increased borrowings	$ 0	$ 0	$ 0	$ 0	$ 0
Sales of business assets	$ 0	$ 0	$ 0	$ 0	$ 0
A/P increases	$ 8,717	$ 10,897	$ 11,769	$ 12,204	$ 43,587
Total other cash inflows	**$ 8,717**	**$ 10,897**	**$ 11,769**	**$ 12,204**	**$ 43,587**
Total cash inflow	**$ 72,020**	**$ 90,025**	**$ 97,227**	**$100,828**	**$360,100**
Cash outflows					
Repayment of principal	$ 2,136	$ 2,184	$ 2,233	$ 2,284	$ 8,837
A/P decreases	$ 5,975	$ 7,469	$ 8,067	$ 8,365	$ 29,876
A/R increases	$ 0	$ 0	$ 0	$ 0	$ 0
Asset purchases	$ 15,826	$ 19,782	$ 21,365	$ 22,156	$ 79,128
Dividends	$ 44,312	$ 55,390	$ 59,821	$ 62,036	$221,559
Total cash outflows	**$ 68,248**	**$ 84,825**	**$ 91,486**	**$ 94,842**	**$339,401**
Net cash flow	**$ 3,772**	**$ 5,200**	**$ 5,741**	**$ 5,986**	**$ 20,699**
Cash balance	**$125,101**	**$130,301**	**$136,042**	**$142,028**	**$142,028**

Cash flow analysis (third year)

Quarter	Q1	Q2	Q3	Q4	3
Cash from operations	$ 81,614	$102,017	$110,178	$114,259	$408,068
Cash from receivables	$ 0	$ 0	$ 0	$ 0	$ 0
Operating cash inflow	**$ 81,614**	**$102,017**	**$110,178**	**$114,259**	**$408,068**
Other cash inflows					
Equity investment	$ 0	$ 0	$ 0	$ 0	$ 0
Increased borrowings	$ 0	$ 0	$ 0	$ 0	$ 0
Sales of business assets	$ 0	$ 0	$ 0	$ 0	$ 0
A/P increases	$ 10,025	$ 12,531	$ 13,534	$ 14,035	$ 50,125
Total other cash inflows	**$ 10,025**	**$ 12,531**	**$ 13,534**	**$ 14,035**	**$ 50,125**
Total cash inflow	**$ 91,639**	**$114,548**	**$123,712**	**$128,294**	**$458,193**
Cash outflows					
Repayment of principal	$ 2,336	$ 2,389	$ 2,443	$ 2,498	$ 9,666
A/P decreases	$ 7,170	$ 8,963	$ 9,680	$ 10,038	$ 35,852
A/R increases	$ 0	$ 0	$ 0	$ 0	$ 0
Asset purchases	$ 20,403	$ 25,504	$ 27,545	$ 28,565	$102,017
Dividends	$ 57,130	$ 71,412	$ 77,125	$ 79,981	$285,648
Total cash outflows	**$ 87,039**	**$108,268**	**$116,792**	**$121,083**	**$433,182**
Net cash flow	**$ 4,600**	**$ 6,280**	**$ 6,920**	**$ 7,211**	**$ 25,011**
Cash balance	**$146,628**	**$152,908**	**$159,828**	**$167,039**	**$167,039**

Self Storage Business

Tulsa StorageMaster Inc.

78 Regan Ave.
Tulsa, Oklahoma 71405

Paul Greenland

Tulsa StorageMaster is a new business, established for the purpose of acquiring an existing self storage facility in Tulsa, Oklahoma.

EXECUTIVE SUMMARY

Business Overview

Tulsa StorageMaster is a new business, established for the purpose of acquiring an existing self storage facility in Tulsa, Oklahoma. The company includes four partners, all of whom reside in Tulsa. Bill Smith is a general contractor who owns Smith Construction Co. Kirk Bradfield is the owner of Bradfield's Bar & Grill. Terry Marciano is an independent attorney. Finally, George Anderson is the owner of Anderson Ford, a local Ford dealership. The owners all have excellent reputations within the community and are members of the Better Business Bureau and the Tulsa Metro Chamber.

Constructed in 1990, the 24,000-square-foot facility includes 220 storage units of varying sizes. The majority of the units (180) are indoors, offering climate control. The remaining 40 units are located outside, with convenient garage door access. The facility is made of poured concrete. It is clean, well-lit, and is equipped with a security video system and code-access security gate. The property includes an undeveloped area that could be used for an additional building, or fenced off for boat and RV storage at a later time. In addition, the facility includes a small, on-site apartment for a facility manager.

MARKET ANALYSIS

Tulsa StorageMaster will serve customers who live, or need to store their belongings in, Tulsa, Oklahoma. According to data from DemographicsNow, this area included nearly 398,187 people in 2010, and was projected to grow 3.5 percent by 2015, reaching about 412,171. The average household income in our primary market was $64,220 in 2010. This figure is expected to grow 8.5 percent by 2015, reaching $69,660.

Tulsa StorageMaster will concentrate its marketing efforts on several specific market segments:

1. *Renter-occupied Housing:* Individuals in this category (especially those dwelling in apartments) will likely have a greater need for off-site storage than those who live in owner-occupied housing.

2. *New Movers:* Those who have recently relocated to Tulsa may discover that they have inadequate storage space for their belongings, or they may need a short-term storage solution while sorting through various items.

3. *Foreclosures:* Economic hardship has forced many homeowners to foreclose on their property and seek residence elsewhere (either in a small apartment or with family). Faced with the need to find a place for their belongings before the bank repossesses their property, we will offer them an affordable storage solution.

INDUSTRY ANALYSIS

According to information from the non-profit Self Storage Association (SSA), in 2010 the U.S. self storage industry generated revenues of more than $20 billion and included approximately 46,500 facilities. For more than 30 years, this "recession-resistant" industry has been recognized as the commercial real estate sector's fastest-growing category.

Many business owners in this industry are members of the SSA, which was established in 1975. The SSA bills itself as "the official trade organization and voice of the U.S. and international self storage industry." The association has affiliations with approximately 27 state and regional associations, as well as four international organizations.

According to the SSA, it has several areas of focus, including: "Collecting and dissemination of industry data, advocacy and lobbying at the federal, state and local levels, conducting conventions, trade shows and seminars, issuing periodic membership communications and publishing a magazine (SSA Globe with a monthly circulation of 15,000), conducting executive education and employee training programs, conducting research, maintaining an internationally utilized web site and relations with more than 29 other industry associations, publishing books, manuals and various industry studies, providing legal education and information."

PERSONNEL

Bill Smith

Bill Smith will serve as president of Tulsa StorageMaster. He is a general contractor who owns Smith Construction Co., a fixture in Tulsa since 1987. Smith Construction Co. focuses on residential construction, specializing in custom home building. His company is known for creating unique floorplans and offering customers the latest energy-efficient designs. In addition, his company handles remodeling jobs and projects such as home additions and basement finishing.

Terry Marciano

A well-known Tulsa attorney, Terry has represented thousands of clients over the years. His law office specializes in the areas of family law, bankruptcy, DUI, traffic, criminal, and civil litigation. The local legal community recognizes his firm for its attention to detail and professionalism in legal proceedings. Terry earned his law degree from the University of Oklahoma College of Law in 1992. After practicing for another firm in Oklahoma City, Terry moved back to his hometown of Tulsa and established his own practice in 2000.

Kirk Bradfield

When the Tulsa community wants to enjoy a night on the town, Bradfield's Bar & Grill tops their list of places to go. Owned and operated by Tulsa native Kirk Bradfield since 2004, Bradfield's not only is a full service bar and grill, it's a hotspot for live music and entertainment. Over the years, Kirk's establishment has developed a reputation for its delicious food, including the signature Bradfield Buffalo Burger.

George Anderson

George Anderson is the owner of Anderson Ford, a local Ford dealership that has been in operation since 1985. Started by his father, Peter, Anderson Ford offers a full selection of new vehicles, as well as quality used vehicles. In addition to departments devoted to functions such as service, parts, finance, and rentals, the dealership also operates a fleet service division.

Smith, Marciano, Bradfield, and Anderson all have excellent reputations within the community and are members of the Better Business Bureau and the Tulsa Metro Chamber.

Paul Stansberry

Paul Stansberry has served as the general manager of Tulsa Action Storage Co. (the business operating the facilities being acquired by Tulsa StorageMaster) since 2005. The owners have decided to retain Paul because of his excellent track record. In addition to having a business management degree from Tulsa Community College, Paul has exceptional customer service skills. He is a fast thinker and understands what needs to be done to operate a successful business. Limited by the previous owners, Paul will be a tremendous asset to the new owners as they focus on growing the business.

Professional and Advisory Support

Tulsa StorageMaster has selected Tulsa Accounting LLC to provide bookkeeping and tax assistance. A commercial checking account has been established with the Bank of Oklahoma, which has agreed to provide merchant accounts so that the business can accept credit card and debit card payments. Legal services will be provided by Terry Marciano. His firm has reviewed and modified the rental agreements utilized by the previous owner and will handle any disputes and litigation moving forward.

BUSINESS STRATEGY

Tulsa StorageMaster Inc. has been established to acquire the assets of Tulsa Action Storage Co. (Tulsa Action), a subsidiary of the publicly traded Nationwide Action Storage Co. (Nationwide). In 2010 Nationwide announced plans to streamline its network of corporately owned storage businesses. As part of this larger initiative, Nationwide announced plans to dissolve Tulsa Action.

Despite having an excellent on-site general manager, the new owners are convinced that Tulsa Action never reached its fullest potential, because its parent company did not provide an adequate level of support in the areas of capital investment and marketing. With this in mind, Tulsa StorageMaster plans to take a good business operation and make it a great one.

Presently, the occupancy level of the storage facility is 76 percent. By developing a strong marketing plan (see below), the new owners are confident that occupancy can grow to near full-capacity by 2014.

The owners plan to devote the first three years of operation to increasing occupancy, based on the following targets:

2012: 85%

2013: 90%

2014: 95%

In year four (2015), the owners will plan to add either an access-controlled, fenced area for boat and RV storage, or an additional structure offering a mix of indoor and outdoor storage units. This decision will be based on customer demand and market conditions. The owners will conduct basic market research during 2014, the results of which will be used during the decision-making process.

SERVICES

Tulsa StorageMaster offers storage units of varying sizes.

Indoor Storage Units

The majority of our storage units (180) are indoors, offering climate control. Unit sizes and prices are as follows:

5 × 10 (50 units)	$ 70/month
10 × 10 (50 units)	$ 95/month
10 × 15 (30 units)	$135/month
10 × 20 (30 units)	$150/month
10 × 30 (20 units)	$165/month

Outdoor Storage Units

The remaining 40 units are located outside, with convenient garage door access. Unit sizes and prices are as follows:

10 × 15 (20 units)	$ 70/month
10 × 20 (10 units)	$ 85/month
10 × 30 (10 units)	$100/month

All customers receive a security code that they enter via a keypad to operate a security gate that controls access to our facility.

We provide complimentary hand trucks and dollies for our customers to use.

MARKETING & SALES

A marketing plan has been developed for Tulsa StorageMaster that includes these main tactics:

Web Site: Tulsa StorageMaster will offer customers a Web site that lists information about our available rental units (e.g., sizes, prices, terms, etc.). In addition, customers will be able to reserve units online, and make payments via credit card or PayPal. The previous owners of the business did not offer these attractive options, which should be very effective in terms of increasing occupancy.

Promotional Signage: New, eye-catching exterior signage will be developed for Tulsa StorageMaster. In addition, we will install an electronic marquee sign that can be preprogrammed with information about rental specials, etc.

Direct Marketing: Tulsa StorageMaster will develop a basic four-color postcard, which will be mailed to "new movers" (individuals who have recently moved into the community), those who have recently foreclosed on a property, and individuals living in rental properties. Mailing lists will be obtained from Brubaker Mailings, a list broker in Oklahoma City. In addition, Robinson Mail Works, a local letter shop, will handle mailings for us on a monthly basis.

Advertising: Tulsa StorageMaster will maintain a regular advertising presence in *The Tulsa World,* a newspaper which has been locally owned since 1917. In addition, we will run a large ad in the Yellow Pages.

We will evaluate our marketing plan on a semi-annual basis during our first three years of operations, and annually thereafter.

OPERATIONS

Hours

Customers will have access to their storage unit 24 hours per day, seven days per week. Our on-site manager will be available to assist customers in person and via phone Tuesday through Friday from 9 AM-5 PM, and on Saturdays from 9 AM-3 PM. Rental payments will be accepted on-site during these hours. Customers also will be able to make online payments and reservations via our Web site at any time.

Payment

Customers will be required to pay in advance for each month of storage. No long-term leases are required; we rent storage units on a month-to-month basis. Credit/debit card payments, PayPal, checks, and cash will be accepted.

Insurance

Customers must insure the belongings they store at our facility. For those without an insurance agent, we provide a listing of several insurance companies that provide appropriate coverage (available upon request).

Legal

The Law Firm of Terry Marciano has developed a complete set of policies and procedures pertaining to the operation of Tulsa StorageMaster. In addition, a comprehensive rental agreement, specifying terms and the responsibilities of all parties involved, has been drafted. These documents are available upon request.

Facility and Location

Constructed in 1990, the 24,000-square-foot facility includes 220 storage units of varying sizes. The majority of the units (180) are indoors, offering climate control. The remaining 40 units are located outside, with convenient garage door access. The facility is made of poured concrete. It is clean, well-lit, and is equipped with a security video system and code-access security gate. The property includes an undeveloped area that could be used for an additional building, or fenced off for boat and RV storage at a later time. In addition, the facility includes a small, on-site apartment for a facility manager.

FINANCIAL ANALYSIS

During fiscal year 2011, the previous owners (Tulsa Action Storage Co.) generated net income of $65,075 on gross revenues of $155,575, with operating expenses of $90,500.

Detailed financial projections, prepared in cooperation with Tulsa Accounting LLC, are available for review. However, based on the occupancy growth targets outlined in the Business Strategy section of this plan, Tulsa StorageMaster is projecting the following:

Year	Gross revenue	Operating expenses	Net income
2012	$169,577	$95,025	$74,552
2013	$177,356	$97,401	$79,955
2014	$185,134	$99,836	$85,298

Each owner is contributing $50,000 of funding to the business. Following their collective $200,000 investment, the owners are seeking a 30-year mortgage for the storage facility in the amount of $625,000.

Used Car Business

Budget Cars

145 Water Street
Alpena, Michigan 49707

The mission of Budget Cars is to buy and sell a desirable mix of quality used cars, trucks, and vans, and to create a friendly atmosphere where Budget Cars will be known as the family used car center of choice.

This plan originally appeared in Business Plans Handbook, Volume 6. It has been updated for this edition.

SUMMARY

Description of the business

Mission—The mission of Budget Cars is to buy and sell a desirable mix of quality used cars, trucks, and vans, and to create a friendly atmosphere where Budget Cars will be known as the family used car center of choice.

Legal Status—The legal status of Budget Cars is a subchapter "S" corporation.

Location—The location is in Alpena, Michigan.

Products and Services

The products that Budget Cars will offer are quality used cars, trucks, and vans at below market value. The services that will be offered are in-house financing provided by area banks (with approved credit) and a full automotive detail center that will recondition all units for sale.

Market and Sales Strategy

Due to several different factors (season changes, market changes, opening date, etc.), our advertising strategies are going to vary accordingly. We are going to be consistent with our advertising in the "Out and About" section that runs every other week in the *Alpena Journal* and at least one ad once a month in the *Daily Herald*.

January 15, 2012—Our goal is to open the doors and start our advertising in the "Out and About" section of the Alpena Journal, $55 each run, reaching 5,100 homes, and an ad in the *Daily Herald*. In addition, we will buy online banner ads with each paper (approximately $60 per week), and will establish a Web site listing details on all of the cars we have for sale, as well as a contact form prospective customers can use to initiate conversations with our salespeople.

February—First week, buy the front page of the *Daily Herald*, $724, reaching 17,364 homes and continue with every other week in the *Alpena Journal*. We also will maintain our online banner ads with each paper.

March—This month we'll continue our "Out and About" section ad, online banner ads, and at least one ad in the *Daily Herald* to keep in contact with the outer areas of the county.

April—"Grand Opening" will be held this month. With the snow gone and everyone ready for a cookout, we'll have our "Family Festival." Included in this will be a tent, hot dogs on the grill, and a classic car show on our lot. Also, we'll run an ad in the "Out and About" section, continue the online advertisements, and place a spot in the *Daily Herald*.

May, June, and July—We will begin radio advertising, maybe sponsoring a morning weather program, and continue with our online advertising, the spot in the "Out and About" section, and an ad in the *Daily Herald*.

August, September, and October—We will maintain the online and radio advertising, and consider sponsoring a local high school sport. In addition, we'll continue the "Out and About" section and an ad in the *Daily Herald*.

November—We'll keep running the online advertising, spots in the "Out and About" section and the ad in the *Daily Herald* and determine if it's time to consider advertising on Facebook, which would allow us to reach customers based on specific criteria, including geography.

December—Have a coloring contest for the kids, with prizes that tie in with the holidays, and continue print/online advertising in the *Alpena Journal* and the *Daily Herald*.

Budgeting $800 a month, a total of $9,600 a year, this should be a realistic dollar amount and provide us with plenty of exposure.

Management Team and Responsibilities

The management team members are Ben Heath, Margerie Heath, and Peter James, with Ben ultimately being the leader. Margerie's responsibilities will include bookkeeping, maintaining our Web site, responding to e-mail inquiries, answering and routing phone calls and payroll. Peter will be maintaining and operating the automotive detail center. Ben will be responsible for the buying and selling of automobiles and overseeing all operations. The number one responsibility of our management team is to create a friendly atmosphere where our customers come first. They will always be courteously acknowledged with a friendly smile and a handshake.

Objectives of the Management Team

Our main objective is to buy and sell 180 quality used vehicles in the first year of operation, with an increase of 60 vehicles annually, ultimately reaching an average of 300 cars per year.

We project $270,000 in gross profit for the first year, making that a $1,500 per unit gross after marketing sales expense ($500) is deducted, increasing accordingly with the number of units sold per year to reach our goal of $450,000 gross profit by the fourth year.

Financial Considerations

- Profit Projections—Budget Cars will have a net profit in the first year of operations.

- Balance Sheet Projections—We are projecting an increase of net worth of the business by $53,993.43.

PRODUCTS AND SERVICES

Initial Products and Services

When we first open in January 2012, if the weather is typically like most northern Michigan winters, there will be snow on the ground. Purposely the inventory will be minimal and focus on 4x4 trucks, utility units, and a family budget row of used cars that will satisfy both first and the second car needs.

Need for the Product and Service

With the prices of new vehicles reaching an average of $30,000 plus, and the difficult economic conditions in Michigan and the rest of the United States, the used car, truck, and van market has become stronger. That's why Budget Cars is opening its doors in January 2012.

Major Suppliers

A majority of the vehicles that Budget Cars will offer will come from auctions and new car dealerships. The auctions will be our major suppliers of late model vehicles and the new car dealerships will be an access to the vehicles we can offer between $5,000 and $10,500. Other vehicles will come from trade-ins and private purchase units.

INDUSTRY DESCRIPTION

Background of the Industry

Immediately following World War II, there were roughly nine buyers for every new car produced. Sales personnel merely had to find out who could afford a new car. "Afford" was defined as paying cash. This condition existed until the early 1950s when some new terms were creeping into the retail salesperson's vocabulary. Words like "over-allowance," "discount," "deal," and "terms." The emphasis, however, was still not on product but on price. In addition, the asking price was no longer final. There was also, if you could haggle a little, a taking price. It was possible to bargain with the dealer for the first time.

During the 1960s, other new merchandising techniques were introduced. "Sticker price," "fleet price," "hard sell," "50 over invoice," "high-powered advertising," and "free" accessories were but a few new innovations. The buyer was becoming better educated, better able to buy—thanks to 24- and 36-month payments—but still confused and fearful of price. "Good deals" became "bad deals" after talking to friends and neighbors. Caution became the watchword when buying a car.

The advent of the 1970s brought more confusion to buyers with new procedures like leasing, 48-month payments, credit unions, rebates, and consumer advocates. However, in defense of the consumer, books on "How to Buy a Car," "Invoice Prices U.S. Cars," and "Used Car Buyers Guide," were published and sold by the millions.

During the 1970s automobile salespeople became conditioned to the notion that customers were interested in only one thing—the very lowest price. The automobile showroom atmosphere didn't change very much from the 1970s to the 1980s. Most retail salespeople saw the business of selling automobile as an "us against them" hard-sell game. Those who sold popular Japanese products became arrogant and insensitive to their customers and those of us who sold American vehicles continued with the approach that price, and price alone, sells vehicles.

As the 1980s came to a close, however, the winds of change began to impact the retail automobile marketplace. During the late 1980s and early 1990s, new car dealers began ramping up their participation in the nation's auction network, which previously had been attended almost exclusively by used car dealers. Weak economic conditions during the early 1990s caused used-car sales to surge. Used car and truck sales surpassed sales of new vehicles at new car dealerships for the first time since World War II.

During the 2000s the Internet began to play an important role in used car sales. Dealers began posting vehicles for sale on their Web sites for consumers to view from the convenience of their home or business. The Internet also made consumers more informed. For example, by 2006 JD power and Associates reported that 34 percent of used car buyers checked out a vehicle history report prior to purchase. By the late 2000s leading car manufacturers such as Chrysler and General Motors were in dire straits during one of the worst economic recessions in U.S. history. New car sales fell to near-record lows, and demand for more affordable used cars surged, although sales were challenging industry-wide.

Trade Association Assistance

Federal Register offers assistance with compliance guidelines for used car rules and the National Auto Dealers Association (NADA) also offers assistance.

Industry Trends

Vehicle sales seem to trend with our Michigan seasons. While the sun is shining and the temperatures are warm, outdoor family activities become more popular, encouraging camping, vacations, and sightseeing. These activities increase the demand for minivans, station wagons, and sport utility vehicles. As the kids head back to school and the weather turns cold, road conditions deteriorate. This creates demand for a more rugged, durable unit such as light duty trucks and vans. The extra security of four-wheel drive is also more popular during this season.

Number and Kind of Businesses in the Area in the Industry

There are four new car dealerships in Alpena that offer a line of used vehicles. There are also three used car lots in town offering a very limited selection of units.

Major Influences on the Industry

Government Regulations—An important regulation of the government is to obtain and maintain a class "B" license. The Federal Trade Commission also publishes rules and regulations for operating a used car lot. The used car rule has four basic components. (1) Prepare and display a Buyers Guide on each used vehicle offered to the consumer. (2) To include a special disclosure in the contract of sale. (3) To identify the final warranty terms in the contract of sale. (4) To give the purchaser a copy of the Buyers Guide that includes the final warranty terms.

Business Cycle—Ups and downs go with any industry, but with the sale of used vehicles there seems to be more of a plateau. When the economy is good, sales are great. When the economy is sluggish, used cars are still in demand because of their price factor.

MARKET DEFINITION

Customer Profile—Budget Cars will be focusing on three customer profiles. One being a first-time buyer, age 16-25, next being the middle-class family looking for a second car, and third, age 50 and over low-income adults.

Buying Decision Determinants—After presenting to the customer quality used vehicles that have been safety checked, backed with a warranty and a competitive low price, the main determinant that we believe will bring the customer to the close is working one on one with the owners and their honesty and reputations.

Customer Awareness of Product/Service—Our advertising campaign and Web site will ensure that the customer knows who and where we are. Our up close and personal interview process will be a thorough, detailed, step-by-step explanation of our product and commitment to our customers' needs.

Market Size

Geographic—Our primary source of customer base will come from the local and surrounding counties. Starting from our location in Alpena, all of the counties are within a thirty-mile radius.

Population—The total population of our targeted customer base is 47,465 people. Using Alpena as a comparison, according to data from DemographicsNow, the total population of Alpena County was such 29,297 in the spring of 2010. The number of 20-to-24-year-olds was 1,867; the number of people 25-34 was 3,418; those aged 35-44 totaled 3,176; and those in the 45-54 age bracket totaled 4,549. This leaves a total of 9,678 people over the age of 55.

Sales—A statistic taken in 2010 determined the number of vehicles per occupied housing unit in Alpena County. That year, 704 households (5.3%) had no means of motorized transportation, 4,787 owned one vehicle, and 7,751 owned two vehicles or more. In order for Budget Cars to reach its projected first-year goal of 15 units per month, only a small percentage of the Alpena market needs to be cornered. Any units sold to customers within the rest of the targeted counties will be additional business.

Market Growth—Alpena's population is expected to remain steady for the foreseeable future. For example, total households are projected to increase from 13,242 in the spring of 2010 to 13,349 in the spring of 2015 (a 0.8% increase). This means that the area will have a continued need for reliable transportation.

Competition

New and Used Car Dealerships

- Jenson's Sales and Service—Dodge, Chrysler, Jeep, and used vehicles

- Alpena Ford Kia—Ford, Kia and used vehicles

- Boji Nissan, Mazda, Suzuki—Nissan, Mazda, Suzuki, and used vehicles

- Miller Chevrolet Cadillac—Chevrolet, Cadillac, and used vehicles

Used Vehicle Dealers Only

- Car Trade Center

- Thunderbird Auto

- Jake's Auto Parts

Strengths and Weaknesses of the Competition

Jenson's Sales and Service is selling new and used cars on a more relaxed approach. Alpena Ford Kia is aggressive in both new and used vehicle sales, with the majority of their used cars being higher-priced program cars. Boji's is focused on new car sales. Miller offers new and used vehicles but is not very aggressive. There are three older used car lots in town that maintain a "B" license. Selling cars is not their main source of income. Very little, if any, priority is given to car sales.

Pricing

Budget Cars is in a better position than our larger competitors because the overhead is much lower. All deals will be conducted between the owner and customer with no commission paid salesperson taking a cut from the profit made on the deal. The clean-up and reconditioning of all vehicles will be completed in-house. This way we will be able to beat the larger dealers' prices every time and still make enough profit to maintain business expenses and build capital for future expansion. Our main goal will be to sell more for less and be known as "Your Family Used Car Center."

MARKETING PLAN

Marketing Overview

Budget Cars plans to focus on young first-time auto buyers, families with second car needs, and low-income adults aged 50 and over. To capture this market we plan to advertise online, with the local newspaper, and on the radio. However, more important is the support and participation that we will show in community activities.

Marketing Objectives

Budget Cars' main marketing objective is to focus on the customers' wants and needs and, at the same time, maintain a marketable selection of vehicles at all times. This will allow us to effectively influence and persuade them to buy.

Marketing Strategy

Advertising—Our main advertising strategy is to let our potential customer know that we are aware of their wants and needs and have quality inventory and prices. To prove it, we will let them know that if we don't have what they're looking for, we'll get it.

Marketing Budget—From the time that Budget Cars takes possession, until the point of sale, the marketing budget will average $500 per unit. This includes the driver's expense, a safety check, repair work, if needed, reconditioning, and all forms and documents used to track market trends.

OPERATIONS

Facility Requirements

The ideal facility for Budget Cars is a highly visible location with a lot large enough to hold 30 units and enough space for customer parking. Also, we will need a building large enough to house a reconditioning center and a sales floor with several private offices.

Equipment Requirements

Reconditioning Department—The equipment needed for this area will be a rug doctor, shop vacuum, stripping wheel, six-foot ladder, hose and nozzle, buffer, heat gun, miscellaneous small tools, and a plow vehicle for snow removal.

Office and Sales Department—The equipment needed for this area will be two desks, nine chairs, three computers and printers, one fax machine, two phones, copy machine, two calculators, and a coffee machine.

Labor Requirements

Budget Cars will have two salaried owners as their main operators. Ben will be manning the sales and Peter will take care of the reconditioning department. Margerie, a full-time employee, will be handling the office duties.

COMPANY STRUCTURE

Legal Status—Budget Cars will be a subchapter "S" corporation.

Business Advisors

Accountant—William P. Johnson of William P. Johnson Company PC CPAs, Alpena, Michigan, will be Budget Cars' accountant.

Insurance—Cheryl Booker and Robert Ordowski of The Floyd Agency, Alpena, Michigan, will be Budget Cars' insurance agents.

Consultant—Phillip J. West of Alpena Community College, Alpena, Michigan, has been a consultant for Budget Cars.

FINANCIAL PLAN

Start-Up Costs

The start-up cost for Budget Cars will be $15,585. This figure includes office supplies, $510; marketing and reconditioning, $5,812; accounting and legal, $1,861; rental security deposit, $1,517; insurances, $2,171; gas expenses, $414; smartphones with data plans, $2,000; Chamber of Commerce dues, $200; and improvements to location, $1,100.

Sources/Uses of Funds

- Personal funds
- $35,000 five-year loan
- $205,000 of floor plan will be used to operate the business

Summary of Financial Projections

Detailed financial projections (available upon request) have been prepared with the assistance of our accountant, William P. Johnson. These include a projection of our monthly cash flow after expenses, as well as a chart showing average gross profit per unit, and the profit potential with volume, for a period of four years. Following are some key findings from the projections:

- Cash Flow Projections—Budget Cars foresees no cash flow projection problems.
- Profit/Loss Projections/Breakeven Analysis—The Company expects to have a gross profit the first year of $83,127.
- Balance Sheet Projections—Budget Cars projects an increase of net worth the first year to be $53,993.43.

LOCATION

Business Location

Budget Cars will be located in Alpena, Michigan.

Location Costs

The lease of the building will be $850 per month for two years.

Licenses, Permits and other Regulations

Budget Cars will need a class "B" dealership license, a sales tax I.D. number, and a city permit for the opening.

Insurance Needs

Budget Cars will need Fleet Insurance, Workman's Compensation, Renters' Insurance, and will be carrying health insurance for the shareholders.

Projected monthly material expenses

This chart shows the materials required monthly for the clean-up and reconditioning of 15 safety-checked units.
Projected monthly material expenses based on 15 units.

Amount required	Item description	Price each	Total
2 gallons	Tire dressing	34.50/gallon	69.00
2 gallons	Interior cleaner	14.50/gallon	29.00
2 gallons	Mag wheel cleaner	21.50/gallon	43.00
1 gallon	Window cleaner	12.50/gallon	12.50
1/4 gallon	Miracle Wax	33.00/gallon	8.25
1/4 gallon	Rubbing compound	22.00/gallon	5.50
1/2 gallon	Bug remover	14.50/gallon	7.25
4 each	Buffing pads	6.00/each	24.00
3 each	Stripping pads	12.00/each	36.00
6 each	Interior paint	6.00/each	36.00
6 each	Semi gloss paint	4.00/each	24.00
1/4 gallon	Interior deodorant	29.00/gallon	7.25
3 gallons	Wash soap	17.00/gallon	51.00
1 each	Chamois	27.50/each	27.50
2 gallons	Mineral spirits	7.00/gallon	14.00
1/4 package	Razor blades	16.50/each	4.13
1 case	Paper towels	25.00/case	25.00
5 each	Wax applicator	3.00/each	15.00
1/2 roll	Polishing cloth	41.50/roll	20.75
6 each	Touch up paint	5.50/each	33.00
Total			**492.13**

(These figures are included in the Sales Marketing Expense.)

Class "B" Licensing Requirements

This list includes the necessary steps to take when acquiring a Class "B" Dealers License, based on information provided by the Michigan Secretary of State.

• $75 License Fee

• Repair Facility Registration or Service Agreement

• Zoning and Municipality Approval

• Fleet Insurance Certificate

• 2 Dealer Plates (Minimum)

• $10,000 Vehicle Dealer Surety Bond

Number of Vehicles Available per Household

According to the latest data on average vehicle ownership per household in Alpena County, in the spring of 2010 the market was as follows:

0 vehicles	704 households	5.3%
1 vehicle	4,787 households	36.2%
2+ vehicles	7,751 households	58.5%

By 2015, the number of households with no vehicles is expected to fall 14.8 percent, while the number of households with one vehicle is projected to increase by 4.6 percent. The number of households with two or more vehicles is expected to remain relatively unchanged.

RESUMES AND STAFF PROFILES

Resumes and personality profiles of Budget Cars's management team.

BEN HEATH

Career Goal

To own and operate a successful used-car dealership that I can devote all my energy and enthusiasm to.

Work Experience

Pine Country Ford, August 2000—October 2004/July 2009—Present (Sales Manager / Consultant)

- Create and maintain a diverse customer base
- Conduct telephone interviews with potential customers
- Maintain a thorough knowledge of all current inventory
- Determine which inventory is marketable and contact buyers that may be interested
- Persuade buyers into a one-on-one meeting
- Recognize and satisfy customers' wants and needs
- Assist customers in determining which vehicle and financing terms best fit their needs
- Be the connecting link between the buyer and dealer while settling on a price which satisfies all parties involved

Alpena Ford Kia, January 2005—June 2009 (Sales Consultant / Sales Manager)

- Oversee all sales operations to include showroom, display lot, and reconditioning shop
- Appraise trade-in vehicles and offer a fair price that will encourage a sale and create a marketable trade-in
- Order new vehicles from factory for retail and dealership inventory
- Create a positive, enthusiastic atmosphere for the subordinate sales consultants that will promote increasing sales and high morale
- Devise and carry out marketing plans to include advertising & promotions that will ensure growth and sales
- Recognize customer needs and limitations through brief descriptions provided by sales consultants
- Request and accept dealer trades that will satisfy a multitude of parties involved
- Interact with the public on a daily basis in a positive, friendly, honest manner
- Create and maintain a consistent marketable lot that will stimulate sales and growth through consumer tracking, market trends, and analyzing area economic status

United States Marines, March 1996—July 2000 (Medical Administration Specialist)

- Decipher doctor-prepared patient charts and type them for future reference
- Monitor, maintain, file, and organize patient records to ensure quality care
- Operate all office equipment to include multi-line telephone, computer, printer, copy machine, facsimile machine

Educational Background

University of Miami, Miami, Florida–December 2003, Used Vehicle Management

Ford Division Increasing Sales through Prospecting Course–April 2001

Ford Division Compact and Full-Size Light Truck Selling Course–March 2001

Ford Division National Walk Around Course (First place in competition)–February 2001

Roger Bolt Advance Sales Course–October 2000

Roger Bolt Professional Sales Course–November 2000

Alpena Community College, Alpena, Michigan–September 1994—June 1995, Business Management

- Psychology

- Public Speaking

Central High School, New York, New York (graduated June 1994)

Special Qualifications

- Ford Division Legend Leaders 300/500 Leadership Recognition Award 2004

- Top 10% Customer Satisfaction Diplomat Society Honors 2005, 2006, 2007, and 2008

- Ford Division Recognition for being the Top Salesperson for Alpena Ford 2004, 2005, 2006, 2007, promoted to Sales Manager in 2008

- Ford Division Recognition for being the Top Salesperson for Pine Country Ford 2000, 2001, promoted to Sales Manager in 2002 and in 2003 won Ford Division Professional Sales Managers Award, Top 10%

Outside Interests

- Sunday School Teaching

- Camping

- Horseback Riding

- Participating in Outdoor Activities

- Gardening

- Handy Work

References available upon request.

Summary of Predictive Index Results

Name: Ben Heath

Survey Date: June 12, 2010

Report Date: June 24, 2010

Ben is an engaging, stimulating communicator, poised and capable of projecting enthusiasm and warmth, and of motivating other people.

He has a strong sense of urgency, initiative, and competitive drive to get things done, an emphasis on working with people in the process. He understands people well and uses that understanding effectively in influencing and persuading others to act.

Focused on results, and impatient with details and routines, Ben is a confident and venturesome "doer" and decision-maker who will delegate details and can also delegate responsibility and authority when necessary. Ben is a self-starter who is skillful at training and developing others. He applies pressure for results, but in doing so, his style is more "selling" than "telling."

At ease and self-assured with groups or in making new contacts, Ben is gregarious and extroverted, has an invigorating impact on people, and is always "selling" in a general sense. He learns and reacts quickly and works at a faster-than-average pace. Able to adapt quickly to change and variety in his work, he will become impatient and less effective if required to work primarily with repetitive routines and details.

In general terms, Ben is an ambitious and driving person who is motivated by opportunity for advancement to levels of responsibility where he can use his skills as team builder, motivator, and mover.

Management Strategies

To maximize his effectiveness, productivity, and job satisfaction, consider providing Ben with the following:

- Opportunities for involvement and interaction with people

- Some independence and flexibility in his activities

- Freedom from repetitive routine and details in work that provide variety and change of pace

- Opportunities to learn and advance at a fairly fast pace

- Recognition and reward for communications and leadership skills demonstrated

- Social and status recognition as rewards for achievement.

PETER JAMES

Career Goal

Seeking employment with a professional establishment that provides a challenging and stimulating work atmosphere for individuals who demonstrate a positive, self-starting attitude.

Work Experience

Alpena Ford Mercury, 1/17/2009—Present (Automotive Appearance Enhancement Technician)

- Clean and detail engine compartments

- Strip excess finishes and imperfections with low RPM power wheel

- Repair minor scratches and discolorations of surface paints

- Rustproof over spray removal

- Paint Protection application

- Apply new finishes

- Perform interior cleaning and minor repair

- Apply dye to carpets and upholstery

- Operate industrial debris extractor

- Apply after market and OEM accessories

American Waste Systems, 1/14/2008—11/9/2008 (Route Coordinator)

- Maintain continuity of 10 collection routes by filling in and training new drivers for routes with short callings

- Organize route changes for maximum efficiency and make changes in computer automated route sheets

- Complete route audits and analysis

Jackson's Disposal Service Inc, 1/6/2005—1/13/2008 (Collection Route Driver)

- Operate manual and automatic transmission heavy trucks

- Operate Clark Pneumatic Forklift

- Operate industrial recycling equipment such as cardboard baler, paper shredder, and glass crusher

- Operate FCC licensed two-way radios

- Operate front end loaders

Holiday Inn of Alpena, 7/11/2004—10/12/2004 (Night Auditor)

- Investigate cashier discrepancies
- Credit card collection
- Complete computer automated audits
- Computer interfacing
- Accounts Payable/Receivable
- Word processing
- Fax/e-mail communications
- Automated telephone switchboard operation

United States Marines, 8/9/1998—2/23/2004 (Food Service Shift Leader, 4/1/2003—2/20/2004) (Shift Supervisor 3/10/2002—4/1/2003) (Night Auditor 1/1/2000—3/10/2002) (Desk Clerk 10/15/1998—1/1/2000)

- Computer operation
- Operate NCR cash register
- Utilize computerized telephone switchboards
- Prepare city ledger accounts
- Accounts payable/receivable
- Bank deposits
- Assign duties
- Prepare schedules
- Train personnel on computer
- Complete employee performance reports
- Meal preparation and stock ordering
- Calculate amount of food required for each day's consumption

Educational Background

ASB Leadership School, June 7, 2003—July 6, 2003

- People/Resource Management

Alpena Community College, August 28, 2002—June 1, 2003

- Mathematics
- Music

Community College of the Marines, October 15, 1998—February 23, 2004

- Hotel/Restaurant Management

Alpena High School (graduated June 1, 1998, 3.5 GPA)

Special Qualifications

- Proficient with leading productivity software applications
- Clean driving record with a commercial Class B endorsement
- Own & operate various audio recording next and equipment
- Perform extensive automobile repair & car stereo installations

Outside Interests

- Playing Guitar

- Sound Recording

- Computer Upgrades/Repair

- Electronics

- Automobiles

- Home Remodeling

References available upon request.

Summary of Predictive Index Results

Name: Peter James

Survey Date: September 11, 2010

Report Date: September 11, 2010

Peter is an intense, results-oriented, self-starter, whose drive and sense of urgency are tempered and disciplined by his concern for the accuracy and quality of his work. His approach to anything he does, or is responsible for, will be carefully thought-out, based on thorough analysis and detailed knowledge of all pertinent facts.

Strongly technically oriented, he has confidence in his professional knowledge and ability to get things done quickly and correctly. With experience, he will develop a high level of expertise in his work and will be very aware of mistakes made either by himself or anybody doing work under his supervision. Peter takes his work and responsibilities very seriously and expects others to do the same.

In social matters, Peter is reserved and private, with little interest in small talk. His interest and his energy will be focused primarily on his work and, in general, he is more comfortable and open in the work environment than he is in purely social situations. In expressing himself in his work environment he is factual, direct, and authoritative.

Imaginative and venturesome, Peter is a creative person, capable of developing new ideas, systems, plans, or technology, or of analyzing and improving old ones. He relies primarily on his own knowledge and thinking, with little reference to others, relying as much as possible on himself alone to get things done. He will find it difficult to delegate, feeling strongly that if he is to be sure that something is done right, he must do it himself.

When, as a supervisor, it may be necessary for Peter to delegate details, he will follow up very closely and will be quick to spot and correct mistakes. His primary concern is to get things done right and quickly, and in accomplishing that goal he will be demanding of himself and others. While he may be perceived by other people as a rather aloof person, he will earn their respect for his knowledge and the soundness of his decisions.

Management Strategies

To maximize his effectiveness, productivity, and job satisfaction, consider providing Peter with the following:

- Opportunities to broaden the technical knowledge of his work with learning experience in increasingly responsible positions

- As much autonomy as possible in expressing his ideas and putting them into action

- Recognition for tangible results obtained, rather than for political or selling skills

MARGERIE HEATH

Career Goal

To contribute the skills and abilities needed in the successful formation and continued operation of a profitable business.

Work Experience

Henderson Real Estate, June 2010—Present—Smith Realty, May 2001—June 2003 (Receptionist/Sales Agent)

- Receive and route phone calls
- Maintain Web site and customer database
- Answer customer inquiries received via e-mail, and company Web site
- Arrange and store of documents
- Prepare legal documents and business forms
- Greet customers
- Build and maintain a customer base
- Identify the needs of customer requests
- Present a list of available options
- Conduct tours of properties
- Act as liaison between seller and buyer

Hidden Valley Resort, June 1998—May 2010—Duchess Inn, July 2001—January 2003 (Waitress/Hostess/Bartender/Supervision)

- Provide people a with warm, friendly atmosphere
- Take orders and relay them to the kitchen staff
- Fulfill orders and beverage requests in a quick and orderly manner
- Monitor dining area and recognizing patrons' needs
- Prepare guest check on computer
- Process payment and provide correct change to guest
- Recognize personnel shortages and take necessary action
- Delegate responsibilities to co-workers
- Train new personnel
- Credit card collection
- Prepare bank deposits

Educational Background

Michigan State University, September 1998—February 2001

- Business Administration
- Psychology

Northern High School (graduated June 1998)

Special Qualifications

- Maintain a valid real estate license
- Teach Sunday school courses
- Full-time parent
- Outgoing
- 6-year cheerleader

- Awarded for top monthly sales, October 2009

- Caring

- Enthusiastic

Outside Interests

- Camping

- Riding bike

- Outdoor sports

- Cooking

- Playing cards

- Gardening

References available upon request.

Summary of Predictive Index Results

Name: Margerie Heath

Survey Date: July 10, 2010

Report Date: July 10, 2010

Margerie is a patient, stable, and cooperative person who will do her work as instructed and will depend on management and professional training to provide the necessary guidelines. She has the patience and tolerance required for routine work and can be relied on to do such work consistently and in a relaxed manner.

She will focus on the details of her work and will handle them with somewhat better-than average accuracy. In work involving repeated contact with people, Margerie will be pleasant and agreeable, helpful and cooperative. She derives satisfaction from being of service to others, works comfortably under close supervision, and likes to feel part of a secure team.

Fairly easygoing, Margerie works at a steady, relatively unhurried pace and is comfortable doing the same things in the same way repeatedly. In the event of change in her work and responsibility, she needs to be given time to learn the new work thoroughly, which is best done with some opportunity for practice. Once having learned, she retains well.

In social terms, Margerie is unassuming, friendly and pleasant in general contact. She is a patient and willing listener, particularly with people she knows well and with whom she feels at ease.

Dependably consistent and steady in her work habits, Margerie will need close support and encouragement from supervision when she is required to work under pressure or in changing conditions.

Management Strategies

To maximize her effectiveness, productivity, and job satisfaction, consider providing Margerie with the following:

- Thorough, careful training in all detailed aspects and routines of her job

- Opportunity for repetitive practice doing what she has been trained to do

- A stable, familiar work environment and organization, with assurance of security provided by helpful, supportive management

- Expressions of recognition for long service, cooperation, and work well done

- Assurances of stability, security, and continuity of relations with familiar coworkers

Business Plan Template

USING THIS TEMPLATE

A business plan carefully spells out a company's projected course of action over a period of time, usually the first two to three years after the start-up. In addition, banks, lenders, and other investors examine the information and financial documentation before deciding whether or not to finance a new business venture. Therefore, a business plan is an essential tool in obtaining financing and should describe the business itself in detail as well as all important factors influencing the company, including the market, industry, competition, operations and management policies, problem solving strategies, financial resources and needs, and other vital information. The plan enables the business owner to anticipate costs, plan for difficulties, and take advantage of opportunities, as well as design and implement strategies that keep the company running as smoothly as possible.

This template has been provided as a model to help you construct your own business plan. Please keep in mind that there is no single acceptable format for a business plan, and that this template is in no way comprehensive, but serves as an example.

The business plans provided in this section are fictional and have been used by small business agencies as models for clients to use in compiling their own business plans.

GENERIC BUSINESS PLAN

Main headings included below are topics that should be covered in a comprehensive business plan. They include:

Business Summary

Purpose
Provides a brief overview of your business, succinctly highlighting the main ideas of your plan.

Includes

- Name and Type of Business
- Description of Product/Service
- Business History and Development
- Location
- Market
- Competition
- Management
- Financial Information
- Business Strengths and Weaknesses
- Business Growth

Table of Contents

Purpose
Organized in an Outline Format, the Table of Contents illustrates the selection and arrangement of information contained in your plan.

Includes

- Topic Headings and Subheadings
- Page Number References

Business History and Industry Outlook

Purpose

Examines the conception and subsequent development of your business within an industry specific context.

Includes

- Start-up Information
- Owner/Key Personnel Experience
- Location
- Development Problems and Solutions
- Investment/Funding Information

- Future Plans and Goals
- Market Trends and Statistics
- Major Competitors
- Product/Service Advantages
- National, Regional, and Local Economic Impact

Product/Service

Purpose

Introduces, defines, and details the product and/or service that inspired the information of your business.

Includes

- Unique Features
- Niche Served
- Market Comparison
- Stage of Product/Service Development

- Production
- Facilities, Equipment, and Labor
- Financial Requirements
- Product/Service Life Cycle
- Future Growth

Market Examination

Purpose

Assessment of product/service applications in relation to consumer buying cycles.

Includes

- Target Market
- Consumer Buying Habits
- Product/Service Applications
- Consumer Reactions
- Market Factors and Trends

- Penetration of the Market
- Market Share
- Research and Studies
- Cost
- Sales Volume and Goals

Competition

Purpose

Analysis of Competitors in the Marketplace.

Includes

- Competitor Information
- Product/Service Comparison
- Market Niche

- Product/Service Strengths and Weaknesses
- Future Product/Service Development

Marketing

Purpose

Identifies promotion and sales strategies for your product/service.

Includes

- Product/Service Sales Appeal
- Special and Unique Features
- Identification of Customers
- Sales and Marketing Staff
- Sales Cycles
- Type of Advertising/ Promotion
- Pricing
- Competition
- Customer Services

Operations

Purpose

Traces product/service development from production/inception to the market environment.

Includes

- Cost Effective Production Methods
- Facility
- Location
- Equipment
- Labor
- Future Expansion

Administration and Management

Purpose

Offers a statement of your management philosophy with an in-depth focus on processes and procedures.

Includes

- Management Philosophy
- Structure of Organization
- Reporting System
- Methods of Communication
- Employee Skills and Training
- Employee Needs and Compensation
- Work Environment
- Management Policies and Procedures
- Roles and Responsibilities

Key Personnel

Purpose

Describes the unique backgrounds of principle employees involved in business.

Includes

- Owner(s)/Employee Education and Experience
- Positions and Roles
- Benefits and Salary
- Duties and Responsibilities
- Objectives and Goals

Potential Problems and Solutions

Purpose

Discussion of problem solving strategies that change issues into opportunities.

Includes

- Risks
- Litigation
- Future Competition
- Economic Impact
- Problem Solving Skills

Financial Information

Purpose

Secures needed funding and assistance through worksheets and projections detailing financial plans, methods of repayment, and future growth opportunities.

Includes

- Financial Statements
- Bank Loans
- Methods of Repayment
- Tax Returns

- Start-up Costs
- Projected Income (3 years)
- Projected Cash Flow (3 Years)
- Projected Balance Statements (3 years)

Appendices

Purpose

Supporting documents used to enhance your business proposal.

Includes

- Photographs of product, equipment, facilities, etc.
- Copyright/Trademark Documents
- Legal Agreements
- Marketing Materials
- Research and or Studies

- Operation Schedules
- Organizational Charts
- Job Descriptions
- Resumes
- Additional Financial Documentation

Fictional Food Distributor

Commercial Foods, Inc.

3003 Avondale Ave.
Knoxville, TN 37920

This plan demonstrates how a partnership can have a positive impact on a new business. It demonstrates how two individuals can carve a niche in the specialty foods market by offering gourmet foods to upscale restaurants and fine hotels. This plan is fictional and has not been used to gain funding from a bank or other lending institution.

STATEMENT OF PURPOSE

Commercial Foods, Inc. seeks a loan of $75,000 to establish a new business. This sum, together with $5,000 equity investment by the principals, will be used as follows:

- Merchandise inventory $25,000
- Office fixture/equipment $12,000
- Warehouse equipment $14,000
- One delivery truck $10,000
- Working capital $39,000
- Total $100,000

DESCRIPTION OF THE BUSINESS

Commercial Foods, Inc. will be a distributor of specialty food service products to hotels and upscale restaurants in the geographical area of a 50 mile radius of Knoxville. Richard Roberts will direct the sales effort and John Williams will manage the warehouse operation and the office. One delivery truck will be used initially with a second truck added in the third year. We expect to begin operation of the business within 30 days after securing the requested financing.

MANAGEMENT

A. Richard Roberts is a native of Memphis, Tennessee. He is a graduate of Memphis State University with a Bachelor's degree from the School of Business. After graduation, he worked for a major manufacturer of specialty food service products as a detail sales person for five years, and, for the past three years, he has served as a product sales manager for this firm.

B. John Williams is a native of Nashville, Tennessee. He holds a B.S. Degree in Food Technology from the University of Tennessee. His career includes five years as a product development chemist in gourmet food products and five years as operations manager for a food service distributor.

Both men are healthy and energetic. Their backgrounds complement each other, which will ensure the success of Commercial Foods, Inc. They will set policies together and personnel decisions will be made jointly. Initial salaries for the owners will be $1,000 per month for the first few years. The spouses of both principals are successful in the business world and earn enough to support the families.

They have engaged the services of Foster Jones, CPA, and William Hale, Attorney, to assist them in an advisory capacity.

PERSONNEL

The firm will employ one delivery truck driver at a wage of $8.00 per hour. One office worker will be employed at $7.50 per hour. One part-time employee will be used in the office at $5.00 per hour. The driver will load and unload his own trucks. Mr. Williams will assist in the warehouse operation as needed to assist one stock person at $7.00 per hour. An additional delivery truck and driver will be added the third year.

LOCATION

The firm will lease a 20,000 square foot building at 3003 Avondale Ave., in Knoxville, which contains warehouse and office areas equipped with two-door truck docks. The annual rental is $9,000. The building was previously used as a food service warehouse and very little modification to the building will be required.

PRODUCTS AND SERVICES

The firm will offer specialty food service products such as soup bases, dessert mixes, sauce bases, pastry mixes, spices, and flavors, normally used by upscale restaurants and nice hotels. We are going after a niche in the market with high quality gourmet products. There is much less competition in this market than in standard run of the mill food service products. Through their work experiences, the principals have contacts with supply sources and with local chefs.

THE MARKET

We know from our market survey that there are over 200 hotels and upscale restaurants in the area we plan to serve. Customers will be attracted by a direct sales approach. We will offer samples of our products and product application data on use of our products in the finished prepared foods. We will cultivate the chefs in these establishments. The technical background of John Williams will be especially useful here.

COMPETITION

We find that we will be only distributor in the area offering a full line of gourmet food service products. Other foodservice distributors offer only a few such items in conjunction with their standard product line. Our survey shows that many of the chefs are ordering products from Atlanta and Memphis because of a lack of adequate local supply.

SUMMARY

Commercial Foods, Inc. will be established as a foodservice distributor of specialty food in Knoxville. The principals, with excellent experience in the industry, are seeking a $75,000 loan to establish the business. The principals are investing $25,000 as equity capital.

The business will be set up as an S Corporation with each principal owning 50% of the common stock in the corporation.

Fictional Hardware Store

OSHKOSH HARDWARE, Inc.

123 Main St.
Oshkosh, WI 54901

The following plan outlines how a small hardware store can survive competition from large discount chains by offering products and providing expert advice in the use of any product it sells. This plan is fictional and has not been used to gain funding from a bank or other lending institution.

EXECUTIVE SUMMARY

Oshkosh Hardware, Inc. is a new corporation that is going to establish a retail hardware store in a strip mall in Oshkosh, Wisconsin. The store will sell hardware of all kinds, quality tools, paint, and housewares. The business will make revenue and a profit by servicing its customers not only with needed hardware but also with expert advice in the use of any product it sells.

Oshkosh Hardware, Inc. will be operated by its sole shareholder, James Smith. The company will have a total of four employees. It will sell its products in the local market. Customers will buy our products because we will provide free advice on the use of all of our products and will also furnish a full refund warranty.

Oshkosh Hardware, Inc. will sell its products in the Oshkosh store staffed by three sales representatives. No additional employees will be needed to achieve its short and long range goals. The primary short range goal is to open the store by October 1, 1994. In order to achieve this goal a lease must be signed by July 1, 1994 and the complete inventory ordered by August 1, 1994.

Mr. James Smith will invest $30,000 in the business. In addition, the company will have to borrow $150,000 during the first year to cover the investment in inventory, accounts receivable, and furniture and equipment. The company will be profitable after six months of operation and should be able to start repayment of the loan in the second year.

THE BUSINESS

The business will sell hardware of all kinds, quality tools, paint, and housewares. We will purchase our products from three large wholesale buying groups.

In general our customers are homeowners who do their own repair and maintenance, hobbyists, and housewives. Our business is unique in that we will have a complete line of all hardware items and will be able to get special orders by overnight delivery. The business makes revenue and profits by servicing our customers not only with needed hardware but also with expert advice in the use of any product we sell. Our major costs for bringing our products to market are cost of merchandise of 36%, salaries of $45,000, and occupancy costs of $60,000.

Oshkosh Hardware, Inc.'s retail outlet will be located at 1524 Frontage Road, which is in a newly developed retail center of Oshkosh. Our location helps facilitate accessibility from all parts of town and reduces our delivery costs. The store will occupy 7500 square feet of space. The major equipment involved in our business is counters and shelving, a computer, a paint mixing machine, and a truck.

THE MARKET

Oshkosh Hardware, Inc. will operate in the local market. There are 15,000 potential customers in this market area. We have three competitors who control approximately 98% of the market at present. We feel we can capture 25% of the market within the next four years. Our major reason for believing this is that our staff is technically competent to advise our customers in the correct use of all products we sell.

After a careful market analysis, we have determined that approximately 60% of our customers are men and 40% are women. The percentage of customers that fall into the following age categories are:

Under 16: 0%
17-21: 5%
22-30: 30%
31-40: 30%
41-50: 20%
51-60: 10%
61-70: 5%
Over 70: 0%

The reasons our customers prefer our products is our complete knowledge of their use and our full refund warranty.

We get our information about what products our customers want by talking to existing customers. There seems to be an increasing demand for our product. The demand for our product is increasing in size based on the change in population characteristics.

SALES

At Oshkosh Hardware, Inc. we will employ three sales people and will not need any additional personnel to achieve our sales goals. These salespeople will need several years experience in home repair and power tool usage. We expect to attract 30% of our customers from newspaper ads, 5% of our customers from local directories, 5% of our customers from the yellow pages, 10% of our customers from family and friends, and 50% of our customers from current customers. The most cost effect source will be current customers. In general our industry is growing.

MANAGEMENT

We would evaluate the quality of our management staff as being excellent. Our manager is experienced and very motivated to achieve the various sales and quality assurance objectives we have set. We will use a management information system that produces key inventory, quality assurance, and sales data on a weekly basis. All data is compared to previously established goals for that week, and deviations are the primary focus of the management staff.

GOALS IMPLEMENTATION

The short term goals of our business are:

1. Open the store by October 1, 1994
2. Reach our breakeven point in two months
3. Have sales of $100,000 in the first six months

In order to achieve our first short term goal we must:

1. Sign the lease by July 1, 1994
2. Order a complete inventory by August 1, 1994

In order to achieve our second short term goal we must:

1. Advertise extensively in Sept. and Oct.
2. Keep expenses to a minimum

In order to achieve our third short term goal we must:

1. Promote power tool sales for the Christmas season
2. Keep good customer traffic in Jan. and Feb.

The long term goals for our business are:

1. Obtain sales volume of $600,000 in three years
2. Become the largest hardware dealer in the city
3. Open a second store in Fond du Lac

The most important thing we must do in order to achieve the long term goals for our business is to develop a highly profitable business with excellent cash flow.

FINANCE

Oshkosh Hardware, Inc. Faces some potential threats or risks to our business. They are discount house competition. We believe we can avoid or compensate for this by providing quality products complimented by quality advice on the use of every product we sell. The financial projections we have prepared are located at the end of this document.

JOB DESCRIPTION-GENERAL MANAGER

The General Manager of the business of the corporation will be the president of the corporation. He will be responsible for the complete operation of the retail hardware store which is owned by the corporation. A detailed description of his duties and responsibilities is as follows.

Sales

Train and supervise the three sales people. Develop programs to motivate and compensate these employees. Coordinate advertising and sales promotion effects to achieve sales totals as outlined in budget. Oversee purchasing function and inventory control procedures to insure adequate merchandise at all times at a reasonable cost.

Finance

Prepare monthly and annual budgets. Secure adequate line of credit from local banks. Supervise office personnel to insure timely preparation of records, statements, all government reports, control of receivables and payables, and monthly financial statements.

Administration

Perform duties as required in the areas of personnel, building leasing and maintenance, licenses and permits, and public relations.

Organizations, Agencies, & Consultants

A listing of Associations and Consultants of interest to entrepreneurs, followed by the ten Small Business Administration Regional Offices, Small Business Development Centers, Service Corps of Retired Executives offices, and Venture Capital and Finance Companies.

Associations

This section contains a listing of associations and other agencies of interest to the small business owner. Entries are listed alphabetically by organization name.

American Business Women's Association
9100 Ward Pkwy.
PO Box 8728
Kansas City, MO 64114-0728
(800)228-0007
E-mail: abwa@abwa.org
Website: http://www.abwa.org
Jeanne Banks, National President

American Franchisee Association
53 W Jackson Blvd., Ste. 1157
Chicago, IL 60604
(312)431-0545
E-mail: info@franchisee.org
Website: http://www.franchisee.org
Susan P. Kezios, President

American Independent Business Alliance
222 S Black Ave.
Bozeman, MT 59715
(406)582-1255
E-mail: info@amiba.net
Website: http://www.amiba.net
Jennifer Rockne, Director

American Small Businesses Association
206 E College St., Ste. 201
Grapevine, TX 76051
800-942-2722
E-mail: info@asbaonline.org
Website: http://www.asbaonline.org/

American Women's Economic Development Corporation
216 East 45th St., 10th Floor
New York, NY 10017
(917)368-6100

Fax: (212)986-7114
E-mail: info@awed.org
Website: http://www.awed.org
Roseanne Antonucci, Exec. Dir.

Association for Enterprise Opportunity
1601 N Kent St., Ste. 1101
Arlington, VA 22209
(703)841-7760
Fax: (703)841-7748
E-mail: aeo@assoceo.org
Website: http://www.micro enterpriseworks.org
Bill Edwards, Exec.Dir.

Association of Small Business Development Centers
c/o Don Wilson
8990 Burke Lake Rd.
Burke, VA 22015
(703)764-9850
Fax: (703)764-1234
E-mail: info@asbdc-us.org
Website: http://www.asbdc-us.org
Don Wilson, Pres./CEO

BEST Employers Association
2505 McCabe Way
Irvine, CA 92614
(949)253-4080
800-433-0088
Fax: (714)553-0883
E-mail: info@bestlife.com
Website: http://www.bestlife.com
Donald R. Lawrenz, CEO

Center for Family Business
PO Box 24219
Cleveland, OH 44124
(440)460-5409
E-mail: grummi@aol.com
Dr. Leon A. Danco, Chm.

Coalition for Government Procurement
1990 M St. NW, Ste. 400
Washington, DC 20036
(202)331-0975
E-mail: info@thecgp.org
Website: http://www.coalgovpro.org
Paul Caggiano, Pres.

Employers of America
PO Box 1874
Mason City, IA 50402-1874
(641)424-3187
800-728-3187
Fax: (641)424-1673
E-mail: employer@employerhelp.org
Website: http://www.employerhelp.org
Jim Collison, Pres.

Family Firm Institute
200 Lincoln St., Ste. 201
Boston, MA 02111
(617)482-3045
Fax: (617)482-3049
E-mail: ffi@ffi.org
Website: http://www.ffi.org
Judy L. Green, Ph.D., Exec.Dir.

Independent Visually Impaired Enterprisers
500 S 3rd St., Apt. H
Burbank, CA 91502
(818)238-9321
E-mail: abazyn@bazyn communications.com
http://www.acb.org/affiliates
Adris Bazyn, Pres.

International Association for Business Organizations
3 Woodthorn Ct., Ste. 12
Owings Mills, MD 21117
(410)581-1373
E-mail: nahbb@msn.com
Rudolph Lewis, Exec. Officer

International Council for Small Business
The George Washington University
School of Business and Public
Management
2115 G St. NW, Ste. 403
Washington, DC 20052
(202)994-0704
Fax: (202)994-4930
E-mail: icsb@gwu.edu
Website: http://www.icsb.org
Susan G. Duffy. Admin.

International Small Business Consortium
3309 Windjammer St.
Norman, OK 73072
E-mail: sb@isbc.com
Website: http://www.isbc.com

Kauffman Center for Entrepreneurial Leadership
4801 Rockhill Rd.
Kansas City, MO 64110-2046
(816)932-1000
E-mail: info@kauffman.org
Website: http://www.entreworld.org

National Alliance for Fair Competition
3 Bethesda Metro Center, Ste. 1100
Bethesda, MD 20814
(410)235-7116
Fax: (410)235-7116
E-mail: ampesq@aol.com
Tony Ponticelli, Exec.Dir.

National Association for the Self-Employed
PO Box 612067
DFW Airport
Dallas, TX 75261-2067
(800)232-6273
E-mail: mpetron@nase.org
Website: http://www.nase.org
Robert Hughes, Pres.

National Association of Business Leaders
4132 Shoreline Dr., Ste. J & H
Earth City, MO 63045
Fax: (314)298-9110
E-mail: nabl@nabl.com
Website: http://www.nabl.com/
Gene Blumenthal, Contact

National Association of Private Enterprise
PO Box 15550
Long Beach, CA 90815
888-224-0953

Fax: (714)844-4942
Website: http://www.napeonline.net
Laura Squiers, Exec.Dir.

National Association of Small Business Investment Companies
666 11th St. NW, Ste. 750
Washington, DC 20001
(202)628-5055
Fax: (202)628-5080
E-mail: nasbic@nasbic.org
Website: http://www.nasbic.org
Lee W. Mercer, Pres.

National Business Association
PO Box 700728
5151 Beltline Rd., Ste. 1150
Dallas, TX 75370
(972)458-0900
800-456-0440
Fax: (972)960-9149
E-mail: info@nationalbusiness.org
Website: http://www.national
business.org
Raj Nisankarao, Pres.

National Business Owners Association
PO Box 111
Stuart, VA 24171
(276)251-7500
(866)251-7505
Fax: (276)251-2217
E-mail: membershipservices@nboa.org
Website: http://www.rvmdb.com.nboa
Paul LaBarr, Pres.

National Center for Fair Competition
PO Box 220
Annandale, VA 22003
(703)280-4622
Fax: (703)280-0942
E-mail: kentonp1@aol.com
Kenton Pattie, Pres.

National Family Business Council
1640 W. Kennedy Rd.
Lake Forest, IL 60045
(847)295-1040
Fax: (847)295-1898
E-mail: lmsnfbc@email.msn.com
Jogn E. Messervey, Pres.

National Federation of Independent Business
53 Century Blvd., Ste. 250
Nashville, TN 37214
(615)872-5800
800-NFIBNOW
Fax: (615)872-5353
Website: http://www.nfib.org
Jack Faris, Pres. and CEO

National Small Business Association
1156 15th St. NW, Ste. 1100
Washington, DC 20005
(202)293-8830
800-345-6728
Fax: (202)872-8543
E-mail: press@nsba.biz
Website: http://www.nsba.biz
Rob Yunich, Dir. of Communications

PUSH Commercial Division
930 E 50th St.
Chicago, IL 60615-2702
(773)373-3366
Fax: (773)373-3571
E-mail: info@rainbowpush.org
Website: http://www.rainbowpush.org
Rev. Willie T. Barrow, Co-Chm.

Research Institute for Small and Emerging Business
722 12th St. NW
Washington, DC 20005
(202)628-8382
Fax: (202)628-8392
E-mail: info@riseb.org
Website: http://www.riseb.org
Allan Neece, Jr., Chm.

Sales Professionals USA
PO Box 149
Arvada, CO 80001
(303)534-4937
888-736-7767
E-mail: salespro@salesprofessionals-usa.com
Website: http://www.salesprofessionals-usa.com
Sharon Herbert, Natl. Pres.

Score Association - Service Corps of Retired Executives
409 3rd St. SW, 6th Fl.
Washington, DC 20024
(202)205-6762
800-634-0245
Fax: (202)205-7636
E-mail: media@score.org
Website: http://www.score.org
W. Kenneth Yancey, Jr., CEO

Small Business and Entrepreneurship Council
1920 L St. NW, Ste. 200
Washington, DC 20036
(202)785-0238
Fax: (202)822-8118
E-mail: membership@sbec.org
Website: http://www.sbecouncil.org
Karen Kerrigan, Pres./CEO

Small Business in Telecommunications
1331 H St. NW, Ste. 500
Washington, DC 20005
(202)347-4511
Fax: (202)347-8607
E-mail: sbt@sbthome.org
Website: http://www.sbthome.org
Lonnie Danchik, Chm.

Small Business Legislative Council
1010 Massachusetts Ave. NW, Ste. 540
Washington, DC 20005
(202)639-8500
Fax: (202)296-5333
E-mail: email@sblc.org
Website: http://www.sblc.org
John Satagaj, Pres.

Small Business Service Bureau
554 Main St.
PO Box 15014
Worcester, MA 01615-0014
(508)756-3513
800-343-0939
Fax: (508)770-0528
E-mail: membership@sbsb.com
Website: http://www.sbsb.com
Francis R. Carroll, Pres.

**Small Publishers Association
of North America**
1618 W COlorado Ave.
Colorado Springs, CO 80904
(719)475-1726
Fax: (719)471-2182
E-mail: span@spannet.org
Website: http://www.spannet.org
Scott Flora, Exec. Dir.

SOHO America
PO Box 941
Hurst, TX 76053-0941
800-495-SOHO
E-mail: soho@1sas.com
Website: http://www.soho.org

**Structured Employment Economic
Development Corporation**
915 Broadway, 17th Fl.
New York, NY 10010
(212)473-0255
Fax: (212)473-0357
E-mail: info@seedco.org
Website: http://www.seedco.org
William Grinker, CEO

Support Services Alliance
107 Prospect St.
Schoharie, NY 12157
800-836-4772

E-mail: info@ssamembers.com
Website: http://www.ssainfo.com
Steve COle, Pres.

**United States Association for Small
Business and Entrepreneurship**
975 University Ave., No. 3260
Madison, WI 53706
(608)262-9982
Fax: (608)263-0818
E-mail: jgillman@wisc.edu
Website: http://www.ususbe.org
Joan Gillman, Exec. Dir.

Consultants

This section contains a listing of consultants specializing in small business development. It is arranged alphabetically by country, then by state or province, then by city, then by firm name.

Canada

Alberta

Common Sense Solutions
3405 16A Ave.
Edmonton, AB, Canada
(403)465-7330
Fax: (403)465-7380
E-mail: gcoulson@comsense
solutions.com
Website: http://www.comsense
solutions.com

Varsity Consulting Group
School of Business
University of Alberta
Edmonton, AB, Canada T6G 2R6
(780)492-2994
Fax: (780)492-5400
Website: http://www.bus.ualberta.ca/vcg

Viro Hospital Consulting
42 Commonwealth Bldg., 9912 - 106
St. NW
Edmonton, AB, Canada T5K 1C5
(403)425-3871
Fax: (403)425-3871
E-mail: rpb@freenet.edmonton.ab.ca

British Columbia

SRI Strategic Resources Inc.
4330 Kingsway, Ste. 1600
Burnaby, BC, Canada V5H 4G7
(604)435-0627
Fax: (604)435-2782

E-mail: inquiry@sri.bc.ca
Website: http://www.sri.com

Andrew R. De Boda Consulting
1523 Milford Ave.
Coquitlam, BC, Canada V3J 2V9
(604)936-4527
Fax: (604)936-4527
E-mail: deboda@intergate.bc.ca
Website: http://www.ourworld.
compuserve.com/homepages/deboda

The Sage Group Ltd.
980 - 355 Burrard St.
744 W Haistings, Ste. 410
Vancouver, BC, Canada V6C 1A5
(604)669-9269
Fax: (604)669-6622

Tikkanen-Bradley
1345 Nelson St., Ste. 202
Vancouver, BC, Canada V6E 1J8
(604)669-0583
E-mail: webmaster@tikkanen
bradley.com
Website: http://www.tikkanenbradley.com

Ontario

The Cynton Co.
17 Massey St.
Brampton, ON, Canada L6S 2V6
(905)792-7769
Fax: (905)792-8116
E-mail: cynton@home.com
Website: http://www.cynton.com

Begley & Associates
RR 6
Cambridge, ON, Canada N1R 5S7
(519)740-3629
Fax: (519)740-3629
E-mail: begley@in.on.ca
Website: http://www.in.on.ca/~begley/
index.htm

CRO Engineering Ltd.
1895 William Hodgins Ln.
Carp, ON, Canada K0A 1L0
(613)839-1108
Fax: (613)839-1406
E-mail: J.Grefford@ieee.ca
Website: http://www.geocities.com/
WallStreet/District/7401/

Task Enterprises
Box 69, RR 2 Hamilton
Flamborough, ON, Canada L8N 2Z7
(905)659-0153
Fax: (905)659-0861

HST Group Ltd.
430 Gilmour St.
Ottawa, ON, Canada K2P 0R8
(613)236-7303
Fax: (613)236-9893

Harrison Associates
BCE Pl.
181 Bay St., Ste. 3740
PO Box 798
Toronto, ON, Canada M5J 2T3
(416)364-5441
Fax: (416)364-2875

TCI Convergence Ltd. Management Consultants
99 Crown's Ln.
Toronto, ON, Canada M5R 3P4
(416)515-4146
Fax: (416)515-2097
E-mail: tci@inforamp.net
Website: http://tciconverge.com/index.1.html

Ken Wyman & Associates Inc.
64B Shuter St., Ste. 200
Toronto, ON, Canada M5B 1B1
(416)362-2926
Fax: (416)362-3039
E-mail: kenwyman@compuserve.com

JPL Business Consultants
82705 Metter Rd.
Wellandport, ON, Canada L0R 2J0
(905)386-7450
Fax: (905)386-7450
E-mail: plamarch@freenet.npiec.on.ca

Quebec

The Zimmar Consulting Partnership Inc.
Westmount
PO Box 98
Montreal, QC, Canada H3Z 2T1
(514)484-1459
Fax: (514)484-3063

Saskatchewan

Trimension Group
No. 104-110 Research Dr.
Innovation Place, SK, Canada S7N 3R3
(306)668-2560
Fax: (306)975-1156
E-mail: trimension@trimension.ca
Website: http://www.trimension.ca

Corporate Management Consultants
40 Government Road - PO Box 185
Prud Homme, SK, Canada, S0K 3K0
(306)654-4569
Fax: (650)618-2742

E-mail: cmccorporatemanagement@shaw.ca
Website: http://www.Corporate managementconsultants.com
Gerald Rekve

United States

Alabama

Business Planning Inc.
300 Office Park Dr.
Birmingham, AL 35223-2474
(205)870-7090
Fax: (205)870-7103

Tradebank of Eastern Alabama
546 Broad St., Ste. 3
Gadsden, AL 35901
(205)547-8700
Fax: (205)547-8718
E-mail: mansion@webex.com
Website: http://www.webex.com/~tea

Alaska

AK Business Development Center
3335 Arctic Blvd., Ste. 203
Anchorage, AK 99503
(907)562-0335
Free: 800-478-3474
Fax: (907)562-6988
E-mail: abdc@gci.net
Website: http://www.abdc.org

Business Matters
PO Box 287
Fairbanks, AK 99707
(907)452-5650

Arizona

Carefree Direct Marketing Corp.
8001 E Serene St.
PO Box 3737
Carefree, AZ 85377-3737
(480)488-4227
Fax: (480)488-2841

Trans Energy Corp.
1739 W 7th Ave.
Mesa, AZ 85202
(480)827-7915
Fax: (480)967-6601
E-mail: aha@clean-air.org
Website: http://www.clean-air.org

CMAS
5125 N 16th St.
Phoenix, AZ 85016

(602)395-1001
Fax: (602)604-8180

Comgate Telemanagement Ltd.
706 E Bell Rd., Ste. 105
Phoenix, AZ 85022
(602)485-5708
Fax: (602)485-5709
E-mail: comgate@netzone.com
Website: http://www.comgate.com

Moneysoft Inc.
1 E Camelback Rd. #550
Phoenix, AZ 85012
Free: 800-966-7797
E-mail: mbray@moneysoft.com

Harvey C. Skoog
PO Box 26439
Prescott Valley, AZ 86312
(520)772-1714
Fax: (520)772-2814

LMC Services
8711 E Pinnacle Peak Rd., No. 340
Scottsdale, AZ 85255-3555
(602)585-7177
Fax: (602)585-5880
E-mail: louws@earthlink.com

Sauerbrun Technology Group Ltd.
7979 E Princess Dr., Ste. 5
Scottsdale, AZ 85255-5878
(602)502-4950
Fax: (602)502-4292
E-mail: info@sauerbrun.com
Website: http://www.sauerbrun.com

Gary L. McLeod
PO Box 230
Sonoita, AZ 85637
Fax: (602)455-5661

Van Cleve Associates
6932 E 2nd St.
Tucson, AZ 85710
(520)296-2587
Fax: (520)296-3358

California

Acumen Group Inc.
(650)949-9349
Fax: (650)949-4845
E-mail: acumen-g@ix.netcom.com
Website: http://pw2.netcom.com/~janed/acumen.html

On-line Career and Management Consulting
420 Central Ave., No. 314
Alameda, CA 94501

(510)864-0336
Fax: (510)864-0336
E-mail: career@dnai.com
Website: http://www.dnai.com/~career

Career Paths-Thomas E. Church & Associates Inc.
PO Box 2439
Aptos, CA 95001
(408)662-7950
Fax: (408)662-7955
E-mail: church@ix.netcom.com
Website: http://www.careerpaths-tom.com

Keck & Co. Business Consultants
410 Walsh Rd.
Atherton, CA 94027
(650)854-9588
Fax: (650)854-7240
E-mail: info@keckco.com
Website: http://www.keckco.com

Ben W. Laverty III, PhD, REA, CEI
4909 Stockdale Hwy., Ste. 132
Bakersfield, CA 93309
(661)283-8300
Free: 800-833-0373
Fax: (661)283-8313
E-mail: cstc@cstcsafety.com
Website: http://www.cstcsafety.com/cstc

Lindquist Consultants-Venture Planning
225 Arlington Ave.
Berkeley, CA 94707
(510)524-6685
Fax: (510)527-6604

Larson Associates
PO Box 9005
Brea, CA 92822
(714)529-4121
Fax: (714)572-3606
E-mail: ray@consultlarson.com
Website: http://www.consultlarson.com

Kremer Management Consulting
PO Box 500
Carmel, CA 93921
(408)626-8311
Fax: (408)624-2663
E-mail: ddkremer@aol.com

W and J PARTNERSHIP
PO Box 2499
18876 Edwin Markham Dr.
Castro Valley, CA 94546
(510)583-7751
Fax: (510)583-7645
E-mail: wamorgan@wjpartnership.com
Website: http://www.wjpartnership.com

JB Associates
21118 Gardena Dr.
Cupertino, CA 95014
(408)257-0214
Fax: (408)257-0216
E-mail: semarang@sirius.com

House Agricultural Consultants
PO Box 1615
Davis, CA 95617-1615
(916)753-3361
Fax: (916)753-0464
E-mail: infoag@houseag.com
Website: http://www.houseag.com/

3C Systems Co.
16161 Ventura Blvd., Ste. 815
Encino, CA 91436
(818)907-1302
Fax: (818)907-1357
E-mail: mark@3CSysCo.com
Website: http://www.3CSysCo.com

Technical Management Consultants
3624 Westfall Dr.
Encino, CA 91436-4154
(818)784-0626
Fax: (818)501-5575
E-mail: tmcrs@aol.com

RAINWATER-GISH & Associates, Business Finance & Development
317 3rd St., Ste. 3
Eureka, CA 95501
(707)443-0030
Fax: (707)443-5683

Global Tradelinks
451 Pebble Beach Pl.
Fullerton, CA 92835
(714)441-2280
Fax: (714)441-2281
E-mail: info@globaltradelinks.com
Website: http://www.globaltradelinks.com

Strategic Business Group
800 Cienaga Dr.
Fullerton, CA 92835-1248
(714)449-1040
Fax: (714)525-1631

Burnes Consulting
20537 Wolf Creek Rd.
Grass Valley, CA 95949
(530)346-8188
Free: 800-949-9021
Fax: (530)346-7704
E-mail: kent@burnesconsulting.com
Website: http://www.burnesconsulting.com

Pioneer Business Consultants
9042 Garfield Ave., Ste. 312
Huntington Beach, CA 92646
(714)964-7600

Beblie, Brandt & Jacobs Inc.
16 Technology, Ste. 164
Irvine, CA 92618
(714)450-8790
Fax: (714)450-8799
E-mail: darcy@bbjinc.com
Website: http://198.147.90.26

Fluor Daniel Inc.
3353 Michelson Dr.
Irvine, CA 92612-0650
(949)975-2000
Fax: (949)975-5271
E-mail: sales.consulting@fluordaniel.com
Website: http://www.fluordaniel consulting.com

MCS Associates
18300 Von Karman, Ste. 710
Irvine, CA 92612
(949)263-8700
Fax: (949)263-0770
E-mail: info@mcsassociates.com
Website: http://www.mcsassociates.com

Inspired Arts Inc.
4225 Executive Sq., Ste. 1160
La Jolla, CA 92037
(619)623-3525
Free: 800-851-4394
Fax: (619)623-3534
E-mail: info@inspiredarts.com
Website: http://www.inspiredarts.com

The Laresis Companies
PO Box 3284
La Jolla, CA 92038
(619)452-2720
Fax: (619)452-8744

RCL & Co.
PO Box 1143
737 Pearl St., Ste. 201
La Jolla, CA 92038
(619)454-8883
Fax: (619)454-8880

Comprehensive Business Services
3201 Lucas Cir.
Lafayette, CA 94549
(925)283-8272
Fax: (925)283-8272

The Ribble Group
27601 Forbes Rd., Ste. 52
Laguna Niguel, CA 92677

(714)582-1085
Fax: (714)582-6420
E-mail: ribble@deltanet.com

Norris Bernstein, CMC
9309 Marina Pacifica Dr. N
Long Beach, CA 90803
(562)493-5458
Fax: (562)493-5459
E-mail: norris@ctecomputer.com
Website: http://foodconsultants.com/
bernstein/

Horizon Consulting Services
1315 Garthwick Dr.
Los Altos, CA 94024
(415)967-0906
Fax: (415)967-0906

Brincko Associates Inc.
1801 Avenue of the Stars, Ste. 1054
Los Angeles, CA 90067
(310)553-4523
Fax: (310)553-6782

**Rubenstein/Justman Management
Consultants**
2049 Century Park E, 24th Fl.
Los Angeles, CA 90067
(310)282-0800
Fax: (310)282-0400
E-mail: info@rjmc.net
Website: http://www.rjmc.net

F.J. Schroeder & Associates
1926 Westholme Ave.
Los Angeles, CA 90025
(310)470-2655
Fax: (310)470-6378
E-mail: fjsacons@aol.com
Website: http://www.mcninet.com/
GlobalLook/Fjschroe.html

Western Management Associates
5959 W Century Blvd., Ste. 565
Los Angeles, CA 90045-6506
(310)645-1091
Free: (888)788-6534
Fax: (310)645-1092
E-mail: gene@cfoforrent.com
Website: http://www.cfoforrent.com

Darrell Sell and Associates
Los Gatos, CA 95030
(408)354-7794
E-mail: darrell@netcom.com

Leslie J. Zambo
3355 Michael Dr.
Marina, CA 93933
(408)384-7086

Fax: (408)647-4199
E-mail: 104776.1552@compuserve.com

Marketing Services Management
PO Box 1377
Martinez, CA 94553
(510)370-8527
Fax: (510)370-8527
E-mail: markserve@biotechnet.com

William M. Shine Consulting Service
PO Box 127
Moraga, CA 94556-0127
(510)376-6516

Palo Alto Management Group Inc.
2672 Bayshore Pky., Ste. 701
Mountain View, CA 94043
(415)968-4374
Fax: (415)968-4245
E-mail: mburwen@pamg.com

BizplanSource
1048 Irvine Ave., Ste. 621
Newport Beach, CA 92660
Free: 888-253-0974
Fax: 800-859-8254
E-mail: info@bizplansource.com
Website: http://www.bizplansource.com
Adam Greengrass, President

The Market Connection
4020 Birch St., Ste. 203
Newport Beach, CA 92660
(714)731-6273
Fax: (714)833-0253

Muller Associates
PO Box 7264
Newport Beach, CA 92658
(714)646-1169
Fax: (714)646-1169

International Health Resources
PO Box 329
North San Juan, CA 95960-0329
(530)292-1266
Fax: (530)292-1243
Website: http://www.futureof
healthcare.com

NEXUS - Consultants to Management
PO Box 1531
Novato, CA 94948
(415)897-4400
Fax: (415)898-2252
E-mail: jimnexus@aol.com

Aerospcace.Org
PO Box 28831
Oakland, CA 94604-8831

(510)530-9169
Fax: (510)530-3411
Website: http://www.aerospace.org

Intelequest Corp.
722 Gailen Ave.
Palo Alto, CA 94303
(415)968-3443
Fax: (415)493-6954
E-mail: frits@iqix.com

McLaughlin & Associates
66 San Marino Cir.
Rancho Mirage, CA 92270
(760)321-2932
Fax: (760)328-2474
E-mail: jackmcla@msn.com

**Carrera Consulting Group, a division
of Maximus**
2110 21st St., Ste. 400
Sacramento, CA 95818
(916)456-3300
Fax: (916)456-3306
E-mail: central@carreraconsulting.com
Website: http://www.carreraconsulting.com

**Bay Area Tax Consultants and Bayhill
Financial Consultants**
1150 Bayhill Dr., Ste. 1150
San Bruno, CA 94066-3004
(415)952-8786
Fax: (415)588-4524
E-mail: baytax@compuserve.com
Website: http://www.baytax.com/

AdCon Services, LLC
8871 Hillery Dr.
Dan Diego, CA 92126
(858)433-1411
E-mail: adam@adconservices.com
Website: http://www.adconservices.com
Adam Greengrass

California Business Incubation Network
101 W Broadway, No. 480
San Diego, CA 92101
(619)237-0559
Fax: (619)237-0521

G.R. Gordetsky Consultants Inc.
11414 Windy Summit Pl.
San Diego, CA 92127
(619)487-4939
Fax: (619)487-5587
E-mail: gordet@pacbell.net

Freeman, Sullivan & Co.
131 Steuart St., Ste. 500
San Francisco, CA 94105
(415)777-0707

Free: 800-777-0737
Fax: (415)777-2420
Website: http://www.fsc-research.com

Ideas Unlimited
2151 California St., Ste. 7
San Francisco, CA 94115
(415)931-0641
Fax: (415)931-0880

Russell Miller Inc.
300 Montgomery St., Ste. 900
San Francisco, CA 94104
(415)956-7474
Fax: (415)398-0620
E-mail: rmi@pacbell.net
Website: http://www.rmisf.com

PKF Consulting
425 California St., Ste. 1650
San Francisco, CA 94104
(415)421-5378
Fax: (415)956-7708
E-mail: callahan@pkfc.com
Website: http://www.pkfonline.com

Welling & Woodard Inc.
1067 Broadway
San Francisco, CA 94133
(415)776-4500
Fax: (415)776-5067

Highland Associates
16174 Highland Dr.
San Jose, CA 95127
(408)272-7008
Fax: (408)272-4040

ORDIS Inc.
6815 Trinidad Dr.
San Jose, CA 95120-2056
(408)268-3321
Free: 800-446-7347
Fax: (408)268-3582
E-mail: ordis@ordis.com
Website: http://www.ordis.com

Stanford Resources Inc.
20 Great Oaks Blvd., Ste. 200
San Jose, CA 95119
(408)360-8400
Fax: (408)360-8410
E-mail: sales@stanfordsources.com
Website: http://www.stanfordresources.com

Technology Properties Ltd. Inc.
PO Box 20250
San Jose, CA 95160
(408)243-9898
Fax: (408)296-6637
E-mail: sanjose@tplnet.com

Helfert Associates
1777 Borel Pl., Ste. 508
San Mateo, CA 94402-3514
(650)377-0540
Fax: (650)377-0472

Mykytyn Consulting Group Inc.
185 N Redwood Dr., Ste. 200
San Rafael, CA 94903
(415)491-1770
Fax: (415)491-1251
E-mail: info@mcgi.com
Website: http://www.mcgi.com

Omega Management Systems Inc.
3 Mount Darwin Ct.
San Rafael, CA 94903-1109
(415)499-1300
Fax: (415)492-9490
E-mail: omegamgt@ix.netcom.com

The Information Group Inc.
4675 Stevens Creek Blvd., Ste. 100
Santa Clara, CA 95051
(408)985-7877
Fax: (408)985-2945
E-mail: dvincent@tig-usa.com
Website: http://www.tig-usa.com

Cast Management Consultants
1620 26th St., Ste. 2040N
Santa Monica, CA 90404
(310)828-7511
Fax: (310)453-6831

Cuma Consulting Management
Box 724
Santa Rosa, CA 95402
(707)785-2477
Fax: (707)785-2478

The E-Myth Academy
131B Stony Cir., Ste. 2000
Santa Rosa, CA 95401
(707)569-5600
Free: 800-221-0266
Fax: (707)569-5700
E-mail: info@e-myth.com
Website: http://www.e-myth.com

Reilly, Connors & Ray
1743 Canyon Rd.
Spring Valley, CA 91977
(619)698-4808
Fax: (619)460-3892
E-mail: davidray@adnc.com

Management Consultants
Sunnyvale, CA 94087-4700
(408)773-0321

RJR Associates
1639 Lewiston Dr.
Sunnyvale, CA 94087
(408)737-7720
E-mail: bobroy@rjrassoc.com
Website: http://www.rjrassoc.com

Schwafel Associates
333 Cobalt Way, Ste. 21
Sunnyvale, CA 94085
(408)720-0649
Fax: (408)720-1796
E-mail: schwafel@ricochet.net
Website: http://www.patca.org

Staubs Business Services
23320 S Vermont Ave.
Torrance, CA 90502-2940
(310)830-9128
Fax: (310)830-9128
E-mail: Harry_L_Staubs@Lamg.com

Out of Your Mind...and Into the Marketplace
13381 White Sands Dr.
Tustin, CA 92780-4565
(714)544-0248
Free: 800-419-1513
Fax: (714)730-1414
E-mail: lpinson@aol.com
Website: http://www.business-plan.com

Independent Research Services
PO Box 2426
Van Nuys, CA 91404-2426
(818)993-3622

Ingman Company Inc.
7949 Woodley Ave., Ste. 120
Van Nuys, CA 91406-1232
(818)375-5027
Fax: (818)894-5001

Innovative Technology Associates
3639 E Harbor Blvd., Ste. 203E
Ventura, CA 93001
(805)650-9353

Grid Technology Associates
20404 Tufts Cir.
Walnut, CA 91789
(909)444-0922
Fax: (909)444-0922
E-mail: grid_technology@msn.com

Ridge Consultants Inc.
100 Pringle Ave., Ste. 580
Walnut Creek, CA 94596
(925)274-1990
Fax: (510)274-1956
E-mail: info@ridgecon.com
Website: http://www.ridgecon.com

Bell Springs Publishing
PO Box 1240
Willits, CA 95490
(707)459-6372
E-mail: bellsprings@sabernet
Website: http://www.bellsprings.com

Hutchinson Consulting and Appraisal
23245 Sylvan St., Ste. 103
Woodland Hills, CA 91367
(818)888-8175
Free: 800-977-7548
Fax: (818)888-8220
E-mail: r.f.hutchinson-cpa@worldnet.att.net

Colorado

Sam Boyer & Associates
4255 S Buckley Rd., No. 136
Aurora, CO 80013
Free: 800-785-0485
Fax: (303)766-8740
E-mail: samboyer@samboyer.com
Website: http://www.samboyer.com/

Ameriwest Business Consultants Inc.
PO Box 26266
Colorado Springs, CO 80936
(719)380-7096
Fax: (719)380-7096
E-mail: email@abchelp.com
Website: http://www.abchelp.com

GVNW Consulting Inc.
2270 La Montana Way
Colorado Springs, CO 80936
(719)594-5800
Fax: (719)594-5803
Website: http://www.gvnw.com

M-Squared Inc.
755 San Gabriel Pl.
Colorado Springs, CO 80906
(719)576-2554
Fax: (719)576-2554

Thornton Financial FNIC
1024 Centre Ave., Bldg. E
Fort Collins, CO 80526-1849
(970)221-2089
Fax: (970)484-5206

TenEyck Associates
1760 Cherryville Rd.
Greenwood Village, CO 80121-1503
(303)758-6129
Fax: (303)761-8286

Associated Enterprises Ltd.
13050 W Ceder Dr., Unit 11
Lakewood, CO 80228

(303)988-6695
Fax: (303)988-6739
E-mail: ael1@classic.msn.com

The Vincent Company Inc.
200 Union Blvd., Ste. 210
Lakewood, CO 80228
(303)989-7271
Free: 800-274-0733
Fax: (303)989-7570
E-mail: vincent@vincentco.com
Website: http://www.vincentco.com

Johnson & West Management Consultants Inc.
7612 S Logan Dr.
Littleton, CO 80122
(303)730-2810
Fax: (303)730-3219

Western Capital Holdings Inc.
10050 E Applwood Dr.
Parker, CO 80138
(303)841-1022
Fax: (303)770-1945

Connecticut

Stratman Group Inc.
40 Tower Ln.
Avon, CT 06001-4222
(860)677-2898
Free: 800-551-0499
Fax: (860)677-8210

Cowherd Consulting Group Inc.
106 Stephen Mather Rd.
Darien, CT 06820
(203)655-2150
Fax: (203)655-6427

Greenwich Associates
8 Greenwich Office Park
Greenwich, CT 06831-5149
(203)629-1200
Fax: (203)629-1229
E-mail: lisa@greenwich.com
Website: http://www.greenwich.com

Follow-up News
185 Pine St., Ste. 818
Manchester, CT 06040
(860)647-7542
Free: 800-708-0696
Fax: (860)646-6544
E-mail: Followupnews@aol.com

Lovins & Associates Consulting
309 Edwards St.
New Haven, CT 06511
(203)787-3367

Fax: (203)624-7599
E-mail: Alovinsphd@aol.com
Website: http://www.lovinsgroup.com

JC Ventures Inc.
4 Arnold St.
Old Greenwich, CT 06870-1203
(203)698-1990
Free: 800-698-1997
Fax: (203)698-2638

Charles L. Hornung Associates
52 Ned's Mountain Rd.
Ridgefield, CT 06877
(203)431-0297

Manus
100 Prospect St., S Tower
Stamford, CT 06901
(203)326-3880
Free: 800-445-0942
Fax: (203)326-3890
E-mail: manus1@aol.com
Website: http://www.RightManus.com

RealBusinessPlans.com
156 Westport Rd.
Wilton, CT 06897
(914)837-2886
E-mail: ct@realbusinessplans.com
Website: http://www.RealBusinessPlans.com
Tony Tecce

Delaware

Focus Marketing
61-7 Habor Dr.
Claymont, DE 19703
(302)793-3064

Daedalus Ventures Ltd.
PO Box 1474
Hockessin, DE 19707
(302)239-6758
Fax: (302)239-9991
E-mail: daedalus@mail.del.net

The Formula Group
PO Box 866
Hockessin, DE 19707
(302)456-0952
Fax: (302)456-1354
E-mail: formula@netaxs.com

Selden Enterprises Inc.
2502 Silverside Rd., Ste. 1
Wilmington, DE 19810-3740
(302)529-7113
Fax: (302)529-7442
E-mail: selden2@bellatlantic.net
Website: http://www.seldenenterprises.com

District of Columbia

Bruce W. McGee and Associates
7826 Eastern Ave. NW, Ste. 30
Washington, DC 20012
(202)726-7272
Fax: (202)726-2946

McManis Associates Inc.
1900 K St. NW, Ste. 700
Washington, DC 20006
(202)466-7680
Fax: (202)872-1898
Website: http://www.mcmanis-mmi.com

Smith, Dawson & Andrews Inc.
1000 Connecticut Ave., Ste. 302
Washington, DC 20036
(202)835-0740
Fax: (202)775-8526
E-mail: webmaster@sda-inc.com
Website: http://www.sda-inc.com

Florida

BackBone, Inc.
20404 Hacienda Court
Boca Raton, FL 33498
(561)470-0965
Fax: 516-908-4038
E-mail: BPlans@backboneinc.com
Website: http://www.backboneinc.com
Charles Epstein, President

Whalen & Associates Inc.
4255 Northwest 26 Ct.
Boca Raton, FL 33434
(561)241-5950
Fax: (561)241-7414
E-mail: drwhalen@ix.netcom.com

E.N. Rysso & Associates
180 Bermuda Petrel Ct.
Daytona Beach, FL 32119
(386)760-3028
E-mail: erysso@aol.com

Virtual Technocrats LLC
560 Lavers Circle, #146
Delray Beach, FL 33444
(561)265-3509
E-mail: josh@virtualtechnocrats.com;
info@virtualtechnocrats.com
Website: http://www.virtualtechno
crats.com
Josh Eikov, Managing Director

Eric Sands Consulting Services
6193 Rock Island Rd., Ste. 412
Fort Lauderdale, FL 33319
(954)721-4767

Fax: (954)720-2815
E-mail: easands@aol.com
Website: http://www.ericsandsconsultig.com

Professional Planning Associates, Inc.
1975 E. Sunrise Blvd. Suite 607
Fort Lauderdale, FL 33304
(954)764-5204
Fax: 954-463-4172
E-mail: Mgoldstein@proplana.com
Website: http://proplana.com
Michael Goldstein, President

Host Media Corp.
3948 S 3rd St., Ste. 191
Jacksonville Beach, FL 32250
(904)285-3239
Fax: (904)285-5618
E-mail: msconsulting@compuserve.com
Website: http://www.media
servicesgroup.com

William V. Hall
1925 Brickell, Ste. D-701
Miami, FL 33129
(305)856-9622
Fax: (305)856-4113
E-mail: williamvhall@compuserve.com

F.A. McGee Inc.
800 Claughton Island Dr., Ste. 401
Miami, FL 33131
(305)377-9123

Taxplan Inc.
Mirasol International Ctr.
2699 Collins Ave.
Miami Beach, FL 33140
(305)538-3303

T.C. Brown & Associates
8415 Excalibur Cir., Apt. B1
Naples, FL 34108
(941)594-1949
Fax: (941)594-0611
E-mail: tcater@naples.net.com

RLA International Consulting
713 Lagoon Dr.
North Palm Beach, FL 33408
(407)626-4258
Fax: (407)626-5772

Comprehensive Franchising Inc.
2465 Ridgecrest Ave.
Orange Park, FL 32065
(904)272-6567
Free: 800-321-6567
Fax: (904)272-6750
E-mail: theimp@cris.com
Website: http://www.franchise411.com

Hunter G. Jackson Jr. - Consulting Environmental Physicist
PO Box 618272
Orlando, FL 32861-8272
(407)295-4188
E-mail: hunterjackson@juno.com

F. Newton Parks
210 El Brillo Way
Palm Beach, FL 33480
(561)833-1727
Fax: (561)833-4541

Avery Business Development Services
2506 St. Michel Ct.
Ponte Vedra Beach, FL 32082
(904)285-6033
Fax: (904)285-6033

Strategic Business Planning Co.
PO Box 821006
South Florida, FL 33082-1006
(954)704-9100
Fax: (954)438-7333
E-mail: info@bizplan.com
Website: http://www.bizplan.com

Dufresne Consulting Group Inc.
10014 N Dale Mabry, Ste. 101
Tampa, FL 33618-4426
(813)264-4775
Fax: (813)264-9300
Website: http://www.dcgconsult.com

Agrippa Enterprises Inc.
PO Box 175
Venice, FL 34284-0175
(941)355-7876
E-mail: webservices@agrippa.com
Website: http://www.agrippa.com

Center for Simplified Strategic Planning Inc.
PO Box 3324
Vero Beach, FL 32964-3324
(561)231-3636
Fax: (561)231-1099
Website: http://www.cssp.com

Georgia

Marketing Spectrum Inc.
115 Perimeter Pl., Ste. 440
Atlanta, GA 30346
(770)395-7244
Fax: (770)393-4071

Business Ventures Corp.
1650 Oakbrook Dr., Ste. 405
Norcross, GA 30093
(770)729-8000
Fax: (770)729-8028

Informed Decisions Inc.
100 Falling Cheek
Sautee Nacoochee, GA 30571
(706)878-1905
Fax: (706)878-1802
E-mail: skylake@compuserve.com

Tom C. Davis & Associates, P.C.
3189 Perimeter Rd.
Valdosta, GA 31602
(912)247-9801
Fax: (912)244-7704
E-mail: mail@tcdcpa.com
Website: http://www.tcdcpa.com/

Illinois

TWD and Associates
431 S Patton
Arlington Heights, IL 60005
(847)398-6410
Fax: (847)255-5095
E-mail: tdoo@aol.com

Management Planning Associates Inc.
2275 Half Day Rd., Ste. 350
Bannockburn, IL 60015-1277
(847)945-2421
Fax: (847)945-2425

Phil Faris Associates
86 Old Mill Ct.
Barrington, IL 60010
(847)382-4888
Fax: (847)382-4890
E-mail: pfaris@meginsnet.net

Seven Continents Technology
787 Stonebridge
Buffalo Grove, IL 60089
(708)577-9653
Fax: (708)870-1220

Grubb & Blue Inc.
2404 Windsor Pl.
Champaign, IL 61820
(217)366-0052
Fax: (217)356-0117

ACE Accounting Service Inc.
3128 N Bernard St.
Chicago, IL 60618
(773)463-7854
Fax: (773)463-7854

AON Consulting Worldwide
200 E Randolph St., 10th Fl.
Chicago, IL 60601
(312)381-4800
Free: 800-438-6487
Fax: (312)381-0240
Website: http://www.aon.com

FMS Consultants
5801 N Sheridan Rd., Ste. 3D
Chicago, IL 60660
(773)561-7362
Fax: (773)561-6274

Grant Thornton
800 1 Prudential Plz.
130 E Randolph St.
Chicago, IL 60601
(312)856-0001
Fax: (312)861-1340
E-mail: gtinfo@gt.com
Website: http://www.grantthornton.com

Kingsbury International Ltd.
5341 N Glenwood Ave.
Chicago, IL 60640
(773)271-3030
Fax: (773)728-7080
E-mail: jetlag@mcs.com
Website: http://www.kingbiz.com

MacDougall & Blake Inc.
1414 N Wells St., Ste. 311
Chicago, IL 60610-1306
(312)587-3330
Fax: (312)587-3699
E-mail: jblake@compuserve.com

James C. Osburn Ltd.
6445 N. Western Ave., Ste. 304
Chicago, IL 60645
(773)262-4428
Fax: (773)262-6755
E-mail: osburnltd@aol.com

Tarifero & Tazewell Inc.
211 S Clark
Chicago, IL 60690
(312)665-9714
Fax: (312)665-9716

Human Energy Design Systems
620 Roosevelt Dr.
Edwardsville, IL 62025
(618)692-0258
Fax: (618)692-0819

China Business Consultants Group
931 Dakota Cir.
Naperville, IL 60563
(630)778-7992
Fax: (630)778-7915
E-mail: cbcq@aol.com

Center for Workforce Effectiveness
500 Skokie Blvd., Ste. 222
Northbrook, IL 60062
(847)559-8777
Fax: (847)559-8778

E-mail: office@cwelink.com
Website: http://www.cwelink.com

Smith Associates
1320 White Mountain Dr.
Northbrook, IL 60062
(847)480-7200
Fax: (847)480-9828

Francorp Inc.
20200 Governors Dr.
Olympia Fields, IL 60461
(708)481-2900
Free: 800-372-6244
Fax: (708)481-5885
E-mail: francorp@aol.com
Website: http://www.francorpinc.com

Camber Business Strategy Consultants
1010 S Plum Tree Ct
Palatine, IL 60078-0986
(847)202-0101
Fax: (847)705-7510
E-mail: camber@ameritech.net

Partec Enterprise Group
5202 Keith Dr.
Richton Park, IL 60471
(708)503-4047
Fax: (708)503-9468

Rockford Consulting Group Ltd.
Century Plz., Ste. 206
7210 E State St.
Rockford, IL 61108
(815)229-2900
Free: 800-667-7495
Fax: (815)229-2612
E-mail: rligus@RockfordConsulting.com
Website: http://www.Rockford
Consulting.com

RSM McGladrey Inc.
1699 E Woodfield Rd., Ste. 300
Schaumburg, IL 60173-4969
(847)413-6900
Fax: (847)517-7067
Website: http://www.rsmmcgladrey.com

A.D. Star Consulting
320 Euclid
Winnetka, IL 60093
(847)446-7827
Fax: (847)446-7827
E-mail: startwo@worldnet.att.net

Indiana

Modular Consultants Inc.
3109 Crabtree Ln.
Elkhart, IN 46514

(219)264-5761
Fax: (219)264-5761
E-mail: sasabo5313@aol.com

Midwest Marketing Research
PO Box 1077
Goshen, IN 46527
(219)533-0548
Fax: (219)533-0540
E-mail: 103365.654@compuserve

Ketchum Consulting Group
8021 Knue Rd., Ste. 112
Indianapolis, IN 46250
(317)845-5411
Fax: (317)842-9941

**MDI Management
Consulting**
1519 Park Dr.
Munster, IN 46321
(219)838-7909
Fax: (219)838-7909

Iowa

McCord Consulting Group Inc.
4533 Pine View Dr. NE
PO Box 11024
Cedar Rapids, IA 52410
(319)378-0077
Fax: (319)378-1577
E-mail: smmccord@hom.com
Website: http://www.mccordgroup.com

Management Solutions L.C.
3815 Lincoln Pl. Dr.
Des Moines, IA 50312
(515)277-6408
Fax: (515)277-3506
E-mail: wasunimers@uswest.net

Grandview Marketing
15 Red Bridge Dr.
Sioux City, IA 51104
(712)239-3122
Fax: (712)258-7578
E-mail: eandrews@pionet.net

Kansas

Assessments in Action
513A N Mur-Len
Olathe, KS 66062
(913)764-6270
Free: (888)548-1504
Fax: (913)764-6495
E-mail: lowdene@qni.com
Website: http://www.assessments-
in-action.com

Maine

Edgemont Enterprises
PO Box 8354
Portland, ME 04104
(207)871-8964
Fax: (207)871-8964

Pan Atlantic Consultants
5 Milk St.
Portland, ME 04101
(207)871-8622
Fax: (207)772-4842
E-mail: pmurphy@mainc.rr.com
Website: http://www.panatlantic.net

Maryland

Clemons & Associates Inc.
5024-R Campbell Blvd.
Baltimore, MD 21236
(410)931-8100
Fax: (410)931-8111
E-mail: info@clemonsmgmt.com
Website: http://www.clemonsmgmt.com

Imperial Group Ltd.
305 Washington Ave., Ste. 204
Baltimore, MD 21204-6009
(410)337-8500
Fax: (410)337-7641

Leadership Institute
3831 Yolando Rd.
Baltimore, MD 21218
(410)366-9111
Fax: (410)243-8478
E-mail: behconsult@aol.com

Burdeshaw Associates Ltd.
4701 Sangamore Rd.
Bethesda, MD 20816-2508
(301)229-5800
Fax: (301)229-5045
E-mail: jstacy@burdeshaw.com
Website: http://www.burdeshaw.com

Michael E. Cohen
5225 Pooks Hill Rd., Ste. 1119 S
Bethesda, MD 20814
(301)530-5738
Fax: (301)530-2988
E-mail: mecohen@crosslink.net

World Development Group Inc.
5272 River Rd., Ste. 650
Bethesda, MD 20816-1405
(301)652-1818
Fax: (301)652-1250
E-mail: wdg@has.com
Website: http://www.worlddg.com

Swartz Consulting
PO Box 4301
Crofton, MD 21114-4301
(301)262-6728

Software Solutions International Inc.
9633 Duffer Way
Gaithersburg, MD 20886
(301)330-4136
Fax: (301)330-4136

Strategies Inc.
8 Park Center Ct., Ste. 200
Owings Mills, MD 21117
(410)363-6669
Fax: (410)363-1231
E-mail: strategies@strat1.com
Website: http://www.strat1.com

Hammer Marketing Resources
179 Inverness Rd.
Severna Park, MD 21146
(410)544-9191
Fax: (305)675-3277
E-mail: info@gohammer.com
Website: http://www.gohammer.com

Andrew Sussman & Associates
13731 Kretsinger
Smithsburg, MD 21783
(301)824-2943
Fax: (301)824-2943

Massachusetts

Geibel Marketing and Public Relations
PO Box 611
Belmont, MA 02478-0005
(617)484-8285
Fax: (617)489-3567
E-mail: jgeibel@geibelpr.com
Website: http://www.geibelpr.com

Bain & Co.
2 Copley Pl.
Boston, MA 02116
(617)572-2000
Fax: (617)572-2427
E-mail: corporate.inquiries@bain.com
Website: http://www.bain.com

Mehr & Co.
62 Kinnaird St.
Cambridge, MA 02139
(617)876-3311
Fax: (617)876-3023
E-mail: mehrco@aol.com

Monitor Company Inc.
2 Canal Park
Cambridge, MA 02141

(617)252-2000
Fax: (617)252-2100
Website: http://www.monitor.com

Information & Research Associates
PO Box 3121
Framingham, MA 01701
(508)788-0784

Walden Consultants Ltd.
252 Pond St.
Hopkinton, MA 01748
(508)435-4882
Fax: (508)435-3971
Website: http://www.waldencon
sultants.com

Jeffrey D. Marshall
102 Mitchell Rd.
Ipswich, MA 01938-1219
(508)356-1113
Fax: (508)356-2989

Consulting Resources Corp.
6 Northbrook Park
Lexington, MA 02420
(781)863-1222
Fax: (781)863-1441
E-mail: res@consultingresources.net
Website: http://www.consulting
resources.net

Planning Technologies Group L.L.C.
92 Hayden Ave.
Lexington, MA 02421
(781)778-4678
Fax: (781)861-1099
E-mail: ptg@plantech.com
Website: http://www.plantech.com

Kalba International Inc.
23 Sandy Pond Rd.
Lincoln, MA 01773
(781)259-9589
Fax: (781)259-1460
E-mail: info@kalbainternational.com
Website: http://www.kalbainter
national.com

VMB Associates Inc.
115 Ashland St.
Melrose, MA 02176
(781)665-0623
Fax: (425)732-7142
E-mail: vmbinc@aol.com

The Company Doctor
14 Pudding Stone Ln.
Mendon, MA 01756
(508)478-1747
Fax: (508)478-0520

Data and Strategies Group Inc.
190 N Main St.
Natick, MA 01760
(508)653-9990
Fax: (508)653-7799
E-mail: dsginc@dsggroup.com
Website: http://www.dsggroup.com

The Enterprise Group
73 Parker Rd.
Needham, MA 02494
(617)444-6631
Fax: (617)433-9991
E-mail: lsacco@world.std.com
Website: http://www.enterprise-group.com

PSMJ Resources Inc.
10 Midland Ave.
Newton, MA 02458
(617)965-0055
Free: 800-537-7765
Fax: (617)965-5152
E-mail: psmj@tiac.net
Website: http://www.psmj.com

Scheur Management Group Inc.
255 Washington St., Ste. 100
Newton, MA 02458-1611
(617)969-7500
Fax: (617)969-7508
E-mail: smgnow@scheur.com
Website: http://www.scheur.com

I.E.E.E., Boston Section
240 Bear Hill Rd., 202B
Waltham, MA 02451-1017
(781)890-5294
Fax: (781)890-5290

Business Planning and Consulting Services
20 Beechwood Ter.
Wellesley, MA 02482
(617)237-9151
Fax: (617)237-9151

Michigan

Walter Frederick Consulting
1719 South Blvd.
Ann Arbor, MI 48104
(313)662-4336
Fax: (313)769-7505

Fox Enterprises
6220 W Freeland Rd.
Freeland, MI 48623
(517)695-9170
Fax: (517)695-9174
E-mail: foxjw@concentric.net
Website: http://www.cris.com/~foxjw

G.G.W. and Associates
1213 Hampton
Jackson, MI 49203
(517)782-2255
Fax: (517)782-2255

Altamar Group Ltd.
6810 S Cedar, Ste. 2-B
Lansing, MI 48911
(517)694-0910
Free: 800-443-2627
Fax: (517)694-1377

Sheffieck Consultants Inc.
23610 Greening Dr.
Novi, MI 48375-3130
(248)347-3545
Fax: (248)347-3530
E-mail: cfsheff@concentric.net

Rehmann, Robson PC
5800 Gratiot
Saginaw, MI 48605
(517)799-9580
Fax: (517)799-0227
Website: http://www.rrpc.com

Francis & Co.
17200 W 10 Mile Rd., Ste. 207
Southfield, MI 48075
(248)559-7600
Fax: (248)559-5249

Private Ventures Inc.
16000 W 9 Mile Rd., Ste. 504
Southfield, MI 48075
(248)569-1977
Free: 800-448-7614
Fax: (248)569-1838
E-mail: pventuresi@aol.com

JGK Associates
14464 Kerner Dr.
Sterling Heights, MI 48313
(810)247-9055
Fax: (248)822-4977
E-mail: kozlowski@home.com

Minnesota

Health Fitness Corp.
3500 W 80th St., Ste. 130
Bloomington, MN 55431
(612)831-6830
Fax: (612)831-7264

Consatech Inc.
PO Box 1047
Burnsville, MN 55337
(612)953-1088
Fax: (612)435-2966

Robert F. Knotek
14960 Ironwood Ct.
Eden Prairie, MN 55346
(612)949-2875

DRI Consulting
7715 Stonewood Ct.
Edina, MN 55439
(612)941-9656
Fax: (612)941-2693
E-mail: dric@dric.com
Website: http://www.dric.com

Markin Consulting
12072 87th Pl. N
Maple Grove, MN 55369
(612)493-3568
Fax: (612)493-5744
E-mail: markin@markinconsulting.com
Website: http://www.markin
consulting.com

**Minnesota Cooperation Office for
Small Business & Job Creation Inc.**
5001 W 80th St., Ste. 825
Minneapolis, MN 55437
(612)830-1230
Fax: (612)830-1232
E-mail: mncoop@msn.com
Website: http://www.mnco.org

Enterprise Consulting Inc.
PO Box 1111
Minnetonka, MN 55345
(612)949-5909
Fax: (612)906-3965

Amdahl International
724 1st Ave. SW
Rochester, MN 55902
(507)252-0402
Fax: (507)252-0402
E-mail: amdahl@best-service.com
Website: http://www.wp.com/amdahl_int

Power Systems Research
1365 Corporate Center Curve, 2nd Fl.
St. Paul, MN 55121
(612)905-8400
Free: (888)625-8612
Fax: (612)454-0760
E-mail: Barb@Powersys.com
Website: http://www.powersys.com

Missouri

**Business Planning and Development
Corp.**
4030 Charlotte St.
Kansas City, MO 64110
(816)753-0495

E-mail: humph@bpdev.demon.co.uk
Website: http://www.bpdev.demon.co.uk

CFO Service
10336 Donoho
St. Louis, MO 63131
(314)750-2940
E-mail: jskae@cfoservice.com
Website: http://www.cfoservice.com

Nebraska

**International Management Consulting
Group Inc.**
1309 Harlan Dr., Ste. 205
Bellevue, NE 68005
(402)291-4545
Free: 800-665-IMCG
Fax: (402)291-4343
E-mail: imcg@neonramp.com
Website: http://www.mgtcon
sulting.com

**Heartland Management Consulting
Group**
1904 Barrington Pky.
Papillion, NE 68046
(402)339-2387
Fax: (402)339-1319

Nevada

The DuBois Group
865 Tahoe Blvd., Ste. 108
Incline Village, NV 89451
(775)832-0550
Free: 800-375-2935
Fax: (775)832-0556
E-mail: DuBoisGrp@aol.com

New Hampshire

Wolff Consultants
10 Buck Rd.
Hanover, NH 03755
(603)643-6015

BPT Consulting Associates Ltd.
12 Parmenter Rd., Ste. B-6
Londonderry, NH 03053
(603)437-8484
Free: (888)278-0030
Fax: (603)434-5388
E-mail: bptcons@tiac.net
Website: http://www.bptconsulting.com

New Jersey

Bedminster Group Inc.
1170 Rte. 22 E
Bridgewater, NJ 08807

(908)500-4155
Fax: (908)766-0780
E-mail: info@bedminstergroup.com
Website: http://www.bedminster
group.com
Fax: (202)806-1777
Terry Strong, Acting Regional Dir.

Delta Planning Inc.
PO Box 425
Denville, NJ 07834
(913)625-1742
Free: 800-672-0762
Fax: (973)625-3531
E-mail: DeltaP@worldnet.att.net
Website: http://deltaplanning.com

Kumar Associates Inc.
1004 Cumbermeade Rd.
Fort Lee, NJ 07024
(201)224-9480
Fax: (201)585-2343
E-mail: mail@kumarassociates.com
Website: http://kumarassociates.com

John Hall & Company Inc.
PO Box 187
Glen Ridge, NJ 07028
(973)680-4449
Fax: (973)680-4581
E-mail: jhcompany@aol.com

Market Focus
PO Box 402
Maplewood, NJ 07040
(973)378-2470
Fax: (973)378-2470
E-mail: mcs366@marketfocus.com

Vanguard Communications Corp.
100 American Rd.
Morris Plains, NJ 07950
(973)605-8000
Fax: (973)605-8329
Website: http://www.vanguard.net/

ConMar International Ltd.
1901 US Hwy. 130
North Brunswick, NJ 08902
(732)940-8347
Fax: (732)274-1199

KLW New Products
156 Cedar Dr.
Old Tappan, NJ 07675
(201)358-1300
Fax: (201)664-2594
E-mail: lrlarsen@usa.net
Website: http://www.klwnew
products.com

PA Consulting Group
315A Enterprise Dr.
Plainsboro, NJ 08536
(609)936-8300
Fax: (609)936-8811
E-mail: info@paconsulting.com
Website: http://www.pa-consulting.com

Aurora Marketing Management Inc.
66 Witherspoon St., Ste. 600
Princeton, NJ 08542
(908)904-1125
Fax: (908)359-1108
E-mail: aurora2@voicenet.com
Website: http://www.auroramarketing.net

Smart Business Supersite
88 Orchard Rd., CN-5219
Princeton, NJ 08543
(908)321-1924
Fax: (908)321-5156
E-mail: irv@smartbiz.com
Website: http://www.smartbiz.com

Tracelin Associates
1171 Main St., Ste. 6K
Rahway, NJ 07065
(732)381-3288

Schkeeper Inc.
130-6 Bodman Pl.
Red Bank, NJ 07701
(732)219-1965
Fax: (732)530-3703

Henry Branch Associates
2502 Harmon Cove Twr.
Secaucus, NJ 07094
(201)866-2008
Fax: (201)601-0101
E-mail: hbranch161@home.com

Robert Gibbons & Company Inc.
46 Knoll Rd.
Tenafly, NJ 07670-1050
(201)871-3933
Fax: (201)871-2173
E-mail: crisisbob@aol.com

PMC Management Consultants Inc.
6 Thistle Ln.
Three Bridges, NJ 08887-0332
(908)788-1014
Free: 800-PMC-0250
Fax: (908)806-7287
E-mail: int@pmc-management.com
Website: http://www.pmc-management.com

R.W. Bankart & Associates
20 Valley Ave., Ste. D-2
Westwood, NJ 07675-3607
(201)664-7672

New Mexico

Vondle & Associates Inc.
4926 Calle de Tierra, NE
Albuquerque, NM 87111
(505)292-8961
Fax: (505)296-2790
E-mail: vondle@aol.com

InfoNewMexico
2207 Black Hills Rd., NE
Rio Rancho, NM 87124
(505)891-2462
Fax: (505)896-8971

New York

Powers Research and Training Institute
PO Box 78
Bayville, NY 11709
(516)628-2250
Fax: (516)628-2252
E-mail: powercocch@compuserve.com
Website: http://www.nancypowers.com

Consortium House
296 Wittenberg Rd.
Bearsville, NY 12409
(845)679-8867
Fax: (845)679-9248
E-mail: eugenegs@aol.com
Website: http://www.chpub.com

Progressive Finance Corp.
3549 Tiemann Ave.
Bronx, NY 10469
(718)405-9029
Free: 800-225-8381
Fax: (718)405-1170

Wave Hill Associates Inc.
2621 Palisade Ave., Ste. 15-C
Bronx, NY 10463
(718)549-7368
Fax: (718)601-9670
E-mail: pepper@compuserve.com

Management Insight
96 Arlington Rd.
Buffalo, NY 14221
(716)631-3319
Fax: (716)631-0203
E-mail: michalski@foodservice insight.com
Website: http://www.foodservice insight.com

Samani International Enterprises, Marions Panyaught Consultancy
2028 Parsons
Flushing, NY 11357-3436
(917)287-8087
Fax: 800-873-8939
E-mail: vjp2@biostrategist.com
Website: http://www.biostrategist.com

Marketing Resources Group
71-58 Austin St.
Forest Hills, NY 11375
(718)261-8882

Mangabay Business Plans & Development Subsidiary of Innis Asset Allocation
125-10 Queens Blvd., Ste. 2202
Kew Gardens, NY 11415
(905)527-1947
Fax: 509-472-1935
E-mail: mangabay@mangabay.com
Website: http://www.mangabay.com
Lee Toh, Managing Partner

ComputerEase Co.
1301 Monmouth Ave.
Lakewood, NY 08701
(212)406-9464
Fax: (914)277-5317
E-mail: crawfordc@juno.com

Boice Dunham Group
30 W 13th St.
New York, NY 10011
(212)924-2200
Fax: (212)924-1108

Elizabeth Capen
27 E 95th St.
New York, NY 10128
(212)427-7654
Fax: (212)876-3190

Haver Analytics
60 E 42nd St., Ste. 2424
New York, NY 10017
(212)986-9300
Fax: (212)986-5857
E-mail: data@haver.com
Website: http://www.haver.com

The Jordan, Edmiston Group Inc.
150 E 52nd Ave., 18th Fl.
New York, NY 10022
(212)754-0710
Fax: (212)754-0337

KPMG International
345 Park Ave.
New York, NY 10154-0102
(212)758-9700

Fax: (212)758-9819
Website: http://www.kpmg.com

Mahoney Cohen Consulting Corp.
111 W 40th St., 12th Fl.
New York, NY 10018
(212)490-8000
Fax: (212)790-5913

Management Practice Inc.
342 Madison Ave.
New York, NY 10173-1230
(212)867-7948
Fax: (212)972-5188
Website: http://www.mpiweb.com

Moseley Associates Inc.
342 Madison Ave., Ste. 1414
New York, NY 10016
(212)213-6673
Fax: (212)687-1520

Practice Development Counsel
60 Sutton Pl. S
New York, NY 10022
(212)593-1549
Fax: (212)980-7940
E-mail: pwhaserot@pdcounsel.com
Website: http://www.pdcounsel.com

Unique Value International Inc.
575 Madison Ave., 10th Fl.
New York, NY 10022-1304
(212)605-0590
Fax: (212)605-0589

The Van Tulleken Co.
126 E 56th St.
New York, NY 10022
(212)355-1390
Fax: (212)755-3061
E-mail: newyork@vantulleken.com

Vencon Management Inc.
301 W 53rd St.
New York, NY 10019
(212)581-8787
Fax: (212)397-4126
Website: http://www.venconinc.com

Werner International Inc.
55 E 52nd, 29th Fl.
New York, NY 10055
(212)909-1260
Fax: (212)909-1273
E-mail: richard.downing@rgh.com
Website: http://www.wernertex.com

Zimmerman Business Consulting Inc.
44 E 92nd St., Ste. 5-B
New York, NY 10128

(212)860-3107
Fax: (212)860-7730
E-mail: ljzzbci@aol.com
Website: http://www.zbcinc.com

Overton Financial
7 Allen Rd.
Peekskill, NY 10566
(914)737-4649
Fax: (914)737-4696

Stromberg Consulting
2500 Westchester Ave.
Purchase, NY 10577
(914)251-1515
Fax: (914)251-1562
E-mail: strategy@stromberg_consul
ting.com
Website: http://www.stromberg_
consulting.com

Innovation Management Consulting Inc.
209 Dewitt Rd.
Syracuse, NY 13214-2006
(315)425-5144
Fax: (315)445-8989
E-mail: missonneb@axess.net

M. Clifford Agress
891 Fulton St.
Valley Stream, NY 11580
(516)825-8955
Fax: (516)825-8955

Destiny Kinal Marketing Consultancy
105 Chemung St.
Waverly, NY 14892
(607)565-8317
Fax: (607)565-4083

Valutis Consulting Inc.
5350 Main St., Ste. 7
Williamsville, NY 14221-5338
(716)634-2553
Fax: (716)634-2554
E-mail: valutis@localnet.com
Website: http://www.valutisconsulting.com

North Carolina

Best Practices L.L.C.
6320 Quadrangle Dr., Ste. 200
Chapel Hill, NC 27514
(919)403-0251
Fax: (919)403-0144
E-mail: best@best:in/class
Website: http://www.best-in-class.com

Norelli & Co.
Bank of America Corporate Ctr.
100 N Tyron St., Ste. 5160

Charlotte, NC 28202-4000
(704)376-5484
Fax: (704)376-5485
E-mail: consult@norelli.com
Website: http://www.norelli.com

North Dakota

Center for Innovation
4300 Dartmouth Dr.
PO Box 8372
Grand Forks, ND 58202
(701)777-3132
Fax: (701)777-2339
E-mail: bruce@innovators.net
Website: http://www.innovators.net

Ohio

Transportation Technology Services
208 Harmon Rd.
Aurora, OH 44202
(330)562-3596

Empro Systems Inc.
4777 Red Bank Expy., Ste. 1
Cincinnati, OH 45227-1542
(513)271-2042
Fax: (513)271-2042

Alliance Management International Ltd.
1440 Windrow Ln.
Cleveland, OH 44147-3200
(440)838-1922
Fax: (440)838-0979
E-mail: bgruss@amiltd.com
Website: http://www.amiltd.com

Bozell Kamstra Public Relations
1301 E 9th St., Ste. 3400
Cleveland, OH 44114
(216)623-1511
Fax: (216)623-1501
E-mail: jfeniger@cleveland.bozellk
amstra.com
Website: http://www.bozellk
amstra.com

Cory Dillon Associates
111 Schreyer Pl. E
Columbus, OH 43214
(614)262-8211
Fax: (614)262-3806

Holcomb Gallagher Adams
300 Marconi, Ste. 303
Columbus, OH 43215
(614)221-3343
Fax: (614)221-3367
E-mail: riadams@acme.freenet.oh.us

Young & Associates
PO Box 711
Kent, OH 44240
(330)678-0524
Free: 800-525-9775
Fax: (330)678-6219
E-mail: online@younginc.com
Website: http://www.younginc.com

Robert A. Westman & Associates
8981 Inversary Dr. SE
Warren, OH 44484-2551
(330)856-4149
Fax: (330)856-2564

Oklahoma

Innovative Partners L.L.C.
4900 Richmond Sq., Ste. 100
Oklahoma City, OK 73118
(405)840-0033
Fax: (405)843-8359
E-mail: ipartners@juno.com

Oregon

INTERCON - The International Converting Institute
5200 Badger Rd.
Crooked River Ranch, OR 97760
(541)548-1447
Fax: (541)548-1618
E-mail: johnbowler@
crookedriverranch.com

Talbott ARM
HC 60, Box 5620
Lakeview, OR 97630
(541)635-8587
Fax: (503)947-3482

Management Technology Associates Ltd.
2768 SW Sherwood Dr, Ste. 105
Portland, OR 97201-2251
(503)224-5220
Fax: (503)224-5334
E-mail: lcuster@mta-ltd.com
Website: http://www.mgmt-tech.com

Pennsylvania

Healthscope Inc.
400 Lancaster Ave.
Devon, PA 19333
(610)687-6199
Fax: (610)687-6376
E-mail: health@voicenet.com
Website: http://www.healthscope.net/

Elayne Howard & Associates Inc.
3501 Masons Mill Rd., Ste. 501

Huntingdon Valley, PA 19006-3509
(215)657-9550

GRA Inc.
115 West Ave., Ste. 201
Jenkintown, PA 19046
(215)884-7500
Fax: (215)884-1385
E-mail: gramail@gra-inc.com
Website: http://www.gra-inc.com

Mifflin County Industrial Development Corp.
Mifflin County Industrial Plz.
6395 SR 103 N
Bldg. 50
Lewistown, PA 17044
(717)242-0393
Fax: (717)242-1842
E-mail: mcide@acsworld.net

Autech Products
1289 Revere Rd.
Morrisville, PA 19067
(215)493-3759
Fax: (215)493-9791
E-mail: autech4@yahoo.com

Advantage Associates
434 Avon Dr.
Pittsburgh, PA 15228
(412)343-1558
Fax: (412)362-1684
E-mail: ecocba1@aol.com

Regis J. Sheehan & Associates
Pittsburgh, PA 15220
(412)279-1207

James W. Davidson Company Inc.
23 Forest View Rd.
Wallingford, PA 19086
(610)566-1462

Puerto Rico

Diego Chevere & Co.
Metro Parque 7, Ste. 204
Metro Office
Caparra Heights, PR 00920
(787)774-9595
Fax: (787)774-9566
E-mail: dcco@coqui.net

Manuel L. Porrata and Associates
898 Munoz Rivera Ave., Ste. 201
San Juan, PR 00927
(787)765-2140
Fax: (787)754-3285
E-mail: m_porrata@manuelporrata.com
Website: http://manualporrata.com

South Carolina

Aquafood Business Associates
PO Box 13267
Charleston, SC 29422
(843)795-9506
Fax: (843)795-9477
E-mail: rraba@aol.com

Profit Associates Inc.
PO Box 38026
Charleston, SC 29414
(803)763-5718
Fax: (803)763-5719
E-mail: bobrog@awod.com
Website: http://www.awod.com/gallery/business/proasc

Strategic Innovations International
12 Executive Ct.
Lake Wylie, SC 29710
(803)831-1225
Fax: (803)831-1177
E-mail: stratinnov@aol.com
Website: http://www.
strategicinnovations.com

Minus Stage
Box 4436
Rock Hill, SC 29731
(803)328-0705
Fax: (803)329-9948

Tennessee

Daniel Petchers & Associates
8820 Fernwood CV
Germantown, TN 38138
(901)755-9896

Business Choices
1114 Forest Harbor, Ste. 300
Hendersonville, TN 37075-9646
(615)822-8692
Free: 800-737-8382
Fax: (615)822-8692
E-mail: bz-ch@juno.com

RCFA Healthcare Management Services L.L.C.
9648 Kingston Pke., Ste. 8
Knoxville, TN 37922
(865)531-0176
Free: 800-635-4040
Fax: (865)531-0722
E-mail: info@rcfa.com
Website: http://www.rcfa.com

Growth Consultants of America
3917 Trimble Rd.
Nashville, TN 37215

(615)383-0550
Fax: (615)269-8940
E-mail: 70244.451@compuserve.com

Texas

**Integrated Cost Management
Systems Inc.**
2261 Brookhollow Plz. Dr., Ste. 104
Arlington, TX 76006
(817)633-2873
Fax: (817)633-3781
E-mail: abm@icms.net
Website: http://www.icms.net

Lori Williams
1000 Leslie Ct.
Arlington, TX 76012
(817)459-3934
Fax: (817)459-3934

Business Resource Software Inc.
2013 Wells Branch Pky., Ste. 305
Austin, TX 78728
Free: 800-423-1228
Fax: (512)251-4401
E-mail: info@brs-inc.com
Website: http://www.brs-inc.com

Erisa Adminstrative Services Inc.
12325 Hymeadow Dr., Bldg. 4
Austin, TX 78750-1847
(512)250-9020
Fax: (512)250-9487
Website: http://www.cserisa.com

R. Miller Hicks & Co.
1011 W 11th St.
Austin, TX 78703
(512)477-7000
Fax: (512)477-9697
E-mail: millerhicks@rmhicks.com
Website: http://www.rmhicks.com

Pragmatic Tactics Inc.
3303 Westchester Ave.
College Station, TX 77845
(409)696-5294
Free: 800-570-5294
Fax: (409)696-4994
E-mail: ptactics@aol.com
Website: http://www.ptatics.com

Perot Systems
12404 Park Central Dr.
Dallas, TX 75251
(972)340-5000
Free: 800-688-4333
Fax: (972)455-4100
E-mail: corp.comm@ps.net
Website: http://www.perotsystems.com

ReGENERATION Partners
3838 Oak Lawn Ave.
Dallas, TX 75219
(214)559-3999
Free: 800-406-1112
E-mail: info@regeneration-partner.com
Website: http://www.regeneration-partners.com

**High Technology Associates - Division
of Global Technologies Inc.**
1775 St. James Pl., Ste. 105
Houston, TX 77056
(713)963-9300
Fax: (713)963-8341
E-mail: hta@infohwy.com

MasterCOM
103 Thunder Rd.
Kerrville, TX 78028
(830)895-7990
Fax: (830)443-3428
E-mail: jmstubblefield@master
training.com
Website: http://www.mastertraining.com

PROTEC
4607 Linden Pl.
Pearland, TX 77584
(281)997-9872
Fax: (281)997-9895
E-mail: p.oman@ix.netcom.com

Alpha Quadrant Inc.
10618 Auldine
San Antonio, TX 78230
(210)344-3330
Fax: (210)344-8151
E-mail: mbussone@sbcglobal.net
Website:http://www.a-quadrant.com
Michele Bussone

Bastian Public Relations
614 San Dizier
San Antonio, TX 78232
(210)404-1839
E-mail: lisa@bastianpr.com
Website: http://www.bastianpr.com
Lisa Bastian CBC

**Business Strategy Development
Consultants**
PO Box 690365
San Antonio, TX 78269
(210)696-8000
Free: 800-927-BSDC
Fax: (210)696-8000

Tom Welch, CPC
6900 San Pedro Ave., Ste. 147
San Antonio, TX 78216-6207

(210)737-7022
Fax: (210)737-7022
E-mail: bplan@iamerica.net
Website: http://www.moneywords.com

Utah

Business Management Resource
PO Box 521125
Salt Lake City, UT 84152-1125
(801)272-4668
Fax: (801)277-3290
E-mail: pingfong@worldnet.att.net

Virginia

Tindell Associates
209 Oxford Ave.
Alexandria, VA 22301
(703)683-0109
Fax: 703-783-0219
E-mail: scott@tindell.net
Website: http://www.tindell.net
Scott Lockett, President

Elliott B. Jaffa
2530-B S Walter Reed Dr.
Arlington, VA 22206
(703)931-0040
E-mail: thetrainingdoctor@excite.com
Website: http://www.tregistry.com/
jaffa.htm

Koach Enterprises - USA
5529 N 18th St.
Arlington, VA 22205
(703)241-8361
Fax: (703)241-8623

Federal Market Development
5650 Chapel Run Ct.
Centreville, VA 20120-3601
(703)502-8930
Free: 800-821-5003
Fax: (703)502-8929

Huff, Stuart & Carlton
2107 Graves Mills Rd., Ste. C
Forest, VA 24551
(804)316-9356
Free: (888)316-9356
Fax: (804)316-9357
Website: http://www.wealthmgt.net

AMX International Inc.
1420 Spring Hill Rd. , Ste. 600
McLean, VA 22102-3006
(703)690-4100
Fax: (703)643-1279
E-mail: amxmail@amxi.com
Website: http://www.amxi.com

Charles Scott Pugh (Investor)
4101 Pittaway Dr.
Richmond, VA 23235-1022
(804)560-0979
Fax: (804)560-4670

John C. Randall and Associates Inc.
PO Box 15127
Richmond, VA 23227
(804)746-4450
Fax: (804)730-8933
E-mail: randalljcx@aol.com
Website: http://www.johncrandall.com

McLeod & Co.
410 1st St.
Roanoke, VA 24011
(540)342-6911
Fax: (540)344-6367
Website: http://www.mcleodco.com/

Salzinger & Company Inc.
8000 Towers Crescent Dr., Ste. 1350
Vienna, VA 22182
(703)442-5200
Fax: (703)442-5205
E-mail: info@salzinger.com
Website: http://www.salzinger.com

The Small Business Counselor
12423 Hedges Run Dr., Ste. 153
Woodbridge, VA 22192
(703)490-6755
Fax: (703)490-1356

Washington

Burlington Consultants
10900 NE 8th St., Ste. 900
Bellevue, WA 98004
(425)688-3060
Fax: (425)454-4383
E-mail: partners@burlington
consultants.com
Website: http://www.burlington
consultants.com

Perry L. Smith Consulting
800 Bellevue Way NE, Ste. 400
Bellevue, WA 98004-4208
(425)462-2072
Fax: (425)462-5638

St. Charles Consulting Group
1420 NW Gilman Blvd.
Issaquah, WA 98027
(425)557-8708
Fax: (425)557-8731
E-mail: info@stcharlesconsulting.com
Website: http://www.stcharlescon
sulting.com

Independent Automotive Training Services
PO Box 334
Kirkland, WA 98083
(425)822-5715
E-mail: ltunney@autosvccon.com
Website: http://www.autosvccon.com

Kahle Associate Inc.
6203 204th Dr. NE
Redmond, WA 98053
(425)836-8763
Fax: (425)868-3770
E-mail: randykahle@kahleassociates.com
Website: http://www.kahleassociates.com

Dan Collin
3419 Wallingord Ave N, No. 2
Seattle, WA 98103
(206)634-9469
E-mail: dc@dancollin.com
Website: http://members.home.net/
dcollin/

ECG Management Consultants Inc.
1111 3rd Ave., Ste. 2700
Seattle, WA 98101-3201
(206)689-2200
Fax: (206)689-2209
E-mail: ecg@ecgmc.com
Website: http://www.ecgmc.com

Northwest Trade Adjustment Assistance Center
900 4th Ave., Ste. 2430
Seattle, WA 98164-1001
(206)622-2730
Free: 800-667-8087
Fax: (206)622-1105
E-mail: matchingfunds@nwtaac.org
Website: http://www.taacenters.org

Business Planning Consultants
S 3510 Ridgeview Dr.
Spokane, WA 99206
(509)928-0332
Fax: (509)921-0842
E-mail: bpci@nextdim.com

West Virginia

**Stanley & Associates Inc./
BusinessandMarketingPlans.com**
1687 Robert C. Byrd Dr.
Beckley, WV 25801
(304)252-0324
Free: 888-752-6720
Fax: (304)252-0470
E-mail: cclay@charterinternet.com

Website: http://www.Businessand
MarketingPlans.com
Christopher Clay

Wisconsin

White & Associates Inc.
5349 Somerset Ln. S
Greenfield, WI 53221
(414)281-7373
Fax: (414)281-7006
E-mail: wnaconsult@aol.com

Small business administration regional offices

This section contains a listing of Small Business Administration offices arranged numerically by region. Service areas are provided. Contact the appropriate office for a referral to the nearest field office, or visit the Small Business Administration online at www.sba.gov.

Region 1

U.S. Small Business Administration
Region I Office
10 Causeway St., Ste. 812
Boston, MA 02222-1093
Phone: (617)565-8415
Fax: (617)565-8420
Serves Connecticut, Maine, Massachusetts, New Hampshire, Rhode Island, and Vermont.

Region 2

U.S. Small Business Administration
Region II Office
26 Federal Plaza, Ste. 3108
New York, NY 10278
Phone: (212)264-1450
Fax: (212)264-0038
Serves New Jersey, New York, Puerto Rico, and the Virgin Islands.

Region 3

U.S. Small Business Administration
Region III Office
Robert N C Nix Sr. Federal Building
900 Market St., 5th Fl.
Philadelphia, PA 19107
(215)580-2807
Serves Delaware, the District of Columbia, Maryland, Pennsylvania, Virginia, and West Virginia.

Region 4

U.S. Small Business Administration
Region IV Office
233 Peachtree St. NE
Harris Tower 1800
Atlanta, GA 30303
Phone: (404)331-4999
Fax: (404)331-2354
Serves Alabama, Florida, Georgia, Kentucky, Mississippi, North Carolina, South Carolina, and Tennessee.

Region 5

U.S. Small Business Administration
Region V Office
500 W. Madison St.
Citicorp Center, Ste. 1240
Chicago, IL 60661-2511
Phone: (312)353-0357
Fax: (312)353-3426
Serves Illinois, Indiana, Michigan, Minnesota, Ohio, and Wisconsin.

Region 6

U.S. Small Business Administration
Region VI Office
4300 Amon Carter Blvd., Ste. 108
Fort Worth, TX 76155
Phone: (817)684-5581
Fax: (817)684-5588
Serves Arkansas, Louisiana, New Mexico, Oklahoma, and Texas.

Region 7

U.S. Small Business Administration
Region VII Office
323 W. 8th St., Ste. 307
Kansas City, MO 64105-1500
Phone: (816)374-6380
Fax: (816)374-6339
Serves Iowa, Kansas, Missouri, and Nebraska.

Region 8

U.S. Small Business Administration
Region VIII Office
721 19th St., Ste. 400
Denver, CO 80202
Phone: (303)844-0500
Fax: (303)844-0506
Serves Colorado, Montana, North Dakota, South Dakota, Utah, and Wyoming.

Region 9

U.S. Small Business Administration
Region IX Office
330 N Brand Blvd., Ste. 1270
Glendale, CA 91203-2304
Phone: (818)552-3434
Fax: (818)552-3440
Serves American Samoa, Arizona, California, Guam, Hawaii, Nevada, and the Trust Territory of the Pacific Islands.

Region 10

U.S. Small Business Administration
Region X Office
2401 Fourth Ave., Ste. 400
Seattle, WA 98121
Phone: (206)553-5676
Fax: (206)553-4155
Serves Alaska, Idaho, Oregon, and Washington.

Small business development centers

This section contains a listing of all Small Business Development Centers, organized alphabetically by state/U.S. territory, then by city, then by agency name.

Alabama

Alabama SBDC
UNIVERSITY OF ALABAMA
2800 Milan Court Suite 124
Birmingham, AL 35211-6908
Phone: 205-943-6750
Fax: 205-943-6752
E-Mail: wcampbell@provost.uab.edu
Website: http://www.asbdc.org
Mr. William Campbell Jr, State Director

Alaska

Alaska SBDC
UNIVERSITY OF ALASKA - ANCHORAGE
430 West Seventh Avenue, Suite 110
Anchorage, AK 99501
Phone: 907-274 7232
Fax: 907-274-9524
E-Mail: anerw@uaa.alaska.edu
Website: http://www.aksbdc.org
Ms. Jean R. Wall, State Director

American Samoa

American Samoa SBDC
AMERICAN SAMOA COMMUNITY COLLEGE
P.O. Box 2609
Pago Pago, American Samoa 96799
Phone: 011-684-699-4830
Fax: 011-684-699-6132
E-Mail: htalex@att.net
Mr. Herbert Thweatt, Director

Arizona

Arizona SBDC
MARICOPA COUNTY COMMUNITY COLLEGE
2411 West 14th Street, Suite 132
Tempe, AZ 85281
Phone: 480-731-8720
Fax: 480-731-8729
E-Mail: mike.york@domail.maricopa.edu
Website: http://www.dist.maricopa.edu.sbdc
Mr. Michael York, State Director

Arkansas

Arkansas SBDC
UNIVERSITY OF ARKANSAS
2801 South University Avenue
Little Rock, AR 72204
Phone: 501-324-9043
Fax: 501-324-9049
E-Mail: jmroderick@ualr.edu
Website: http://asbdc.ualr.edu
Ms. Janet M. Roderick, State Director

California

California - San Francisco SBDC
Northern California SBDC Lead Center
HUMBOLDT STATE UNIVERSITY
Office of Economic Development
1 Harpst Street 2006A, Siemens Hall
Arcata, CA, 95521
Phone: 707-826-3922
Fax: 707-826-3206
E-Mail: gainer@humboldt.edu
Ms. Margaret A. Gainer, Regional Director

California - Sacramento SBDC
CALIFORNIA STATE UNIVERSITY - CHICO
Chico, CA 95929-0765
Phone: 530-898-4598
Fax: 530-898-4734

E-Mail: dripke@csuchico.edu
Website: http://gsbdc.csuchico.edu
Mr. Dan Ripke, Interim Regional Director

California - San Diego SBDC
SOUTHWESTERN COMMUNITY
COLLEGE DISTRICT
900 Otey Lakes Road
Chula Vista, CA 91910
Phone: 619-482-6388
Fax: 619-482-6402
E-Mail: dtrujillo@swc.cc.ca.us
Website: http://www.sbditc.org
Ms. Debbie P. Trujillo, Regional Director

California - Fresno SBDC
UC Merced Lead Center
UNIVERSITY OF CALIFORNIA -
MERCED
550 East Shaw, Suite 105A
Fresno, CA 93710
Phone: 559-241-6590
Fax: 559-241-7422
E-Mail: crosander@ucmerced.edu
Website: http://sbdc.ucmerced.edu
Mr. Chris Rosander, State Director

California - Santa Ana SBDC
Tri-County Lead SBDC
CALIFORNIA STATE UNIVERSITY -
FULLERTON
800 North State College Boulevard, LH640
Fullerton, CA 92834
Phone: 714-278-2719
Fax: 714-278-7858
E-Mail: vpham@fullerton.edu
Website: http://www.leadsbdc.org
Ms. Vi Pham, Lead Center Director

California - Los Angeles Region SBDC
LONG BEACH COMMUNITY
COLLEGE DISTRICT
3950 Paramount Boulevard, Ste 101
Lakewood, CA 90712
Phone: 562-938-5004
Fax: 562-938-5030
E-Mail: ssloan@lbcc.edu
Ms. Sheneui Sloan, Interim Lead Center
Director

Colorado

Colorado SBDC
OFFICE OF ECONOMIC
DEVELOPMENT
1625 Broadway, Suite 170
Denver, CO 80202
Phone: 303-892-3864
Fax: 303-892-3848
E-Mail: Kelly.Manning@state.co.us

Website: http://www.state.co.us/oed/sbdc
Ms. Kelly Manning, State Director

Connecticut

Connecticut SBDC
UNIVERSITY OF CONNECTICUT
1376 Storrs Road, Unit 4094
Storrs, CT 06269-1094
Phone: 860-870-6370
Fax: 860-870-6374
E-Mail: richard.cheney@uconn.edu
Website: http://www.sbdc.uconn.edu
Mr. Richard Cheney, Interim State Director

Delaware

Delaware SBDC
DELAWARE TECHNOLOGY PARK
1 Innovation Way, Suite 301
Newark, DE 19711
Phone: 302-831-2747
Fax: 302-831-1423
E-Mail: Clinton.tymes@mvs.udel.edu
Website: http://www.delawaresbdc.org
Mr. Clinton Tymes, State Director

District of Columbia

District of Columbia SBDC
HOWARD UNIVERSITY
2600 6th Street, NW Room 128
Washington, DC 20059
Phone: 202-806-1550
Fax: 202-806-1777
E-Mail: hturner@howard.edu
Website: http://www.dcsbdc.com/
Mr. Henry Turner, Executive Director

Florida

Florida SBDC
UNIVERSITY OF WEST FLORIDA
401 East Chase Street, Suite 100
Pensacola, FL 32502
Phone: 850-473-7800
Fax: 850-473-7813
E-Mail: jcartwri@uwf.edu
Website: http://www.floridasbdc.com
Mr. Jerry Cartwright, State Director

Georgia

Georgia SBDC
UNIVERSITY OF GEORGIA
1180 East Broad Street
Athens, GA 30602
Phone: 706-542-6762
Fax: 706-542-6776
E-mail: aadams@sbdc.uga.edu

Website: http://www.sbdc.uga.edu
Mr. Allan Adams, Interim State Director

Guam

Guam Small Business Development
Center
UNIVERSITY OF GUAM
Pacific Islands SBDC
P.O. Box 5014 - U.O.G. Station
Mangilao, GU 96923
Phone: 671-735-2590
Fax: 671-734-2002
E-mail: casey@pacificsbdc.com
Website: http://www.uog.edu/sbdc
Mr. Casey Jeszenka, Director

Hawaii

Hawaii SBDC
UNIVERSITY OF HAWAII - HILO
308 Kamehameha Avenue, Suite 201
Hilo, HI 96720
Phone: 808-974-7515
Fax: 808-974-7683
E-Mail: darrylm@interpac.net
Website: http://www.hawaii-sbdc.org
Mr. Darryl Mleynek, State Director

Idaho

Idaho SBDC
BOISE STATE UNIVERSITY
1910 University Drive
Boise, ID 83725
Phone: 208-426-3799
Fax: 208-426-3877
E-mail: jhogge@boisestate.edu
Website: http://www.idahosbdc.org
Mr. Jim Hogge, State Director

Illinois

Illinois SBDC
DEPARTMENT OF COMMERCE
AND ECONOMIC OPPORTUNITY
620 E. Adams, S-4
Springfield, IL 62701
Phone: 217-524-5700
Fax: 217-524-0171
E-mail: mpatrilli@ildceo.net
Website: http://www.ilsbdc.biz
Mr. Mark Petrilli, State Director

Indiana

Indiana SBDC
INDIANA ECONOMIC
DEVELOPMENT CORPORATION
One North Capitol, Suite 900
Indianapolis, IN 46204

Phone: 317-234-8872
Fax: 317-232-8874
E-mail: dtrocha@isbdc.org
Website: http://www.isbdc.org
Ms. Debbie Bishop Trocha, State
Director

Iowa

Iowa SBDC
IOWA STATE UNIVERSITY
340 Gerdin Business Bldg.
Ames, IA 50011-1350
Phone: 515-294-2037
Fax: 515-294-6522
E-mail: jonryan@iastate.edu
Website: http://www.iabusnet.org
Mr. Jon Ryan, State Director

Kansas

Kansas SBDC
FORT HAYS STATE UNIVERSITY
214 SW Sixth Street, Suite 301
Topeka, KS 66603
Phone: 785-296-6514
Fax: 785-291-3261
E-mail: ksbdc.wkearns@fhsu.edu
Website: http://www.fhsu.edu/ksbdc
Mr. Wally Kearns, State Director

Kentucky

Kentucky SBDC
UNIVERSITY OF KENTUCKY
225 Gatton College of Business
Economics Building
Lexington, KY 40506 0034
Phone: 859-257-7668
Fax: 859-323-1907
E-mail: lrnaug0@pop.uky.edu
Website: http://www.ksbdc.org
Ms. Becky Naugle, State Director

Louisiana

Louisiana SBDC
UNIVERSITY OF LOUISIANA -
MONROE
College of Business Administration
700 University Avenue
Monroe, LA 71209
Phone: 318-342-5506
Fax: 318-342-5510
E-mail: wilkerson@ulm.edu
Website: http://www.lsbdc.org
Ms. Mary Lynn Wilkerson, State
Director

Maine

Maine SBDC
UNIVERSITY OF SOUTHERN
MAINE
96 Falmouth Street P.O. Box 9300
Portland, ME 04103
Phone: 207-780-4420
Fax: 207-780-4810
E-mail: jrmassaua@maine.edu
Website: http://www.mainesbdc.org
Mr. John Massaua, State Director

Maryland

Maryland SBDC
UNIVERSITY OF MARYLAND
7100 Baltimore Avenue, Suite 401
College Park, MD 20742
Phone: 301-403-8300
Fax: 301-403-8303
E-mail: rsprow@mdsbdc.umd.edu
Website: http://www.mdsbdc.umd.edu
Ms. Renee Sprow, State Director

Massachusetts

Massachusetts SBDC
UNIVERSITY OF MASSACHUSETTS
School of Management, Room 205
Amherst, MA 01003-4935
Phone: 413-545-6301
Fax: 413-545-1273
E-mail: gep@msbdc.umass.edu
Website: http://msbdc.som.umass.edu
Ms. Georgianna Parkin, State Director

Michigan

Michigan SBTDC
GRAND VALLEY STATE
UNIVERSITY
510 West Fulton Avenue
Grand Rapids, MI 49504
Phone: 616-331-7485
Fax: 616-331-7389
E-mail: lopuckic@gvsu.edu
Website: http://www.misbtdc.org
Ms. Carol Lopucki, State Director

Minnesota

Minnesota SBDC
MINNESOTA SMALL BUSINESS
DEVELOPMENT CENTER
1st National Bank Building
332 Minnesota Street, Suite E200
St. Paul, MN 55101-1351
Phone: 651-297-5773
Fax: 651-296-5287

E-mail: michael.myhre@state.mn.us
Website: http://www.mnsbdc.com
Mr. Michael Myhre, State Director

Mississippi

Mississippi SBDC
UNIVERSITY OF MISSISSIPPI
B-19 Jeanette Phillips Drive
P.O. Box 1848
University, MS 38677
Phone: 662-915-5001
Fax: 662-915-5650
E-mail: wgurley@olemiss.edu
Website: http://www.olemiss.edu/depts/
mssbdc
Mr. Doug Gurley, Jr., State Director

Missouri

Missouri SBDC
UNIVERSITY OF MISSOURI
1205 University Avenue, Suite 300
Columbia, MO 65211
Phone: 573-882-1348
Fax: 573-884-4297
E-mail: summersm@missouri.edu
Website: http://www.mo-sbdc.org/
index.shtml
Mr. Max Summers, State Director

Montana

Montana SBDC
DEPARTMENT OF COMMERCE
301 South Park Avenue, Room 114 /
P.O. Box 200505
Helena, MT 59620
Phone: 406-841-2746
Fax: 406-444-1872
E-mail: adesch@state.mt.us
Website: http://commerce.state.mt.us/
brd/BRD_SBDC.html
Ms. Ann Desch, State Director

Nebraska

Nebraska SBDC
UNIVERSITY OF NEBRASKA -
OMAHA
60th & Dodge Street, CBA Room 407
Omaha, NE 68182
Phone: 402-554-2521
Fax: 402-554-3473
E-mail: rbernier@unomaha.edu
Website: http://nbdc.unomaha.edu
Mr. Robert Bernier, State Director

Nevada

Nevada SBDC
UNIVERSITY OF NEVADA - RENO
Reno College of Business
Administration, Room 411
Reno, NV 89557-0100
Phone: 775-784-1717
Fax: 775-784-4337
E-mail: males@unr.edu
Website: http://www.nsbdc.org
Mr. Sam Males, State Director

New Hampshire

New Hampshire SBDC
UNIVERSITY OF NEW HAMPSHIRE
108 McConnell Hall
Durham, NH 03824-3593
Phone: 603-862-4879
Fax: 603-862-4876
E-mail: Mary.Collins@unh.edu
Website: http://www.nhsbdc.org
Ms. Mary Collins, State Director

New Jersey

New Jersey SBDC
RUTGERS UNIVERSITY
49 Bleeker Street
Newark, NJ 07102-1993
Phone: 973-353-5950
Fax: 973-353-1110
E-mail: bhopper@njsbdc.com
Website: http://www.njsbdc.com/home
Ms. Brenda Hopper, State Director

New Mexico

New Mexico SBDC
SANTA FE COMMUNITY COLLEGE
6401 Richards Avenue
Santa Fe, NM 87505
Phone: 505-428-1362
Fax: 505-471-9469
E-mail: rmiller@santa-fe.cc.nm.us
Website: http://www.nmsbdc.org
Mr. Roy Miller, State Director

New York

New York SBDC
STATE UNIVERSITY OF NEW YORK
SUNY Plaza, S-523
Albany, NY 12246
Phone: 518-443-5398
Fax: 518-443-5275
E-mail: j.king@nyssbdc.org
Website: http://www.nyssbdc.org
Mr. Jim King, State Director

North Carolina

North Carolina SBDTC
UNIVERSITY OF NORTH CAROLINA
5 West Hargett Street, Suite 600
Raleigh, NC 27601
Phone: 919-715-7272
Fax: 919-715-7777
E-mail: sdaugherty@sbtdc.org
Website: http://www.sbtdc.org
Mr. Scott Daugherty, State Director

North Dakota

North Dakota SBDC
UNIVERSITY OF NORTH DAKOTA
1600 E. Century Avenue, Suite 2
Bismarck, ND 58503
Phone: 701-328-5375
Fax: 701-328-5320
E-mail: christine.martin@und.nodak.edu
Website: http://www.ndsbdc.org
Ms. Christine Martin-Goldman, State
Director

Ohio

Ohio SBDC
OHIO DEPARTMENT
OF DEVELOPMENT
77 South High Street
Columbus, OH 43216
Phone: 614-466-5102
Fax: 614-466-0829
E-mail: mabraham@odod.state.oh.us
Website: http://www.ohiosbdc.org
Ms. Michele Abraham, State Director

Oklahoma

Oklahoma SBDC
SOUTHEAST OKLAHOMA STATE
UNIVERSITY
517 University, Box 2584, Station A
Durant, OK 74701
Phone: 580-745-7577
Fax: 580-745-7471
E-mail: gpennington@sosu.edu
Website: http://www.osbdc.org
Mr. Grady Pennington, State Director

Oregon

Oregon SBDC
LANE COMMUNITY COLLEGE
99 West Tenth Avenue, Suite 390
Eugene, OR 97401-3021
Phone: 541-463-5250
Fax: 541-345-6006
E-mail: carterb@lanecc.edu

Website: http://www.bizcenter.org
Mr. William Carter, State Director

Pennsylvania

Pennsylvania SBDC
UNIVERSITY OF PENNSYLVANIA
The Wharton School
3733 Spruce Street
Philadelphia, PA 19104-6374
Phone: 215-898-1219
Fax: 215-573-2135
E-mail: ghiggins@wharton.upenn.edu
Website: http://pasbdc.org
Mr. Gregory Higgins, State Director

Puerto Rico

Puerto Rico SBDC
INTER-AMERICAN UNIVERSITY
OF PUERTO RICO
416 Ponce de Leon Avenue, Union Plaza,
Seventh Floor
Hato Rey, PR 00918
Phone: 787-763-6811
Fax: 787-763-4629
E-mail: cmarti@prsbdc.org
Website: http://www.prsbdc.org
Ms. Carmen Marti, Executive Director

Rhode Island

Rhode Island SBDC
BRYANT UNIVERSITY
1150 Douglas Pike
Smithfield, RI 02917
Phone: 401-232-6923
Fax: 401-232-6933
E-mail: adawson@bryant.edu
Website: http://www.risbdc.org
Ms. Diane Fournaris, Interim State Director

South Carolina

South Carolina SBDC
UNIVERSITY OF SOUTH CAROLINA
College of Business Administration
1710 College Street
Columbia, SC 29208
Phone: 803-777-4907
Fax: 803-777-4403
E-mail: lenti@moore.sc.edu
Website: http://scsbdc.moore.sc.edu
Mr. John Lenti, State Director

South Dakota

South Dakota SBDC
UNIVERSITY OF SOUTH DAKOTA
414 East Clark Street, Patterson Hall
Vermillion, SD 57069

Phone: 605-677-6256
Fax: 605-677-5427
E-mail: jshemmin@usd.edu
Website: http://www.sdsbdc.org
Mr. John S. Hemmingstad, State
Director

Tennessee

Tennessee SBDC
TENNESSEE BOARD OF REGENTS
1415 Murfressboro Road, Suite 540
Nashville, TN 37217-2833
Phone: 615-898-2745
Fax: 615-893-7089
E-mail: pgeho@mail.tsbdc.org
Website: http://www.tsbdc.org
Mr. Patrick Geho, State Director

Texas

Texas-North SBDC
**DALLAS COUNTY COMMUNITY
COLLEGE**
1402 Corinth Street
Dallas, TX 75215
Phone: 214-860-5835
Fax: 214-860-5813
E-mail: emk9402@dcccd.edu
Website: http://www.ntsbdc.org
Ms. Liz Klimback, Region Director

Texas-Houston SBDC
UNIVERSITY OF HOUSTON
2302 Fannin, Suite 200
Houston, TX 77002
Phone: 713-752-8425
Fax: 713-756-1500
E-mail: fyoung@uh.edu
Website: http://sbdcnetwork.uh.edu
Mr. Mike Young, Executive Director

Texas-NW SBDC
TEXAS TECH UNIVERSITY
2579 South Loop 289, Suite 114
Lubbock, TX 79423
Phone: 806-745-3973
Fax: 806-745-6207
E-mail: c.bean@nwtsbdc.org
Website: http://www.nwtsbdc.org
Mr. Craig Bean, Executive Director

**Texas-South-West Texas Border
Region SBDC**
**UNIVERSITY OF TEXAS -
SAN ANTONIO**
501 West Durango Boulevard
San Antonio, TX 78207-4415
Phone: 210-458-2742
Fax: 210-458-2464

E-mail: albert.salgado@utsa.edu
Website: http://www.iedtexas.org
Mr. Alberto Salgado, Region Director

Utah

Utah SBDC
SALT LAKE COMMUNITY COLLEGE
9750 South 300 West
Sandy, UT 84070
Phone: 801-957-3493
Fax: 801-957-3488
E-mail: Greg.Panichello@slcc.edu
Website: http://www.slcc.edu/sbdc
Mr. Greg Panichello, State Director

Vermont

Vermont SBDC
VERMONT TECHNICAL COLLEGE
PO Box 188, 1 Main Street
Randolph Center, VT 05061-0188
Phone: 802-728-9101
Fax: 802-728-3026
E-mail: lquillen@vtc.edu
Website: http://www.vtsbdc.org
Ms. Lenae Quillen-Blume, State Director

Virgin Islands

Virgin Islands SBDC
**UNIVERSITY OF THE VIRGIN
ISLANDS**
8000 Nisky Center, Suite 720
St. Thomas, VI 00802-5804
Phone: 340-776-3206
Fax: 340-775-3756
E-mail: wbush@webmail.uvi.edu
Website: http://rps.uvi.edu/SBDC
Mr. Warren Bush, State Director

Virginia

Virginia SBDC
GEORGE MASON UNIVERSITY
4031 University Drive, Suite 200
Fairfax, VA 22030-3409
Phone: 703-277-7727
Fax: 703-352-8515
E-mail: jkeenan@gmu.edu
Website: http://www.virginiasbdc.org
Ms. Jody Keenan, Director

Washington

Washington SBDC
WASHINGTON STATE UNIVERSITY
534 E. Trent Avenue
P.O. Box 1495
Spokane, WA 99210-1495

Phone: 509-358-7765
Fax: 509-358-7764
E-mail: barogers@wsu.edu
Website: http://www.wsbdc.org
Mr. Brett Rogers, State Director

West Virginia

West Virginia SBDC
**WEST VIRGINIA DEVELOPMENT
OFFICE**
Capital Complex, Building 6, Room 652
Charleston, WV 25301
Phone: 304-558-2960
Fax: 304-558-0127
E-mail: csalyer@wvsbdc.org
Website: http://www.wvsbdc.org
Mr. Conley Salyor, State Director

Wisconsin

Wisconsin SBDC
UNIVERSITY OF WISCONSIN
432 North Lake Street, Room 423
Madison, WI 53706
Phone: 608-263-7794
Fax: 608-263-7830
E-mail: erica.kauten@uwex.edu
Website: http://www.wisconsinsbdc.org
Ms. Erica Kauten, State Director

Wyoming

Wyoming SBDC
UNIVERSITY OF WYOMING
P.O. Box 3922
Laramie, WY 82071-3922
Phone: 307-766-3505
Fax: 307-766-3406
E-mail: DDW@uwyo.edu
Website: http://www.uwyo.edu/sbdc
Ms. Debbie Popp, Acting State Director

Service corps of retired executives (score) offices

*This section contains a listing of all
SCORE offices organized alphabetically by
state/U.S. territory, then by city, then by
agency name.*

Alabama

SCORE Office (Northeast Alabama)
1330 Quintard Ave.
Anniston, AL 36202
(256)237-3536

SCORE Office (North Alabama)
901 South 15th St, Rm. 201
Birmingham, AL 35294-2060
(205)934-6868
Fax: (205)934-0538

SCORE Office (Baldwin County)
29750 Larry Dee Cawyer Dr.
Daphne, AL 36526
(334)928-5838

SCORE Office (Shoals)
612 S. COurt
Florence, AL 35630
(256)764-4661
Fax: (256)766-9017
E-mail: shoals@shoalschamber.com

SCORE Office (Mobile)
600 S Court St.
Mobile, AL 36104
(334)240-6868
Fax: (334)240-6869

SCORE Office (Alabama Capitol City)
600 S. Court St.
Montgomery, AL 36104
(334)240-6868
Fax: (334)240-6869

SCORE Office (East Alabama)
601 Ave. A
Opelika, AL 36801
(334)745-4861
E-mail: score636@hotmail.com
Website: http://www.angelfire.com/sc/score636/

SCORE Office (Tuscaloosa)
2200 University Blvd.
Tuscaloosa, AL 35402
(205)758-7588

Alaska

SCORE Office (Anchorage)
510 L St., Ste. 310
Anchorage, AK 99501
(907)271-4022
Fax: (907)271-4545

Arizona

SCORE Office (Lake Havasu)
10 S. Acoma Blvd.
Lake Havasu City, AZ 86403
(520)453-5951
E-mail: SCORE@ctaz.com
Website: http://www.scorearizona.org/lake_havasu/

SCORE Office (East Valley)
Federal Bldg., Rm. 104
26 N. MacDonald St.
Mesa, AZ 85201
(602)379-3100
Fax: (602)379-3143
E-mail: 402@aol.com
Website: http://www.scorearizona.org/mesa/

SCORE Office (Phoenix)
2828 N. Central Ave., Ste. 800
Central & One Thomas
Phoenix, AZ 85004
(602)640-2329
Fax: (602)640-2360
E-mail: e-mail@SCORE-phoenix.org
Website: http://www.score-phoenix.org/

SCORE Office (Prescott Arizona)
1228 Willow Creek Rd., Ste. 2
Prescott, AZ 86301
(520)778-7438
Fax: (520)778-0812
E-mail: score@northlink.com
Website: http://www.scorearizona.org/prescott/

SCORE Office (Tucson)
110 E. Pennington St.
Tucson, AZ 85702
(520)670-5008
Fax: (520)670-5011
E-mail: score@azstarnet.com
Website: http://www.scorearizona.org/tucson/

SCORE Office (Yuma)
281 W. 24th St., Ste. 116
Yuma, AZ 85364
(520)314-0480
E-mail: score@C2i2.com
Website: http://www.scorearizona.org/yuma

Arkansas

SCORE Office (South Central)
201 N. Jackson Ave.
El Dorado, AR 71730-5803
(870)863-6113
Fax: (870)863-6115

SCORE Office (Ozark)
Fayetteville, AR 72701
(501)442-7619

SCORE Office (Northwest Arkansas)
Glenn Haven Dr., No. 4
Ft. Smith, AR 72901
(501)783-3556

SCORE Office (Garland County)
Grand & Ouachita
PO Box 6012
Hot Springs Village, AR 71902
(501)321-1700

SCORE Office (Little Rock)
2120 Riverfront Dr., Rm. 100
Little Rock, AR 72202-1747
(501)324-5893
Fax: (501)324-5199

SCORE Office (Southeast Arkansas)
121 W. 6th
Pine Bluff, AR 71601
(870)535-7189
Fax: (870)535-1643

California

SCORE Office (Golden Empire)
1706 Chester Ave., No. 200
Bakersfield, CA 93301
(805)322-5881
Fax: (805)322-5663

SCORE Office (Greater Chico Area)
1324 Mangrove St., Ste. 114
Chico, CA 95926
(916)342-8932
Fax: (916)342-8932

SCORE Office (Concord)
2151-A Salvio St., Ste. B
Concord, CA 94520
(510)685-1181
Fax: (510)685-5623

SCORE Office (Covina)
935 W. Badillo St.
Covina, CA 91723
(818)967-4191
Fax: (818)966-9660

SCORE Office (Rancho Cucamonga)
8280 Utica, Ste. 160
Cucamonga, CA 91730
(909)987-1012
Fax: (909)987-5917

SCORE Office (Culver City)
PO Box 707
Culver City, CA 90232-0707
(310)287-3850
Fax: (310)287-1350

SCORE Office (Danville)
380 Diablo Rd., Ste. 103
Danville, CA 94526
(510)837-4400

SCORE Office (Downey)
11131 Brookshire Ave.
Downey, CA 90241
(310)923-2191
Fax: (310)864-0461

SCORE Office (El Cajon)
109 Rea Ave.
El Cajon, CA 92020
(619)444-1327
Fax: (619)440-6164

SCORE Office (El Centro)
1100 Main St.
El Centro, CA 92243
(619)352-3681
Fax: (619)352-3246

SCORE Office (Escondido)
720 N. Broadway
Escondido, CA 92025
(619)745-2125
Fax: (619)745-1183

SCORE Office (Fairfield)
1111 Webster St.
Fairfield, CA 94533
(707)425-4625
Fax: (707)425-0826

SCORE Office (Fontana)
17009 Valley Blvd., Ste. B
Fontana, CA 92335
(909)822-4433
Fax: (909)822-6238

SCORE Office (Foster City)
1125 E. Hillsdale Blvd.
Foster City, CA 94404
(415)573-7600
Fax: (415)573-5201

SCORE Office (Fremont)
2201 Walnut Ave., Ste. 110
Fremont, CA 94538
(510)795-2244
Fax: (510)795-2240

SCORE Office (Central California)
2719 N. Air Fresno Dr., Ste. 200
Fresno, CA 93727-1547
(559)487-5605
Fax: (559)487-5636

SCORE Office (Gardena)
1204 W. Gardena Blvd.
Gardena, CA 90247
(310)532-9905
Fax: (310)515-4893

SCORE Office (Lompoc)
330 N. Brand Blvd., Ste. 190
Glendale, CA 91203-2304

(818)552-3206
Fax: (818)552-3323

SCORE Office (Los Angeles)
330 N. Brand Blvd., Ste. 190
Glendale, CA 91203-2304
(818)552-3206
Fax: (818)552-3323

SCORE Office (Glendora)
131 E. Foothill Blvd.
Glendora, CA 91740
(818)963-4128
Fax: (818)914-4822

SCORE Office (Grover Beach)
177 S. 8th St.
Grover Beach, CA 93433
(805)489-9091
Fax: (805)489-9091

SCORE Office (Hawthorne)
12477 Hawthorne Blvd.
Hawthorne, CA 90250
(310)676-1163
Fax: (310)676-7661

SCORE Office (Hayward)
22300 Foothill Blvd., Ste. 303
Hayward, CA 94541
(510)537-2424

SCORE Office (Hemet)
1700 E. Florida Ave.
Hemet, CA 92544-4679
(909)652-4390
Fax: (909)929-8543

SCORE Office (Hesperia)
16367 Main St.
PO Box 403656
Hesperia, CA 92340
(619)244-2135

SCORE Office (Holloster)
321 San Felipe Rd., No. 11
Hollister, CA 95023

SCORE Office (Hollywood)
7018 Hollywood Blvd.
Hollywood, CA 90028
(213)469-8311
Fax: (213)469-2805

SCORE Office (Indio)
82503 Hwy. 111
PO Drawer TTT
Indio, CA 92202
(619)347-0676

SCORE Office (Inglewood)
330 Queen St.

Inglewood, CA 90301
(818)552-3206

SCORE Office (La Puente)
218 N. Grendanda St. D.
La Puente, CA 91744
(818)330-3216
Fax: (818)330-9524

SCORE Office (La Verne)
2078 Bonita Ave.
La Verne, CA 91750
(909)593-5265
Fax: (714)929-8475

SCORE Office (Lake Elsinore)
132 W. Graham Ave.
Lake Elsinore, CA 92530
(909)674-2577

SCORE Office (Lakeport)
PO Box 295
Lakeport, CA 95453
(707)263-5092

SCORE Office (Lakewood)
5445 E. Del Amo Blvd., Ste. 2
Lakewood, CA 90714
(213)920-7737

SCORE Office (Long Beach)
1 World Trade Center
Long Beach, CA 90831

SCORE Office (Los Alamitos)
901 W. Civic Center Dr., Ste. 160
Los Alamitos, CA 90720

SCORE Office (Los Altos)
321 University Ave.
Los Altos, CA 94022
(415)948-1455

SCORE Office (Manhattan Beach)
PO Box 3007
Manhattan Beach, CA 90266
(310)545-5313
Fax: (310)545-7203

SCORE Office (Merced)
1632 N. St.
Merced, CA 95340
(209)725-3800
Fax: (209)383-4959

SCORE Office (Milpitas)
75 S. Milpitas Blvd., Ste. 205
Milpitas, CA 95035
(408)262-2613
Fax: (408)262-2823

SCORE Office (Yosemite)
1012 11th St., Ste. 300
Modesto, CA 95354
(209)521-9333

SCORE Office (Montclair)
5220 Benito Ave.
Montclair, CA 91763

SCORE Office (Monterey Bay)
380 Alvarado St.
PO Box 1770
Monterey, CA 93940-1770
(408)649-1770

SCORE Office (Moreno Valley)
25480 Alessandro
Moreno Valley, CA 92553

SCORE Office (Morgan Hill)
25 W. 1st St.
PO Box 786
Morgan Hill, CA 95038
(408)779-9444
Fax: (408)778-1786

SCORE Office (Morro Bay)
880 Main St.
Morro Bay, CA 93442
(805)772-4467

SCORE Office (Mountain View)
580 Castro St.
Mountain View, CA 94041
(415)968-8378
Fax: (415)968-5668

SCORE Office (Napa)
1556 1st St.
Napa, CA 94559
(707)226-7455
Fax: (707)226-1171

SCORE Office (North Hollywood)
5019 Lankershim Blvd.
North Hollywood, CA 91601
(818)552-3206

SCORE Office (Northridge)
8801 Reseda Blvd.
Northridge, CA 91324
(818)349-5676

SCORE Office (Novato)
807 De Long Ave.
Novato, CA 94945
(415)897-1164
Fax: (415)898-9097

SCORE Office (East Bay)
519 17th St.
Oakland, CA 94612

(510)273-6611
Fax: (510)273-6015
E-mail: webmaster@eastbayscore.org
Website: http://www.eastbayscore.org

SCORE Office (Oceanside)
928 N. Coast Hwy.
Oceanside, CA 92054
(619)722-1534

SCORE Office (Ontario)
121 West B. St.
Ontario, CA 91762
Fax: (714)984-6439

SCORE Office (Oxnard)
PO Box 867
Oxnard, CA 93032
(805)385-8860
Fax: (805)487-1763

SCORE Office (Pacifica)
450 Dundee Way, Ste. 2
Pacifica, CA 94044
(415)355-4122

SCORE Office (Palm Desert)
72990 Hwy. 111
Palm Desert, CA 92260
(619)346-6111
Fax: (619)346-3463

SCORE Office (Palm Springs)
650 E. Tahquitz Canyon Way Ste. D
Palm Springs, CA 92262-6706
(760)320-6682
Fax: (760)323-9426

SCORE Office (Lakeside)
2150 Low Tree
Palmdale, CA 93551
(805)948-4518
Fax: (805)949-1212

SCORE Office (Palo Alto)
325 Forest Ave.
Palo Alto, CA 94301
(415)324-3121
Fax: (415)324-1215

SCORE Office (Pasadena)
117 E. Colorado Blvd., Ste. 100
Pasadena, CA 91105
(818)795-3355
Fax: (818)795-5663

SCORE Office (Paso Robles)
1225 Park St.
Paso Robles, CA 93446-2234
(805)238-0506
Fax: (805)238-0527

SCORE Office (Petaluma)
799 Baywood Dr., Ste. 3
Petaluma, CA 94954
(707)762-2785
Fax: (707)762-4721

SCORE Office (Pico Rivera)
9122 E. Washington Blvd.
Pico Rivera, CA 90660

SCORE Office (Pittsburg)
2700 E. Leland Rd.
Pittsburg, CA 94565
(510)439-2181
Fax: (510)427-1599

SCORE Office (Pleasanton)
777 Peters Ave.
Pleasanton, CA 94566
(510)846-9697

SCORE Office (Monterey Park)
485 N. Garey
Pomona, CA 91769

SCORE Office (Pomona)
485 N. Garey Ave.
Pomona, CA 91766
(909)622-1256

SCORE Office (Antelope Valley)
4511 West Ave. M-4
Quartz Hill, CA 93536
(805)272-0087
E-mail: avscore@ptw.com
Website: http://www.score.av.org/

SCORE Office (Shasta)
737 Auditorium Dr.
Redding, CA 96099
(916)225-2770

SCORE Office (Redwood City)
1675 Broadway
Redwood City, CA 94063
(415)364-1722
Fax: (415)364-1729

SCORE Office (Richmond)
3925 MacDonald Ave.
Richmond, CA 94805

SCORE Office (Ridgecrest)
PO Box 771
Ridgecrest, CA 93555
(619)375-8331
Fax: (619)375-0365

SCORE Office (Riverside)
3685 Main St., Ste. 350
Riverside, CA 92501
(909)683-7100

SCORE Office (Sacramento)
9845 Horn Rd., 260-B
Sacramento, CA 95827
(916)361-2322
Fax: (916)361-2164
E-mail: sacchapter@directcon.net

SCORE Office (Salinas)
PO Box 1170
Salinas, CA 93902
(408)424-7611
Fax: (408)424-8639

SCORE Office (Inland Empire)
777 E. Rialto Ave.
Purchasing
San Bernardino, CA 92415-0760
(909)386-8278

SCORE Office (San Carlos)
San Carlos Chamber of Commerce
PO Box 1086
San Carlos, CA 94070
(415)593-1068
Fax: (415)593-9108

SCORE Office (Encinitas)
550 W. C St., Ste. 550
San Diego, CA 92101-3540
(619)557-7272
Fax: (619)557-5894

SCORE Office (San Diego)
550 West C. St., Ste. 550
San Diego, CA 92101-3540
(619)557-7272
Fax: (619)557-5894
Website: http://www.score
sandiego.org

SCORE Office (Menlo Park)
1100 Merrill St.
San Francisco, CA 94105
(415)325-2818
Fax: (415)325-0920

SCORE Office (San Francisco)
455 Market St., 6th Fl.
San Francisco, CA 94105
(415)744-6827
Fax: (415)744-6750
E-mail: sfscore@sfscore.
Website: http://www.sfscore.com

SCORE Office (San Gabriel)
401 W. Las Tunas Dr.
San Gabriel, CA 91776
(818)576-2525
Fax: (818)289-2901

SCORE Office (San Jose)
Deanza College
208 S. 1st. St., Ste. 137
San Jose, CA 95113
(408)288-8479
Fax: (408)535-5541

SCORE Office (Silicon Valley)
84 W. Santa Clara St., Ste. 100
San Jose, CA 95113
(408)288-8479
Fax: (408)535-5541
E-mail: info@svscore.org
Website: http://www.svscore.org

SCORE Office (San Luis Obispo)
3566 S. Hiquera, No. 104
San Luis Obispo, CA 93401
(805)547-0779

SCORE Office (San Mateo)
1021 S. El Camino, 2nd Fl.
San Mateo, CA 94402
(415)341-5679

SCORE Office (San Pedro)
390 W. 7th St.
San Pedro, CA 90731
(310)832-7272

SCORE Office (Orange County)
200 W. Santa Anna Blvd., Ste. 700
Santa Ana, CA 92701
(714)550-7369
Fax: (714)550-0191
Website: http://www.score114.org

SCORE Office (Santa Barbara)
3227 State St.
Santa Barbara, CA 93130
(805)563-0084

SCORE Office (Central Coast)
509 W. Morrison Ave.
Santa Maria, CA 93454
(805)347-7755

SCORE Office (Santa Maria)
614 S. Broadway
Santa Maria, CA 93454-5111
(805)925-2403
Fax: (805)928-7559

SCORE Office (Santa Monica)
501 Colorado, Ste. 150
Santa Monica, CA 90401
(310)393-9825
Fax: (310)394-1868

SCORE Office (Santa Rosa)
777 Sonoma Ave., Rm. 115E
Santa Rosa, CA 95404

(707)571-8342
Fax: (707)541-0331
Website: http://www.pressdemo.com/
community/score/score.html

SCORE Office (Scotts Valley)
4 Camp Evers Ln.
Scotts Valley, CA 95066
(408)438-1010
Fax: (408)438-6544

SCORE Office (Simi Valley)
40 W. Cochran St., Ste. 100
Simi Valley, CA 93065
(805)526-3900
Fax: (805)526-6234

SCORE Office (Sonoma)
453 1st St. E
Sonoma, CA 95476
(707)996-1033

SCORE Office (Los Banos)
222 S. Shepard St.
Sonora, CA 95370
(209)532-4212

SCORE Office (Tuolumne County)
39 North Washington St.
Sonora, CA 95370
(209)588-0128
E-mail: score@mlode.com

SCORE Office (South San Francisco)
445 Market St., Ste. 6th Fl.
South San Francisco, CA 94105
(415)744-6827
Fax: (415)744-6812

SCORE Office (Stockton)
401 N. San Joaquin St., Rm. 215
Stockton, CA 95202
(209)946-6293

SCORE Office (Taft)
314 4th St.
Taft, CA 93268
(805)765-2165
Fax: (805)765-6639

SCORE Office (Conejo Valley)
625 W. Hillcrest Dr.
Thousand Oaks, CA 91360
(805)499-1993
Fax: (805)498-7264

SCORE Office (Torrance)
3400 Torrance Blvd., Ste. 100
Torrance, CA 90503
(310)540-5858
Fax: (310)540-7662

SCORE Office (Truckee)
PO Box 2757
Truckee, CA 96160
(916)587-2757
Fax: (916)587-2439

SCORE Office (Visalia)
113 S. M St,
Tulare, CA 93274
(209)627-0766
Fax: (209)627-8149

SCORE Office (Upland)
433 N. 2nd Ave.
Upland, CA 91786
(909)931-4108

SCORE Office (Vallejo)
2 Florida St.
Vallejo, CA 94590
(707)644-5551
Fax: (707)644-5590

SCORE Office (Van Nuys)
14540 Victory Blvd.
Van Nuys, CA 91411
(818)989-0300
Fax: (818)989-3836

SCORE Office (Ventura)
5700 Ralston St., Ste. 310
Ventura, CA 93001
(805)658-2688
Fax: (805)658-2252
E-mail: scoreven@jps.net
Website: http://www.jps.net/scoreven

SCORE Office (Vista)
201 E. Washington St.
Vista, CA 92084
(619)726-1122
Fax: (619)226-8654

SCORE Office (Watsonville)
PO Box 1748
Watsonville, CA 95077
(408)724-3849
Fax: (408)728-5300

SCORE Office (West Covina)
811 S. Sunset Ave.
West Covina, CA 91790
(818)338-8496
Fax: (818)960-0511

SCORE Office (Westlake)
30893 Thousand Oaks Blvd.
Westlake Village, CA 91362
(805)496-5630
Fax: (818)991-1754

Colorado

SCORE Office (Colorado Springs)
2 N. Cascade Ave., Ste. 110
Colorado Springs, CO 80903
(719)636-3074
Website: http://www.cscc.org/score02/index.html

SCORE Office (Denver)
US Custom's House, 4th Fl.
721 19th St.
Denver, CO 80201-0660
(303)844-3985
Fax: (303)844-6490
E-mail: score62@csn.net
Website: http://www.sni.net/score62

SCORE Office (Tri-River)
1102 Grand Ave.
Glenwood Springs, CO 81601
(970)945-6589

SCORE Office (Grand Junction)
2591 B & 3/4 Rd.
Grand Junction, CO 81503
(970)243-5242

SCORE Office (Gunnison)
608 N. 11th
Gunnison, CO 81230
(303)641-4422

SCORE Office (Montrose)
1214 Peppertree Dr.
Montrose, CO 81401
(970)249-6080

SCORE Office (Pagosa Springs)
PO Box 4381
Pagosa Springs, CO 81157
(970)731-4890

SCORE Office (Rifle)
0854 W. Battlement Pky., Apt. C106
Parachute, CO 81635
(970)285-9390

SCORE Office (Pueblo)
302 N. Santa Fe
Pueblo, CO 81003
(719)542-1704
Fax: (719)542-1624
E-mail: mackey@iex.net
Website: http://www.pueblo.org/score

SCORE Office (Ridgway)
143 Poplar Pl.
Ridgway, CO 81432

SCORE Office (Silverton)
PO Box 480

Silverton, CO 81433
(303)387-5430

SCORE Office (Minturn)
PO Box 2066
Vail, CO 81658
(970)476-1224

Connecticut

SCORE Office (Greater Bridgeport)
230 Park Ave.
Bridgeport, CT 06601-0999
(203)576-4369
Fax: (203)576-4388

SCORE Office (Bristol)
10 Main St. 1st. Fl.
Bristol, CT 06010
(203)584-4718
Fax: (203)584-4722

SCORE office (Greater Danbury)
246 Federal Rd.
Unit LL2, Ste. 7
Brookfield, CT 06804
(203)775-1151

SCORE Office (Greater Danbury)
246 Federal Rd., Unit LL2, Ste. 7
Brookfield, CT 06804
(203)775-1151

SCORE Office (Eastern Connecticut)
Administration Bldg., Rm. 313
PO 625
61 Main St. (Chapter 579)
Groton, CT 06475
(203)388-9508

SCORE Office (Greater Hartford County)
330 Main St.
Hartford, CT 06106
(860)548-1749
Fax: (860)240-4659
Website: http://www.score56.org

SCORE Office (Manchester)
20 Hartford Rd.
Manchester, CT 06040
(203)646-2223
Fax: (203)646-5871

SCORE Office (New Britain)
185 Main St., Ste. 431
New Britain, CT 06051
(203)827-4492
Fax: (203)827-4480

SCORE Office (New Haven)
25 Science Pk., Bldg. 25, Rm. 366

New Haven, CT 06511
(203)865-7645

SCORE Office (Fairfield County)
24 Beldon Ave., 5th Fl.
Norwalk, CT 06850
(203)847-7348
Fax: (203)849-9308

SCORE Office (Old Saybrook)
146 Main St.
Old Saybrook, CT 06475
(860)388-9508

SCORE Office (Simsbury)
Box 244
Simsbury, CT 06070
(203)651-7307
Fax: (203)651-1933

SCORE Office (Torrington)
23 North Rd.
Torrington, CT 06791
(203)482-6586

Delaware

SCORE Office (Dover)
Treadway Towers
PO Box 576
Dover, DE 19903
(302)678-0892
Fax: (302)678-0189

SCORE Office (Lewes)
PO Box 1
Lewes, DE 19958
(302)645-8073
Fax: (302)645-8412

SCORE Office (Milford)
204 NE Front St.
Milford, DE 19963
(302)422-3301

SCORE Office (Wilmington)
824 Market St., Ste. 610
Wilmington, DE 19801
(302)573-6652
Fax: (302)573-6092
Website: http://www.scoredelaware.com

District of Columbia

SCORE Office (George Mason University)
409 3rd St. SW, 4th Fl.
Washington, DC 20024
800-634-0245

SCORE Office (Washington DC)
1110 Vermont Ave. NW, 9th Fl.

Washington, DC 20043
(202)606-4000
Fax: (202)606-4225
E-mail: dcscore@hotmail.com
Website: http://www.scoredc.org/

Florida

SCORE Office (Desota County Chamber of Commerce)
16 South Velucia Ave.
Arcadia, FL 34266
(941)494-4033

SCORE Office (Suncoast/Pinellas)
Airport Business Ctr.
4707 - 140th Ave. N, No. 311
Clearwater, FL 33755
(813)532-6800
Fax: (813)532-6800

SCORE Office (DeLand)
336 N. Woodland Blvd.
DeLand, FL 32720
(904)734-4331
Fax: (904)734-4333

SCORE Office (South Palm Beach)
1050 S. Federal Hwy., Ste. 132
Delray Beach, FL 33483
(561)278-7752
Fax: (561)278-0288

SCORE Office (Ft. Lauderdale)
Federal Bldg., Ste. 123
299 E. Broward Blvd.
Ft. Lauderdale, FL 33301
(954)356-7263
Fax: (954)356-7145

SCORE Office (Southwest Florida)
The Renaissance
8695 College Pky., Ste. 345 & 346
Ft. Myers, FL 33919
(941)489-2935
Fax: (941)489-1170

SCORE Office (Treasure Coast)
Professional Center, Ste. 2
3220 S. US, No. 1
Ft. Pierce, FL 34982
(561)489-0548

SCORE Office (Gainesville)
101 SE 2nd Pl., Ste. 104
Gainesville, FL 32601
(904)375-8278

SCORE Office (Hialeah Dade Chamber)
59 W. 5th St.
Hialeah, FL 33010

(305)887-1515
Fax: (305)887-2453

SCORE Office (Daytona Beach)
921 Nova Rd., Ste. A
Holly Hills, FL 32117
(904)255-6889
Fax: (904)255-0229
E-mail: score87@dbeach.com

SCORE Office (South Broward)
3475 Sheridian St., Ste. 203
Hollywood, FL 33021
(305)966-8415

SCORE Office (Citrus County)
5 Poplar Ct.
Homosassa, FL 34446
(352)382-1037

SCORE Office (Jacksonville)
7825 Baymeadows Way, Ste. 100-B
Jacksonville, FL 32256
(904)443-1911
Fax: (904)443-1980
E-mail: scorejax@juno.com
Website: http://www.scorejax.org/

SCORE Office (Jacksonville Satellite)
3 Independent Dr.
Jacksonville, FL 32256
(904)366-6600
Fax: (904)632-0617

SCORE Office (Central Florida)
5410 S. Florida Ave., No. 3
Lakeland, FL 33801
(941)687-5783
Fax: (941)687-6225

SCORE Office (Lakeland)
100 Lake Morton Dr.
Lakeland, FL 33801
(941)686-2168

SCORE Office (St. Petersburg)
800 W. Bay Dr., Ste. 505
Largo, FL 33712
(813)585-4571

SCORE Office (Leesburg)
9501 US Hwy. 441
Leesburg, FL 34788-8751
(352)365-3556
Fax: (352)365-3501

SCORE Office (Cocoa)
1600 Farno Rd., Unit 205
Melbourne, FL 32935
(407)254-2288

SCORE Office (Melbourne)
Melbourne Professional Complex
1600 Sarno, Ste. 205
Melbourne, FL 32935
(407)254-2288
Fax: (407)245-2288

SCORE Office (Merritt Island)
1600 Sarno Rd., Ste. 205
Melbourne, FL 32935
(407)254-2288
Fax: (407)254-2288

SCORE Office (Space Coast)
Melbourn Professional Complex
1600 Sarno, Ste. 205
Melbourne, FL 32935
(407)254-2288
Fax: (407)254-2288

SCORE Office (Dade)
49 NW 5th St.
Miami, FL 33128
(305)371-6889
Fax: (305)374-1882
E-mail: score@netrox.net
Website: http://www.netrox.net/~score/

SCORE Office (Naples of Collier)
International College
2654 Tamiami Trl. E
Naples, FL 34112
(941)417-1280
Fax: (941)417-1281
E-mail: score@naples.net
Website: http://www.naples.net/clubs/
score/index.htm

SCORE Office (Pasco County)
6014 US Hwy. 19, Ste. 302
New Port Richey, FL 34652
(813)842-4638

SCORE Office (Southeast Volusia)
115 Canal St.
New Smyrna Beach, FL 32168
(904)428-2449
Fax: (904)423-3512

SCORE Office (Ocala)
110 E. Silver Springs Blvd.
Ocala, FL 34470
(352)629-5959

Clay County SCORE Office
Clay County Chamber of Commerce
1734 Kingsdey Ave.
PO Box 1441
Orange Park, FL 32073
(904)264-2651
Fax: (904)269-0363

SCORE Office (Orlando)
80 N. Hughey Ave.
Rm. 445 Federal Bldg.
Orlando, FL 32801
(407)648-6476
Fax: (407)648-6425

SCORE Office (Emerald Coast)
19 W. Garden St., No. 325
Pensacola, FL 32501
(904)444-2060
Fax: (904)444-2070

SCORE Office (Charlotte County)
201 W. Marion Ave., Ste. 211
Punta Gorda, FL 33950
(941)575-1818
E-mail: score@gls3c.com
Website: http://www.charlotte-
florida.com/business/scorepg01.htm

SCORE Office (St. Augustine)
1 Riberia St.
St. Augustine, FL 32084
(904)829-5681
Fax: (904)829-6477

SCORE Office (Bradenton)
2801 Fruitville, Ste. 280
Sarasota, FL 34237
(813)955-1029

SCORE Office (Manasota)
2801 Fruitville Rd., Ste. 280
Sarasota, FL 34237
(941)955-1029
Fax: (941)955-5581
E-mail: score116@gte.net
Website: http://www.score-suncoast.org/

SCORE Office (Tallahassee)
200 W. Park Ave.
Tallahassee, FL 32302
(850)487-2665

SCORE Office (Hillsborough)
4732 Dale Mabry Hwy. N, Ste. 400
Tampa, FL 33614-6509
(813)870-0125

SCORE Office (Lake Sumter)
122 E. Main St.
Tavares, FL 32778-3810
(352)365-3556

SCORE Office (Titusville)
2000 S. Washington Ave.
Titusville, FL 32780
(407)267-3036
Fax: (407)264-0127

SCORE Office (Venice)
257 N. Tamiami Trl.
Venice, FL 34285
(941)488-2236
Fax: (941)484-5903

SCORE Office (Palm Beach)
500 Australian Ave. S, Ste. 100
West Palm Beach, FL 33401
(561)833-1672
Fax: (561)833-1712

SCORE Office (Wildwood)
103 N. Webster St.
Wildwood, FL 34785

Georgia

SCORE Office (Atlanta)
Harris Tower, Suite 1900
233 Peachtree Rd., NE
Atlanta, GA 30309
(404)347-2442
Fax: (404)347-1227

SCORE Office (Augusta)
3126 Oxford Rd.
Augusta, GA 30909
(706)869-9100

SCORE Office (Columbus)
School Bldg.
PO Box 40
Columbus, GA 31901
(706)327-3654

SCORE Office (Dalton-Whitfield)
305 S. Thorton Ave.
Dalton, GA 30720
(706)279-3383

SCORE Office (Gainesville)
PO Box 374
Gainesville, GA 30503
(770)532-6206
Fax: (770)535-8419

SCORE Office (Macon)
711 Grand Bldg.
Macon, GA 31201
(912)751-6160

SCORE Office (Brunswick)
4 Glen Ave.
St. Simons Island, GA 31520
(912)265-0620
Fax: (912)265-0629

SCORE Office (Savannah)
111 E. Liberty St., Ste. 103
Savannah, GA 31401
(912)652-4335

Fax: (912)652-4184
E-mail: info@scoresav.org
Website: http://www.coastalempire.com/
score/index.htm

Guam

SCORE Office (Guam)
Pacific News Bldg., Rm. 103
238 Archbishop Flores St.
Agana, GU 96910-5100
(671)472-7308

Hawaii

SCORE Office (Hawaii, Inc.)
1111 Bishop St., Ste. 204
PO Box 50207
Honolulu, HI 96813
(808)522-8132
Fax: (808)522-8135
E-mail: hnlscore@juno.com

SCORE Office (Kahului)
250 Alamaha, Unit N16A
Kahului, HI 96732
(808)871-7711

SCORE Office (Maui, Inc.)
590 E. Lipoa Pkwy., Ste. 227
Kihei, HI 96753
(808)875-2380

Idaho

SCORE Office (Treasure Valley)
1020 Main St., No. 290
Boise, ID 83702
(208)334-1696
Fax: (208)334-9353

SCORE Office (Eastern Idaho)
2300 N. Yellowstone, Ste. 119
Idaho Falls, ID 83401
(208)523-1022
Fax: (208)528-7127

Illinois

SCORE Office (Fox Valley)
40 W. Downer Pl.
PO Box 277
Aurora, IL 60506
(630)897-9214
Fax: (630)897-7002

SCORE Office (Greater Belvidere)
419 S. State St.
Belvidere, IL 61008
(815)544-4357
Fax: (815)547-7654

SCORE Office (Bensenville)
1050 Busse Hwy. Suite 100
Bensenville, IL 60106
(708)350-2944
Fax: (708)350-2979

SCORE Office (Central Illinois)
402 N. Hershey Rd.
Bloomington, IL 61704
(309)644-0549
Fax: (309)663-8270
E-mail: webmaster@central-illinois-
score.org
Website: http://www.central-illinois-
score.org/

SCORE Office (Southern Illinois)
150 E. Pleasant Hill Rd.
Box 1
Carbondale, IL 62901
(618)453-6654
Fax: (618)453-5040

SCORE Office (Chicago)
Northwest Atrium Ctr.
500 W. Madison St., No. 1250
Chicago, IL 60661
(312)353-7724
Fax: (312)886-5688
Website: http://www.mcs.net/~bic/

SCORE Office (Chicago–Oliver Harvey College)
Pullman Bldg.
1000 E. 11th St., 7th Fl.
Chicago, IL 60628
Fax: (312)468-8086

SCORE Office (Danville)
28 W. N. Street
Danville, IL 61832
(217)442-7232
Fax: (217)442-6228

SCORE Office (Decatur)
Milliken University
1184 W. Main St.
Decatur, IL 62522
(217)424-6297
Fax: (217)424-3993
E-mail: charding@mail.millikin.edu
Website: http://www.millikin.edu/
academics/Tabor/score.html

SCORE Office (Downers Grove)
925 Curtis
Downers Grove, IL 60515
(708)968-4050
Fax: (708)968-8368

SCORE Office (Elgin)
24 E. Chicago, 3rd Fl.
PO Box 648
Elgin, IL 60120
(847)741-5660
Fax: (847)741-5677

SCORE Office (Freeport Area)
26 S. Galena Ave.
Freeport, IL 61032
(815)233-1350
Fax: (815)235-4038

SCORE Office (Galesburg)
292 E. Simmons St.
PO Box 749
Galesburg, IL 61401
(309)343-1194
Fax: (309)343-1195

SCORE Office (Glen Ellyn)
500 Pennsylvania
Glen Ellyn, IL 60137
(708)469-0907
Fax: (708)469-0426

SCORE Office (Greater Alton)
Alden Hall
5800 Godfrey Rd.
Godfrey, IL 62035-2466
(618)467-2280
Fax: (618)466-8289
Website: http://www.altonweb.com/
score/

SCORE Office (Grayslake)
19351 W. Washington St.
Grayslake, IL 60030
(708)223-3633
Fax: (708)223-9371

SCORE Office (Harrisburg)
303 S. Commercial
Harrisburg, IL 62946-1528
(618)252-8528
Fax: (618)252-0210

SCORE Office (Joliet)
100 N. Chicago
Joliet, IL 60432
(815)727-5371
Fax: (815)727-5374

SCORE Office (Kankakee)
101 S. Schuyler Ave.
Kankakee, IL 60901
(815)933-0376
Fax: (815)933-0380

SCORE Office (Macomb)
216 Seal Hall, Rm. 214

Macomb, IL 61455
(309)298-1128
Fax: (309)298-2520

SCORE Office (Matteson)
210 Lincoln Mall
Matteson, IL 60443
(708)709-3750
Fax: (708)503-9322

SCORE Office (Mattoon)
1701 Wabash Ave.
Mattoon, IL 61938
(217)235-5661
Fax: (217)234-6544

SCORE Office (Quad Cities)
622 19th St.
Moline, IL 61265
(309)797-0082
Fax: (309)757-5435
E-mail: score@qconline.com
Website: http://www.qconline.com/
business/score/

SCORE Office (Naperville)
131 W. Jefferson Ave.
Naperville, IL 60540
(708)355-4141
Fax: (708)355-8355

SCORE Office (Northbrook)
2002 Walters Ave.
Northbrook, IL 60062
(847)498-5555
Fax: (847)498-5510

SCORE Office (Palos Hills)
10900 S. 88th Ave.
Palos Hills, IL 60465
(847)974-5468
Fax: (847)974-0078

SCORE Office (Peoria)
124 SW Adams, Ste. 300
Peoria, IL 61602
(309)676-0755
Fax: (309)676-7534

SCORE Office (Prospect Heights)
1375 Wolf Rd.
Prospect Heights, IL 60070
(847)537-8660
Fax: (847)537-7138

SCORE Office (Quincy Tri-State)
300 Civic Center Plz., Ste. 245
Quincy, IL 62301
(217)222-8093
Fax: (217)222-3033

SCORE Office (River Grove)
2000 5th Ave.
River Grove, IL 60171
(708)456-0300
Fax: (708)583-3121

SCORE Office (Northern Illinois)
515 N. Court St.
Rockford, IL 61103
(815)962-0122
Fax: (815)962-0122

SCORE Office (St. Charles)
103 N. 1st Ave.
St. Charles, IL 60174-1982
(847)584-8384
Fax: (847)584-6065

SCORE Office (Springfield)
511 W. Capitol Ave., Ste. 302
Springfield, IL 62704
(217)492-4416
Fax: (217)492-4867

SCORE Office (Sycamore)
112 Somunak St.
Sycamore, IL 60178
(815)895-3456
Fax: (815)895-0125

SCORE Office (University)
Hwy. 50 & Stuenkel Rd. Ste. C3305
University Park, IL 60466
(708)534-5000
Fax: (708)534-8457

Indiana

SCORE Office (Anderson)
205 W. 11th St.
Anderson, IN 46015
(317)642-0264

SCORE Office (Bloomington)
Star Center
216 W. Allen
Bloomington, IN 47403
(812)335-7334
E-mail: wtfische@indiana.edu
Website: http://www.brainfreezemedia.
com/score527/

SCORE Office (South East Indiana)
500 Franklin St.
Box 29
Columbus, IN 47201
(812)379-4457

SCORE Office (Corydon)
310 N. Elm St.
Corydon, IN 47112

(812)738-2137
Fax: (812)738-6438

SCORE Office (Crown Point)
Old Courthouse Sq. Ste. 206
PO Box 43
Crown Point, IN 46307
(219)663-1800

SCORE Office (Elkhart)
418 S. Main St.
Elkhart, IN 46515
(219)293-1531
Fax: (219)294-1859

SCORE Office (Evansville)
1100 W. Lloyd Expy., Ste. 105
Evansville, IN 47708
(812)426-6144

SCORE Office (Fort Wayne)
1300 S. Harrison St.
Ft. Wayne, IN 46802
(219)422-2601
Fax: (219)422-2601

SCORE Office (Gary)
973 W. 6th Ave., Rm. 326
Gary, IN 46402
(219)882-3918

SCORE Office (Hammond)
7034 Indianapolis Blvd.
Hammond, IN 46324
(219)931-1000
Fax: (219)845-9548

SCORE Office (Indianapolis)
429 N. Pennsylvania St., Ste. 100
Indianapolis, IN 46204-1873
(317)226-7264
Fax: (317)226-7259
E-mail: inscore@indy.net
Website: http://www.score-
indianapolis.org/

SCORE Office (Jasper)
PO Box 307
Jasper, IN 47547-0307
(812)482-6866

**SCORE Office (Kokomo/Howard
Counties)**
106 N. Washington St.
Kokomo, IN 46901
(765)457-5301
Fax: (765)452-4564

SCORE Office (Logansport)
300 E. Broadway, Ste. 103
Logansport, IN 46947
(219)753-6388

SCORE Office (Madison)
301 E. Main St.
Madison, IN 47250
(812)265-3135
Fax: (812)265-2923

SCORE Office (Marengo)
Rt. 1 Box 224D
Marengo, IN 47140
Fax: (812)365-2793

SCORE Office (Marion/Grant Counties)
215 S. Adams
Marion, IN 46952
(765)664-5107

SCORE Office (Merrillville)
255 W. 80th Pl.
Merrillville, IN 46410
(219)769-8180
Fax: (219)736-6223

SCORE Office (Michigan City)
200 E. Michigan Blvd.
Michigan City, IN 46360
(219)874-6221
Fax: (219)873-1204

SCORE Office (South Central Indiana)
4100 Charleston Rd.
New Albany, IN 47150-9538
(812)945-0066

SCORE Office (Rensselaer)
104 W. Washington
Rensselaer, IN 47978

SCORE Office (Salem)
210 N. Main St.
Salem, IN 47167
(812)883-4303
Fax: (812)883-1467

SCORE Office (South Bend)
300 N. Michigan St.
South Bend, IN 46601
(219)282-4350
E-mail: chair@southbend-score.org
Website: http://www.southbend-score.org/

SCORE Office (Valparaiso)
150 Lincolnway
Valparaiso, IN 46383
(219)462 1105
Fax: (219)469-5710

SCORE Office (Vincennes)
27 N. 3rd
PO Box 553
Vincennes, IN 47591
(812)882-6440
Fax: (812)882-6441

SCORE Office (Wabash)
PO Box 371
Wabash, IN 46992
(219)563-1168
Fax: (219)563-6920

Iowa

SCORE Office (Burlington)
Federal Bldg.
300 N. Main St.
Burlington, IA 52601
(319)752-2967

SCORE Office (Cedar Rapids)
2750 1st Ave. NE, Ste 350
Cedar Rapids, IA 52401-1806
(319)362-6405
Fax: (319)362-7861
E:mail: score@scorecr.org
Website: http://www.scorecr.org

SCORE Office (Illowa)
333 4th Ave. S
Clinton, IA 52732
(319)242-5702

SCORE Office (Council Bluffs)
7 N. 6th St.
Council Bluffs, IA 51502
(712)325-1000

SCORE Office (Northeast Iowa)
3404 285th St.
Cresco, IA 52136
(319)547-3377

SCORE Office (Des Moines)
Federal Bldg., Rm. 749
210 Walnut St.
Des Moines, IA 50309-2186
(515)284-4760

SCORE Office (Ft. Dodge)
Federal Bldg., Rm. 436
205 S. 8th St.
Ft. Dodge, IA 50501
(515)955-2622

SCORE Office (Independence)
110 1st. St. east
Independence, IA 50644
(319)334-7178
Fax: (319)334-7179

SCORE Office (Iowa City)
210 Federal Bldg.
PO Box 1853
Iowa City, IA 52240-1853
(319)338-1662

SCORE Office (Keokuk)
401 Main St.
Pierce Bldg., No. 1
Keokuk, IA 52632
(319)524-5055

SCORE Office (Central Iowa)
Fisher Community College
709 S. Center
Marshalltown, IA 50158
(515)753-6645

SCORE Office (River City)
15 West State St.
Mason City, IA 50401
(515)423-5724

SCORE Office (South Central)
SBDC, Indian Hills Community College
525 Grandview Ave.
Ottumwa, IA 52501
(515)683-5127
Fax: (515)683-5263

SCORE Office (Dubuque)
10250 Sundown Rd.
Peosta, IA 52068
(319)556-5110

SCORE Office (Southwest Iowa)
614 W. Sheridan
Shenandoah, IA 51601
(712)246-3260

SCORE Office (Sioux City)
Federal Bldg.
320 6th St.
Sioux City, IA 51101
(712)277-2324
Fax: (712)277-2325

SCORE Office (Iowa Lakes)
122 W. 5th St.
Spencer, IA 51301
(712)262-3059

SCORE Office (Vista)
119 W. 6th St.
Storm Lake, IA 50588
(712)732-3780

SCORE Office (Waterloo)
215 E. 4th
Waterloo, IA 50703
(319)233-8431

Kansas

SCORE Office (Southwest Kansas)
501 W. Spruce
Dodge City, KS 67801
(316)227-3119

SCORE Office (Emporia)
811 Homewood
Emporia, KS 66801
(316)342-1600

SCORE Office (Golden Belt)
1307 Williams
Great Bend, KS 67530
(316)792-2401

SCORE Office (Hays)
PO Box 400
Hays, KS 67601
(913)625-6595

SCORE Office (Hutchinson)
1 E. 9th St.
Hutchinson, KS 67501
(316)665-8468
Fax: (316)665-7619

SCORE Office (Southeast Kansas)
404 Westminster Pl.
PO Box 886
Independence, KS 67301
(316)331-4741

SCORE Office (McPherson)
306 N. Main
PO Box 616
McPherson, KS 67460
(316)241-3303

SCORE Office (Salina)
120 Ash St.
Salina, KS 67401
(785)243-4290
Fax: (785)243-1833

SCORE Office (Topeka)
1700 College
Topeka, KS 66621
(785)231-1010

SCORE Office (Wichita)
100 E. English, Ste. 510
Wichita, KS 67202
(316)269-6273
Fax: (316)269-6499

SCORE Office (Ark Valley)
205 E. 9th St.
Winfield, KS 67156
(316)221-1617

Kentucky

SCORE Office (Ashland)
PO Box 830
Ashland, KY 41105
(606)329-8011
Fax: (606)325-4607

SCORE Office (Bowling Green)
812 State St.
PO Box 51
Bowling Green, KY 42101
(502)781-3200
Fax: (502)843-0458

SCORE Office (Tri-Lakes)
508 Barbee Way
Danville, KY 40422-1548
(606)231-9902

SCORE Office (Glasgow)
301 W. Main St.
Glasgow, KY 42141
(502)651-3161
Fax: (502)651-3122

SCORE Office (Hazard)
B & I Technical Center
100 Airport Gardens Rd.
Hazard, KY 41701
(606)439-5856
Fax: (606)439-1808

SCORE Office (Lexington)
410 W. Vine St., Ste. 290, Civic C
Lexington, KY 40507
(606)231-9902
Fax: (606)253-3190
E-mail: scorelex@uky.campus.mci.net

SCORE Office (Louisville)
188 Federal Office Bldg.
600 Dr. Martin L. King Jr. Pl.
Louisville, KY 40202
(502)582-5976

SCORE Office (Madisonville)
257 N. Main
Madisonville, KY 42431
(502)825-1399
Fax: (502)825-1396

SCORE Office (Paducah)
Federal Office Bldg.
501 Broadway, Rm. B-36
Paducah, KY 42001
(502)442-5685

Louisiana

SCORE Office (Central Louisiana)
802 3rd St.
Alexandria, LA 71309
(318)442-6671

SCORE Office (Baton Rouge)
564 Laurel St.
PO Box 3217
Baton Rouge, LA 70801

(504)381-7130
Fax: (504)336-4306

SCORE Office (North Shore)
2 W. Thomas
Hammond, LA 70401
(504)345-4457
Fax: (504)345-4749

SCORE Office (Lafayette)
804 St. Mary Blvd.
Lafayette, LA 70505-1307
(318)233-2705
Fax: (318)234-8671
E-mail: score302@aol.com

SCORE Office (Lake Charles)
120 W. Pujo St.
Lake Charles, LA 70601
(318)433-3632

SCORE Office (New Orleans)
365 Canal St., Ste. 3100
New Orleans, LA 70130
(504)589-2356
Fax: (504)589-2339

SCORE Office (Shreveport)
400 Edwards St.
Shreveport, LA 71101
(318)677-2536
Fax: (318)677-2541

Maine

SCORE Office (Augusta)
40 Western Ave.
Augusta, ME 04330
(207)622-8509

SCORE Office (Bangor)
Peabody Hall, Rm. 229
One College Cir.
Bangor, ME 04401
(207)941-9707

SCORE Office (Central & Northern Arroostock)
111 High St.
Caribou, ME 04736
(207)492-8010
Fax: (207)492-8010

SCORE Office (Penquis)
South St.
Dover Foxcroft, ME 04426
(207)564-7021

SCORE Office (Maine Coastal)
Mill Mall
Box 1105
Ellsworth, ME 04605-1105

(207)667-5800
E-mail: score@arcadia.net

SCORE Office (Lewiston-Auburn)
BIC of Maine-Bates Mill Complex
35 Canal St.
Lewiston, ME 04240-7764
(207)782-3708
Fax: (207)783-7745

SCORE Office (Portland)
66 Pearl St., Rm. 210
Portland, ME 04101
(207)772-1147
Fax: (207)772-5581
E-mail: Score53@score.maine.org
Website: http://www.score.maine.org/
chapter53/

SCORE Office (Western Mountains)
255 River St.
PO Box 252
Rumford, ME 04257-0252
(207)369-9976

SCORE Office (Oxford Hills)
166 Main St.
South Paris, ME 04281
(207)743-0499

Maryland

SCORE Office (Southern Maryland)
2525 Riva Rd., Ste. 110
Annapolis, MD 21401
(410)266-9553
Fax: (410)573-0981
E-mail: score390@aol.com
Website: http://members.aol.com/
score390/index.htm

SCORE Office (Baltimore)
The City Crescent Bldg., 6th Fl.
10 S. Howard St.
Baltimore, MD 21201
(410)962-2233
Fax: (410)962-1805

SCORE Office (Bel Air)
108 S. Bond St.
Bel Air, MD 21014
(410)838-2020
Fax: (410)893-4715

SCORE Office (Bethesda)
7910 Woodmont Ave., Ste. 1204
Bethesda, MD 20814
(301)652-4900
Fax: (301)657-1973

SCORE Office (Bowie)
6670 Race Track Rd.
Bowie, MD 20715
(301)262-0920
Fax: (301)262-0921

SCORE Office (Dorchester County)
203 Sunburst Hwy.
Cambridge, MD 21613
(410)228-3575

SCORE Office (Upper Shore)
210 Marlboro Ave.
Easton, MD 21601
(410)822-4606
Fax: (410)822-7922

SCORE Office (Frederick County)
43A S. Market St.
Frederick, MD 21701
(301)662-8723
Fax: (301)846-4427

SCORE Office (Gaithersburg)
9 Park Ave.
Gaithersburg, MD 20877
(301)840-1400
Fax: (301)963-3918

SCORE Office (Glen Burnie)
103 Crain Hwy. SE
Glen Burnie, MD 21061
(410)766-8282
Fax: (410)766-9722

SCORE Office (Hagerstown)
111 W. Washington St.
Hagerstown, MD 21740
(301)739-2015
Fax: (301)739-1278

SCORE Office (Laurel)
7901 Sandy Spring Rd. Ste. 501
Laurel, MD 20707
(301)725-4000
Fax: (301)725-0776

SCORE Office (Salisbury)
300 E. Main St.
Salisbury, MD 21801
(410)749-0185
Fax: (410)860-9925

Massachusetts

SCORE Office (NE Massachusetts)
100 Cummings Ctr., Ste. 101 K
Beverly, MA 01923
(978)922-9441
Website: http://www1.shore.net/~score/

SCORE Office (Boston)
10 Causeway St., Rm. 265
Boston, MA 02222-1093
(617)565-5591
Fax: (617)565-5598
E-mail: boston-score-20@worldnet.att.net
Website: http://www.scoreboston.org/

SCORE office (Bristol/Plymouth County)
53 N. 6th St., Federal Bldg.
Bristol, MA 02740
(508)994-5093

SCORE Office (SE Massachusetts)
60 School St.
Brockton, MA 02401
(508)587-2673
Fax: (508)587-1340
Website: http://www.metrosouth
chamber.com/score.html

SCORE Office (North Adams)
820 N. State Rd.
Cheshire, MA 01225
(413)743-5100

SCORE Office (Clinton Satellite)
1 Green St.
Clinton, MA 01510
Fax: (508)368-7689

SCORE Office (Greenfield)
PO Box 898
Greenfield, MA 01302
(413)773-5463
Fax: (413)773-7008

SCORE Office (Haverhill)
87 Winter St.
Haverhill, MA 01830
(508)373-5663
Fax: (508)373-8060

SCORE Office (Hudson Satellite)
PO Box 578
Hudson, MA 01749
(508)568-0360
Fax: (508)568-0360

SCORE Office (Cape Cod)
Independence Pk., Ste. 5B
270 Communications Way
Hyannis, MA 02601
(508)775-4884
Fax: (508)790-2540

SCORE Office (Lawrence)
264 Essex St.
Lawrence, MA 01840
(508)686-0900
Fax: (508)794-9953

SCORE Office (Leominster Satellite)
110 Erdman Way
Leominster, MA 01453
(508)840-4300
Fax: (508)840-4896

SCORE Office (Bristol/Plymouth Counties)
53 N. 6th St., Federal Bldg.
New Bedford, MA 02740
(508)994-5093

SCORE Office (Newburyport)
29 State St.
Newburyport, MA 01950
(617)462-6680

SCORE Office (Pittsfield)
66 West St.
Pittsfield, MA 01201
(413)499-2485

SCORE Office (Haverhill-Salem)
32 Derby Sq.
Salem, MA 01970
(508)745-0330
Fax: (508)745-3855

SCORE Office (Springfield)
1350 Main St.
Federal Bldg.
Springfield, MA 01103
(413)785-0314

SCORE Office (Carver)
12 Taunton Green, Ste. 201
Taunton, MA 02780
(508)824-4068
Fax: (508)824-4069

SCORE Office (Worcester)
33 Waldo St.
Worcester, MA 01608
(508)753-2929
Fax: (508)754-8560

Michigan

SCORE Office (Allegan)
PO Box 338
Allegan, MI 49010
(616)673-2479

SCORE Office (Ann Arbor)
425 S. Main St., Ste. 103
Ann Arbor, MI 48104
(313)665-4433

SCORE Office (Battle Creek)
34 W. Jackson Ste. 4A
Battle Creek, MI 49017-3505

(616)962-4076
Fax: (616)962-6309

SCORE Office (Cadillac)
222 Lake St.
Cadillac, MI 49601
(616)775-9776
Fax: (616)768-4255

SCORE Office (Detroit)
477 Michigan Ave., Rm. 515
Detroit, MI 48226
(313)226-7947
Fax: (313)226-3448

SCORE Office (Flint)
708 Root Rd., Rm. 308
Flint, MI 48503
(810)233-6846

SCORE Office (Grand Rapids)
111 Pearl St. NW
Grand Rapids, MI 49503-2831
(616)771-0305
Fax: (616)771-0328
E-mail: scoreone@iserv.net
Website: http://www.iserv.net/
~scoreone/

SCORE Office (Holland)
480 State St.
Holland, MI 49423
(616)396-9472

SCORE Office (Jackson)
209 East Washington
PO Box 80
Jackson, MI 49204
(517)782-8221
Fax: (517)782-0061

SCORE Office (Kalamazoo)
345 W. Michigan Ave.
Kalamazoo, MI 49007
(616)381-5382
Fax: (616)384-0096
E-mail: score@nucleus.net

SCORE Office (Lansing)
117 E. Allegan
PO Box 14030
Lansing, MI 48901
(517)487-6340
Fax: (517)484-6910

SCORE Office (Livonia)
15401 Farmington Rd.
Livonia, MI 48154
(313)427-2122
Fax: (313)427-6055

SCORE Office (Madison Heights)
26345 John R
Madison Heights, MI 48071
(810)542-5010
Fax: (810)542-6821

SCORE Office (Monroe)
111 E. 1st
Monroe, MI 48161
(313)242-3366
Fax: (313)242-7253

SCORE Office (Mt. Clemens)
58 S/B Gratiot
Mt. Clemens, MI 48043
(810)463-1528
Fax: (810)463-6541

SCORE Office (Muskegon)
PO Box 1087
230 Terrace Plz.
Muskegon, MI 49443
(616)722-3751
Fax: (616)728-7251

SCORE Office (Petoskey)
401 E. Mitchell St.
Petoskey, MI 49770
(616)347-4150

SCORE Office (Pontiac)
Executive Office Bldg.
1200 N. Telegraph Rd.
Pontiac, MI 48341
(810)975-9555

SCORE Office (Pontiac)
PO Box 430025
Pontiac, MI 48343
(810)335-9600

SCORE Office (Port Huron)
920 Pinegrove Ave.
Port Huron, MI 48060
(810)985-7101

SCORE Office (Rochester)
71 Walnut Ste. 110
Rochester, MI 48307
(810)651-6700
Fax: (810)651-5270

SCORE Office (Saginaw)
901 S. Washington Ave.
Saginaw, MI 48601
(517)752-7161
Fax: (517)752-9055

SCORE Office (Upper Peninsula)
2581 I-75 Business Spur
Sault Ste. Marie, MI 49783
(906)632-3301

SCORE Office (Southfield)
21000 W. 10 Mile Rd.
Southfield, MI 48075
(810)204-3050
Fax: (810)204-3099

SCORE Office (Traverse City)
202 E. Grandview Pkwy.
PO Box 387
Traverse City, MI 49685
(616)947-5075
Fax: (616)946-2565

SCORE Office (Warren)
30500 Van Dyke, Ste. 118
Warren, MI 48093
(810)751-3939

Minnesota

SCORE Office (Aitkin)
Aitkin, MN 56431
(218)741-3906

SCORE Office (Albert Lea)
202 N. Broadway Ave.
Albert Lea, MN 56007
(507)373-7487

SCORE Office (Austin)
PO Box 864
Austin, MN 55912
(507)437-4561
Fax: (507)437-4869

SCORE Office (South Metro)
Ames Business Ctr.
2500 W. County Rd., No. 42
Burnsville, MN 55337
(612)898-5645
Fax: (612)435-6972
E-mail: southmetro@scoreminn.org
Website: http://www.scoreminn.org/southmetro/

SCORE Office (Duluth)
1717 Minnesota Ave.
Duluth, MN 55802
(218)727-8286
Fax: (218)727-3113
E-mail: duluth@scoreminn.org
Website: http://www.scoreminn.org

SCORE Office (Fairmont)
PO Box 826
Fairmont, MN 56031
(507)235-5547
Fax: (507)235-8411

SCORE Office (Southwest Minnesota)
112 Riverfront St.

Box 999
Mankato, MN 56001
(507)345-4519
Fax: (507)345-4451
Website: http://www.scoreminn.org/

SCORE Office (Minneapolis)
North Plaza Bldg., Ste. 51
5217 Wayzata Blvd.
Minneapolis, MN 55416
(612)591-0539
Fax: (612)544-0436
Website: http://www.scoreminn.org/

SCORE Office (Owatonna)
PO Box 331
Owatonna, MN 55060
(507)451-7970
Fax: (507)451-7972

SCORE Office (Red Wing)
2000 W. Main St., Ste. 324
Red Wing, MN 55066
(612)388-4079

SCORE Office (Southeastern Minnesota)
220 S. Broadway, Ste. 100
Rochester, MN 55901
(507)288-1122
Fax: (507)282-8960
Website: http://www.scoreminn.org/

SCORE Office (Brainerd)
St. Cloud, MN 56301

SCORE Office (Central Area)
1527 Northway Dr.
St. Cloud, MN 56301
(320)240-1332
Fax: (320)255-9050
Website: http://www.scoreminn.org/

SCORE Office (St. Paul)
350 St. Peter St., No. 295
Lowry Professional Bldg.
St. Paul, MN 55102
(651)223-5010
Fax: (651)223-5048
Website: http://www.scoreminn.org/

SCORE Office (Winona)
Box 870
Winona, MN 55987
(507)452-2272
Fax: (507)454-8814

SCORE Office (Worthington)
1121 3rd Ave.
Worthington, MN 56187
(507)372-2919
Fax: (507)372-2827

Mississippi

SCORE Office (Delta)
915 Washington Ave.
PO Box 933
Greenville, MS 38701
(601)378-3141

SCORE Office (Gulfcoast)
1 Government Plaza
2909 13th St., Ste. 203
Gulfport, MS 39501
(228)863-0054

SCORE Office (Jackson)
1st Jackson Center, Ste. 400
101 W. Capitol St.
Jackson, MS 39201
(601)965-5533

SCORE Office (Meridian)
5220 16th Ave.
Meridian, MS 39305
(601)482-4412

Missouri

SCORE Office (Lake of the Ozark)
University Extension
113 Kansas St.
PO Box 1405
Camdenton, MO 65020
(573)346-2644
Fax: (573)346-2694
E-mail: score@cdoc.net
Website: http://sites.cdoc.net/score/

Chamber of Commerce (Cape Girardeau)
PO Box 98
Cape Girardeau, MO 63702-0098
(314)335-3312

SCORE Office (Mid-Missouri)
1705 Halstead Ct.
Columbia, MO 65203
(573)874-1132

SCORE Office (Ozark-Gateway)
1486 Glassy Rd.
Cuba, MO 65453-1640
(573)885-4954

SCORE Office (Kansas City)
323 W. 8th St., Ste. 104
Kansas City, MO 64105
(816)374-6675
Fax: (816)374-6692
E-mail: SCOREBIC@AOL.COM
Website: http://www.crn.org/score/

SCORE Office (Sedalia)
Lucas Place
323 W. 8th St., Ste.104
Kansas City, MO 64105
(816)374-6675

SCORE office (Tri-Lakes)
PO Box 1148
Kimberling, MO 65686
(417)739-3041

SCORE Office (Tri-Lakes)
HCRI Box 85
Lampe, MO 65681
(417)858-6798

SCORE Office (Mexico)
111 N. Washington St.
Mexico, MO 65265
(314)581-2765

SCORE Office (Southeast Missouri)
Rte. 1, Box 280
Neelyville, MO 63954
(573)989-3577

SCORE office (Poplar Bluff Area)
806 Emma St.
Poplar Bluff, MO 63901
(573)686-8892

SCORE Office (St. Joseph)
3003 Frederick Ave.
St. Joseph, MO 64506
(816)232-4461

SCORE Office (St. Louis)
815 Olive St., Rm. 242
St. Louis, MO 63101-1569
(314)539-6970
Fax: (314)539-3785
E-mail: info@stlscore.org
Website: http://www.stlscore.org/

SCORE Office (Lewis & Clark)
425 Spencer Rd.
St. Peters, MO 63376
(314)928-2900
Fax: (314)928-2900
E-mail: score01@mail.win.org

SCORE Office (Springfield)
620 S. Glenstone, Ste. 110
Springfield, MO 65802-3200
(417)864-7670
Fax: (417)864-4108

SCORE office (Southeast Kansas)
1206 W. First St.
Webb City, MO 64870
(417)673-3984

Montana

SCORE Office (Billings)
815 S. 27th St.
Billings, MT 59101
(406)245-4111

SCORE Office (Bozeman)
1205 E. Main St.
Bozeman, MT 59715
(406)586-5421

SCORE Office (Butte)
1000 George St.
Butte, MT 59701
(406)723-3177

SCORE Office (Great Falls)
710 First Ave. N
Great Falls, MT 59401
(406)761-4434
E-mail: scoregtf@in.tch.com

SCORE Office (Havre, Montana)
518 First St.
Havre, MT 59501
(406)265-4383

SCORE Office (Helena)
Federal Bldg.
301 S. Park
Helena, MT 59626-0054
(406)441-1081

SCORE Office (Kalispell)
2 Main St.
Kalispell, MT 59901
(406)756-5271
Fax: (406)752-6665

SCORE Office (Missoula)
723 Ronan
Missoula, MT 59806
(406)327-8806
E-mail: score@safeshop.com
Website: http://missoula.bigsky.net/
score/

Nebraska

SCORE Office (Columbus)
Columbus, NE 68601
(402)564-2769

SCORE Office (Fremont)
92 W. 5th St.
Fremont, NE 68025
(402)721-2641

SCORE Office (Hastings)
Hastings, NE 68901
(402)463-3447

SCORE Office (Lincoln)
8800 O St.
Lincoln, NE 68520
(402)437-2409

SCORE Office (Panhandle)
150549 CR 30
Minatare, NE 69356
(308)632-2133
Website: http://www.tandt.com/
SCORE

SCORE Office (Norfolk)
3209 S. 48th Ave.
Norfolk, NE 68106
(402)564-2769

SCORE Office (North Platte)
3301 W. 2nd St.
North Platte, NE 69101
(308)532-4466

SCORE Office (Omaha)
11145 Mill Valley Rd.
Omaha, NE 68154
(402)221-3606
Fax: (402)221-3680
E-mail: infoctr@ne.uswest.net
Website: http://www.tandt.com/score/

Nevada

SCORE Office (Incline Village)
969 Tahoe Blvd.
Incline Village, NV 89451
(702)831-7327
Fax: (702)832-1605

SCORE Office (Carson City)
301 E. Stewart
PO Box 7527
Las Vegas, NV 89125
(702)388-6104

SCORE Office (Las Vegas)
300 Las Vegas Blvd. S, Ste. 1100
Las Vegas, NV 89101
(702)388-6104

SCORE Office (Northern Nevada)
SBDC, College of Business
Administration
Univ. of Nevada
Reno, NV 89557-0100
(702)784-4436
Fax: (702)784-4337

New Hampshire

SCORE Office (North Country)
PO Box 34

Berlin, NH 03570
(603)752-1090

SCORE Office (Concord)
143 N. Main St., Rm. 202A
PO Box 1258
Concord, NH 03301
(603)225-1400
Fax: (603)225-1409

SCORE Office (Dover)
299 Central Ave.
Dover, NH 03820
(603)742-2218
Fax: (603)749-6317

SCORE Office (Monadnock)
34 Mechanic St.
Keene, NH 03431-3421
(603)352-0320

SCORE Office (Lakes Region)
67 Water St., Ste. 105
Laconia, NH 03246
(603)524-9168

SCORE Office (Upper Valley)
Citizens Bank Bldg., Rm. 310
20 W. Park St.
Lebanon, NH 03766
(603)448-3491
Fax: (603)448-1908
E-mail: billt@valley.net
Website: http://www.valley.net/~score/

SCORE Office (Merrimack Valley)
275 Chestnut St., Rm. 618
Manchester, NH 03103
(603)666-7561
Fax: (603)666-7925

SCORE Office (Mt. Washington Valley)
PO Box 1066
North Conway, NH 03818
(603)383-0800

SCORE Office (Seacoast)
195 Commerce Way, Unit-A
Portsmouth, NH 03801-3251
(603)433-0575

New Jersey

SCORE Office (Somerset)
Paritan Valley Community College,
Rte. 28
Branchburg, NJ 08807
(908)218-8874
E-mail: nj-score@grizbiz.com.
Website: http://www.nj-score.org/

SCORE Office (Chester)
5 Old Mill Rd.
Chester, NJ 07930
(908)879-7080

**SCORE Office
(Greater Princeton)**
4 A George Washington Dr.
Cranbury, NJ 08512
(609)520-1776

SCORE Office (Freehold)
36 W. Main St.
Freehold, NJ 07728
(908)462-3030
Fax: (908)462-2123

SCORE Office (North West)
Picantinny Innovation Ctr.
3159 Schrader Rd.
Hamburg, NJ 07419
(973)209-8525
Fax: (973)209-7252
E-mail: nj-score@grizbiz.com
Website: http://www.nj-score.org/

SCORE Office (Monmouth)
765 Newman Springs Rd.
Lincroft, NJ 07738
(908)224-2573
E-mail: nj-score@grizbiz.com
Website: http://www.nj-score.org/

SCORE Office (Manalapan)
125 Symmes Dr.
Manalapan, NJ 07726
(908)431-7220

SCORE Office (Jersey City)
2 Gateway Ctr., 4th Fl.
Newark, NJ 07102
(973)645-3982
Fax: (973)645-2375

SCORE Office (Newark)
2 Gateway Center, 15th Fl.
Newark, NJ 07102-5553
(973)645-3982
Fax: (973)645-2375
E-mail: nj-score@grizbiz.com
Website: http://www.nj-score.org

SCORE Office (Bergen County)
327 E. Ridgewood Ave.
Paramus, NJ 07652
(201)599-6090
E-mail: nj-score@grizbiz.com
Website: http://www.nj-score.org/

SCORE Office (Pennsauken)
4900 Rte. 70

Pennsauken, NJ 08109
(609)486-3421

SCORE Office (Southern New Jersey)
4900 Rte. 70
Pennsauken, NJ 08109
(609)486-3421
E-mail: nj-score@grizbiz.com
Website: http://www.nj-score.org/

SCORE Office (Greater Princeton)
216 Rockingham Row
Princeton Forrestal Village
Princeton, NJ 08540
(609)520-1776
Fax: (609)520-9107
E-mail: nj-score@grizbiz.com
Website: http://www.nj-score.org/

SCORE Office (Shrewsbury)
Hwy. 35
Shrewsbury, NJ 07702
(908)842-5995
Fax: (908)219-6140

SCORE Office (Ocean County)
33 Washington St.
Toms River, NJ 08754
(732)505-6033
E-mail: nj-score@grizbiz.com
Website: http://www.nj-score.org/

SCORE Office (Wall)
2700 Allaire Rd.
Wall, NJ 07719
(908)449-8877

SCORE Office (Wayne)
2055 Hamburg Tpke.
Wayne, NJ 07470
(201)831-7788
Fax: (201)831-9112

New Mexico

SCORE Office (Albuquerque)
525 Buena Vista, SE
Albuquerque, NM 87106
(505)272-7999
Fax: (505)272-7963

SCORE Office (Las Cruces)
Loretto Towne Center
505 S. Main St., Ste. 125
Las Cruces, NM 88001
(505)523-5627
Fax: (505)524-2101
E-mail: score.397@zianet.com

SCORE Office (Roswell)
Federal Bldg., Rm. 237

Roswell, NM 88201
(505)625-2112
Fax: (505)623-2545

SCORE Office (Santa Fe)
Montoya Federal Bldg.
120 Federal Place, Rm. 307
Santa Fe, NM 87501
(505)988-6302
Fax: (505)988-6300

New York

SCORE Office (Northeast)
1 Computer Dr. S
Albany, NY 12205
(518)446-1118
Fax: (518)446-1228

SCORE Office (Auburn)
30 South St.
PO Box 675
Auburn, NY 13021
(315)252-7291

SCORE Office (South Tier Binghamton)
Metro Center, 2nd Fl.
49 Court St.
PO Box 995
Binghamton, NY 13902
(607)772-8860

SCORE Office (Queens County City)
12055 Queens Blvd., Rm. 333
Borough Hall, NY 11424
(718)263-8961

SCORE Office (Buffalo)
Federal Bldg., Rm. 1311
111 W. Huron St.
Buffalo, NY 14202
(716)551-4301
Website: http://www2.pcom.net/score/buf45.html

SCORE Office (Canandaigua)
Chamber of Commerce Bldg.
113 S. Main St.
Canandaigua, NY 14424
(716)394-4400
Fax: (716)394-4546

SCORE Office (Chemung)
333 E. Water St., 4th Fl.
Elmira, NY 14901
(607)734-3358

SCORE Office (Geneva)
Chamber of Commerce Bldg.
PO Box 587

Geneva, NY 14456
(315)789-1776
Fax: (315)789-3993

SCORE Office (Glens Falls)
84 Broad St.
Glens Falls, NY 12801
(518)798-8463
Fax: (518)745-1433

SCORE Office (Orange County)
40 Matthews St.
Goshen, NY 10924
(914)294-8080
Fax: (914)294-6121

SCORE Office (Huntington Area)
151 W. Carver St.
Huntington, NY 11743
(516)423-6100

SCORE Office (Tompkins County)
904 E. Shore Dr.
Ithaca, NY 14850
(607)273-7080

SCORE Office (Long Island City)
120-55 Queens Blvd.
Jamaica, NY 11424
(718)263-8961
Fax: (718)263-9032

SCORE Office (Chatauqua)
101 W. 5th St.
Jamestown, NY 14701
(716)484-1103

SCORE Office (Westchester)
2 Caradon Ln.
Katonah, NY 10536
(914)948-3907
Fax: (914)948-4645
E-mail: score@w-w-w.com
Website: http://w-w-w.com/score/

SCORE Office (Queens County)
Queens Borough Hall
120-55 Queens Blvd. Rm. 333
Kew Gardens, NY 11424
(718)263-8961
Fax: (718)263-9032

SCORE Office (Brookhaven)
3233 Rte. 112
Medford, NY 11763
(516)451-6563
Fax: (516)451-6925

SCORE Office (Melville)
35 Pinelawn Rd., Rm. 207-W
Melville, NY 11747
(516)454-0771

SCORE Office (Nassau County)
400 County Seat Dr., No. 140
Mineola, NY 11501
(516)571-3303
E-mail: Counse1998@aol.com
Website: http://members.aol.com/Counse1998/Default.htm

SCORE Office (Mt. Vernon)
4 N. 7th Ave.
Mt. Vernon, NY 10550
(914)667-7500

SCORE Office (New York)
26 Federal Plz., Rm. 3100
New York, NY 10278
(212)264-4507
Fax: (212)264-4963
E-mail: score1000@erols.com
Website: http://users.erols.com/score-nyc/

SCORE Office (Newburgh)
47 Grand St.
Newburgh, NY 12550
(914)562-5100

SCORE Office (Owego)
188 Front St.
Owego, NY 13827
(607)687-2020

SCORE Office (Peekskill)
1 S. Division St.
Peekskill, NY 10566
(914)737-3600
Fax: (914)737-0541

SCORE Office (Penn Yan)
2375 Rte. 14A
Penn Yan, NY 14527
(315)536-3111

SCORE Office (Dutchess)
110 Main St.
Poughkeepsie, NY 12601
(914)454-1700

SCORE Office (Rochester)
601 Keating Federal Bldg., Rm. 410
100 State St.
Rochester, NY 14614
(716)263-6473
Fax: (716)263-3146
Website: http://www.ggw.org/score/

SCORE Office (Saranac Lake)
30 Main St.
Saranac Lake, NY 12983
(315)448-0415

SCORE Office (Suffolk)
286 Main St.
Setauket, NY 11733
(516)751-3886

SCORE Office (Staten Island)
130 Bay St.
Staten Island, NY 10301
(718)727-1221

SCORE Office (Ulster)
Clinton Bldg., Rm. 107
Stone Ridge, NY 12484
(914)687-5035
Fax: (914)687-5015
Website: http://www.scoreulster.org/

SCORE Office (Syracuse)
401 S. Salina, 5th Fl.
Syracuse, NY 13202
(315)471-9393

SCORE Office (Utica)
SUNY Institute of Technology, Route 12
Utica, NY 13504-3050
(315)792-7553

SCORE Office (Watertown)
518 Davidson St.
Watertown, NY 13601
(315)788-1200
Fax: (315)788-8251

North Carolina

SCORE office (Asheboro)
317 E. Dixie Dr.
Asheboro, NC 27203
(336)626-2626
Fax: (336)626-7077

SCORE Office (Asheville)
Federal Bldg., Rm. 259
151 Patton
Asheville, NC 28801-5770
(828)271-4786
Fax: (828)271-4009

SCORE Office (Chapel Hill)
104 S. Estes Dr.
PO Box 2897
Chapel Hill, NC 27514
(919)967-7075

SCORE Office (Coastal Plains)
PO Box 2897
Chapel Hill, NC 27515
(919)967-7075
Fax: (919)968-6874

SCORE Office (Charlotte)
200 N. College St., Ste. A-2015

Charlotte, NC 28202
(704)344-6576
Fax: (704)344-6769
E-mail: CharlotteSCORE47@AOL.com
Website: http://www.charweb.org/
business/score/

SCORE Office (Durham)
411 W. Chapel Hill St.
Durham, NC 27707
(919)541-2171

SCORE Office (Gastonia)
PO Box 2168
Gastonia, NC 28053
(704)864-2621
Fax: (704)854-8723

SCORE Office (Greensboro)
400 W. Market St., Ste. 103
Greensboro, NC 27401-2241
(910)333-5399

SCORE Office (Henderson)
PO Box 917
Henderson, NC 27536
(919)492-2061
Fax: (919)430-0460

SCORE Office (Hendersonville)
Federal Bldg., Rm. 108
W. 4th Ave. & Church St.
Hendersonville, NC 28792
(828)693-8702
E-mail: score@circle.net
Website: http://www.wncguide.com/
score/Welcome.html

SCORE Office (Unifour)
PO Box 1828
Hickory, NC 28603
(704)328-6111

SCORE Office (High Point)
1101 N. Main St.
High Point, NC 27262
(336)882-8625
Fax: (336)889-9499

SCORE Office (Outer Banks)
Collington Rd. and Mustain
Kill Devil Hills, NC 27948
(252)441-8144

SCORE Office (Down East)
312 S. Front St., Ste. 6
New Bern, NC 28560
(252)633-6688
Fax: (252)633-9608

SCORE Office (Kinston)
PO Box 95

New Bern, NC 28561
(919)633-6688

SCORE Office (Raleigh)
Century Post Office Bldg., Ste. 306
300 Federal St. Mall
Raleigh, NC 27601
(919)856-4739
E-mail: jendres@ibm.net
Website: http://www.intrex.net/score96/
score96.htm

SCORE Office (Sanford)
1801 Nash St.
Sanford, NC 27330
(919)774-6442
Fax: (919)776-8739

SCORE Office (Sandhills Area)
1480 Hwy. 15-501
PO Box 458
Southern Pines, NC 28387
(910)692-3926

SCORE Office (Wilmington)
Corps of Engineers Bldg.
96 Darlington Ave., Ste. 207
Wilmington, NC 28403
(910)815-4576
Fax: (910)815-4658

North Dakota

**SCORE Office
(Bismarck-Mandan)**
700 E. Main Ave., 2nd Fl.
PO Box 5509
Bismarck, ND 58506-5509
(701)250-4303

SCORE Office (Fargo)
657 2nd Ave., Rm. 225
Fargo, ND 58108-3083
(701)239-5677

SCORE Office (Upper Red River)
4275 Technology Dr., Rm. 156
Grand Forks, ND 58202-8372
(701)777-3051

SCORE Office (Minot)
100 1st St. SW
Minot, ND 58701-3846
(701)852-6883
Fax: (701)852-6905

Ohio

SCORE Office (Akron)
1 Cascade Plz., 7th Fl.
Akron, OH 44308

(330)379-3163
Fax: (330)379-3164

SCORE Office (Ashland)
Gill Center
47 W. Main St.
Ashland, OH 44805
(419)281-4584

SCORE Office (Canton)
116 Cleveland Ave. NW, Ste. 601
Canton, OH 44702-1720
(330)453-6047

SCORE Office (Chillicothe)
165 S. Paint St.
Chillicothe, OH 45601
(614)772-4530

SCORE Office (Cincinnati)
Ameritrust Bldg., Rm. 850
525 Vine St.
Cincinnati, OH 45202
(513)684-2812
Fax: (513)684-3251
Website: http://www.score.
chapter34.org/

SCORE Office (Cleveland)
Eaton Center, Ste. 620
1100 Superior Ave.
Cleveland, OH 44114-2507
(216)522-4194
Fax: (216)522-4844

SCORE Office (Columbus)
2 Nationwide Plz., Ste. 1400
Columbus, OH 43215-2542
(614)469-2357
Fax: (614)469-2391
E-mail: info@scorecolumbus.org
Website: http://www.scorecolumbus.org/

SCORE Office (Dayton)
Dayton Federal Bldg., Rm. 505
200 W. Second St.
Dayton, OH 45402-1430
(513)225-2887
Fax: (513)225-7667

SCORE Office (Defiance)
615 W. 3rd St.
PO Box 130
Defiance, OH 43512
(419)782-7946

SCORE Office (Findlay)
123 E. Main Cross St.
PO Box 923
Findlay, OH 45840
(419)422-3314

SCORE Office (Lima)
147 N. Main St.
Lima, OH 45801
(419)222-6045
Fax: (419)229-0266

SCORE Office (Mansfield)
55 N. Mulberry St.
Mansfield, OH 44902
(419)522-3211

SCORE Office (Marietta)
Thomas Hall
Marietta, OH 45750
(614)373-0268

SCORE Office (Medina)
County Administrative Bldg.
144 N. Broadway
Medina, OH 44256
(216)764-8650

SCORE Office (Licking County)
50 W. Locust St.
Newark, OH 43055
(614)345-7458

SCORE Office (Salem)
2491 State Rte. 45 S
Salem, OH 44460
(216)332-0361

SCORE Office (Tiffin)
62 S. Washington St.
Tiffin, OH 44883
(419)447-4141
Fax: (419)447-5141

SCORE Office (Toledo)
608 Madison Ave, Ste. 910
Toledo, OH 43624
(419)259-7598
Fax: (419)259-6460

SCORE Office (Heart of Ohio)
377 W. Liberty St.
Wooster, OH 44691
(330)262-5735
Fax: (330)262-5745

SCORE Office (Youngstown)
306 Williamson Hall
Youngstown, OH 44555
(330)746-2687

Oklahoma

SCORE Office (Anadarko)
PO Box 366
Anadarko, OK 73005
(405)247-6651

SCORE Office (Ardmore)
410 W. Main
Ardmore, OK 73401
(580)226-2620

SCORE Office (Northeast Oklahoma)
210 S. Main
Grove, OK 74344
(918)787-2796
Fax: (918)787-2796
E-mail: Score595@greencis.net

SCORE Office (Lawton)
4500 W. Lee Blvd., Bldg. 100, Ste. 107
Lawton, OK 73505
(580)353-8727
Fax: (580)250-5677

SCORE Office (Oklahoma City)
210 Park Ave., No. 1300
Oklahoma City, OK 73102
(405)231-5163
Fax: (405)231-4876
E-mail: score212@usa.net

SCORE Office (Stillwater)
439 S. Main
Stillwater, OK 74074
(405)372-5573
Fax: (405)372-4316

SCORE Office (Tulsa)
616 S. Boston, Ste. 406
Tulsa, OK 74119
(918)581-7462
Fax: (918)581-6908
Website: http://www.ionet.net/~tulscore/

Oregon

SCORE Office (Bend)
63085 N. Hwy. 97
Bend, OR 97701
(541)923-2849
Fax: (541)330-6900

SCORE Office (Willamette)
1401 Willamette St.
PO Box 1107
Eugene, OR 97401-4003
(541)465-6600
Fax: (541)484-4942

SCORE Office (Florence)
3149 Oak St.
Florence, OR 97439
(503)997-8444
Fax: (503)997-8448

SCORE Office (Southern Oregon)
33 N. Central Ave., Ste. 216

Medford, OR 97501
(541)776-4220
E-mail: pgr134f@prodigy.com

SCORE Office (Portland)
1515 SW 5th Ave., Ste. 1050
Portland, OR 97201
(503)326-3441
Fax: (503)326-2808
E-mail: gr134@prodigy.com

SCORE Office (Salem)
416 State St. (corner of Liberty)
Salem, OR 97301
(503)370-2896

Pennsylvania

SCORE Office (Altoona-Blair)
1212 12th Ave.
Altoona, PA 16601-3493
(814)943-8151

SCORE Office (Lehigh Valley)
Rauch Bldg. 37
Lehigh University
621 Taylor St.
Bethlehem, PA 18015
(610)758-4496
Fax: (610)758-5205

SCORE Office (Butler County)
100 N. Main St.
PO Box 1082
Butler, PA 16003
(412)283-2222
Fax: (412)283-0224

SCORE Office (Harrisburg)
4211 Trindle Rd.
Camp Hill, PA 17011
(717)761-4304
Fax: (717)761-4315

SCORE Office (Cumberland Valley)
75 S. 2nd St.
Chambersburg, PA 17201
(717)264-2935

SCORE Office (Monroe County-Stroudsburg)
556 Main St.
East Stroudsburg, PA 18301
(717)421-4433

SCORE Office (Erie)
120 W. 9th St.
Erie, PA 16501
(814)871-5650
Fax: (814)871-7530

SCORE Office (Bucks County)
409 Hood Blvd.
Fairless Hills, PA 19030
(215)943-8850
Fax: (215)943-7404

SCORE Office (Hanover)
146 Broadway
Hanover, PA 17331
(717)637-6130
Fax: (717)637-9127

SCORE Office (Harrisburg)
100 Chestnut, Ste. 309
Harrisburg, PA 17101
(717)782-3874

SCORE Office (East Montgomery County)
Baederwood Shopping Center
1653 The Fairways, Ste. 204
Jenkintown, PA 19046
(215)885-3027

SCORE Office (Kittanning)
2 Butler Rd.
Kittanning, PA 16201
(412)543-1305
Fax: (412)543-6206

SCORE Office (Lancaster)
118 W. Chestnut St.
Lancaster, PA 17603
(717)397-3092

SCORE Office (Westmoreland County)
300 Fraser Purchase Rd.
Latrobe, PA 15650-2690
(412)539-7505
Fax: (412)539-1850

SCORE Office (Lebanon)
252 N. 8th St.
PO Box 899
Lebanon, PA 17042-0899
(717)273-3727
Fax: (717)273-7940

SCORE Office (Lewistown)
3 W. Monument Sq., Ste. 204
Lewistown, PA 17044
(717)248-6713
Fax: (717)248-6714

SCORE Office (Delaware County)
602 E. Baltimore Pike
Media, PA 19063
(610)565-3677
Fax: (610)565-1606

SCORE Office (Milton Area)
112 S. Front St.
Milton, PA 17847

(717)742-7341
Fax: (717)792-2008

SCORE Office (Mon-Valley)
435 Donner Ave.
Monessen, PA 15062
(412)684-4277
Fax: (412)684-7688

SCORE Office (Monroeville)
William Penn Plaza
2790 Mosside Blvd., Ste. 295
Monroeville, PA 15146
(412)856-0622
Fax: (412)856-1030

SCORE Office (Airport Area)
986 Brodhead Rd.
Moon Township, PA 15108-2398
(412)264-6270
Fax: (412)264-1575

SCORE Office (Northeast)
8601 E. Roosevelt Blvd.
Philadelphia, PA 19152
(215)332-3400
Fax: (215)332-6050

SCORE Office (Philadelphia)
1315 Walnut St., Ste. 500
Philadelphia, PA 19107
(215)790-5050
Fax: (215)790-5057
E-mail: score46@bellatlantic.net
Website: http://www.pgweb.net/score46/

SCORE Office (Pittsburgh)
1000 Liberty Ave., Rm. 1122
Pittsburgh, PA 15222
(412)395-6560
Fax: (412)395-6562

SCORE Office (Tri-County)
801 N. Charlotte St.
Pottstown, PA 19464
(610)327-2673

SCORE Office (Reading)
601 Penn St.
Reading, PA 19601
(610)376-3497

SCORE Office (Scranton)
Oppenheim Bldg.
116 N. Washington Ave., Ste. 650
Scranton, PA 18503
(717)347-4611
Fax: (717)347-4611

SCORE Office (Central Pennsylvania)
200 Innovation Blvd., Ste. 242-B
State College, PA 16803

(814)234-9415
Fax: (814)238-9686
Website: http://countrystore.org/
business/score.htm

SCORE Office (Monroe-Stroudsburg)
556 Main St.
Stroudsburg, PA 18360
(717)421-4433

SCORE Office (Uniontown)
Federal Bldg.
Pittsburg St.
PO Box 2065 DTS
Uniontown, PA 15401
(412)437-4222
E-mail: uniontownscore@lcsys.net

SCORE Office (Warren County)
315 2nd Ave.
Warren, PA 16365
(814)723-9017

SCORE Office (Waynesboro)
323 E. Main St.
Waynesboro, PA 17268
(717)762-7123
Fax: (717)962-7124

SCORE Office (Chester County)
Government Service Center, Ste. 281
601 Westtown Rd.
West Chester, PA 19382-4538
(610)344-6910
Fax: (610)344-6919
E-mail: score@locke.ccil.org

SCORE Office (Wilkes-Barre)
7 N. Wilkes-Barre Blvd.
Wilkes Barre, PA 18702-5241
(717)826-6502
Fax: (717)826-6287

SCORE Office (North Central Pennsylvania)
240 W. 3rd St., Rm. 227
PO Box 725
Williamsport, PA 17703
(717)322-3720
Fax: (717)322-1607
E-mail: score234@mail.csrlink.net
Website: http://www.lycoming.org/
score/

SCORE Office (York)
Cyber Center
2101 Pennsylvania Ave.
York, PA 17404
(717)845-8830
Fax: (717)854-9333

Puerto Rico

SCORE Office (Puerto Rico & Virgin Islands)
PO Box 12383-96
San Juan, PR 00914-0383
(787)726-8040
Fax: (787)726-8135

Rhode Island

SCORE Office (Barrington)
281 County Rd.
Barrington, RI 02806
(401)247-1920
Fax: (401)247-3763

SCORE Office (Woonsocket)
640 Washington Hwy.
Lincoln, RI 02865
(401)334-1000
Fax: (401)334-1009

SCORE Office (Wickford)
8045 Post Rd.
North Kingstown, RI 02852
(401)295-5566
Fax: (401)295-8987

SCORE Office (J.G.E. Knight)
380 Westminster St.
Providence, RI 02903
(401)528-4571
Fax: (401)528-4539
Website: http://www.riscore.org

SCORE Office (Warwick)
3288 Post Rd.
Warwick, RI 02886
(401)732-1100
Fax: (401)732-1101

SCORE Office (Westerly)
74 Post Rd.
Westerly, RI 02891
(401)596-7761
800-732-7636
Fax: (401)596-2190

South Carolina

SCORE Office (Aiken)
PO Box 892
Aiken, SC 29802
(803)641-1111
800-542-4536
Fax: (803)641-4174

SCORE Office (Anderson)
Anderson Mall
3130 N. Main St.

Anderson, SC 29621
(864)224-0453

SCORE Office (Coastal)
284 King St.
Charleston, SC 29401
(803)727-4778
Fax: (803)853-2529

SCORE Office (Midlands)
Strom Thurmond Bldg., Rm. 358
1835 Assembly St., Rm 358
Columbia, SC 29201
(803)765-5131
Fax: (803)765-5962
Website: http://www.scoremid
lands.org/

SCORE Office (Piedmont)
Federal Bldg., Rm. B-02
300 E. Washington St.
Greenville, SC 29601
(864)271-3638

SCORE Office (Greenwood)
PO Drawer 1467
Greenwood, SC 29648
(864)223-8357

SCORE Office (Hilton Head Island)
52 Savannah Trail
Hilton Head, SC 29926
(803)785-7107
Fax: (803)785-7110

SCORE Office (Grand Strand)
937 Broadway
Myrtle Beach, SC 29577
(803)918-1079
Fax: (803)918-1083
E-mail: score381@aol.com

SCORE Office (Spartanburg)
PO Box 1636
Spartanburg, SC 29304
(864)594-5000
Fax: (864)594-5055

South Dakota

SCORE Office (West River)
Rushmore Plz. Civic Ctr.
444 Mount Rushmore Rd., No. 209
Rapid City, SD 57701
(605)394-5311
E-mail: score@gwtc.net

SCORE Office (Sioux Falls)
First Financial Center
110 S. Phillips Ave., Ste. 200
Sioux Falls, SD 57104-6727

(605)330-4231
Fax: (605)330-4231

Tennessee

SCORE Office (Chattanooga)
Federal Bldg., Rm. 26
900 Georgia Ave.
Chattanooga, TN 37402
(423)752-5190
Fax: (423)752-5335

SCORE Office (Cleveland)
PO Box 2275
Cleveland, TN 37320
(423)472-6587
Fax: (423)472-2019

SCORE Office (Upper Cumberland Center)
1225 S. Willow Ave.
Cookeville, TN 38501
(615)432-4111
Fax: (615)432-6010

SCORE Office (Unicoi County)
PO Box 713
Erwin, TN 37650
(423)743-3000
Fax: (423)743-0942

SCORE Office (Greeneville)
115 Academy St.
Greeneville, TN 37743
(423)638-4111
Fax: (423)638-5345

SCORE Office (Jackson)
194 Auditorium St.
Jackson, TN 38301
(901)423-2200

SCORE Office (Northeast Tennessee)
1st Tennessee Bank Bldg.
2710 S. Roan St., Ste. 584
Johnson City, TN 37601
(423)929-7686
Fax: (423)461-8052

SCORE Office (Kingsport)
151 E. Main St.
Kingsport, TN 37662
(423)392-8805

SCORE Office (Greater Knoxville)
Farragot Bldg., Ste. 224
530 S. Gay St.
Knoxville, TN 37902
(423)545-4203
E-mail: scoreknox@ntown.com
Website: http://www.scoreknox.org/

SCORE Office (Maryville)
201 S. Washington St.
Maryville, TN 37804-5728
(423)983-2241
800-525-6834
Fax: (423)984-1386

SCORE Office (Memphis)
Federal Bldg., Ste. 390
167 N. Main St.
Memphis, TN 38103
(901)544-3588

SCORE Office (Nashville)
50 Vantage Way, Ste. 201
Nashville, TN 37228-1500
(615)736-7621

Texas

SCORE Office (Abilene)
2106 Federal Post Office and Court Bldg.
Abilene, TX 79601
(915)677-1857

SCORE Office (Austin)
2501 S. Congress
Austin, TX 78701
(512)442-7235
Fax: (512)442-7528

SCORE Office (Golden Triangle)
450 Boyd St.
Beaumont, TX 77704
(409)838-6581
Fax: (409)833-6718

SCORE Office (Brownsville)
3505 Boca Chica Blvd., Ste. 305
Brownsville, TX 78521
(210)541-4508

SCORE Office (Brazos Valley)
3000 Briarcrest, Ste. 302
Bryan, TX 77802
(409)776-8876
E-mail: 102633.2612@compuserve.com

SCORE Office (Cleburne)
Watergarden Pl., 9th Fl., Ste. 400
Cleburne, TX 76031
(817)871-6002

SCORE Office (Corpus Christi)
651 Upper North Broadway, Ste. 654
Corpus Christi, TX 78477
(512)888-4322
Fax: (512)888-3418

SCORE Office (Dallas)
6260 E. Mockingbird
Dallas, TX 75214-2619

(214)828-2471
Fax: (214)821-8033

SCORE Office (El Paso)
10 Civic Center Plaza
El Paso, TX 79901
(915)534-0541
Fax: (915)534-0513

SCORE Office (Bedford)
100 E. 15th St., Ste. 400
Ft. Worth, TX 76102
(817)871-6002

SCORE Office (Ft. Worth)
100 E. 15th St., No. 24
Ft. Worth, TX 76102
(817)871-6002
Fax: (817)871-6031
E-mail: fwbac@onramp.net

SCORE Office (Garland)
2734 W. Kingsley Rd.
Garland, TX 75041
(214)271-9224

SCORE Office (Granbury Chamber of Commerce)
416 S. Morgan
Granbury, TX 76048
(817)573-1622
Fax: (817)573-0805

SCORE Office (Lower Rio Grande Valley)
222 E. Van Buren, Ste. 500
Harlingen, TX 78550
(956)427-8533
Fax: (956)427-8537

SCORE Office (Houston)
9301 Southwest Fwy., Ste. 550
Houston, TX 77074
(713)773-6565
Fax: (713)773-6550

SCORE Office (Irving)
3333 N. MacArthur Blvd., Ste. 100
Irving, TX 75062
(214)252-8484
Fax: (214)252-6710

SCORE Office (Lubbock)
1205 Texas Ave., Rm. 411D
Lubbock, TX 79401
(806)472-7462
Fax: (806)472-7487

SCORE Office (Midland)
Post Office Annex
200 E. Wall St., Rm. P121
Midland, TX 79701
(915)687-2649

SCORE Office (Orange)
1012 Green Ave.
Orange, TX 77630-5620
(409)883-3536
800-528-4906
Fax: (409)886-3247

SCORE Office (Plano)
1200 E. 15th St.
PO Drawer 940287
Plano, TX 75094-0287
(214)424-7547
Fax: (214)422-5182

SCORE Office (Port Arthur)
4749 Twin City Hwy., Ste. 300
Port Arthur, TX 77642
(409)963-1107
Fax: (409)963-3322

SCORE Office (Richardson)
411 Belle Grove
Richardson, TX 75080
(214)234-4141
800-777-8001
Fax: (214)680-9103

SCORE Office (San Antonio)
Federal Bldg., Rm. A527
727 E. Durango
San Antonio, TX 78206
(210)472-5931
Fax: (210)472-5935

SCORE Office (Texarkana State College)
819 State Line Ave.
Texarkana, TX 75501
(903)792-7191
Fax: (903)793-4304

SCORE Office (East Texas)
RTDC
1530 SSW Loop 323, Ste. 100
Tyler, TX 75701
(903)510-2975
Fax: (903)510-2978

SCORE Office (Waco)
401 Franklin Ave.
Waco, TX 76701
(817)754-8898
Fax: (817)756-0776
Website: http://www.brc-waco.com/

SCORE Office (Wichita Falls)
Hamilton Bldg.
900 8th St.
Wichita Falls, TX 76307
(940)723-2741
Fax: (940)723-8773

Utah

SCORE Office (Northern Utah)
160 N. Main
Logan, UT 84321
(435)746-2269

SCORE Office (Ogden)
1701 E. Windsor Dr.
Ogden, UT 84604
(801)629-8613
E-mail: score158@netscape.net

SCORE Office (Central Utah)
1071 E. Windsor Dr.
Provo, UT 84604
(801)373-8660

SCORE Office (Southern Utah)
225 South 700 East
St. George, UT 84770
(435)652-7751

SCORE Office (Salt Lake)
310 S Main St.
Salt Lake City, UT 84101
(801)746-2269
Fax: (801)746-2273

Vermont

SCORE Office (Champlain Valley)
Winston Prouty Federal Bldg.
11 Lincoln St., Rm. 106
Essex Junction, VT 05452
(802)951-6762

SCORE Office (Montpelier)
87 State St., Rm. 205
PO Box 605
Montpelier, VT 05601
(802)828-4422
Fax: (802)828-4485

SCORE Office (Marble Valley)
256 N. Main St.
Rutland, VT 05701-2413
(802)773-9147

SCORE Office (Northeast Kingdom)
20 Main St.
PO Box 904
St. Johnsbury, VT 05819
(802)748-5101

Virgin Islands

SCORE Office (St. Croix)
United Plaza Shopping Center
PO Box 4010, Christiansted
St. Croix, VI 00822
(809)778-5380

SCORE Office (St. Thomas-St. John)
Federal Bldg., Rm. 21
Veterans Dr.
St. Thomas, VI 00801
(809)774-8530

Virginia

SCORE Office (Arlington)
2009 N. 14th St., Ste. 111
Arlington, VA 22201
(703)525-2400

SCORE Office (Blacksburg)
141 Jackson St.
Blacksburg, VA 24060
(540)552-4061

SCORE Office (Bristol)
20 Volunteer Pkwy.
Bristol, VA 24203
(540)989-4850

SCORE Office (Central Virginia)
1001 E. Market St., Ste. 101
Charlottesville, VA 22902
(804)295-6712
Fax: (804)295-7066

SCORE Office (Alleghany Satellite)
241 W. Main St.
Covington, VA 24426
(540)962-2178
Fax: (540)962-2179

SCORE Office (Central Fairfax)
3975 University Dr., Ste. 350
Fairfax, VA 22030
(703)591-2450

SCORE Office (Falls Church)
PO Box 491
Falls Church, VA 22040
(703)532-1050
Fax: (703)237-7904

SCORE Office (Glenns)
Glenns Campus
Box 287
Glenns, VA 23149
(804)693-9650

SCORE Office (Peninsula)
6 Manhattan Sq.
PO Box 7269
Hampton, VA 23666
(757)766-2000
Fax: (757)865-0339
E-mail: score100@seva.net

SCORE Office (Tri-Cities)
108 N. Main St.

Hopewell, VA 23860
(804)458-5536

SCORE Office (Lynchburg)
Federal Bldg.
1100 Main St.
Lynchburg, VA 24504-1714
(804)846-3235

SCORE Office (Greater Prince William)
8963 Center St
Manassas, VA 20110
(703)368-4813
Fax: (703)368-4733

SCORE Office (Martinsvile)
115 Broad St.
Martinsville, VA 24112-0709
(540)632-6401
Fax: (540)632-5059

SCORE Office (Hampton Roads)
Federal Bldg., Rm. 737
200 Grandby St.
Norfolk, VA 23510
(757)441-3733
Fax: (757)441-3733
E-mail: scorehr60@juno.com

SCORE Office (Norfolk)
Federal Bldg., Rm. 737
200 Granby St.
Norfolk, VA 23510
(757)441-3733
Fax: (757)441-3733

SCORE Office (Virginia Beach)
Chamber of Commerce
200 Grandby St., Rm 737
Norfolk, VA 23510
(804)441-3733

SCORE Office (Radford)
1126 Norwood St.
Radford, VA 24141
(540)639-2202

SCORE Office (Richmond)
Federal Bldg.
400 N. 8th St., Ste. 1150
PO Box 10126
Richmond, VA 23240-0126
(804)771-2400
Fax: (804)771-8018
E-mail: scorechapter12@yahoo.com
Website: http://www.cvco.org/score/

SCORE Office (Roanoke)
Federal Bldg., Rm. 716
250 Franklin Rd.
Roanoke, VA 24011

(540)857-2834
Fax: (540)857-2043
E-mail: scorerva@juno.com
Website: http://hometown.aol.com/
scorerv/Index.html

SCORE Office (Fairfax)
8391 Old Courthouse Rd., Ste. 300
Vienna, VA 22182
(703)749-0400

SCORE Office (Greater Vienna)
513 Maple Ave. West
Vienna, VA 22180
(703)281-1333
Fax: (703)242-1482

SCORE Office (Shenandoah Valley)
301 W. Main St.
Waynesboro, VA 22980
(540)949-8203
Fax: (540)949-7740
E-mail: score427@intelos.net

SCORE Office (Williamsburg)
201 Penniman Rd.
Williamsburg, VA 23185
(757)229-6511
E-mail: wacc@williamsburgcc.com

SCORE Office (Northern Virginia)
1360 S. Pleasant Valley Rd.
Winchester, VA 22601
(540)662-4118

Washington

SCORE Office (Gray's Harbor)
506 Duffy St.
Aberdeen, WA 98520
(360)532-1924
Fax: (360)533-7945

SCORE Office (Bellingham)
101 E. Holly St.
Bellingham, WA 98225
(360)676-3307

SCORE Office (Everett)
2702 Hoyt Ave.
Everett, WA 98201-3556
(206)259-8000

SCORE Office (Gig Harbor)
3125 Judson St.
Gig Harbor, WA 98335
(206)851-6865

SCORE Office (Kennewick)
PO Box 6986
Kennewick, WA 99336
(509)736-0510

SCORE Office (Puyallup)
322 2nd St. SW
PO Box 1298
Puyallup, WA 98371
(206)845-6755
Fax: (206)848-6164

SCORE Office (Seattle)
1200 6th Ave., Ste. 1700
Seattle, WA 98101
(206)553-7320
Fax: (206)553-7044
E-mail: score55@aol.com
Website: http://www.scn.org/civic/score-
online/index55.html

SCORE Office (Spokane)
801 W. Riverside Ave., No. 240
Spokane, WA 99201
(509)353-2820
Fax: (509)353-2600
E-mail: score@dmi.net
Website: http://www.dmi.net/score/

SCORE Office (Clover Park)
PO Box 1933
Tacoma, WA 98401-1933
(206)627-2175

SCORE Office (Tacoma)
1101 Pacific Ave.
Tacoma, WA 98402
(253)274-1288
Fax: (253)274-1289

SCORE Office (Fort Vancouver)
1701 Broadway, S-1
Vancouver, WA 98663
(360)699-1079

SCORE Office (Walla Walla)
500 Tausick Way
Walla Walla, WA 99362
(509)527-4681

SCORE Office (Mid-Columbia)
1113 S. 14th Ave.
Yakima, WA 98907
(509)574-4944
Fax: (509)574-2943
Website: http://www.ellensburg.com/
~score/

West Virginia

SCORE Office (Charleston)
1116 Smith St.
Charleston, WV 25301
(304)347-5463
E-mail: score256@juno.com

SCORE Office (Virginia Street)
1116 Smith St., Ste. 302
Charleston, WV 25301
(304)347-5463

SCORE Office (Marion County)
PO Box 208
Fairmont, WV 26555-0208
(304)363-0486

SCORE Office (Upper Monongahela Valley)
1000 Technology Dr., Ste. 1111
Fairmont, WV 26555
(304)363-0486
E-mail: score537@hotmail.com

SCORE Office (Huntington)
1101 6th Ave., Ste. 220
Huntington, WV 25701-2309
(304)523-4092

SCORE Office (Wheeling)
1310 Market St.
Wheeling, WV 26003
(304)233-2575
Fax: (304)233-1320

Wisconsin

SCORE Office (Fox Cities)
227 S. Walnut St.
Appleton, WI 54913
(920)734-7101
Fax: (920)734-7161

SCORE Office (Beloit)
136 W. Grand Ave., Ste. 100
PO Box 717
Beloit, WI 53511
(608)365-8835
Fax: (608)365-9170

SCORE Office (Eau Claire)
Federal Bldg., Rm. B11
510 S. Barstow St.
Eau Claire, WI 54701
(715)834-1573
E-mail: score@ecol.net
Website: http://www.ecol.net/~score/

SCORE Office (Fond du Lac)
207 N. Main St.
Fond du Lac, WI 54935
(414)921-9500
Fax: (414)921-9559

SCORE Office (Green Bay)
835 Potts Ave.
Green Bay, WI 54304
(414)496-8930
Fax: (414)496-6009

SCORE Office (Janesville)
20 S. Main St., Ste. 11
PO Box 8008
Janesville, WI 53547
(608)757-3160
Fax: (608)757-3170

SCORE Office (La Crosse)
712 Main St.
La Crosse, WI 54602-0219
(608)784-4880

SCORE Office (Madison)
505 S. Rosa Rd.
Madison, WI 53719
(608)441-2820

SCORE Office (Manitowoc)
1515 Memorial Dr.
PO Box 903
Manitowoc, WI 54221-0903
(414)684-5575
Fax: (414)684-1915

SCORE Office (Milwaukee)
310 W. Wisconsin Ave., Ste. 425
Milwaukee, WI 53203
(414)297-3942
Fax: (414)297-1377

SCORE Office (Central Wisconsin)
1224 Lindbergh Ave.
Stevens Point, WI 54481
(715)344-7729

SCORE Office (Superior)
Superior Business Center Inc.
1423 N. 8th St.
Superior, WI 54880
(715)394-7388
Fax: (715)393-7414

SCORE Office (Waukesha)
223 Wisconsin Ave.
Waukesha, WI 53186-4926
(414)542-4249

SCORE Office (Wausau)
300 3rd St., Ste. 200
Wausau, WI 54402-6190
(715)845-6231

SCORE Office (Wisconsin Rapids)
2240 Kingston Rd.
Wisconsin Rapids, WI 54494
(715)423-1830

Wyoming

SCORE Office (Casper)
Federal Bldg., No. 2215
100 East B St.

Casper, WY 82602
(307)261-6529
Fax: (307)261-6530

Venture capital & financing companies

This section contains a listing of financing and loan companies in the United States and Canada. These listing are arranged alphabetically by country, then by state or province, then by city, then by organization name.

Canada

Alberta

Launchworks Inc.
1902J 11th St., S.E.
Calgary, AB, Canada T2G 3G2
(403)269-1119
Fax: (403)269-1141
Website: http://www.launchworks.com

Native Venture Capital Company, Inc.
21 Artist View Point, Box 7
Site 25, RR 12
Calgary, AB, Canada T3E 6W3
(903)208-5380

Miralta Capital Inc.
4445 Calgary Trail South
888 Terrace Plaza Alberta
Edmonton, AB, Canada T6H 5R7
(780)438-3535
Fax: (780)438-3129

Vencap Equities Alberta Ltd.
10180-101st St., Ste. 1980
Edmonton, AB, Canada T5J 3S4
(403)420-1171
Fax: (403)429-2541

British Columbia

Discovery Capital
5th Fl., 1199 West Hastings
Vancouver, BC, Canada V6E 3T5
(604)683-3000
Fax: (604)662-3457
E-mail: info@discoverycapital.com
Website: http://www.discoverycapital.com

Greenstone Venture Partners
1177 West Hastings St.
Ste. 400
Vancouver, BC, Canada V6E 2K3
(604)717-1977
Fax: (604)717-1976
Website: http://www.greenstonevc.com

Growthworks Capital
2600-1055 West Georgia St.
Box 11170 Royal Centre
Vancouver, BC, Canada V6E 3R5
(604)895-7259
Fax: (604)669-7605
Website: http://www.wofund.com

MDS Discovery Venture Management, Inc.
555 W. Eighth Ave., Ste. 305
Vancouver, BC, Canada V5Z 1C6
(604)872-8464
Fax: (604)872-2977
E-mail: info@mds-ventures.com

Ventures West Management Inc.
1285 W. Pender St., Ste. 280
Vancouver, BC, Canada V6E 4B1
(604)688-9495
Fax: (604)687-2145
Website: http://www.ventureswest.com

Nova Scotia

ACF Equity Atlantic Inc.
Purdy's Wharf Tower II
Ste. 2106
Halifax, NS, Canada B3J 3R7
(902)421-1965
Fax: (902)421-1808

Montgomerie, Huck & Co.
146 Bluenose Dr.
PO Box 538
Lunenburg, NS, Canada B0J 2C0
(902)634-7125
Fax: (902)634-7130

Ontario

IPS Industrial Promotion Services Ltd.
60 Columbia Way, Ste. 720
Markham, ON, Canada L3R 0C9
(905)475-9400
Fax: (905)475-5003

Betwin Investments Inc.
Box 23110
Sault Ste. Marie, ON, Canada P6A 6W6
(705)253-0744
Fax: (705)253-0744

Bailey & Company, Inc.
594 Spadina Ave.
Toronto, ON, Canada M5S 2H4
(416)921-6930
Fax: (416)925-4670

BCE Capital
200 Bay St.

South Tower, Ste. 3120
Toronto, ON, Canada M5J 2J2
(416)815-0078
Fax: (416)941-1073
Website: http://www.bcecapital.com

Castlehill Ventures
55 University Ave., Ste. 500
Toronto, ON, Canada M5J 2H7
(416)862-8574
Fax: (416)862-8875

CCFL Mezzanine Partners of Canada
70 University Ave.
Ste. 1450
Toronto, ON, Canada M5J 2M4
(416)977-1450
Fax: (416)977-6764
E-mail: info@ccfl.com
Website: http://www.ccfl.com

Celtic House International
100 Simcoe St., Ste. 100
Toronto, ON, Canada M5H 3G2
(416)542-2436
Fax: (416)542-2435
Website: http://www.celtic-house.com

Clairvest Group Inc.
22 St. Clair Ave. East
Ste. 1700
Toronto, ON, Canada M4T 2S3
(416)925-9270
Fax: (416)925-5753

Crosbie & Co., Inc.
One First Canadian Place
9th Fl.
PO Box 116
Toronto, ON, Canada M5X 1A4
(416)362-7726
Fax: (416)362-3447
E-mail: info@crosbieco.com
Website: http://www.crosbieco.com

Drug Royalty Corp.
Eight King St. East
Ste. 202
Toronto, ON, Canada M5C 1B5
(416)863-1865
Fax: (416)863-5161

Grieve, Horner, Brown & Asculai
8 King St. E, Ste. 1704
Toronto, ON, Canada M5C 1B5
(416)362-7668
Fax: (416)362-7660

Jefferson Partners
77 King St. West
Ste. 4010

PO Box 136
Toronto, ON, Canada M5K 1H1
(416)367-1533
Fax: (416)367-5827
Website: http://www.jefferson.com

J.L. Albright Venture Partners
Canada Trust Tower, 161 Bay St.
Ste. 4440
PO Box 215
Toronto, ON, Canada M5J 2S1
(416)367-2440
Fax: (416)367-4604
Website: http://www.jlaventures.com

McLean Watson Capital Inc.
One First Canadian Place
Ste. 1410
PO Box 129
Toronto, ON, Canada M5X 1A4
(416)363-2000
Fax: (416)363-2010
Website: http://www.mcleanwatson.com

Middlefield Capital Fund
One First Canadian Place
85th Fl.
PO Box 192
Toronto, ON, Canada M5X 1A6
(416)362-0714
Fax: (416)362-7925
Website: http://www.middlefield.com

Mosaic Venture Partners
24 Duncan St.
Ste. 300
Toronto, ON, Canada M5V 3M6
(416)597-8889
Fax: (416)597-2345

Onex Corp.
161 Bay St.
PO Box 700
Toronto, ON, Canada M5J 2S1
(416)362-7711
Fax: (416)362-5765

Penfund Partners Inc.
145 King St. West
Ste. 1920
Toronto, ON, Canada M5H 1J8
(416)865-0300
Fax: (416)364-6912
Website: http://www.penfund.com

Primaxis Technology Ventures Inc.
1 Richmond St. West, 8th Fl.
Toronto, ON, Canada M5H 3W4
(416)313-5210
Fax: (416)313-5218
Website: http://www.primaxis.com

Priveq Capital Funds
240 Duncan Mill Rd., Ste. 602
Toronto, ON, Canada M3B 3P1
(416)447-3330
Fax: (416)447-3331
E-mail: priveq@sympatico.ca

Roynat Ventures
40 King St. West, 26th Fl.
Toronto, ON, Canada M5H 1H1
(416)933-2667
Fax: (416)933-2783
Website: http://www.roynatcapital.com

Tera Capital Corp.
366 Adelaide St. East, Ste. 337
Toronto, ON, Canada M5A 3X9
(416)368-1024
Fax: (416)368-1427

Working Ventures Canadian Fund Inc.
250 Bloor St. East, Ste. 1600
Toronto, ON, Canada M4W 1E6
(416)934-7718
Fax: (416)929-0901
Website: http://www.workingventures.ca

Quebec

Altamira Capital Corp.
202 University
Niveau de Maisoneuve, Bur. 201
Montreal, QC, Canada H3A 2A5
(514)499-1656
Fax: (514)499-9570

Federal Business Development Bank
Venture Capital Division
Five Place Ville Marie, Ste. 600
Montreal, QC, Canada H3B 5E7
(514)283-1896
Fax: (514)283-5455

Hydro-Quebec Capitech Inc.
75 Boul, Rene Levesque Quest
Montreal, QC, Canada H2Z 1A4
(514)289-4783
Fax: (514)289-5420
Website: http://www.hqcapitech.com

Investissement Desjardins
2 complexe Desjardins
C.P. 760
Montreal, QC, Canada H5B 1B8
(514)281-7131
Fax: (514)281-7808
Website: http://www.desjardins.com/id

Marleau Lemire Inc.
One Place Ville-Marie, Ste. 3601
Montreal, QC, Canada H3B 3P2

(514)877-3800
Fax: (514)875-6415

Speirs Consultants Inc.
365 Stanstead
Montreal, QC, Canada H3R 1X5
(514)342-3858
Fax: (514)342-1977

Tecnocap Inc.
4028 Marlowe
Montreal, QC, Canada H4A 3M2
(514)483-6009
Fax: (514)483-6045
Website: http://www.technocap.com

Telsoft Ventures
1000, Rue de la Gauchetiere
Quest, 25eme Etage
Montreal, QC, Canada H3B 4W5
(514)397-8450
Fax: (514)397-8451

Saskatchewan

Saskatchewan Government Growth Fund
1801 Hamilton St., Ste. 1210
Canada Trust Tower
Regina, SK, Canada S4P 4B4
(306)787-2994
Fax: (306)787-2086

United states

Alabama

FHL Capital Corp.
600 20th Street North
Suite 350
Birmingham, AL 35203
(205)328-3098
Fax: (205)323-0001

Harbert Management Corp.
One Riverchase Pkwy. South
Birmingham, AL 35244
(205)987-5500
Fax: (205)987-5707
Website: http://www.harbert.net

Jefferson Capital Fund
PO Box 13129
Birmingham, AL 35213
(205)324-7709

Private Capital Corp.
100 Brookwood Pl., 4th Fl.
Birmingham, AL 35209
(205)879-2722
Fax: (205)879-5121

21st Century Health Ventures
One Health South Pkwy.
Birmingham, AL 35243
(256)268-6250
Fax: (256)970-8928

FJC Growth Capital Corp.
200 W. Side Sq., Ste. 340
Huntsville, AL 35801
(256)922-2918
Fax: (256)922-2909

Hickory Venture Capital Corp.
301 Washington St. NW
Suite 301
Huntsville, AL 35801
(256)539-1931
Fax: (256)539-5130
E-mail: hvcc@hvcc.com
Website: http://www.hvcc.com

Southeastern Technology Fund
7910 South Memorial Pkwy., Ste. F
Huntsville, AL 35802
(256)883-8711
Fax: (256)883-8558

Cordova Ventures
4121 Carmichael Rd., Ste. 301
Montgomery, AL 36106
(334)271-6011
Fax: (334)260-0120
Website: http://www.cordova
ventures.com

**Small Business Clinic of Alabama/AG
Bartholomew & Associates**
PO Box 231074
Montgomery, AL 36123-1074
(334)284-3640

Arizona

Miller Capital Corp.
4909 E. McDowell Rd.
Phoenix, AZ 85008
(602)225-0504
Fax: (602)225-9024
Website: http://www.themiller
group.com

The Columbine Venture Funds
9449 North 90th St., Ste. 200
Scottsdale, AZ 85258
(602)661-9222
Fax: (602)661-6262

Koch Ventures
17767 N. Perimeter Dr., Ste. 101
Scottsdale, AZ 85255
(480)419-3600

Fax: (480)419-3606
Website: http://www.kochventures.com

McKee & Co.
7702 E. Doubletree Ranch Rd.
Suite 230
Scottsdale, AZ 85258
(480)368-0333
Fax: (480)607-7446

Merita Capital Ltd.
7350 E. Stetson Dr., Ste. 108-A
Scottsdale, AZ 85251
(480)947-8700
Fax: (480)947-8766

Valley Ventures / Arizona Growth Partners L.P.
6720 N. Scottsdale Rd., Ste. 208
Scottsdale, AZ 85253
(480)661-6600
Fax: (480)661-6262

Estreetcapital.com
660 South Mill Ave., Ste. 315
Tempe, AZ 85281
(480)968-8400
Fax: (480)968-8480
Website: http://www.estreetcapital.com

Coronado Venture Fund
PO Box 65420
Tucson, AZ 85728-5420
(520)577-3764
Fax: (520)299-8491

Arkansas

Arkansas Capital Corp.
225 South Pulaski St.
Little Rock, AR 72201
(501)374-9247
Fax: (501)374-9425
Website: http://www.arcapital.com

California

Sundance Venture Partners, L.P.
100 Clocktower Place, Ste. 130
Carmel, CA 93923
(831)625-6500
Fax: (831)625-6590

Westar Capital (Costa Mesa)
949 South Coast Dr., Ste. 650
Costa Mesa, CA 92626
(714)481-5160
Fax: (714)481-5166
E-mail: mailbox@westarcapital.com
Website: http://www.westarcapital.com

Alpine Technology Ventures
20300 Stevens Creek Boulevard, Ste. 495
Cupertino, CA 95014
(408)725-1810
Fax: (408)725-1207
Website: http://www.alpineventures.com

Bay Partners
10600 N. De Anza Blvd.
Cupertino, CA 95014-2031
(408)725-2444
Fax: (408)446-4502
Website: http://www.baypartners.com

Novus Ventures
20111 Stevens Creek Blvd., Ste. 130
Cupertino, CA 95014
(408)252-3900
Fax: (408)252-1713
Website: http://www.novusventures.com

Triune Capital
19925 Stevens Creek Blvd., Ste. 200
Cupertino, CA 95014
(310)284-6800
Fax: (310)284-3290

Acorn Ventures
268 Bush St., Ste. 2829
Daly City, CA 94014
(650)994-7801
Fax: (650)994-3305
Website: http://www.acornventures.com

Digital Media Campus
2221 Park Place
El Segundo, CA 90245
(310)426-8000
Fax: (310)426-8010
E-mail: info@thecampus.com
Website: http://www.digital
mediacampus.com

BankAmerica Ventures / BA Venture Partners
950 Tower Ln., Ste. 700
Foster City, CA 94404
(650)378-6000
Fax: (650)378-6040
Website: http://
www.baventurepartners.com

Starting Point Partners
666 Portofino Lane
Foster City, CA 94404
(650)722-1035
Website: http://www.startingpoint
partners.com

Opportunity Capital Partners
2201 Walnut Ave., Ste. 210

Fremont, CA 94538
(510)795-7000
Fax: (510)494-5439
Website: http://www.ocpcapital.com

Imperial Ventures Inc.
9920 S. La Cienega Boulevar, 14th Fl.
Inglewood, CA 90301
(310)417-5409
Fax: (310)338-6115

Ventana Global (Irvine)
18881 Von Karman Ave., Ste. 1150
Irvine, CA 92612
(949)476-2204
Fax: (949)752-0223
Website: http://www.ventanaglobal.com

Integrated Consortium Inc.
50 Ridgecrest Rd.
Kentfield, CA 94904
(415)925-0386
Fax: (415)461-2726

Enterprise Partners
979 Ivanhoe Ave., Ste. 550
La Jolla, CA 92037
(858)454-8833
Fax: (858)454-2489
Website: http://www.epvc.com

Domain Associates
28202 Cabot Rd., Ste. 200
Laguna Niguel, CA 92677
(949)347-2446
Fax: (949)347-9720
Website: http://www.domainvc.com

Cascade Communications Ventures
60 E. Sir Francis Drake Blvd., Ste. 300
Larkspur, CA 94939
(415)925-6500
Fax: (415)925-6501

Allegis Capital
One First St., Ste. Two
Los Altos, CA 94022
(650)917-5900
Fax: (650)917-5901
Website: http://www.allegiscapital.com

Aspen Ventures
1000 Fremont Ave., Ste. 200
Los Altos, CA 94024
(650)917-5670
Fax: (650)917-5677
Website: http://www.aspenventures.com

AVI Capital L.P.
1 First St., Ste. 2
Los Altos, CA 94022

ORGANIZATIONS, AGENCIES, & CONSULTANTS

(650)949-9862
Fax: (650)949-8510
Website: http://www.avicapital.com

Bastion Capital Corp.
1999 Avenue of the Stars, Ste. 2960
Los Angeles, CA 90067
(310)788-5700
Fax: (310)277-7582
E-mail: ga@bastioncapital.com
Website: http://www.bastioncapital.com

Davis Group
PO Box 69953
Los Angeles, CA 90069-0953
(310)659-6327
Fax: (310)659-6337

Developers Equity Corp.
1880 Century Park East, Ste. 211
Los Angeles, CA 90067
(213)277-0300

Far East Capital Corp.
350 S. Grand Ave., Ste. 4100
Los Angeles, CA 90071
(213)687-1361
Fax: (213)617-7939
E-mail: free@fareastnationalbank.com

Kline Hawkes & Co.
11726 San Vicente Blvd., Ste. 300
Los Angeles, CA 90049
(310)442-4700
Fax: (310)442-4707
Website: http://www.klinehawkes.com

Lawrence Financial Group
701 Teakwood
PO Box 491773
Los Angeles, CA 90049
(310)471-4060
Fax: (310)472-3155

Riordan Lewis & Haden
300 S. Grand Ave., 29th Fl.
Los Angeles, CA 90071
(213)229-8500
Fax: (213)229-8597

Union Venture Corp.
445 S. Figueroa St., 9th Fl.
Los Angeles, CA 90071
(213)236-4092
Fax: (213)236-6329

Wedbush Capital Partners
1000 Wilshire Blvd.
Los Angeles, CA 90017
(213)688-4545
Fax: (213)688-6642
Website: http://www.wedbush.com

Advent International Corp.
2180 Sand Hill Rd., Ste. 420
Menlo Park, CA 94025
(650)233-7500
Fax: (650)233-7515
Website: http://www.adventinternational.com

Altos Ventures
2882 Sand Hill Rd., Ste. 100
Menlo Park, CA 94025
(650)234-9771
Fax: (650)233-9821
Website: http://www.altosvc.com

Applied Technology
1010 El Camino Real, Ste. 300
Menlo Park, CA 94025
(415)326-8622
Fax: (415)326-8163

APV Technology Partners
535 Middlefield, Ste. 150
Menlo Park, CA 94025
(650)327-7871
Fax: (650)327-7631
Website: http://www.apvtp.com

August Capital Management
2480 Sand Hill Rd., Ste. 101
Menlo Park, CA 94025
(650)234-9900
Fax: (650)234-9910
Website: http://www.augustcap.com

Baccharis Capital Inc.
2420 Sand Hill Rd., Ste. 100
Menlo Park, CA 94025
(650)324-6844
Fax: (650)854-3025

Benchmark Capital
2480 Sand Hill Rd., Ste. 200
Menlo Park, CA 94025
(650)854-8180
Fax: (650)854-8183
E-mail: info@benchmark.com
Website: http://www.benchmark.com

Bessemer Venture Partners (Menlo Park)
535 Middlefield Rd., Ste. 245
Menlo Park, CA 94025
(650)853-7000
Fax: (650)853-7001
Website: http://www.bvp.com

The Cambria Group
1600 El Camino Real Rd., Ste. 155
Menlo Park, CA 94025
(650)329-8600

Fax: (650)329-8601
Website: http://www.cambriagroup.com

Canaan Partners
2884 Sand Hill Rd., Ste. 115
Menlo Park, CA 94025
(650)854-8092
Fax: (650)854-8127
Website: http://www.canaan.com

Capstone Ventures
3000 Sand Hill Rd., Bldg. One, Ste. 290
Menlo Park, CA 94025
(650)854-2523
Fax: (650)854-9010
Website: http://www.capstonevc.com

Comdisco Venture Group (Silicon Valley)
3000 Sand Hill Rd., Bldg. 1, Ste. 155
Menlo Park, CA 94025
(650)854-9484
Fax: (650)854-4026

Commtech International
535 Middlefield Rd., Ste. 200
Menlo Park, CA 94025
(650)328-0190
Fax: (650)328-6442

Compass Technology Partners
1550 El Camino Real, Ste. 275
Menlo Park, CA 94025-4111
(650)322-7595
Fax: (650)322-0588
Website: http://www.compasstechpartners.com

Convergence Partners
3000 Sand Hill Rd., Ste. 235
Menlo Park, CA 94025
(650)854-3010
Fax: (650)854-3015
Website: http://www.convergencepartners.com

The Dakota Group
PO Box 1025
Menlo Park, CA 94025
(650)853-0600
Fax: (650)851-4899
E-mail: info@dakota.com

Delphi Ventures
3000 Sand Hill Rd.
Bldg. One, Ste. 135
Menlo Park, CA 94025
(650)854-9650
Fax: (650)854-2961
Website: http://www.delphiventures.com

El Dorado Ventures
2884 Sand Hill Rd., Ste. 121
Menlo Park, CA 94025
(650)854-1200
Fax: (650)854-1202
Website: http://www.eldorado
ventures.com

Glynn Ventures
3000 Sand Hill Rd., Bldg. 4, Ste. 235
Menlo Park, CA 94025
(650)854-2215

Indosuez Ventures
2180 Sand Hill Rd., Ste. 450
Menlo Park, CA 94025
(650)854-0587
Fax: (650)323-5561
Website: http://www.indosuez
ventures.com

Institutional Venture Partners
3000 Sand Hill Rd., Bldg. 2, Ste. 290
Menlo Park, CA 94025
(650)854-0132
Fax: (650)854-5762
Website: http://www.ivp.com

Interwest Partners (Menlo Park)
3000 Sand Hill Rd., Bldg. 3, Ste. 255
Menlo Park, CA 94025-7112
(650)854-8585
Fax: (650)854-4706
Website: http://www.interwest.com

**Kleiner Perkins Caufield & Byers
(Menlo Park)**
2750 Sand Hill Rd.
Menlo Park, CA 94025
(650)233-2750
Fax: (650)233-0300
Website: http://www.kpcb.com

Magic Venture Capital LLC
1010 El Camino Real, Ste. 300
Menlo Park, CA 94025
(650)325-4149

Matrix Partners
2500 Sand Hill Rd., Ste. 113
Menlo Park, CA 94025
(650)854-3131
Fax: (650)854-3296
Website: http://www.matrixpartners.com

Mayfield Fund
2800 Sand Hill Rd.
Menlo Park, CA 94025
(650)854-5560
Fax: (650)854-5712
Website: http://www.mayfield.com

**McCown De Leeuw and Co. (Menlo
Park)**
3000 Sand Hill Rd., Bldg. 3, Ste. 290
Menlo Park, CA 94025-7111
(650)854-6000
Fax: (650)854-0853
Website: http://www.mdcpartners.com

Menlo Ventures
3000 Sand Hill Rd., Bldg. 4, Ste. 100
Menlo Park, CA 94025
(650)854-8540
Fax: (650)854-7059
Website: http://www.menloventures.com

Merrill Pickard Anderson & Eyre
2480 Sand Hill Rd., Ste. 200
Menlo Park, CA 94025
(650)854-8600
Fax: (650)854-0345

**New Enterprise Associates (Menlo
Park)**
2490 Sand Hill Rd.
Menlo Park, CA 94025
(650)854-9499
Fax: (650)854-9397
Website: http://www.nea.com

Onset Ventures
2400 Sand Hill Rd., Ste. 150
Menlo Park, CA 94025
(650)529-0700
Fax: (650)529-0777
Website: http://www.onset.com

Paragon Venture Partners
3000 Sand Hill Rd., Bldg. 1, Ste. 275
Menlo Park, CA 94025
(650)854-8000
Fax: (650)854-7260

**Pathfinder Venture Capital Funds
(Menlo Park)**
3000 Sand Hill Rd., Bldg. 3, Ste. 255
Menlo Park, CA 94025
(650)854-0650
Fax: (650)854-4706

Rocket Ventures
3000 Sandhill Rd., Bldg. 1, Ste. 170
Menlo Park, CA 94025
(650)561-9100
Fax: (650)561-9183
Website: http://www.rocketventures.com

Sequoia Capital
3000 Sand Hill Rd., Bldg. 4, Ste. 280
Menlo Park, CA 94025
(650)854-3927
Fax: (650)854-2977

E-mail: sequoia@sequioacap.com
Website: http://www.sequoiacap.com

Sierra Ventures
3000 Sand Hill Rd., Bldg. 4, Ste. 210
Menlo Park, CA 94025
(650)854-1000
Fax: (650)854-5593
Website: http://www.sierraventures.com

Sigma Partners
2884 Sand Hill Rd., Ste. 121
Menlo Park, CA 94025-7022
(650)853-1700
Fax: (650)853-1717
E-mail: info@sigmapartners.com
Website: http://www.sigmapartners.com

Sprout Group (Menlo Park)
3000 Sand Hill Rd.
Bldg. 3, Ste. 170
Menlo Park, CA 94025
(650)234-2700
Fax: (650)234-2779
Website: http://www.sproutgroup.com

TA Associates (Menlo Park)
70 Willow Rd., Ste. 100
Menlo Park, CA 94025
(650)328-1210
Fax: (650)326-4933
Website: http://www.ta.com

Thompson Clive & Partners Ltd.
3000 Sand Hill Rd., Bldg. 1, Ste. 185
Menlo Park, CA 94025-7102
(650)854-0314
Fax: (650)854-0670
E-mail: mail@tcvc.com
Website: http://www.tcvc.com

Trinity Ventures Ltd.
3000 Sand Hill Rd., Bldg. 1, Ste. 240
Menlo Park, CA 94025
(650)854-9500
Fax: (650)854-9501
Website: http://www.trinityventures.com

U.S. Venture Partners
2180 Sand Hill Rd., Ste. 300
Menlo Park, CA 94025
(650)854-9080
Fax: (650)854-3018
Website: http://www.usvp.com

USVP-Schlein Marketing Fund
2180 Sand Hill Rd., Ste. 300
Menlo Park, CA 94025
(415)854-9080
Fax: (415)854-3018
Website: http://www.usvp.com

Venrock Associates
2494 Sand Hill Rd., Ste. 200
Menlo Park, CA 94025
(650)561-9580
Fax: (650)561-9180
Website: http://www.venrock.com

Brad Peery Capital Inc.
145 Chapel Pkwy.
Mill Valley, CA 94941
(415)389-0625
Fax: (415)389-1336

Dot Edu Ventures
650 Castro St., Ste. 270
Mountain View, CA 94041
(650)575-5638
Fax: (650)325-5247
Website: http://www.dotedu
ventures.com

Forrest, Binkley & Brown
840 Newport Ctr. Dr., Ste. 480
Newport Beach, CA 92660
(949)729-3222
Fax: (949)729-3226
Website: http://www.fbbvc.com

Marwit Capital LLC
180 Newport Center Dr., Ste. 200
Newport Beach, CA 92660
(949)640-6234
Fax: (949)720-8077
Website: http://www.marwit.com

Kaiser Permanente / National Venture Development
1800 Harrison St., 22nd Fl.
Oakland, CA 94612
(510)267-4010
Fax: (510)267-4036
Website: http://www.kpventures.com

Nu Capital Access Group, Ltd.
7677 Oakport St., Ste. 105
Oakland, CA 94621
(510)635-7345
Fax: (510)635-7068

Inman and Bowman
4 Orinda Way, Bldg. D, Ste. 150
Orinda, CA 94563
(510)253-1611
Fax: (510)253-9037

Accel Partners (San Francisco)
428 University Ave.
Palo Alto, CA 94301
(650)614-4800
Fax: (650)614-4880
Website: http://www.accel.com

Advanced Technology Ventures
485 Ramona St., Ste. 200
Palo Alto, CA 94301
(650)321-8601
Fax: (650)321-0934
Website: http://www.atvcapital.com

Anila Fund
400 Channing Ave.
Palo Alto, CA 94301
(650)833-5790
Fax: (650)833-0590
Website: http://www.anila.com

Asset Management Company Venture Capital
2275 E. Bayshore, Ste. 150
Palo Alto, CA 94303
(650)494-7400
Fax: (650)856-1826
E-mail: postmaster@assetman.com
Website: http://www.assetman.com

BancBoston Capital / BancBoston Ventures
435 Tasso St., Ste. 250
Palo Alto, CA 94305
(650)470-4100
Fax: (650)853-1425
Website: http://www.bancboston
capital.com

Charter Ventures
525 University Ave., Ste. 1400
Palo Alto, CA 94301
(650)325-6953
Fax: (650)325-4762
Website: http://www.charterventures.com

Communications Ventures
505 Hamilton Avenue, Ste. 305
Palo Alto, CA 94301
(650)325-9600
Fax: (650)325-9608
Website: http://www.comven.com

HMS Group
2468 Embarcadero Way
Palo Alto, CA 94303-3313
(650)856-9862
Fax: (650)856-9864

Jafco America Ventures, Inc.
505 Hamilton Ste. 310
Palto Alto, CA 94301
(650)463-8800
Fax: (650)463-8801
Website: http://www.jafco.com

New Vista Capital
540 Cowper St., Ste. 200

Palo Alto, CA 94301
(650)329-9333
Fax: (650)328-9434
E-mail: fgreene@nvcap.com
Website: http://www.nvcap.com

Norwest Equity Partners (Palo Alto)
245 Lytton Ave., Ste. 250
Palo Alto, CA 94301-1426
(650)321-8000
Fax: (650)321-8010
Website: http://www.norwestvp.com

Oak Investment Partners
525 University Ave., Ste. 1300
Palo Alto, CA 94301
(650)614-3700
Fax: (650)328-6345
Website: http://www.oakinv.com

Patricof & Co. Ventures, Inc. (Palo Alto)
2100 Geng Rd., Ste. 150
Palo Alto, CA 94303
(650)494-9944
Fax: (650)494-6751
Website: http://www.patricof.com

RWI Group
835 Page Mill Rd.
Palo Alto, CA 94304
(650)251-1800
Fax: (650)213-8660
Website: http://www.rwigroup.com

Summit Partners (Palo Alto)
499 Hamilton Ave., Ste. 200
Palo Alto, CA 94301
(650)321-1166
Fax: (650)321-1188
Website: http://www.summit
partners.com

Sutter Hill Ventures
755 Page Mill Rd., Ste. A-200
Palo Alto, CA 94304
(650)493-5600
Fax: (650)858-1854
E-mail: shv@shv.com

Vanguard Venture Partners
525 University Ave., Ste. 600
Palo Alto, CA 94301
(650)321-2900
Fax: (650)321-2902
Website: http://www.vanguard
ventures.com

Venture Growth Associates
2479 East Bayshore St., Ste. 710
Palo Alto, CA 94303

(650)855-9100
Fax: (650)855-9104

Worldview Technology Partners
435 Tasso St., Ste. 120
Palo Alto, CA 94301
(650)322-3800
Fax: (650)322-3880
Website: http://www.worldview.com

Draper, Fisher, Jurvetson / Draper Associates
400 Seaport Ct., Ste.250
Redwood City, CA 94063
(415)599-9000
Fax: (415)599-9726
Website: http://www.dfj.com

Gabriel Venture Partners
350 Marine Pkwy., Ste. 200
Redwood Shores, CA 94065
(650)551-5000
Fax: (650)551-5001
Website: http://www.gabrielvp.com

Hallador Venture Partners, L.L.C.
740 University Ave., Ste. 110
Sacramento, CA 95825-6710
(916)920-0191
Fax: (916)920-5188
E-mail: chris@hallador.com

Emerald Venture Group
12396 World Trade Dr., Ste. 116
San Diego, CA 92128
(858)451-1001
Fax: (858)451-1003
Website: http://www.emerald
venture.com

Forward Ventures
9255 Towne Centre Dr.
San Diego, CA 92121
(858)677-6077
Fax: (858)452-8799
E-mail: info@forwardventure.com
Website: http://www.forward
venture.com

Idanta Partners Ltd.
4660 La Jolla Village Dr., Ste. 850
San Diego, CA 92122
(619)452-9690
Fax: (619)452-2013
Website: http://www.idanta.com

Kingsbury Associates
3655 Nobel Dr., Ste. 490
San Diego, CA 92122
(858)677-0600
Fax: (858)677-0800

Kyocera International Inc.
Corporate Development
8611 Balboa Ave.
San Diego, CA 92123
(858)576-2600
Fax: (858)492-1456

Sorrento Associates, Inc.
4370 LaJolla Village Dr., Ste. 1040
San Diego, CA 92122
(619)452-3100
Fax: (619)452-7607
Website: http://www.sorrento
ventures.com

Western States Investment Group
9191 Towne Ctr. Dr., Ste. 310
San Diego, CA 92122
(619)678-0800
Fax: (619)678-0900

Aberdare Ventures
One Embarcadero Center, Ste. 4000
San Francisco, CA 94111
(415)392-7442
Fax: (415)392-4264
Website: http://www.aberdare.com

Acacia Venture Partners
101 California St., Ste. 3160
San Francisco, CA 94111
(415)433-4200
Fax: (415)433-4250
Website: http://www.acaciavp.com

Access Venture Partners
319 Laidley St.
San Francisco, CA 94131
(415)586-0132
Fax: (415)392-6310
Website: http://www.access
venturepartners.com

Alta Partners
One Embarcadero Center, Ste. 4050
San Francisco, CA 94111
(415)362-4022
Fax: (415)362-6178
E-mail: alta@altapartners.com
Website: http://www.altapartners.com

Bangert Dawes Reade Davis & Thom
220 Montgomery St., Ste. 424
San Francisco, CA 94104
(415)954-9900
Fax: (415)954-9901
E-mail: bdrdt@pacbell.net

Berkeley International Capital Corp.
650 California St., Ste. 2800
San Francisco, CA 94108-2609

(415)249-0450
Fax: (415)392-3929
Website: http://www.berkeleyvc.com

Blueprint Ventures LLC
456 Montgomery St., 22nd Fl.
San Francisco, CA 94104
(415)901-4000
Fax: (415)901-4035
Website: http://www.blue
printventures.com

Blumberg Capital Ventures
580 Howard St., Ste. 401
San Francisco, CA 94105
(415)905-5007
Fax: (415)357-5027
Website: http://www.blumberg-
capital.com

Burr, Egan, Deleage, and Co. (San Francisco)
1 Embarcadero Center, Ste. 4050
San Francisco, CA 94111
(415)362-4022
Fax: (415)362-6178

Burrill & Company
120 Montgomery St., Ste. 1370
San Francisco, CA 94104
(415)743-3160
Fax: (415)743-3161
Website: http://www.burrillandco.com

CMEA Ventures
235 Montgomery St., Ste. 920
San Francisco, CA 94401
(415)352-1520
Fax: (415)352-1524
Website: http://www.cmeaventures.com

Crocker Capital
1 Post St., Ste. 2500
San Francisco, CA 94101
(415)956-5250
Fax: (415)959-5710

Dominion Ventures, Inc.
44 Montgomery St., Ste. 4200
San Francisco, CA 94104
(415)362-4890
Fax: (415)394-9245

Dorset Capital
Pier 1
Bay 2
San Francisco, CA 94111
(415)398-7101
Fax: (415)398-7141
Website: http://www.dorsetcapital.com

Gatx Capital
Four Embarcadero Center, Ste. 2200
San Francisco, CA 94904
(415)955-3200
Fax: (415)955-3449

IMinds
135 Main St., Ste. 1350
San Francisco, CA 94105
(415)547-0000
Fax: (415)227-0300
Website: http://www.iminds.com

LF International Inc.
360 Post St., Ste. 705
San Francisco, CA 94108
(415)399-0110
Fax: (415)399-9222
Website: http://www.lfvc.com

Newbury Ventures
535 Pacific Ave., 2nd Fl.
San Francisco, CA 94133
(415)296-7408
Fax: (415)296-7416
Website: http://www.newburyven.com

Quest Ventures (San Francisco)
333 Bush St., Ste. 1750
San Francisco, CA 94104
(415)782-1414
Fax: (415)782-1415

Robertson-Stephens Co.
555 California St., Ste. 2600
San Francisco, CA 94104
(415)781-9700
Fax: (415)781-2556
Website: http://www.omegaad
ventures.com

Rosewood Capital, L.P.
One Maritime Plaza, Ste. 1330
San Francisco, CA 94111-3503
(415)362-5526
Fax: (415)362-1192
Website: http://www.rosewoodvc.com

Ticonderoga Capital Inc.
555 California St., No. 4950
San Francisco, CA 94104
(415)296-7900
Fax: (415)296-8956

21st Century Internet Venture Partners
Two South Park
2nd Floor
San Francisco, CA 94107
(415)512-1221
Fax: (415)512-2650
Website: http://www.21vc.com

VK Ventures
600 California St., Ste.1700
San Francisco, CA 94111
(415)391-5600
Fax: (415)397-2744

Walden Group of Venture Capital Funds
750 Battery St., Seventh Floor
San Francisco, CA 94111
(415)391-7225
Fax: (415)391-7262

Acer Technology Ventures
2641 Orchard Pkwy.
San Jose, CA 95134
(408)433-4945
Fax: (408)433-5230

Authosis
226 Airport Pkwy., Ste. 405
San Jose, CA 95110
(650)814-3603
Website: http://www.authosis.com

Western Technology Investment
2010 N. First St., Ste. 310
San Jose, CA 95131
(408)436-8577
Fax: (408)436-8625
E-mail: mktg@westerntech.com

Drysdale Enterprises
177 Bovet Rd., Ste. 600
San Mateo, CA 94402
(650)341-6336
Fax: (650)341-1329
E-mail: drysdale@aol.com

Greylock
2929 Campus Dr., Ste. 400
San Mateo, CA 94401
(650)493-5525
Fax: (650)493-5575
Website: http://www.greylock.com

Technology Funding
2000 Alameda de las Pulgas, Ste. 250
San Mateo, CA 94403
(415)345-2200
Fax: (415)345-1797

2M Invest Inc.
1875 S. Grant St.
Suite 750
San Mateo, CA 94402
(650)655-3765
Fax: (650)372-9107
E-mail: 2minfo@2minvest.com
Website: http://www.2minvest.com

Phoenix Growth Capital Corp.
2401 Kerner Blvd.
San Rafael, CA 94901
(415)485-4569
Fax: (415)485-4663

NextGen Partners LLC
1705 East Valley Rd.
Santa Barbara, CA 93108
(805)969-8540
Fax: (805)969-8542
Website: http://www.nextgen
partners.com

Denali Venture Capital
1925 Woodland Ave.
Santa Clara, CA 95050
(408)690-4838
Fax: (408)247-6979
E-mail: wael@denaliventurecapital.com
Website: http://www.denali
venturecapital.com

Dotcom Ventures LP
3945 Freedom Circle, Ste. 740
Santa Clara, CA 95045
(408)919-9855
Fax: (408)919-9857
Website: http://www.dotcom
venturesatl.com

Silicon Valley Bank
3003 Tasman
Santa Clara, CA 95054
(408)654-7400
Fax: (408)727-8728

Al Shugart International
920 41st Ave.
Santa Cruz, CA 95062
(831)479-7852
Fax: (831)479-7852
Website: http://www.alshugart.com

Leonard Mautner Associates
1434 Sixth St.
Santa Monica, CA 90401
(213)393-9788
Fax: (310)459-9918

Palomar Ventures
100 Wilshire Blvd., Ste. 450
Santa Monica, CA 90401
(310)260-6050
Fax: (310)656-4150
Website: http://www.palomar
ventures.com

Medicus Venture Partners
12930 Saratoga Ave., Ste. D8
Saratoga, CA 95070

(408)447-8600
Fax: (408)447-8599
Website: http://www.medicusvc.com

Redleaf Venture Management
14395 Saratoga Ave., Ste. 130
Saratoga, CA 95070
(408)868-0800
Fax: (408)868-0810
E-mail: nancy@redleaf.com
Website: http://www.redleaf.com

Artemis Ventures
207 Second St., Ste. E
3rd Fl.
Sausalito, CA 94965
(415)289-2500
Fax: (415)289-1789
Website: http://www.artemisventures.com

Deucalion Venture Partners
19501 Brooklime
Sonoma, CA 95476
(707)938-4974
Fax: (707)938-8921

Windward Ventures
PO Box 7688
Thousand Oaks, CA 91359-7688
(805)497-3332
Fax: (805)497-9331

National Investment Management, Inc.
2601 Airport Dr., Ste.210
Torrance, CA 90505
(310)784-7600
Fax: (310)784-7605

Southern California Ventures
406 Amapola Ave. Ste. 125
Torrance, CA 90501
(310)787-4381
Fax: (310)787-4382

Sandton Financial Group
21550 Oxnard St., Ste. 300
Woodland Hills, CA 91367
(818)702-9283

Woodside Fund
850 Woodside Dr.
Woodside, CA 94062
(650)368-5545
Fax: (650)368-2416
Website: http://www.woodsidefund.com

Colorado

Colorado Venture Management
Ste. 300
Boulder, CO 80301

(303)440-4055
Fax: (303)440-4636

Dean & Associates
4362 Apple Way
Boulder, CO 80301
Fax: (303)473-9900

Roser Ventures LLC
1105 Spruce St.
Boulder, CO 80302
(303)443-6436
Fax: (303)443-1885
Website: http://www.roserventures.com

Sequel Venture Partners
4430 Arapahoe Ave., Ste. 220
Boulder, CO 80303
(303)546-0400
Fax: (303)546-9728
E-mail: tom@sequelvc.com
Website: http://www.sequelvc.com

New Venture Resources
445C E. Cheyenne Mtn. Blvd.
Colorado Springs, CO 80906-4570
(719)598-9272
Fax: (719)598-9272

The Centennial Funds
1428 15th St.
Denver, CO 80202-1318
(303)405-7500
Fax: (303)405-7575
Website: http://www.centennial.com

Rocky Mountain Capital Partners
1125 17th St., Ste. 2260
Denver, CO 80202
(303)291-5200
Fax: (303)291-5327

Sandlot Capital LLC
600 South Cherry St., Ste. 525
Denver, CO 80246
(303)893-3400
Fax: (303)893-3403
Website: http://www.sandlotcapital.com

Wolf Ventures
50 South Steele St., Ste. 777
Denver, CO 80209
(303)321-4800
Fax: (303)321-4848
E-mail: businessplan@wolf
ventures.com
Website: http://www.wolfventures.com

The Columbine Venture Funds
5460 S. Quebec St., Ste. 270
Englewood, CO 80111

(303)694-3222
Fax: (303)694-9007

Investment Securities of Colorado, Inc.
4605 Denice Dr.
Englewood, CO 80111
(303)796-9192

Kinship Partners
6300 S. Syracuse Way, Ste. 484
Englewood, CO 80111
(303)694-0268
Fax: (303)694-1707
E-mail: block@vailsys.com

Boranco Management, L.L.C.
1528 Hillside Dr.
Fort Collins, CO 80524-1969
(970)221-2297
Fax: (970)221-4787

Aweida Ventures
890 West Cherry St., Ste. 220
Louisville, CO 80027
(303)664-9520
Fax: (303)664-9530
Website: http://www.aweida.com

Access Venture Partners
8787 Turnpike Dr., Ste. 260
Westminster, CO 80030
(303)426-8899
Fax: (303)426-8828

Medmax Ventures LP
1 Northwestern Dr., Ste. 203
Bloomfield, CT 06002
(860)286-2960
Fax: (860)286-9960

James B. Kobak & Co.
Four Mansfield Place
Darien, CT 06820
(203)656-3471
Fax: (203)655-2905

Orien Ventures
1 Post Rd.
Fairfield, CT 06430
(203)259-9933
Fax: (203)259-5288

ABP Acquisition Corporation
115 Maple Ave.
Greenwich, CT 06830
(203)625-8287
Fax: (203)447-6187

Catterton Partners
9 Greenwich Office Park
Greenwich, CT 06830
(203)629-4901

Fax: (203)629-4903
Website: http://www.cpequity.com

Consumer Venture Partners
3 Pickwick Plz.
Greenwich, CT 06830
(203)629-8800
Fax: (203)629-2019

Insurance Venture Partners
31 Brookside Dr., Ste. 211
Greenwich, CT 06830
(203)861-0030
Fax: (203)861-2745

The NTC Group
Three Pickwick Plaza
Ste. 200
Greenwich, CT 06830
(203)862-2800
Fax: (203)622-6538

Regulus International Capital Co., Inc.
140 Greenwich Ave.
Greenwich, CT 06830
(203)625-9700
Fax: (203)625-9706

Axiom Venture Partners
City Place II
185 Asylum St., 17th Fl.
Hartford, CT 06103
(860)548-7799
Fax: (860)548-7797
Website: http://www.axiomventures.com

Conning Capital Partners
City Place II
185 Asylum St.
Hartford, CT 06103-4105
(860)520-1289
Fax: (860)520-1299
E-mail: pe@conning.com
Website: http://www.conning.com

First New England Capital L.P.
100 Pearl St.
Hartford, CT 06103
(860)293-3333
Fax: (860)293-3338
E-mail: info@firstnewenglandcapital.com
Website: http://www.firstnewengland
capital.com

Northeast Ventures
One State St., Ste. 1720
Hartford, CT 06103
(860)547-1414
Fax: (860)246-8755

Windward Holdings
38 Sylvan Rd.
Madison, CT 06443
(203)245-6870
Fax: (203)245-6865

Advanced Materials Partners, Inc.
45 Pine St.
PO Box 1022
New Canaan, CT 06840
(203)966-6415
Fax: (203)966-8448
E-mail: wkb@amplink.com

RFE Investment Partners
36 Grove St.
New Canaan, CT 06840
(203)966-2800
Fax: (203)966-3109
Website: http://www.rfeip.com

Connecticut Innovations, Inc.
999 West St.
Rocky Hill, CT 06067
(860)563-5851
Fax: (860)563-4877
E-mail: pamela.hartley@ctin
novations.com
Website: http://www.ctinnovations.com

Canaan Partners
105 Rowayton Ave.
Rowayton, CT 06853
(203)855-0400
Fax: (203)854-9117
Website: http://www.canaan.com

Landmark Partners, Inc.
10 Mill Pond Ln.
Simsbury, CT 06070
(860)651-9760
Fax: (860)651-8890
Website: http://
www.landmarkpartners.com

Sweeney & Company
PO Box 567
Southport, CT 06490
(203)255-0220
Fax: (203)255-0220
E-mail: sweeney@connix.com

Baxter Associates, Inc.
PO Box 1333
Stamford, CT 06904
(203)323-3143
Fax: (203)348-0622

Beacon Partners Inc.
6 Landmark Sq., 4th Fl.
Stamford, CT 06901-2792

(203)359-5776
Fax: (203)359-5876

Collinson, Howe, and Lennox, LLC
1055 Washington Blvd., 5th Fl.
Stamford, CT 06901
(203)324-7700
Fax: (203)324-3636
E-mail: info@chlmedical.com
Website: http://www.chlmedical.com

Prime Capital Management Co.
550 West Ave.
Stamford, CT 06902
(203)964-0642
Fax: (203)964-0862

Saugatuck Capital Co.
1 Canterbury Green
Stamford, CT 06901
(203)348-6669
Fax: (203)324-6995
Website: http://www.sauga
tuckcapital.com

Soundview Financial Group Inc.
22 Gatehouse Rd.
Stamford, CT 06902
(203)462-7200
Fax: (203)462-7350
Website: http://www.sndv.com

TSG Ventures, L.L.C.
177 Broad St., 12th Fl.
Stamford, CT 06901
(203)406-1500
Fax: (203)406-1590

Whitney & Company
177 Broad St.
Stamford, CT 06901
(203)973-1400
Fax: (203)973-1422
Website: http://www.jhwhitney.com

Cullinane & Donnelly Venture Partners L.P.
970 Farmington Ave.
West Hartford, CT 06107
(860)521-7811

The Crestview Investment and Financial Group
431 Post Rd. E, Ste. 1
Westport, CT 06880-4403
(203)222-0333
Fax: (203)222-0000

Marketcorp Venture Associates, L.P. (MCV)
274 Riverside Ave.
Westport, CT 06880

(203)222-3030
Fax: (203)222-3033

Oak Investment Partners (Westport)
1 Gorham Island
Westport, CT 06880
(203)226-8346
Fax: (203)227-0372
Website: http://www.oakinv.com

Oxford Bioscience Partners
315 Post Rd. W
Westport, CT 06880-5200
(203)341-3300
Fax: (203)341-3309
Website: http://www.oxbio.com

Prince Ventures (Westport)
25 Ford Rd.
Westport, CT 06880
(203)227-8332
Fax: (203)226-5302

LTI Venture Leasing Corp.
221 Danbury Rd.
Wilton, CT 06897
(203)563-1100
Fax: (203)563-1111
Website: http://www.ltileasing.com

Delaware

Blue Rock Capital
5803 Kennett Pike, Ste. A
Wilmington, DE 19807
(302)426-0981
Fax: (302)426-0982
Website: http://www.bluerockcapital.com

District of Columbia

Allied Capital Corp.
1919 Pennsylvania Ave. NW
Washington, DC 20006-3434
(202)331-2444
Fax: (202)659-2053
Website: http://www.alliedcapital.com

Atlantic Coastal Ventures, L.P.
3101 South St. NW
Washington, DC 20007
(202)293-1166
Fax: (202)293-1181
Website: http://www.atlanticcv.com

Columbia Capital Group, Inc.
1660 L St. NW, Ste. 308
Washington, DC 20036
(202)775-8815
Fax: (202)223-0544

Core Capital Partners
901 15th St., NW
9th Fl.
Washington, DC 20005
(202)589-0090
Fax: (202)589-0091
Website: http://www.core-capital.com

Next Point Partners
701 Pennsylvania Ave. NW, Ste. 900
Washington, DC 20004
(202)661-8703
Fax: (202)434-7400
E-mail: mf@nextpoint.vc
Website: http://www.nextpointvc.com

Telecommunications Development Fund
2020 K. St. NW
Ste. 375
Washington, DC 20006
(202)293-8840
Fax: (202)293-8850
Website: http://www.tdfund.com

Wachtel & Co., Inc.
1101 4th St. NW
Washington, DC 20005-5680
(202)898-1144

Winslow Partners LLC
1300 Connecticut Ave. NW
Washington, DC 20036-1703
(202)530-5000
Fax: (202)530-5010
E-mail: winslow@winslowpartners.com

Women's Growth Capital Fund
1054 31st St., NW
Ste. 110
Washington, DC 20007
(202)342-1431
Fax: (202)341-1203
Website: http://www.wgcf.com

Sigma Capital Corp.
22668 Caravelle Circle
Boca Raton, FL 33433
(561)368-9783

North American Business Development Co., L.L.C.
111 East Las Olas Blvd.
Ft. Lauderdale, FL 33301
(305)463-0681
Fax: (305)527-0904
Website: http://
www.northamericanfund.com

Chartwell Capital Management Co. Inc.
1 Independent Dr., Ste. 3120

Jacksonville, FL 32202
(904)355-3519
Fax: (904)353-5833
E-mail: info@chartwellcap.com

CEO Advisors
1061 Maitland Center Commons
Ste. 209
Maitland, FL 32751
(407)660-9327
Fax: (407)660-2109

Henry & Co.
8201 Peters Rd., Ste. 1000
Plantation, FL 33324
(954)797-7400

Avery Business Development Services
2506 St. Michel Ct.
Ponte Vedra, FL 32082
(904)285-6033

New South Ventures
5053 Ocean Blvd.
Sarasota, FL 34242
(941)358-6000
Fax: (941)358-6078
Website: http://www.newsouth
ventures.com

Venture Capital Management Corp.
PO Box 2626
Satellite Beach, FL 32937
(407)777-1969

Florida Capital Venture Ltd.
325 Florida Bank Plaza
100 W. Kennedy Blvd.
Tampa, FL 33602
(813)229-2294
Fax: (813)229-2028

Quantum Capital Partners
339 South Plant Ave.
Tampa, FL 33606
(813)250-1999
Fax: (813)250-1998
Website: http://www.quantum
capitalpartners.com

South Atlantic Venture Fund
614 W. Bay St.
Tampa, FL 33606-2704
(813)253-2500
Fax: (813)253-2360
E-mail: venture@southatlantic.com
Website: http://www.southatlantic.com

LM Capital Corp.
120 S. Olive, Ste. 400
West Palm Beach, FL 33401

(561)833-9700
Fax: (561)655-6587
Website: http://www.lmcapital
securities.com

Georgia

Venture First Associates
4811 Thornwood Dr.
Acworth, GA 30102
(770)928-3733
Fax: (770)928-6455

Alliance Technology Ventures
8995 Westside Pkwy., Ste. 200
Alpharetta, GA 30004
(678)336-2000
Fax: (678)336-2001
E-mail: info@atv.com
Website: http://www.atv.com

Cordova Ventures
2500 North Winds Pkwy., Ste. 475
Alpharetta, GA 30004
(678)942-0300
Fax: (678)942-0301
Website: http://www.cordovaventures.
com

**Advanced Technology Development
Fund**
1000 Abernathy, Ste. 1420
Atlanta, GA 30328-5614
(404)668-2333
Fax: (404)668-2333

CGW Southeast Partners
12 Piedmont Center, Ste. 210
Atlanta, GA 30305
(404)816-3255
Fax: (404)816-3258
Website: http://www.cgwlp.com

Cyberstarts
1900 Emery St., NW
3rd Fl.
Atlanta, GA 30318
(404)267-5000
Fax: (404)267-5200
Website: http://www.cyberstarts.com

EGL Holdings, Inc.
10 Piedmont Center, Ste. 412
Atlanta, GA 30305
(404)949-8300
Fax: (404)949-8311

Equity South
1790 The Lenox Bldg.
3399 Peachtree Rd. NE
Atlanta, GA 30326

(404)237-6222
Fax: (404)261-1578

Five Paces
3400 Peachtree Rd., Ste. 200
Atlanta, GA 30326
(404)439-8300
Fax: (404)439-8301
Website: http://www.fivepaces.com

Frontline Capital, Inc.
3475 Lenox Rd., Ste. 400
Atlanta, GA 30326
(404)240-7280
Fax: (404)240-7281

Fuqua Ventures LLC
1201 W. Peachtree St. NW, Ste. 5000
Atlanta, GA 30309
(404)815-4500
Fax: (404)815-4528
Website: http://www.fuquaventures.com

Noro-Moseley Partners
4200 Northside Pkwy., Bldg. 9
Atlanta, GA 30327
(404)233-1966
Fax: (404)239-9280
Website: http://www.noro-moseley.com

Renaissance Capital Corp.
34 Peachtree St. NW, Ste. 2230
Atlanta, GA 30303
(404)658-9061
Fax: (404)658-9064

River Capital, Inc.
Two Midtown Plaza
1360 Peachtree St. NE, Ste. 1430
Atlanta, GA 30309
(404)873-2166
Fax: (404)873-2158

State Street Bank & Trust Co.
3414 Peachtree Rd. NE, Ste. 1010
Atlanta, GA 30326
(404)364-9500
Fax: (404)261-4469

UPS Strategic Enterprise Fund
55 Glenlake Pkwy. NE
Atlanta, GA 30328
(404)828-8814
Fax: (404)828-8088
E-mail: jcacyce@ups.com
Website: http://www.ups.com/sef/
sef_home

Wachovia
191 Peachtree St. NE, 26th Fl.
Atlanta, GA 30303

(404)332-1000
Fax: (404)332-1392
Website: http://www.wachovia.com/wca

Brainworks Ventures
4243 Dunwoody Club Dr.
Chamblee, GA 30341
(770)239-7447

First Growth Capital Inc.
Best Western Plaza, Ste. 105
PO Box 815
Forsyth, GA 31029
(912)781-7131

Financial Capital Resources, Inc.
21 Eastbrook Bend, Ste. 116
Peachtree City, GA 30269
(404)487-6650

Hawaii

HMS Hawaii Management Partners
Davies Pacific Center
841 Bishop St., Ste. 860
Honolulu, HI 96813
(808)545-3755
Fax: (808)531-2611

Idaho

Sun Valley Ventures
160 Second St.
Ketchum, ID 83340
(208)726-5005
Fax: (208)726-5094

Illinois

Open Prairie Ventures
115 N. Neil St., Ste. 209
Champaign, IL 61820
(217)351-7000
Fax: (217)351-7051
E-mail: inquire@openprairie.com
Website: http://www.openprairie.com

ABN AMRO Private Equity
208 S. La Salle St., 10th Fl.
Chicago, IL 60604
(312)855-7079
Fax: (312)553-6648
Website: http://www.abnequity.com

Alpha Capital Partners, Ltd.
122 S. Michigan Ave., Ste. 1700
Chicago, IL 60603
(312)322-9800
Fax: (312)322-9808
E-mail: acp@alphacapital.com

Ameritech Development Corp.
30 S. Wacker Dr., 37th Fl.
Chicago, IL 60606
(312)750-5083
Fax: (312)609-0244

Apex Investment Partners
225 W. Washington, Ste. 1450
Chicago, IL 60606
(312)857-2800
Fax: (312)857-1800
E-mail: apex@apexvc.com
Website: http://www.apexvc.com

Arch Venture Partners
8725 W. Higgins Rd., Ste. 290
Chicago, IL 60631
(773)380-6600
Fax: (773)380-6606
Website: http://www.archventure.com

The Bank Funds
208 South LaSalle St., Ste. 1680
Chicago, IL 60604
(312)855-6020
Fax: (312)855-8910

Batterson Venture Partners
303 W. Madison St., Ste. 1110
Chicago, IL 60606-3309
(312)269-0300
Fax: (312)269-0021
Website: http://www.battersonvp.com

William Blair Capital Partners, L.L.C.
222 W. Adams St., Ste. 1300
Chicago, IL 60606
(312)364-8250
Fax: (312)236-1042
E-mail: privateequity@wmblair.com
Website: http://www.wmblair.com

Bluestar Ventures
208 South LaSalle St., Ste. 1020
Chicago, IL 60604
(312)384-5000
Fax: (312)384-5005
Website: http://www.bluestarventures.com

The Capital Strategy Management Co.
233 S. Wacker Dr.
Box 06334
Chicago, IL 60606
(312)444-1170

DN Partners
77 West Wacker Dr., Ste. 4550
Chicago, IL 60601
(312)332-7960
Fax: (312)332-7979

Dresner Capital Inc.
29 South LaSalle St., Ste. 310
Chicago, IL 60603
(312)726-3600
Fax: (312)726-7448

Eblast Ventures LLC
11 South LaSalle St., 5th Fl.
Chicago, IL 60603
(312)372-2600
Fax: (312)372-5621
Website: http://www.eblastventures.com

Essex Woodlands Health Ventures, L.P.
190 S. LaSalle St., Ste. 2800
Chicago, IL 60603
(312)444-6040
Fax: (312)444-6034
Website: http://www.essexwoodlands.com

First Analysis Venture Capital
233 S. Wacker Dr., Ste. 9500
Chicago, IL 60606
(312)258-1400
Fax: (312)258-0334
Website: http://www.firstanalysis.com

Frontenac Co.
135 S. LaSalle St., Ste.3800
Chicago, IL 60603
(312)368-0044
Fax: (312)368-9520
Website: http://www.frontenac.com

GTCR Golder Rauner, LLC
6100 Sears Tower
Chicago, IL 60606
(312)382-2200
Fax: (312)382-2201
Website: http://www.gtcr.com

High Street Capital LLC
311 South Wacker Dr., Ste. 4550
Chicago, IL 60606
(312)697-4990
Fax: (312)697-4994
Website: http://www.highstr.com

IEG Venture Management, Inc.
70 West Madison
Chicago, IL 60602
(312)644-0890
Fax: (312)454-0369
Website: http://www.iegventure.com

JK&B Capital
180 North Stetson, Ste. 4500
Chicago, IL 60601
(312)946-1200
Fax: (312)946-1103

E-mail: gspencer@jkbcapital.com
Website: http://www.jkbcapital.com

Kettle Partners L.P.
350 W. Hubbard, Ste. 350
Chicago, IL 60610
(312)329-9300
Fax: (312)527-4519
Website: http://www.kettlevc.com

Lake Shore Capital Partners
20 N. Wacker Dr., Ste. 2807
Chicago, IL 60606
(312)803-3536
Fax: (312)803-3534

LaSalle Capital Group Inc.
70 W. Madison St., Ste. 5710
Chicago, IL 60602
(312)236-7041
Fax: (312)236-0720

Linc Capital, Inc.
303 E. Wacker Pkwy., Ste. 1000
Chicago, IL 60601
(312)946-2670
Fax: (312)938-4290
E-mail: bdemars@linccap.com

Madison Dearborn Partners, Inc.
3 First National Plz., Ste. 3800
Chicago, IL 60602
(312)895-1000
Fax: (312)895-1001
E-mail: invest@mdcp.com
Website: http://www.mdcp.com

Mesirow Private Equity Investments Inc.
350 N. Clark St.
Chicago, IL 60610
(312)595-6950
Fax: (312)595-6211
Website: http://www.meisrowfinancial.com

Mosaix Ventures LLC
1822 North Mohawk
Chicago, IL 60614
(312)274-0988
Fax: (312)274-0989
Website: http://www.mosaixventures.com

Nesbitt Burns
111 West Monroe St.
Chicago, IL 60603
(312)416-3855
Fax: (312)765-8000
Website: http://www.harrisbank.com

Polestar Capital, Inc.
180 N. Michigan Ave., Ste. 1905
Chicago, IL 60601
(312)984-9090
Fax: (312)984-9877
E-mail: wl@polestarvc.com
Website: http://www.polestarvc.com

Prince Ventures (Chicago)
10 S. Wacker Dr., Ste. 2575
Chicago, IL 60606-7407
(312)454-1408
Fax: (312)454-9125

Prism Capital
444 N. Michigan Ave.
Chicago, IL 60611
(312)464-7900
Fax: (312)464-7915
Website: http://www.prismfund.com

Third Coast Capital
900 N. Franklin St., Ste. 700
Chicago, IL 60610
(312)337-3303
Fax: (312)337-2567
E-mail: manic@earthlink.com
Website: http://www.third
coastcapital.com

Thoma Cressey Equity Partners
4460 Sears Tower, 92nd Fl.
233 S. Wacker Dr.
Chicago, IL 60606
(312)777-4444
Fax: (312)777-4445
Website: http://www.thomacressey.com

Tribune Ventures
435 N. Michigan Ave., Ste. 600
Chicago, IL 60611
(312)527-8797
Fax: (312)222-5993
Website: http://www.tribuneventures.com

Wind Point Partners (Chicago)
676 N. Michigan Ave., Ste. 330
Chicago, IL 60611
(312)649-4000
Website: http://www.wppartners.com

Marquette Venture Partners
520 Lake Cook Rd., Ste. 450
Deerfield, IL 60015
(847)940-1700
Fax: (847)940-1724
Website: http://www.marquette
ventures.com

Duchossois Investments Limited, LLC
845 Larch Ave.
Elmhurst, IL 60126

(630)530-6105
Fax: (630)993-8644
Website: http://www.duchtec.com

Evanston Business Investment Corp.
1840 Oak Ave.
Evanston, IL 60201
(847)866-1840
Fax: (847)866-1808
E-mail: t-parkinson@nwu.com
Website: http://www.ebic.com

Inroads Capital Partners L.P.
1603 Orrington Ave., Ste. 2050
Evanston, IL 60201-3841
(847)864-2000
Fax: (847)864-9692

The Cerulean Fund/WGC Enterprises
1701 E. Lake Ave., Ste. 170
Glenview, IL 60025
(847)657-8002
Fax: (847)657-8168

Ventana Financial Resources, Inc.
249 Market Sq.
Lake Forest, IL 60045
(847)234-3434

Beecken, Petty & Co.
901 Warrenville Rd., Ste. 205
Lisle, IL 60532
(630)435-0300
Fax: (630)435-0370
E-mail: hep@bpcompany.com
Website: http://www.bpcompany.com

Allstate Private Equity
3075 Sanders Rd., Ste. G5D
Northbrook, IL 60062-7127
(847)402-8247
Fax: (847)402-0880

KB Partners
1101 Skokie Blvd., Ste. 260
Northbrook, IL 60062-2856
(847)714-0444
Fax: (847)714-0445
E-mail: keith@kbpartners.com
Website: http://www.kbpartners.com

Transcap Associates Inc.
900 Skokie Blvd., Ste. 210
Northbrook, IL 60062
(847)753-9600
Fax: (847)753-9090

**Graystone Venture Partners, L.L.C. /
Portage Venture Partners**
One Northfield Plaza, Ste. 530
Northfield, IL 60093

(847)446-9460
Fax: (847)446-9470
Website: http://www.portage
ventures.com

Motorola Inc.
1303 E. Algonquin Rd.
Schaumburg, IL 60196-1065
(847)576-4929
Fax: (847)538-2250
Website: http://www.mot.com/mne

Indiana

Irwin Ventures LLC
500 Washington St.
Columbus, IN 47202
(812)373-1434
Fax: (812)376-1709
Website: http://www.irwinventures.com

Cambridge Venture Partners
4181 East 96th St., Ste. 200
Indianapolis, IN 46240
(317)814-6192
Fax: (317)944-9815

CID Equity Partners
One American Square, Ste. 2850
Box 82074
Indianapolis, IN 46282
(317)269-2350
Fax: (317)269-2355
Website: http://www.cidequity.com

Gazelle Techventures
6325 Digital Way, Ste. 460
Indianapolis, IN 46278
(317)275-6800
Fax: (317)275-1101
Website: http://www.gazellevc.com

Monument Advisors Inc.
Bank One Center/Circle
111 Monument Circle, Ste. 600
Indianapolis, IN 46204-5172
(317)656-5065
Fax: (317)656-5060
Website: http://www.monumentadv.com

MWV Capital Partners
201 N. Illinois St., Ste. 300
Indianapolis, IN 46204
(317)237-2323
Fax: (317)237-2325
Website: http://www.mwvcapital.com

First Source Capital Corp.
100 North Michigan St.
PO Box 1602
South Bend, IN 46601

(219)235-2180
Fax: (219)235-2227

Iowa

Allsop Venture Partners
118 Third Ave. SE, Ste. 837
Cedar Rapids, IA 52401
(319)368-6675
Fax: (319)363-9515

InvestAmerica Investment Advisors, Inc.
101 2nd St. SE, Ste. 800
Cedar Rapids, IA 52401
(319)363-8249
Fax: (319)363-9683

Pappajohn Capital Resources
2116 Financial Center
Des Moines, IA 50309
(515)244-5746
Fax: (515)244-2346
Website: http://www.pappajohn.com

Berthel Fisher & Company Planning Inc.
701 Tama St.
PO Box 609
Marion, IA 52302
(319)497-5700
Fax: (319)497-4244

Kansas

Enterprise Merchant Bank
7400 West 110th St., Ste. 560
Overland Park, KS 66210
(913)327-8500
Fax: (913)327-8505

Kansas Venture Capital, Inc. (Overland Park)
6700 Antioch Plz., Ste. 460
Overland Park, KS 66204
(913)262-7117
Fax: (913)262-3509
E-mail: jdalton@kvci.com

Child Health Investment Corp.
6803 W. 64th St., Ste. 208
Shawnee Mission, KS 66202
(913)262-1436
Fax: (913)262-1575
Website: http://www.chca.com

Kansas Technology Enterprise Corp.
214 SW 6th, 1st Fl.
Topeka, KS 66603-3719
(785)296-5272
Fax: (785)296-1160

E-mail: ktec@ktec.com
Website: http://www.ktec.com

Kentucky

Kentucky Highlands Investment Corp.
362 Old Whitley Rd.
London, KY 40741
(606)864-5175
Fax: (606)864-5194
Website: http://www.khic.org

Chrysalis Ventures, L.L.C.
1850 National City Tower
Louisville, KY 40202
(502)583-7644
Fax: (502)583-7648
E-mail: bobsany@chrysalisventures.com
Website: http://www.chrysalis
ventures.com

Humana Venture Capital
500 West Main St.
Louisville, KY 40202
(502)580-3922
Fax: (502)580-2051
E-mail: gemont@humana.com
George Emont, Director

Summit Capital Group, Inc.
6510 Glenridge Park Pl., Ste. 8
Louisville, KY 40222
(502)332-2700

Louisiana

Bank One Equity Investors, Inc.
451 Florida St.
Baton Rouge, LA 70801
(504)332-4421
Fax: (504)332-7377

Advantage Capital Partners
LLE Tower
909 Poydras St., Ste. 2230
New Orleans, LA 70112
(504)522-4850
Fax: (504)522-4950
Website: http://www.advantagecap.com

Maine

CEI Ventures / Coastal Ventures LP
2 Portland Fish Pier, Ste. 201
Portland, ME 04101
(207)772-5356
Fax: (207)772-5503
Website: http://www.ceiventures.com

Commwealth Bioventures, Inc.
4 Milk St.
Portland, ME 04101

(207)780-0904
Fax: (207)780-0913

Maryland

Annapolis Ventures LLC
151 West St., Ste. 302
Annapolis, MD 21401
(443)482-9555
Fax: (443)482-9565
Website: http://www.annapolis
ventures.com

Delmag Ventures
220 Wardour Dr.
Annapolis, MD 21401
(410)267-8196
Fax: (410)267-8017
Website: http://www.delmag
ventures.com

Abell Venture Fund
111 S. Calvert St., Ste. 2300
Baltimore, MD 21202
(410)547-1300
Fax: (410)539-6579
Website: http://www.abell.org

ABS Ventures (Baltimore)
1 South St., Ste. 2150
Baltimore, MD 21202
(410)895-3895
Fax: (410)895-3899
Website: http://www.absventures.com

Anthem Capital, L.P.
16 S. Calvert St., Ste. 800
Baltimore, MD 21202-1305
(410)625-1510
Fax: (410)625-1735
Website: http://www.anthemcapital.com

Catalyst Ventures
1119 St. Paul St.
Baltimore, MD 21202
(410)244-0123
Fax: (410)752-7721

Maryland Venture Capital Trust
217 E. Redwood St., Ste. 2200
Baltimore, MD 21202
(410)767-6361
Fax: (410)333-6931

New Enterprise Associates (Baltimore)
1119 St. Paul St.
Baltimore, MD 21202
(410)244-0115
Fax: (410)752-7721
Website: http://www.nea.com

T. Rowe Price Threshold Partnerships
100 E. Pratt St., 8th Fl.
Baltimore, MD 21202
(410)345-2000
Fax: (410)345-2800

Spring Capital Partners
16 W. Madison St.
Baltimore, MD 21201
(410)685-8000
Fax: (410)727-1436
E-mail: mailbox@springcap.com

Arete Corporation
3 Bethesda Metro Ctr., Ste. 770
Bethesda, MD 20814
(301)657-6268
Fax: (301)657-6254
Website: http://www.arete-
microgen.com

Embryon Capital
7903 Sleaford Place
Bethesda, MD 20814
(301)656-6837
Fax: (301)656-8056

Potomac Ventures
7920 Norfolk Ave., Ste. 1100
Bethesda, MD 20814
(301)215-9240
Website: http://www.potomac
ventures.com

Toucan Capital Corp.
3 Bethesda Metro Center, Ste. 700
Bethesda, MD 20814
(301)961-1970
Fax: (301)961-1969
Website: http://www.toucancapital.com

Kinetic Ventures LLC
2 Wisconsin Cir., Ste. 620
Chevy Chase, MD 20815
(301)652-8066
Fax: (301)652-8310
Website: http://www.kineticventures.com

Boulder Ventures Ltd.
4750 Owings Mills Blvd.
Owings Mills, MD 21117
(410)998-3114
Fax: (410)356-5492
Website: http://www.boulderventures.com

Grotech Capital Group
9690 Deereco Rd., Ste. 800
Timonium, MD 21093
(410)560-2000
Fax: (410)560-1910
Website: http://www.grotech.com

Massachusetts

Adams, Harkness & Hill, Inc.
60 State St.
Boston, MA 02109
(617)371-3900

Advent International
75 State St., 29th Fl.
Boston, MA 02109
(617)951-9400
Fax: (617)951-0566
Website: http://www.adventiner
national.com

American Research and Development
30 Federal St.
Boston, MA 02110-2508
(617)423-7500
Fax: (617)423-9655

Ascent Venture Partners
255 State St., 5th Fl.
Boston, MA 02109
(617)270-9400
Fax: (617)270-9401
E-mail: info@ascentvp.com
Website: http://www.ascentvp.com

Atlas Venture
222 Berkeley St.
Boston, MA 02116
(617)488-2200
Fax: (617)859-9292
Website: http://www.atlasventure.com

Axxon Capital
28 State St., 37th Fl.
Boston, MA 02109
(617)722-0980
Fax: (617)557-6014
Website: http://www.axxoncapital.com

BancBoston Capital/BancBoston Ventures
175 Federal St., 10th Fl.
Boston, MA 02110
(617)434-2509
Fax: (617)434-6175
Website: http://
www.bancbostoncapital.com

Boston Capital Ventures
Old City Hall
45 School St.
Boston, MA 02108
(617)227-6550
Fax: (617)227-3847
E-mail: info@bcv.com
Website: http://www.bcv.com

Boston Financial & Equity Corp.
20 Overland St.
PO Box 15071
Boston, MA 02215
(617)267-2900
Fax: (617)437-7601
E-mail: debbie@bfec.com

Boston Millennia Partners
30 Rowes Wharf
Boston, MA 02110
(617)428-5150
Fax: (617)428-5160
Website: http://www.millennia
partners.com

Bristol Investment Trust
842A Beacon St.
Boston, MA 02215-3199
(617)566-5212
Fax: (617)267-0932

Brook Venture Management LLC
50 Federal St., 5th Fl.
Boston, MA 02110
(617)451-8989
Fax: (617)451-2369
Website: http://www.brookventure.com

Burr, Egan, Deleage, and Co. (Boston)
200 Clarendon St., Ste. 3800
Boston, MA 02116
(617)262-7770
Fax: (617)262-9779

Cambridge/Samsung Partners
One Exeter Plaza
Ninth Fl.
Boston, MA 02116
(617)262-4440
Fax: (617)262-5562

Chestnut Street Partners, Inc.
75 State St., Ste. 2500
Boston, MA 02109
(617)345-7220
Fax: (617)345-7201
E-mail: chestnut@chestnutp.com

Claflin Capital Management, Inc.
10 Liberty Sq., Ste. 300
Boston, MA 02109
(617)426-6505
Fax: (617)482-0016
Website: http://www.claflincapital.com

Copley Venture Partners
99 Summer St., Ste. 1720
Boston, MA 02110
(617)737-1253
Fax: (617)439-0699

Corning Capital / Corning Technology Ventures
121 High Street, Ste. 400
Boston, MA 02110
(617)338-2656
Fax: (617)261-3864
Website: http://www.corningventures.com

Downer & Co.
211 Congress St.
Boston, MA 02110
(617)482-6200
Fax: (617)482-6201
E-mail: cdowner@downer.com
Website: http://www.downer.com

Fidelity Ventures
82 Devonshire St.
Boston, MA 02109
(617)563-6370
Fax: (617)476-9023
Website: http://www.fidelityventures.com

Greylock Management Corp. (Boston)
1 Federal St.
Boston, MA 02110-2065
(617)423-5525
Fax: (617)482-0059

Gryphon Ventures
222 Berkeley St., Ste.1600
Boston, MA 02116
(617)267-9191
Fax: (617)267-4293
E-mail: all@gryphoninc.com

Halpern, Denny & Co.
500 Boylston St.
Boston, MA 02116
(617)536-6602
Fax: (617)536-8535

Harbourvest Partners, LLC
1 Financial Center, 44th Fl.
Boston, MA 02111
(617)348-3707
Fax: (617)350-0305
Website: http://www.hvpllc.com

Highland Capital Partners
2 International Pl.
Boston, MA 02110
(617)981-1500
Fax: (617)531-1550
E-mail: info@hcp.com
Website: http://www.hcp.com

Lee Munder Venture Partners
John Hancock Tower T-53
200 Clarendon St.
Boston, MA 02103

(617)380-5600
Fax: (617)380-5601
Website: http://www.leemunder.com

M/C Venture Partners
75 State St., Ste. 2500
Boston, MA 02109
(617)345-7200
Fax: (617)345-7201
Website: http://www.mcventure
partners.com

Massachusetts Capital Resources Co.
420 Boylston St.
Boston, MA 02116
(617)536-3900
Fax: (617)536-7930

Massachusetts Technology Development Corp. (MTDC)
148 State St.
Boston, MA 02109
(617)723-4920
Fax: (617)723-5983
E-mail: jhodgman@mtdc.com
Website: http://www.mtdc.com

New England Partners
One Boston Place, Ste. 2100
Boston, MA 02108
(617)624-8400
Fax: (617)624-8999
Website: http://www.nepartners.com

North Hill Ventures
Ten Post Office Square
11th Fl.
Boston, MA 02109
(617)788-2112
Fax: (617)788-2152
Website: http://www.northhill
ventures.com

OneLiberty Ventures
150 Cambridge Park Dr.
Boston, MA 02140
(617)492-7280
Fax: (617)492-7290
Website: http://www.oneliberty.com

Schroder Ventures
Life Sciences
60 State St., Ste. 3650
Boston, MA 02109
(617)367-8100
Fax: (617)367-1590
Website: http://www.shroderventures.com

Shawmut Capital Partners
75 Federal St., 18th Fl.
Boston, MA 02110

(617)368-4900
Fax: (617)368-4910
Website: http://www.shawmutcapital.com

Solstice Capital LLC
15 Broad St., 3rd Fl.
Boston, MA 02109
(617)523-7733
Fax: (617)523-5827
E-mail: solticecapital@solcap.com

Spectrum Equity Investors
One International Pl., 29th Fl.
Boston, MA 02110
(617)464-4600
Fax: (617)464-4601
Website: http://www.spectrumequity.com

Spray Venture Partners
One Walnut St.
Boston, MA 02108
(617)305-4140
Fax: (617)305-4144
Website: http://www.sprayventure.com

The Still River Fund
100 Federal St., 29th Fl.
Boston, MA 02110
(617)348-2327
Fax: (617)348-2371
Website: http://www.stillriverfund.com

Summit Partners
600 Atlantic Ave., Ste. 2800
Boston, MA 02210-2227
(617)824-1000
Fax: (617)824-1159
Website: http://www.summitpartners.com

TA Associates, Inc. (Boston)
High Street Tower
125 High St., Ste. 2500
Boston, MA 02110
(617)574-6700
Fax: (617)574-6728
Website: http://www.ta.com

TVM Techno Venture Management
101 Arch St., Ste. 1950
Boston, MA 02110
(617)345-9320
Fax: (617)345-9377
E-mail: info@tvmvc.com
Website: http://www.tvmvc.com

UNC Ventures
64 Burough St.
Boston, MA 02130-4017
(617)482-7070
Fax: (617)522-2176

Venture Investment Management Company (VIMAC)
177 Milk St.
Boston, MA 02190-3410
(617)292-3300
Fax: (617)292-7979
E-mail: bzeisig@vimac.com
Website: http://www.vimac.com

MDT Advisers, Inc.
125 Cambridge Park Dr.
Cambridge, MA 02140-2314
(617)234-2200
Fax: (617)234-2210
Website: http://www.mdtai.com

TTC Ventures
One Main St., 6th Fl.
Cambridge, MA 02142
(617)528-3137
Fax: (617)577-1715
E-mail: info@ttcventures.com

Zero Stage Capital Co. Inc.
101 Main St., 17th Fl.
Cambridge, MA 02142
(617)876-5355
Fax: (617)876-1248
Website: http://www.zerostage.com

Atlantic Capital
164 Cushing Hwy.
Cohasset, MA 02025
(617)383-9449
Fax: (617)383-6040
E-mail: info@atlanticcap.com
Website: http://www.atlanticcap.com

Seacoast Capital Partners
55 Ferncroft Rd.
Danvers, MA 01923
(978)750-1300
Fax: (978)750-1301
E-mail: gdeli@seacoastcapital.com
Website: http://www.seacoast capital.com

Sage Management Group
44 South Street
PO Box 2026
East Dennis, MA 02641
(508)385-7172
Fax: (508)385-7272
E-mail: sagemgt@capecod.net

Applied Technology
1 Cranberry Hill
Lexington, MA 02421-7397
(617)862-8622
Fax: (617)862-8367

Royalty Capital Management
5 Downing Rd.
Lexington, MA 02421-6918
(781)861-8490

Argo Global Capital
210 Broadway, Ste. 101
Lynnfield, MA 01940
(781)592-5250
Fax: (781)592-5230
Website: http://www.gsmcapital.com

Industry Ventures
6 Bayne Lane
Newburyport, MA 01950
(978)499-7606
Fax: (978)499-0686
Website: http://www.industryventures.com

Softbank Capital Partners
10 Langley Rd., Ste. 202
Newton Center, MA 02459
(617)928-9300
Fax: (617)928-9305
E-mail: clax@bvc.com

Advanced Technology Ventures (Boston)
281 Winter St., Ste. 350
Waltham, MA 02451
(781)290-0707
Fax: (781)684-0045
E-mail: info@atvcapital.com
Website: http://www.atvcapital.com

Castile Ventures
890 Winter St., Ste. 140
Waltham, MA 02451
(781)890-0060
Fax: (781)890-0065
Website: http://www.castileventures.com

Charles River Ventures
1000 Winter St., Ste. 3300
Waltham, MA 02451
(781)487-7060
Fax: (781)487-7065
Website: http://www.crv.com

Comdisco Venture Group (Waltham)
Totton Pond Office Center
400-1 Totten Pond Rd.
Waltham, MA 02451
(617)672-0250
Fax: (617)398-8099

Marconi Ventures
890 Winter St., Ste. 310
Waltham, MA 02451
(781)839-7177

Fax: (781)522-7477
Website: http://www.marconi.com

Matrix Partners
Bay Colony Corporate Center
1000 Winter St., Ste.4500
Waltham, MA 02451
(781)890-2244
Fax: (781)890-2288
Website: http://www.matrix partners.com

North Bridge Venture Partners
950 Winter St. Ste. 4600
Waltham, MA 02451
(781)290-0004
Fax: (781)290-0999
E-mail: eta@nbvp.com

Polaris Venture Partners
Bay Colony Corporate Ctr.
1000 Winter St., Ste. 3500
Waltham, MA 02451
(781)290-0770
Fax: (781)290-0880
E-mail: partners@polarisventures.com
Website: http://www.polar isventures.com

Seaflower Ventures
Bay Colony Corporate Ctr.
1000 Winter St. Ste. 1000
Waltham, MA 02451
(781)466-9552
Fax: (781)466-9553
E-mail: moot@seaflower.com
Website: http://www.seaflower.com

Ampersand Ventures
55 William St., Ste. 240
Wellesley, MA 02481
(617)239-0700
Fax: (617)239-0824
E-mail: info@ampersandventures.com
Website: http://www.ampersand ventures.com

Battery Ventures (Boston)
20 William St., Ste. 200
Wellesley, MA 02481
(781)577-1000
Fax: (781)577-1001
Website: http://www.battery.com

Commonwealth Capital Ventures, L.P.
20 William St., Ste.225
Wellesley, MA 02481
(781)237-7373
Fax: (781)235-8627
Website: http://www.ccvlp.com

Fowler, Anthony & Company
20 Walnut St.
Wellesley, MA 02481
(781)237-4201
Fax: (781)237-7718

Gemini Investors
20 William St.
Wellesley, MA 02481
(781)237-7001
Fax: (781)237-7233

Grove Street Advisors Inc.
20 William St., Ste. 230
Wellesley, MA 02481
(781)263-6100
Fax: (781)263-6101
Website: http://www.groves
treetadvisors.com

Mees Pierson Investeringsmaat B.V.
20 William St., Ste. 210
Wellesley, MA 02482
(781)239-7600
Fax: (781)239-0377

Norwest Equity Partners
40 William St., Ste. 305
Wellesley, MA 02481-3902
(781)237-5870
Fax: (781)237-6270
Website: http://www.norwestvp.com

Bessemer Venture Partners (Wellesley Hills)
83 Walnut St.
Wellesley Hills, MA 02481
(781)237-6050
Fax: (781)235-7576
E-mail: travis@bvpny.com
Website: http://www.bvp.com

Venture Capital Fund of New England
20 Walnut St., Ste. 120
Wellesley Hills, MA 02481-2175
(781)239-8262
Fax: (781)239-8263

Prism Venture Partners
100 Lowder Brook Dr., Ste. 2500
Westwood, MA 02090
(781)302-4000
Fax: (781)302-4040
E-mail: dwbaum@prismventure.com

Palmer Partners LP
200 Unicorn Park Dr.
Woburn, MA 01801
(781)933-5445
Fax: (781)933-0698

Michigan

Arbor Partners, L.L.C.
130 South First St.
Ann Arbor, MI 48104
(734)668-9000
Fax: (734)669-4195
Website: http://www.arborpartners.com

EDF Ventures
425 N. Main St.
Ann Arbor, MI 48104
(734)663-3213
Fax: (734)663-7358
E-mail: edf@edfvc.com
Website: http://www.edfvc.com

White Pines Management, L.L.C.
2401 Plymouth Rd., Ste. B
Ann Arbor, MI 48105
(734)747-9401
Fax: (734)747-9704
E-mail: ibund@whitepines.com
Website: http://www.whitepines.com

Wellmax, Inc.
3541 Bendway Blvd., Ste. 100
Bloomfield Hills, MI 48301
(248)646-3554
Fax: (248)646-6220

Venture Funding, Ltd.
Fisher Bldg.
3011 West Grand Blvd., Ste. 321
Detroit, MI 48202
(313)871-3606
Fax: (313)873-4935

Investcare Partners L.P. / GMA Capital LLC
32330 W. Twelve Mile Rd.
Farmington Hills, MI 48334
(248)489-9000
Fax: (248)489-8819
E-mail: gma@gmacapital.com
Website: http://www.gmacapital.com

Liberty Bidco Investment Corp.
30833 Northwestern Highway, Ste. 211
Farmington Hills, MI 48334
(248)626-6070
Fax: (248)626-6072

Seaflower Ventures
5170 Nicholson Rd.
PO Box 474
Fowlerville, MI 48836
(517)223-3335
Fax: (517)223-3337
E-mail: gibbons@seaflower.com
Website: http://www.seaflower.com

Ralph Wilson Equity Fund LLC
15400 E. Jefferson Ave.
Gross Pointe Park, MI 48230
(313)821-9122
Fax: (313)821-9101
Website: http://www.Ralph
WilsonEquityFund.com
J. Skip Simms, President

Minnesota

Development Corp. of Austin
1900 Eighth Ave., NW
Austin, MN 55912
(507)433-0346
Fax: (507)433-0361
E-mail: dca@smig.net
Website: http://www.spamtownusa.com

Northeast Ventures Corp.
802 Alworth Bldg.
Duluth, MN 55802
(218)722-9915
Fax: (218)722-9871

Medical Innovation Partners, Inc.
6450 City West Pkwy.
Eden Prairie, MN 55344-3245
(612)828-9616
Fax: (612)828-9596

St. Paul Venture Capital, Inc.
10400 Vicking Dr., Ste. 550
Eden Prairie, MN 55344
(612)995-7474
Fax: (612)995-7475
Website: http://www.stpaulvc.com

Cherry Tree Investments, Inc.
7601 France Ave. S, Ste. 150
Edina, MN 55435
(612)893-9012
Fax: (612)893-9036
Website: http://www.cherrytree.com

Shared Ventures, Inc.
6550 York Ave. S
Edina, MN 55435
(612)925-3411

Sherpa Partners LLC
5050 Lincoln Dr., Ste. 490
Edina, MN 55436
(952)942-1070
Fax: (952)942-1071
Website: http://www.sherpapartners.com

Affinity Capital Management
901 Marquette Ave., Ste. 1810
Minneapolis, MN 55402
(612)252-9900

Fax: (612)252-9911
Website: http://www.affinitycapital.com

Artesian Capital
1700 Foshay Tower
821 Marquette Ave.
Minneapolis, MN 55402
(612)334-5600
Fax: (612)334-5601
E-mail: artesian@artesian.com

Coral Ventures
60 S. 6th St., Ste. 3510
Minneapolis, MN 55402
(612)335-8666
Fax: (612)335-8668
Website: http://www.coralventures.com

Crescendo Venture Management, L.L.C.
800 LaSalle Ave., Ste. 2250
Minneapolis, MN 55402
(612)607-2800
Fax: (612)607-2801
Website: http://www.crescendo
ventures.com

Gideon Hixon Venture
1900 Foshay Tower
821 Marquette Ave.
Minneapolis, MN 55402
(612)904-2314
Fax: (612)204-0913

Norwest Equity Partners
3600 IDS Center
80 S. 8th St.
Minneapolis, MN 55402
(612)215-1600
Fax: (612)215-1601
Website: http://www.norwestvp.com

Oak Investment Partners (Minneapolis)
4550 Norwest Center
90 S. 7th St.
Minneapolis, MN 55402
(612)339-9322
Fax: (612)337-8017
Website: http://www.oakinv.com

Pathfinder Venture Capital Funds (Minneapolis)
7300 Metro Blvd., Ste. 585
Minneapolis, MN 55439
(612)835-1121
Fax: (612)835-8389
E-mail: jahrens620@aol.com

U.S. Bancorp Piper Jaffray Ventures, Inc.
800 Nicollet Mall, Ste. 800
Minneapolis, MN 55402

(612)303-5686
Fax: (612)303-1350
Website: http://www.paperjaffrey
ventures.com

The Food Fund, Ltd. Partnership
5720 Smatana Dr., Ste. 300
Minnetonka, MN 55343
(612)939-3950
Fax: (612)939-8106

Mayo Medical Ventures
200 First St. SW
Rochester, MN 55905
(507)266-4586
Fax: (507)284-5410
Website: http://www.mayo.edu

Missouri

Bankers Capital Corp.
3100 Gillham Rd.
Kansas City, MO 64109
(816)531-1600
Fax: (816)531-1334

Capital for Business, Inc. (Kansas City)
1000 Walnut St., 18th Fl.
Kansas City, MO 64106
(816)234-2357
Fax: (816)234-2952
Website: http://
www.capitalforbusiness.com

De Vries & Co. Inc.
800 West 47th St.
Kansas City, MO 64112
(816)756-0055
Fax: (816)756-0061

InvestAmerica Venture Group Inc. (Kansas City)
Commerce Tower
911 Main St., Ste. 2424
Kansas City, MO 64105
(816)842-0114
Fax: (816)471-7339

Kansas City Equity Partners
233 W. 47th St.
Kansas City, MO 64112
(816)960-1771
Fax: (816)960-1777
Website: http://www.kcep.com

Bome Investors, Inc.
8000 Maryland Ave., Ste. 1190
St. Louis, MO 63105
(314)721-5707
Fax: (314)721-5135

Website: http://www.gateway
ventures.com

Capital for Business, Inc. (St. Louis)
11 S. Meramac St., Ste. 1430
St. Louis, MO 63105
(314)746-7427
Fax: (314)746-8739
Website: http://www.capitalfor
business.com

Crown Capital Corp.
540 Maryville Centre Dr., Ste. 120
Saint Louis, MO 63141
(314)576-1201
Fax: (314)576-1525
Website: http://www.crown-
cap.com

Gateway Associates L.P.
8000 Maryland Ave., Ste. 1190
St. Louis, MO 63105
(314)721-5707
Fax: (314)721-5135

Harbison Corp.
8112 Maryland Ave., Ste. 250
Saint Louis, MO 63105
(314)727-8200
Fax: (314)727-0249

Heartland Capital Fund, Ltd.
PO Box 642117
Omaha, NE 68154
(402)778-5124
Fax: (402)445-2370
Website: http://www.heartland
capitalfund.com

Odin Capital Group
1625 Farnam St., Ste. 700
Omaha, NE 68102
(402)346-6200
Fax: (402)342-9311
Website: http://www.odincapital.com

Nevada

Edge Capital Investment Co. LLC
1350 E. Flamingo Rd., Ste. 3000
Las Vegas, NV 89119
(702)438-3343
E-mail: info@edgecapital.net
Website: http://www.edgecapital.net

The Benefit Capital Companies Inc.
PO Box 542
Logandale, NV 89021
(702)398-3222
Fax: (702)398-3700

Millennium Three Venture Group LLC
6880 South McCarran Blvd., Ste. A-11
Reno, NV 89509
(775)954-2020
Fax: (775)954-2023
Website: http://www.m3vg.com

New Jersey

Alan I. Goldman & Associates
497 Ridgewood Ave.
Glen Ridge, NJ 07028
(973)857-5680
Fax: (973)509-8856

CS Capital Partners LLC
328 Second St., Ste. 200
Lakewood, NJ 08701
(732)901-1111
Fax: (212)202-5071
Website: http://www.cs-capital.com

Edison Venture Fund
1009 Lenox Dr., Ste. 4
Lawrenceville, NJ 08648
(609)896-1900
Fax: (609)896-0066
E-mail: info@edisonventure.com
Website: http://www.edisonventure.com

Tappan Zee Capital Corp. (New Jersey)
201 Lower Notch Rd.
PO Box 416
Little Falls, NJ 07424
(973)256-8280
Fax: (973)256-2841

The CIT Group/Venture Capital, Inc.
650 CIT Dr.
Livingston, NJ 07039
(973)740-5429
Fax: (973)740-5555
Website: http://www.cit.com

Capital Express, L.L.C.
1100 Valleybrook Ave.
Lyndhurst, NJ 07071
(201)438-8228
Fax: (201)438-5131
E-mail: niles@capitalexpress.com
Website: http://www.capitalexpress.com

Westford Technology Ventures, L.P.
17 Academy St.
Newark, NJ 07102
(973)624-2131
Fax: (973)624-2008

Accel Partners
1 Palmer Sq.
Princeton, NJ 08542

(609)683-4500
Fax: (609)683-4880
Website: http://www.accel.com

Cardinal Partners
221 Nassau St.
Princeton, NJ 08542
(609)924-6452
Fax: (609)683-0174
Website: http://www.cardinal
healthpartners.com

Domain Associates L.L.C.
One Palmer Sq., Ste. 515
Princeton, NJ 08542
(609)683-5656
Fax: (609)683-9789
Website: http://www.domainvc.com

Johnston Associates, Inc.
181 Cherry Valley Rd.
Princeton, NJ 08540
(609)924-3131
Fax: (609)683-7524
E-mail: jaincorp@aol.com

Kemper Ventures
Princeton Forrestal Village
155 Village Blvd.
Princeton, NJ 08540
(609)936-3035
Fax: (609)936-3051

Penny Lane Parnters
One Palmer Sq., Ste. 309
Princeton, NJ 08542
(609)497-4646
Fax: (609)497-0611

Early Stage Enterprises L.P.
995 Route 518
Skillman, NJ 08558
(609)921-8896
Fax: (609)921-8703
Website: http://www.esevc.com

MBW Management Inc.
1 Springfield Ave.
Summit, NJ 07901
(908)273-4060
Fax: (908)273-4430

BCI Advisors, Inc.
Glenpointe Center W.
Teaneck, NJ 07666
(201)836-3900
Fax: (201)836-6368
E-mail: info@bciadvisors.com
Website: http://www.bci
partners.com

**Demuth, Folger & Wetherill / DFW
Capital Partners**
Glenpointe Center E., 5th Fl.
300 Frank W. Burr Blvd.
Teaneck, NJ 07666
(201)836-2233
Fax: (201)836-5666
Website: http://www.dfwcapital.com

First Princeton Capital Corp.
189 Berdan Ave., No. 131
Wayne, NJ 07470-3233
(973)278-3233
Fax: (973)278-4290
Website: http://www.lytellcatt.net

Edelson Technology Partners
300 Tice Blvd.
Woodcliff Lake, NJ 07675
(201)930-9898
Fax: (201)930-8899
Website: http://www.edelsontech.com

New Mexico

Bruce F. Glaspell & Associates
10400 Academy Rd. NE, Ste. 313
Albuquerque, NM 87111
(505)292-4505
Fax: (505)292-4258

High Desert Ventures, Inc.
6101 Imparata St. NE, Ste. 1721
Albuquerque, NM 87111
(505)797-3330
Fax: (505)338-5147

New Business Capital Fund, Ltd.
5805 Torreon NE
Albuquerque, NM 87109
(505)822-8445

SBC Ventures
10400 Academy Rd. NE, Ste. 313
Albuquerque, NM 87111
(505)292-4505
Fax: (505)292-4528

Technology Ventures Corp.
1155 University Blvd. SE
Albuquerque, NM 87106
(505)246-2882
Fax: (505)246-2891

New York

**New York State Science & Technology
Foundation
Small Business Technology Investment
Fund**
99 Washington Ave., Ste. 1731
Albany, NY 12210

(518)473-9741
Fax: (518)473-6876

Rand Capital Corp.
2200 Rand Bldg.
Buffalo, NY 14203
(716)853-0802
Fax: (716)854-8480
Website: http://www.randcapital.com

Seed Capital Partners
620 Main St.
Buffalo, NY 14202
(716)845-7520
Fax: (716)845-7539
Website: http://www.seedcp.com

Coleman Venture Group
5909 Northern Blvd.
PO Box 224
East Norwich, NY 11732
(516)626-3642
Fax: (516)626-9722

Vega Capital Corp.
45 Knollwood Rd.
Elmsford, NY 10523
(914)345-9500
Fax: (914)345-9505

Herbert Young Securities, Inc.
98 Cuttermill Rd.
Great Neck, NY 11021
(516)487-8300
Fax: (516)487-8319

Sterling/Carl Marks Capital, Inc.
175 Great Neck Rd., Ste. 408
Great Neck, NY 11021
(516)482-7374
Fax: (516)487-0781
E-mail: stercrlmar@aol.com
Website: http://www.serling
carlmarks.com

Impex Venture Management Co.
PO Box 1570
Green Island, NY 12183
(518)271-8008
Fax: (518)271-9101

Corporate Venture Partners L.P.
200 Sunset Park
Ithaca, NY 14850
(607)257-6323
Fax: (607)257-6128

Arthur P. Gould & Co.
One Wilshire Dr.
Lake Success, NY 11020
(516)773-3000
Fax: (516)773-3289

Dauphin Capital Partners
108 Forest Ave.
Locust Valley, NY 11560
(516)759-3339
Fax: (516)759-3322
Website: http://www.dauphincapital.com

550 Digital Media Ventures
555 Madison Ave., 10th Fl.
New York, NY 10022
Website: http://www.550dmv.com

Aberlyn Capital Management Co., Inc.
500 Fifth Ave.
New York, NY 10110
(212)391-7750
Fax: (212)391-7762

Adler & Company
342 Madison Ave., Ste. 807
New York, NY 10173
(212)599-2535
Fax: (212)599-2526

Alimansky Capital Group, Inc.
605 Madison Ave., Ste. 300
New York, NY 10022-1901
(212)832-7300
Fax: (212)832-7338

Allegra Partners
515 Madison Ave., 29th Fl.
New York, NY 10022
(212)826-9080
Fax: (212)759-2561

The Argentum Group
The Chyrsler Bldg.
405 Lexington Ave.
New York, NY 10174
(212)949-6262
Fax: (212)949-8294
Website: http://www.argentum
group.com

Axavision Inc.
14 Wall St., 26th Fl.
New York, NY 10005
(212)619-4000
Fax: (212)619-7202

Bedford Capital Corp.
18 East 48th St., Ste. 1800
New York, NY 10017
(212)688-5700
Fax: (212)754-4699
E-mail: info@bedfordnyc.com
Website: http://www.bedfordnyc.com

Bloom & Co.
950 Third Ave.

New York, NY 10022
(212)838-1858
Fax: (212)838-1843

Bristol Capital Management
300 Park Ave., 17th Fl.
New York, NY 10022
(212)572-6306
Fax: (212)705-4292

**Citicorp Venture Capital Ltd.
(New York City)**
399 Park Ave., 14th Fl.
Zone 4
New York, NY 10043
(212)559-1127
Fax: (212)888-2940

CM Equity Partners
135 E. 57th St.
New York, NY 10022
(212)909-8428
Fax: (212)980-2630

Cohen & Co., L.L.C.
800 Third Ave.
New York, NY 10022
(212)317-2250
Fax: (212)317-2255
E-mail: nlcohen@aol.com

Cornerstone Equity Investors, L.L.C.
717 5th Ave., Ste. 1100
New York, NY 10022
(212)753-0901
Fax: (212)826-6798
Website: http://www.cornerstone-
equity.com

CW Group, Inc.
1041 3rd Ave., 2nd fl.
New York, NY 10021
(212)308-5266
Fax: (212)644-0354
Website: http://www.cwventures.com

DH Blair Investment Banking Corp.
44 Wall St., 2nd Fl.
New York, NY 10005
(212)495-5000
Fax: (212)269-1438

Dresdner Kleinwort Capital
75 Wall St.
New York, NY 10005
(212)429-3131
Fax: (212)429-3139
Website: http://www.dresdnerkb.com

East River Ventures, L.P.
645 Madison Ave., 22nd Fl.

New York, NY 10022
(212)644-2322
Fax: (212)644-5498

Easton Hunt Capital Partners
641 Lexington Ave., 21st Fl.
New York, NY 10017
(212)702-0950
Fax: (212)702-0952
Website: http://www.eastoncapital.com

Elk Associates Funding Corp.
747 3rd Ave., Ste. 4C
New York, NY 10017
(212)355-2449
Fax: (212)759-3338

EOS Partners, L.P.
320 Park Ave., 22nd Fl.
New York, NY 10022
(212)832-5800
Fax: (212)832-5815
E-mail: mfirst@eospartners.com
Website: http://www.eospartners.com

Euclid Partners
45 Rockefeller Plaza, Ste. 3240
New York, NY 10111
(212)218-6880
Fax: (212)218-6877
E-mail: graham@euclidpartners.com
Website: http://www.euclidpartners.com

Evergreen Capital Partners, Inc.
150 East 58th St.
New York, NY 10155
(212)813-0758
Fax: (212)813-0754

Exeter Capital L.P.
10 E. 53rd St.
New York, NY 10022
(212)872-1172
Fax: (212)872-1198
E-mail: exeter@usa.net

Financial Technology Research Corp.
518 Broadway
Penthouse
New York, NY 10012
(212)625-9100
Fax: (212)431-0300
E-mail: fintek@financier.com

4C Ventures
237 Park Ave., Ste. 801
New York, NY 10017
(212)692-3680
Fax: (212)692-3685
Website: http://www.4cventures.com

Fusient Ventures
99 Park Ave., 20th Fl.
New York, NY 10016
(212)972-8999
Fax: (212)972-9876
E-mail: info@fusient.com
Website: http://www.fusient.com

Generation Capital Partners
551 Fifth Ave., Ste. 3100
New York, NY 10176
(212)450-8507
Fax: (212)450-8550
Website: http://www.genpartners.com

Golub Associates, Inc.
555 Madison Ave.
New York, NY 10022
(212)750-6060
Fax: (212)750-5505

Hambro America Biosciences Inc.
650 Madison Ave., 21st Floor
New York, NY 10022
(212)223-7400
Fax: (212)223-0305

Hanover Capital Corp.
505 Park Ave., 15th Fl.
New York, NY 10022
(212)755-1222
Fax: (212)935-1787

Harvest Partners, Inc.
280 Park Ave, 33rd Fl.
New York, NY 10017
(212)559-6300
Fax: (212)812-0100
Website: http://www.harvpart.com

Holding Capital Group, Inc.
10 E. 53rd St., 30th Fl.
New York, NY 10022
(212)486-6670
Fax: (212)486-0843

Hudson Venture Partners
660 Madison Ave., 14th Fl.
New York, NY 10021-8405
(212)644-9797
Fax: (212)644-7430
Website: http://www.hudsonptr.com

IBJS Capital Corp.
1 State St., 9th Fl.
New York, NY 10004
(212)858-2018
Fax: (212)858-2768

InterEquity Capital Partners, L.P.
220 5th Ave.
New York, NY 10001

(212)779-2022
Fax: (212)779-2103
Website: http://www.interequity-capital.com

The Jordan Edmiston Group Inc.
150 East 52nd St., 18th Fl.
New York, NY 10022
(212)754-0710
Fax: (212)754-0337

Josephberg, Grosz and Co., Inc.
633 3rd Ave., 13th Fl.
New York, NY 10017
(212)974-9926
Fax: (212)397-5832

J.P. Morgan Capital Corp.
60 Wall St.
New York, NY 10260-0060
(212)648-9000
Fax: (212)648-5002
Website: http://www.jpmorgan.com

The Lambda Funds
380 Lexington Ave., 54th Fl.
New York, NY 10168
(212)682-3454
Fax: (212)682-9231

Lepercq Capital Management Inc.
1675 Broadway
New York, NY 10019
(212)698-0795
Fax: (212)262-0155

Loeb Partners Corp.
61 Broadway, Ste. 2400
New York, NY 10006
(212)483-7000
Fax: (212)574-2001

Madison Investment Partners
660 Madison Ave.
New York, NY 10021
(212)223-2600
Fax: (212)223-8208

MC Capital Inc.
520 Madison Ave., 16th Fl.
New York, NY 10022
(212)644-0841
Fax: (212)644-2926

McCown, De Leeuw and Co. (New York)
65 E. 55th St., 36th Fl.
New York, NY 10022
(212)355-5500
Fax: (212)355-6283
Website: http://www.mdcpartners.com

Morgan Stanley Venture Partners
1221 Avenue of the Americas, 33rd Fl.
New York, NY 10020
(212)762-7900
Fax: (212)762-8424
E-mail: msventures@ms.com
Website: http://www.msvp.com

Nazem and Co.
645 Madison Ave., 12th Fl.
New York, NY 10022
(212)371-7900
Fax: (212)371-2150

Needham Capital Management, L.L.C.
445 Park Ave.
New York, NY 10022
(212)371-8300
Fax: (212)705-0299
Website: http://www.needhamco.com

Norwood Venture Corp.
1430 Broadway, Ste. 1607
New York, NY 10018
(212)869-5075
Fax: (212)869-5331
E-mail: nvc@mail.idt.net
Website: http://www.norven.com

Noveltek Venture Corp.
521 Fifth Ave., Ste. 1700
New York, NY 10175
(212)286-1963

Paribas Principal, Inc.
787 7th Ave.
New York, NY 10019
(212)841-2005
Fax: (212)841-3558

**Patricof & Co. Ventures, Inc.
(New York)**
445 Park Ave.
New York, NY 10022
(212)753-6300
Fax: (212)319-6155
Website: http://www.patricof.com

The Platinum Group, Inc.
350 Fifth Ave, Ste. 7113
New York, NY 10118
(212)736-4300
Fax: (212)736-6086
Website: http://www.platinumgroup.com

Pomona Capital
780 Third Ave., 28th Fl.
New York, NY 10017
(212)593-3639
Fax: (212)593-3987
Website: http://www.pomonacapital.com

Prospect Street Ventures
10 East 40th St., 44th Fl.
New York, NY 10016
(212)448-0702
Fax: (212)448-9652
E-mail: wkohler@prospectstreet.com
Website: http://www.prospectstreet.com

Regent Capital Management
505 Park Ave., Ste. 1700
New York, NY 10022
(212)735-9900
Fax: (212)735-9908

Rothschild Ventures, Inc.
1251 Avenue of the Americas, 51st Fl.
New York, NY 10020
(212)403-3500
Fax: (212)403-3652
Website: http://www.nmrothschild.com

Sandler Capital Management
767 Fifth Ave., 45th Fl.
New York, NY 10153
(212)754-8100
Fax: (212)826-0280

Siguler Guff & Company
630 Fifth Ave., 16th Fl.
New York, NY 10111
(212)332-5100
Fax: (212)332-5120

Spencer Trask Ventures Inc.
535 Madison Ave.
New York, NY 10022
(212)355-5565
Fax: (212)751-3362
Website: http://www.spencertrask.com

Sprout Group (New York City)
277 Park Ave.
New York, NY 10172
(212)892-3600
Fax: (212)892-3444
E-mail: info@sproutgroup.com
Website: http://www.sproutgroup.com

US Trust Private Equity
114 W.47th St.
New York, NY 10036
(212)852-3949
Fax: (212)852-3759
Website: http://www.ustrust.com/
privateequity

Vencon Management Inc.
301 West 53rd St., Ste. 10F
New York, NY 10019
(212)581-8787
Fax: (212)397-4126
Website: http://www.venconinc.com

Venrock Associates
30 Rockefeller Plaza, Ste. 5508
New York, NY 10112
(212)649-5600
Fax: (212)649-5788
Website: http://www.venrock.com

Venture Capital Fund of America, Inc.
509 Madison Ave., Ste. 812
New York, NY 10022
(212)838-5577
Fax: (212)838-7614
E-mail: mail@vcfa.com
Website: http://www.vcfa.com

Venture Opportunities Corp.
150 E. 58th St.
New York, NY 10155
(212)832-3737
Fax: (212)980-6603

Warburg Pincus Ventures, Inc.
466 Lexington Ave., 11th Fl.
New York, NY 10017
(212)878-9309
Fax: (212)878-9200
Website: http://www.warburgpincus.com

Wasserstein, Perella & Co. Inc.
31 W. 52nd St., 27th Fl.
New York, NY 10019
(212)702-5691
Fax: (212)969-7879

Welsh, Carson, Anderson, & Stowe
320 Park Ave., Ste. 2500
New York, NY 10022-6815
(212)893-9500
Fax: (212)893-9575

Whitney and Co. (New York)
630 Fifth Ave. Ste. 3225
New York, NY 10111
(212)332-2400
Fax: (212)332-2422
Website: http://www.jhwitney.com

Winthrop Ventures
74 Trinity Place, Ste. 600
New York, NY 10006
(212)422-0100

The Pittsford Group
8 Lodge Pole Rd.
Pittsford, NY 14534
(716)223-3523

Genesee Funding
70 Linden Oaks, 3rd Fl.
Rochester, NY 14625
(716)383-5550
Fax: (716)383-5305

Gabelli Multimedia Partners
One Corporate Center
Rye, NY 10580
(914)921-5395
Fax: (914)921-5031

Stamford Financial
108 Main St.
Stamford, NY 12167
(607)652-3311
Fax: (607)652-6301
Website: http://www.stamford
financial.com

Northwood Ventures LLC
485 Underhill Blvd., Ste. 205
Syosset, NY 11791
(516)364-5544
Fax: (516)364-0879
E-mail: northwood@northwood.com
Website: http://www.north
woodventures.com

Exponential Business Development Co.
216 Walton St.
Syracuse, NY 13202-1227
(315)474-4500
Fax: (315)474-4682
E-mail: dirksonn@aol.com
Website: http://www.exponential-ny.com

Onondaga Venture Capital Fund Inc.
714 State Tower Bldg.
Syracuse, NY 13202
(315)478-0157
Fax: (315)478-0158

Bessemer Venture Partners (Westbury)
1400 Old Country Rd., Ste. 109
Westbury, NY 11590
(516)997-2300
Fax: (516)997-2371
E-mail: bob@bvpny.com
Website: http://www.bvp.com

Ovation Capital Partners
120 Bloomingdale Rd., 4th Fl.
White Plains, NY 10605
(914)258-0011
Fax: (914)684-0848
Website: http://www.ovation
capital.com

North Carolina

Carolinas Capital Investment Corp.
1408 Biltmore Dr.
Charlotte, NC 28207
(704)375-3888
Fax: (704)375-6226

First Union Capital Partners
1st Union Center, 12th Fl.
301 S. College St.
Charlotte, NC 28288-0732
(704)383-0000
Fax: (704)374-6711
Website: http://www.fucp.com

Frontier Capital LLC
525 North Tryon St., Ste. 1700
Charlotte, NC 28202
(704)414-2880
Fax: (704)414-2881
Website: http://www.frontierfunds.com

Kitty Hawk Capital
2700 Coltsgate Rd., Ste. 202
Charlotte, NC 28211
(704)362-3909
Fax: (704)362-2774
Website: http://www.kittyhawk
capital.com

Piedmont Venture Partners
One Morrocroft Centre
6805 Morisson Blvd., Ste. 380
Charlotte, NC 28211
(704)731-5200
Fax: (704)365-9733
Website: http://www.piedmontvp.com

Ruddick Investment Co.
1800 Two First Union Center
Charlotte, NC 28282
(704)372-5404
Fax: (704)372-6409

The Shelton Companies Inc.
3600 One First Union Center
301 S. College St.
Charlotte, NC 28202
(704)348-2200
Fax: (704)348-2260

Wakefield Group
1110 E. Morehead St.
PO Box 36329
Charlotte, NC 28236
(704)372-0355
Fax: (704)372-8216
Website: http://www.wakefiel
dgroup.com

Aurora Funds, Inc.
2525 Meridian Pkwy., Ste. 220
Durham, NC 27713
(919)484-0400
Fax: (919)484-0444
Website: http://www.aurora
funds.com

Intersouth Partners
3211 Shannon Rd., Ste. 610
Durham, NC 27707
(919)493-6640
Fax: (919)493-6649
E-mail: info@intersouth.com
Website: http://www.intersouth.com

Geneva Merchant Banking Partners
PO Box 21962
Greensboro, NC 27420
(336)275-7002
Fax: (336)275-9155
Website: http://www.geneva
merchantbank.com

The North Carolina Enterprise Fund, L.P.
3600 Glenwood Ave., Ste. 107
Raleigh, NC 27612
(919)781-2691
Fax: (919)783-9195
Website: http://www.ncef.com

Ohio

Senmend Medical Ventures
4445 Lake Forest Dr., Ste. 600
Cincinnati, OH 45242
(513)563-3264
Fax: (513)563-3261

The Walnut Group
312 Walnut St., Ste. 1151
Cincinnati, OH 45202
(513)651-3300
Fax: (513)929-4441
Website: http://www.thewal
nutgroup.com

Brantley Venture Partners
20600 Chagrin Blvd., Ste. 1150
Cleveland, OH 44122
(216)283-4800
Fax: (216)283-5324

Clarion Capital Corp.
1801 E. 9th St., Ste. 1120
Cleveland, OH 44114
(216)687-1096
Fax: (216)694-3545

Crystal Internet Venture Fund, L.P.
1120 Chester Ave., Ste. 418
Cleveland, OH 44114
(216)263-5515
Fax: (216)263-5518
E-mail: jf@crystalventure.com
Website: http://www.crystal
venture.com

Key Equity Capital Corp.
127 Public Sq., 28th Fl.
Cleveland, OH 44114
(216)689-3000
Fax: (216)689-3204
Website: http://www.keybank.com

Morgenthaler Ventures
Terminal Tower
50 Public Square, Ste. 2700
Cleveland, OH 44113
(216)416-7500
Fax: (216)416-7501
Website: http://www.morgenthaler.com

National City Equity Partners Inc.
1965 E. 6th St.
Cleveland, OH 44114
(216)575-2491
Fax: (216)575-9965
E-mail: nccap@aol.com
Website: http://www.nccapital.com

Primus Venture Partners, Inc.
5900 LanderBrook Dr., Ste. 2000
Cleveland, OH 44124-4020
(440)684-7300
Fax: (440)684-7342
E-mail: info@primusventure.com
Website: http://www.primusventure.com

Banc One Capital Partners (Columbus)
150 East Gay St., 24th Fl.
Columbus, OH 43215
(614)217-1100
Fax: (614)217-1217

Battelle Venture Partners
505 King Ave.
Columbus, OH 43201
(614)424-7005
Fax: (614)424-4874

Ohio Partners
62 E. Board St., 3rd Fl.
Columbus, OH 43215
(614)621-1210
Fax: (614)621-1240

Capital Technology Group, L.L.C.
400 Metro Place North, Ste. 300
Dublin, OH 43017
(614)792-6066
Fax: (614)792-6036
E-mail: info@capitaltech.com
Website: http://www.capitaltech.com

Northwest Ohio Venture Fund
4159 Holland-Sylvania R., Ste. 202
Toledo, OH 43623
(419)824-8144

Fax: (419)882-2035
E-mail: bwalsh@novf.com

Oklahoma

Moore & Associates
1000 W. Wilshire Blvd., Ste. 370
Oklahoma City, OK 73116
(405)842-3660
Fax: (405)842-3763

Chisholm Private Capital Partners
100 West 5th St., Ste. 805
Tulsa, OK 74103
(918)584-0440
Fax: (918)584-0441
Website: http://www.chisholmvc.com

Davis, Tuttle Venture Partners (Tulsa)
320 S. Boston, Ste. 1000
Tulsa, OK 74103-3703
(918)584-7272
Fax: (918)582-3404
Website: http://www.davistuttle.com

RBC Ventures
2627 E. 21st St.
Tulsa, OK 74114
(918)744-5607
Fax: (918)743-8630

Oregon

Utah Ventures II LP
10700 SW Beaverton-Hillsdale Hwy.,
Ste. 548
Beaverton, OR 97005
(503)574-4125
E-mail: adishlip@uven.com
Website: http://www.uven.com

Orien Ventures
14523 SW Westlake Dr.
Lake Oswego, OR 97035
(503)699-1680
Fax: (503)699-1681

OVP Venture Partners (Lake Oswego)
340 Oswego Pointe Dr., Ste. 200
Lake Oswego, OR 97034
(503)697-8766
Fax: (503)697-8863
E-mail: info@ovp.com
Website: http://www.ovp.com

**Oregon Resource and Technology
Development Fund**
4370 NE Halsey St., Ste. 233
Portland, OR 97213-1566
(503)282-4462
Fax: (503)282-2976

Shaw Venture Partners
400 SW 6th Ave., Ste. 1100
Portland, OR 97204-1636
(503)228-4884
Fax: (503)227-2471
Website: http://www.shawventures.com

Pennsylvania

Mid-Atlantic Venture Funds
125 Goodman Dr.
Bethlehem, PA 18015
(610)865-6550
Fax: (610)865-6427
Website: http://www.mavf.com

Newspring Ventures
100 W. Elm St., Ste. 101
Conshohocken, PA 19428
(610)567-2380
Fax: (610)567-2388
Website: http://www.news
printventures.com

Patricof & Co. Ventures, Inc.
455 S. Gulph Rd., Ste. 410
King of Prussia, PA 19406
(610)265-0286
Fax: (610)265-4959
Website: http://www.patricof.com

Loyalhanna Venture Fund
527 Cedar Way, Ste. 104
Oakmont, PA 15139
(412)820-7035
Fax: (412)820-7036

Innovest Group Inc.
2000 Market St., Ste. 1400
Philadelphia, PA 19103
(215)564-3960
Fax: (215)569-3272

**Keystone Venture Capital
Management Co.**
1601 Market St., Ste. 2500
Philadelphia, PA 19103
(215)241-1200
Fax: (215)241-1211
Website: http://www.keystonevc.com

Liberty Venture Partners
2005 Market St., Ste. 200
Philadelphia, PA 19103
(215)282-4484
Fax: (215)282-4485
E-mail: info@libertyvp.com
Website: http://www.libertyvp.com

Penn Janney Fund, Inc.
1801 Market St., 11th Fl.
Philadelphia, PA 19103

(215)665-4447
Fax: (215)557-0820

Philadelphia Ventures, Inc.
The Bellevue
200 S. Broad St.
Philadelphia, PA 19102
(215)732-4445
Fax: (215)732-4644

Birchmere Ventures Inc.
2000 Technology Dr.
Pittsburgh, PA 15219-3109
(412)803-8000
Fax: (412)687-8139
Website: http://www.birchmerevc.com

CEO Venture Fund
2000 Technology Dr., Ste. 160
Pittsburgh, PA 15219-3109
(412)687-3451
Fax: (412)687-8139
E-mail: ceofund@aol.com
Website: http://www.ceoventure
fund.com

Innovation Works Inc.
2000 Technology Dr., Ste. 250
Pittsburgh, PA 15219
(412)681-1520
Fax: (412)681-2625
Website: http://www.innovation
works.org

Keystone Minority Capital Fund L.P.
1801 Centre Ave., Ste. 201
Williams Sq.
Pittsburgh, PA 15219
(412)338-2230
Fax: (412)338-2224

Mellon Ventures, Inc.
One Mellon Bank Ctr., Rm. 3500
Pittsburgh, PA 15258
(412)236-3594
Fax: (412)236-3593
Website: http://www.mellon
ventures.com

Pennsylvania Growth Fund
5850 Ellsworth Ave., Ste. 303
Pittsburgh, PA 15232
(412)661-1000
Fax: (412)361-0676

Point Venture Partners
The Century Bldg.
130 Seventh St., 7th Fl.
Pittsburgh, PA 15222
(412)261-1966
Fax: (412)261-1718

Cross Atlantic Capital Partners
5 Radnor Corporate Center, Ste. 555
Radnor, PA 19087
(610)995-2650
Fax: (610)971-2062
Website: http://www.xacp.com

Meridian Venture Partners (Radnor)
The Radnor Court Bldg., Ste. 140
259 Radnor-Chester Rd.
Radnor, PA 19087
(610)254-2999
Fax: (610)254-2996
E-mail: mvpart@ix.netcom.com

TDH
919 Conestoga Rd., Bldg. 1, Ste. 301
Rosemont, PA 19010
(610)526-9970
Fax: (610)526-9971

Adams Capital Management
500 Blackburn Ave.
Sewickley, PA 15143
(412)749-9454
Fax: (412)749-9459
Website: http://www.acm.com

S.R. One, Ltd.
Four Tower Bridge
200 Barr Harbor Dr., Ste. 250
W. Conshohocken, PA 19428
(610)567-1000
Fax: (610)567-1039

Greater Philadelphia Venture Capital Corp.
351 East Conestoga Rd.
Wayne, PA 19087
(610)688-6829
Fax: (610)254-8958

PA Early Stage
435 Devon Park Dr., Bldg. 500, Ste. 510
Wayne, PA 19087
(610)293-4075
Fax: (610)254-4240
Website: http://www.paearlystage.com

The Sandhurst Venture Fund, L.P.
351 E. Constoga Rd.
Wayne, PA 19087
(610)254-8900
Fax: (610)254-8958

TL Ventures
700 Bldg.
435 Devon Park Dr.
Wayne, PA 19087-1990
(610)975-3765
Fax: (610)254-4210
Website: http://www.tlventures.com

Rockhill Ventures, Inc.
100 Front St., Ste. 1350
West Conshohocken, PA 19428
(610)940-0300
Fax: (610)940-0301

Puerto Rico

Advent-Morro Equity Partners
Banco Popular Bldg.
206 Tetuan St., Ste. 903
San Juan, PR 00902
(787)725-5285
Fax: (787)721-1735

North America Investment Corp.
Mercantil Plaza, Ste. 813
PO Box 191831
San Juan, PR 00919
(787)754-6178
Fax: (787)754-6181

Rhode Island

Manchester Humphreys, Inc.
40 Westminster St., Ste. 900
Providence, RI 02903
(401)454-0400
Fax: (401)454-0403

Navis Partners
50 Kennedy Plaza, 12th Fl.
Providence, RI 02903
(401)278-6770
Fax: (401)278-6387
Website: http://www.navis
partners.com

South Carolina

Capital Insights, L.L.C.
PO Box 27162
Greenville, SC 29616-2162
(864)242-6832
Fax: (864)242-6755
E-mail: jwarner@capitalinsights.com
Website: http://www.capitalin
sights.com

Transamerica Mezzanine Financing
7 N. Laurens St., Ste. 603
Greenville, SC 29601
(864)232-6198
Fax: (864)241-4444

Tennessee

Valley Capital Corp.
Krystal Bldg.
100 W. Martin Luther King Blvd.,
Ste. 212

Chattanooga, TN 37402
(423)265-1557
Fax: (423)265-1588

Coleman Swenson Booth Inc.
237 2nd Ave. S
Franklin, TN 37064-2649
(615)791-9462
Fax: (615)791-9636
Website: http://
www.colemanswenson.com

Capital Services & Resources, Inc.
5159 Wheelis Dr., Ste. 106
Memphis, TN 38117
(901)761-2156
Fax: (907)767-0060

Paradigm Capital Partners LLC
6410 Poplar Ave., Ste. 395
Memphis, TN 38119
(901)682-6060
Fax: (901)328-3061

SSM Ventures
845 Crossover Ln., Ste. 140
Memphis, TN 38117
(901)767-1131
Fax: (901)767-1135
Website: http://www.ssm
ventures.com

Capital Across America L.P.
501 Union St., Ste. 201
Nashville, TN 37219
(615)254-1414
Fax: (615)254-1856
Website: http://
www.capitalacrossamerica.com

Equitas L.P.
2000 Glen Echo Rd., Ste. 101
PO Box 158838
Nashville, TN 37215-8838
(615)383-8673
Fax: (615)383-8693

Massey Burch Capital Corp.
One Burton Hills Blvd., Ste. 350
Nashville, TN 37215
(615)665-3221
Fax: (615)665-3240
E-mail: tcalton@masseyburch.com
Website: http://www.masseyburch.com

Nelson Capital Corp.
3401 West End Ave., Ste. 300
Nashville, TN 37203
(615)292-8787
Fax: (615)385-3150

Texas

Phillips-Smith Specialty Retail Group
5080 Spectrum Dr., Ste. 805 W
Addison, TX 75001
(972)387-0725
Fax: (972)458-2560
E-mail: pssrg@aol.com
Website: http://www.phillips-smith.com

Austin Ventures, L.P.
701 Brazos St., Ste. 1400
Austin, TX 78701
(512)485-1900
Fax: (512)476-3952
E-mail: info@ausven.com
Website: http://www.austinventures.com

The Capital Network
3925 West Braker Lane, Ste. 406
Austin, TX 78759-5321
(512)305-0826
Fax: (512)305-0836

Techxas Ventures LLC
5000 Plaza on the Lake
Austin, TX 78746
(512)343-0118
Fax: (512)343-1879
E-mail: bruce@techxas.com
Website: http://www.techxas.com

Alliance Financial of Houston
218 Heather Ln.
Conroe, TX 77385-9013
(936)447-3300
Fax: (936)447-4222

Amerimark Capital Corp.
1111 W. Mockingbird, Ste. 1111
Dallas, TX 75247
(214)638-7878
Fax: (214)638-7612
E-mail: amerimark@amcapital.com
Website: http://www.amcapital.com

AMT Venture Partners / AMT Capital Ltd.
5220 Spring Valley Rd., Ste. 600
Dallas, TX 75240
(214)905-9757
Fax: (214)905-9761
Website: http://www.amtcapital.com

Arkoma Venture Partners
5950 Berkshire Lane, Ste. 1400
Dallas, TX 75225
(214)739-3515
Fax: (214)739-3572
E-mail: joelf@arkomavp.com

Capital Southwest Corp.
12900 Preston Rd., Ste. 700
Dallas, TX 75230
(972)233-8242
Fax: (972)233-7362
Website: http://
www.capitalsouthwest.com

Dali, Hook Partners
One Lincoln Center, Ste. 1550
5400 LBJ Freeway
Dallas, TX 75240
(972)991-5457
Fax: (972)991-5458
E-mail: dhook@hookpartners.com
Website: http://www.hookpartners.com

HO2 Partners
Two Galleria Tower
13455 Noel Rd., Ste. 1670
Dallas, TX 75240
(972)702-1144
Fax: (972)702-8234
Website: http://www.ho2.com

Interwest Partners (Dallas)
2 Galleria Tower
13455 Noel Rd., Ste. 1670
Dallas, TX 75240
(972)392-7279
Fax: (972)490-6348
Website: http://www.interwest.com

Kahala Investments, Inc.
8214 Westchester Dr., Ste. 715
Dallas, TX 75225
(214)987-0077
Fax: (214)987-2332

MESBIC Ventures Holding Co.
2435 North Central Expressway, Ste. 200
Dallas, TX 75080
(972)991-1597
Fax: (972)991-4770
Website: http://www.mvhc.com

North Texas MESBIC, Inc.
9500 Forest Lane, Ste. 430
Dallas, TX 75243
(214)221-3565
Fax: (214)221-3566

Richard Jaffe & Company, Inc,
7318 Royal Cir.
Dallas, TX 75230
(214)265-9397
Fax: (214)739-1845

Sevin Rosen Management Co.
13455 Noel Rd., Ste. 1670
Dallas, TX 75240

(972)702-1100
Fax: (972)702-1103
E-mail: info@srfunds.com
Website: http://www.srfunds.com

Stratford Capital Partners, L.P.
300 Crescent Ct., Ste. 500
Dallas, TX 75201
(214)740-7377
Fax: (214)720-7393
E-mail: stratcap@hmtf.com

Sunwestern Investment Group
12221 Merit Dr., Ste. 935
Dallas, TX 75251
(972)239-5650
Fax: (972)701-0024

Wingate Partners
750 N. St. Paul St., Ste. 1200
Dallas, TX 75201
(214)720-1313
Fax: (214)871-8799

Buena Venture Associates
201 Main St., 32nd Fl.
Fort Worth, TX 76102
(817)339-7400
Fax: (817)390-8408
Website: http://www.buenaventure.com

The Catalyst Group
3 Riverway, Ste. 770
Houston, TX 77056
(713)623-8133
Fax: (713)623-0473
E-mail: herman@thecatalystgroup.net
Website: http://www.thecatalyst
group.net

Cureton & Co., Inc.
1100 Louisiana, Ste. 3250
Houston, TX 77002
(713)658-9806
Fax: (713)658-0476

Davis, Tuttle Venture Partners (Dallas)
8 Greenway Plaza, Ste. 1020
Houston, TX 77046
(713)993-0440
Fax: (713)621-2297
Website: http://www.davistuttle.com

Houston Partners
401 Louisiana, 8th Fl.
Houston, TX 77002
(713)222-8600
Fax: (713)222-8932

Southwest Venture Group
10878 Westheimer, Ste. 178

Houston, TX 77042
(713)827-8947
(713)461-1470

AM Fund
4600 Post Oak Place, Ste. 100
Houston, TX 77027
(713)627-9111
Fax: (713)627-9119

Ventex Management, Inc.
3417 Milam St.
Houston, TX 77002-9531
(713)659-7870
Fax: (713)659-7855

MBA Venture Group
1004 Olde Town Rd., Ste. 102
Irving, TX 75061
(972)986-6703

First Capital Group Management Co.
750 East Mulberry St., Ste. 305
PO Box 15616
San Antonio, TX 78212
(210)736-4233
Fax: (210)736-5449

The Southwest Venture Partnerships
16414 San Pedro, Ste. 345
San Antonio, TX 78232
(210)402-1200
Fax: (210)402-1221
E-mail: swvp@aol.com

Medtech International Inc.
1742 Carriageway
Sugarland, TX 77478
(713)980-8474
Fax: (713)980-6343

Utah

First Security Business Investment Corp.
15 East 100 South, Ste. 100
Salt Lake City, UT 84111
(801)246-5737
Fax: (801)246-5740

Utah Ventures II, L.P.
423 Wakara Way, Ste. 206
Salt Lake City, UT 84108
(801)583-5922
Fax: (801)583-4105
Website: http://www.uven.com

Wasatch Venture Corp.
1 S. Main St., Ste. 1400
Salt Lake City, UT 84133
(801)524-8939

Fax: (801)524-8941
E-mail: mail@wasatchvc.com

Vermont

North Atlantic Capital Corp.
76 Saint Paul St., Ste. 600
Burlington, VT 05401
(802)658-7820
Fax: (802)658-5757
Website: http://www.north
atlanticcapital.com

Green Mountain Advisors Inc.
PO Box 1230
Quechee, VT 05059
(802)296-7800
Fax: (802)296-6012
Website: http://www.gmtcap.com

Virginia

Oxford Financial Services Corp.
Alexandria, VA 22314
(703)519-4900
Fax: (703)519-4910
E-mail: oxford133@aol.com

Continental SBIC
4141 N. Henderson Rd.
Arlington, VA 22203
(703)527-5200
Fax: (703)527-3700

Novak Biddle Venture Partners
1750 Tysons Blvd., Ste. 1190
McLean, VA 22102
(703)847-3770
Fax: (703)847-3771
E-mail: roger@novakbiddle.com
Website: http://www.novakbiddle.com

Spacevest
11911 Freedom Dr., Ste. 500
Reston, VA 20190
(703)904-9800
Fax: (703)904-0571
E-mail: spacevest@spacevest.com
Website: http://www.spacevest.com

Virginia Capital
1801 Libbie Ave., Ste. 201
Richmond, VA 23226
(804)648-4802
Fax: (804)648-4809
E-mail: webmaster@vacapital.com
Website: http://www.vacapital.com

Calvert Social Venture Partners
402 Maple Ave. W
Vienna, VA 22180

(703)255-4930
Fax: (703)255-4931
E-mail: calven2000@aol.com

Fairfax Partners
8000 Towers Crescent Dr., Ste. 940
Vienna, VA 22182
(703)847-9486
Fax: (703)847-0911

Global Internet Ventures
8150 Leesburg Pike, Ste. 1210
Vienna, VA 22182
(703)442-3300
Fax: (703)442-3388
Website: http://www.givinc.com

Walnut Capital Corp. (Vienna)
8000 Towers Crescent Dr., Ste. 1070
Vienna, VA 22182
(703)448-3771
Fax: (703)448-7751

Washington

Encompass Ventures
777 108th Ave. NE, Ste. 2300
Bellevue, WA 98004
(425)486-3900
Fax: (425)486-3901
E-mail: info@evpartners.com
Website: http://www.encom
passventures.com

Fluke Venture Partners
11400 SE Sixth St., Ste. 230
Bellevue, WA 98004
(425)453-4590
Fax: (425)453-4675
E-mail: gabelein@flukeventures.com
Website: http://www.flukeventures.com

Pacific Northwest Partners SBIC, L.P.
15352 SE 53rd St.
Bellevue, WA 98006
(425)455-9967
Fax: (425)455-9404

Materia Venture Associates, L.P.
3435 Carillon Pointe
Kirkland, WA 98033-7354
(425)822-4100
Fax: (425)827-4086

OVP Venture Partners (Kirkland)
2420 Carillon Pt.
Kirkland, WA 98033
(425)889-9192
Fax: (425)889-0152
E-mail: info@ovp.com
Website: http://www.ovp.com

Digital Partners
999 3rd Ave., Ste. 1610
Seattle, WA 98104
(206)405-3607
Fax: (206)405-3617
Website: http://www.digitalpartners.com

Frazier & Company
601 Union St., Ste. 3300
Seattle, WA 98101
(206)621-7200
Fax: (206)621-1848
E-mail: jon@frazierco.com

Kirlan Venture Capital, Inc.
221 First Ave. W, Ste. 108
Seattle, WA 98119-4223
(206)281-8610
Fax: (206)285-3451
Website: http://www.kirlanventure.com

Phoenix Partners
1000 2nd Ave., Ste. 3600
Seattle, WA 98104
(206)624-8968
Fax: (206)624-1907

Voyager Capital
800 5th St., Ste. 4100
Seattle, WA 98103
(206)470-1180
Fax: (206)470-1185
E-mail: info@voyagercap.com
Website: http://www.voyagercap.com

Northwest Venture Associates
221 N. Wall St., Ste. 628
Spokane, WA 99201
(509)747-0728
Fax: (509)747-0758
Website: http://www.nwva.com

Wisconsin

Venture Investors Management, L.L.C.
University Research Park
505 S. Rosa Rd.
Madison, WI 53719
(608)441-2700
Fax: (608)441-2727
E-mail: roger@ventureinvestors.com
Website: http://www.venture
investers.com

Capital Investments, Inc.
1009 West Glen Oaks Lane, Ste. 103
Mequon, WI 53092
(414)241-0303
Fax: (414)241-8451
Website: http://
www.capitalinvestmentsinc.com

Future Value Venture, Inc.
2745 N. Martin Luther King
Dr., Ste. 204
Milwaukee, WI 53212-2300
(414)264-2252
Fax: (414)264-2253
E-mail: fvvventures@aol.com
William Beckett, President

Lubar and Co., Inc.
700 N. Water St., Ste. 1200
Milwaukee, WI 53202
(414)291-9000
Fax: (414)291-9061

GCI
20875 Crossroads Cir., Ste. 100
Waukesha, WI 53186
(262)798-5080
Fax: (262)798-5087

Glossary of Small Business Terms

Absolute liability
Liability that is incurred due to product defects or negligent actions. Manufacturers or retail establishments are held responsible, even though the defect or action may not have been intentional or negligent.

ACE
See Active Corps of Executives

Accident and health benefits
Benefits offered to employees and their families in order to offset the costs associated with accidental death, accidental injury, or sickness.

Account statement
A record of transactions, including payments, new debt, and deposits, incurred during a defined period of time.

Accounting system
System capturing the costs of all employees and/or machinery included in business expenses.

Accounts payable
See Trade credit

Accounts receivable
Unpaid accounts which arise from unsettled claims and transactions from the sale of a company's products or services to its customers.

Active Corps of Executives (ACE)
A group of volunteers for a management assistance program of the U.S. Small Business Administration; volunteers provide one-on-one counseling and teach workshops and seminars for small firms.

ADA
See Americans with Disabilities Act

Adaptation
The process whereby an invention is modified to meet the needs of users.

Adaptive engineering
The process whereby an invention is modified to meet the manufacturing and commercial requirements of a targeted market.

Adverse selection
The tendency for higher-risk individuals to purchase health care and more comprehensive plans, resulting in increased costs.

Advertising
A marketing tool used to capture public attention and influence purchasing decisions for a product or service. Utilizes various forms of media to generate consumer response, such as flyers, magazines, newspapers, radio, and television.

Age discrimination
The denial of the rights and privileges of employment based solely on the age of an individual.

Agency costs
Costs incurred to insure that the lender or investor maintains control over assets while allowing the borrower or entrepreneur to use them. Monitoring and information costs are the two major types of agency costs.

Agribusiness
The production and sale of commodities and products from the commercial farming industry.

America Online
An online service which is accessible by computer modem. The service features Internet access, bulletin boards, online periodicals, electronic mail, and other services for subscribers.

Americans with Disabilities Act (ADA)
Law designed to ensure equal access and opportunity to handicapped persons.

Annual report
Yearly financial report prepared by a business that adheres to the requirements set forth by the Securities and Exchange Commission (SEC).

Antitrust immunity
Exemption from prosecution under antitrust laws. In the transportation industry, firms with antitrust immunity are permitted under certain conditions to set schedules and sometimes prices for the public benefit.

Applied research
Scientific study targeted for use in a product or process.

Asians
A minority category used by the U.S. Bureau of the Census to represent a diverse group that includes Aleuts, Eskimos, American Indians, Asian Indians, Chinese, Japanese, Koreans, Vietnamese, Filipinos, Hawaiians, and other Pacific Islanders.

Assets
Anything of value owned by a company.

Audit
The verification of accounting records and business procedures conducted by an outside accounting service.

Average cost
Total production costs divided by the quantity produced.

Balance Sheet
A financial statement listing the total assets and liabilities of a company at a given time.

Bankruptcy
The condition in which a business cannot meet its debt obligations and petitions a federal district court either for reorganization of its debts (Chapter 11) or for liquidation of its assets (Chapter 7).

Basic research
Theoretical scientific exploration not targeted to application.

Basket clause
A provision specifying the amount of public pension funds that may be placed in investments not included on a state's legal list (see separate citation).

BBS
See Bulletin Board Service

BDC
See Business development corporation

Benefit
Various services, such as health care, flextime, day care, insurance, and vacation, offered to employees as part of a hiring package. Typically subsidized in whole or in part by the business.

BIDCO
See Business and industrial development company

Billing cycle
A system designed to evenly distribute customer billing throughout the month, preventing clerical backlogs.

Birth
See Business birth

Blue chip security
A low-risk, low-yield security representing an interest in a very stable company.

Blue sky laws
A general term that denotes various states' laws regulating securities.

Bond
A written instrument executed by a bidder or contractor (the principal) and a second party (the surety or sureties) to assure fulfillment of the principal's obligations to a third party (the obligee or government) identified in the bond. If the principal's obligations are not met, the bond assures payment to the extent stipulated of any loss sustained by the obligee.

Bonding requirements
Terms contained in a bond (see separate citation).

Bonus
An amount of money paid to an employee as a reward for achieving certain business goals or objectives.

Brainstorming
A group session where employees contribute their ideas for solving a problem or meeting a company objective without fear of retribution or ridicule.

Brand name
The part of a brand, trademark, or service mark that can be spoken. It can be a word, letter, or group of words or letters.

Bridge financing
A short-term loan made in expectation of intermediateterm or long-term financing. Can be used when a company plans to go public in the near future.

Broker
One who matches resources available for innovation with those who need them.

Budget
An estimate of the spending necessary to complete a project or offer a service in comparison to cash-on-hand and expected earnings for the coming year, with an emphasis on cost control.

Bulletin Board Service (BBS)
An online service enabling users to communicate with each other about specific topics.

Business and industrial development company (BIDCO)
A private, for-profit financing corporation chartered by the state to provide both equity and long-term debt capital to small business owners (see separate citations for equity and debt capital).

Business birth
The formation of a new establishment or enterprise. The appearance of a new establishment or enterprise in the Small Business Data Base (see separate citation).

Business conditions
Outside factors that can affect the financial performance of a business.

Business contractions
The number of establishments that have decreased in employment during a specified time.

Business cycle
A period of economic recession and recovery. These cycles vary in duration.

Business death
The voluntary or involuntary closure of a firm or establishment. The disappearance of an establishment or enterprise from the Small Business Data Base (see separate citation).

Business development corporation (BDC)
A business financing agency, usually composed of the financial institutions in an area or state, organized to assist in financing businesses unable to obtain assistance through normal channels; the risk is spread among various members of the business development corporation, and interest rates may vary somewhat from those charged by member institutions. A venture capital firm in which shares of ownership are publicly held and to which the Investment Act of 1940 applies.

Business dissolution
For enumeration purposes, the absence of a business that was present in the prior time period from any current record.

Business entry
See Business birth

Business ethics
Moral values and principles espoused by members of the business community as a guide to fair and honest business practices.

Business exit
See Business death

Business expansions
The number of establishments that added employees during a specified time.

Business failure
Closure of a business causing a loss to at least one creditor.

Business format franchising
The purchase of the name, trademark, and an ongoing business plan of the parent corporation or franchisor by the franchisee.

Business license
A legal authorization issued by municipal and state governments and required for business operations.

Business name
Enterprises must register their business names with local governments usually on a "doing business as" (DBA) form. (This name is sometimes referred to as a "fictional name.") The procedure is part of the business licensing process and prevents any other business from using that same name for a similar business in the same locality.

Business norms
See Financial ratios

Business permit
See Business license

Business plan
A document that spells out a company's expected course of action for a specified period, usually including a detailed listing and analysis of risks and uncertainties. For the small business, it should examine the proposed products, the market, the industry, the management policies, the marketing policies, production needs, and financial needs. Frequently, it is used as a prospectus for potential investors and lenders.

Business proposal
See Business plan

Business service firm
An establishment primarily engaged in rendering services to other business organizations on a fee or contract basis.

Business start
For enumeration purposes, a business with a name or similar designation that did not exist in a prior time period.

Cafeteria plan
See Flexible benefit plan

Capacity
Level of a firm's, industry's, or nation's output corresponding to full practical utilization of available resources.

Capital
Assets less liabilities, representing the ownership interest in a business. A stock of accumulated goods, especially at a specified time and in contrast to income received during a specified time period. Accumulated goods devoted to production. Accumulated possessions calculated to bring income.

Capital expenditure
Expenses incurred by a business for improvements that will depreciate over time.

Capital gain
The monetary difference between the purchase price and the selling price of capital. Capital gains are taxed at a rate of 28% by the federal government.

Capital intensity
The relative importance of capital in the production process, usually expressed as the ratio of capital to labor but also sometimes as the ratio of capital to output.

Capital resource
The equipment, facilities and labor used to create products and services.

Caribbean Basin Initiative
An interdisciplinary program to support commerce among the businesses in the nations of the Caribbean Basin and the United States. Agencies involved include: the Agency for International Development, the U.S. Small Business Administration, the International Trade Administration of the U.S. Department of Commerce, and various private sector groups.

Catastrophic care
Medical and other services for acute and long-term illnesses that cost more than insurance coverage limits or that cost the amount most families may be expected to pay with their own resources.

CDC
See Certified development corporation

CD-ROM
Compact disc with read-only memory used to store large amounts of digitized data.

Certified development corporation (CDC)
A local area or statewide corporation or authority (for profit or nonprofit) that packages U.S. Small Business Administration (SBA), bank, state, and/or private money into financial assistance for existing business capital improvements. The SBA holds the second lien on its maximum share of 40 percent involvement. Each state has at least one certified development corporation. This program is called the SBA 504 Program.

Certified lenders
Banks that participate in the SBA guaranteed loan program (see separate citation). Such banks must have a good track record with the U.S. Small Business Administration (SBA) and must agree to certain conditions set forth by the agency. In return, the SBA agrees to process any guaranteed loan application within three business days.

Champion
An advocate for the development of an innovation.

Channel of distribution
The means used to transport merchandise from the manufacturer to the consumer.

Chapter 7 of the 1978 Bankruptcy Act
Provides for a court-appointed trustee who is responsible for liquidating a company's assets in order to settle outstanding debts.

Chapter 11 of the 1978 Bankruptcy Act
Allows the business owners to retain control of the company while working with their creditors to reorganize their finances and establish better business practices to prevent liquidation of assets.

Closely held corporation
A corporation in which the shares are held by a few persons, usually officers, employees, or others close to the management; these shares are rarely offered to the public.

Code of Federal Regulations
Codification of general and permanent rules of the federal government published in the Federal Register.

Code sharing
See Computer code sharing

Coinsurance
Upon meeting the deductible payment, health insurance participants may be required to make additional health care cost-sharing payments. Coinsurance is a payment of a fixed percentage of the cost of each service; copayment is usually a fixed amount to be paid with each service.

Collateral
Securities, evidence of deposit, or other property pledged by a borrower to secure repayment of a loan.

Collective ratemaking
The establishment of uniform charges for services by a group of businesses in the same industry.

Commercial insurance plan
See Underwriting

Commercial loans
Short-term renewable loans used to finance specific capital needs of a business.

Commercialization
The final stage of the innovation process, including production and distribution.

Common stock
The most frequently used instrument for purchasing ownership in private or public companies. Common stock generally carries the right to vote on certain corporate actions and may pay dividends, although it rarely does in venture investments. In liquidation, common stockholders are the last to share in the proceeds from the sale of a corporation's assets; bondholders and preferred shareholders have priority. Common stock is often used in firstround start-up financing.

Community development corporation
A corporation established to develop economic programs for a community and, in most cases, to provide financial support for such development.

Competitor
A business whose product or service is marketed for the same purpose/use and to the same consumer group as the product or service of another.

Computer code sharing
An arrangement whereby flights of a regional airline are identified by the two-letter code of a major carrier in the computer reservation system to help direct passengers to new regional carriers.

Consignment
A merchandising agreement, usually referring to secondhand shops, where the dealer pays the owner of an item a percentage of the profit when the item is sold.

Consortium
A coalition of organizations such as banks and corporations for ventures requiring large capital resources.

Consultant
An individual that is paid by a business to provide advice and expertise in a particular area.

Consumer price index
A measure of the fluctuation in prices between two points in time.

Consumer research
Research conducted by a business to obtain information about existing or potential consumer markets.

Continuation coverage
Health coverage offered for a specified period of time to employees who leave their jobs and to their widows, divorced spouses, or dependents.

Contractions
See Business contractions

Convertible preferred stock
A class of stock that pays a reasonable dividend and is convertible into common stock (see separate citation). Generally the convertible feature may only be exercised after being held for a stated period of time. This arrangement is usually considered second-round financing when a company needs equity to maintain its cash flow.

Convertible securities
A feature of certain bonds, debentures, or preferred stocks that allows them to be exchanged by the owner for another class of securities at a future date and in accordance with any other terms of the issue.

Copayment
See Coinsurance

Copyright
A legal form of protection available to creators and authors to safeguard their works from unlawful use or claim of ownership by others. Copyrights may be acquired for works of art, sculpture, music, and published or unpublished manuscripts. All copyrights should be registered at the Copyright Office of the Library of Congress.

Corporate financial ratios
The relationship between key figures found in a company's financial statement expressed as a numeric value. Used to evaluate risk and company performance. Also known as Financial averages, Operating ratios, and Business ratios.

Corporation
A legal entity, chartered by a state or the federal government, recognized as a separate entity having its own rights, privileges, and liabilities distinct from those of its members.

Cost containment
Actions taken by employers and insurers to curtail rising health care costs; for example, increasing

employee cost sharing (see separate citation), requiring second opinions, or preadmission screening.

Cost sharing
The requirement that health care consumers contribute to their own medical care costs through deductibles and coinsurance (see separate citations). Cost sharing does not include the amounts paid in premiums. It is used to control utilization of services; for example, requiring a fixed amount to be paid with each health care service.

Cottage industry
Businesses based in the home in which the family members are the labor force and family-owned equipment is used to process the goods.

Credit Rating
A letter or number calculated by an organization (such as Dun & Bradstreet) to represent the ability and disposition of a business to meet its financial obligations.

Customer service
Various techniques used to ensure the satisfaction of a customer.

Cyclical peak
The upper turning point in a business cycle.

Cyclical trough
The lower turning point in a business cycle.

DBA
See Business name

Death
See Business death

Debenture
A certificate given as acknowledgment of a debt (see separate citation) secured by the general credit of the issuing corporation. A bond, usually without security, issued by a corporation and sometimes convertible to common stock.

Debt
Something owed by one person to another. Financing in which a company receives capital that must be repaid; no ownership is transferred.

Debt capital
Business financing that normally requires periodic interest payments and repayment of the principal within a specified time.

Debt financing
See Debt capital

Debt securities
Loans such as bonds and notes that provide a specified rate of return for a specified period of time.

Deductible
A set amount that an individual must pay before any benefits are received.

Demand shock absorbers
A term used to describe the role that some small firms play by expanding their output levels to accommodate a transient surge in demand.

Demographics
Statistics on various markets, including age, income, and education, used to target specific products or services to appropriate consumer groups.

Demonstration
Showing that a product or process has been modified sufficiently to meet the needs of users.

Deregulation
The lifting of government restrictions; for example, the lifting of government restrictions on the entry of new businesses, the expansion of services, and the setting of prices in particular industries.

Desktop Publishing
Using personal computers and specialized software to produce camera-ready copy for publications.

Disaster loans
Various types of physical and economic assistance available to individuals and businesses through the U.S. Small Business Administration (SBA). This is the only SBA loan program available for residential purposes.

Discrimination
The denial of the rights and privileges of employment based on factors such as age, race, religion, or gender.

Diseconomies of scale
The condition in which the costs of production increase faster than the volume of production.

Dissolution
See Business dissolution

Distribution
Delivering a product or process to the user.

Distributor
One who delivers merchandise to the user.

Diversified company
A company whose products and services are used by several different markets.

Doing business as (DBA)
See Business name

Dow Jones
An information services company that publishes the Wall Street Journal and other sources of financial information.

Dow Jones Industrial Average
An indicator of stock market performance.

Earned income
A tax term that refers to wages and salaries earned by the recipient, as opposed to monies earned through interest and dividends.

Economic efficiency
The use of productive resources to the fullest practical extent in the provision of the set of goods and services that is most preferred by purchasers in the economy.

Economic indicators
Statistics used to express the state of the economy. These include the length of the average work week, the rate of unemployment, and stock prices.

Economically disadvantaged
See Socially and economically disadvantaged

Economies of scale
See Scale economies

EEOC
See Equal Employment Opportunity Commission

8(a) Program
A program authorized by the Small Business Act that directs federal contracts to small businesses owned and

Glossary

operated by socially and economically disadvantaged individuals.

Electronic mail (e-mail)
The electronic transmission of mail via phone lines.

E-mail
See Electronic mail

Employee leasing
A contract by which employers arrange to have their workers hired by a leasing company and then leased back to them for a management fee. The leasing company typically assumes the administrative burden of payroll and provides a benefit package to the workers.

Employee tenure
The length of time an employee works for a particular employer.

Employer identification number
The business equivalent of a social security number. Assigned by the U.S. Internal Revenue Service.

Enterprise
An aggregation of all establishments owned by a parent company. An enterprise may consist of a single, independent establishment or include subsidiaries and other branches under the same ownership and control.

Enterprise zone
A designated area, usually found in inner cities and other areas with significant unemployment, where businesses receive tax credits and other incentives to entice them to establish operations there.

Entrepreneur
A person who takes the risk of organizing and operating a new business venture.

Entry
See Business entry

Equal Employment Opportunity Commission (EEOC)
A federal agency that ensures nondiscrimination in the hiring and firing practices of a business.

Equal opportunity employer
An employer who adheres to the standards set by the Equal Employment Opportunity Commission (see separate citation).

Equity
The ownership interest. Financing in which partial or total ownership of a company is surrendered in exchange for capital. An investor's financial return comes from dividend payments and from growth in the net worth of the business.

Equity capital
See Equity; Equity midrisk venture capital

Equity financing
See Equity; Equity midrisk venture capital

Equity midrisk venture capital
An unsecured investment in a company. Usually a purchase of ownership interest in a company that occurs in the later stages of a company's development.

Equity partnership
A limited partnership arrangement for providing start-up and seed capital to businesses.

Equity securities
See Equity

Equity-type
Debt financing subordinated to conventional debt.

Establishment
A single-location business unit that may be independent (a single-establishment enterprise) or owned by a parent enterprise.

Establishment and Enterprise Microdata File
See U.S. Establishment and Enterprise Microdata File

Establishment birth
See Business birth

Establishment Longitudinal Microdata File
See U.S. Establishment Longitudinal Microdata File

Ethics
See Business ethics

Evaluation
Determining the potential success of translating an invention into a product or process.

Exit
See Business exit

Experience rating
See Underwriting

Export
A product sold outside of the country.

Export license
A general or specific license granted by the U.S. Department of Commerce required of anyone wishing to export goods. Some restricted articles need approval from the U.S. Departments of State, Defense, or Energy.

Failure
See Business failure

Fair share agreement
An agreement reached between a franchisor and a minority business organization to extend business ownership to minorities by either reducing the amount of capital required or by setting aside certain marketing areas for minority business owners.

Feasibility study
A study to determine the likelihood that a proposed product or development will fulfill the objectives of a particular investor.

Federal Trade Commission (FTC)
Federal agency that promotes free enterprise and competition within the U.S.

Federal Trade Mark Act of 1946
See Lanham Act

Fictional name
See Business name

Fiduciary
An individual or group that hold assets in trust for a beneficiary.

Financial analysis
The techniques used to determine money needs in a business. Techniques include ratio analysis, calculation of return on investment, guides for measuring profitability, and break-even analysis to determine ultimate success.

Financial intermediary
A financial institution that acts as the intermediary between borrowers and lenders. Banks, savings and loan associations, finance companies, and venture capital companies are major financial intermediaries in the United States.

Financial ratios
See Corporate financial ratios; Industry financial ratios

Financial statement
A written record of business finances, including balance sheets and profit and loss statements.

Financing
See First-stage financing; Second-stage financing; Thirdstage financing

First-stage financing
Financing provided to companies that have expended their initial capital, and require funds to start full-scale manufacturing and sales. Also known as First-round financing.

Fiscal year
Any twelve-month period used by businesses for accounting purposes.

504 Program
See Certified development corporation

Flexible benefit plan
A plan that offers a choice among cash and/or qualified benefits such as group term life insurance, accident and health insurance, group legal services, dependent care assistance, and vacations.

FOB
See Free on board

Format franchising
See Business format franchising; Franchising

401(k) plan
A financial plan where employees contribute a percentage of their earnings to a fund that is invested in stocks, bonds, or money markets for the purpose of saving money for retirement.

Four Ps
Marketing terms referring to Product, Price, Place, and Promotion.

Franchising
A form of licensing by which the owner-the franchisor distributes or markets a product, method, or service through affiliated dealers called franchisees. The product, method, or service being marketed is identified by a brand name, and the franchisor

maintains control over the marketing methods employed. The franchisee is often given exclusive access to a defined geographic area.

Free on board (FOB)
A pricing term indicating that the quoted price includes the cost of loading goods into transport vessels at a specified place.

Frictional unemployment
See Unemployment

FTC
See Federal Trade Commission

Fulfillment
The systems necessary for accurate delivery of an ordered item, including subscriptions and direct marketing.

Full-time workers
Generally, those who work a regular schedule of more than 35 hours per week.

Garment registration number
A number that must appear on every garment sold in the U.S. to indicate the manufacturer of the garment, which may or may not be the same as the label under which the garment is sold. The U.S. Federal Trade Commission assigns and regulates garment registration numbers.

Gatekeeper
A key contact point for entry into a network.

GDP
See Gross domestic product

General obligation bond
A municipal bond secured by the taxing power of the municipality. The Tax Reform Act of 1986 limits the purposes for which such bonds may be issued and establishes volume limits on the extent of their issuance.

GNP
See Gross national product

Good Housekeeping Seal
Seal appearing on products that signifies the fulfillment of the standards set by the Good Housekeeping Institute to protect consumer interests.

Goods sector
All businesses producing tangible goods, including agriculture, mining, construction, and manufacturing businesses.

GPO
See Gross product originating

Gross domestic product (GDP)
The part of the nation's gross national product (see separate citation) generated by private business using resources from within the country.

Gross national product (GNP)
The most comprehensive single measure of aggregate economic output. Represents the market value of the total output of goods and services produced by a nation's economy.

Gross product originating (GPO)
A measure of business output estimated from the income or production side using employee compensation, profit income, net interest, capital consumption, and indirect business taxes.

HAL
See Handicapped assistance loan program

Handicapped assistance loan program (HAL)
Low-interest direct loan program through the U.S. Small Business Administration (SBA) for handicapped persons. The SBA requires that these persons demonstrate that their disability is such that it is impossible for them to secure employment, thus making it necessary to go into their own business to make a living.

Health maintenance organization (HMO)
Organization of physicians and other health care professionals that provides health services to subscribers and their dependents on a prepaid basis.

Health provider
An individual or institution that gives medical care. Under Medicare, an institutional provider is a hospital, skilled nursing facility, home health agency, or provider of certain physical therapy services.

Hispanic
A person of Cuban, Mexican, Puerto Rican, Latin American (Central or South American), European Spanish, or other Spanish-speaking origin or ancestry.

HMO
See Health maintenance organization

Home-based business
A business with an operating address that is also a residential address (usually the residential address of the proprietor).

Hub-and-spoke system
A system in which flights of an airline from many different cities (the spokes) converge at a single airport (the hub). After allowing passengers sufficient time to make connections, planes then depart for different cities.

Human Resources Management
A business program designed to oversee recruiting, pay, benefits, and other issues related to the company's work force, including planning to determine the optimal use of labor to increase production, thereby increasing profit.

Idea
An original concept for a new product or process.

Import
Products produced outside the country in which they are consumed.

Income
Money or its equivalent, earned or accrued, resulting from the sale of goods and services.

Income statement
A financial statement that lists the profits and losses of a company at a given time.

Incorporation
The filing of a certificate of incorporation with a state's secretary of state, thereby limiting the business owner's liability.

Incubator
A facility designed to encourage entrepreneurship and minimize obstacles to new business formation and growth, particularly for high-technology firms, by housing a number of fledgling enterprises that share an array of services, such as meeting areas, secretarial services, accounting, research library, on-site financial and management counseling, and word processing facilities.

Independent contractor
An individual considered self-employed (see separate citation) and responsible for paying Social Security taxes and income taxes on earnings.

Indirect health coverage
Health insurance obtained through another individual's health care plan; for example, a spouse's employersponsored plan.

Industrial development authority
The financial arm of a state or other political subdivision established for the purpose of financing economic development in an area, usually through loans to nonprofit organizations, which in turn provide facilities for manufacturing and other industrial operations.

Industry financial ratios
Corporate financial ratios averaged for a specified industry. These are used for comparison purposes and reveal industry trends and identify differences between the performance of a specific company and the performance of its industry. Also known as Industrial averages, Industry ratios, Financial averages, and Business or Industrial norms.

Inflation
Increases in volume of currency and credit, generally resulting in a sharp and continuing rise in price levels.

Informal capital
Financing from informal, unorganized sources; includes informal debt capital such as trade credit or loans from friends and relatives and equity capital from informal investors.

Initial public offering (IPO)
A corporation's first offering of stock to the public.

Innovation
The introduction of a new idea into the marketplace in the form of a new product or service or an improvement in organization or process.

Intellectual property
Any idea or work that can be considered proprietary in nature and is thus protected from infringement by others.

Glossary

Internal capital
Debt or equity financing obtained from the owner or through retained business earnings.

Internet
A government-designed computer network that contains large amounts of information and is accessible through various vendors for a fee.

Intrapreneurship
The state of employing entrepreneurial principles to nonentrepreneurial situations.

Invention
The tangible form of a technological idea, which could include a laboratory prototype, drawings, formulas, etc.

IPO
See Initial public offering

Job description
The duties and responsibilities required in a particular position.

Job tenure
A period of time during which an individual is continuously employed in the same job.

Joint marketing agreements
Agreements between regional and major airlines, often involving the coordination of flight schedules, fares, and baggage transfer. These agreements help regional carriers operate at lower cost.

Joint venture
Venture in which two or more people combine efforts in a particular business enterprise, usually a single transaction or a limited activity, and agree to share the profits and losses jointly or in proportion to their contributions.

Keogh plan
Designed for self-employed persons and unincorporated businesses as a tax-deferred pension account.

Labor force
Civilians considered eligible for employment who are also willing and able to work.

Labor force participation rate
The civilian labor force as a percentage of the civilian population.

Labor intensity
The relative importance of labor in the production process, usually measured as the capital-labor ratio; i.e., the ratio of units of capital (typically, dollars of tangible assets) to the number of employees. The higher the capital-labor ratio exhibited by a firm or industry, the lower the capital intensity of that firm or industry is said to be.

Labor surplus area
An area in which there exists a high unemployment rate. In procurement (see separate citation), extra points are given to firms in counties that are designated a labor surplus area; this information is requested on procurement bid sheets.

Labor union
An organization of similarly-skilled workers who collectively bargain with management over the conditions of employment.

Laboratory prototype
See Prototype

LAN
See Local Area Network

Lanham Act
Refers to the Federal Trade Mark Act of 1946. Protects registered trademarks, trade names, and other service marks used in commerce.

Large business-dominated industry
Industry in which a minimum of 60 percent of employment or sales is in firms with more than 500 workers.

LBO
See Leveraged buy-out

Leader pricing
A reduction in the price of a good or service in order to generate more sales of that good or service.

Legal list
A list of securities selected by a state in which certain institutions and fiduciaries (such as pension funds, insurance companies, and banks) may invest. Securities not on the list are not eligible for investment. Legal lists typically restrict investments to high quality securities meeting certain specifications. Generally, investment is

limited to U.S. securities and investment-grade blue chip securities (see separate citation).

Leveraged buy-out (LBO)
The purchase of a business or a division of a corporation through a highly leveraged financing package.

Liability
An obligation or duty to perform a service or an act. Also defined as money owed.

License
A legal agreement granting to another the right to use a technological innovation.

Limited partnerships
See Venture capital limited partnerships

Liquidity
The ability to convert a security into cash promptly.

Loans
See Commercial loans; Disaster loans; SBA direct loans; SBA guaranteed loans; SBA special lending institution categories Local Area Network (LAN) Computer networks contained within a single building or small area; used to facilitate the sharing of information.

Local development corporation
An organization, usually made up of local citizens of a community, designed to improve the economy of the area by inducing business and industry to locate and expand there. A local development corporation establishes a capability to finance local growth.

Long-haul rates
Rates charged by a transporter in which the distance traveled is more than 800 miles.

Long-term debt
An obligation that matures in a period that exceeds five years.

Low-grade bond
A corporate bond that is rated below investment grade by the major rating agencies (Standard and Poor's, Moody's).

Macro-efficiency
Efficiency as it pertains to the operation of markets and market systems.

Managed care
A cost-effective health care program initiated by employers whereby low-cost health care is made available to the employees in return for exclusive patronage to program doctors.

Management Assistance Programs
See SBA Management Assistance Programs

Management and technical assistance
A term used by many programs to mean business (as opposed to technological) assistance.

Mandated benefits
Specific treatments, providers, or individuals required by law to be included in commercial health plans.

Market evaluation
The use of market information to determine the sales potential of a specific product or process.

Market failure
The situation in which the workings of a competitive market do not produce the best results from the point of view of the entire society.

Market information
Data of any type that can be used for market evaluation, which could include demographic data, technology forecasting, regulatory changes, etc.

Market research
A systematic collection, analysis, and reporting of data about the market and its preferences, opinions, trends, and plans; used for corporate decision-making.

Market share
In a particular market, the percentage of sales of a specific product.

Marketing
Promotion of goods or services through various media.

Master Establishment List (MEL)
A list of firms in the United States developed by the U.S. Small Business Administration; firms can be selected by industry, region, state, standard metropolitan statistical area (see separate citation), county, and zip code.

Maturity
The date upon which the principal or stated value of a bond or other indebtedness becomes due and payable.

Medicaid (Title XIX)
A federally aided, state-operated and administered program that provides medical benefits for certain low income persons in need of health and medical care who are eligible for one of the government's welfare cash payment programs, including the aged, the blind, the disabled, and members of families with dependent children where one parent is absent, incapacitated, or unemployed.

Medicare (Title XVIII)
A nationwide health insurance program for disabled and aged persons. Health insurance is available to insured persons without regard to income. Monies from payroll taxes cover hospital insurance and monies from general revenues and beneficiary premiums pay for supplementary medical insurance.

MEL
See Master Establishment List

MESBIC
See Minority enterprise small business investment corporation

MET
See Multiple employer trust

Metropolitan statistical area (MSA)
A means used by the government to define large population centers that may transverse different governmental jurisdictions. For example, the Washington, D.C. MSA includes the District of Columbia and contiguous parts of Maryland and Virginia because all of these geopolitical areas comprise one population and economic operating unit.

Mezzanine financing
See Third-stage financing

Micro-efficiency
Efficiency as it pertains to the operation of individual firms.

Microdata
Information on the characteristics of an individual business firm.

Mid-term debt
An obligation that matures within one to five years.

Midrisk venture capital
See Equity midrisk venture capital

Minimum premium plan
A combination approach to funding an insurance plan aimed primarily at premium tax savings. The employer self-funds a fixed percentage of estimated monthly claims and the insurance company insures the excess.

Minimum wage
The lowest hourly wage allowed by the federal government.

Minority Business Development Agency
Contracts with private firms throughout the nation to sponsor Minority Business Development Centers which provide minority firms with advice and technical assistance on a fee basis.

Minority Enterprise Small Business Investment Corporation (MESBIC)
A federally funded private venture capital firm licensed by the U.S. Small Business Administration to provide capital to minority-owned businesses (see separate citation).

Minority-owned business
Businesses owned by those who are socially or economically disadvantaged (see separate citation).

Mom and Pop business
A small store or enterprise having limited capital, principally employing family members.

Moonlighter
A wage-and-salary worker with a side business.

MSA
See Metropolitan statistical area

Multi-employer plan
A health plan to which more than one employer is required to contribute and that may be maintained through a collective bargaining agreement and required to meet standards prescribed by the U.S. Department of Labor.

Multi-level marketing
A system of selling in which you sign up other people to assist you and they, in turn, recruit others to help them. Some entrepreneurs have built successful

companies on this concept because the main focus of their activities is their product and product sales.

Multimedia
The use of several types of media to promote a product or service. Also, refers to the use of several different types of media (sight, sound, pictures, text) in a CD-ROM (see separate citation) product.

Multiple employer trust (MET)
A self-funded benefit plan generally geared toward small employers sharing a common interest.

NAFTA
See North American Free Trade Agreement

NASDAQ
See National Association of Securities Dealers Automated Quotations

National Association of Securities Dealers Automated Quotations
Provides price quotes on over-the-counter securities as well as securities listed on the New York Stock Exchange.

National income
Aggregate earnings of labor and property arising from the production of goods and services in a nation's economy.

Net assets
See Net worth

Net income
The amount remaining from earnings and profits after all expenses and costs have been met or deducted. Also known as Net earnings.

Net profit
Money earned after production and overhead expenses (see separate citations) have been deducted.

Net worth
The difference between a company's total assets and its total liabilities.

Network
A chain of interconnected individuals or organizations sharing information and/or services.

New York Stock Exchange (NYSE)
The oldest stock exchange in the U.S. Allows for trading in stocks, bonds, warrants, options, and rights that meet listing requirements.

Niche
A career or business for which a person is well-suited. Also, a product which fulfills one need of a particular market segment, often with little or no competition.

Nodes
One workstation in a network, either local area or wide area (see separate citations).

Nonbank bank
A bank that either accepts deposits or makes loans, but not both. Used to create many new branch banks.

Noncompetitive awards
A method of contracting whereby the federal government negotiates with only one contractor to supply a product or service.

Nonmember bank
A state-regulated bank that does not belong to the federal bank system.

Nonprofit
An organization that has no shareholders, does not distribute profits, and is without federal and state tax liabilities.

Norms
See Financial ratios

North American Free Trade Agreement (NAFTA)
Passed in 1993, NAFTA eliminates trade barriers among businesses in the U.S., Canada, and Mexico.

NYSE
See New York Stock Exchange

Occupational Safety & Health Administration (OSHA)
Federal agency that regulates health and safety standards within the workplace.

Optimal firm size
The business size at which the production cost per unit of output (average cost) is, in the long run, at its minimum.

Glossary

Organizational chart
A hierarchical chart tracking the chain of command within an organization.

OSHA
See Occupational Safety & Health Administration

Overhead
Expenses, such as employee benefits and building utilities, incurred by a business that are unrelated to the actual product or service sold.

Owner's capital
Debt or equity funds provided by the owner(s) of a business; sources of owner's capital are personal savings, sales of assets, or loans from financial institutions.

P & L
See Profit and loss statement

Part-time workers
Normally, those who work less than 35 hours per week. The Tax Reform Act indicated that part-time workers who work less than 17.5 hours per week may be excluded from health plans for purposes of complying with federal nondiscrimination rules.

Part-year workers
Those who work less than 50 weeks per year.

Partnership
Two or more parties who enter into a legal relationship to conduct business for profit. Defined by the U.S. Internal Revenue Code as joint ventures, syndicates, groups, pools, and other associations of two or more persons organized for profit that are not specifically classified in the IRS code as corporations or proprietorships.

Patent
A grant made by the government assuring an inventor the sole right to make, use, and sell an invention for a period of 17 years.

PC
See Professional corporation

Peak
See Cyclical peak

Pension
A series of payments made monthly, semiannually, annually, or at other specified intervals during the lifetime of the pensioner for distribution upon retirement. The term is sometimes used to denote the portion of the retirement allowance financed by the employer's contributions.

Pension fund
A fund established to provide for the payment of pension benefits; the collective contributions made by all of the parties to the pension plan.

Performance appraisal
An established set of objective criteria, based on job description and requirements, that is used to evaluate the performance of an employee in a specific job.

Permit
See Business license

Plan
See Business plan

Pooling
An arrangement for employers to achieve efficiencies and lower health costs by joining together to purchase group health insurance or self-insurance.

PPO
See Preferred provider organization

Preferred lenders program
See SBA special lending institution categories

Preferred provider organization (PPO)
A contractual arrangement with a health care services organization that agrees to discount its health care rates in return for faster payment and/or a patient base.

Premiums
The amount of money paid to an insurer for health insurance under a policy. The premium is generally paid periodically (e.g., monthly), and often is split between the employer and the employee. Unlike deductibles and coinsurance or copayments, premiums are paid for coverage whether or not benefits are actually used.

Prime-age workers
Employees 25 to 54 years of age.

Prime contract
A contract awarded directly by the U.S. Federal Government.

Private company
See Closely held corporation

Private placement
A method of raising capital by offering for sale an investment or business to a small group of investors (generally avoiding registration with the Securities and Exchange Commission or state securities registration agencies). Also known as Private financing or Private offering.

Pro forma
The use of hypothetical figures in financial statements to represent future expenditures, debts, and other potential financial expenses.

Proactive
Taking the initiative to solve problems and anticipate future events before they happen, instead of reacting to an already existing problem or waiting for a difficult situation to occur.

Procurement
A contract from an agency of the federal government for goods or services from a small business.

Prodigy
An online service which is accessible by computer modem. The service features Internet access, bulletin boards, online periodicals, electronic mail, and other services for subscribers.

Product development
The stage of the innovation process where research is translated into a product or process through evaluation, adaptation, and demonstration.

Product franchising
An arrangement for a franchisee to use the name and to produce the product line of the franchisor or parent corporation.

Production
The manufacture of a product.

Production prototype
See Prototype

Productivity
A measurement of the number of goods produced during a specific amount of time.

Professional corporation (PC)
Organized by members of a profession such as medicine, dentistry, or law for the purpose of conducting their professional activities as a corporation. Liability of a member or shareholder is limited in the same manner as in a business corporation.

Profit and loss statement (P & L)
The summary of the incomes (total revenues) and costs of a company's operation during a specific period of time. Also known as Income and expense statement.

Proposal
See Business plan

Proprietorship
The most common legal form of business ownership; about 85 percent of all small businesses are proprietorships. The liability of the owner is unlimited in this form of ownership.

Prospective payment system
A cost-containment measure included in the Social Security Amendments of 1983 whereby Medicare payments to hospitals are based on established prices, rather than on cost reimbursement.

Prototype
A model that demonstrates the validity of the concept of an invention (laboratory prototype); a model that meets the needs of the manufacturing process and the user (production prototype).

Prudent investor rule or standard
A legal doctrine that requires fiduciaries to make investments using the prudence, diligence, and intelligence that would be used by a prudent person in making similar investments. Because fiduciaries make investments on behalf of third-party beneficiaries, the standard results in very conservative investments. Until recently, most state regulations required the fiduciary to apply this standard to each investment. Newer, more progressive regulations permit fiduciaries to apply this standard to the portfolio taken as a whole, thereby allowing a fiduciary to balance a portfolio with higher-yield, higher-risk investments. In states with more progressive regulations, practically every type of security is eligible for inclusion in the portfolio of investments made by a fiduciary, provided that the

portfolio investments, in their totality, are those of a prudent person.

Public equity markets
Organized markets for trading in equity shares such as common stocks, preferred stocks, and warrants. Includes markets for both regularly traded and nonregularly traded securities.

Public offering
General solicitation for participation in an investment opportunity. Interstate public offerings are supervised by the U.S. Securities and Exchange Commission (see separate citation).

Quality control
The process by which a product is checked and tested to ensure consistent standards of high quality.

Rate of return
The yield obtained on a security or other investment based on its purchase price or its current market price. The total rate of return is current income plus or minus capital appreciation or depreciation.

Real property
Includes the land and all that is contained on it.

Realignment
See Resource realignment

Recession
Contraction of economic activity occurring between the peak and trough (see separate citations) of a business cycle.

Regulated market
A market in which the government controls the forces of supply and demand, such as who may enter and what price may be charged.

Regulation D
A vehicle by which small businesses make small offerings and private placements of securities with limited disclosure requirements. It was designed to ease the burdens imposed on small businesses utilizing this method of capital formation.

Regulatory Flexibility Act
An act requiring federal agencies to evaluate the impact of their regulations on small businesses before the regulations are issued and to consider less burdensome alternatives.

Research
The initial stage of the innovation process, which includes idea generation and invention.

Research and development financing
A tax-advantaged partnership set up to finance product development for start-ups as well as more mature companies.

Resource mobility
The ease with which labor and capital move from firm to firm or from industry to industry.

Resource realignment
The adjustment of productive resources to interindustry changes in demand.

Resources
The sources of support or help in the innovation process, including sources of financing, technical evaluation, market evaluation, management and business assistance, etc.

Retained business earnings
Business profits that are retained by the business rather than being distributed to the shareholders as dividends.

Revolving credit
An agreement with a lending institution for an amount of money, which cannot exceed a set maximum, over a specified period of time. Each time the borrower repays a portion of the loan, the amount of the repayment may be borrowed yet again.

Risk capital
See Venture capital

Risk management
The act of identifying potential sources of financial loss and taking action to minimize their negative impact.

Routing
The sequence of steps necessary to complete a product during production.

S corporations
See Sub chapter S corporations

SBA
See Small Business Administration

SBA direct loans
Loans made directly by the U.S. Small Business Administration (SBA); monies come from funds appropriated specifically for this purpose. In general, SBA direct loans carry interest rates slightly lower than those in the private financial markets and are available only to applicants unable to secure private financing or an SBA guaranteed loan.

SBA 504 Program
See Certified development corporation

SBA guaranteed loans
Loans made by lending institutions in which the U.S. Small Business Administration (SBA) will pay a prior agreed-upon percentage of the outstanding principal in the event the borrower of the loan defaults. The terms of the loan and the interest rate are negotiated between theborrower and the lending institution, within set parameters.

SBA loans
See Disaster loans; SBA direct loans; SBA guaranteed loans; SBA special lending institution categories

SBA Management Assistance Programs
Classes, workshops, counseling, and publications offered by the U.S. Small Business Administration.

SBA special lending institution categories
U.S. Small Business Administration (SBA) loan program in which the SBA promises certified banks a 72-hour turnaround period in giving its approval for a loan, and in which preferred lenders in a pilot program are allowed to write SBA loans without seeking prior SBA approval.

SBDB
See Small Business Data Base

SBDC
See Small business development centers

SBI
See Small business institutes program

SBIC
See Small business investment corporation

SBIR Program
See Small Business Innovation Development Act of 1982

Scale economies
The decline of the production cost per unit of output (average cost) as the volume of output increases.

Scale efficiency
The reduction in unit cost available to a firm when producing at a higher output volume.

SCORE
See Service Corps of Retired Executives

SEC
See Securities and Exchange Commission

SECA
See Self-Employment Contributions Act

Second-stage financing
Working capital for the initial expansion of a company that is producing, shipping, and has growing accounts receivable and inventories. Also known as Second-round financing.

Secondary market
A market established for the purchase and sale of outstanding securities following their initial distribution.

Secondary worker
Any worker in a family other than the person who is the primary source of income for the family.

Secondhand capital
Previously used and subsequently resold capital equipment (e.g., buildings and machinery).

Securities and Exchange Commission (SEC)
Federal agency charged with regulating the trade of securities to prevent unethical practices in the investor market.

Securitized debt
A marketing technique that converts long-term loans to marketable securities.

Seed capital
Venture financing provided in the early stages of the innovation process, usually during product development.

Self-employed person
One who works for a profit or fees in his or her own business, profession, or trade, or who operates a farm.

Self-Employment Contributions Act (SECA)
Federal law that governs the self-employment tax (see separate citation).

Self-employment income
Income covered by Social Security if a business earns a net income of at least $400.00 during the year. Taxes are paid on earnings that exceed $400.00.

Self-employment retirement plan
See Keogh plan

Self-employment tax
Required tax imposed on self-employed individuals for the provision of Social Security and Medicare. The tax must be paid quarterly with estimated income tax statements.

Self-funding
A health benefit plan in which a firm uses its own funds to pay claims, rather than transferring the financial risks of paying claims to an outside insurer in exchange for premium payments.

Service Corps of Retired Executives (SCORE)
Volunteers for the SBA Management Assistance Program who provide one-on-one counseling and teach workshops and seminars for small firms.

Service firm
See Business service firm

Service sector
Broadly defined, all U.S. industries that produce intangibles, including the five major industry divisions of transportation, communications, and utilities; wholesale trade; retail trade; finance, insurance, and real estate; and services.

Set asides
See Small business set asides

Short-haul service
A type of transportation service in which the transporter supplies service between cities where the maximum distance is no more than 200 miles.

Short-term debt
An obligation that matures in one year.

SIC codes
See Standard Industrial Classification codes

Single-establishment enterprise
See Establishment

Small business
An enterprise that is independently owned and operated, is not dominant in its field, and employs fewer than 500 people. For SBA purposes, the U.S. Small Business Administration (SBA) considers various other factors (such as gross annual sales) in determining size of a business.

Small Business Administration (SBA)
An independent federal agency that provides assistance with loans, management, and advocating interests before other federal agencies.

Small Business Data Base
A collection of microdata (see separate citation) files on individual firms developed and maintained by the U.S. Small Business Administration.

Small business development centers (SBDC)
Centers that provide support services to small businesses, such as individual counseling, SBA advice, seminars and conferences, and other learning center activities. Most services are free of charge, or available at minimal cost.

Small business development corporation
See Certified development corporation

Small business-dominated industry
Industry in which a minimum of 60 percent of employment or sales is in firms with fewer than 500 employees.

Small Business Innovation Development Act of 1982
Federal statute requiring federal agencies with large extramural research and development budgets to allocate a certain percentage of these funds to small research and development firms. The program, called the Small Business Innovation Research (SBIR) Program, is designed to stimulate technological innovation and make greater use of small businesses in meeting national innovation needs.

Small business institutes (SBI) program
Cooperative arrangements made by U.S. Small Business Administration district offices and local colleges and

universities to provide small business firms with graduate students to counsel them without charge.

Small business investment corporation (SBIC)
A privately owned company licensed and funded through the U.S. Small Business Administration and private sector sources to provide equity or debt capital to small businesses.

Small business set asides
Procurement (see separate citation) opportunities required by law to be on all contracts under $10,000 or a certain percentage of an agency's total procurement expenditure.

Smaller firms
For U.S. Department of Commerce purposes, those firms not included in the Fortune 1000.

SMSA
See Metropolitan statistical area

Socially and economically disadvantaged
Individuals who have been subjected to racial or ethnic prejudice or cultural bias without regard to their qualities as individuals, and whose abilities to compete are impaired because of diminished opportunities to obtain capital and credit.

Sole proprietorship
An unincorporated, one-owner business, farm, or professional practice.

Special lending institution categories
See SBA special lending institution categories

Standard Industrial Classification (SIC) codes
Four-digit codes established by the U.S. Federal Government to categorize businesses by type of economic activity; the first two digits correspond to major groups such as construction and manufacturing, while the last two digits correspond to subgroups such as home construction or highway construction.

Standard metropolitan statistical area (SMSA)
See Metropolitan statistical area

Start-up
A new business, at the earliest stages of development and financing.

Start-up costs
Costs incurred before a business can commence operations.

Start-up financing
Financing provided to companies that have either completed product development and initial marketing or have been in business for less than one year but have not yet sold their product commercially.

Stock
A certificate of equity ownership in a business.

Stop-loss coverage
Insurance for a self-insured plan that reimburses the company for any losses it might incur in its health claims beyond a specified amount.

Strategic planning
Projected growth and development of a business to establish a guiding direction for the future. Also used to determine which market segments to explore for optimal sales of products or services.

Structural unemployment
See Unemployment

Sub chapter S corporations
Corporations that are considered noncorporate for tax purposes but legally remain corporations.

Subcontract
A contract between a prime contractor and a subcontractor, or between subcontractors, to furnish supplies or services for performance of a prime contract (see separate citation) or a subcontract.

Surety bonds
Bonds providing reimbursement to an individual, company, or the government if a firm fails to complete a contract. The U.S. Small Business Administration guarantees surety bonds in a program much like the SBA guaranteed loan program (see separate citation).

Swing loan
See Bridge financing

Target market
The clients or customers sought for a business' product or service.

Targeted Jobs Tax Credit
Federal legislation enacted in 1978 that provides a tax credit to an employer who hires structurally unemployed individuals.

Tax number
A number assigned to a business by a state revenue department that enables the business to buy goods without paying sales tax.

Taxable bonds
An interest-bearing certificate of public or private indebtedness. Bonds are issued by public agencies to finance economic development.

Technical assistance
See Management and technical assistance

Technical evaluation
Assessment of technological feasibility.

Technology
The method in which a firm combines and utilizes labor and capital resources to produce goods or services; the application of science for commercial or industrial purposes.

Technology transfer
The movement of information about a technology or intellectual property from one party to another for use.

Tenure
See Employee tenure

Term
The length of time for which a loan is made.

Terms of a note
The conditions or limits of a note; includes the interest rate per annum, the due date, and transferability and convertibility features, if any.

Third-party administrator
An outside company responsible for handling claims and performing administrative tasks associated with health insurance plan maintenance.

Third-stage financing
Financing provided for the major expansion of a company whose sales volume is increasing and that is breaking even or profitable. These funds are used for further plant expansion, marketing, working capital, or development of an improved product. Also known as Third-round or Mezzanine financing.

Time deposit
A bank deposit that cannot be withdrawn before a specified future time.

Time management
Skills and scheduling techniques used to maximize productivity.

Trade credit
Credit extended by suppliers of raw materials or finished products. In an accounting statement, trade credit is referred to as "accounts payable."

Trade name
The name under which a company conducts business, or by which its business, goods, or services are identified. It may or may not be registered as a trademark.

Trade periodical
A publication with a specific focus on one or more aspects of business and industry.

Trade secret
Competitive advantage gained by a business through the use of a unique manufacturing process or formula.

Trade show
An exhibition of goods or services used in a particular industry. Typically held in exhibition centers where exhibitors rent space to display their merchandise.

Trademark
A graphic symbol, device, or slogan that identifies a business. A business has property rights to its trademark from the inception of its use, but it is still prudent to register all trademarks with the Trademark Office of the U.S. Department of Commerce.

Translation
See Product development

Treasury bills
Investment tender issued by the Federal Reserve Bank in amounts of $10,000 that mature in 91 to 182 days.

Treasury bonds
Long-term notes with maturity dates of not less than seven and not more than twenty-five years.

Treasury notes
Short-term notes maturing in less than seven years.

Trend
A statistical measurement used to track changes that occur over time.

Trough
See Cyclical trough

UCC
See Uniform Commercial Code

UL
See Underwriters Laboratories

Underwriters Laboratories (UL)
One of several private firms that tests products and processes to determine their safety. Although various firms can provide this kind of testing service, many local and insurance codes specify UL certification.

Underwriting
A process by which an insurer determines whether or not and on what basis it will accept an application for insurance. In an experience-rated plan, premiums are based on a firm's or group's past claims; factors other than prior claims are used for community-rated or manually rated plans.

Unfair competition
Refers to business practices, usually unethical, such as using unlicensed products, pirating merchandise, or misleading the public through false advertising, which give the offending business an unequitable advantage over others.

Unfunded accrued liability
The excess of total liabilities, both present and prospective, over present and prospective assets.

Unemployment
The joblessness of individuals who are willing to work, who are legally and physically able to work, and who are seeking work. Unemployment may represent the temporary joblessness of a worker between jobs (frictional unemployment) or the joblessness of a worker whose skills are not suitable for jobs available in the labor market (structural unemployment).

Uniform Commercial Code (UCC)
A code of laws governing commercial transactions across the U.S., except Louisiana. Their purpose is to bring uniformity to financial transactions.

Uniform product code (UPC symbol)
A computer-readable label comprised of ten digits and stripes that encodes what a product is and how much it costs. The first five digits are assigned by the Uniform Product Code Council, and the last five digits by the individual manufacturer.

Unit cost
See Average cost

UPC symbol
See Uniform product code

U.S. Establishment and Enterprise Microdata (USEEM) File
A cross-sectional database containing information on employment, sales, and location for individual enterprises and establishments with employees that have a Dun & Bradstreet credit rating.

U.S. Establishment Longitudinal Microdata (USELM) File
A database containing longitudinally linked sample microdata on establishments drawn from the U.S. Establishment and Enterprise Microdata file (see separate citation).

U.S. Small Business Administration 504 Program
See Certified development corporation

USEEM
See U.S. Establishment and Enterprise Microdata File

USELM
See U.S. Establishment Longitudinal Microdata File

VCN
See Venture capital network

Venture capital
Money used to support new or unusual business ventures that exhibit above-average growth rates, significant potential for market expansion, and are in need of additional financing to sustain growth or further research and development; equity or equity-type financing traditionally provided at the

Glossary

commercialization stage, increasingly available prior to commercialization.

Venture capital company

A company organized to provide seed capital to a business in its formation stage, or in its first or second stage of expansion. Funding is obtained through public or private pension funds, commercial banks and bank holding companies, small business investment corporations licensed by the U.S. Small Business Administration, private venture capital firms, insurance companies, investment management companies, bank trust departments, industrial companies seeking to diversify their investment, and investment bankers acting as intermediaries for other investors or directly investing on their own behalf.

Venture capital limited partnerships

Designed for business development, these partnerships are an institutional mechanism for providing capital for young, technology-oriented businesses. The investors' money is pooled and invested in money market assets until venture investments have been selected. The general partners are experienced investment managers who select and invest the equity and debt securities of firms with high growth potential and the ability to go public in the near future.

Venture capital network (VCN)

A computer database that matches investors with entrepreneurs.

WAN

See Wide Area Network

Wide Area Network (WAN)

Computer networks linking systems throughout a state or around the world in order to facilitate the sharing of information.

Withholding

Federal, state, social security, and unemployment taxes withheld by the employer from employees' wages; employers are liable for these taxes and the corporate umbrella and bankruptcy will not exonerate an employer from paying back payroll withholding. Employers should escrow these funds in a separate account and disperse them quarterly to withholding authorities.

Workers' compensation

A state-mandated form of insurance covering workers injured in job-related accidents. In some states, the state is the insurer; in other states, insurance must be acquired from commercial insurance firms. Insurance rates are based on a number of factors, including salaries, firm history, and risk of occupation.

Working capital

Refers to a firm's short-term investment of current assets, including cash, short-term securities, accounts receivable, and inventories.

Yield

The rate of income returned on an investment, expressed as a percentage. Income yield is obtained by dividing the current dollar income by the current market price of the security. Net yield or yield to maturity is the current income yield minus any premium above par or plus any discount from par in purchase price, with the adjustment spread over the period from the date of purchase to the date of maturity.

Index

Index